The Taste
of Britain

The Taste of Britain

Laura Mason and Catherine Brown
Foreword by Hugh Fearnley-Whittingstall

 Harper Press
An imprint of HarperCollinsPublishers

Harper Press
An imprint of HarperCollins*Publishers*
77–85 Fulham Palace Road
Hammersmith, London W6 8JB
www.harpercollins.co.uk

Published by Harper Press in 2006

First published in Great Britain in 1999
as *Traditional Foods of Britain*
by Prospect Books
 Allaleigh House, Blackawton, Totnes, Devon TQ9 7DL
Copyright © 1999, 2004, edition and arrangement, Prospect Books

Copyright © 1999, text, GEIE/Euroterroirs, Paris
Copyright © 2006, edition and arrangement, Harper Press
Copyright © 2006, Foreword, Hugh Fearnely-Whittingstall
Copyright © 2006, Preface, Laura Mason and Catherine Brown
Copyright © contributions on pp. 17/31/66/75/119/130-1/149/171/193/212
239/280-1/338-9/342-3/366/380-1/ individual authors (see Acknowledgements)

9 8 7 6 5 4 3 2 1

A catalogue record for this book
is available from the British Library

ISBN-13 978-0-00-724132-3
ISBN-10 0-00-724132-1

Design by ′OMEDESIGN

Printed and bound in Italy by L.E.G.O. SpA

Contents

Foreword

Much is made these days of British food culture. Chefs and food writers, myself included, are keen to tell you that it's thriving, it should be celebrated, it's as good as anything our Continental cousins enjoy. Yet sometimes it seems as if our words come rolling back to us, as if bouncing off some distant land mass, unheard and unheeded along the way, so that we begin to have trouble persuading ourselves, let alone others, that there is something here worth fighting for.

The fact is that if you spend much time in supermarkets, or amongst the proliferation of branded fast foods on any high street, or if you eat in any but a handful of UK restaurants or pubs, then the concept of regional British food can seem a bit like Father Christmas, or Nirvana. A lovely romantic idea, but it doesn't really exist, does it?

Well, yes, it does. And if you're having trouble finding it, it may just be because you are looking in the wrong place. The problem, in part at least, is that the best, most uplifting stories about British food culture are being drowned out by the cacophony of mediocrity, and worse. The Turkey Twizzler is front page news – and rightly so, when it is making pre-basted, additive-laced butterballs of our children themselves. Shavings of Turkey 'ham' – 98 per cent fat free, of course – are filling the sandwiches of figure-conscious office workers the length and breadth of the nation. But the Norfolk Black, a real turkey slow-grown and bred for flavour, is out there, too – waiting to show you what he's worth. He's not making a song and dance – just gobbling quietly to himself. Track him down, and you're in for a revelation.

That's why this book is so timely, so necessary – and so brilliantly useful. It's a map, an investigative tool that will enable you to leave behind the homogenous and the bland, and set off on an exciting journey to find Britain's edible treasure – some of which may turn out to be hidden on your very doorstep.

And I urge you not merely to browse it, but to use it. Because if you can get out there and discover for yourself some of our great British specialities – whether it's traditional sage Derby cheese, or the Yorkshire teacakes known as Fat Rascals, or a properly aged Suffolk cider vinegar – then you will discover, or at least remind yourself, that food can be so much more than fuel. That it can, several times a day, every day of our lives, relax us, stimulate us, and give us pleasure.

The foods described in this book can all work that small daily miracle of exciting our passions. Not all of them, for all of us. But each of them for some of us. They have been made and honed over generations – sometimes centuries – and they are still with us because enough of us – sometimes only just enough of us – love them. Of course, in many instances, we have yet to discover whether we love them or not. And that is why this book is so loaded with fantastic potential. Everybody has a new favourite food waiting for them in the pages ahead.

I've travelled fairly widely, if somewhat randomly, around Britain, and tracking down and tasting local foods has become an increasing priority for me. Very uplifting it is, too. Approach our regional food culture with a true sense of curiosity, and you can never become an old hand, or a jaded palate. I still feel a great sense of excitement and discovery when I finally get to eat a classic local dish on its own home turf. You can't easily deconstruct the magic formula of a well-made Lancashire Hot Pot, or a Dorset apple cake. It is in the nature of such dishes that their sum is greater than their parts. But you can, when you find a version that hits the spot, instantly appreciate how such dishes have survived the harsh natural selection of public taste, and come to delight, comfort and sustain families and groups of friends for so long.

Recently, for instance, I managed to track down my very first proper Yorkshire curd tart, its delectable filling made from colostrum – the very rich milk produced by a cow for her newborn calf. It was baked for me by a farmer's wife at home in her own kitchen, using the method passed down to her through her family, and it was wonderful – very rich, curdy and slightly crumbly – having a hint of cakiness without the flouriness (I told you deconstruction was a vain enterprise). Anyway, it was a world away from any 'regular' custard tart I'd tried before. What I learnt from that experience, and from many similar ones, is that regionality really does matter. If that tart had been made in Dorset or in the Highlands, it wouldn't have tasted the same. And if it had not been made at all, the world – and on that drizzly autumn day, me – would have been the poorer for it.

There are so many factors that affect the way a food turns out. Cheese is the best example. I love cheese – 'milk's leap toward immortality' as someone once said – and it never ceases to amaze me. It's made from milk, of course, plus something that will make the milk curdle (usually rennet, but sometimes quirkier coagulants, like nettle juice). Two basic ingredients. Yet cheese is one of the most diverse foods known to man. There are hundreds of varieties in the British Isles alone – and a bowlful of fresh, pillowy Scottish crowdie differs so greatly from a nutty Somerset cheddar that it's hard to believe they're basically the same stuff. The breed of cattle and their diet, the local water and pasture, the yeasts and bacteria that live locally in the air, the techniques used to curdle the milk, the way the cheese is pressed, turned, and aged – all these things affect the outcome.

That's why it seems absolutely right to me that only cheese made in a handful of Midlands dairies can be called Stilton, and that beer brewed with the gypsum-rich water in Burton-upon-Trent is labelled as such. What's more, if you understand why regional products are unique – that it's high temperatures and seaweed fertiliser that make Jersey Royals taste different to any other potatoes, for instance – then you know more about food in general. An understanding of regional diversity can only make us more intelligent and appreciative eaters.

This understanding is not always easy to come by. Most other European countries have long taken for granted that local foods should be protected, their unique identity preserved. Hence the French AOC and the Italian DOC systems. But it's an idea not everyone in this country is comfortable with. I put this down to two things, and the first is the creeping curse of supermarket culture. The big multiple retailers try to tell us that we can eat whatever we want, whenever we want and indeed wherever we want. If you understand the seasonal nature of fresh produce, you know this is neither true nor desirable – and the same goes for regionality. You might not be able to buy genuine Arbroath smokies in every shop in the land, but that is precisely what makes them special when you do find them.

The second reason for resistance to regional labelling is illustrated by the pork pie issue. The pie makers of Melton Mowbray are currently battling to have their product awarded PGI (Protected Geographic Indication) status. That would mean only pies made in the area, to a traditional recipe, could carry the name. Other pork pie makers, from other areas, object to this. They want to call their products Melton Mowbray pies, too, arguing that their recipe is much the same. That's nonsense, of course: a recipe is only the beginning of a dish, a mere framework. The where, the how and the who of its making are just as important. But why would you even want to call your pie a Mowbray pie if it comes from London, or Swansea? Only, perhaps, if you know the real Mowbray pies taste better, and you can't be bothered to make your own recipe good enough to compete.

All of which goes to show why the issue of regionality is as relevent today as it ever has been. It's important not to see *The Taste of Britain* as a history book, a compendium of nostalgic culinary whimsy. The food included here is alive and well, and there is nothing described in these pages that you can't eat today, as long as you go to the right place. That's perhaps the most important criterion for inclusion because our regional food traditions are just as much part of the future as the past. At least, they had better be, or we will be in serious trouble.

The implications for our health, and the health of our environment, are far-reaching. If we eat, say, fruit that's produced locally, not only do we reduce the food miles that are wrecking our climate, but that fruit will be fresher and richer in nutrients. If we can go to a butcher's shop to buy meat that's been raised nearby, we can ask the butcher how it was farmed, and how it was slaughtered. And perhaps we can take our children with us, so they learn something too. In the end, a local food culture, supplied in the main by contiguous communities, militates against secrecy, adulteration – cruelty even – and in favour of transparency, accountability and good practice. What could be more reassuring than knowing the names and addresses of the people who produce your food?

I don't think it's overstating the case, either, to say that a knowledge of regional cooking promotes resourcefulness and a renewed respect for food in all of us. Regional dishes are, by their very nature, simple things. This is folk cooking – a 'nose to tail' approach that uses whatever's available and makes it go as far as possible. For a while now – since conspicuous consumption has become practically an end in itself – our predecessors' abhorrence of throwing away anything may have seemed at best, quaint, at worst, laughable. But as we begin to come to terms with the consequences of our 'have it all now' culture, it is becoming clear that ethical production, good husbandry, environmental responsibility and kitchen thrift all go hand in hand. The frugal culture that gave birth to chitterlings and lardy cake, Bath chaps and bread pudding is something we should be proud to belong to. To re-embrace it can only do us good.

Aside from their currency, the foods in this book have had to prove themselves in other ways. They must be unique to a specific region and they must have longevity, having been made or produced for at least 75 years. Finally, they must be, to use a rather ugly word, 'artisanal'. That means that special knowledge and skills are required to make them properly. Which brings me to one crucial element of good food that should never be forgotten: the people who make it. Almost without exception, the brewers, bakers, cooks, farmers and fishermen who produce traditional foods are what you might call 'characters'. This doesn't mean they are yokels caught in a yesteryear time warp. They are people of passion and commitment, intelligence and good humour, and often extraordinary specialist knowledge. And they know more than most of us about the meaning of life.

Not a single one of them goes to work in the morning in order to make lots of money –

you certainly don't choose to devote your life to bannock-making in the hope it will furnish you with a swimming pool and a Ferrari. They do it because they believe in it and, ultimately, feel it is worthwhile. In their own quiet and industrious way, they understand just how much is at stake. The future of civilized, communal, respectful life on our islands? It is not preposterous to suggest it. Use your regular custom and generously expressed enthusiasm to support this modest army of dedicated souls, working away in their kitchens, gardens, orchards breweries and smokehouses all over Britain, and you do a great deal more than simply save a cheese, or a beer, for posterity. You help save the next generation from the tyranny of industrial mediocrity.

Amid this talk of pride and principles, it's crucial not to lose sight of the fact that this is food to be enjoyed, celebrated – and shared with friends. Dishes don't survive down the centuries unless they taste good. You may not need much persuasion to try some of the buttery cakes or fabulously fresh fruit and veg described in these pages. But you will perhaps need a sense of adventure to rediscover the charms of some of the entries. Be ready to cast your squeamishness aside and sample some tripe, some tongue, some trotters as well. If the experience of visitors to our River Cottage events here in Dorset is anything to go by, I'm betting you'll be pleasantly surprised. You'll be taking a pig's head home from the butcher's and making your own brawn before you can say, 'Er, not for me, thanks.'

One element of this book to be richly savoured is the language. It is written, by Laura Mason and Catherine Brown, without hyperbole, but with a precision and clarity that far better express its authors' underlying passion and purpose. Another thing that makes it a joy to read is its embrace of the regional food vernacular: Dorset knobs, Puggie Buns, Singin' Hinnnies, Black Bullets and Mendip Wallfish are all to be revelled in for their names alone. Indeed, some might be tempted to enjoy *The Taste of Britain* chiefly as a glorious catalogue of eccentricity, a celebration of the cowsheel and the careless gooseberry, of the head cheese and the damson cheese (neither of which are actually cheese) that make British food so charming and idiosyncratic.

But to do so would be to miss out. Now that this book exists, now that it is in your hands, use it to bring about change. It should not be taken as a slice of the past, in aspic, but as a well-stocked store cupboard, with the potential to enrich our future food culture. See it not as a preservation order for British regional foods, but a call to action. Use this book as a guide, not merely to seek out delicious things that you've never tried before, but also to recreate some of them in your own kitchen. Do that and you'll be actively participating in a great food culture that has always been with us, that is often hidden beneath the mass-produced, homogenous, seasonless food we are so frequently offered, but which may yet have a vibrant future.

This book is a thorough and splendid answer to the question 'What is British food?' Use it well, and it may help to ensure that is still a meaningful question a hundred years from now.

Hugh Fearnley-Whittingstall

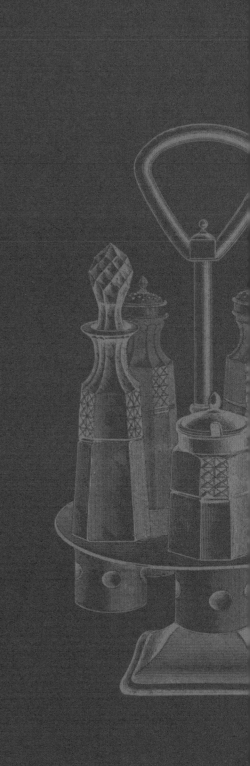

Preface

In 1994 we embarked on a mission to describe as many British foods with regional affiliations as we could find. We were part of a Europe-wide project working within a framework – handed down from Brussels – which demanded a link to the *terroir* (soil). In fact the project, named Euroterroir, was more suited to rural southern Europe than industrialized, urbanized Britain. How do you link Yorkshire Relish to the soil? But ultimately we succeeded in writing up some four hundred British entries. And along the way we asked some broader questions – what are our traditional foods? What is the character of British taste?

We've discovered that many rural treasures had survived against the odds. That sometimes foods with traditional or regional affiliations languished unloved. That sometimes British foods, though not always linking directly to the *terroir*, did have other powerful historical influences which made them special, and distinct, from the rest of Europe. No other country in Europe has a history of spicing to match the British.

Yet our homogenized food supply was clearly inflicting a far-reaching loss of local distinctiveness and quality. The idea, inherent in the project, that foods should be the property of a place and its community (*terroir*, in the context of food in France, carries implications of regionality, cultural groupings and the influence of trade and climate), rather than the trademarked possession of an individual or company, was especially alien.

Our initial research complete, we felt confident that either the Ministry of Agriculture or Food from Britain would take up the cause and publish a book based on the work which had taken us two years to complete. Instead, it was a small publisher in Devon (Tom Jaine of Prospect Books) who kept the flag flying and *Traditional Foods of Britain* was published in 1999. Seven years on, we welcome this new publication by HarperCollins.

We also welcome signs of change. Now, there is more awareness of commercial dilution, and dishonest imitation and therefore the need to protect food names, though the application process for producers is slow and difficult. There are certainly more small producers working locally, but they have to cope with numerous barriers. However much they protest otherwise, powerful supermarket central distribution systems and cut-throat pricing polices are not designed to foster local produce. And consumers do not always pause to consider the more subtle and elusive nuances of foods from closer to home.

Of course the ties of regionality do not suit foodstuffs, and in any case should be just one of many avenues open to British farmers and food producers. But it would be good to see more raw local ingredients transformed into distinctive foods since records show their rich variety in the past. Shops and markets bursting with colourful and varied local produce are one of the great pleasures of shopping for food on the continent. They exist because national policies and local custom support them. They should not be impossible in Britain. This book is not an end, but a beginning.

Laura Mason and Catherine Brown 2006

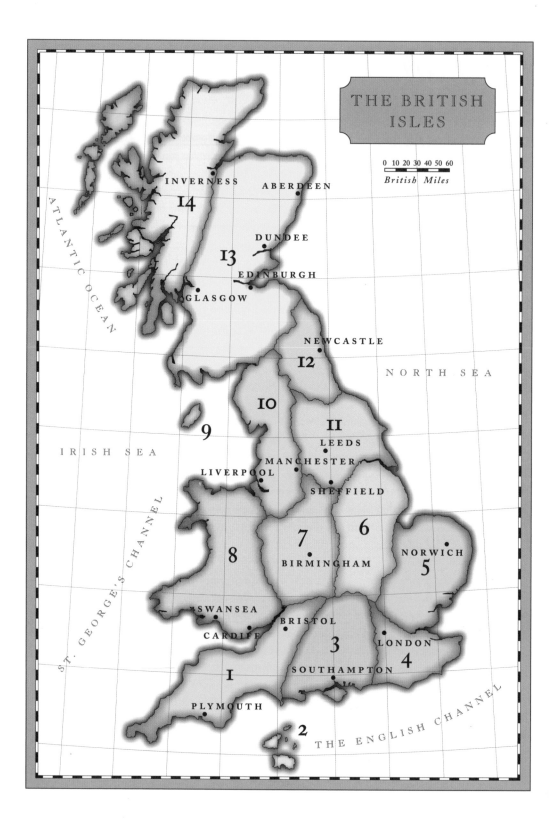

THE BRITISH
ISLES

0 10 20 30 40 50 60
British Miles

ATLANTIC OCEAN

INVERNESS   ABERDEEN

14

DUNDEE

13

EDINBURGH

GLASGOW

NEWCASTLE

12

NORTH SEA

10

11

9   LEEDS

IRISH SEA   MANCHESTER

LIVERPOOL

SHEFFIELD

7   6

BIRMINGHAM   NORWICH

8   5

ST. GEORGE'S CHANNEL

SWANSEA

BRISTOL

CARDIFF   LONDON

3   4

1   SOUTHAMPTON

PLYMOUTH

2   THE ENGLISH CHANNEL

Regions

South West England

Dittisham Plum

DESCRIPTION:
A MEDIUM-LARGE RED DESSERT PLUM, OF OVAL-OBLONG SHAPE; IT HAS GOLDEN YELLOW FLESH AND AN EXCELLENT RICH FLAVOUR. THE HARVEST IS VERY SHORT, FROM THE SECOND TO THIRD WEEKS IN AUGUST.

HISTORY:
This is a localized plum variety, grown in and around one village in Devon. It is sometimes known as the Dittisham Small Red and, locally, as the Dittisham Ploughman. It is a chance seedling, appreciated in the locality and propagated by suckers. This process (see Cambridge Gage, p.112) is common to a number of plum varieties in England. The Kea in Cornwall is very like the Dittisham although smaller and with a slightly later season.

A number of myths luxuriate around the supposed origin of this plum: that they were grown from a cargo of fruit or from seedlings dumped by a ship, the villagers planting trees in their gardens; or that the original plum came from Holland or Germany, and that the name 'ploughman' is a corruption of the German for plum, *Pflaume*; or that the nuns of the Priory of Cornworthy, nearby, brought them to the district in centuries past. There is nothing to substantiate any of these beliefs.

Oral tradition is that before motor transport, people from towns as far away as Plymouth came by horse and cart (a journey of several hours) to collect large quantities of plums. The variety was received at the National Fruit Trials in 1949. A liqueur based on these plums is now available locally. The fruit is macerated in grain spirit.

TECHNIQUE:
Dittisham lies at sea level on the estuary of the River Dart, a wide, drowned valley which opens on to the south coast of Devon. The climate is mild and sheltered, protected from the north and west winds by high hills. The soil is slightly acid and shaley. Local people claim that this plum will not flourish anywhere but Dittisham. It is propagated from suckers, and most cottage gardens in the area contain an example. There are also orchards, which generally receive little attention except at fruiting time. Under normal circumstances, the plums flower and fruit without difficulty, but easterly winds during the flowering season may adversely affect the blossoms and, therefore, the crop.

REGION OF PRODUCTION:
SOUTH WEST ENGLAND.

Bath Cheese

DESCRIPTION:
UNPASTEURIZED, SOFT COW'S MILK CHEESE. DIMENSIONS: 8CM SQUARE, 2CM DEEP. WEIGHT: 250G. COLOUR: CREAM, WITH WHITE MOULD SURFACE. FLAVOUR AND TEXTURE: MILD, WITH SLIGHT ACID FLAVOUR, MELLOWING WITH AGE, CREAMY TEXTURE.

HISTORY:

Bath cheese is mentioned in several late-Victorian texts. *Law's Grocer's Manual* (*c.* 1895) said it was 'a noted kind of soft creamy cheese'. Conditions imposed upon farm cheese-makers during the first half of the twentieth century were unfavourable for the soft, moist category of cheese to which this belongs. It was not made for many years until the current maker revived it in the 1980s.

TECHNIQUE:

Unpasteurized milk from one herd of Friesian cattle is used. Starter is added to milk at about 32°C, then animal rennet, and it is allowed to coagulate. The curd is cut to encourage whey separation to begin, and the curds and whey ladled into moulds placed on rush mats. The cheeses stand overnight. The surface is dry-salted, after which the cheese is left to dry 2 days at about 15°C. It is ripened in cooler conditions for 3–4 weeks. The cheese is made all year but is best in the autumn.

REGION OF PRODUCTION:

SOUTH WEST ENGLAND, BATH (SOMERSET).

Baydon Hill Cheese

DESCRIPTION:

AN UNPASTEURIZED COW'S AND SHEEP'S MILK CHEESE. WEIGHT: 2 SIZES, THE LARGER WEIGHS ABOUT 2.3KG; THE SMALLER ABOUT 450G. FORM: THE LARGER IS A TRUCKLE (TALL CYLINDER); THE SMALLER IS A ROUND OR LOAF, AS SUCH CHEESES ARE KNOWN LOCALLY. COLOUR: THAT OF THE COW'S MILK CHEESE IS GOLDEN YELLOW; THE SHEEP'S MILK VERSION IS A PALER, BUTTERY COLOUR; BOTH ARE WAXED WITH NATURAL BEESWAX. FLAVOUR AND TEXTURE: THE COW'S MILK CHEESE IS MILD AND CREAMY; THE SHEEP'S MILK CHEESE IS DENSER, WITH A SWEET RICH FLAVOUR.

HISTORY:

This is a modern version of a cheese formerly known as Wiltshire. Its history over the past 200 years is fairly well documented. It is related by method to Cheddar and Gloucester cheeses; as with the latter, both a thick and a thin version were known in the past. Val Cheke (1959) estimates that in 1798 5,000 tons of North Wiltshire cheese were made. This was said to be of excellent quality and in part was attributed to the particular method of dairying in Wiltshire which allowed for consistency in temperature and method. At this time, the milk of Longhorn cattle was used; these have long since been replaced by modern dairy breeds. As with Cheddar, there is some evidence for communal cheese-making. Small cheeses, known as Wiltshire loaves, and larger ones, similar to Gloucesters, are both recorded. A sheep's milk cheese is now made to the same recipe.

The local cheese-making industry declined rapidly after 1914–18 and remained a memory until Jo Hale, a farmer's wife, began her research in the late 1980s. She located a family recipe for North Wiltshire Cheese and has developed it for both sheep's and cow's milk under the name of Baydon Hill, where she lives.

TECHNIQUE:

The milk comes from a flock of British Friesland sheep, pastured in the valley of the River Avon, or from the maker's herd of cattle, mostly Friesians with a little Guernsey, feeding on semi-permanent ley pasture. It is not pasteurized. The method is the same for both cheeses.

Starter is added, plus annatto, followed shortly afterwards by a vegetarian rennet, and the milk left for the curd to form. It is cut into cubes of roughly 1cm. The temperature is raised slightly and the curd stirred for about 100 minutes until the correct acidity is reached; then it is allowed to settle for a few minutes and the whey is drained off. The curd is cut in blocks and turned up to 5 times; the number of turns varies according to the state of the milk, and fewer turns may be required with the sheep's milk curd. The curd is milled, salted and put into moulds. It is pressed for about 2 days, the cheeses being turned once. The cheeses are removed from their moulds; the larger ones are larded and bandaged, the smaller ones simply larded. They are stored for 4 months, turned daily for the first 6 weeks and once a week thereafter; then they are washed, dried, waxed and distributed.

REGION OF PRODUCTION:
SOUTH WEST, WILTSHIRE.

Beenleigh Blue Cheese

DESCRIPTION:
THERE ARE 3 CHEESES IN THIS GROUP: DEVON BLUE (COW'S MILK); HARBOURNE BLUE (GOAT'S MILK), AND BEENLEIGH BLUE (SHEEP'S MILK). DIMENSIONS: BEENLEIGH BLUE: 14CM DIAMETER, 12CM DEEP; DEVON BLUE: 16CM DIAMETER, 12CM DEEP; HARBOURNE BLUE: ABOUT 16CM DIAMETER, 12CM DEEP. WEIGHT: 2.5–3KG. COLOUR: BEENLEIGH BLUE: VERY PALE CREAMY YELLOW, WITH GREEN-BLUE VEINING; DEVON BLUE: VERY PALE CREAM, ALMOST WHITE, WITH PALE GREEN-GREY VEINING; HARBOURNE BLUE: ALMOST WHITE, WITH VERY SLIGHT GREEN TINT, GREY-GREEN VEINING. FLAVOUR AND TEXTURE: BEENLEIGH BLUE, RICH VELVETY TEXTURE, WELL-BALANCED FLAVOUR NOTES OF BLUE, SALT AND SHEEP, WITH UNDERLYING SWEETNESS; DEVON BLUE, FIRM TEXTURED AND SALTY, CARAMEL-LEATHER FLAVOUR NOTE; HARBOURNE BLUE, FIRM TEXTURE, INITIAL GOAT TANG, DEVELOPING INTO A RICH BLUE FLAVOUR.

HISTORY:
This cheese originated in the late 1970s in Devon. It arose in part from necessity, as the producer sought new markets for sheep's milk; one answer was to make a blue cheese. The person who developed Beenleigh Blue and its sister cheeses, Robin Congdon, was one of a handful of pioneers in the artisan manufacture of fine cheeses. This tradition, once vibrant in the British Isles, had almost died out during the 1940s under the impact of strict rationing.

Sheep's milk cheese may once have been made in southern England – indeed, it was the dominant type – but Beenleigh Blue was the first blue sheep's milk cheese to be made in the area for many years. The milk comes from 2 flocks kept nearby the dairy. Devon Blue, made from milk of a designated herd not far distant, was developed in the mid-1980s; Harbourne Blue is a new addition to the range, made from goat's milk from a single farm on the edge of Dartmoor.

TECHNIQUE:
Beenleigh Blue: the milk is heat-treated for 30 minutes before cheese-making commences. Starter is added, followed by vegetarian rennet and a culture of *penicillium roquefortii*; the curd is left for about 45 minutes, the exact time depending on the season, as this affects the quality of the milk. After cutting, the curd is stirred gently, then allowed to settle for about 15 minutes.

The curd is broken by hand and packed into moulds, in which it remains for 2 days. The cheese is surface-salted, spiked after a few days, allowed to blue, and then wrapped in foil to stop the rind. The cheese is matured for up to 6 months. The methods for making Devon and Harbourne are very similar, but the first is matured for about 3 months. Season: Beenleigh Blue, made January–July, available September–February; Devon Blue, all year; Harbourne Blue, made all year, but the largest quantities are produced in the spring and early summer.
REGION OF PRODUCTION:
SOUTH WEST ENGLAND, DEVON.

Cheddar Cheese

DESCRIPTION:
PRESSED COW'S MILK CHEESE. CHEDDAR IS PRODUCED IN MANY DIFFERENT SIZES WEIGHING 500G–30KG. THE TRADITIONAL SHAPE IS A CYLINDER. SMALL ONES ARE KNOWN AS TRUCKLES. CHEDDAR CHEESES WERE BANDAGED AND SMEARED WITH LARD TO PREVENT THE RIND FROM CRACKING AND TO REDUCE EVAPORATION, A PRACTICE WHICH SOME PRODUCERS STILL FOLLOW, ALTHOUGH OTHERS NOW DIP THE CHEESES IN YELLOW WAX. RINDLESS CHEESE, MADE BY THE CHEDDAR METHOD IN BLOCKS OF ABOUT 19KG, IS NOW COMMONLY AVAILABLE. COLOUR: GOOD CHEDDAR IS AN EVEN PALE YELLOW. FLAVOUR: DEPENDS ON MATURITY. IN GENERAL IT IS RICH WITH A SHARP NOTE AND A NUTTY AFTERTASTE; SHARPNESS STRENGTHENS WITH AGE. SOME MANUFACTURERS OFFER SMOKED CHEESES OR ADD HERBS.

HISTORY:
The name is taken from the village of Cheddar on the southern edge of the Mendips. Points to note are a long history, the apparently consistent excellence of the cheese, a cooperative system for its production, and the way in which the techniques associated with it have spread around the world, though often abused. The name may mislead, however. Although first-class in the parish of Cheddar itself, this cheese was from the outset made throughout the county and the wider region. The name, it is suggested, was attached to the cheese because the fame of Cheddar Gorge defined the district of origin.

Medieval records demonstrate that cheese-making was already undertaken in the region, but more precise information is not forthcoming until the modern period. In the seventeenth century, the communal pooling of milk to make very large truckles was a matter of remark, although few of them can have been as large as the cheese made for Lord Weymouth that 'was big enough to hold a girl of 13'. All the milk was contributed to a common dairy, or 'cheddar club' which meant each cheese could be much larger than those from small, individual herds, so making them fit for long maturing, which accounts for their excellent flavour. This set Cheddar cheese apart from much of the competition. Already, by 1662, they were 'so few and so dear [that they are] hardly to be met with, save at some great man's table' (Rance, 1982). The system was also sufficiently scouted to be hinted at in a play by Aphra Behn in the late seventeenth century. Its high reputation continued. Rance notes that in the early eighteenth century, Cheddar was described as 'the most noted place in England for making large, fine, rich and pleasant cheese' and that milk was brought into the common dairy and the quantities noted down in a book kept for the purpose. Profit from selling cheese was given back in proportion to the amount of milk each person contributed. Cooperative cheese-making continued until the First World War. Cheeses were indeed very large, weighing 90–120 pounds (45–60kg); cheeses of up to one and a half hundredweight (about 90kg) were noted in *Law's Grocer's Manual* in the late nineteenth century.

Detailed accounts of the Cheddar method date from an agricultural report of the late eighteenth century, but an exact recipe was not written down (or has not survived) for another 50 years. None the less, the routines associated with the cheese may have spread beyond the region earlier than this implies. Improvements in agriculture in the late nineteenth century benefited the cheese-makers, who made advances in both techniques and equipment, including the invention of the cheese mill and careful work on time, temperature and hygiene. Once perfected, the method became so identified with the cheese that it was known as 'cheddaring'. This was generously exported around the world by the British, who left a trail of upstart 'Cheddars' whenever they colonized an area deemed suitable for production.

The centralization of cheese-making during 1939–45 had significant effects on Cheddar. Firstly, official requirements for cheese to be of a specified moisture content (to enhance keeping qualities) led to the elimination of moister types. Secondly, the number of farms who resumed production after the war was greatly reduced. The introduction of rindless, block cheeses and frequent use of pasteurized milk further reduced the unique characteristics of Cheddar made in South Western England. Proliferation of *soi-disant* Cheddars blurred the popular concept of the real thing.

Farmhouse cheese-making survives in the area, although some of the operations are semi-industrial in scale. Some makers still use unpasteurized milk to make truckle cheeses. A recent development is the introduction of rennet of vegetable origin, to cope with the increased demand for vegetarian foods.

The designation Cheddar is unprotected, and much inferior cheese is made elsewhere under this name. 'West Country Farmhouse Cheddar Cheese' has been awarded Protected Designation of Origin (PDO).

TECHNIQUE:
Cheddar cheese is produced by many manufacturers, large and small, using the basic recipe with slight individual variations. Both pasteurized and unpasteurized milk are used, according to the maker's preference. The milk is heated to about 21°C and inoculated with starter culture (1–2 per cent, 5–15 minutes ripening); rennet is added and stirred in. After 30–40 minutes, cutting is begun, gently, to give curd pieces the size of wheat grains; once cut, stirring begins as the heat is raised. The curds and whey are thoroughly heated in the vat, and the temperature increased to 40°C over 40–50 minutes; the curd is continuously stirred until the correct firmness is achieved (judging this can only be achieved by experience). Acidity at this point is crucial; once the correct level is achieved, stirring ceases; the curd starts to mat, and the whey is run off. Cutting and turning, or cheddaring, is carried out either in the vat, or on a shallow tray or cooler. The object is to expel as much whey as possible. Firstly a centre portion of curd is removed to create a drainage channel; then the remainder is cut into large blocks which are turned; after 5–10 minutes the blocks are cut into smaller strips which are turned and piled higher; this process of cutting and turning continues for up to 90 minutes until the curd is judged sufficiently cool, well drained and acid. The curd is put through a curd mill to break it up. The curd is turned with a

fork to keep it friable and allow salt to be mixed evenly (1kg salt to 45kg curd). The curd is broken into small pieces and put into cloth-lined moulds. The moulds are piled on top of each other to commence pressing, then placed in horizontal gang presses (in which several cheeses are pressed at once); when the whey starts to be expelled, the pressure is increased for 24–48 hours; the cheese is turned out 2–4 hours after the first pressing; the cloth wrung out in warm water and replaced and the cheese returned to the press; the next day the cheese is bathed for 5–10 seconds in warm water and returned to the press with light pressure; later the same day, the cheese is changed into a dry cloth and greased with melted lard which is rubbed thoroughly into the surface of the cheese; then the cheese is pressed for another 24 hours; after removal from the press, another bandage is applied. Ripening is at 8–9°C and a relative humidity of 86°; the cheeses are turned every day and cleaned to remove mould.

The production of block cheddar is similar until the moulding stage is reached. Then it is pressed into blocks. On removal from the press, it is wrapped in film to exclude air, and the cheeses are then strapped under pressure and transferred to the ripening room.

Cheddars sell at various degrees of maturity: mild (6 months after making); mature (9–12 months); extra-mature (over 12 months).

REGION OF PRODUCTION:
SOUTH WEST ENGLAND.

Clotted Cream and Clotted-Cream Butter

DESCRIPTION:
CLOTTED CREAM IS THICK, WITH A SOLID, PALE GOLDEN CRUST. IT CONTAINS 55–60 PER CENT BUTTERFAT.

HISTORY:
Clotting cream is really a means of lightly preserving it; when ordinary cream has been transformed into clotted cream it will keep in a cool place for about 2 weeks, as opposed to a few days. The method is probably very ancient and similar products are known in western Asia. Early references to clotted, or clouted, cream can be found in English texts from the sixteenth century onwards. The first mention cited by the *Oxford English Dictionary* is Boorde's *Dyetary of Helth* (1542). A multitude of descriptions and references exist from the seventeenth century and later. Even the earliest references make clear that it was a regional product. Recipes show that the method for making it has remained essentially unchanged for 400 years.

This is a region with a mild climate, rich pasture lands, and a traditional cattle breed yielding milk with a high butterfat content, all factors conducive to the development of specialist dairy produce. *Law's Grocer's Manual* (*c.* 1895) remarks on 'the increasing fancy for this delicacy'; that a regular sale for it was springing up in all large towns, and that the best was thought to come from Devon, notably the area around Ilfracombe. The cream was packed in small glazed pots for export to other parts of the country. Although the presumption is that clotted cream comes from Devon, it is equally known and long-established in Cornwall. The Devon connection probably took first place simply because it was the larger county, with wider connections to the country at large.

Once clotted, it was claimed the crust was sometimes solid enough to support a pound

weight without breaking. Clotted cream has been used in the cookery of its region of origin (in breads, cakes, pastries, with fish, or as other regions might use cream); it is more generally thought of as a delicacy in its own right.

Clotting cream was also a very good way to turn milk into a flavourous butter. The heat-treatment required to make scalded cream and transforming the result into butter are 2 consecutive steps in preserving and adding value to a local raw material. 'This cream was stirred by hand, the maid putting her arm into the pot and stirring it until the butter came. In hot weather when the hand was too warm, a bottle was sometimes used' (Fussell, 1966). The existence of this butter was acknowledged by the author of the *General View of the Agriculture of the County of Devon* (1813) and, a century later, White (1932) writes about a Devonshire farmer's wife demonstrating making butter by beating clotted cream with her hand. There is a view current that this form of butter-making is now more known in Cornwall than Devon. Small amounts are still produced in the West Country for local consumption. No other region of Britain has developed clotted cream, or butter made from it, as a speciality. Awarded Protected Designation of Origin (PDO).

TECHNIQUE:
Clotted cream requires long slow heating at a moderate temperature. The craft method is as follows: both unpasteurized and pasteurized milk are used. Traditionalists prefer the excellent flavour of unpasteurized milk from Channel Island cattle which has a high butterfat content. The cream is separated from the milk and kept overnight; it may be ripened if desired. The cream, contained in enamel pans, is placed in a bain-marie and heated gently for about 2 hours. This process is crucial; the time and temperature must be correct; only experience will teach the right combination. The temperature of the bain-marie is maintained at below boiling, about 82°C. Once the correct golden, honeycomb crust has formed, the pans are removed from the heat. Industrial methods work on the same principle, but heating takes place either in an oven or in steam cabinets.

Before the advent of milk separators, cream would be clotted on the whole milk. First, the cream would be allowed to rise naturally on the pan of milk saved from one of the day's milkings. If the morning milk, it would be left until late in the afternoon; if the evening's, then left overnight. The pan was placed carefully over the fire and it was scalded, as described above. In small farmhouses, the pan would be placed over the kitchen hearth; in larger households, the dairy might have a special stove constructed from a stone slab pierced with holes big enough to accommodate the pans safely. A charcoal brazier could be placed beneath each pan. These pans were of brass or of earthenware. Once the cream was scalded and had clotted, it was skimmed off the milk and stored in flat dishes. Brears (1998) provides illustrations.

Clotted-cream butter is made on a small scale by craft producers. Instead of stirring the cream by hand, as was done in the past, an electric whisk is now used. The cream is whipped until crumbly and worked by hand to squeeze out as much moisture as possible. It is washed in cold water, then beaten with a boiled cloth on a wooden platter. It is pressed by hand into a mould to make round pats.

REGION OF PRODUCTION:
SOUTH WEST ENGLAND, DEVON AND CORNWALL.

Cornish Yarg Cheese

DESCRIPTION:

Pressed cow's milk cheese, with nettle leaves as a wrapping, made in 2 sizes, 15cm diameter and 25cm; both roughly 7cm high. Weight: 1kg and 3kg. Form: a truckle and a flat wheel. Colour: almost white curd, with a powdery grey rind that shows a pattern derived from the nettle leaves in which it is wrapped. Flavour and texture: a young Yarg cheese has a fresh, lemony flavour and a moist, crumbly curd; it softens as it matures, developing a deeper flavour.

HISTORY:

The use of leaves of common plants such as nettles as substrata for draining cheeses, or wrappings for the finished product, has a long history, though now unusual. 'Nettle Cheese' was mentioned in the seventeenth century by Gervase Markham, who considered that a new milk cheese ripened on nettles was 'the finest of all summer cheeses which can be eaten'.

Although Cornwall was never famous for cheese in the way of counties to the east, some was made. A recipe 'to make our good Cornish cheese' was published in *Farmhouse Fare*, a collection of recipes from farmers' wives all over the country. The details suggest that modern Cornish Yarg is not dissimilar. It was developed in the 1970s by Alan and Jennie Gray ('Yarg' is simply 'Gray' spelt backwards). It has been awarded a Protected Designation of Origin (PDO).

TECHNIQUE:

Milk from designated herds of local Friesian cattle is used; the milk is pasteurized. Starter is added, and the milk left for about an hour, before renneting with vegetarian rennet. It is then left for another hour. The curd is cut by hand, drained gradually and the mass stirred, recut and turned until considered dry enough. It is milled through a peg mill into pieces of about 50mm then filled into moulds. It is left under medium pressure for about 18 hours, after which it is unmoulded. Brining is for 6 hours. The cheeses are wrapped in nettle leaves; these encourage the growth of penicillium moulds essential for ripening. The cheeses are stacked in controlled humidity and temperature for 3 weeks, turned daily.

REGION OF PRODUCTION:

South West England, Cornwall.

Curworthy Cheese

DESCRIPTION:

Pressed, pasteurized and unpasteurized cow's milk cheese. There are 3 cheeses in this group, Curworthy, Devon Oke (the largest) and Belstone. Dimensions: 10cm diameter, 4.5cm deep (450g, Curworthy only); 12cm diameter, 5cm deep (1.1kg, Curworthy and Belstone); 15cm diameter, 6cm deep (2.3kg, Curworthy and Belstone); 16cm diameter, 10cm deep (4.7kg, Devon Oke). Colour: buttery yellow, darker towards the edges, with a few small holes. Texture and flavour: smooth, sweet, with overtones of dried grass and sharp afternote.

HISTORY:

The Curworthy recipe was devised in the early 1980s using old instructions for 'quick' cheeses from the South West combined with local expertise. Sources included Gervase Markham's *Country Contentments* (1620), Baxter's *Library of Agriculture* (1846) and Dorothy Hartley's recipe for slipcoat or slipcote (1954). Slipcoat is a term which was used quite widely in England until the beginning of the last century meaning either a cheese which burst its coat and was eaten young because it would never mature properly (usually referring to a Stilton), or a creamy, light-textured cheese to be eaten young, made with only a light, brief pressing – a category to which Curworthy belongs. The initial development was carried out by the *Farmer's Weekly* (the main trade journal for the farming community), Wanda and David Morton (farm managers working for the magazine) and the staff of the local Agricultural Development and Advisory Service. Curworthy is an emergent product; it began initially as an experiment in diversification. Having proved successful, the farm and recipe were acquired by the current makers in 1987 and output has increased steadily.

TECHNIQUE:
The same method is employed for all 3 cheeses. Animal rennet is used for Curworthy and Devon Oke, both of which can be of pasteurized or unpasteurized milk; Belstone is always made from unpasteurized, using vegetable rennet. Milk from a designated herd of Friesian cattle is used. The milk is pasteurized if required and then brought to the temperature necessary for cheese-making; starter and rennet are added. The curd is cut 2 ways, stirred and scalded to about 38°C, then drained and piled at one end of the vat, before being filled into the mould. It is pressed for about 2.5 hours, after which the cheese is removed and brined. Maturing varies with size, but is a minimum of 6 weeks for the smallest Curworthy and up to 6 months for Devon Oke.

REGION OF PRODUCTION:
SOUTH WEST ENGLAND, OKEHAMPTON (DEVON).

'Bachelor's fare: bread and cheese, and kisses.'

JONATHAN SWIFT

Dorset Blue Vinney Cheese

DESCRIPTION:
BLUE MOULD, HARD, SKIMMED COW'S MILK CHEESE, MADE IN CYLINDERS OF 1.35–2.3KG AND 6KG. COLOUR: CREAM OR YELLOW, WITH FINE BLUE-GREEN VEINS. FLAVOUR AND TEXTURE: STRONG, SHARP BLUE FLAVOUR; HARD TEXTURE.

HISTORY:
The word vinney derives from an archaic word vinew, which meant mould. It was in general use until the sixteenth century but was subsequently confined to South West dialect. Here, it was associated with a blue-mould cheese made in Dorset. This was certainly known in the eighteenth and nineteenth centuries as a cheese made by the wives of dairymen, using milk

left after the cream had been removed for sale or conversion into butter. Thus it was always a very low-fat, rather hard cheese (Rance, 1982). Numerous recipes survive. The growth of blue mould in the cheese was regarded as the defining characteristic, and was encouraged by various methods, including placing the cheeses in barns or harness rooms to mature.

In the twentieth century, several factors adversely affected production: the secure market for whole, fresh milk provided by the Milk Marketing Board; the invention of efficient mechanical devices for separating milk and cream, which left no residual fat, producing a very hard cheese; and limits on cheese-makers imposed by the Ministry of Food during 1939–45. Until the 1970s, output remained low and the cheese was hard to find. A true Blue Vinney is once again available commercially.

TECHNIQUE:

The milk from morning milking is skimmed by hand. Skimmed-milk powder is added to adjust the fat content, to make a cheese suitable for modern taste. Starter culture, rennet from vegetable sources and penicillin mould are added. The curd is cut into 2cm cubes and left overnight. Next day, the curd is drained, cut into blocks, milled, salted and packed into moulds. These remain in a warm dairy for 5 days. The cheeses are unmoulded, spread with a paste of flour and blue mould, and ripened for 10 weeks to 5 months, with spiking after 1 month to encourage the spread of mould through the cheese. Dorset Blue has been awarded Protected Geographical Indication (PGI).

REGION OF PRODUCTION:
SOUTH WEST ENGLAND, DORSET.

Double Gloucester Cheese

DESCRIPTION:
HARD, PRESSED, UNPASTEURIZED AND PASTEURIZED COW'S MILK CHEESE. DOUBLE GLOUCESTER IS MADE IN A FLAT WHEEL ABOUT 30CM DIAMETER, 12CM HIGH, WEIGHING ABOUT 11KG. COLOUR: PALE ORANGE TO DEEP RED-ORANGE. SOME CHEESES HAVE ANNATTO ADDED TO THE CURD. FLAVOUR AND TEXTURE: MELLOW, ROUND FLAVOUR AND CLOSE CREAMY TEXTURE.

HISTORY:
Two cheeses are associated with Gloucestershire: Double Gloucester, and the less common, lower fat Single (see below). Despite a common heritage, they are separate. The differences of method are subtle and the origin of the terms double and single obscure. They evolved in the late eighteenth century, when the traditional method for making 'best' cheese developed into one calling for the whole milk of 2 milkings, or the cream from an evening milking plus the whole milk from a morning milking (Rance, 1982). Double may refer to this use of 2 lots of milk. Alternatively, the terms may have meant nothing more than double being twice as thick as single (Black, 1989).

Gloucestershire, which includes both the Cotswolds and the low-lying land in the valley of the River Severn, has certainly produced cheese for a long time. Rance (1982) states that a regional cheese was exported in the eighth century AD. It is impossible to know what this was like. Fourteenth-century records show a Cotswold manor making cow's and sheep's milk

cheeses and sending them to the nuns who owned the farm, in Caen in Normandy. If Gloucester cheese did incorporate sheep's milk, no trace of this habit has been found beyond this isolated record.

Evidence for cheese-making throughout the county during the early modern period can be seen in the tall farmhouses which contain a cheese-room on the third storey; domestic inventories also mention much cheese-making equipment. One area, the Vale of Berkeley, in the south, became very important. Possibly the local Gloucester breed of cattle, whose milk is particularly good for cheese-making, contributed to the excellence of their cheese.

At first, Gloucester was a coloured cheese made from the full-cream milk of a single milking. These were known as 'best' until Double Gloucester was recognized as a separate type at the end of the eighteenth century. The cheeses continued to have a high reputation, although disease reduced the population of Gloucester cattle and they were replaced by 'improved' breeds from the Midlands. Cheese production became factory-centred in the twentieth century. A little farmhouse cheese survived and renewed interest in old breeds led to the revival of Gloucester cattle and the use of their milk in cheese from the 1970s onwards.

Several folk customs are associated with cheeses in this region. One is the 'cheese rolling' on Whit Monday at Cooper's Hill, between Gloucester and Cheltenham. Four cheeses are rolled down the hill and chased by an assembled crowd. A similar merriment was recorded at Randwick.

TECHNIQUE:

Current practice is to make Double Gloucester from the whole milk of 2 milkings. It is heated to 28°C and starter is added. Annatto is mixed through the milk and then rennet is added and the milk left 45–60 minutes. The curd is cut into cubes of about 3mm and stirred for 20–40 minutes whilst the heat is raised to about 37°C. Stirring continues until the correct acidity is reached. The curd is allowed to settle and the whey drained off slowly. It is cut into fairly large blocks, piled and turned every 15 minutes as the acidity develops. Milling is through a fine curd mill; then salt is added (about 750g for each 45kg), stirred in thoroughly and allowed to dissolve. The curd is placed in moulds lined with cheese-cloth. Pressing continues for 2 days; the cheese is removed and turned once during this time, and increasing pressure is used on the second day. The cheese is ripened at 8°C and turned daily; then matured for 3–8 months.

REGION OF PRODUCTION:
WEST ENGLAND, GLOUCESTERSHIRE.

Single Gloucester Cheese

DESCRIPTION:
PRESSED, COW'S MILK CHEESE, ORIGINALLY MADE IN A WHEEL 6.5CM THICK, ABOUT 40CM DIAMETER, WEIGHING ABOUT 7KG. NOW MADE IN VARYING WEIGHTS, 900G–3.5KG. COLOUR: PALE LEMON. FLAVOUR: MILD, SWEET-SHARP, WITH CREAMY FINISH.

HISTORY:
Single Gloucester became distinct from the closely related Double Gloucester (see the entry above) at the end of the eighteenth century. Patrick Rance (1982) said that they were praised

by William Marshall in 1796, who considered them equal to 'whole-milk cheeses from counties with poorer soil and less admirable cattle,' even though they were made partially from skimmed milk. Single Gloucester evolved as a lower-fat cheese, smaller in size. Unlike Double, it was not coloured. The making of Double Gloucester flourished in the Vale of Berkeley, whilst the Single was made on farms in the north and east of the county. They were more seasonal, some only made during the spring, and they were only matured for 2 months. They have never been as widely marketed as Double Gloucester and for much of the twentieth century only small amounts were made. Interest was renewed in the 1970s and it is now on sale again. Awarded Protected Designation of Origin.

TECHNIQUE:

This cheese uses a mixture of whole and skimmed milk. It is heated to 19°C and starter added, followed by a vegetarian rennet. The curd is left to set for about 1 hour and 40 minutes. The curd is cut, stirred to break it up further, and the heat is raised to 34°C. The curd is drained, cut into relatively small squares and turned. It is recut and turned at least twice more to make very small pieces. It is then sliced and milled through a Cheshire mill, and salt is added. It is filled into cheese-cloth-lined moulds. Pressing is for 48 hours, during which the cheese is removed, turned and put back in the cloth, then given a final pressing for 2 hours without the cloth. Maturing: 3–12 weeks.

REGION OF PRODUCTION:

WEST ENGLAND, GLOUCESTERSHIRE, DEVON.

Sharpham Cheese

DESCRIPTION:

MOULD-RIPENED, SOFT, UNPASTEURIZED COW'S MILK CHEESE IN 3 SIZES. WEIGHT: 250G; 500G; OR 1KG. FORM: THE SMALLEST CHEESE IS SQUARE; THE LARGER ROUND. COLOUR: WHITE MOULD CRUST WITH STRIPES FROM STRAW MAT; DEEP RICH YELLOW-CREAM. FLAVOUR AND TEXTURE: SHARP AND CHALKY WHEN YOUNG, RIPENING TO A SOFT CREAMY TEXTURE WITH MILD MUSHROOM FLAVOUR.

HISTORY:

Sharpham cheese belongs to the new cheeses which have arisen during the last 40 years as the artisan side of the industry began to revive from the damage inflicted by rationing during and after World War II. Several craftsmen have become well established in Devon, a county traditionally famous for dairy produce – in the early eighteenth century, the traveller Celia Fiennes noted that the dairy market in Exeter occupied 3 streets.

Experiments were carried on for some years at Sharpham House, near Totnes, before the present recipe was evolved. The particular type of milk used – from Jersey cattle – has a high butterfat content. Much background research was undertaken in France and, eventually, a Coulommiers type (widely taught in Britain and popular with small cheese-makers throughout the last century) proved successful. Sharpham has been sold since the early 1980s.

TECHNIQUE:

Milk from the Sharpham Estate Jersey herd is first flash-heated and cooled. Starter is added, and the milk ripened, vegetable rennet and a penicillin strain are added. The curd is cut by hand and separated from the whey; some of the whey is scooped off after a few minutes and the curd cut again; then it is hand-ladled into moulds and drained. The cheeses are turned, drained further and salted. Maturing is at a relatively warm temperature for about a week; then they are left for the mould to develop. They are wrapped and transferred to cooler temperatures to finish ripening.

REGION OF PRODUCTION:
SOUTH WEST ENGLAND, TOTNES (DEVON).

Vulscombe Cheese

DESCRIPTION:
SOFT GOAT'S CHEESE, IN ROUNDS 6CM DIAMETER, 4CM DEEP. WEIGHT: ABOUT 180G. COLOUR: WHITE. FLAVOUR: CREAMY, DENSE, SLIGHT LEMON TANG, VERY MILD GOAT FLAVOUR. VARIANTS ARE FLAVOURED WITH HERBS AND GARLIC, OR WITH CRUSHED BLACK PEPPERCORNS.

HISTORY:
This is one of many goat's milk cheeses which have become so important in British artisan manufacture during the last 40 years. Before, with the exception of a few families who kept milking-goats as a hobby or to provide milk for children allergic to that of cows, not many paid attention to making goat's cheese and none reached the market place. During the 1960s and 1970s, interest in self-sufficiency and small-holding led to the greater popularity of goat's milk products. This was given extra momentum by changes in agriculture and the necessity for diversification in the 1980s. There are now many well-established makers of goat's cheese, spread throughout Britain, with concentrations in Kent and Sussex, North Yorkshire, Cumbria and the Scottish Borders. Though receiving little support from government and small in volume, this is a dynamic and creative sector. Recipes may be inspired by French examples or British originals evolved through trial and error. It is impossible to list them all. British taste generally leans towards young, cream-textured cheeses characterized by a mild goat flavour and slightly acid freshness, although some people do make mould-ripened, soft cheeses, or hard, pressed cheese, or blue cheeses using goat's milk. Vulscombe is based on the acid curd method, used by cottagers and farmers' wives during the eighteenth and nineteenth centuries to make small quantities of fresh soft cheese for immediate consumption.

TECHNIQUE:
British goat cheeses are a diverse subject and it is impossible to discuss them all. One which represents the general taste for mild creaminess has been selected. Vulscombe is named for the valley where it is made. The area has a mixed farming economy in which dairy products are important. The cheese derives from the milk of one herd of goats grazing old-established, flower-rich pastures at an altitude of about 250 metres in central Devon. Supplementary hay and silage are fed in winter and a grain-based concentrate is used for lactating animals. Cheese-making begins once 3 milkings have been accumulated. The temperature is raised to 10°C and a cultured starter added. Then it rises to 32°C over some hours and incubation continues until the milk has separated into curds and whey. Straining is through muslin and cheese-cloth for about 36 hours, then the curd is salted and herbs or peppercorns added if

appropriate. It is ladled into moulds and pressed lightly for 24 hours.

REGION OF PRODUCTION:
SOUTH WEST ENGLAND, DEVON.

Whey Butter

DESCRIPTION:
BUTTER MADE FROM THE WHEY. IN COLOUR IT IS PALE GOLD; IN FLAVOUR, IT IS DESCRIBED
AS 'NUTTY' OR SLIGHTLY CHEESY, THIS DEEPENS WITH AGE.

HISTORY:
Whey butter has probably been produced by cheese-makers in Britain for many centuries.
Whey is the by-product of cheese-making, a thin liquid separated from the curd in the early
stages. Depending on the type of cheese, the whey carries with it a small proportion of butter-fat and, in some areas, this is collected and churned into butter. Val Cheke (1959) states
that, in the early medieval period, one of the duties of the dairy maid was to make whey butter and there are many references from later centuries relating to this practice. Maria Rundell
(1807) gave details of how to manage cream for whey butter, a process which required the
whey to stand a day and a night before it was skimmed, then boiled, poured into a pan of cold
water and skimmed again 'as the cream rises' – this is not unlike making clotted cream. She
remarks, 'Where new-milk cheese is made daily, whey-butter for common and present use
may be made to advantage.' This statement still holds true today, and it is made in many
cheese-making areas.

TECHNIQUE:
Ordinary butter produced in Britain is made from cream separated from fresh milk. In contrast to this, the butterfat used for whey butter goes through the initial processes of cheese-
making. The exact details of these vary from region to region, but include the steps of adding
starter and rennet, and allowing the milk to ripen and curdle with the temperature at about
32°C. Once the curd has set, it is cut and stirred while the temperature is increased by a few
degrees. After a certain time, which varies according to the type of cheese being made, the
whey is drained off. It is this part of the process which gives the distinctive flavour to the butter. The whey, which has a fat content of about 0.5–1 per cent, is then put through a mechanical separator (centrifuge), yielding up the fat in the form of cream which is then churned by
conventional methods, lightly salted (about 1 per cent), and packed for sale.

REGION OF PRODUCTION:
SOUTH WEST ENGLAND.

Elver

DESCRIPTION:

YOUNG EELS ABOUT 4CM LONG, SLENDER AND THREAD-LIKE. COLOUR: TRANSPARENT, PALE AMBER. FLAVOUR: MILDLY FISHY.

HISTORY:

Eels were once a staple of fish-day diet. Medieval household accounts devote more entries to them than almost any other species of fish (Woolgar, 1992). Small wonder, therefore, that their fry should be esteemed as delicacies. The River Severn has long been noted for the vast numbers of elvers it attracts. Neufville Taylor (1965) mentions an elver net in a domestic inventory dated 1587 and Daniel Defoe (1724–6) remarked on elver-cakes sold at Bath and Bristol. White (1932) states elvers in large baskets were being cried through the streets of Gloucester even after the First World War. The fish products of the Severn estuary were important regional symbols, whether the salmon, the elvers or the lampreys – the Corporation of Gloucester sent a lamprey pie to the reigning monarch every year until 1836. Elvers are caught from the Somerset Levels up the Severn as far north as Tewkesbury. Villages some way from the bank have memories of elver cookery. FitzGibbon (1972) records instructions for elver pie (made as a sort of pasty) from the village of Keynsham, half way between Bristol and Bath on the River Avon.

Elvers have remained a popular food in the region, but they are now very expensive, and much of the catch is exported, some going as stock for eel-farms (Green, 1993). Furthermore, a study undertaken by Brian Knights to investigate the declining catch of elvers from the Severn in the 1980s concluded that oceanic cycles had affected numbers.

There are several local methods for cooking elvers, including flouring and deep frying; and frying in bacon fat then adding eggs to make a type of omelette. Alternatively, they are steamed to make a loaf. There are elver-eating contests in the villages on the lower reaches of the Severn on Easter Monday. During the season, between the spring tides of March and April, fresh elvers can be bought from local markets.

TECHNIQUE:

The elvers are caught at night by inhabitants who have rights to particular places on the river where swift-moving water comes close to the bank. They take up station some time before the 'bore', a high wave formed by the incoming tide in the Severn estuary as it narrows, and warn each other of its arrival by shouting a message along the river, marking its progress. As the tide begins to ebb, nets are put into the water with their mouth facing downstream to catch the elvers as they swim upstream against the flow; after a few minutes a net is removed and emptied, then dipped again. A suspended light can be used to attract the fish. If the run is poor, the net may be 'tealed', pegged in position for some time, in an attempt to maximize the catch.

REGION OF PRODUCTION:

WEST ENGLAND, SEVERN ESTUARY AND TRIBUTARIES.

Smoked Mackerel

DESCRIPTION:
SINGLE FILLETS OF SMOKED MACKEREL WITH SKIN. COLOUR: CHESTNUT BROWN ON FLESH
SURFACE, CREAM INTERNAL FLESH. FLAVOUR: WOODY-OILY, LIGHTLY SALTY.

HISTORY:
Similar to the herring, with a high oil content, mackerel flesh spoils rapidly when fresh and
the hot-smoking process over oak chips was a method of processing which the curers have
developed and which has become as popular as kippers. Mackerel is fished all around the
British coasts, and has long been a mainstay of the South West. In the early twentieth century, the catch was preserved by canning (in Cornwall) or salting (in parts of Scotland). When
the herring fishery declined in the 1970s, processors turned their attention to mackerel as an
alternative. Particularly good catches were made off the Cornish coast and a substantial
smoking industry developed, using both whole fish and fillets.

When the Scottish herring fisheries were closed in 1977 to conserve stocks, attitudes there
(where mackerel had hitherto been regarded as inferior) changed and catches began to
increase; smoking was also taken up as a means of using the catch.

TECHNIQUE:
Made with fish caught mostly during December–February when they have an oil content of
about 23 per cent. They are filleted to remove head and bone. Single fillets with the skin on are
cured in a brine, placed on stainless-steel trays and cold-smoked for an hour then hot-smoked
for 2 hours. Flavourings (pepper, herbs and spices) are sprinkled over before they are smoked.

REGION OF PRODUCTION:
SOUTH WEST ENGLAND; ALSO SCOTLAND; EAST ANGLIA.

Bath Chaps

DESCRIPTION:
WEIGHT: 400–600G, DEPENDING ON THE AGE AND BREED OF PIG. COLOUR: BATH CHAP HAS
THE APPEARANCE OF A CONE CUT IN HALF VERTICALLY; THE CURVED UPPER SURFACE IS COV-
ERED WITH LIGHT BROWN OR ORANGE BREAD CRUMBS; WHEN CUT, THE CHAP IS STREAKED
IN LAYERS OF PINK LEAN AND WHITE FAT. FLAVOUR: SIMILAR TO ENGLISH COOKED HAMS OF
THE YORK TYPE.

HISTORY:
A Bath chap is the cheek of a pig, boned, brined and cooked. Why this delicacy should be
associated with the town of Bath is not clear, except that it lies in an area which has been a
centre of bacon curing.

Pig's cheeks have probably been cured and dried for as long as any other part of the animal.
The word chap is simply a variant on chop which, in the sixteenth century, meant the jaws and
cheeks of an animal. These are probably what Mrs Raffald (1769) intended when she gave a
recipe 'To salt chops' with salt, saltpetre, bay salt and brown sugar. This called for the meat to
be dried afterwards; it would be expected to keep for several months. A century later, Mrs
Beeton gave a method for drying and smoking pig's cheeks, observing that 'A pig's cheek, or
Bath chap, will take about 2 hours after the water boils.' *Law's Grocer's Manual* (*c.* 1895) notes

I am passionate about the use of local food and the high quality of produce to be found in Devon is one of the main reasons I chose to move here to start my latest venture. I have spent a lot of my time driving around the county, sourcing suppliers, going to farmers markets, visiting smallholders, speaking to day-boat fishermen and building up a network of people who are as passionate and mad about food as we are here at the New Angel. I love anticipating what produce is going to be brought into the restaurant on any given day. Take asparagus for example: because the season only lasts for six weeks, there is always an air of anticipation around their delivery. Devon asparagus is excellent and dishes containing my favourite vegetable always fly out of the door. Likewise, it's great when Anthony Buscombe and his brother come straight in from their boat to the restaurant with a big box of freshly caught crab – 80 per cent of all of Britain's crab comes from the Dartmouth and Salcombe coast, and it's the best there is. The delicate, sweet meat needs only a little butter and spice, and I'm very lucky to be able to source such quality from my own doorstep. I regard this county as a centre of excellence for locally produced food. No other area can match Devon's variety of produce, and that is why I believe it is so important to promote and support local food producers, suppliers and small farming businesses.

John Burton Race

CHEF AND PROPRIETOR, THE NEW ANGEL, DARTMOUTH

both upper and lower jaws were used, the lower, which was meatier and contained the tongue, selling at about twice the price of the upper. Several manufacturers are recorded, including Hilliers of Stroud and the Wiltshire Bacon Company (founded at the end of the nineteenth century). However, today, only 2 producers have been located.

Bath chaps are eaten at main meals, usually with mustard. They are sold already cooked.

TECHNIQUE:

Bath chaps are no longer dried, merely lightly brined. They are cut from the pig's heads, cleaned, and boned. They are brined for a short time, after which they are cooked. Subsequently, they are pressed in a mould to give the cone shape; when cold and set, the chaps are removed from their moulds and dusted with crumbs.

REGION OF PRODUCTION:

WILTSHIRE AND SOMERSET; SOUTH ENGLAND

Bradenham Ham (Fortnum Black Ham)

DESCRIPTION:

AN UNSMOKED CURED HAM FOR COOKING. WEIGHT: ABOUT 14KG. COLOUR: THE SKIN IS BLACK, THE FAT BROWN-TINTED. FLAVOUR: DELICATE, SWEET, MILD.

HISTORY:

The Bradenham Ham Company of Wiltshire produced hams according to a recipe dated 1781 (Simon, 1960). The recipe is thought to be named for the last Lord Bradenham. It emanated from Bradenham in Buckinghamshire. The secret is in the immersion in molasses and spices, resulting in a sweet-tasting meat. Recipes for treacle-cured hams appeared in domestic cookery books at this time, and the developing West India trade provided molasses a-plenty. The hams were hung and matured for a longer period than other, less exclusive products. In the novel *A Rebours* (1884), the decadent hero visits an English restaurant in Paris, passing at the entrance a counter displaying 'hams the mellow brown of old violins'.

The curing method and the trademark of a flying horse were the exclusive property of the Bradenham Ham Co. which was awarded a Royal Warrant in 1888. In 1897 the Wiltshire Bacon Company took over Bradenham Ham but continued to produce at Chippenham in Wiltshire. When that company closed in its turn, production was moved to Yorkshire. Similar recipes are used by other curers; Brunham, made in Wiltshire, is one example.

TECHNIQUE:

The legs, cut from bacon pigs, must carry a specified level of fat otherwise they become dry; they are long-cut, giving a rounded shape. Curing begins in dry salt with saltpetre and sugar but, after an unspecified time, the hams are removed and placed in a marinade of molasses and spices, after which they are hung to mature. The process from fresh meat to fully matured ham takes 5–6 months.

REGION OF PRODUCTION:

SOUTH WEST ENGLAND, WILTSHIRE.

Brawn

DESCRIPTION:

SMALL PIECES OF BRINED PORK, USUALLY FROM THE HEAD AND SHOULDER, SET IN A JELLY. IN APPEARANCE, IT IS A TRANSLUCENT, PALE GOLD-BROWN WITH PIECES OF PALE MEAT AND SOMETIMES CHOPPED HERBS; THE MEAT IS BRINED AND FINELY SHREDDED FOR SOME VERSIONS, GIVING AN OPAQUE, PINK APPEARANCE; IN THE NORTH-EAST, BRAWN IS COLOURED A BRIGHT ORANGE-RED. BRAWN SHOULD BE HIGHLY FLAVOURED; SAGE AND BLACK PEPPER ARE FAVOURITE SEASONINGS.

HISTORY:

One element of the history of brawn is constant right down to the present day and this is not the composition of the dish itself but the habit of serving it with mustard. 'Furst set forth the mustard and brawne of boore ye wild swyne,' instructed the *Boke of Nurture* in 1460.

'Good bread and good drinke,
a good fier in the hall,
brawne, pudding and souse,
and good mustard withall'

was Thomas Tusser's (1573) prescription for a husbandman's Christmas. Later recipes for brawn sauce made of mustard, sugar and vinegar abound (e.g. Dallas, 1877).

Brawn originally meant muscle or meat of any description; by the fifteenth century the word was particularly, although not exclusively, associated with the flesh of wild boar. The Tudor physician Thomas Cogan stated that the flesh of wild swine was better for you than any tame animal and that brawn, which is the flesh 'of a boare long fedde in the stie,' was difficult of digestion. He counselled that it should be eaten at the start of a meal – advice that seems to have been followed, even if unconsciously, unto the present day (O'Hara May, 1977). Because the word applied exclusively to flesh or muscle meat, it followed that brawn developed the restricted meaning of the boned flesh, fat and skin, as opposed to the whole joint, bone-in. The way such a floppy joint was best dealt with was that it would be collared. It would be rolled up tight, wrapped in cloth and tied round [collared] with tape or string before boiling. Collaring was normally done to sides of pig, rather than hams. In the sixteenth-century accounts of the Star Chamber brawn appears almost monotonously as collars or rounds. Martha Bradley (1756) has instructions on choosing brawn. Her definition of the word was meat that came from an uncastrated boar (not necessarily wild). The best was from a young animal: old boar was too tough and the rind too thick, meat from a sow too soft. Her namesake, Richard Bradley, writing 20 years earlier (1736), disagreed. His brawn was the collared flitches of 'an old boar, for the older he is, the more horny will the brawn be'. He thought brawn rather insipid; horny was probably a good thing.

A collar was a convenient package that could be cooked and sliced. The method was also a way of preserving unwieldy and quick-spoiling food, in other words, pickling. Collared meats (and fish) were usually brined and spiced, boiled, pressed and sliced. Brawn came to mean almost exclusively pork cooked in this manner. If the meat was pressed and cooled in its liquor, it would indeed begin to look like the jellied brawn we have today.

Whereas at the outset brawn applied to most parts of the pig apart from the valuable hams, by the 1800s, in the southern part of England, it had come to mean a dish based on pigs' heads, collared. This appears under the title 'Tonbridge Brawn' in Eliza Acton (1845). As the head was the boniest (and least vendible) part of the animal, it was a natural candidate for collaring and repackaging, leaving the rest for bacon, ham or roasting joints. A dish that was also common in Georgian recipe books was 'mock brawn': a flank of pork rolled around morsels from calves' feet and pig's head, cooked, pressed and cooled. Gradually, as brawn was relegated to a dish of the poor and country people who killed their own pigs, the dish was simplified into a highly seasoned, moulded, meat jelly containing small pieces of pork.

Pork cheese, once commonly termed head cheese, is a similar dish made from finely minced meat rather than chopped scraps. In some regions, especially the North, brawn-type dishes are made from beef.

Brawn is still widely made, and is a profitable by-product of pork butchery. It is a component of salad lunches and still eaten with mustard or strong condiments. Although it may be found in many parts of the country, it is most often sold in the South West, where a number of relics of a once important industry survive, such as Bath chaps, chitterlings and the like.

TECHNIQUE:

The meat for brawn, usually pigs' heads, is cleaned thoroughly and brined for a few hours. It is boiled with seasonings, bones and feet until very well cooked. The mixture is strained, the meat picked off the bones and placed in moulds, the stock reduced and poured over, and the whole allowed to set. Where a colour is given to the brawn, suppliers would once have offered 'Indian Red' colouring agent.

REGION OF PRODUCTION:

SOUTH WEST ENGLAND.

Cornish Pasty

DESCRIPTION:

A BAKED PASTY WITH MANY DIFFERENT FILLINGS WHICH ARE INVARIABLY RAW WHEN THE PASTY IS MADE UP. THE SHAPE IS A POINTED OVAL, WITH A SEAM OF CRIMPED PASTRY RUNNING THE LENGTH OF THE PASTY ABOUT ONE-THIRD OF THE WAY IN FROM THE EDGE. INDIVIDUAL VERSIONS VARY IN THEIR FORMS; INDUSTRIALLY PRODUCED ONES ARE MORE LIKELY TO BE SEMI-CIRCULAR. A MEAN SIZE MIGHT BE 20CM LONG, 10CM WIDE, AND 4CM DEEP, WEIGHING 330G. COLOUR: GOLDEN PASTRY (EGG-WASHED). FLAVOUR: BEEF AND POTATO PREDOMINATE.

HISTORY:

'A bit of pastry is everything to a Cornish household. I can remember the sense of shock when I visited my up-country in-laws for the first time and neither they nor their five daughters had a rolling pin' (Merrick, 1990).

Pasty is an old English word for a pie of venison or other meat baked without a dish (*OED*). Samuel Pepys consumed great numbers of them, as his diary relates. However, the use of the word declined in a large part of England and the only region where it survives is that stronghold of pastry, the South West, especially Cornwall. Here, the form settled into a fixed type: a pie that was food for the working man and his family. Spicer (1948), collecting regional recipes in the 1940s, remarked that pasties were originally baked on an iron plate set on the hearth, covered with an iron bowl, with ashes and embers heaped around. The Cornish were part of the English highland tradition which used a bakestone and pot-oven rather than the masonry or brick oven of champion country. Under the dialect name fuggan, references to pasties can be traced back to the mid-nineteenth century (Wright, 1896–1905), defined as 'an old Cornish dish... which is a pasty of very thick crust filled with potatoes'.

Tradition states that such food was the portable midday meal of miners and farm labourers, and that the Cornish will put anything in a pasty – meat, fish, bacon, cheese, vegetables, eggs or, in times of dearth, wild herbs. Potatoes, onions, leeks and turnips are allowed, but carrots are not customary; nor is minced, as opposed to chopped, meat. Fishermen, ideal beneficiaries of the convenience of the pasty, in fact eschew it. It is thought bad luck to bring one on a boat (Merrick, 1990). Pasties were often made too large to consume at a single sitting, and their ingredients were varied according to individual preference. Cooks would therefore mark each pasty with the initials of each intended recipient so that they could take up the relic they left off, and avoid a nasty surprise at the first bite.

The pasty's success has been contagious since World War II. There are manufacturers everywhere. This may lead to variations, for example Priddy Oggie, sometimes quoted as a long-standing regional dish, is a pork-filled pasty with a cheese pastry which was invented in the late 1960s in Somerset.

TECHNIQUE:

A shortcrust pastry is usual, although some makers prefer something very like puff. This is rolled and cut to a circle 20cm across. A mixture of roughly equal quantities of raw, chopped beef steak and thinly sliced, raw potato, plus half as much chopped onion and turnip is well seasoned with salt and pepper. The filling is placed on one side of the pastry, the edge brushed with egg and excess pastry folded over to enclose it. The edge is crimped to seal, the outside egg-washed. It is baked at 200°C for 20 minutes, then 180°C for 40 more.

REGION OF PRODUCTION:
SOUTH WEST ENGLAND.

COMPARE WITH:
Forfar Bridie, Scotland (p. 310); Bedforshire Clanger, South England (p. 67)

Devon Cattle

DESCRIPTION:
DRESSED CARCASS WEIGHT FOR STEERS AGED 500 DAYS IS 190–300KG; FOR HEIFERS, 160–300KG. THE DEVON IS A FAIRLY LONG ANIMAL. THE FLESH IS FINELY GRAINED, WELL-MARBLED AND TENDER, WITH AN EXCELLENT FLAVOUR.

HISTORY:
These cattle, which gain two alternative names, Red Devon or Ruby Red, from their dark, red-brown pelts, are traditional to Exmoor – hence a third, North Devons. Even in the Domesday Book (1086), the density of cattle recorded in north-west Devon was exceptional. This may hint, perhaps, at the emergence of a distinctive breed, although the first known mention of red cattle in the West Country was in correspondence of the late sixteenth century.

In the eighteenth century, detailed descriptions of Devon cattle were given by several agricul-turists. By this time the breed was improved to produce a stronger animal for heavy draught work. The foundations for these changes were laid by the Quartly family, who had acquired a farm on Exmoor. Comment thereafter stresses both the docility of the cattle and the quality of the beef. The Breed Society was formed in the late nineteenth century.

There is another Devon breed, the South Devon, which is recognized as distinct; it is a dual-purpose cow which provides excellent rich milk and good beef. Although coming from the same original strain, it is a heavier beast than the Ruby Red. It is touched upon in the entry for Channel Island milk, below, p.52.

TECHNIQUE:

The Red Devon cattle of Exmoor, where the breed was developed, are on the small side; this is because they were expected to fatten on sparse moorland pasture which is susceptible to trampling into mud (the rainfall is very high) and responds well to the lightness of the Red Devons' feet. Exmoor is now an Environmentally Sensitive Area. Breeders on the lower, lush-er pastures of Somerset selected for larger cattle.

Recently, new blood from the French Saler breed (known sometimes as French Devons) has been used to improve conformation, particularly the quantity of fat carried on the brisket and at the top of the tail. The two strains have been interbred in the past, the Devon con-tributing genes to the Salers in the 1800s.

Animals destined for beef are slaughtered from the age of 18 months. Some butchers pre-fer an older animal, of about 3 years. Older cattle were favoured for beef production in Britain in the past, but in previous centuries they worked as draught animals for some years prior to slaughter. At present, the returns for keeping cattle at pasture longer than absolutely necessary are low. Devons are cross-bred with various dairy cattle including Friesians, whose offspring are known as black steers or heifers.

REGION OF PRODUCTION:

SOUTH WEST ENGLAND, DEVON.

Devonshire Ham

DESCRIPTION:

A SMOKED OR UNSMOKED CURED HAM FOR COOKING. WEIGHT: 3.5–5.5KG. FORM: HAMS MADE IN DEVON WERE LONG-CUT; THE CURRENT MAKER TRIMS THE BROAD ENDS OF THE HAMS FOLLOWING A NATURAL CURVE IN THE MEAT, AND REMOVES THE SKIN, EXCEPT AT THE KNUCKLE END WHERE IT IS CUT INTO A ZIG-ZAG PATTERN IN A STYLE KNOWN AS FLORENTINE. COLOUR: WHITE FAT, DEEP ROSE LEAN. FLAVOUR: A SUCCULENT TEXTURE AND CLEAN, PURE HAM FLAVOUR, WITH A LIGHT, FRAGRANT OAK SMOKE.

HISTORY:

Devonshire hams have been known for well over 150 years, and there is evidence that a par-ticular ham cure existed in the area for a century before that. White (1932) quotes a Devon recipe for salting hams from the 1700s. Mrs Beeton (1861) gives a recipe for bacon or hams the Devonshire way, which shows the cure to have begun with dry-salting for 2 days, followed by brining in a pickle based on salt and sugar in proportions roughly 2:1. The hams were smoked for keeping and the pickle boiled and fortified with more salt and some black treacle before re-use. Anne Petch, the most prominent maker of hams currently working in this area, remarks that sugar or treacle in the cure helped to act as preservative and flavouring before saltpetre was available in a reliable form; it also counteracted the effects on flavour and texture which large quantities of salt had on the ham. *Law's Grocer's Manual* (*c.*1895) mentions that 'Devonshire long cut hams – smoked or pale dried, and produced in the district round Plymouth – are also highly popular.' By the 1930s, the Devonshire cure, whilst remaining a brine cure, had lost much of its sweetness. A recipe collected from a farmer's wife between the world wars requires only a little treacle added to a salt and water brine.

TECHNIQUE:
Devonshire's rural economy places emphasis on dairy products, apple orchards, and pig-rearing. The climate is damp and mild and, consequently, the local ham cure is brine-based. The hams now made in Devon are by a producer who uses English breeds of pig, and oversees the entire process from raising the animal to marketing. The animals are farmed extensively, on open pasture, finished with a mixed grain feed of barley and wheat, and slaughtered at 6–7 months. After cutting from the carcass, the hams are trimmed, then brined for 12 days in a 60 per cent brine. They are smoked, if required, in cold smoke from oak, plus a little beech. The hams are aged for 3–4 weeks. They may be dispatched raw, boiled plain, or cooked with cider and spices, a local method.

REGION OF PRODUCTION:
SOUTH WEST ENGLAND, DEVON.

Dorset Horn Sheep

DESCRIPTION:
DRESSED CARCASS WEIGHT ABOUT 18–19KG.

HISTORY:
The Dorset Horn is indeed a Dorset sheep. This sparsely populated area, dominated by rolling chalk hills, has a long connection with the beast. The breed may have evolved from the now-rare Portland, a relic of the old tan-faced primitives once widely known in Britain and centred in the South West (Hall & Clutton-Brock, 1989). Further details are mysterious, although the influence of Merino blood is postulated. For a long time, the Dorset has been favoured for its extended breeding season. This was exploited to provide out-of-season lamb. In the mid-1700s, a manual of husbandry described the production of 'Dorset House Lambs' in Essex during late autumn for the London Christmas market. Such meat was associated with status; William Kitchiner (1817) remarked, 'House lamb is ... prized merely because it is unseasonable and expensive,' and Mrs Beeton (1861) commented on the system of intensive rearing pursued 'to please the appetite of luxury'. A flock book was established in 1892 and the breed has continued to be valued. The intensive rearing system was abandoned before the First World War, but the Dorset Horn and the relatively new Polled Dorset are still used to provide young, new-season's lamb.

TECHNIQUE:
Lambing time can be adjusted to the demands of the market. The ewes breed from a young age and are excellent milkers. On mixed farms where lamb is just one part of the business,

'Methinks sometimes I have no more wit than a Christian or an ordinary man has; but I am a great eater of beef, and I believe that does harm to my wit.'

WILLIAM SHAKESPEARE, *TWELFTH NIGHT*

farmers tend to concentrate on producing meat for Christmas and New Year and then through to Easter. The lambs are born between mid-September and November; the flocks may be housed at lambing for ease of management and protection from predators. Shelter is otherwise unnecessary. Soon after lambing, the flocks are turned out to graze on the flush of autumn grass which follows hay- and silage-making. Sheep farmers who keep Dorset Horns produce 3 crops of lambs every 2 years.

REGION OF PRODUCTION:
SOUTH WEST ENGLAND.

Gloucestershire Old Spots Pig

DESCRIPTION:
USUALLY SLAUGHTERED TO YIELD A PORKER OF 50–55KG AFTER DRESSING; IT IS A DUAL-PURPOSE ANIMAL WHICH CAN, IF DESIRED, BE GROWN TO REACH BACON WEIGHT. IT IS CHARACTERIZED BY LARGE, IRREGULAR BLACK SPOTS ON THE SKIN WHICH LEAVE MARKS AFTER THE BRISTLES HAVE BEEN REMOVED; OTHERWISE, THE MEAT IS DEEP PINK, WELL-MARBLED, WITH WHITE FAT AND A PALE SKIN. FLESH IS TENDER, SUCCULENT, WITH AN EXCELLENT FLAVOUR. HERE IS PIG WHICH MAKES EXCELLENT CRACKLING.

HISTORY:
The breed developed in response to farming conditions of the 1800s which required a hardy animal that could flourish on a varied diet. The Severn Valley in which the race evolved is a cheese and cider region and excess whey and windfall apples formed part of its diet, as well as household and garden waste. It is sometimes referred to as an orchard pig, because of where it prospered. Gloucestershire Old Spots were first noted in the early twentieth century, when the Breed Society was formed. It was then talked of as an ancient breed and the word 'Old' has always been part of the name, implying a long history. A Gloucester pig was noted in the 1850s but was described as white with large wattles. It is possible the breed arose from these Gloucesters crossed with Saddle-backs or unimproved Berkshires, black animals whose genes may have contributed the spots.

A drive towards home production of bacon by the British government in the 1930s led to a decline in numbers of Old Spots. It is slower maturing than improved animals and the spots were disliked. A trend towards leaner meat also worked against its use for pork. Breeders have eliminated all but a token spot. In the 1970s, renewed interest in rare breeds led to conservation of breeding stocks and reintroduction of old strains to modern farming and the food chain. This has been quite successful with Gloucestershire Old Spots.

TECHNIQUE:
The breed has a strong following in the Severn valley and environs. It is popular with hobby farmers who keep a few animals. The blotched skin is currently thought less of a problem and the spots have been bred back in. The pigs now resemble those known earlier last century. It is still used to forage apple and pear orchards by some farmers; whey, generated by West-Country cheese-making, is also available. These are supplemented with grain-based rations; the pigs may also be turned out to feed on residues of arable crops or on specially grown forage crops. It is still renowned as hardy, requiring minimal accommodation. The

sows are good mothers. The breed is slow to mature, reaching a weight for slaughter as pork at 18–22 weeks.

REGION OF PRODUCTION:
SOUTH WEST ENGLAND.

Gloucester Sausage

DESCRIPTION:
UNCOOKED, FRESH PORK SAUSAGE, WEIGHING 75–100G – LARGER THAN OTHER FRESH SAUSAGES; PALE PINK; SHORT LINKS; GOOD, RICH FLAVOUR, WITH HERBS.

HISTORY:
Many Gloucester butchers include 'Gloster sausages' in their display. No early references have been located, but oral tradition is that they have been made for as long as anyone can remember. One factor in their excellence is the distinctive pig, Gloucestershire Old Spots. This produces fine fresh pork, hence also sausages. In a letter dated 1766, the Georgian man of fashion, Gilly Williams, wrote to his friend George Selwyn anticipating a meeting near the city. 'We shall eat Gloucester chine together,' he mused. Here, at least, there is a conjunction of Gloucester and pork that goes back a while.

TECHNIQUE:
Gloucestershire Old Spots are raised extensively on grain, dairy by-products and windfall apples, resulting in succulent, well-flavoured meat with good marbling, excellent for sausage making. The Gloucester recipe is not exceptional, using minced lean and fat pork, plus cereal (in the form of rusk) and a seasoning of herbs, salt and pepper. They are filled into natural casings.

REGION OF PRODUCTION:
WEST ENGLAND, GLOUCESTER.

Hog's Pudding

DESCRIPTION:
A COOKED PORK AND CEREAL SAUSAGE; ABOUT 3 CM DIAMETER AND OF VARYING LENGTHS. COLOUR: A GREYISH-WHITE OR MOTTLED PINK AND WHITE; IN SOME TYPES THE CEREAL CAN BE SEEN AS WHOLE GRAINS. FLAVOUR: A BLAND COMBINATION OF PORK AND CEREAL, OVERLAID BY THE SPICES FAVOURED BY THE MAKER; SOME CONTAIN DRIED FRUIT.

HISTORY:
The first specific reference to hog's pudding in the *Oxford English Dictionary* is from the early eighteenth century. However, the word hog (used in English to mean a bacon pig since at least the fourteenth century), combined with recipes including spices and currants in a savoury dish, suggests the tradition is far older, with roots in medieval practice. White puddings of cereal, spices and dried fruit were known in the 1500s, and were probably made throughout southern England. Much later, Flora Thompson (1939) describes how the country dwellers of Oxfordshire used the various parts of a pig when it was killed in the winter months – hog's puddings bulked large.

Recipes varied; often they would have formerly included lights and spleen. Others emphasize the cereal content: a quotation from Hampshire (Wright, 1896–1905) describes it as 'the entrail of a pig stuffed with pudding composed of flour, currants and spice'. A late Victorian recipe from Sussex describes hog's puddings as small ball-like sausages, stuffed with pork, flour, spices and currants (White, 1932). Modern puddings have evolved from these heavily cereal-based, sweetish products. Although some containing fruit are still made, other examples are closer to a sausage, with groats (hulled, crushed cereal grains), lean pork and savoury spices, especially black pepper. In the past, they were used for any meal but now tend to be served at breakfast. The customary method of reheating was in simmering water, but they can be baked, fried or grilled.

TECHNIQUE:
Groats are soaked and cooked until soft, then mixed with minced pork, dried fruit and seasonings. This is filled into wide casings and tied in rings which are blanched in simmering water, just enough to cook the sausage through.

REGION OF PRODUCTION:
SOUTH ENGLAND, ESPECIALLY SOUTH WEST.

Mendip Wallfish

DESCRIPTION:
'WALLFISH' IS A SOMERSET NAME FOR SNAILS. THE GARDEN SNAIL IS THE COMMONEST VARIETY; IT HAS A BROWNISH-OCHRE SHELL, ABOUT 3.5CM DIAMETER.

HISTORY:
The use of snails as food is generally regarded by the British as curious and outlandish – more specifically, French. Evidence for their consumption in the past is patchy. Recipes used snails medicinally, to ease chest ailments. They are often found in early books of household remedies. A handful of culinary recipes were given by John Nott (1726). Roy Groves, who developed methods for the indoor farming of snails during the 1980s, states there is some oral evidence for snail eating in areas such as the North-East of England, where glass-blowing was an occupation. Snails reputedly have a beneficial effect on the respiratory system. Oral tradition also states that 'wallfish' are part of the diet in the West Country, particularly in the area around the Mendips. Here, for about 50 years, the Miner's Arms (a pub and restaurant) at Priddy, has served snails as a house speciality.

Both the Roman snail (*Helix pomatia*) and the smaller garden snail (*Helix aspersa*) are found wild in Britain. *Law's Grocer's Manual* (c. 1895) remarked that both species were collected in England for the Paris market. Recent initiatives in agricultural diversification have also led to the foundation of a snail-farming industry with several producers of *Helix aspersa* in the Somerset area. Another species which is farmed is the African land snail.

TECHNIQUE:
Snails are collected from the wild in Somerset, but rarely reach the market, being consumed at home or sold to restaurants. The snails are collected in the autumn, and a proportion are frozen for use throughout the winter at the Miner's Arms. Snail farming is carried out at several locations, including at least one where the snails are reared outdoors in poly-tunnels. These enclose forage crops such as stubble turnips, to provide cover and help retain moisture. The snails take approximately a year to become fully grown. During winter they hibernate, when they are kept

in boxes in barns, safe from predators. They are collected as required and sold alive.

REGION OF PRODUCTION:
SOUTH WEST ENGLAND, SOMERSET.

Wiltshire Bacon

DESCRIPTION:
SMOKED OR UNSMOKED CURED PORK FOR COOKING; A SIDE WEIGHS 29–31KG; THIS REPRE-
SENTS HALF A PIG, TRIMMED AND CURED. COLOUR: DEEP ROSE-PINK LEAN, WHITE FAT.
FLAVOUR: A MILD CURE.

HISTORY:
A reference dated 1794 which mentions the 'old' Wiltshire bacon, implies the area had been long known for this product (*OED*). The trade was based on both pigs native to the region and imported ones from Ireland which were driven across the county on their way to London markets. Mrs Beeton (1861) states the Wiltshire cure used dry salt and coarse sugar, the flitches lying in the pickle for a month before being hung to dry. One of the largest bacon curing companies in Britain, Harris of Calne, was started by a local butcher who took advantage of the herds of pigs passing his doorstep. In the mid-nineteenth century, the company began to use ice to chill the premises in the summer, an innovation allowing production the year round and the amount of salt in the cure to be reduced, making for sweeter, milder bacon. About this time a switch from dry to brine curing took place, to give the modern form of the cure, now practised in many areas outside its place of origin.

The bacon was sold after drying (when it was called green bacon in the South, and pale dried bacon in the north of England). If smoking took place, it was carried out by the wholesaler or retailer to suit their market. The south of the country showed a preference for smoked bacon. Large quantities of bacon are now imported into Britain. Until their Calne factory closed, Harris still produced Wiltshire bacon in its home region, but now there are only 2 commercial curers left in the area.

It should be noted that some bacon experts, for instance William Hogan (1978), use the term Wiltshire to refer to a cut as well as the cure. In this case it indicates half a pig, with the ham left on and the ribs intact but the blade bone removed.

TECHNIQUE:
A local manufacturer uses pigs reared on his own farm, fed on home-grown wheat and whey from the cheese industry in neighbouring Somerset. After cutting, the sides are immersed in a salt, saltpetre and water brine for 4–5 days. They are then stacked and drained for 14 days. The bacon may be smoked over hardwood sawdust. It is dispatched whole, in smaller joints, or sliced into rashers.

REGION OF PRODUCTION:
SOUTH WEST ENGLAND, WILTSHIRE.

COMPARE WITH:
Suffolk Sweet-Cured Bacon, East Anglia (p. 128); Ayrshire Bacon, Scotland (p. 306); Welsh Bacon, Wales (p. 190).

Apple Cake

DESCRIPTION:

APPLE CAKE, SOMETIMES CALLED APPLE PUDDING, AND OFTEN GIVEN A COUNTY PREFIX DEPENDING ON THE PLACE OF ITS MAKING, IS USUALLY OBLONG OR SQUARE, BAKED IN A TRAY. ITS FLAVOUR PLAYS ON SWEET–ACID BALANCE, WHICH DEPENDS ON VARIETY OF APPLE USED: COOKING APPLES GIVE A MOISTER CAKE WITH AN ACID NOTE, DESSERT APPLES SWEETER AND MORE AROMATIC.

HISTORY:

Several modern recipes are found. They vary in concept; one from Cornwall is similar to a French *tarte Tatin*; one from Cambridgeshire appears related to German *Streusel*. However, a distinctively English version does exist in the South West, especially Dorset, Devon and Somerset. Here, raw apples are added to a plain cake at the outset, as if they were raisins or currants in a fruit cake. Apples have always been added to various cakes and puddings in apple country, but little documentary evidence survives. An example is a farmhouse recipe from Somerset (Webb, *c.* 1930). One from Dorset, 'one of the most famous of all English tea cakes', is in Spicer (1949). A modern collection asserts that Dorset apple cake is distinguished from others by being baked in separate tins before being sandwiched with butter (Raffael, 1997).

While popular in domestic circles and often made for sale in cafés, it can also be found in many craft bakeries in the region.

TECHNIQUE:

Apple cakes from the South West have minor variations in detail, such as addition of dried fruit and candied peel in a recipe from Dorset. They call for apples, flour, butter and caster sugar in the proportions 4:2:1:1. Chemical leavening is used. The apples (sour cooking apples are generally required, although some prefer eating apples because they are drier) are peeled, cored and sliced into segments. The butter is rubbed into the flour until the mixture resembles fine breadcrumbs. The sugar is stirred in, followed by sliced raw apple, and dried fruit and spices if required; the mixture is bound with egg and milk. It is scaled off into greased tins. The surface is levelled and sprinkled with granulated sugar. Baking takes 1 hour at 180°C.

REGION OF PRODUCTION:

SOUTH WEST ENGLAND.

Bath Bun

DESCRIPTION:

A CIRCULAR BUN WITH NIB SUGAR ON THE TOP AND A HIGHLY GLAZED SURFACE; DIAMETER 60–70MM, DEPTH 50MM. WEIGHT: ABOUT 75G. COLOUR: GOLDEN BROWN WITH SHINY GLAZE, SPRINKLED WITH CURRANTS AND SUGAR. FLAVOUR AND TEXTURE: LIGHTLY SPICED AND SWEETENED, CLOSE TEXTURED, WITH LUMP SUGAR UNDERNEATH.

HISTORY:

Bath has long been an important pleasure and health resort. Bath buns are one of several distinctive foods which became famous as the town grew during the eighteenth century. The Bath cook and author Martha Bradley (1756) gave a recipe for a Bath seed cake which

appears different to other seed cakes in its use of wine and rose water. This instruction came, in fact, from Bradley's lengthy quotation of an earlier household manuscript, possibly dating from the seventeenth century. Elizabeth Raffald (1769) tells how to cook 'Bath Cakes', which are caraway (seed) cakes shaped into buns. The light, yeast-leavened rolls were enriched with cream and butter, but no eggs. Some caraway comfits were worked into the dough and more were strewn over the top. This recipe is repeated in Farley (1783) – a work largely derivative of Raffald – and Henderson (c. 1790), a work largely derivative of Farley. When Henderson was re-edited by J.C. Schnebbelie (1804) the title of the recipe was transformed to 'Bath Cakes or Buns'. While Raffald sent her cakes in 'hot for breakfast', Farley, Henderson and Schnebbelie suggested they be eaten at either breakfast or tea. A cookery book produced in the Midlands in 1807 calls them Bath buns (Simon, 1960). The proportions are very similar to those in Raffald, except some of the cream is replaced by egg. It, too, deploys caraway, a defining ingredient in these early recipes.

That Bath buns were not universal in the city during the Georgian era may be inferred from the letters of a visitor who never stinted his descriptions of food and drink. John Penrose wrote in 1766 (Penrose, 1983): '…with our Tea Cambridge-Cakes buttered. We have had these too ourselves. They are round thick Cakes, a penny apiece, hardly an Ounce weight; look like Dow [dough], all white and soft: these we toast a little by the fire, just to warm them through, and then butter them; they eat exceedingly well.' Were his Cambridge cakes the forerunners of Bath buns? Jane Austen refers to 'disordering her stomach with Bath bunns' in a letter of 1801 (Austen, 1995).

Meg Dods (1826) included recipes for both Bath cake and Bath buns in her description of English specialities. She likened the dough to the French *brioche* (it included eggs and butter) and suggested caraway seeds for the cake and caraway comfits (sugar-coated) for the buns. Neither cake nor buns were described in the Victorian cookery bibles of Eliza Acton and Isabella Beeton, although the buns occur in Mrs Marshall (1887), retaining their spicing with caraway. The nineteenth century, however, does seem to be the period when Bath buns underwent considerable change and normalization, losing for the most part their distinctive caraway flavour and gaining the now-accepted adornment of nib sugar as well as candied peel or grated citrus zest and dried fruit.

The defining moment appears to have been the Great Exhibition of 1851. The catering contractors served Bath buns in their tens of thousands (David, 1977). This led to the development of a 'Cheap Bath or London bun' described by Kirkland (1907) which was little more than a bun with eggs, orange peel, sultanas and a final ornament of nib sugar. The fat used was lard.

The general move away from caraway is confirmed by Dallas (1877), who suggests a plain brioche dough for Bath buns and Skuse (1892), who advises lemon zest.

In the town of Bath, buns made from a recipe adapted from one dated 1679 are still available. It was used by James Cobb, who founded his bakery in 1866. It does not deploy caraway, except in a residual addition of a pinch of mixed ground spice. The firm of Cobb's continued to trade until the late 1980s, when the business and recipe were acquired by Mountstevens Ltd, who continue to make the buns and have several shops in Bath itself. Beyond the town, it is largely the 'cheap or London' variety that is produced.

T he sun is shining at Stroud Farmers Market. It is shining on four fruit and vegetable stalls, three of them organic, piled high with broad beans; tufted carrots; young beetroot complete with emerald tops; red-skinned potatoes, white-skinned potatoes, yellow potatoes, potatoes blotched pink and white, with their names scrawled on bits of cardboard – Pink Fir Apple, Desiree, Pentland Javelin, Charlotte, Duke of York; shaggy, multifarious salad leaves; onions and shallots; crisp cabbages. It is shining on boxes of white cherries, Merton Glory, blushed down one side, and others of gooseberries as green as opals. It is shining on seven meat stalls, among them offering Gloucester Old Spot and Tamworth pork, Gloucester Long Horn and Hereford beef, Cotswold lamb, free-range chickens from Chepstow and Aylesbury ducklings, and game – rabbit as well as fallow and muntjack venison from the countryside about. It shines on two bread stalls, two cake stalls, two stalls selling apple juice, perry and cider; another with fresh trout, trout pâté and watercress; and on three cheese stalls, one of which has sheeps' milk cheeses coated in ash stacked up like so many small square turrets.

I lurch away up, laden with a couple of chickens from Chepstow, belly pork from Minchinhampton, green back rashers from Dursley, a kilo of carrots from Highrove, kale tops from Wotten, a bag of cherries, a large lump of extra mature Double Gloucester and a Dublin loaf from the WI stall. Second helpings anybody?

Matthew Fort

COOKERY WRITER AND BROADCASTER

The recipe used by Cobb's was quoted by Grigson (1984). Strong white flour, eggs, butter and crushed lump sugar are used, roughly in the proportions 3:2:1:1, and to the following method. A ferment of yeast, sugar and water is allowed to work for 10 minutes and then eggs and a little flour are added; this is covered and left for about an hour. The ferment is kneaded with the remaining flour, butter, crushed lump sugar, and a little additional granulated sugar, plus small quantities of lemon juice and mixed spice. It is left to rise, then knocked back and shaped and proved. The buns are baked for 20 minutes at 220°C, glazed with sugar syrup and sprinkled with crushed sugar lumps.

REGION OF PRODUCTION:
SOUTH WEST ENGLAND, BATH (SOMERSET).

Bath Oliver

DESCRIPTION:
A ROUND BISCUIT, 75MM DIAMETER, 3MM THICK. WEIGHT: 10G. COLOUR: PALE CREAM. FLAVOUR AND TEXTURE: NEUTRAL, SLIGHTLY SALTY; VERY CRISP. A CHOCOLATE-COATED VERSION IS MADE, KNOWN AS A CHOCOLATE OLIVER, 40MM DIAMETER, WITH A THICK COATING OF BITTER CHOCOLATE.

HISTORY:
Bath Olivers are named for William Oliver, a doctor who was born in Penzance in 1695. He lived most of his life in Bath and was the city's most important practitioner during the time of its greatest expansion. The accepted account is that Dr Oliver created a recipe for thin, palatable, easily digested biscuits, to be eaten by those who came to Bath to take the waters and recover from excessively rich diets. The story continues that Dr Oliver set up his coachman as a baker; providing some premises, 10 bags of flour, £100 and the recipe. This recipe passed by a sort of apostolic succession from Atkins, the original coachman, to Norris, to Carter, to Munday, to Ashman, until it finally came into the possession of Cater, Stoffell & Fortt, who had a shop in Bath until the mid-1960s. The biscuits were always known as Dr Oliver's, then, when in the hands of Fortt, as Original Bath Olivers. Olivers or Bath Olivers were quite possibly a similar biscuit, but not produced by those with the sacred recipe. Nor did they have the distinctive packaging and stamp of the good doctor's head. Although today they come in paper packets with the familiar livery, for many decades they were sold in tall tins.

Although there is this apparently cogent account of an early origin for the biscuits, the earliest reference so far discovered to Olivers is given by Maria Rundell (1807), herself a resident of the city; she gives a recipe which shows them to have been a plain yeast-leavened biscuit. Similar recipes, for example one for 'Bath biscuits' in *The Family Cookery Book* (1812) can be found from the same period.

Law's Grocer's Manual (*c.* 1895) commented that there were several makers of Bath Olivers, and John Kirkland (1907) noted the biscuits were a speciality 'still made in great quantities in Bath, and in which some of the leading houses take great pride'. He observes that there was considerable diversity in the recipes and methods of manufacture, and that the biscuits should be very thin and rich, made with butter only. These statements confirm the biscuits were not as exclusive as legend instructs and cast some doubt on the notion that they were an early version of a health food.

The modern biscuits, still manufactured under the name of Fortt's Original Bath Olivers, but no longer owned by Cater, Stoffell & Fortt, are probably rather different to those known at the beginning of the last century. Various sources agree that they required great care, and possessed distinctive characteristics: they wanted a well-leavened dough, thorough kneading, and were dried in a warm cupboard for 30 minutes, then baked in a slack (cool) oven (Simon, 1960); a special bowed rolling pin was used, so that the biscuits were thinner in the middle than at the edge; there was a singular method for docking (pricking) the dough which required 2 biscuits placed faces together, pricked, and pulled apart again; they should burn a little in the middle during baking 'which is correct for a good Oliver' (Law, *c.* 1895).

The chocolate-coated version has been made since at least the 1960s.

TECHNIQUE:
The recipe used for Fortt's Bath Olivers is a trade secret; the ingredient list shows the biscuits are still yeast-leavened and contain butter; other ingredients are wheat flour, milk, animal fat, salt, malt extract, hops, and an antioxidant (E320). A commercial recipe for craft bakers calls for flour and butter in the ratio 4:1. The flour and butter are rubbed together and made into a stiff dough with milk in which a little sugar and yeast have been dissolved; a little salt is added. They rise for 90 minutes; the dough is kneaded with a brake until smooth; it is rested before being rolled to a thickness of about 3mm and cut into rounds of the appropriate size; these are docked and allowed to rest. They are baked at 190°C until gold and crisp.

REGION OF PRODUCTION:
SOUTH ENGLAND, FORMERLY BATH (SOMERSET).

Blueberry Pie (Double-Crust Fruit Pie)

DESCRIPTION:
DOUBLE-CRUST PIES MADE WITH SHORT-CRUST PASTRY AND A FRUIT FILLING ARE DISTINCT-IVELY BRITISH. DIMENSIONS, FLAVOUR AND APPEARANCE WILL DEPEND ENTIRELY ON THE MAKER: WHETHER LARGE OR INDIVIDUAL PIES, COOKED ON A PLATE OR IN A DEEP DISH, IN FOIL CASINGS, AND SO ON. A WIDE RANGE OF FRUITS MAY BE USED AS FILLING: THE COMMONEST ARE APPLE, ALONE OR COMBINED WITH SPICES, DRIED FRUIT OR BLACKBERRIES; OTHERS, ESPECIALLY RHUBARB, GOOSEBERRIES, PLUMS AND CHERRIES, ARE USED. IN THE NORTH, THIS IS SOME-TIMES MADE IN A THINNER VERSION CALLED A 'PLATE PIE', OR IT MAY BE MADE RELATIVELY DEEP AND A THIRD LAYER OF PASTRY ADDED BETWEEN 2 FRUIT LAYERS IN THE FILLING.

HISTORY:
Pies have long been a favourite dish in Britain. The word has been in the language since at least the start of the fourteenth century. There are many recipes and almost any edible item seems at one time or another, to have been put between 2 layers of pastry and baked in the oven. Sweet fruit pies have been known since at least the seventeenth century, when Murrell (1638) gave recipes for 'tarts' of pippins (apples) flavoured with spices, orange zest and rose water; tarts of gooseberries or cherries are also cited. These were similar to modern pies, requiring a double crust, with sugar scattered over the surface before baking.

Fillings varied according to availability of fruit. Apple was probably the most popular; cherries were used in Kent and Buckinghamshire (Mabey, 1978). The blueberry pies now available in Dorset come within this genus of dishes, although their fruit filling is of a more recent tradition, imported in fact from North America (Davidson, 1991). The bilberry (Vaccinium myrtillus) is a bush that grows on acid soils in northern Europe. In Scotland it is known as whinberry (because it grows amidst whin, or gorse) or blaeberry and in Ireland, and in North-East England it is also known as blaeberry (blae means blue). Whortleberries are closely related.

Florence White (1932) records bilberry pies in Yorkshire. Bilberries were available for anyone who cared to pick them in many heathland areas along the south coast, in Wales, the Pennines and in Scotland. Gathering bilberries from the wild is time-consuming and the preserve of enthusiasts; recently, interest in using them as a local speciality in hotels has been rekindled in mid-Wales.

TECHNIQUE:
Short-crust pastry is prepared from flour and fat in the ratio 2:1. Lard is the preferred fat, making a crisp pastry. A mixture of lard and butter is sometimes used to give more flavour whilst retaining the shortness. Fruit is prepared; a portion of pastry is rolled 5mm thick and used to line the pie dish; the fruit, sugar and any other flavourings are placed in this; another disc of pastry is used to cover the top, and the edges are sealed. The top may be sugared or decorated. Pies are baked at 220°C for 10–15 minutes, then at 180°C for 30 minutes.

REGION OF PRODUCTION:
SOUTH WEST ENGLAND, DORSET, THOUGH DOUBLE-CRUST PIE MADE WITH FRUIT OTHER THAN BLUEBERRIES IS PRODUCED NATIONWIDE.

Colston Bun

DESCRIPTION:
A ROUND BUN RING MARKED INTO 8 WEDGES; 140MM DIAMETER, 30–40MM DEEP. WEIGHT: ABOUT 250–300G. COLOUR: GOLDEN BROWN, WITH A GLAZED SURFACE, CREAM INTERIOR. FLAVOUR: SWEET, WITH LEMON AND SPICE.

HISTORY:

The Colston bun is a popular teabread in Bristol. It is said to have gained its name from Edward Colston (1636–1721), a merchant who made a fortune trading with the West Indies. He founded an almshouse and a school, now a charitable trust administered by the Society of Merchant Venturers. The connection between Colston and the bun is through this trust. Each November, to commemorate the grant of the Charter to the Merchant Venturers, a service is held in the Cathedral attended by the pupils of Colston School. After the service, they are given a small currant bun (called the ha'penny starver), a Colston bun, and a 10 pence piece (the modern British coin based on the old silver florin). Of the 2 buns, it is said the smaller is for the child to consume immediately, and the larger to be taken home to share among the family.

The marked divisions on the top of the bun suggests a connection with the old-fashioned enriched breads known as wigs or whigs (see Hawkshead wigs p. 232), which were also marked in sections. Variant names are Colston ring or ring bun. The ha'penny starver was made with the same dough. They are made today by most craft bakers in the city.

The recipe calls for flour and butter in the proportions 8:1. The yeast is set to work with sugar and flour in a little warm milk for about 30 minutes; in the meantime, the butter is rubbed into the flour, together with a little sweet spice (cinnamon, allspice and nutmeg), plus grated lemon rind and a little dried fruit and candied peel; then the yeast mixture is stirred in, plus enough warm milk to produce a coherent dough. After rising, shaping, proving and marking, the buns are baked at 220°C for 20–25 minutes. They are glazed with sugar syrup whilst still warm.

REGION OF PRODUCTION:
SOUTH WEST ENGLAND, BRISTOL.

Cornish Fairing

DESCRIPTION:
A ROUGHLY CIRCULAR BISCUIT, 50MM DIAMETER, 7MM THICK. WEIGHT: 20G. COLOUR: DARK BROWN WITH AN IRREGULAR, ROUGH SURFACE. FLAVOUR: SWEET, DISTINCTLY SPICY.

HISTORY:
A Cornish fairing is a ginger biscuit of a type long associated with fairs in the South West. Some speculate that the name fairing means a ring-shaped biscuit sold at a fair, but most authorities agree that it actually means objects (not necessarily edible) which could be bought at fairs and were popular as gifts. As we come home with a goldfish in a bowl and candy-floss, so our forebears returned with a little packet of goodies. Florence White (1932) quotes information from Cornwall that 'a proper and complete fairing' included gingerbread biscuits, lamb's tails (caraway dragées), candied angelica, almond comfits and macaroons. Early in the nineteenth century, the poet Keats mentioned the 'gingerbread wives' of Barnstaple (Devon). Recipes for Barnstaple Fair gingerbread are still to be found, even if the sweetmeat itself is no longer available. Almost every fair and festivity in Britain probably had some edible keepsake: in Nottingham it was the cock-on-a-stick, in Bath the gingerbread Valentines, and so on. In more cases than not, the memento was spiced bread, cake or biscuit – the consequence of the medieval love affair with spices. Just the same process can be seen across the water in continental Europe.

The history of the specific biscuits now called Cornish fairing is largely unrecorded. All that is known is that they have been made for many years by a baker's firm called Furniss, which was founded in 1886 in Truro.

TECHNIQUE:
Furniss's recipe is a trade secret. The ingredients include flour, syrup, sugar and shortening (a vegetable fat is now favoured), plus spices and a raising agent. The biscuits are cut with a wire cutter to give a rough surface. Published recipes have flour, butter and sugar in the proportions 2:1:1. The flour is combined with baking powder and bicarbonate of soda, spices – ginger, cinnamon, mixed spice and lemon zest – and granulated sugar. These are bound with a little Golden Syrup to form a coherent dough.

REGION OF PRODUCTION:
SOUTH WEST ENGLAND, CORNWALL.

Cornish Heavy Cake

DESCRIPTION:

HEAVY CAKE IS A FLAT PASTRY BAKED IN A ROUGH SQUARE ABOUT 10MM THICK, LIGHTLY SWEETENED, WITH CURRANTS IN THE DOUGH. IT HAS A DISTINCTIVE CRISS-CROSS PATTERN CUT IN THE TOP.

HISTORY:

The dialect name 'fuggan' is the one for which the earliest references have been found. It is given in Joseph Wright (1896–1905) attached to quotations dating from the mid-nineteenth century. At this time the word could indicate 3 or 4 different things. Sources agree that these were all based on a heavy pastry: one definition specifies 'a cake made of flour and raisins, often eaten by miners for dinner', which sounds very similar to the modern heavy cake. Alternative versions include cakes with either potatoes in the dough or a slice of pork pressed into the top of the pastry before baking, in which case the dish might also be known as a 'hoggan'.

Nowadays, heavy cake or fuggan seems to refer more to a pastry-like cake containing dried fruit. Recipes vary: one by Dorothy Hartley calls for flour, a little salt and currants, mixed to a paste with clotted cream, rolled out to 20mm thick; another contains flour, sugar, currants and lard; a third is like puff pastry, made with equal quantities of butter and flour (Boyd, 1982). The constants are currants and the criss-cross top. Martin (1993) notes that heavy cake could be quickly made in fishing villages when the boats were seen returning to port, and that the pattern cut in the top was supposed to represent the fishing nets.

TECHNIQUE:

Flour, lard and sugar are used in the proportions 3:2:1, with the same weight of currants as lard. A little candied peel can be added. The flour, salt and sugar are mixed roughly, the lard and currants added. Milk or water may be used to hold the dough together. The dough is rolled out, slashed with a knife and baked at 190°C for 30 minutes.

REGION OF PRODUCTION:

SOUTH WEST ENGLAND, CORNWALL.

Cornish Saffron Cake

DESCRIPTION:

AN OBLONG LOAF, 200MM LONG, 140MM WIDE, 120MM DEEP, WEIGHING ABOUT 500G. COLOUR: DEEP GOLDEN CRUST, SPECKLED WITH FRUIT; A PRONOUNCED YELLOW CRUMB. FLAVOUR: LIGHTLY SWEETENED, SLIGHT ASTRINGENT SAFFRON FLAVOUR.

HISTORY:

The use of saffron in sweet breads and buns is now thought typical of Cornwall. Formerly the spice was more widely used in British cookery, and was quite often called for in cakes of the seventeenth and eighteenth centuries (Glasse, 1747). Thereafter, it is found very rarely, although it crops up here and there in recipes collected in Northumberland. Its chief survival was in Cornwall at the other end of the country. It may have lingered here because saffron was still grown. Carolyn Martin (1993) notes that 'various wills and documents refer to "saffron meadows"', and there is a reference to saffron growing at Launcells, near Bude, in the 1870s.

Originally, saffron buns were eaten with clotted cream on Good Friday. The saffron, an expensive spice, is now sometimes replaced with yellow colouring. David (1977) observed that in the past, saffron filaments were infused to produce the colour and they were not strained out before the water was mixed with the other ingredients. She also noted that eggs were not usually added, although the recipe quoted below, collected recently, does include them.

TECHNIQUE:

Recipes for saffron doughs vary in the combinations of spices and dried fruit used. The results are generally light and bread-like. The saffron is mixed into water, which is whisked with a little flour, sugar, whey powder, yeast and eggs. The mixture is allowed to work for 30 minutes. After mixing and bulk fermentation, the dough is scaled off and shaped into buns or loaves. Saffron bread (a variant name for saffron cake) is baked at 175°C: 12 minutes for buns, 30 minutes for cakes.

REGION OF PRODUCTION:

SOUTH WEST ENGLAND, CORNWALL.

Devonshire Split

DESCRIPTION:

A SMALL ROUNDED BUN ABOUT 80MM DIAMETER, 40MM HIGH. WEIGHT: APPROXIMATELY 40G. COLOUR AND TEXTURE: PALE GOLD CRUST FADING TO WHITE AT LOWER EDGE, SPRINKLED WITH ICING SUGAR; INSIDE PALE, CREAM CRUMB; VERY LIGHT BREAD. FLAVOUR: SLIGHTLY SWEET.

HISTORY:

Cassell's Dictionary of Cookery (1875) defines Devonshire buns as ordinary bun dough using cream instead of milk. The result would have been a soft, light, yet rich dough. The use of split to describe a bun or roll that has been split to receive jam, cream or filling is first recorded in 1905 (*OED*). The reason why these buns carried the alternative name of Chudleighs is unknown. The fact that this small market town in Devonshire was visited by a catastrophic fire in 1807 that started in a bakehouse in Mill Lane is doubtless coincidental. The first reference to this name is in the collections made by Florence White as founder of the English Folk Cookery Association during the 1920s. Here, it is suggested that Chudleighs be rubbed over with butter paper for a gloss, and wrapped in a warm cloth after baking, which gave a soft crust – something found also for Scottish baps. The second record is also in White (1932). White's recipes did not call for cream, only for milk. She also notes the existence of Cornish splits (which were the same but larger) and the alternative name (in Devon and east Cornwall) of tuffs.

The popularity of these buns is reinforced by the tourist industry and the vast quantity of Devon or Cornish cream teas that are served each summer (clotted cream, of course). Most of these may come today with scones, but there are sufficient to keep the Chudleigh living.

TECHNIQUE:

Before the Second World War, small rolls made in Devonshire and Cornwall, known as splits (or sometimes Chudleighs, in Devon) were yeast-leavened and lightly enriched with a mixture of butter and lard (3lbs flour, 8 ounces butter and 2 ounces lard mixed with water and a little milk). The dough was mixed in a conventional manner, divided into small rounds, proved and baked. On removal from the oven, the hot rolls were rubbed with a butter paper to give them a slight gloss, and covered with a cloth or blanket whilst cooling, giving a soft crust. Sadly, modern practice veers towards the use of margarine and milk powder.

REGION OF PRODUCTION:
SOUTH WEST ENGLAND, DEVON AND CORNWALL.

Dorset Knob

DESCRIPTION:
A DOMED RUSK, 40MM DIAMETER, 35MM HIGH. WEIGHT: ABOUT 10G. COLOUR: PALE GOLD, DARKER ON TOP, A PALER CRUMB. FLAVOUR AND TEXTURE: BREADY, SLIGHTLY SWEET, DRY, VERY CRISP.

HISTORY:
Dorset Knobs (a type of rusk) have been baked by the firm of Moore's since the late nineteenth century. Originally, they are said to have been made from leftover bread dough mixed with butter and sugar and baked in the falling heat of the oven after the bread was removed. It is impossible to say, without further evidence, if the tradition is older than stated. Unlike the similar hollow biscuits made in East Anglia, no surviving domestic recipes have appeared. *Law's Grocer's Manual* (*c.* 1895) merely remarks that there were several species of rusk, mixed from flour, milk, butter and sugar, very light and spongy, cut into 'particular shapes and sizes', first baked on both sides, then dried in a low oven for 3–4 hours.

Around 1939–45, Knobs became the main business of the firm. Today, they make other biscuit specialities. This rusk was sold as a breakfast roll, when it would be dipped in tea to soften; it is also eaten with butter and cheese.

TECHNIQUE:
The exact recipe and method are trade secrets. A dough includes flour, sugar, fat, yeast and water. After kneading and an initial rising, small pieces of dough are nipped off the bulk, shaped and proved for about an hour. They are baked at a high temperature for 20 minutes, turned over and baked a further 10. They are separated by hand, and put in a low oven for 3 hours to desiccate completely.

REGION OF PRODUCTION:
SOUTH WEST ENGLAND, BRIDPORT (DORSET).

COMPARE WITH:
Norfolk Knob, East Anglia (p. 132).

Dough Cake

DESCRIPTION:
A ROUND FRUIT DOUGH CAKE – AN EXAMPLE BOUGHT IN BANBURY WAS ABOUT 200MM DIAMETER, 50MM DEEP. WEIGHT: ABOUT 500G. COLOUR: PALE BROWN WITH A SPONGY APPEARANCE (IT IS THE UNDERSIDE OF THE CAKE WHICH IS EXPOSED TO THE BUYER) AND A FEW CURRANTS SHOWING ON THE SURFACE; THE BASE (WHICH WAS THE TOP DURING BAKING) IS SMOOTH, FLAT AND A DEEPER GOLDEN BROWN; THE INSIDE HAS A FINE-TEXTURED, OFF-WHITE CRUMB, SPECKLED WITH FRUIT. FLAVOUR AND TEXTURE: SWEETISH, WITH A

'He may live without books – what is knowledge but grieving?
He may live without hope – what is hope but deceiving?
He may live without love – what is passion but pining?
But where is the man that can live without dining?'

EDWARD R. BULWER-LYTTON, 'LUCILLE'

SLIGHT SOURDOUGH TASTE AND A SOFT, CLINGING TEXTURE.

HISTORY:

An early literary reference to the dough cake is dated to the mid-eighteenth century, comes from Devon, and is recorded as a term of affectionate abuse for a thick-headed person (*OED*). This suggests dough cakes were well known, but gives little indication of the recipe. Dough cakes in modern England are similar in composition to lardy cakes, but the added ingredients are evenly distributed through the dough rather than being carefully folded in. A tradition mentioned by Flora Thompson (1939) may have some bearing on this. In rural Oxfordshire, amongst poor households who had no ovens for baking, a 'baker's cake' was made for harvest teas. 'The housewife provided all the ingredients excepting the dough, putting raisins and currants, lard, sugar and spice in a basin which she gave to the baker, who added the dough, made and baked the cake, and returned it, beautifully browned, in his big oven. The charge was the same as that for a loaf of the same size, and the result was delicious.' Since the price of this cake was no more than the cost of the dough, it had to be simpler than lardy cakes which require laborious rolling and folding; presumably the baker simply kneaded the additions through the dough after bulk fermentation, much as today. Dough cakes are made in the same general area as lardy cakes. In Devon, they are most often found on the eastern side of the county. Just over the county border in Dorset may be found the Portland dough cake – described by the WI earlier in the century (Raffael, 1997).

TECHNIQUE:

As with lardy cakes, proportions vary. Cakes made domestically are likely to be richer than those in commerce. A typical baker's recipe would use dough, dried fruit, lard and sugar in the ratio 4:1:1:1. The dough for the cake is removed from a batch for bread after bulk fermentation; the extras are kneaded through; the mixture is scaled off, shaped and placed in tins. Proving times are variable, but can be up to 18 hours. They are baked for 60 minutes at 220°C. After baking, dough cakes are turned out and displayed upside down. The reason for this may be to demonstrate that they are fully cooked or, as with lardy cakes, in consequence of a belief that the lard permeates evenly through the warm cake. Some recipes call for butter, not lard, and some add spices.

REGION OF PRODUCTION:
SOUTH WEST ENGLAND; SOUTH ENGLAND

COMPARE WITH:
Lardy Cake, South England (p. 73)

Easter Biscuit

DESCRIPTION:

A CIRCULAR BISCUIT WITH A FLUTED EDGE, 50–90MM DIAMETER, 5MM THICK; WEIGHT: 12–20G. COLOUR: PALE GOLD IRREGULARLY FLECKED WITH CURRANTS. FLAVOUR: SWEET, LIGHTLY SPICED. SHORT TEXTURE.

HISTORY:

In the past, the British made many special foods for Easter, including various breads and biscuits and things like tansy puddings. In the twenty-first century, only hot cross buns and simnel

cakes are well-known, but a few others survive. One is the Easter biscuit, known also as Easter cake, in South Western England. Old recipes show them to belong to the same type as Shrewsbury cakes (p. 176), based on a rich shortbread mixed with currants and flavoured with spices and peel. Harris and Borella (c. 1900) say there were many varieties, that they were rather large, cut with a fluted cutter and sugared on top. They give 2 recipes. Firstly, 'the usual', made with butter or margarine and flavoured with oil of lemon; and a 'recommended' one, for which butter and Vostizza currants are specified and lemon zest used to flavour. They comment on a method used by an old-fashioned pastry cook's shop in London where the biscuit was pressed out with the thumbs to give an irregularly shaped biscuit with an uneven surface. The appearance was ugly, but the butter and flavouring of orange and lemon zest made them very good. These recipes are similar to 2 collected by Florence White in the 1930s. One, called a Sedgemoor Easter cake, came from Somerset. According to Bristol baker John Williams, Easter biscuits are still very popular in the city of Bristol and throughout much of the South West; he regards the flavouring of oil of cassia (a form of cinnamon) as the defining characteristic.

TECHNIQUE:
Easter biscuits are a shortbread type. A commercial recipe (c. 1925–30) calls for flour, butter, sugar and currants roughly in the proportions 4:2:2:1. They are mixed with eggs and baking powder, nutmeg and oil of cassia. They are baked at 195–205°C until lightly browned. Other recorded recipes may include mixed sweet spice, cinnamon and brandy (Sedgemoor) or lemon zest (London).

REGION OF PRODUCTION:
SOUTH WEST ENGLAND, BRISTOL.

Mothering Bun

DESCRIPTION:
A CIRCULAR BUN 90MM ACROSS, 30–40MM DEEP. WEIGHT: 60G. COLOUR: GOLDEN CRUST, DECORATED WITH WHITE GLACÉ ICING AND A THICK COATING OF HUNDREDS-AND-THOU-SANDS (NONPAREILS). FLAVOUR: LIGHT, SLIGHTLY ENRICHED BREAD, WITH SWEET ICING.

HISTORY:
Mothering buns are a speciality of Bristol made on the Saturday immediately preceding Mothering Sunday (Mid-Lent Sunday). This is a day on which the Lenten fast was relaxed to allow consumption of richer foods. In the past, it was also associated with the better-known custom of the Simnel Cake (see below). The buns are small and rather plain, and the cakes large, rich and elaborate, although there is evidence for plainer, yeast-raised simnels in various places.

John Williams, a baker who has taken an interest in Bristol specialities, comments that mothering buns have been made for as long as anyone can remember, and that at the beginning of the twentieth century, they were coated with caraway or aniseed comfits, rather than the hundreds-and-thousands now used. This links them to the tradition of Bath buns which once incorporated caraway comfits, and to the many other bun and wig recipes of 200 years ago which used the same flavouring. All bakers in Bristol make mothering buns, only on the Saturday before Mothering Sunday.

A plain dough is made using flour, fat and sugar in the proportions 10:1:1. A ferment works for about 30 minutes at 32°C. The fat – usually lard, butter is used in particularly rich buns – is rubbed into the flour, sugar and a little salt and the ferment are added. After fermentation, it is knocked back and kneaded again. It is baked at 220°C for 20 minutes. The tops are given a plain icing, followed immediately by dipping in a dish of hundreds-and-thousands.

REGION OF PRODUCTION:

SOUTH WEST ENGLAND, BRISTOL.

Oldbury Tart

DESCRIPTION:

A SMALL CIRCULAR PIE ABOUT 90MM DIAMETER, 20MM DEEP. THE EDGE OF THE PIE IS NIPPED INTO LITTLE POINTS, GIVING A CROWN EFFECT. WEIGHT: APPROXIMATELY 100G.

HISTORY:

These tarts were also known (more accurately perhaps) as pies. They are distinctive in their use of hot-water pastry, usually associated with savoury pies, in combination with sweet filling. See also Cumnock tarts, below. Gooseberries are the common filling, but black currants are also known. A very similar gooseberry pie was made for Mansfield Fair in Nottinghamshire. No other fruit pies using this type of pastry are mentioned by authorities on British food.

Both the Oldbury and Mansfield pies were noted at the end of the last century. The Nottinghamshire affairs involved melted apple jelly being poured into the warm pies to set as it cooled. This is just like adding jellied stock to savoury pork pies. White (1932) records that the pies were still being sold at Mansfield Fair. Surviving recipes for Oldbury tarts are of more recent date, but the use of brown sugar as a sweetener suggests a tradition stretching well into the nineteenth century before white sugar became cheap and easily available (about 1840). Pauline Gazard, one of the few people who now keeps the dish alive, quotes oral traditions to do with the pies. They should be eaten from the hand, and a good pie is full of juice which runs out when bitten. The pastry should be thin, and the decorative edge is important; there should be 21 points to the crown. They are more difficult to make than ordinary pies, which discourages many. This most interesting tradition appears to be declining. They are still available in small numbers at local fêtes and fairs in July.

TECHNIQUE:

The proportion of flour to fat is slightly more than double the weight. The fat is butter and lard in equal quantities. The dough is made like any other hot-water paste. To shape the cases the dough is rolled out thinly and cut in circles of 160mm diameter. These are hand-raised by pleating the sides 4 or 5 times. They are filled with small gooseberries and soft brown sugar. A pastry lid is nipped with the case to give the pointed effect; a small hole is cut in the centre. At this stage, the pies are sometimes left to stand overnight, allowing the pastry to firm. They are baked at about 200°C for 25–30 minutes.

REGION OF PRODUCTION:

WEST ENGLAND, GLOUCESTERSHIRE.

Sally Lunn

DESCRIPTION:

A LOW CIRCULAR LOAF; A USUAL SIZE IS ABOUT 140MM DIAMETER, ABOUT 80MM DEEP. WEIGHT: APPROXIMATELY 200G. COLOUR AND TEXTURE: A DEEP GOLD CRUST ON TOP, FADING TO CREAM UNDERNEATH, WITH A RICH, CREAM, CLOSE-TEXTURED, LIGHT AND MELTING CRUMB.

HISTORY:

This light yeast cake is a speciality of the spa town of Bath. There are several theories as to its origin. An early reference in a Bath guidebook of 1780 is to 'a spungy hot roll'. In 1798, they were again said to be hot rolls, 'not long ago in vogue in Bath'. Hot bread was much loved at Bath breakfasts (see Bath buns, above). In 1827 there was an account of how Sally Lunns were named after the girl who cried them for sale ('about thirty years ago'). She and her recipe were adopted and commercialized (*OED*).

There is a charming but probably apocryphal legend that a Huguenot refugee called Solange Luyon, a name corrupted to Sally Lunn, first made the cakes famous. A building, dating originally from the fifteenth century, is supposed to be the place where she worked. It still houses a restaurant and shop baking Sally Lunns. Bath historian Trevor Fawcett observes that no documentation has ever been produced to support this story.

A completely different hare was started by Eliza Acton (1845). She described her recipe for a 'solimemne' as a 'rich French breakfast cake or Sally Lunn'. Hartley (1954) produced other uses of the word solimemne, variously spelled, and suggests it is a corruption of the French *soleil lune*, sun and moon. In fact, solimemne is a misspelling of *solilem* or *solimeme* which is the name of an enriched brioche from Alsace. The distinguishing feature of *solimemes* (Larousse, 1938) is that they are split horizontally soon after baking, soaked with melted butter which is absorbed by the dough, then reassembled. Whether they made the transition from Alsace to Bath is not known, but maybe the Huguenot has a place. An alternative proposal is that Sally Lunns were discovered by a French chef when travelling in the West Country – Carême is suggested – and he exported the idea to his homeland, where the name was completely garbled into *solimeme*. All this is speculation.

The main characteristics, a light richness derived from a high proportion of eggs and cream or butter in the dough, are consistent through the years. Some recipes are lightly spiced or flavoured with lemon peel. However, Maria Eliza Rundell (1807), herself a resident of Bath, likens a plain but light roll to a Sally Lunn. It is split, whilst still warm, into 2 or 3 horizontal slices and spread with butter or clotted cream, then reassembled for immediate consumption. If more than 24 hours old, the cake is usually toasted before eating.

TECHNIQUE:

The recipe used by the Sally Lunn shop is a trade secret. Other versions are published, for example by David (1978). It calls for flour, cream and eggs in the proportions 2:1:1 and is flavoured with lemon peel.

REGION OF PRODUCTION:

SOUTH WEST ENGLAND, BATH (SOMERSET).

Cider (West Country)

DESCRIPTION:

PALE GOLD-YELLOW TO THE EYE; SOME MAY BE CLOUDY, BUT MUCH PRODUCED COMMERCIALLY IS USUALLY CLARIFIED. FERMENTED UNTIL DRY, WEST-COUNTRY CIDER IS ROBUST AND ASTRINGENT WITH PERFUMED APPLE OVERTONES. TYPICALLY 6 PER CENT ALCOHOL BY VOLUME.

HISTORY:

Although it must remain uncertain, it does appear that the Anglo-Saxon word *beor* refers to an alcoholic apple-based beverage. In Norman-French dialect, the word *bère* for cider survives to this day. Whether cider existed in early England or not, it is thought the art was stimulated by contacts with Normandy after the Conquest, and that cider-making was at first strongest in the South-Eastern counties of Sussex and Kent (Davies, 1993). But there are also many early references to cider in the West Country, including from the 1100s in Gloucestershire and the 1200s in Devon.

Cider from western Britain is distinguished by the use of apples specifically grown for cider-making. This practice has been current for at least 400 years. During the seventeenth century cider became a gentleman's drink, equated with wine. In Herefordshire, much attention was paid to cider apples and methods. Advances at this time included greater selection of apples, refinement of storage and crushing techniques, and the invention of glass bottles strong enough to withstand a secondary fermentation. Celia Fiennes, travelling through Britain in the late seventeenth century, noted the good quality of Hereford cider.

In the eighteenth century cider sank on the social scale: there was increased competition from imported wine; middlemen sold inferior weak brews; and an epidemic of lead poisoning attracted opprobrium (French, 1982). Competition from wine may have been the most influential and long-lasting cause of cider's drop in standing. Cider became a drink associated with the labouring poor; the quality was uneven and the flavour sharp. The juice was mixed with water, giving 'ciderkin' with an alcohol content comparable to that of small beer, a servants' drink. It was this, not the fine ciders of the seventeenth century, that survived. In the late nineteenth century, there was renewed interest. Businesses that are still important today were established. Cider apples were classified according to acidity and tannin content into sweet, bittersweet, and bittersharp. Hereford and Worcester were known for cider made from bittersharps, Devon was known for sweet ciders and Somerset for ciders made from bittersweets (Morgan, 1993). Some of the larger cider-makers established their own orchards.

Advances in knowledge of fermentation, plus expanding urban markets, benefited small factory-based cider-makers but farm production diminished after 1930. English cider generally developed into a consistent, uniform product in which alcoholic strength was considered important (although western cider is generally less strong than that made on the eastern side of the country) and the process was standardized with added yeast cultures.

Since the 1970s, distinct trends have emerged: new planting of orchards of cider apples to better supply the industry; a renewed interest in on-farm cider-making and methods of production. For instance, ciders from single varieties such as Kingston Black, Yarlington Mill, Dabinett, Sweet Coppin and Brown's Apple are now available.

Scrumpy is a name colloquially applied to farmhouse ciders which have been produced by traditional methods, but it has no fixed definition and is frowned upon by cider-lovers.

Gloucestershire, Herefordshire and Worcestershire ciders have Protected Designations of Origin (PDO).

TECHNIQUE:

Ciders vary between makers and harvests, as do wines. Methods of production are at heart identical; it is variations in soils, micro-climate and fruit varieties which most affect the flavour. As yet, little systematic attempt to classify these has been made in respect of cider, and the necessary vocabulary is underdeveloped in English.

The hallowed routine followed for making farmhouse cider began with the harvest. The apples were either allowed to fall naturally or were shaken off the tree with a long pole; then they were taken into an apple loft and allowed to mellow. The stored apples of different varieties were blended. They were crushed in a horse-driven stone wheel-mill or, at the end of the nineteenth century, in a powered rotary press. Sometimes the crushed apple pulp (pomace) was left to stand to allow flavour to develop. It would then be pressed. It was placed in 4–6cm layers on hairs, or thick horsehair cloths which were folded over to envelop the pulp, and then built up into a cheese consisting of about 10 filled cloths. Pressure was applied from above by screwing a plate down on to the cheese. In Devon and Dorset, barley straw was used in place of the hairs, but this is no longer practised. As the juice flowed from the press, it was poured into barrels, loosely stoppered, and left to work under the action of naturally present yeasts. Once fermentation had ceased, the cider was racked off the spent yeast.

Modern production follows the same sequence but with refinements. The fruit may be dislodged and harvested mechanically. It is blended, picked over and cleaned before mechanical crushing. Hydraulically operated presses, with layers of fruit packed in polypropylene cloths, similar to the old-fashioned screw presses, are used to extract juice by small producers; big horizontal or continuous presses are used for factory operations. The juice may be sterilized with sulphur dioxide and yeast cultures added. Other additions are sugar if the year has been poor, and water by some makers. Fermentation takes place in large vats. The result is generally still, strong and dry. If sweet is required it is usually obtained by adding sugar. Royal cider, where fermentation is stopped by the addition of strong alcohol – which will give a sweeter finish – is not pursued as it used to be in the classic period. Some cider apples have sufficiently well-balanced acid and tannin to produce good cider without further blending. A few makers offer cider produced from single varieties. Otherwise, the apples may be blended before milling or after fermentation. Large companies have turned cider-making into a year-round activity by holding part of the year's apple juice in a concentrated form until required; they may also use concentrated apple juice from abroad.

REGION OF PRODUCTION:

WEST AND SOUTH WEST ENGLAND.

Plymouth Gin

DESCRIPTION:

PLYMOUTH GIN IS COLOURLESS AND TRANSPARENT. ITS FLAVOUR IS AROMATIC WITH CITRUS AND CORIANDER OVERTONES. TWO STRENGTHS ARE AVAILABLE: 37 AND 57 PER CENT ALCOHOL BY VOLUME.

HISTORY:

Gin has been distilled in Plymouth since at least the eighteenth century. Coates, the only company now allowed to use the name Plymouth Gin, began production in 1793 in the building which still houses the distillery. It has continued with little interruption. The 57 per cent spirit was made only for the Royal Navy but a quantity was released to celebrate the bicentenary of the company's foundation. Coates is now marketed by Hiram Walker Agencies, a subsidiary of Allied Lyons.

TECHNIQUE:

A neutral grain alcohol is distilled through a rectifying still to remove odours. This yields a very pure spirit which is 95 per cent alcohol; to this are added the 'botanicals': juniper, coriander seed, orange and lemon peel, angelica, orris root and cardamom. Coates's formula lays greater emphasis on the roots (angelica and orris) than other gins, giving it a distinctive aroma. The mixture is distilled once more in a pot still, checked in a spirit safe, and bottled.

REGION OF PRODUCTION:

SOUTH WEST ENGLAND.

Shrub

DESCRIPTION:

THIS IS PALE GOLD IN COLOUR; ITS TASTE IS SWEET, WITH CITRUS AND CARAMEL NOTES. IT IS 5.3 PER CENT ALCOHOL BY VOLUME.

HISTORY:

The word shrub derives from the Arabic root *sharab*, meaning a sweetened drink. The word and various drinks and confections associated with it are discussed in detail by Alan Davidson (1993). Since the mid-eighteenth century it has been applied to a sweetened drink of rum and oranges, lemons or other acid fruit such as currants. Athough it was clearly old-fashioned by the late 1800s, it was well enough known for *Law's Grocer's Manual* to give a recipe. The taste for it has survived in the South West of Britain, where its manufacture is associated with Bristol. This town carried on an important trade with both the West Indies and the wine- and brandy-producing areas of France and Spain. Rum or cognac were vital ingredients for the drink. The Bristol company that now produces it, J.R. Phillips, makes several other alcoholic cordials, including lovage, peppermint and aniseed.

TECHNIQUE:

The commercial recipe and method are trade secrets, but published recipes state that either brandy or rum can be used as a base. Lemon and orange peel are mixed with the liquor and fresh lemon juice. The mixture is infused for several weeks, it is then sweetened with syrup, strained and bottled.

REGION OF PRODUCTION:

SOUTH WEST ENGLAND.

Sparkling Cider

DESCRIPTION:

THIS CIDER HAS A STRONG APPLE BOUQUET, WITH THE DRY, SPICY FLAVOUR TYPICAL OF ENGLISH CIDERS. IT IS NORMALLY 5–8 PER CENT ALCOHOL BY VOLUME.

HISTORY:

Sparkling cider was made in Herefordshire in the 1600s. It had been made possible by the development of glass bottles strong enough to withstand the secondary fermentation. Their invention is credited to Sir Kenelm Digby, a man with a deep interest in the arts of brewing and fermenting, whose collection of recipes for food and especially meads, metheglins and other drinks was posthumously published as *The Closet of … Sir Kenelme Digbie, Kt., Opened* (1669). This is a charming myth, for he was a charming man, but the more likely explanation is that Lord Scudamore, whose family was foremost in improving varieties of apples suitable for cider, began to bottle and lay down cider in the reign of Charles I (Davies, 1993). Glass strong enough to hold the explosive liquid was developed as a result of hotter-burning coal furnaces being used by the glassworkers when the use of charcoal was curtailed after 1615. By the end of the century, there was such a trade with London in bottled cider (sent down the Thames from Lechlade) that 5 or 6 glasshouses had been built in the area to supply the bottles.

The tradition suffered in the eighteenth century when cider became the drink of the poor but was revived towards the end of the reign of Queen Victoria. In 1895, *Law's Grocer's Manual* stated that, 'Champagne cider is, or should be, the best mellow or sweet cider bottled before it has fermented or worked much … it is quite frequently made by charging common cider that is deficient in spirit and sparkle with carbonic acid gas.' Over the last century, both secondary fermentation and carbon dioxide have been used by various manufacturers to give sparkling ciders. Since the late 1970s, an increasing interest in the art of making fine cider has led several specialists to experiment once more with sparkling ciders made by secondary fermentation. At least 7 makers produce a naturally sparkling cider.

TECHNIQUE:

A cider produced by the standard English method is used. After initial fermentation, it is allowed to undergo a secondary fermentation in the bottle. A few producers clear the cider by allowing the yeast to settle in the necks of the bottles, freezing them and disgorging it before corking. Others leave the yeast in the bottom of the bottle.

Much commercially produced cider is sparkling but it is carbonated.

REGION OF PRODUCTION:

SOUTH WEST ENGLAND.

Original Urchfont Chilli Mustard

DESCRIPTION:

THIS GRAIN MUSTARD IS DARK YELLOW-ORANGE, WITH CRUSHED YELLOW MUSTARD SEEDS VISIBLE AND SPECKS OF RED AND DARK BROWN. ITS TASTE IS ACID, MILD MUSTARD WITH A POWERFUL CHILLI KICK.

HISTORY:

Originally, all mustard must have been fairly coarsely ground. It was only in the early 1700s that the fine, sieved flour now thought of as English mustard became widely known. During the late 1960s, there was a general revival of interest in early recipes and methods for producing various foods. This, combined with a desire to make interesting condiments for meat, led to the invention in 1970 by the Wiltshire Tracklement Company of a whole-grain, chilli-spiced mustard called Urchfont (originally made in Urchfont, Wiltshire). It was the first whole-grain mustard to be marketed in England for many years. Its success led to an expansion of the company's range and its emulation by other small and larger concerns.

TECHNIQUE:
Locally-grown mustard seeds are used. They are blended, ground and mixed and left to stand in drums for up to 14 days (depending on the weather, the colder it is, the longer the process takes). Ingredients: mustard, cider and wine vinegars, black peppercorns, allspice, chillies.

REGION OF PRODUCTION:
SOUTH WEST ENGLAND, WILTSHIRE.

Tewkesbury Mustard

DESCRIPTION:
THE COLOUR IS DULL OCHRE, WITH COARSELY CRUSHED MUSTARD SEED AND HUSKS VISIBLE. FLAVOUR IS SHARP WITH A SWEET, DISTINCT HORSERADISH AFTERTASTE.

HISTORY:
Tewkesbury Mustard was famous in the 1500s, so famous that it was a byword for a particular kind of stupidity – 'His wit's as thick as Tewkesbury Mustard!' exclaimed Sir John Falstaff in *Henry IV*. The mustard seed was ground in a mortar or crushed with a cannon ball, sifted, combined with an infusion of horseradish, well mixed for at least an hour, made into balls and dried. It was sold and kept until reconstituted with various substances – vinegar, verjuice, cider and red wine are all quoted. No trace of this early industry has remained in Tewkesbury; only the name recalls the association (Man and Weir, 1988).

A habit of mixing horseradish and mustard persisted. References can be found in a recipe by John Nott (1726), and Eliza Acton (1845) gave instructions for making 'Tartar Mustard', a mixture of mustard powder, horseradish vinegar and chilli vinegar. These compounds were made at home, instead of being dried and marketed. Increased interest in the production of speciality foods by small independent producers led to the revival of Tewkesbury mustard in the late twentieth century.

TECHNIQUE:
The ingredients are mustard seed, horseradish root, wine vinegar and acetic acid. The spices are ground, mixed to a paste with the other ingredients and allowed to mature for several days before bottling.

REGION OF PRODUCTION:
WEST ENGLAND.

***

Also produced in South West England
CAERPHILLY CHEESE (P. 186)
CHITTERLINGS (P.68)
CIDER BRANDY (P. 181)
PERRY (P. 182)
SPICED BEEF (P. 154)

Also produced in South England
BATH CHAPS (P. 16)

Channel Islands

Jersey Royal Potato

DESCRIPTION:

JERSEY ROYALS ARE SMALL, KIDNEY-SHAPED POTATOES (THEY ARE ALSO CALLED INTERNATIONAL KIDNEYS) WITH A THIN WHITE SKIN AND CREAMY WHITE FLESH; THEY ARE GRADED BY SIZE INTO 'WARE' OR 'MIDS'. THEY ARE A WAXY POTATO WITH A DELICATE SWEET, EARTHY TASTE.

HISTORY:

These potatoes owe their origin to a single seed bought from a local shop by Jersey farmer Hugh de la Haye in 1880. The potato, which had 16 sprouts, was divided up and planted, yielding a good crop of early potatoes. The de la Hayes nurtured the variety until they had enough to trade with. A Jersey newspaper editor, Charles le Feuvre, was responsible for the name 'Royal Jersey Fluke'; the potatoes are now known as Jersey Royals.

A Protected Designation of Origin has been applied for. Marketing of Jersey Royals is intense and tends to exclude the word 'potato' from the name. The aim is to build up brand identity attached to the variety alone. Jersey is well suited to production of early potatoes because of its higher mean temperature. Other districts which have entered the early market are Cornwall and the South-West. Jersey Royals attain a premium price, although there is competition and undercutting from less flavourous tubers from Cyprus and Egypt.

TECHNIQUE:

The seed potatoes are dug and selected in late June. The first shoots are removed, then the roots stored until October. The seed potatoes are arranged by hand, upright in boxes. They are left for about 4 weeks, during which they send out another 3 shoots. Planting is done by hand, sprouting-side uppermost, working from the fields closest to the sea towards the centre of the island. The fields are covered with perforated polythene. Lifting is by mechanical diggers, about 12 weeks after planting; samples are dug daily to ascertain the correct moment. To qualify for the grade of 'mids', they must either be no longer than 45mm prior to a specified date or, after that date, be mechanically graded and be of a diameter not less than 19mm and not more than 32mm.

The fields used for potatoes are mostly dressed with seaweed. Jersey Royals are also grown indoors, hand-graded and packed in oyster kegs holding 5.8kg.

REGION OF PRODUCTION:

CHANNEL ISLANDS, JERSEY.

'Though the potato is an excellent root, deserving to be brought into general use, yet it seems not likely that the use of it should ever be normal in the country.'

DAVID DAVIES, *THE CASE OF THE LABOURERS IN HUSBANDRY*

Channel Island Milk and Channel Island Butter

DESCRIPTION:

CHANNEL ISLAND MILK IS RICHER IN FLAVOUR THAN THAT OF OTHER CATTLE; GUERNSEY IS SLIGHTLY YELLOWER IN COLOUR THAN JERSEY. AVERAGE BUTTERFAT CONTENT, 5.1 PER CENT.

CHANNEL ISLAND BUTTER IS DERIVED FROM THE CHURNED CREAM OF THIS MILK. SOME FARM BUTTERS BEAR THE TRADITIONAL DECORATION OF RIDGES AND DIAMONDS PRODUCED BY USING 'SCOTCH HANDS' (SMALL RIDGED WOODEN BOARDS). THIS BUTTER IS ALSO SOMETIMES SOLD LOOSE. COLOUR VARIES WITH THE SEASON: A RICH CREAM IN WINTER, DEEP CREAM TO GOLD IN SUMMER.

HISTORY:

There are 3 breeds associated with Channel Island milk: Guernsey, Jersey, and South Devon. They evolved in the eighteenth century. South Devon cattle are now counted as rare and only one viable dairy herd exists today. The status of Guernsey and Jersey cattle is much stronger. They are exported from their native islands but once they have left, they are not allowed to return. The emphasis on preserving bloodlines on the island means that the milk is derived from the native breeds only. The closure of Jersey to foreign blood dates from 1789, of Guernsey from 1819. The islands exported stock from at least 1724, the annual rate of import into Britain from Jersey running at 2,000 head in 1878. South Devons are associated with Channel Island cattle because of the presence of the gene for haemoglobin B, a characteristic unique to these 3 breeds. There was much crossing of South Devons with Guernseys in the nineteenth century. This may be the route of entry of this genetic identity (Hall & Clutton-Brock, 1989).

Originally known collectively as Alderneys, the cattle have been valued as producers of rich milk for almost 2 centuries. The English aristocracy gave them wide distribution for at first, in the Victorian period, it was a park and home-farm breed associated with country estates (Hall & Clutton-Brock, 1989). The 2 breeds began to develop separately in the mid-nineteenth century, when the Jersey was especially fashionable. On the British mainland, a number of farms maintain herds of pure-bred Channel Island cattle whose milk is marketed separately.

Butter-making is found on the Channel Islands themselves and is undertaken by many owners of mainland British herds, particularly in Cornwall. During 1939–45, milk and butter production was strictly controlled and much on-farm butter-making ceased. The owners of Channel Island cattle formed an association, Quality Milk Producers, shortly after the war, to promote their milk and products made from it. Butter-making using the milk was, and still is, an activity of one major dairy company in the South-West. A number of smaller creameries and dairy farms began producing butter once more in the 1980s, encouraged by moves towards agricultural diversification.

In law, Channel Island milk is defined as milk solely from Jersey and Guernsey herds. 'Gold Top' and 'Breakfast Milk' are brand names registered by Quality Milk Producers in 1956 and 1984 respectively.

TECHNIQUE:

The use of milk from Channel Island cattle is the crucial point in the production of this butter and, because of this, it is collected and processed separately. Theoretically, Guernseys,

Jerseys and South Devons can be kept in almost any part of Britain, but they thrive best on rich pastures in the dairying area of the South West (the South Devon, of which there are few, is mostly restricted to this area). For butter, the pasteurized milk is separated mechanically. The cream is usually allowed to ripen; some dairies add a lactic acid starter; it is then churned by conventional English methods. The scale will vary with the producer, from small wooden churns holding a few gallons up to very large stainless-steel industrial units. Small producers prefer to use traditional wooden utensils for working the butter.

REGION OF PRODUCTION:
CHANNEL ISLANDS; HERDS EXIST THROUGHOUT BRITAIN, MAINLY SOUTH.

Guernsey Gâche

DESCRIPTION:
GUERNSEY GÂCHES (SPELLED GAUCHE IN SOME ENGLISH SOURCES) COME IN VARIOUS WEIGHTS, INCLUDING ONE OF 500G WHICH IS SHAPED LIKE A WIDE LOAF AND ONE OF 900G, WHICH IS A NARROW OBLONG. ANOTHER, NAMED AFTER THE MAKER'S SHOP, THE MAISON CARRÉ, IS SET IN A SHALLOW OBLONG TIN, ABOVE WHOSE EDGES THE DOUGH RISES TO GIVE A MUSHROOM HEAD. COLOUR: FLAKY, GOLDEN BROWN CRUST, PALE YELLOW CRUMB WITH PROMINENT DRIED FRUIT AND CANDIED PEEL. FLAVOUR: SWEET AND RICH.

HISTORY:
Guernsey has its own variation on the theme of British fruit breads. J.R. Irons (c. 1935) states, 'the one thing they all seemed agreed upon is that it cannot be made without good tough butter' (tough in this instance meaning well-rinsed of water and whey). Recipes show it to be of the enriched dough type which pre-dates the chemically leavened fruit breads now mostly available in Britain. It may be compared to an enriched French brioche. Recipes deriving from eighteenth-century practice have been collected (Cox, 1971). Irons also describes a distinctive shape, certainly universal in the 1930s, stemming from the use of 'flat tins, sides slightly sloping, [which] resembles more the housewife's tin for cooking joints'.

TECHNIQUE:
This bread is heavily enriched: 1 part Guernsey butter, 2 parts sultanas or currants, 2 parts flour. It is yeast-risen.

REGION OF PRODUCTION:
CHANNEL ISLANDS, GUERNSEY.

Black Butter

DESCRIPTION:
A THICK PASTE PACKED IN 500G GLASS JARS; DARK BROWN AND SLIGHTLY GRAINY. SHARPLY APPLE TASTE WITH STRONG LIQUORICE AND CINNAMON NOTES. COMPOSITION: APPLES, CIDER, LEMONS, SPICES.

HISTORY:
Black butter is made on the island of Jersey. Originally a by-product of cider-making, it is a type of apple paste eaten as a spread on bread. The use of the word butter, like 'cheese', is

common for these very thick fruit pastes. Butter describes a mixture that is potted, while cheese is the preferred term for a paste poured into an oiled mould to set, then wrapped in paper or foil for storage. Cheese is sliced with a knife and eaten as an accompaniment to dairy cheese or as a sweetmeat on its own. Butter is spreadable.

At first, these were often known as marmalades, the word deriving from the paste made from quince, which is *marmelo* in Portuguese. In Europe it is most often commercialized as *pâte de coings* in France or *membrillo* in Spain.

English recipes for fruit pastes are to be found from the 1400s. Some included spices as well as fruit pulp and honey or sugar. Many fruits have been used as a base: black currants, red currants, elderberries, gooseberries, damsons, quinces and oranges. It was a useful way to cope with seasonal gluts. However, in the nineteenth century, new methods of preserving made them seem old-fashioned and they went out of favour. In the confectionery industry, they survive as fruit pastilles and jellies.

Apples were the most familiar fruit and were reduced to butters more often than to cheeses. The American cookery writer Della Lutes has an evocative description of her family's way with apple butters at the turn of the century. In England, and still today in Jersey, they were called 'black' butters. The novelist Jane Austen wrote in a letter that some black butter served to her was neither properly set nor sweet enough, remarking that it was probably insufficiently boiled.

There has survived on Jersey a tradition, which must stretch back many generations, of making a black butter heavily flavoured with spices. It has remained a communal task and important social event: much labour is needed, both for preparation and for stirring. This has been maintained by a few people, mostly using the exercise as a means of charitable fundraising. However, production of black butter has declined since the Second World War (Brown, 1986). Interest in the product has lessened. Fewer cider apple trees are now planted and many old ones were uprooted in the storm of October 1987, which affected apple production in general.

TECHNIQUE:

On Jersey, favoured apple varieties include France and Romeril (sweet) and Bramley's (sour). All formulae that survive are for making large batches. One recipe requires 27 barrels of prepared apples, 70 litres of juice, 24 whole lemons, 13kg sugar, 500g cinnamon, 1.5kg mixed spices, 500g nutmeg, plus lemon juice and liquorice. For cooking, a very large, heavy brass cauldron called a *bâchin*, well over a metre in diameter and 30–40cm deep, is needed.

Apples (about 12 parts sweet to 1 part sour) are peeled, cored and cut into small pieces; some are pressed to yield fresh juice. A wood fire is prepared, the *bâchin* put in place and the apple juice first reduced to half by boiling. Three barrels of prepared apples are added and the whole cooked gently. From now on, the mixture must be continuously stirred. Periodically, more fresh apples are added until just over half have been incorporated. Several liquorice sticks (the black dried-juice type) are pounded and added. After the addition of more fresh apple, whole lemons reduced to a pulp are stirred in. Once all the cider apples have been incorporated and cooked down, the Bramley's are added. Cooking continues until the mixture is thought ready for testing; this is done by taking some up on a wooden spoon and slapping it onto a saucer. If the saucer doesn't fall when the spoon is lifted, the butter is deemed ready.

Spices, sugar and lemon juice are stirred through. The mixture is potted and sealed. Cooking can take 24–30 hours and the mixture becomes progressively heavy and stiff. Constant, thorough stirring is essential.

REGION OF PRODUCTION:
CHANNEL ISLANDS, JERSEY.

'Hunger is the best sauce in the world.'

MIGUEL DE CERVANTES, *DON QUIXOTE* (1615)

South England

Blueberry (High Bush)

DESCRIPTION:

BLUEBERRIES ARE SMALL ROUND BERRIES JUST UNDER 1CM DIAMETER; THEY HAVE A THIN BLACK SKIN COVERED IN A POWDERY BLUE BLOOM, GREENISH OR PURPLISH FLESH, AND A DISTINCTIVE SLIGHTLY WINY FLAVOUR.

HISTORY:

High bush blueberries, *Vaccinium corymbosum*, are related to the native British bilberry (*Vaccinium myrtillus*) and flourish in similar conditions. A precedent for the use of blueberries was well established in hill and heathland areas of the British Isles, where the inhabitants were accustomed to using wild blaeberries or bilberries in various sweet dishes. In Scotland, in the hills of Angus and Perthshire, blaeberries were picked by itinerant travellers who used a wooden device which they combed through the small bushes to extract the berries. These they sold in towns and villages to be eaten with cream, used for jam, or made into pies. Since the wild berries are time-consuming to gather, fruit-farmers have been experimenting with the alternative high bush blueberry.

This was developed in New Jersey, USA in 1920, putting to good use acid, boggy soils which had previously been thought worthless for growing. They have been grown in Britain since the 1930s. The first edition of *Law's Grocer's Manual* (*c*. 1895) mentions 'swamp blueberries', which grew on bushes up to 6 feet (2 metres) high, so it is possible that the British growers were aware of this type of plant some decades earlier but no evidence for their cultivation has been found. According to grower Jeremy Trehane, the bushes with which his family began production were offered free to British growers by a Canadian university in the 1940s. Cultivation has spread to other places in the lowland heath areas of the southern counties of England. In Scotland the berries were originally developed at the Scottish Crop Research Institute at Invergowrie as an alternative to blaeberries.

TECHNIQUE:

High bush blueberries grow well in impoverished acid soils (ideally pH 4.3–4.8, although they can tolerate slightly higher pH if dressed with peat) of the type which underlie many of the heathlands of Britain. The ground is cleared and the bushes planted at an appropriate density. Their only major nutrient requirement is potash, but to do well they do need heathland environments, as good growth relies on the presence of a particular micro-organism in the soil, which is not found in land that has been cultivated. They are pruned lightly in winter to remove old wood which has not fruited in the previous season. Protection from birds is necessary.

REGION OF PRODUCTION:

SOUTH ENGLAND.

Borage

BORAGE (*BORAGO OFFICINALIS*) IS A TALL ANNUAL HERB WITH COBALT-BLUE FLOWERS AND STEMS AND LEAVES WHICH ARE COVERED IN COARSE HAIRS; THE LEAVES AND FLOWERS HAVE A FLAVOUR REMINISCENT OF CUCUMBER, AND A NATURALLY COOLING EFFECT WHEN EATEN.

HISTORY:

Borage was probably introduced to Britain by the Romans, and has subsequently spread and naturalized on the chalk hills of southern England. There have been literary references to it since the thirteenth century. It was valued as a medicinal herb, and was made into cordials. Apothecaries considered it promoted cheerfulness and herbalists still use it to ease colds and throat complaints. The herb has also been used to decorate and flavour drinks. Dorothy Hartley (1954) quotes a recipe for claret cup from a Victorian magazine. This gives instructions for each glass to be flavoured with a sprig of borage, commenting on the unique flavour the herb gives and remarking, 'On this account the pretty blue flowers can be had of every gardener during the picnic season, and it is grown under glass all the year round for the express purpose of flavouring claret-cup.'

Borage is grown in gardens on a small scale and produced in larger volumes by market gardeners and specialist herb growers. Several growers who specialize in herbs and salad vegetables, mostly in the southern and eastern part of England, grow borage as part of their mixed crop. Recently, it has been established as a field crop for the sake of the oil that can be extracted. Always recognized as a useful bee-plant, this modern development has allowed some apiarists to produce monofloral borage honey.

The flowers are used to garnish summer drinks, especially Pimm's and claret cups. They are also added alone, or with other edible flowers such as nasturtiums, pot marigolds, chive flowers and heartsease, to salads; the leaves can be added too, if chopped finely. It is also used to flavour vinegars. The seeds can be used for the extraction of oils for food supplements. Until very recently, it was possible to buy borage flowers candied with sugar, although it appears that no-one makes these at present.

Alkanet, a related plant with similar leaves but smaller, rounder flowers is sometimes mistaken for borage; it is edible, although the applications are medicinal rather than culinary.

TECHNIQUE:

Borage is relatively undemanding and although some recommend well-drained calcareous soils, in practice it is tolerant. The plant prefers a sunny aspect. Commercial growers start the plants from seed under glass in about March and plant out in April. Borage is susceptible to frost, and dies back as the weather becomes colder in autumn. Once established, the plants will self-seed and grow again in the same ground year after year. The leaves and flowers wilt easily after picking, and so are generally picked to order for hotels and restaurants. One technique used by cooks for preserving the flowers is to freeze them in ice cubes.

REGION OF PRODUCTION:

SOUTH ENGLAND; EAST ENGLAND.

Cherry

DESCRIPTION:

ALMOST ALL CHERRIES GROWN IN ENGLAND ARE OF THE SWEET TYPE.

HISTORY:

Wild cherries (geans or mazzards) have been eaten in Britain since prehistoric times (Roach, 1985) but the development of cultivated fruit was the work of Mediterranean cultures. Pliny reported: 'Before the victory of Lucullus in the war against Mithridates … there were no cherry trees in Italy. Lucullus first imported them from Pontus [Asia Minor] and in 120 years they have crossed the ocean and got as far as Britain.' This seems pretty firm evidence and it is certain that Roman soldiers were plentifully supplied – perhaps from the precursors of the Kentish orchards. In the Middle Ages cherries were a common occupant of garden plots and sold in street markets. However, Europe was still the chief source of the fruit, where climate and skill combined for a larger harvest.

Kent became a centre of cultivation during the sixteenth century, partly because of good water-transport to London, the main market, partly because there were close links with orchardists and gardeners across the Channel. Most varieties grown came from Europe, especially Flanders and France, but there were early signs of specifically English breeds, notably the 'Duke' cherries, hybrids of the sweet *Prunus avium* and the sour *Prunus cerasus*. This group was known to the French as 'Anglais'.

Several classic varieties were bred by nurserymen in the 1800s, including Frogmore Early and Early Rivers, both introduced in the middle of the century. Two others are Bradbourne Black and Merton Glory, the latter introduced in the 1940s. For technical reasons, most orchards consist of several cherry varieties grown together; of the large number of varieties available, about 12 are commercially important.

The area devoted to cherry orchards has sadly diminished and we rely on imports again, as we used to in the fifteenth century, when they were freighted over from Flanders. Kent, however, has kept its first place among the regions of production.

TECHNIQUE:

The custom was to cultivate cherry trees as tall standards with grass underneath. The orchards are grazed by sheep. Most sweet cherries require pollinators and care is needed to choose a compatible variety. Until the twentieth century, geans or wild cherry seedlings from the woods were used as rootstocks. These produce large trees which require very long ladders to gather the fruit; as there is now some reluctance to pick from these, producers have been experimenting with less vigorous rootstocks. The latter have the advantage that they can be netted to protect them from birds during fruiting. A few farms offer pick-your-own facilities for cherry picking.

REGION OF PRODUCTION:

SOUTH AND WEST ENGLAND, KENT, HEREFORD AND WORCESTER, ESSEX, OXFORDSHIRE.

'One must ask children and birds how cherries and strawberries taste.'

JOHANN WOLFGANG VON GOETHE

Cox's Orange Pippin

DESCRIPTION:

A LATE-SEASON DESSERT APPLE, DESCRIBED BY MORGAN & RICHARDS (1993) AS MEDIUM-SIZED (5–7CM DIAMETER) OF ROUND-CONICAL SHAPE, THE BASIN OF MEDIUM WIDTH AND DEPTH, SLIGHTLY RIBBED, WITH RUSSET USUALLY PRESENT; THE EYE SMALL AND HALF-OPEN, THE SEPALS MEDIUM TO LONG AND NARROW; THE CAVITY MEDIUM BROAD, QUITE DEEP, WITH A LITTLE RUSSET; THE STALK OF MEDIUM LENGTH, AND QUITE THIN; THE COLOUR OF THE SKIN CHARACTERISTICALLY DISPLAYING AN ORANGE RED FLUSH WITH RED STRIPES OVER GREENISH YELLOW TURNING TO GOLD, WITH A LITTLE RUSSETING AS DOTS AND PATCHES; WHEN PERFECTLY RIPE, DELICIOUSLY SWEET AND ENTICING WITH RICH INTENSE AROMATIC FLAVOUR; DEEP CREAM FLESH; SPICY, HONEYED, NUTTY, PEAR-LIKE, BUT WITH A SUBTLE BLEND OF GREAT COMPLEXITY.

HISTORY:

The British have concentrated on the development of a uniquely wide spectrum of flavours and qualities in apple varieties; some of the finest are known as pippins. The word originally denoted an apple raised from seed as opposed to multiplied by scions. Morgan & Richards (1993) remark, 'in time the term "pippin" came to be synonymous with fine-flavoured late-keeping English varieties'. From Tudor times, pippins of various types have been popular and commercially important. At first the Golden Pippin was esteemed for making jellies and tarts. Then, the Ribston Pippin (Yorkshire), the Wyken Pippin (Warwickshire) and the Sturmer Pippin (Suffolk) arose, which remained important through the nineteenth century.

The Cox's Orange Pippin was raised by Richard Cox in Buckinghamshire. It is believed to have been grown from a pip of a Ribston Pippin. Commercialization took place in the 1860s in the neighbouring county of Hertford and it was widely planted in southern England over the next 30 years. Roach (1985) illustrates an orchard of Cox's Orange Pippin on dwarfing rootstocks in 1865. Today, it is the most important British dessert apple. Several clones are grown, including the Queen Cox. As well as being valued for its fruit, the Cox, crossed with other varieties, was the source of various late-season dessert apples, including Ellison's Orange, Epicure, Fortune and Laxton's Superb, several of which are still grown on a small scale.

Other notable varieties classed as late-season dessert types have complex aromatic flavours – sometimes reflected in their names, such as Cornish Gilliflower and Pitmaston Pine Apple (whose honeyed flavour is considered reminiscent of that fruit). These, and many others, were greatly enjoyed by Victorian and Edwardian connoisseurs when fine-flavoured dessert apples were much appreciated by the rich. That wealth of varieties has since reduced as a consequence of the modern emphasis on ease of growth and handling, and the uniform and attractive appearance demanded by supermarkets. However, a renewal of interest in rarities has been prompted by enthusiasts.

Many of these apples are now much grown abroad, including the Cox and the Sturmer. Controlled-atmosphere storage, very important to Cox's and some other late-season apples, has been used in Britain since the 1920s. Cox's Orange Pippin is generally eaten raw, although it can successfully be used in pies, tarts and cooked desserts. Some aromatic dessert apples have been used for single-variety juices.

See Bramley's Seedling (p. 111) for details about rootstocks. Cox's are not suitable for cultivation in the northern half of England, or in areas of high rainfall. They require free-draining soils, and are mostly concentrated in the south-east of Britain. Optimum pollination time is mid-May; the tree is of medium vigour and is a good cropper, but prone to mildew, scab and canker which are controlled by lime sulphur sprays. For commercial production, the fruit is chemically analysed to determine storage potential; picking is then carried out by hand. Cox's are picked in late September and early October. Grading is by diameter (sizes are set according to variety) and by quality (EU standards, for appearance) into Grade 1 or Grade 2. Storage in controlled atmosphere (low in oxygen, high in carbon dioxide) and temperature allows Cox's to be kept until spring.

REGION OF PRODUCTION:
SOUTH ENGLAND.

Egremont Russet Apple

DESCRIPTION:
A MID-SEASON DESSERT APPLE. DESCRIBED BY MORGAN & RICHARDS (1993) AS A MEDIUM-SIZED APPLE (5–7CM DIAMETER), FLAT-ROUND IN SHAPE, THE BASIN BROAD AND QUITE DEEP, THE EYE LARGE AND OPEN, THE SEPALS BROAD-BASED, AND QUITE DOWNY; THE CAVITY NARROW AND SHALLOW, LINED WITH RUSSET; THE STALK VERY SHORT AND QUITE THIN; THE COLOUR IS CHARACTERIZED BY OCHRE RUSSET (ROUGH-TEXTURED AREAS OF SKIN) WITH A SLIGHT ORANGE FLUSH ON GOLD GROUND COLOUR; THE FLESH IS CREAM COLOURED AND THE FLAVOUR IS NUTTY, WITH A SMOKY TANNIC DRYNESS DEVELOPING ON KEEPING.

HISTORY:
Russet pippins were described in the seventeenth century. This may simply have indicated red-flushed apples, as the word russet also carries a meaning of redness. Russet in the sense of rough-skinned does not seem to have been used until late in Victoria's reign. It was in the second half of the nineteenth century that the Egremont Russet was first noted. Exactly where it originated is unknown: it was first recorded in Somerset, but the name suggests a link with the estate of Lord Egremont at Petworth (Sussex). The head gardener from the estate maintained that it was raised there (Morgan & Richards, 1993). It was commercialized in the early twentieth century but suffered from being in season at the same time as the Cox's Orange Pippin. However, demand has continued and the Russet is still available.

The enthusiasm of the British for after-dinner drinking of port accompanied by fruit and nuts is one reason for their affection for the russets as a group. Their especial flavour, reminiscent of nuts and spice, and happy balance of sweetness and acidity matched that of the wine far better than any other style of dessert apple.

TECHNIQUE:
See Bramley's Seedling (p. 111) for details about rootstocks. Optimum pollination time for Egremont Russet is early May; the tree is of medium vigour and upright habit, hardy and a good cropper; it is resistant to scab but prone to bitter pit. Picking is by hand in late

September and early October. Grading is by diameter (sizes are set according to variety) and by quality (EU standards, for appearance) into Grade 1 or Grade 2. Egremont Russet can be stored for only a short time.

REGION OF PRODUCTION:
SOUTH ENGLAND.

Lord Derby Apple

DESCRIPTION:
A MID-SEASON COOKING APPLE, LARGE, ROUND-CONICAL TO OBLONG-CONICAL, GREEN, WITH SLIGHT PINK OR PURPLE ON CHEEK. FLAVOUR: STRONG, ACID, REQUIRES SUGAR.

HISTORY:
This apple was raised in the mid-nineteenth century in Cheshire, and commercialized shortly afterwards. It is possible that the apple originated from a seedling of the older English cooking variety called, because of its profile, the Catshead. This had been known since the early seventeenth century, and was popular for making dumplings in the 1800s. Unlike the codlin type of cooking apples, Lord Derby keeps its shape when cooked. Other cooking apples in season at this time are the old variety known as Harvey, first recorded in the 1600s, and Stirling Castle, both of which cook to a purée. They are now rare and little grown. Lord Derby is especially good in pies.

TECHNIQUE:
See entry on Cox's Orange Pippin for more details of apple growing.

REGION OF PRODUCTION:
SOUTH ENGLAND.

Samphire

DESCRIPTION:
THE LEAVES OF MARSH SAMPHIRE GROW IN BRIGHT GREEN SPEARS, SOMETIMES DESCRIBED AS LOOKING 'LIKE A BRANCH OF CORAL'. FLAVOUR: VERY SALTY.

ROCK SAMPHIRE IS MORE PINNATE, GROWING ON ROCKY CLIFFS AND SLOPES BY THE COAST.

HISTORY:
There are 2 forms of samphire. The first, and original, is rock samphire (*Crithmum maritimum*). The second is marsh samphire, once more commonly known as glasswort (*Salicornia stricta*) because it was used as a source of soda for glassmaking. Glasswort is found on many tidal marshes around the British coast. It is very common, and best known in Norfolk. Spencer (1994) observes that, unlike rock samphire, which was highly esteemed in the past, marsh samphire was historically a food for the poor. In the late nineteenth century it was a substitute for the increasingly rare rock samphire. Since the second half of the twentieth century, marsh samphire has become better known generally.

Rock samphire still grows abundantly on the coasts of southern Britain. It was the subject of a much-quoted line in *King Lear*, when Edgar wishes to deceive blind Gloucester into thinking he is on the cliffs at Dover: 'Half way down hangs one that gathers samphire, dreadful trade!' he exclaims.

Culpeper the herbalist remarked in 1656 that samphire was not as much used as it was, but the statement was no barrier to a battery of seventeenth- and eighteenth-century recipes, especially for pickles, the form that mostly reached the table. Nor was it in such short supply that it could not be hawked on the streets of London as 'Cress marine!' However, the curious intelligence of John Evelyn (1699) wished to pursue the possibility of cultivating the plant, to assure supplies, much as they did, he observed, in France. His venture was of little success and the plant here has remained obstinately wild. Evelyn included a recipe for pickling samphire 'the Dover way' – it was Mr John Bullen of Dover who sent him his experimental seeds, a descendant, perhaps, of Edgar's labourer.

It is possible that there was insufficient rock samphire to maintain a large-scale trade, or the dangers of clifftop gathering were too fatal, but there are signs at the end of the eighteenth century that supplies were running out and a substitute was needed. Here we might bring forward another poet's reference, John Phillips:

> How from a scraggy rock, whose prominence
> Half overshades the ocean, hardy men
> Fearless of rending winds, and dashing waves,
> Cut samphire, to excite the squeamish gust
> Of pamper'd luxury…

Hugh Smythson in *Compleat Family Physician* (1781) lets fall that it was 'not often brought genuine to London'. The more easily gathered glasswort, already the object of industrial exploitation for the glass trade, was a willing candidate, but it is not entirely clear that its offer, or that of its vendors, was ever taken up. There may have been a plethora of early recipes, but there are few in Victoria's reign, implying an acceptance of the scarcity of the original plant (Tee, 1983).

It was different in East Anglia. There, the locals accepted glasswort as samphire and continued to pickle it. Mabey (1978) remarks that the 'old way was to pack the samphire into jars with vinegar and store them in bread ovens which were cooling down on Friday night after the baking was finished. The jars were left until Monday morning … it seems to have been highly valued.' Even this tradition appears to have declined, and may have died out so far as the East Anglian table is concerned. However, the revival of the fresh-fish trade supplying restaurants and commercial kitchens in the South-East, together with an appreciation of wild foods, has led to a reintroduction of samphire (mainly marsh) to fishmongers. It can be bought in many places in London.

The position of rock samphire is less secure. No one gathers it in sufficient quantity to pickle it for sale, but there are commercial kitchens which use it in their recipes in the South-West of England. Pickled samphire is still available in markets in Spain (Stobart, 1980) and in Boulogne – to name but one in France. It can also be eaten raw at the start of the season, or lightly blanched and served with melted butter. It then goes as well with lamb as with fish.

TECHNIQUE:

Marsh samphire is collected by hand from the edges of tidal creeks; it should be cut from the plant just above the base, washed, and used whilst very fresh. Sold from fish stalls, markets and wayside stalls in north Norfolk.

Rock samphire is gathered before it flowers from cliffs and rocks on the coast. After washing and blanching, it may be pickled in vinegar. Evelyn reckoned the best time to pickle it was Michaelmas (29 September); this is thought late in the year by modern cooks.

REGION OF PRODUCTION:
SOUTH ENGLAND.

Watercress

DESCRIPTION:
THE DARK GREEN LEAVES OF WATERCRESS ARE SOLD IN BUNCHES OF ABOUT 100G. FLAVOUR:
PEPPERY.

HISTORY:
Watercress, *Nasturtium officinale*, picked from streams and meadows, was valued for its medicinal qualities. The herbalist John Gerard (1636) and others extolled it as an anti-scorbutic. The Italian Castelvetro in 1614 wrote that it was 'the last green salad of the season which goes on being available all winter provided the streams are not frozen. It makes quite a pleasant salad, but since there is no alternative it always seems better that it really is. Because watercress grows in fast-running water it is very refreshing and is usually eaten raw.' There was confusion, however, between the various sorts of cress and the nasturtium flower (now called *Tropaeolum majus*). John Evelyn (1699) expresses it well: 'Cresses, Nasturtium, garden cresses; to be monthly sown: but above all the Indian [our nasturtium flower], moderately hot and aromatick, quicken the torpent spirits, and purge the brain, and are of singular effect against the scorbute [scurvy] …There is the *Nasturtium Hybernicum* commended also [the winter cress, *Barbarea verna*], and the vulgar watercress, proper in the spring, all of the same nature, tho' of different degrees, and best for raw and cold stomachs, but nourish little.'

This 'vulgar' cress did not receive much notice from cookery writers, it was perhaps beneath their notice or merely formed part of a general category of saladings. The perils of eating plants that grew in near-stagnant water fouled by animal droppings must also have militated against too general an adoption. In Flanders, there was a fondness for watercress soup, and in France 'cooks insist upon sending to table a bunch of cresses with roast fowl – even when there is salad besides' (Dallas, 1877); but neither were British customs.

The general adoption of watercress into the diet, particularly of the urban proletariat, occurred when the hygienic cultivation of watercress began in Kent in the early nineteenth century. In essence, the cress was grown in guaranteed running water. From Kent, it spread to the Thames Valley, and thence, as the expanding rail network enabled speedy transport, to the chalk streams of Hampshire and Dorset with which it is most closely connected today. The railway to these districts was even popularly dubbed 'the Watercress Line'. It was cried in the streets of London, where workmen bought it for breakfast and became as popular for sandwiches as cucumber (Mayhew, 1851).

TECHNIQUE:
The main areas for cultivation are the valleys of the rivers Test and Itchen, in Hampshire.

Cress is also grown in Dorset and Wiltshire. A very little cultivation is still carried on in Hertfordshire and Kent. Watercress requires hard water at constant temperature; the latter is important in winter. In southern England these conditions are provided by the chalk aquifers in the counties of Hampshire, Dorset and Wiltshire; this maintains a temperature of 11°C; the beds have a gravel base and a gradual even slope to ensure the correct flow. The cress is cut by hand or harvested mechanically, cooled, washed, and packed. All watercress seed used in Britain is home-produced; in summer, beds are cleaned and replanted at frequent intervals to ensure a regular supply of young leaves, whilst in winter, crops are grown under protective covering.

REGION OF PRODUCTION:
SOUTH ENGLAND, HAMPSHIRE.

Sussex Slipcote Cheese

DESCRIPTION:
SOFT, UNPASTEURIZED SHEEP'S MILK CHEESE; AS BUTTONS OF 5CM DIAMETER, 2CM DEEP (100G), OR LOGS 18CM LONG, 6CM DEEP (1KG). COLOUR: PALE, ALMOST WHITE. FLAVOUR: LIGHT BUT CREAMY. GARLIC, AND HERB AND BLACK PEPPERCORN-FLAVOURED CHEESES ALSO MADE.

HISTORY:
Slipcote, or slipcoat, cheese has a long history in Britain. Originally, it appears to have been a full-fat cheese, and was widely known. The name may derive from the cheese breaking out of its rind as it ripened (Rance, 1982). Other British cheeses had this reputation, for instance the now-extinct Colwick. *Law's Grocer's Manual* (*c.* 1895) described slipcote as 'a rich and soft kind of cheese made of milk warm from the cow, and often with cream added. It closely resembles white butter.' It was a cheese type, rather than a regional description, though a Victorian writer linked it especially with Yorkshire, and apparently it was known in Rutland until the First World War and, Rance says, 'remembered later as something like a Camembert, sold on straw, with a volatile coat'. Sir Kenelm Digby gave 3 recipes for slipcote from his *Closet* (1669), recalling that 'My Lady of Middlesex makes excellent slippcoat Cheese of good morning milk, putting Cream to it.' It was a soft, fresh cheese, usually wrapped in docks, nettles, grass or reeds.

Rationing discouraged the manufacture of such rich cheeses, but it is now made again, this time with sheep's rather than cow's milk.

TECHNIQUE:
Milk from local flocks is used whenever possible, preferably that from Dorset Horns. It is not pasteurized. The milk is started and vegetarian rennet added; it is left overnight. The curd is gently broken and ladled into moulds. Salt is added, as are herbs or peppercorns if required. Draining depends on season and size of cheese, but lasts 1–5 days.

REGION OF PRODUCTION:
SOUTH ENGLAND, SUSSEX.

As a chef, it is extremely important to me to use the best-tasting, healthiest and freshest food I can find – from pork and beef to fruit and vegetables. For this reason, we at Le Manoir aux Quat'Saisons have always worked closely with our local producers, my favourite of which is Laverstoke Park. For me, farm founder Jody Scheckter and his team, through their uncompromising approach to organic farming, are already achieving excellence in their field. Jody's ambitions are extremely high – compromise doesn't exist in his approach to farming. He has surrounded himself with the best professionals in every facet of his business and he was one of the very first to understand that the quality and variety of the soil are cornerstones of successful organic farming.

The team at Laverstoke Park creates the most natural and healthy environment for their animals and crops to thrive in. They follow nature closely, carefully combining natural processes where appropriate with the latest and best scientific research, techniques and equipment. They also know that to achieve a healthy environment, plant and animal biodiversity is a vital factor, as are slower-growing traditional, older, native and rare breeds of animals.

As a result, Jody is already producing some of the best-tasting and most nutritious food available. We use Hebridean lambs from Laverstoke Park, an ancient breed of sheep originating from the islands off the west coast of Scotland. The small carcass produces the most delicious lamb, and is very tender and succulent.

Raymond Blanc

CHEF AND PROPRIETOR, LE MANOIR AUX QUAT'SAISONS, GREAT MILTON

Bedfordshire Clanger

DESCRIPTION:

AN OBLONG, BAKED PASTY MADE WITH A SUET CRUST, FILLED WITH SAVOURY AND SWEET
INGREDIENTS AT OPPOSITE ENDS. DIMENSIONS: 12–14CM LONG, 6–8CM WIDE. COLOUR:
GOLDEN CRUST. FLAVOUR: A SAVOURY FILLING OF MEAT, USUALLY CURED PORK, AT ONE END
AND A SWEET, OFTEN APPLE, AT THE OTHER.

HISTORY:

The Bedfordshire Clanger has undergone much change in the last century. Today it is a baked
pasty (with a suet crust) which has 2 fillings rather than one. Savoury meat and something
sweet sit at opposite ends of a baked pie. This does not seem to have been the original form.
Clangers were once a boiled suet roll, like plum duff or roly-poly. The roll contained a meat
filling, and the crust was itself studded with fruit. It became a sort of complete meal in one.
Compilations of English country recipes show them to have been plain, substantial food for
farm labourers and other manual workers. Suet pastry enclosed a filling which varied with the
affluence of the family involved (Ayrton, 1982). The poor used the only meat which was readily available, bacon; richer families used good steak or pork. Similar dishes were made in other
parts of central eastern England. Poulson (1977) mentions a bacon clanger, filled with bacon,
sage and onion, from the Thames valley; a similar dish was known in Leicestershire as a
Quorn bacon roll.

No-one has offered a derivation of clanger. Wright (1896–1905) cites 'clang' as a
Northamptonshire dialect word meaning 'to eat voraciously'. The Bedfordshire Clanger may
have developed in response to local employment patterns (Mabey, 1978). Many women were
employed in the straw-hat industry and the clanger, boiling slowly for hours unattended, was
a complete hot meal for those arriving home from work. Clangers are now made because there
is a local taste for them. There are even clanger-eating contests at local fairs and festivities.
Clangers have now evolved into a baked dish. This reflects the evolution of British cooking
methods away from long boiling to dry baking, more convenient once domestic gas or electric
cookers were universally available. Old recipes sometimes called for the boiled rolls to be dried
in a low oven before consumption.

TECHNIQUE:

Bedfordshire Clangers made for sale are less elaborate than those produced at home. The
fillings are prepared first; meat is cut into small dice, onions chopped, apples peeled and sliced.
An English suet crust is made: plain flour and chopped suet (2:1), salt and enough water for
a coherent dough. The pastry is rolled out and cut to oblongs twice the size of the finished
clanger. Small mounds of the savoury and sweet fillings are placed in opposing ends divided
by a strip of pastry. The pastry is folded over to enclose the fillings. The edges and the area
around the central dividing strip are sealed, and the surface glazed with egg. It is baked at
210°C for 30 minutes.

REGION OF PRODUCTION:

SOUTH ENGLAND, BEDFORDSHIRE.

COMPARE WITH:

Forfar Bridie, Scotland (p. 310); Cornish Pasty, South-West England (p. 20).

Berkshire Pig

DESCRIPTION:

Dressed carcass weight 36–45kg. Berkshire pigs have a short, deep body, although the development of longer animals has been recently encouraged. Although the breed has a black skin, this becomes white if the carcass is correctly prepared. When reared extensively, the meat is deeper pink than normal; it is finely textured with a sweet flavour and a high proportion of lean to fat.

HISTORY:

This breed was developed in the Thames valley in the late 1700s. Early specimens are described as large-boned and tawny, red or white spotted with black. Not many years later, it was made more compact, more lightly boned and faster-maturing by interbreeding with Chinese or east Asian stock. The improved Berkshire was entirely black or white.

Mrs Beeton (1861) listed Berkshires among native British stock and praises it for a fine, delicate skin and a great aptitude to fatten. The British Berkshire Society was founded in the 1880s but the fortunes of the race declined in this century when it proved too slow-maturing and fat in comparison with modern bloodlines. Since the 1970s, there has been renewed interest and numbers are slowly recovering.

TECHNIQUE:

The majority of Berkshires are kept outdoors, grubbing for food on grassland. They are hardy, can withstand cold weather and do not suffer sunburn. Although they can feed themselves adequately by foraging, most breeders supplement with barley or oats as well as vitamins. It is especially important that carcasses of Berkshires are carefully scalded as the black hairs and pigment of the skin, considered unsightly when the meat is presented for sale, can be entirely removed by correct treatment. This is important for the British market as pork is almost always roasted with the skin intact. Berkshire is noted as pork with excellent crackling: an English sine qua non.

REGION OF PRODUCTION:
South England.

Chitterlings

DESCRIPTION:

Chitterlings are cooked pigs' intestines; there are several methods of presenting these for sale. They may be made into plaits; or cut in 6–8cm lengths, and sold by weight; or made into slabs, the pieces held together in jelly. The 2 latter often include pieces of pigs' maw (stomach) cut into strips and mixed with the chitterlings. Colour: variable, off-white through pale grey-pink to deep pink; the jellied slabs are cut into slices at right angles to the length of the chitterlings, giving an attractive marbled appearance. Flavour: brined, jellied chitterling tastes similar to lean bacon.

HISTORY:

The word chitterling is of uncertain derivation but has been used in English since at least the thirteenth century for the small intestines of animals, especially pigs, when used for food. At one time it seems to have also referred to a type of sausage made from them (akin to a French *andouillette*), but latterly has come to mean simply the intestines, cleaned and prepared.

Their preparation is not elaborate. Since the late twentieth century they are a minority taste, seen as a poverty food and regarded as old-fashioned. It is recognized that they are more popular in some regions than others. Their stronghold is the South and South-West, where pigs have long been reared in huge numbers.

Chitterlings are sold cooked and can be eaten cold with vinegar or mustard; or they can be heated by frying with bacon, or by boiling.

TECHNIQUE:

Pigs' small intestines are prepared by turning them inside out and cleaning; they are cut into short lengths or plaited. The chitterlings may be soaked in brine overnight if desired. They are cooked in boiling salted water for about 30 minutes. As they give off a pungent smell in the cooking, some butchers now prefer to enclose them in vacuum bags before putting them into the water. After this they are ready for sale. Some manufacturers pressed chitterlings and maw in a mould to cool, the liquor forming a jelly around them. This is sliced and vacuum-packed for sale.

REGION OF PRODUCTION:
SOUTH ENGLAND; SOUTH WEST ENGLAND.

Oxford Sausage

DESCRIPTION:
A FRESH PORK AND VEAL SAUSAGE; 6–8 SAUSAGES TO THE LB (450G). FORM: FAIRLY SHORT AND PLUMP. COLOUR: SLIGHTLY PALER PINK THAN THE AVERAGE, WITH PROMINENT HERB FLECKS. FLAVOUR: A GOOD BALANCE OF LEMON AND HERBS.

HISTORY:
In 1779, the Reverend Dr Warner wrote to his friend George Selwyn, 'I shall also order some New College puddings and Oxford sausages, and hope to bring you a hare.' (Jesse, 1901) These sausages were already famous. In 1726, John Nott gave a recipe for 'Sausages called Oxford Skates' which closely resembles recipes still known. It is a mixture of pork, veal and beef suet, quite highly seasoned. White (1932) has printed similar recipes from the following 200 years. In all of them, the mixture was rolled into cylinders or patties, floured and fried. If Oxford sausages were skinless, it goes without saying that Cambridge sausages (also celebrated in the past) were stuffed into skins.

Mrs Rundell (1807) mentions the addition of a little soaked bread in her instructions, suggesting the recipe had then begun to evolve along lines similar to other British sausages. Dallas (1877) noted that the mixture was pressed 'down close in a pan for use. It may be stuffed in skins like other sausage meat; but is generally rolled out as wanted, and either fried in fresh butter of a brown colour or broiled over a clear fire.' Oxford sausages were less remarked in the twentieth century but were still known, and Florence White records correspondence about them, including the fact they could still be bought in Oxford market in the early 1930s and that a similar skinless sausage was found in Cornwall. Finney's guide for pork

'One can say everything best over a meal.'

GEORGE ELIOT, *ADAM BEDE*

butchers (1915) included an Oxford seasoning which included sage and coriander; he also had recipes for Oxford beef sausages.

In recent years British fresh sausages generally have suffered from the application of mass-production techniques. Recently, more interest has been taken in the subject, and new companies are researching and using recipes based on those from the eighteenth century.

TECHNIQUE:
There are 2 differences between Oxford sausages of the past and those known today. The first is in the composition: beef suet is rarely used now, as it produces a sausage which is dense and heavy to modern taste. Secondly, the sausages are now put into casings. A manufacturer who has recently begun to make Oxford sausages based on old recipes uses shoulder pork from locally produced, extensively farmed pigs. Equal quantities of veal, plus a small amount of cereal form the basis; the meat is minced with a little rusk, and seasoned with herbs, salt, lemon zest and spices, and then filled into narrow hog casings and hand-linked.

REGION OF PRODUCTION:
SOUTH ENGLAND, OXFORD.

Cottage Loaf

DESCRIPTION:
A CIRCULAR LOAF WITH A LARGE TOPKNOT (USUALLY ONE-THIRD THE SIZE OF THE MAIN PART); THE SURFACE IS SOMETIMES SLASHED TO GIVE A ROSETTE EFFECT WHEN RISING IS COMPLETED. A SMALL LOAF IS ABOUT 100MM HIGH, 180–200MM DIAMETER. WEIGHT: 400G (SMALL), 800G (LARGE). COLOUR: DEEP GOLD CRUST WITH PALER, LESS BAKED AREAS IN THE NOTCHES. FLAVOUR: THE SHAPE OF THE LOAF GIVES A HIGHER RATIO OF CRUST TO CRUMB THAN OBTAINED WITH TIN LOAVES.

HISTORY:
The earliest reference to the distinctive shape known as a 'cottage loaf' cited by the *Oxford English Dictionary* comes from the 1840s. How long they were made before then is not obvious, although a description by Edlin (1805) makes it clear that loaves of the cottage type were being made. Until the Second World War, they were perhaps the most common shape available in England. In Scotland, they were only occasionally made but when they were, they were flatter and lighter. By contrast, Welsh loaves and those from the Midlands had a closer, cakier texture.

The moulding of a cottage loaf is not easy. Inadequate craftsmanship could make the halves separate or cause alarming tilts and eccentricities. Perhaps this is why Kirkland (1907) noticed that London cottage loaves had smaller topknots.

No complete explanation of the development of the shape is likely. A parallel may be drawn with the shape of *pain chapeau*, found in the Finistère district of Brittany. The cob loaf was the simplest, round, oven-bottom bread in the English baker's repertoire. Oven-bottom breads were crustier and more flavourful than loaves cooked in tins (as were most often produced in Scotland, for example, and which became almost universal with the industrialization of British breadmaking). The word cob meant nothing more than a small lump. A similar loaf shape was the coburg, a London form named in honour of the marriage of Queen Victoria to Prince Albert of Saxe-Coburg. This was a cob loaf with extra slashes across the top. The cottage loaf could be likened to 2 cobs piled on top of each other. As it became necessary to increase the output of bakeries in the face of growing demand as England industrialized and urbanized, so a cottage loaf would greatly increase the production of each oven load. It is also possible that the shape was fostered by the availability of fine, high-protein white flour with the advent of roller milling and imports of hard wheat from North America.

TECHNIQUE:
No particular dough is reserved to this shape, but it is best if it is stiff in texture. After mixing and bulk fermentation, the dough is scaled off into pieces for the tops and bottoms (top and bottom loaves was a Chichester (Sussex) name for this shape). The top is joined to the bottom by pressing through the centre of the top with the fingers. After a final proof and, if required, slashing the top surface, the loaf is baked on the oven bottom at 230°C for 60 minutes.

REGION OF PRODUCTION:
SOUTH ENGLAND.

Isle of Wight Doughnut

DESCRIPTION:
ROUGHLY SPHERICAL FRIED DOUGH, 70MM DIAMETER. WEIGHT: ABOUT 75G. COLOUR: GOLDEN BROWN OUTSIDE, DUSTED WITH SUGAR; PALE GOLD INSIDE, WITH SULTANAS AND A JAM FILLING. FLAVOUR: SWEETISH, SHORT-TEXTURED.

HISTORY:
Deep-fried pastry and fritters are not well represented in British food traditions. An exception seems to be the Isle of Wight, on the English south coast. Here, there are several variations on the theme including doughnuts filled with currants and tied in the shape of a knot and an apple-filled one in a turnover (half circle) shape. In the mid-nineteenth century a yeast-raised doughnut with a filling of raisins and candied peel was made there; a recipe was given by Eliza Acton (1845). She noted that at certain times they were made in large quantities and were drained of their fat on very clean straw. The dough was flavoured with allspice, cinnamon, cloves and mace. Another recipe was collected by the local Women's Institute in the 1930s. It is similar, apart from a reduction in spices to nutmeg alone. Oral tradition states that until about 30 years ago, a few shops displayed these doughnuts piled up in their windows and sold nothing else. The doughnuts made at present are produced to a recipe belonging to a long-established bakery in Newport.

TECHNIQUE:
Published recipes call for plain flour, butter and sugar in the proportions 6:1:1. The butter is rubbed into the flour, followed by the sugar and grated nutmeg; this is made into a soft yeasted dough with milk and egg. After fermentation, pieces about the size of tangerines are nipped off. A hollow is made which is filled with a few raisins and a piece of candied peel and, in some recipes, lemon zest. The dough is wrapped around and smoothed over to make a ball. They were cooked in lard – now more often vegetable oil – at 160–170°C. They are turned once during cooking, when golden brown. Then they are drained and dusted with icing sugar.

REGION OF PRODUCTION:
SOUTH ENGLAND, ISLE OF WIGHT.

Cider Cake

DESCRIPTION:

A CIRCULAR CAKE (OCCASIONALLY SQUARE), 140–200MM DIAMETER, 30–40MM DEEP. WEIGHT: 450–700G. COLOUR: PALE GOLDEN EXTERIOR, DEEP CREAM CRUMB. FLAVOUR: RICH, WITH AFTERTASTE OF CIDER; SOMETIMES SPICED AND WITH DRIED FRUIT.

HISTORY:

Elizabeth Ayrton (1982) remarks that cider cake is often met in Oxfordshire, Herefordshire, Worcestershire and Gloucestershire, that several recipes from the 1800s are known and that they all use bicarbonate of soda as a raising agent. In this form, the cake cannot date much before the 1850s, when baking soda was first used as a leaven. The technique for mixing the cake is also relatively modern. There is a possible connection between cider cakes and vinegar cakes. These last rely on bicarbonate of soda neutralized by the acetic acid in vinegar to make them rise; English cider, which is very dry and rather acid, makes a good alternative. Cider cakes are made in all cider-producing counties, and are sometimes called after the relevant county. Examples are recorded from Suffolk, Somerset, Dorset, Gloucester, Hereford and Worcester, and Oxford.

TECHNIQUE:

Flour, butter and sugar are used in the proportions 2:1:1. Some add spices; nutmeg is the most common. There are 2 methods of mixing. The first sees the fat rubbed into the flour, the sugar stirred through, and eggs, cider, dried fruit and nuts added as required. The second is more elaborate: the butter and sugar are beaten together until fluffy, mixed with eggs and beaten again. Then half the flour, combined with spice and bicarbonate of soda, is beaten in. The cider is added, and the mixture stirred until it begins to froth. The remaining flour is immediately stirred through. The cake is baked at 200°C for 40–50 minutes.

REGION OF PRODUCTION:

SOUTH ENGLAND.

Lardy Cake

DESCRIPTION:

RECTANGULAR OR ROUND CAKES; ONE FROM OXFORD WAS 180MM LONG, 110MM WIDE, 30MM DEEP; ONE FROM GLOUCESTER WAS A LOOSE SPIRAL 160MM DIAMETER, 40MM DEEP. WEIGHT: THE OXFORD EXAMPLE WAS 500G, THE GLOUCESTER 250G. COLOUR: DEEP GOLD, STICKY AND SHINY UNDERNEATH, SPECKLED WITH DRIED FRUIT, PALE, ALMOST WHITE CRUMB; THE CAKE RANGES FROM LAYERED AND FLAKY PUFF PASTRY TO A SIMPLE, ROLLED SHEET OF DOUGH. FLAVOUR AND TEXTURE: SWEET WITH A FLAKY APPEARANCE WHEN CUT; SOLID, CHEWY.

HISTORY:

This cake is based on lard, the fat most commonly used in pig-rearing regions of Britain, which is incorporated into dough taken from the main batch at bread making. Wright (1896–1905) associates it with Oxfordshire, Berkshire and Wiltshire but it was more widely known than that. Most counties appear to have made a version at one time, and they varied a little according to the fat used. Some called for the 'flead' or 'flare' – the kidney fat – to be used raw. Others used scratchings, the residue after fat has been rendered. Mayhew (1851) records trays of flare cakes for sale on the streets of London. As a food of the poor and of country people, lardy cakes escaped the attention of many early recipe collectors. They are now principally identified with the South, especially north and west of London. There are differences, especially in shape, between counties, but not of basic principle. Variant names include shaley or sharley cake (Wiltshire); dripping cake or 'drips' (Gloucestershire); bread cake (Shropshire). Apples or spices such as cinnamon may be included for variety.

TECHNIQUE:

Home cooks tend to make richer cakes than commercial bakers. Ingredients are dough, sugar, lard and mixed fruit and peel in the ratio of 3 or 4:1:1:1. The dough is taken from the main batch after bulk fermentation and rolled into a rectangle; two thirds of this is spread with one third of the lard, and scattered with one third of the fruit and peel and one third of the sugar; the dough is folded and turned, and the process repeated twice. The final turn is arranged so the dough is shaped into a roll. The cake may then be scored for later cutting. It is proved for 1 hour and baked for 45 minutes at 220°C. It is turned upside down to cool to prevent it sticking; this is said to encourage the lard to run back through the cake.

REGION OF PRODUCTION:
SOUTH ENGLAND, WILTSHIRE.

COMPARE WITH:
Dough Cake, South West England (p. 38).

Barley Wine: Thomas Hardy's Ale

DESCRIPTION:

COLOUR VARIES ACCORDING TO AGE BUT IS OFTEN A DEEP COPPERY BROWN WITH A HEAVY AND MALTY FLAVOUR. THOMAS HARDY'S ALE IS SWEET, HEAVY BODIED, WITH FRUIT AND CHOCOLATE OVERTONES. IT IS 12 PER CENT ALCOHOL BY VOLUME, STRONGER THAN ANY NORMAL BEER AND MANY WINES.

HISTORY:

Earliest references to barley wine by name date from the twentieth century (*OED*). Jackson (1993) considers, 'the romantic term "barley wine" may have been coined by rural home-brewers to describe their most impressively potent efforts'. There is no evidence that the name came from the use of wine yeasts. It is now often employed by brewers to describe their strongest ale, but the style is older than the name. It is kin to the dark beers known earlier as porter. The archaic northern dialect word 'stingo' has also been used. In Scotland, such powerful beers are known as 'wee heavy'.

Dorchester developed as a centre of the brewing industry during the eighteenth century, due partly to a chalk aquifer in the strata below the town. Richard Bradley (1736) wrote of its fine beer with 'a strength of malt and hops in it' to last 4 years. '[It] is esteem'd preferable to most of the Malt-Liquor in England,' he continued, '[for] it is for the most part brew'd of chalky water.'

Hardy himself wrote a lyrical description of Dorchester ale in *The Trumpet Major* (1880). The drink which now bears his name, however, is recent: developed in 1968 to honour the

When I got my first job on a newspaper it was as cookery writer for the *Daily Mail*, and I was lucky not to lose it in the first month. I had written a recipe for Oxford Marmalade – you know the one: made with bitter Seville oranges, chunky and dark with treacle – but I had written it by hand and forgotten to cross the 't' in treacle. This meant that '2 tbs' was printed as '2 lbs'. Since the rest of the ingredients only amounted to ten oranges and a kilo of sugar, this had disaster potential. And a disaster it was.

You would not believe the number of people who just accept what they read in newspapers. The *Daily Mail* switchboard went white-hot with complaints about the black caramel in readers' saucepans. We had to reimburse readers for a lot of ingredient costs and quite a few saucepans which were damaged beyond repair. So when a woman rang up and suggested we let her know how much extra sugar and how many extra oranges she should add to the mixture to get the proportions right again, I thought, 'Good, this is how we rescue the situation – we just get everyone to make extra marmalade for next year, plus a few pots for the village fête and so on.' Until, that is, we worked out that each reader would need to make about eighty jars of marmalade. We reimbursed her like everyone else.

The day after publication I found what looked like a letter bomb on my desk. Well, I knew I'd got the recipe wrong, but I thought bombing was going a bit far. I could tell it was a bomb because, this being the time of the IRA letter bomb campaign, we'd all had bomb training. If you got a suspicious package, especially one like this, which had something squashy in the middle and what felt like wires sticking out each side, you called the security desk and they sent a copper in a flak jacket who took it away.

Eventually the copper brought it back. It contained a piece of marmalade toffee with a dental brace, complete with two teeth embedded in it. And a very large orthodontist's bill.

Prue Leith

Cookery editor, food columnist and broadcaster,
and founder of Leith's Restaurant

then prime minister, Harold Macmillan, whose family was Hardy's publisher. Breweries who produce barley wines often give them names of characters, fictional or real. Eldridge Pope, the brewers of this beer, were founded in 1837.

TECHNIQUE:

A lightly kilned ale malt is used for Thomas Hardy's Ale. The wort is hopped with English varieties, and a top-fermenting yeast is used for a primary fermentation which lasts for approximately 10 days. After this, the beer is re-yeasted for a secondary fermentation and warm-conditioned for 3–6 months, after which the beer is drawn off the sediment and given a further conditioning in cold store for 1–3 months. Yeast is added several times during this time, as the high sugar and alcohol content affect it significantly. When considered ready to leave the brewery, the beer is re-yeasted again and bottled for distribution. It will improve up to its best in the bottle at 5–7 years and will keep for 25 years.

REGION OF PRODUCTION:
SOUTH ENGLAND, DORSET.

Elderflower Cordial

DESCRIPTION:
A PALE STRAW COLOUR AND TRANSPARENT. IT HAS A STRONG AROMA OF ELDERFLOWER AND MUSCAT AND IS BOTH SWEET AND SHARP TO THE TASTE.

HISTORY:
Most British soft drinks are fruit based; this is singular in being made from flowers. Rather aptly, the elder was once considered of value for treating the heart and circulation. Its being used to make a syrup (for it had hitherto flavoured vinegars and wines) was the result of the set of influences mentioned in the entry on elderberry cordial, p. 428.

TECHNIQUE:
Elderflowers, gathered when fully open (late May to late June), are steeped with sugar, lemon and citric acid for 5 days, before the cordial is strained and bottled. Commercial producers use methods which are a scaled-up version of this. There are differences in the treatment of the flowers after picking: one producer mills and presses them to produce a juice which is used to flavour the essence; another stores them in a solution of sugar and citric acid. Dried flowers are also used in some cordials.

REGION OF PRODUCTION:
SOUTH ENGLAND AND NATIONWIDE.

Single-Variety Apple Juice

DESCRIPTION:
FRESH PRESSED APPLE JUICE IS OFTEN PALE YELLOW-GREEN AND CLOUDY. SOME IS FILTERED. THE FLAVOUR DEPENDS ON THE VARIETY OF APPLE. MANY HAVE COMPLEX FLORAL, FRUITY, SPICY AND NUTTY OVERTONES. PRODUCTION FROM INDIGENOUS VARIETIES IS AS PARTICULAR TO BRITAIN AS THE APPLES THEMSELVES.

Apples have been pressed for juice, primarily as the first step in cider-making, for centuries. Commercial juice production in England began in the 1930s and by the 1970s had become a large industry. At this time, most so-called juice was made from concentrate mixed with water. The development of single-variety juices has arisen from a growing interest in the different flavours of apples and from a need to diversify into new markets for agricultural produce. Cox's Orange Pippin and Bramley's Seedling, favourite long-keeping English apples, are much used (and often blended together when a single-variety juice is not required); other varieties are pressed when available.

TECHNIQUE:
All producers begin with milling and pressing the apples as if for cider. The juice may then be left to clear and be filtered before pasteurizing. Both flash-pasteurizing at a high temperature and a lower-temperature, longer method are used. Some add vitamin C as an antioxidant.

REGION OF PRODUCTION:
SOUTH ENGLAND.

***

Also produced in South England
DOUGH CAKE (P. 38)
FAGGOT (P. 146)
HASLET (P. 147)
HOG'S PUDDING (P. 26)
WORCESTER PEARMAIN APPLE (P. 165)

South East England

Blenheim Orange Apple

DESCRIPTION:

A LATE-SEASON APPLE SUITABLE FOR DESSERT AND COOKING. DESCRIBED BY MORGAN & RICHARDS (1993) AS MEDIUM-LARGE (5–8CM DIAMETER); FLAT-ROUND, WITH ROUNDED RIBS, SLIGHTLY CROWNED; HAVING A BROAD DEEP BASIN, WITH A LITTLE RUSSET; THE EYE LARGE AND OPEN, THE SEPALS SEPARATED AT THE BASE; THE CAVITY OF MEDIUM WIDTH AND DEPTH, RUSSET LINED; THE STALK SHORT AND THICK; THE COLOUR IS CHARACTERIZED BY AN ORANGE-RED FLUSH WITH A FEW RED STRIPES OVER GREENISH YELLOW OR GOLD, WITH RUSSET PATCHES AND VEINS; THE FLESH IS PALE CREAM AND SLIGHTLY CRUMBLY; THE FLAVOUR IS DESCRIBED AS ADDICTIVE, PLAIN, FLAVOURED WITH NUTS, QUITE SWEET.

HISTORY:

This apple was discovered in the mid-eighteenth century growing against a boundary wall of Blenheim Park, the seat of the dukes of Marlborough in Oxfordshire. A local workman moved it into his garden and the tree became famous for the colour and quantity of fruit. Initially it was known as Kempster's Pippin but was renamed in the early nineteenth century with the consent of the Duke of the time. It was then widely grown and considered one of the finest of English apple types. It declined in importance when production for market became more methodical as it is biennial in habit. Interest in old varieties has led to new attention being paid to this and other less well-known apples.

Early in its season, in late September, Blenheim Orange is often chosen for cooking: it keeps its shape well and is used for dishes where appearance is important or a firm purée necessary. Later, during the following month, it has developed in flavour sufficiently to be offered as a dessert apple, thought also excellent with cheese.

TECHNIQUE:

Optimum pollination time for this variety is mid-May. The tree is vigorous. Blenheim Orange is described by experts as easy to grow but difficult to crop, as it is biennial in habit, cropping heavily every other year. Fruit buds are produced partly at the tips of new growth. The variety is resistant to mildew. Picking is by hand in late September and early October. Little organized storage of this apple takes place because it is not widely grown on a commercial scale; it used to be stored for use as a dessert apple in late autumn.

REGION OF PRODUCTION:

KENT.

Grenadier Apple

DESCRIPTION:

EARLY-SEASON COOKING APPLE. DESCRIBED BY MORGAN & RICHARDS (1993) AS LARGE (DIAMETER 7.5–8CM); THE SHAPE IS ROUND-CONICAL, QUITE IRREGULAR, FIBBED AND FLAT SIDED, WITH A NARROW, QUITE SHALLOW BASIN THAT IS RIBBED AND PUCKERED; THE EYE SMALL AND CLOSED, THE CORE OPEN, THE CAVITY BROAD AND QUITE DEEP AND THE STALK SHORT AND THICK; THE SKIN IS GREEN-YELLOW WITH SCARF SKIN AT BASE, AND THE FLESH WHITE; IT IS SHARP-FLAVOURED.

HISTORY:

The British apple market is distinctive in having several varieties that are grown specifically for cooking. These disintegrate into a purée more readily than eating apples (having more malic acid). Other countries tend to grow varieties (and develop sympathetic recipes) that are used for both cooking and eating.

The Grenadier is the first cooking apple to reach the market at the start of the English apple season in late summer. Its origin is unknown; it was exhibited in the 1860s by one Charles Turner, a nurseryman in Slough (Buckinghamshire), and was commercialized in the 1880s. It cooks to a purée. Another early-season cooking apple, of the type known as codlin (a sour apple which cooks to a froth), which came to prominence just before the First World War was the Emneth Early, raised at Emneth in Cambridgeshire. It was important for many years, but is now rarely seen for sale.

Grenadier is good for dishes in which a frothy purée is needed. A drink made with codlin apples is 'lambswool', in which the cooked pulp is floated on top of hot spiced ale.

TECHNIQUE:

See Bramley's Seedling (p. 111) for details about root-stocks. Optimum pollination time for Grenadier is early to mid-May; the tree is of medium vigour and is a heavy cropper. Picking is by hand in mid-August. Grading is by diameter (sizes are set according to variety) and by quality (EU standards, for appearance) into Grade 1 or Grade 2. Grenadier can be stored for only about 2 months.

REGION OF PRODUCTION:

SOUTH EAST ENGLAND, KENT.

Kentish Cobnut

DESCRIPTION:

FRESH HAZELNUTS. AT THE START OF THE SEASON, COBNUTS HAVE GREEN HUSKS AND SHELLS, AND PALE MILKY KERNELS; AS IT PROGRESSES, THE SHELLS TURN BROWN AND THE FLAVOUR OF THE KERNELS BECOMES MORE INTENSE. THE KENTISH COB PRODUCES A MEDIUM-LARGE NUT, THIN-SHELLED AND ELONGATED WITH A LONG HUSK, GROWING IN CLUSTERS OF 2–5 FRUITS. THE DIFFERENCES BETWEEN CULTIVARS ARE SHAPE AND SIZE. FLAVOUR: MILKY, SLIGHTLY SWEET, CRUNCHY TEXTURE.

HISTORY:

The hazelnut, *Corylus avallana*, is indigenous to all of Britain and there is evidence of its use for food from archaeological sites from the Neolithic onwards. Hazelnuts have been cultivated since at least the sixteenth century but these seem mainly to have been another species, native to south-eastern Europe, *Corylus maxima*, which is distinguished by the length of its husk. The name filbert seems always to have referred to nuts with long husks which covered the nut itself. Cobnut was used to describe 'our hedge Nut or Hasell Nut Tree', while filberts were 'that which groweth in gardens and orchards' (Gerard, 1597).

Kent was already famous for its Filberts when John Evelyn wrote his great treatise on forestry, Sylva, in 1664. They continued to be grown as part of a mixed husbandry with hops, apples and cherries (Roach, 1985). There were 3 or 4 important varieties: the one known as the 'Kentish' Filbert was the white-skinned.

This was ultimately displaced, either from 1812 or from 1830 (depending which Lambert was in fact responsible for its introduction), by an improved breed called Lambert's Filbert. It was inconvenient that history never guaranteed the identity of its progenitor. Lovers of simplicity will also decry the renaming of Lambert's Filbert as the Kentish Cobnut, but that is what happened around the turn of the century.

Mrs Beeton (1861) wrote, 'It is supposed that, within a few miles of Maidstone, in Kent, there are more Filberts grown than in all England besides; and it is from that place that the London market is supplied.' By the early 1900s, over 7,000 acres (approximately 1,750 hectares), mostly in Kent, was given over to hazelnuts, and substantial quantities were exported to the USA. There had been much experiment with different varieties, although the Kentish Cob reigned supreme. Thereafter, nut production declined greatly, until only a few specialist growers remained. The reasons are largely to do with changes in agricultural and orcharding practice in Kent, as well as the high level of handiwork involved in maintaining the cropping trees. Little research has been undertaken to improve strains. Kent remains the chief centre of production, but there are orchards in Sussex, Devon and Worcestershire.

TECHNIQUE:
Two or three varieties of hazelnut are often grown together to ensure pollination. They require a sheltered, well-drained site. In modern practice, they are grown as bush trees on stems 35–40cm high, and planted in rows 5 metres apart. Older 'plats' (the local term for a hazelnut orchard) may be planted more closely. Close planted trees are pruned by hand; mechanical pruning can be carried out in more widely spaced, modern plats. The trees are routinely treated with fungicide, although experiments are being carried out in the organic production of hazelnuts. Picking is by hand. Some plats are marketed as pick-your-own. A hectare of trees produces about 4 tonnes of nuts per annum.

REGION OF PRODUCTION:
SOUTH EAST ENGLAND.

Leveller Gooseberry

DESCRIPTION:
A DESSERT FRUIT THAT IS LARGE, YELLOW AND SWEET.

HISTORY:
The gooseberry is usually a fruit more suitable for cooking, needing considerable sweetening for palatability unless used as a savoury accompaniment to meat or fish. But Leveller is a variety

raised by J. Greenhalgh in Ashton-under-Lyne (Lancashire) in 1851 that became an important dessert fruit. Roach (1995) remarks that it was, and still is, grown in the Chailey-Newick district of Sussex, 'where the cultivation of large-sized Leveller berries for the dessert trade has reached a very high degree of perfection.' The berries have been grown in this area for the London market since before World War II.

TECHNIQUE:

The area in East Sussex associated with the growing of this variety for the dessert market is sandy and highly suitable, producing a berry which ripens well with a very sweet flavour. The fruit is gathered by hand in late July or early August; it must be picked when it is just ripe and marketed straight away.

Those who grow gooseberries for show prune the bushes severely and strip most of the fruit early in the season, leaving only a few berries to attain the largest possible size.

REGION OF PRODUCTION:

SOUTH EAST ENGLAND, EAST SUSSEX.

COMPARE WITH:

Careless Gooseberry, East Anglia (p. 113)

Medlar

DESCRIPTION:

MEDLARS ARE SMALL FRUIT (3–4CM DIAMETER), WEIGHING ABOUT 15G. THEY LOOK LIKE BROWN-SKINNED APPLES, BUT HAVE A CUP-SHAPED DEPRESSION, KNOWN AS THE EYE, BETWEEN THE CALYX LOBES. COLOUR: GREEN-PURPLE WITH A SLIGHT GLOSS WHEN FRESH; PURPLE-BROWN, DULL AND SOFT WHEN BLETTED. FLAVOUR: SWEET-ACID.

HISTORY:

The medlar, *Mespilus germanica*, is a native of Transcaucasia and made its long journey into northern Europe after its adoption by Greece and Rome. It may even have been brought to Britain by the Romans – a single seed has been excavated at Silchester – and it was certainly cultivated here during the Middle Ages. The hedge-row specimens that are still found, especially in the South-East, are probably escapees from this early cultivation (Roach, 1985).

When English garden varieties were first described and codified, there were not many sorts of medlar held in high esteem – the most celebrated were the Dutch and the Neapolitan. Thus, by and large, it remained until the end of the eighteenth century when a new variety, or so it seemed, was named: the Nottingham. This appears in fact to be a Neapolitan, but muddled or renamed. The re-baptism stuck, and Nottingham it is to this day. There were some new cultivars developed in the Victorian years, but what perhaps makes the medlar quintessentially British was the enjoyment of the bletted (rotten) fruit by drinkers of port at the end of a meal. Not everyone appreciated these 'wineskins of brown morbidity' (D.H. Lawrence, quoted by Davidson, 1991) and their number reduced as time went on, but their use as a jelly which accompanies meats has seen their survival in a sphere wider than the private gardens of a handful of connoisseurs. (See also Medlar Jelly, East Anglia p. 136.)

TECHNIQUE:

Medlars are propagated by grafting or budding. Various species have been used to provide rootstock; today, the quince is most commonly employed. The fruit are left on the trees until late autumn and may be quite hard when hand-picked. At this stage they are considered astringent and inedible. The fruit is stored in moist bran or sawdust until it becomes brown and soft. Effectively, this is a controlled rotting of the fruit. They used to be brought to the table in a dish still covered with bran or sawdust and cleaned off by the diners who scraped out the pulp to eat with sugar and cream, and to accompany port.

REGION OF PRODUCTION:
SOUTH EAST ENGLAND.

Strawberry (Royal Sovereign)

DESCRIPTION:
ROYAL SOVEREIGN HAS SMALL TO MEDIUM ROUNDED BERRIES OF A BRIGHT INTENSE RED, AND IS STILL THOUGHT BY MANY TO HAVE THE BEST FLAVOUR OF ALL BRITISH VARIETIES. MODERN STRAWBERRY VARIETIES TEND TO HAVE MUCH BIGGER, POINTED FRUIT AND A LESS INTENSE FLAVOUR.

HISTORY:
Although wood strawberries, *Fragaria vesca*, are native to Britain, the history of the strawberry in its modern form really begins in the early nineteenth century. At this time, Michael Keen, a market gardener in Isleworth (Middlesex), used the Chilean strawberry (*F. chiloensis*) to produce improved varieties. The first of these was Keen's Imperial; the second which he raised, Keen's Seedling, caused a sensation, and became very important both in its own right and as a parent of other varieties. There was much interest in strawberry growing during the mid-nineteenth century. One of the most influential of Victorian nurserymen, Thomas Laxton at Bedford, bred Royal Sovereign. This was esteemed for its appearance and flavour and for the fact that it cropped early.

Royal Sovereign lost commercial favour around the time of World War II as producers, driven by necessity to cultivate disease-resistant stock and by the changing needs of processors, began using the Cambridge varieties (bred from the 1930s at the Horticultural Research Station of Cambridge University) and their descendants. For many years, Royal Sovereign was grown only by amateurs, but interest is reviving among commercial producers on the south-east coast of England. This region came into its own as a centre of market gardening at the end of the Victorian period. London, its chief customer, had outgrown its eighteenth-century envelope and was fast expanding into land on its western side which had until then been the main area of commercial gardening. Simultaneously, efficient railway transport enabled producers to base themselves further away than those who had depended on waterborne delivery, carriage on foot or by cart, or conveyance in panniers slung each side of a donkey. The counties along the south-eastern coast of England have been noted areas for strawberry production for over 100 years. Hampshire was known for its early strawberries, a trade now severely eroded by foreign imports.

TECHNIQUE:
Strawberries are now grown from virus-free runners produced by specialist growers. The old method was to grow under glass cloches, now superseded by polythene tunnels. Soil sterilization

is also practised to control disease. In the old days, the ground was mulched with straw. The berries are grown both for dessert and processing. Royal Sovereign is a dessert variety which is grown by similar methods to other strawberries, but requires special care in handling as the berries are delicate and soft. Cambridge Favourite is regarded as a good dual-purpose type. The growth of pick-your-own farms has meant that many people have access to supplies of very fresh strawberries.

REGION OF PRODUCTION:
SOUTH EAST ENGLAND.

Victoria Plum

DESCRIPTION:
A VICTORIA PLUM WEIGHS 30–50G AND HAS DARK RED SKIN, PALE GREEN FLESH, AND A GOOD SWEET-ACID BALANCE OF FLAVOUR.

HISTORY:
The cultivated plum has been known in Britain since Roman times. Plums continued to be grown in Britain through the medieval period, with new varieties being introduced in the fifteenth century (Roach, 1985). The development of specifically British varieties is noticed under Dittisham Plum, above, and Cambridge Gage, below. The eighteenth-century varieties, including Fotheringham, Coe's Golden Drop (much used as a parent for good quality, late-season dessert plums), Magnum Bonum, Damascenes, and Gage were delicious and valuable, but it is the work of the Victorian nurserymen that has had most lasting significance. They raised several varieties still grown today, including Early Rivers and Czar. Several local varieties, including Aylesbury Prune, were also widely grown for drying. One of the few local seedlings which has become important in recent years is Marjories, which was discovered growing in Berkshire in 1912.

However, the Victoria plum is the most popular in modern Britain. It was a chance seedling from Alderton in Sussex found in 1840. Development took place in a nursery at Brixton, south London. It soon became established as a commercial variety in the main orcharding areas of southern England. It was used for crossing in experiments to produce new breeds in the early 1900s, especially by the Laxton brothers; although several were introduced, they have failed to maintain a place in commercial production.

Victorias now provide the majority of dessert plums, most of those for commerce grown in Kent. It is also the most ubiquitous breed in English gardens: it is easier and less sensitive than most comparable varieties. Jane Grigson (1982) wrote tellingly of their dangerously bland flavour: 'Victorias are for canning. Victorias are for plums and custard, that crowning moment of the school, hospital, prison and boarding house midday meal: I reflect that Mr Bird invented his powder round about the time that Victoria plums were beginning their career.'

TECHNIQUE:
Plums require shelter from frost and a soil which holds moisture well. Old orchards are on strong rootstocks, giving large trees. Dwarf rootstocks, planted in rows about 6 metres apart are now favoured. Some varieties require pollinators, although Victoria is a variety which is largely

self-fertile. Provided the soil is correct, and the land sheltered from frost, plums do well in Kent and its region. After the first 2 years, little maintenance beyond light pruning is carried out.

REGION OF PRODUCTION:
SOUTH EAST ENGLAND, KENT.

Carolina Cheese

DESCRIPTION:
A PRESSED SHEEP'S MILK CHEESE. DIMENSIONS: TRUCKLES APPROXIMATELY 8CM HIGH, 5CM DIAMETER OR 14CM HIGH, 14CM DIAMETER. WEIGHT: ABOUT 750G (SMALL); 2-2.7KG (LARGE). COLOUR: ALMOST WHITE. FLAVOUR: WELL-ROUNDED, WITH A MILD SHEEP NOTE.

HISTORY:
An ancient origin is claimed for the recipe from which these cheeses were evolved: the monks of a Cistercian abbey near Chard, Somerset. This is not impossible; there are parallels in the north of England, where Wensleydale and related cheeses almost certainly owe their origin to monastic dairy skills.

In its current form, Carolina was developed by John Norman in the Chard area; the name was taken from a field name of land he farmed. In the early 1970s, he began to make a sheep's milk cheese, continuing until ill health prevailed. Ten years later the current maker, Harold Woolley, bought the recipe and transferred production to Kent, where the cheese has been made ever since. He has since evolved 2 similar cheeses – Cecilia (plain and smoked) and Nepicar.

TECHNIQUE:
Carolina, Cecilia and Nepicar are all made from sheep's milk, mostly from Friesland-Romney sheep on permanent pasture. For Carolina, a home-produced starter is incubated overnight and added to the warm milk the next morning followed, about 45 minutes later, by vegetarian rennet. The milk is left for another 45 minutes for the curd to set. The curd is cut, then stirred gently by hand for about 30 minutes, allowed to settle and drained. The curd is cut in blocks and stacked for an hour to drain further. The curd is milled, salted and packed into cloth-lined moulds. The cheeses are pressed individually for 24 hours, being turned once; then they are removed from the moulds, the cloths removed, the cheeses returned to the moulds and pressed a further 24 hours. On removal from the moulds, they are brined for a day. They are matured for 60 days.

Nepicar is made to the same recipe and method, using milk pasteurized by a high-temperature, short-term process, and the cheeses are matured for 90 days. Cecilia is made to a similar recipe, with slight differences in times and temperatures; it is dry-salted rather than brined, and matured in oak barrels over a bed of hops. Frozen milk is stored for use when the sheep stop milking in September.

REGION OF PRODUCTION:
SOUTH EAST ENGLAND, KENT.

Wellington Cheese

DESCRIPTION:

HARD, PRESSED, UNPASTEURIZED COW'S MILK CHEESE IN ROUNDS ABOUT 18CM DIAMETER, 7CM HIGH; A SMALLER ONE IS MADE FOR CHRISTMAS. WEIGHT: 2.5–3KG (LARGE); 750G (SMALL). COLOUR: A RICH YELLOW WITH A NATURAL GREY-BROWN MOTTLED RIND. FLAVOUR AND TEXTURE: RICH CREAMY TEXTURE, VERY SMOOTH; SWEET.

HISTORY:

There is no great history of cheese-making in Berkshire, though Reading University has latterly been a centre for research into dairying. Work carried out by the university led to the development of the recipe for Smallholder Cheese in 1911. It was specifically intended as a recipe for those wishing to make a hard cheese on a limited scale. It enjoyed some success with home cheese-makers, still being made at the end of the 1950s. In the mid-1980s, the maker of Wellington, Anne Wigmore (a microbiologist at the dairy research institute at the university) took the Smallholder recipe and developed it for use with milk from a Guernsey herd kept at Stratfield Saye, the nearby estate belonging to the Duke of Wellington.

TECHNIQUE:

Unpasteurized milk from one designated herd of Guernsey cattle is used. The Smallholder recipe is along the following lines. The milk is heated to 32°C, starter added, followed by vegetarian rennet about 30 minutes later; the top layer is stirred to ensure the cream is mixed in, then left 40 minutes. The curd is cut 3 ways and allowed to settle. The heat is increased to 38°C over 30 minutes, the curd stirred continuously, then the whey is drained off. The curd is cut into strips and stacked and re-stacked until the correct acidity has developed. Milling is into pieces the size of a nutmeg; the curd is salted during this process, then filled into moulds. Pressing is for about 24 hours, the cheese removed from the mould once (at an early stage) and reversed. The cheeses are unmoulded and matured 6 months in the cellars at Stratfield Saye.

Anne Wigmore's interest in cheese-making has also led to the development of Spenwood (named after the Berkshire village of Spencer's Wood, where the work was carried out) and Wigmore, both based on sheep's milk; and Waterloo, a soft cow's milk cheese.

REGION OF PRODUCTION:

SOUTH EAST ENGLAND, BERKSHIRE.

Jellied Eels

DESCRIPTION:

A CLEAR JELLY CONTAINING EEL IN PIECES 2–5CM LONG. COLOUR: THE JELLY IS PALE BROWN-GOLD, THE EEL PIECES HAVE LIGHT GREY-BLUE SKIN WITH WHITE FLESH, THE BEST HAVE A FINE PALE BLUE BLOOM ON THE SKIN. FLAVOUR: DELICATE, MILDLY FISHY.

HISTORY:

Eel is a fish once favoured by Cockneys. Thames eels are more silver in colour and sweeter of taste than those from the Continent (Simon, 1960). Among many early recipes, eel pies were celebrated – not least at Eel Pie Island, near Richmond-upon-Thames; Shakespeare describes a Cockney making a pie in *King Lear*, putting eels 'in the paste alive'. Stews and galantines were also made with plenty of eels.

'The appetite grows with eating.'

FRANÇOIS RABELAIS

Today eel pie has all but vanished even if the shops seem to keep its name alive, but jellied and stewed eels are still made – sold from street stalls and cooked-food shops in London and seaside towns of Essex and Kent. These are the 'Eel, Pie and Mash' shops, which sell steak and kidney pies, mashed potatoes and cooked eels.

Brian Knights, who has made a study of the eel and its fishery in Britain, observes that eels are now caught in the Thames again. Some of them are used by the jelliers who supply the shops, but imported eels are also employed.

TECHNIQUE:

The eels are kept alive in holding tanks then electrically stunned and killed immediately before use. They are chopped into lengths then boiled for 15–20 minutes in salted water. The eels in their cooking liquor are left to go cold in the large white basins from which they are sold.

REGION OF PRODUCTION:

SOUTH EAST ENGLAND, LONDON.

Oyster

DESCRIPTION:

ENGLISH NATIVE OYSTERS ARE GRADED ACCORDING TO WEIGHT INTO: EXTRA LARGE (OVER 160G); 1: 120–160G; 2: 90–120G; 3: 70–90G. FORM: THE SHELL IS DENSE AND HARD, RELATIVELY FLAT AND SMOOTH, WITH A STRONG NACRE ON THE INSIDE. COLOUR: THE MEAT IS A RICH CREAM, BISCUIT COLOUR.

WHITSTABLE OYSTERS ARE SLOW-GROWING WITH HEAVY SHELLS; THEY MAY WEIGH UP TO 240G AND BE UP TO 11CM LONG.

HISTORY:

The first people to exploit the native oyster, *Ostrea edulis*, on a large scale in this part of Britain were the Romans. The shellfish were even exported to Rome itself (Wilson, 1973). In the Middle Ages, the Colchester fishery was granted a charter in 1189.

There were many other beds of native oysters available to the British, Poole in Dorset and Helford in Cornwall to name but two. Trade between the coasts and consumers inland is documented readily from medieval books of account. But there is little doubt that the most important production was concentrated on the Thames estuary: Colchester on the north side and Whitstable on the south. The 'Company of Free Fishers and Dredgers', an association of oyster fishermen from Whitstable, has a history stretching back over 400 years. At their peak, there were more than 800 principals in the fisheries (Neild, 1995). One reason for their pre-eminence was the existence of London on their doorstep, with easy water transport to link them to Billingsgate, the principal point of sale. One has only to read diaries, correspondence and printed accounts to appreciate the scale of the business. Oysters were an important food of the common people in London: the Mayor regulated the price of oysters from at least the fifteenth century, and an early reference to 'Colchesters' from 1625 confirms the identity of the town with the product.

Oysters were apparently unlimited until a moment in the 1860s. The development of beds off the Sussex coast in the English Channel had caused the price to fall through oversupply, but these were soon exhausted, and disease and a sequence of bad weather combined to cause a shortage elsewhere. The oyster ceased to be food of the masses and became a costly delicacy.

Problems first encountered by the Victorians were never properly addressed and the native oyster beds have suffered acute decline in the intervening years. Fears of catching typhoid due to unhygienic storage wiped out demand before the First World War; catastrophic seasons, such as the winter of 1962–3 which killed 95 per cent of marketable stocks; disease; and finally price competition from oyster varieties that were more easily farmed, or more cheaply gathered, were the most potent causes.

Seasalter, the company based in Whitstable which currently does most work on oyster culture in the Thames estuary, has a history which stretches back to the mid-nineteenth century. The fishery of Whitstable did not escape the trials endured by other sites, but recovery has been put in hand. The beds were re-stocked with young natives from other locations, and Pacific oysters were introduced in the 1960s. Both varieties are now farmed at Whitstable. In Colchester, commerce was interrupted by the crises described above, but Colchester Oyster Fishery Ltd was established in 1966 to restore the beds. Stocks were hit badly by the parasite Bonamia in 1982 but are slowly recovering. Whitstable Oysters have been awarded Protected Geographical Indication (PGI).

TECHNIQUE:

Colchester oysters are fattened in the Pyefleet, a creek in the estuary of the River Colne. This is good for the purpose, as it has mildly brackish, nutrient-rich water, containing the phytoplankton on which oysters thrive. The name 'Pyefleet' has always been jealously guarded by Colchester Borough Council. The derelict oyster beds at Pyefleet, just south of the town of Colchester, were cleared of accumulated silt in the 1960s, an operation which was followed by natural re-stocking. New storage tanks were built. Water for these is pumped from settlement ponds into a storage pond and filtered into temperature-controlled, oxygenated tanks. The water for holding oysters is circulated through an ultra-violet treatment plant, and the water composition is monitored daily. After purification, the oysters are graded, packed in tubs with seaweed, and distributed.

In Whitstable, native oysters are gathered by a power dredge towed by a trawler which flicks the oysters into a cage; all oysters sold in England are purified in clean water under ultra-violet light for 2 days; after this they are graded by eye. Some farming of native oysters is also carried out at Whitstable, where Pacifics are farmed in mesh bags on steel tables.

To be called a Whitstable oyster, the shellfish must come from the coast between Shoeburyness and North Foreland, north Kent.

REGION OF PRODUCTION:

COLCHESTER (ESSEX); SOUTH EAST ENGLAND, WHITSTABLE (KENT). ALSO EAST ANGLIA.

COMPARE WITH:

Oyster, Scotland (p. 335)

'Oysters are more beautiful than any religion… There's nothing in Christianity or Buddhism that quite matches the sympathetic unselfish-ness of an oyster.'

SAKI, *THE CHRONICLES OF CLOVIS*

Patum Peperium

DESCRIPTION:

ANCHOVY RELISH IN SMALL FLAT ROUND PLASTIC BOXES OF 42.5G OR 70G; LARGER GLASS AND PORCELAIN POTS ARE ALSO USED. COLOUR: PINK-BROWN; THE COLOUR OF SALTED ANCHOVY. FLAVOUR: SALTY, FISHY, STRONG ANCHOVY FLAVOUR.

HISTORY:

The recipe for Patum Peperium is said to have been 'perfected' by John Osborn, an English provision merchant living in Paris in 1828. At this time, compounds of fish, meat or cheese, with spices and butter, were very popular. Recipes for potted anchovies, the fish rubbed through a sieve to remove the bones, mixed with spices and sealed with clarified butter were made and used for garnishes, or spread on toast. The recipe remained the intellectual property of the Osborn family and was brought back to England in the middle of the nineteenth century. According to the company history (Elsenham, n.d.), it was very successful. To the original name, Patum Peperium (the first word appears to be a fanciful play on the word for paste, or pâté; the second is derived from the Greek for pepper), the phrase 'The Gentleman's Relish' was added, apparently by customers asking for the product. Despite the fact that the paste was first made in France, it became closely identified with pre-war British upper-class tastes and remains so today. The brand was sold by the Osborns on the retirement of the last 2 surviving members of the family from the business in 1971.

REGION OF PRODUCTION:
SOUTH EAST ENGLAND, LONDON.

Smoked Salmon (London cure)

DESCRIPTION:

SMOKED WILD SALMON HAS A REDDER HUE THAN THE FARMED, WHICH IS ORANGE-TINTED, AND SLIGHTLY TRANSLUCENT. FLAVOUR AND TEXTURE: SOFT BUTTERY FLAVOUR, VERY MILD SALT AND SMOKE; YIELDING.

HISTORY:

The light London cure developed from a different tradition to those known in Scotland. These last were intended to preserve the fish for a matter of months and were therefore heavy and intrusively flavoured. Immigrants from eastern Europe, arriving in England at the end of the nineteenth century, brought with them expertise in their own style of curing and began to practise in London using supplies of wild salmon from Scotland. The London cure was a means of enhancing flavour rather than of preservation. The fish is intended for consumption within a few hours of processing: it is more mildly flavoured, with a silkier texture than most Scottish smoked salmon. The most prominent firm, H. Forman and Sons, began curing in 1905. They are the last family firm of East-European origin still working in this field.

TECHNIQUE:

Forman and Sons use both wild and farmed salmon from Scottish waters. The farmed salmon is bought fresh as necessary; the wild is bought in season and supplies are frozen for subsequent use. Much of the fish is smoked to individual orders, the sides selected for size and oil

content to the customer's taste. After filleting and trimming, pure salt is used in a very light, dry cure which emphasizes the natural flavour of the fish, rather than masking it as do heavier cures; the sides are then lightly smoked.

REGION OF PRODUCTION:
SOUTH EAST ENGLAND, LONDON.

COMPARE WITH:
Smoked Salmon, Scotland (p. 369)

Whelk

DESCRIPTION:
AT POINT OF SALE, WHELKS ARE DISPLAYED COOKED AND SHELLED; THOSE FROM WHITSTABLE USED FOR THE ENGLISH MARKET GENERALLY WEIGH ABOUT 100–140 PER KG. THE MEAT IS BROWNISH-YELLOW, FLAVOURFUL AND CHEWY; THEY ARE SOLD BY WEIGHT OR IN PRE-WEIGHED PORTIONS. THERE ARE SIGNIFICANT DISPARITIES OF SIZE BETWEEN WHELKS FROM DIFFERENT AREAS AROUND THE BRITISH COAST.

HISTORY:
Whelks, *Buccinum undatum*, are a common gastropod whose coiled, pointed shells are found on the coasts. Variant names are dog whelk, waved whelk, and buckie (in Scotland). The Romans carried them to various inland sites, and they are mentioned in the accounts of fifteenth-century fishmongers and many medieval households. For instance, 4,000 were used to garnish a salted sturgeon at the enthronement of the Archbishop of Canterbury in the early sixteenth century. The normal medieval procedure was to boil in water and eat with vinegar and parsley (Wilson, 1973).

Fishing grounds for whelks are off the north coast of Norfolk and in the Thames estuary. They formed part of the diet of the London poor, both at home and on holiday on the Kent coast. The phrase, 'he couldn't run a whelk stall', suggests they found a ready sale. However, they were never considered elegant.

When they are bought ready-cooked as street food, the consumer splashes as much vinegar on as he would wish. They remain a seaside staple and as part of the food traditions of the urban poor in Midland cities. The uncooked meat has found a new market in Chinese and Japanese restaurants.

TECHNIQUE:
Whelks are usually fished within a few miles of the shore; the best quality come from open waters. They are carnivorous and plastic barrels or iron baskets baited variously with dead shore crabs, fish offal or salt herring are used to catch them. On the East coast, a number of pots are tied to one rope to form a shank, with a buoy at each end. Weather permitting, the pots are examined, emptied and re-baited daily. Once landed, the fish are boiled in sea-water, shell-on, for 12–16 minutes, then cooled and the meat extracted. The cap (*operculum*) is discarded. Alternatively, some processors crack the shell and remove it, which reduces boiling time to 7–8 minutes. If the whelks are required raw, the shells are crushed and removed before packing.

REGION OF PRODUCTION:
EAST ENGLAND.

Whitebait

DESCRIPTION:

INDIVIDUAL FISH ARE VERY SMALL, 3–4CM IN LENGTH AND SLENDER IN PROPORTION. WEIGHT: TYPICALLY, THERE ARE ABOUT 400 FISH TO A KILO. COLOUR: SEMI-TRANSPARENT, OR SILVER-WHITE. FLAVOUR: WHITEBAIT ARE VALUED AS MUCH FOR THEIR CRUNCHY TEXTURE AS THEIR FLAVOUR, WHICH, WHILST MILDLY FISHY, IS MASKED BY THE FLAVOUR OF HOT FAT DURING FRYING AND THE LEMON JUICE WITH WHICH MOST PEOPLE SEASON THE DISH JUST BEFORE EATING IT.

HISTORY:

Whitebait may be a mixture of the fry of herring (*Clupea harengus*) and sprat (*Sprattus sprattus*), or the fry of sprat alone. Historians have claimed whitebait first appeared on an English menu as long ago as 1612 (Davidson, 1979). The name derives from the use of these small fish as bait for catching other fish (*OED*). It seems that they really became important as food in the mid-eighteenth century. For at least a century after this time, they were a noted speciality of Blackwall and Greenwich, downstream from the City of London (Mars, 1998).

There was much controversy over the exact nature of whitebait, some claiming that it was actually a separate species. This debate was still alive in 1861 when Mrs Beeton stated, 'This highly esteemed little fish appears in innumerable multitudes in the river Thames, near Greenwich and Blackwall, during the month of July, when it forms a tempting dish to vast numbers of Londoners who flock to the various taverns of these places in order to gratify their appetites ... The ministers of the Crown have had a custom, for many years, of having a "whitebait dinner" just before the close of the session.' This ministerial dinner has origins more banal than epicurean delight in fish fry. There used once to be an annual shindig held at Dagenham by the commissioners for embanking the River Thames. To one of these, in the 1790s, Pitt the Younger was invited and brought some of his Cabinet colleagues. The habit stuck but the location was shifted to the more salubrious Greenwich in the early part of the next century. Only then did they start to eat whitebait. The tradition continued until 1894.

Whitebait still shoal in the mouth of the Thames but the fishery has declined. According to one of the few remaining fishermen, demand for the fish has dropped, partly because they are cooked by deep-frying, now considered an unhealthy method, and because imported whitebait are cheaper than fish caught locally, due to the way in which the fishing industries of other countries are subsidized.

The fishing of whitebait is no longer encouraged because of the implications for fish stocks, though the sprat is not under any threat at present. A whitebait festival was held annually at Southend, down the estuary, at the same time as a ceremony of blessing the sea.

TECHNIQUE:

Whitebait were defined by Alan Davidson (1979) as 'the fry of various clupeoid fish, notably the herring and the sprat, and often mixed together'; most authorities now state that they are the fry of the sprat alone. They are caught from boats working in pairs with a fine net stretched between them. The season was considered to be March–August, but now fishing is discouraged when there are immature fish in the river, a period which lasts approximately from June until October.

REGION OF PRODUCTION:

SOUTH EAST ENGLAND.

Aylesbury Duck

DESCRIPTION:

OVEN-READY WEIGHT, 3.5–4KG. WHITE FEATHERS AND PINK BEAK; THE FLESH IS PALE, SOFT AND TENDER, WITH LITTLE GRAIN AND LESS FATTY THAN MOST DUCK TYPES; THE FAT IS LOCATED IN A THIN HARD LAYER UNDER THE SKIN. FLAVOUR IS GOOD, WITH PRONOUNCED GAMINESS.

HISTORY:

The family of the one remaining commercial producer has been rearing Aylesbury ducks since the last quarter of the eighteenth century. Martha Bradley, writing in 1756, thought any breed of duck acceptable for the table, but by the time of Mrs Beeton (1861), Aylesburys were noted for their excellence and the intensive system of rearing then current: 'not on plains or commons … but in the abodes of the cottagers. Round the walls of the living-rooms, and of the bedroom even, are fixed rows of wooden boxes, lined with hay; and it is the business of the wife and children to nurse and comfort the feathered lodgers, to feed the little ducklings, and to take the old ones out for an airing. Sometimes the "stock" ducks are the cottager's own property, but it more frequently happens that they are intrusted to his care by a wholesale breeder who pays him so much per score for all ducklings properly raised.' Transport was a factor in the fame of the birds; Smithfield, the London wholesale meat market, was easily accessible.

The old system of rearing died out before the First World War; at the same time, hybrid ducks with Chinese blood became common. The popularity of the Aylesbury declined in the face of competition from birds of more acceptable conformation. Strict enforcement of EU hygiene regulations have further reduced the number of duck-farmers by vastly reducing the economic viability of the business for small producers.

TECHNIQUE:

The ducklings are now hatched in incubators. They are kept indoors for the first 2 weeks of life, and then allowed access to the open air in fenced runs for the third. After this, they are kept in outdoor enclosures for about 5 weeks. For the first 3 weeks they subsist on a high-protein ration; feeding of this continues once they are outdoors, but they also forage for grass and insects. The ducklings are killed at 8 weeks; they are dry-plucked, waxed, and hung 48 hours before evisceration and trussing. Older ducks of a larger size and more mature flavour are available when the breeding stock is killed at about 14 months.

REGION OF PRODUCTION:

SOUTH EAST ENGLAND, BUCKINGHAMSHIRE.

Romney Sheep

DESCRIPTION:

ABOUT 18–20KG DRESSED WEIGHT FOR A CARCASS AT 3–4 MONTHS; 25KG LATER IN SEASON. HEAVY-BODIED SHEEP WITH GOOD CONFORMATION. MEAT IS DARK, WELL-FLAVOURED, CLOSE-TEXTURED.

HISTORY:

Romneys are white-faced, naturally long-tailed, and related to the Cheviot, Ile de France, Texel and Welsh Mountain. Their name is that of their native district, Romney Marsh. The stock which may have given rise to the breed were imported in about the second century AD by the Romans. Large numbers of sheep were maintained at Romney by the medieval Priory of Canterbury – whose breeding flock was at Thanet – for the sake of their wool, milk and meat. The relative importance of these products to the strain has waxed and waned. At present it is primarily a wool sheep. In the past, they were shorn of wool in the summer of their birth and sold as store lambs to be finished by arable farmers, graziers and butchers. They were slaughtered for meat as hoggets (over a year old). Often they were kept to 2 years, by which time they became very fat.

The Romney was mentioned by Youatt (1837) as crossed with the Southdown, popular further along the coast. The progeny was suited to meat production. The Kent and Romney Marsh Sheep Breeders Association was founded in 1895 and the breed has been much exported.

TECHNIQUE:
The owners of the sheep used to live around the edge of the marsh and paid 'lookers' (people from the marsh itself who could tolerate the brackish well-water and the malarial fevers) to oversee the sheep. Before modern veterinary treatments for parasitic infections, managing the flocks to avoid infestation was skilled.

Romneys can be kept in large flocks and they scatter whilst grazing. Some still graze long-established native pastures on which grass species include perennial rye grass and Kentish wild white clover – which can be very close grazed. The pastures were kept close-cropped by moving the sheep frequently. There is a tradition of moving the ewes to arable land in Surrey and Sussex during the winter to feed on root crops, although nowadays they may be housed indoors on their home farms. The object is to allow an early flush of grass on summer pastures.

The lambs are born outdoors, traditionally from 1 April onwards. They are slaughtered from 3–4 months. Romney lamb reared on the salt marshes is sometimes requested by butchers or restaurants and the breed society has taken an interest in this in the past. However, the British consumer was not willing to pay a premium for the extra flavour, so it was not actively promoted. Romneys are still occasionally crossed with Southdowns to produce lambs for meat, but other lowland breeds such as Suffolk and, lately, Texel, have been favoured.

REGION OF PRODUCTION:
SOUTH EAST ENGLAND.

Southdown Sheep

DESCRIPTION:
DRESSED CARCASS WEIGHT IS ABOUT 17KG. A COMPACT, FLESHY SHEEP WITH FINE BONES AND A HIGH RATIO OF MEAT TO BONE; EXCELLENT, SWEET FLAVOUR, GOOD MARBLING, VERY JUICY.

HISTORY:
The sheep collectively known as 'down' breeds evolved from the native stock of the chalk hills of southern England. This area has been sheep-raising country for many centuries and, by the 1700s, several distinct races had evolved. The first to receive any attention was the Southdown. Improvements were begun by John Ellman of Glynde (Sussex). Thereafter, it was con-

sidered one of the best producers of lamb and mutton. Mrs Beeton (1861) comments on the 'recent improvements', and remarks, 'of all mutton, that furnished by the Southdown sheep is most highly esteemed; it is also the dearest on account of its scarcity, and the great demand for it.'

'From the beginning of the nineteenth century, the fashionable Southdown was increasingly interbred with all the downland breeds and this transformed them,' thus the origin of Oxford Down, Hampshire Down, and Dorset Down (Hall & Clutton-Brock, 1989). It was also used to improve the Shropshire and bred with the Norfolk to produce the ancestors of the modern Suffolk – now much used for meat.

TECHNIQUE:

The Downs consist of several relatively high chalk escarpments with steep faces and dry valleys; the flora is typified by soft, short turf with a great diversity of herbs and flowering plants. Sheep grazing, a part of the area's economy since the Middle Ages, is a vital element in its maintenance. In the nineteenth century, the Southdown was of enormous importance to Sussex farms which practised a system of folding the flocks on arable crops at night with extensive grazing on the short, downland pasture during the day. This survived until recently in a few places. Its drawbacks are that it is labour intensive and less ploughland is now available, partly because of set-aside. Many Southdown sheep are now kept on ley pasture.

Lambing usually begins in February. They are sold for meat from about 16 weeks but many are retained for breeding; Southdown rams are in demand as sires for cross-bred lambs. The value of these has been recognized for well over 150 years, when Mrs Beeton remarked that Southdown crossed with Lincoln or Leicester were used to supply the London meat markets; the crossing breeds may have changed to Cluns, Cotswolds and Dartmoors, but the principle remains the same. A premium is often paid for Southdown lambs; demand is high and there is much direct marketing.

REGION OF PRODUCTION:

SOUTH EAST ENGLAND, SUSSEX.

Sussex Cattle

DESCRIPTION:

SUSSEX PROVIDE COMPACT, FINE-BONED CARCASSES WHICH HAVE A DRESSED WEIGHT OF 250–272KG. THE FLESH HAS AN EXCELLENT, SWEET FLAVOUR; WELL-MARBLED WITH A FINE GRAIN, EXTREMELY TENDER.

HISTORY:

Sussex cattle have red-brown pelts, a characteristic dating back many centuries. Red cattle in the county are mentioned in the Domesday Book (1086). The breed developed from draught oxen (a use which continued into the early 1900s). They were worked for several years before slaughter for beef. By the nineteenth century, they were recognized as fine beef animals. Registration of pedigree began in the mid-Victorian period and the breed society was founded in the 1870s. Sussex have been much exported, especially for beef production in southern Africa.

TECHNIQUE:

The breed has developed to give a hardy foraging animal, capable of remaining outside all

year. In practice, this only happens on the chalk downs where the soils are light and thin; on lower ground, the cattle are housed for the first 3 months of the year to prevent the grassland, which overlies heavy clay soils, being poached. Housed cattle are fed hay, silage and straw and little, if any, concentrate. Animals in fruit-growing areas may be given the excess apples and pears in the autumn. The land on which the animals graze for much of the year includes the long-established and herb-rich grasslands of the chalk downs. Sussex cattle are also kept in the harsh micro-climate of Isle of Sheppey. This place, with a relatively low annual rainfall and exposed to cold north-easterly winds, is categorized as a Site of Special Scientific Interest; consequently restrictions are imposed affecting the date at which the grass can be cut for hay (1 July) and the use of fertilizers, maintaining a unique flora. Calving is arranged to take place in spring or autumn; the calves are suckled until weaning. They are killed at 18–24 months. Whilst some pure-bred Sussex beef reaches the market, the cattle are also crossed with continental breeds to produce large, lean, commercial carcasses.

REGION OF PRODUCTION:
SOUTH EAST ENGLAND.

Sussex Chicken

DESCRIPTION:
A HEAVY BIRD (ABOUT 3KG DRESSED WEIGHT AT 16–20 WEEKS) WITH A BROAD BREAST. WELL-FLAVOURED, WHITE FLESH WITH A JUICY, SUCCULENT TEXTURE. THERE ARE SEVERAL VARIETIES DISTINGUISHED BY THE COLOUR OF THEIR PLUMAGE, WITH PALE FEATHERS GENERALLY BEING FAVOURED IN THE LAST 100 YEARS.

HISTORY:
The history of poultry – for meat or for eggs – is not especially long or glorious in Britain. It was a matter of the barn-door fowl and the farmer's wife tending a small flock, with little specialization or arcane skill. Cookery books often contained instruction on fattening or cramming, but the almost sacerdotal tending of birds for the table undertaken in France or Belgium was not at first widespread in this country. The agriculturalist William Marshall (1796) noticed that none of the poultry of Devon was shut up at night or in any way confined so as to harvest the egg crop. At that time, the district around Berwick-upon-Tweed (Northumbria) was an important source of eggs for the London market. Scottish routines for extending the laying day were more advanced than those of the South-West. Indeed, it was only at the beginning of the twentieth century that a market for 'fresh-laid' eggs was identifiable in any way. More than 2 billion eggs were imported into Britain in the year 1900, some from as far away as Eastern Europe – hardly fresh.

There was no great distinction between breeds of British chicken until the nineteenth century and most of those that were distinguished were of foreign origin. Hence, the Poland was Dutch and the Cochin was from Shanghai, to name two that commanded remarkable prices for their ornamental value. Two varieties represented indigenous English stock: Indian Game and the Dorking. The Dorking fowl was unique in having 5 toes. Its flesh was white, and it was the most famous table bird produced for the London market. There were other Surrey varieties, all related (but none having the extra toes), and this is indication enough that the existence of a large market stimulated the development of breeds specific to its requirements. At the first Poultry Breeders' Show, held in London in 1845, there were classes for Dorkings, Surrey, Kent and Old Sussex fowls.

The Dorking's origins have been pushed back to the time of the Roman occupation, in myth at least. The Roman agricultural writer Columella did indeed give a description of a five-toed bird which closely resembles it in colour and form. A thousand years later, the early history of the race and its place of origin were still in dispute between the poultrymen of Sussex and Surrey: each county claiming to be the motherland. The facts have never been capable of resolution and the likelihood is a common source for most South-Eastern birds. As London spread over the Surrey hills, so the rearing and fattening of fowl extended towards the county of Sussex, particularly the area around Heathfield. There arose a Sussex system of cramming, with oats ground between millstones tooled for the purpose, mixed with hog's grease, sugar and milk – this survived until 1939–45. Not all the birds so fattened were of Dorking, Surrey or Sussex descent. Many were imported from Ireland for finishing closer to the point of sale. The fatteners also surgically caponized some of their flock to produce the famous 'Surrey Capons'.

A breeders' club for Sussex chickens was formed in 1903 and three varieties – light, speckled and red – were standardized. Other plumage colours, some gender-linked, have been developed over the years. The Sussex has also been much crossed with other varieties of British chickens. It was used with the Indian Game (which, despite its name, has been bred in Britain for centuries) in the 1930s to develop the Ixworth, a bird which has been neglected commercially despite having excellent qualities.

The impact of the Second World War on food production in general and the introduction of commercial broiler-chicken systems from the USA started a decline in traditional poultry farming which is not yet arrested.

TECHNIQUE:

A few specialist breeders still keep Sussex fowl. The poultry farms of the past, using caponizing and cramming, have died out and are unlikely to be ever reintroduced; and the casual system in which poultry ranged freely under the care of the farmer's wife, who collected the eggs and dressed table poultry for the market, is on the verge of extinction. The concern of those who now keep Sussex strains is as much to preserve bloodlines and genetic diversity as to produce eggs and meat. Because of this and because of the costs involved in rearing the fowl, they are usually kept under close supervision and a system of fold units, or coops with runs on grass enclosed by wire mesh, is followed. Each unit, containing one cockerel and several hens, is moved daily to allow access to fresh grass. Supplementary feed of protein pellets and grain is given daily. The chickens, hatched in spring, are marked to identify the genetic strain, particularly important in flocks which are kept closed – at least one has been in existence since the 1930s.

All poultry breeders who wish to market their birds as meat now have to observe strictly enforced regulations of hygiene and slaughter, requiring the use of an accredited abattoir. There are relatively few of these. The slaughter-houses are obliged to concentrate on one species of meat animal on any given day, and generally prefer to operate with large throughputs. These factors, added to high transport costs, have had an adverse effect on small poultry breeders.

REGION OF PRODUCTION:

SOUTH EAST ENGLAND.

Chelsea Bun

DESCRIPTION:

A LOOSE SPIRAL BUN, SQUARED OFF AT THE SIDES; APPROXIMATELY 100MM SQUARE BY 40MM DEEP. WEIGHT: 100–120G. COLOUR: GOLD-BROWN ON TOP WHERE WELL-BAKED, FADING TO PALE CREAM AT THE SIDES WHERE THE BUNS HAVE TOUCHED. FLAVOUR: SWEET, LIGHTLY SPICED, WITH DRIED FRUIT.

HISTORY:

Chelsea buns have been known since the eighteenth century. Originally they were sold from a pastry cook's shop known as the Bun House in Chelsea. David (1977) discusses the history of the buns and the Bun House, and speculates that the patronage of the royal family in the 1730s may have helped their popularity. Their earliest occurrence in literature is 1711, when Jonathan Swift reported buying one for a penny and finding that it was stale (*OED*).

The Chelsea bun as made at the Bun House was thought very light, rich and delicate in the early 1800s, but there is no record of what size or shape they were; it can only be assumed that they were the coils we now associate with them. The Bun House in Pimlico Road was demolished in 1839. Kirkland (1907) said that it was 'a popular bun in English confectioners' shops – but, it must be confessed, not so popular as it was at one time.' Observations by Harris and Borella (*c*. 1900) show there were various grades baked, and that bakers did not view Chelsea buns with much regard, a situation which has continued through the century. They are to be found in many bakers' shops and are generally rather large and filling.

TECHNIQUE:

A ferment of milk, sugar, yeast and flour is set. A small proportion of butter is rubbed into the rest of the flour, the ferment is whisked with eggs and more sugar and added to the dough. Once fermented, the dough is rolled into square sheets and the surface brushed with melted butter; brown sugar, mixed with cinnamon or spices, is strewn over the surface, followed by a scatter of currants; then the whole is rolled up and cut in slices about 30mm deep. These are placed cut side down on a greased sheet. The spacing is crucial for, as the buns prove and spread, each should touch its neighbour to give the signature square shape. While still hot from the oven, the buns are glazed with milk and sugar and sometimes dusted with caster sugar. An icing of water and powdered sugar may be used instead of a glaze.

REGION OF PRODUCTION:

SOUTH EAST ENGLAND, LONDON.

Huffkin

DESCRIPTION:

A FLATTISH, CIRCULAR ROLL WITH A DIMPLE IN THE CENTRE, 150MM DIAMETER, 20MM DEEP. WEIGHT: 80–90G. COLOUR AND TEXTURE: PALE CRUST, WHITE CRUMB, LIGHT OPEN TEXTURE, SMOOTH THIN CRUST.

HISTORY:

Florence White (1932) remarked that huffkins (hufkins or uffkins) were particularly associated with east Kent. She described them as 'thick flat oval cakes of light bread with a hole in the middle'. They have been known since at least 1790. Joseph Wright (1896–1905) cites a quotation from this date. A contributor to *Notes & Queries* (1869) expresses it well: 'Most people know what muffins and crumpets are, but in East Kent ... the former are known as uffkins.' Manufacture seems to have declined greatly since World War II; in 1978 David Mabey stated that huffkins had all but disappeared. David Hopper, whose family have been bakers in north-east Kent for several generations, bears this out, but affirms they are still seen occasionally.

TECHNIQUE:

Old recipes show them to be made from a simple flour, water and yeast dough with a little lard, usually in between one-eighth and one-twelfth the quantity of flour. This was kneaded into the dough after the first rise. Spicer (1948) proposes an alternative strategy of melting the lard with hot water at the outset of mixing the dough. After baking, the huffkins are wrapped in a cloth to prevent the crust from hardening. Modern commercial recipes include sugar and milk powder.

REGION OF PRODUCTION:
South East England, Kent.

Bread Pudding

DESCRIPTION:

Bread pudding is baked in large, shallow, square trays and sold in individual portions measuring about 750mm square, 250mm deep and weighing about 150g. Colour: irregular gold-beige; thickly sprinkled with caster sugar. Flavour and texture: dense, moist and sweet, with spices and dried fruit.

HISTORY:

This pudding is one English response to the problem of what to do with leftovers. There are others, such as bread-and-butter pudding (layering thin slices of buttered bread with custard) or Poor Knights of Windsor (deep-frying the slices and serving them with sugar); but bread pudding is the only one which has much history of commercialization. How long it has been sold in the South-East, however, is unknown. The idea can be traced back several centuries. John Nott (1726) gives 3 recipes for puddings based on bread, including one, 'Grateful Pudding', which shares some elements of the modern form, including the additions of eggs and dried fruit, the resulting batter being baked in a dish and served dusted with sugar. Hannah Glasse (1747) gave several, ranging from extremely rich to quite plain. Maria Rundell (1807) included a good selection, with a plainer one requiring suet rather than butter and cream. Mrs Beeton's (1861) are notably spare: the cream has vanished, the butter diminished, and suet more important.

This appears to be a turning point in the history of the product. The essential details of soaked bread mixed with sugar, fat, spice and fruit, poured into a dish and baked are all there, but the more delicate recipes known in the eighteenth century vanish.

TECHNIQUE:

Modern recipes for bread pudding are unsophisticated. Stale bread (baker's bread, not the sliced, white, moist, plastic-wrapped loaves from industrial plant bakeries) is required. This is soaked in water overnight. The water is drained, the bread squeezed dry by hand. The bread is measured, usually by volume, to establish the quantity of other ingredients required, principally suet, sugar and dried fruit which are each added in quantities of one-third the volume of soaked bread. These are mixed into the bread together with a little spice ('mixed' sweet spice

– clove, allspice and cinnamon – is the usual choice); sometimes a little flour is added. This is made into a batter by the addition of milk and eggs and baked.

REGION OF PRODUCTION:
SOUTH EAST ENGLAND.

Ginger Cake

DESCRIPTION:
COLOUR: A VERY DARK RICH BROWN. FLAVOUR: SWEET, WITH BITTER MOLASSES NOTE AND DISTINCT GINGER.

HISTORY:
Ginger cakes are known all over Britain but there is markedly less interest in them in the North and West where there are already distinctive gingerbreads with a strong local following. Ginger has long been an important baking spice in Europe, where it was often associated (as were other spices) with fairings and celebration. The cake described here is a continuation and development of that tradition but peculiar to Britain.

In the 1840s, the *Magazine of Domestic Economy* noted that in London the manufacture of gingerbread was very important, and that it was made into long narrow cakes to export to India. It was based on flour, treacle and ginger, and the author considered that other ingredients added were 'mere supernumeraries imparting flavour and they may therefore be varied at will'. Butter, egg whites, and a leavening of ammonia salts are mentioned in this context. This is the ancestor of modern ginger cakes. A richer, more refined ginger cake, using sugar rather than treacle, is mentioned in the same article. Flour and treacle gingerbread has vanished, but rich ginger cakes are still made by domestic and craft bakers. Their methods are heavily influenced by the nineteenth-century developments in bakery techniques which allowed quick and easy leavening (baking powders) and light sweetening (sugars).

TECHNIQUE:
Ginger cakes are enriched with butter, vegetable fat or lard, and eggs; bicarbonate of soda or baking powder is favoured as leavening agent. Black treacle and Golden Syrup are usually added. The proportions of flour, fat and sugar are 2:1:1, and the weight of black treacle added is usually about three-quarters the weight of sugar. Other ingredients may include chopped candied peel, dried fruit, apple pieces, or chunks of preserved ginger.

REGION OF PRODUCTION:
SOUTH EAST ENGLAND.

Maids Of Honour

DESCRIPTION:
A ROUND OPEN TART, 80MM DIAMETER, 35MM DEEP. WEIGHT: ABOUT 60G. COLOUR: LIGHT BROWN PASTRY, YELLOW FILLING, GOLDEN IN PATCHES. FLAVOUR: SWEET, RICH, ALMONDS.

HISTORY:
These little tarts are of a type widespread in the past but now rare. They resemble simple cheesecakes. The name is first used in the middle of the eighteenth century. It is possible it

derives from the close connections of the royal court with the former palace of Richmond (in which town they appear first to have been made), or with the palace at Kew (now the Royal Botanic Gardens) purchased by Frederick, Prince of Wales and long the home of his son King George III. The recipe in use today in 'The Original Maids of Honour Shop' opposite the walls of Kew Gardens came into the hands of the Newens family, the present owners, in the mid-nineteenth century when an ancestor served an apprenticeship at the Richmond Maids of Honour shop. Production continued in both Richmond and the adjacent village of Kew, but it is in the latter place that the pastries are now made. Other bakers produce variations, but none is authentic. Newens Maids of Honour is a trademark.

TECHNIQUE:
The recipe is a trade secret. Puff pastry is always used for the case and the filling consists of a mixture of milk, breadcrumbs, butter, sugar, grated lemon rind, ground almonds and eggs. The objective is a very well-risen, crisp case filled with a moist, lightly browned filling.

REGION OF PRODUCTION:
South East England, Kew (Surrey).

Bittermints

DESCRIPTION:
A small, thick, disc 45mm diameter, 9mm deep. Weight: 18g. Colour: very dark chocolate coating, with white fondant centre. Flavour: the chocolate is bitter, the fondant powerfully flavoured with mint. Composition: chocolate, sugar, mint. Bittermints are large, with a low sugar content in the coating and a strength of mint flavour contrasting markedly with similar products which are mostly smaller and invariably sweeter.

HISTORY:
Mint has been used as a flavour for grained-sugar sweets in Britain since at least the early 1800s. In 1830, a provincial confectioner S.W. Stavely told his readers how to make candied peppermint. Sugar fondant became popular as a filling for chocolate confectionery about 50 years later. In *The Complete Confectioner* (*c*. 1910) Skuse commented, while giving a recipe for peppermint cream patties, that 'the fondant cream has been of great assistance to the cocoa bean in providing luscious centres'. In 1921, Lousia Thorpe suggested peppermint creams could be coated with chocolate, although she was unlikely to be the first person to have the idea. It was about then that Colonel Benson and Mr Dickinson established 'Bendicks', a chocolatier's, in Mayfair, London. Bittermints were created in 1931. The recipe remains unchanged, and is regarded as the quintessential British mint. No other firm uses the name.

TECHNIQUE:
An unblended mint oil from the American West Coast is specified for the fondant; a relatively high percentage is added. The chocolate is made from a blend of cocoa beans, roasted and refined to produce cocoa liquor of distinctive character; it has an unusually coarse texture. The mint centre is double-coated with the chocolate.

REGION OF PRODUCTION:
South East England.

'It is disgusting to note the increase in the quantity of coffee used by my subjects and the amount of money that goes out of the country in consequence. Everybody is using coffee. If possible, this must be prevented. My people must drink beer.'

FREDERICK THE GREAT

Bitter Beer (Kent)

DESCRIPTION:

THE COLOUR IS FROM TAWNY-GOLD TO COPPERY RED. THE TASTE HAS A HOPPY AND BITTER FINISH TINGED WITH SWEETNESS. ALCOHOL BY VOLUME IS 3.4–5.2 PER CENT.

HISTORY:

Kent was famed as early as the twelfth century for producing the finest ale in England (Wilson, 1973). This was ale in the Old English sense, a fermented drink made from malt without hops, which were unknown in Britain until their introduction in the 1500s by Flemish settlers in this very county.

Hops gradually replaced the other herbs and spices which had been used to flavour beer. They had the double advantage of tasting pleasant and acting as a preservative. They give the bitter note and thus the name to the most widely-drunk beer style. Kent remains a centre of cultivation, with hop gardens and oast houses a feature of the landscape. The freshness of the hops available to brewers in Kent gives distinctive flavour and character to their beer.

Shepherd Neame at Faversham in Kent was founded in the last years of the seventeenth century. It has since been in continuous production: longer than any other in the country.

TECHNIQUE:

Technique does not differ from other British beers. Shepherd Neame makes its strongest bitter (Bishop's Finger) with a mash of crushed malt and liquor drawn from the company's own well bored into an aquifer in the greensand stratum. The wort is strained off into a brew kettle and boiled with Target, Challenger and Goldings hops (all local) for 60–90 minutes. A proportion of the hops is added towards the end of the boil; the wort is strained and cooled and the company's own yeast strain added. Fermentation is for 7 days; more hops are added to ale intended for casks. It is racked into conventional casks to stand for 3–4 days before distribution. If it is to be bottled, it is first filtered and pasteurized. Kentish Ale and Kentish Strong Ale have been awarded Protected Geographical Indication (PGI).

REGION OF PRODUCTION:

SOUTH EAST ENGLAND.

Flag Porter

DESCRIPTION:

IN APPEARANCE, A DEEP MAHOGANY WITH A CREAMY HEAD AND FINE BUBBLES. ITS FLAVOUR IS AROMATIC, SWEETISH, WITH CHARACTERISTIC TOASTED AND FRUITED UNDERTONES. IT IS 5 PER CENT ALCOHOL BY VOLUME.

HISTORY:

Porter and stout owe their distinctive qualities to London water. Jackson (1993) suggests they may have become so closely associated with London and Dublin (Guinness) because the waters of these cities did not lend themselves to the paler beers that became fashionable in the late nineteenth century. Wilson (1973) remarks that by the reign of Elizabeth I, London ale already had a good reputation. The word porter, applied to beer, seems in the mid-eighteenth century to have meant porters' ale, i.e. a beer drunk by porters and other labourers. Quotations from this period attribute its invention to a brewer in Shoreditch in

1722. His beer was called 'entire' because it is said to have included the characteristics of 3 contemporary beer styles, normally mixed in the jug by drawing from different barrels. Originally, the word 'porter' covered several strengths and weights, but then the fuller-bodied 'stouter' examples appear to have become a style in their own right – the modern stout (Jackson, 1993).

A high-temperature roasting process, essential for the malt for these dark beers, was patented in 1817; the grains were roasted in a rotating drum so they could be exposed to the higher temperatures without being burned. Porter was stored in large wooden tuns, giving microflora which lent a characteristic smell.

Porter went out of fashion in the British Isles during the 1960s and production almost ceased, but it was revived in the 1970s and is now popular again. One brand, Flag Porter, is brewed to a nineteenth-century recipe. The yeast for the brew was recovered from sealed bottles found in a ship wrecked in 1825 in the English Channel, and cultured for use in the beer. It is probably the closest in style to the porter of Georgian London. Flag Porter is made by Elgood's in Wisbech, Cambridgeshire; Young's, an old-established London company, still brew a porter in London itself; others make porter-style beers.

TECHNIQUE:
Flag Porter is based on a Whitbread recipe from the mid-nineteenth century. The barley and hops used are grown without pesticides or chemical fertilizers. It is made from pale, crystal, brown and chocolate malts, with Fuggles hops, by the conventional English brewing method. The primary fermentation uses top-fermenting modern yeast; a secondary fermentation uses yeast cultured from the Channel wreck. The beer is then fined, pasteurized and bottled.

REGION OF PRODUCTION:
SOUTH EAST ENGLAND.

Imperial Russian Stout

DESCRIPTION:
THIS STOUT IS ALMOST BLACK, WITH RED GLINTS. ITS FLAVOUR IS VERY COMPLEX, WITH ELEMENTS OF ROASTED, SMOKY, TAR-LIKE FLAVOURS AND BURNT CURRANTS. IT IS GENERALLY 9.5–10.5 PER CENT ALCOHOL BY VOLUME, ALTHOUGH SOME ARE ONLY 7 PER CENT.

HISTORY:
Stout evolved alongside porter as a type of dark beer in eighteenth-century England. Whilst the currency of porter declined, several stouts remained as specialities. One was Imperial Stout, an allusion to its popularity in Tsarist Russia (Jackson, 1993). At least 10 London breweries made this style, particularly in Southwark. From here the beer was shipped to Bremen and the Baltic ports. One of these breweries is now owned by the Courage group which shifted production to John Smith's Brewery, Tadcaster, Yorkshire, despite the London association. Like most dark beers, it is more favoured as a winter drink. Another version, called Vassilinsky's Black Russian Beer, is made by McMullen's, Hertford. There is a third, also brewed in Tadcaster, but by Samuel, not John, Smith's.

TECHNIQUE:
Brewing Imperial Russian stout at the Courage brewery commences with a mash of pale ale,

amber and black malts, plus a proportion of Pilsner malt (included in the recipe since the nineteenth century). The wort is boiled in a brew kettle with Targets hops. Fermentation is at 23–24°C for 5–6 days, using top-fermenting yeast. There follow 2 weeks of warm conditioning in the fermentation tank, then removal to a second tank for several weeks to condition further. Bottling is carried out without filtration or pasteurization. Originally, the beer was kept for 18 months–2 years before being released.

Samuel Smith's brews its Imperial Stout with crystal malts and roasted barley, using the Yorkshire squares method of fermentation, allowing about 24 hours longer than standard bitter for the stout to ferment.

REGION OF PRODUCTION:
SOUTH EAST ENGLAND.

Sloe Gin

DESCRIPTION:
SLOE GIN IS A DEEP, CLEAR RED. IT HAS A RICH, SLIGHTLY BITTER PLUM FLAVOUR.

HISTORY:
From the start of distilling in Britain at the end of the Middle Ages, crude spirits were rectified to eliminate undesirable flavours by redistilling with ingredients such as aniseed before being sweetened and coloured. Alternatively, a good-quality spirit was used to make a cordial by steeping with flavourings like apricot kernels. This set a precedent. During the eighteenth century, many British towns had distilleries to make gin, then a popular new drink. London dry gin is now made by taking a neutral alcohol (triple-distilled through a rectifying still), adding a mixture of 'botanicals' (flavourings such as juniper berries, citrus peels, etc.) and distilling again.

Sloes are a type of wild plum, the fruit of the blackthorn (*Prunus spinosa*) which is native to Britain and grows in hedges and scrubby woodland. An early literary reference to sloe-flavoured gin dates from the 1890s, although 'sloe-juice negus' is mentioned 50 years earlier. It is probable that country people have used sloes as flavouring for many centuries (*OED*). André Simon (1960) calls sloe gin 'one of the oldest and best English liqueurs'. Mabey (1978) states that distiller Thomas Grant, working in Kent in the mid-nineteenth century, made early experiments with sloe gin on a commercial scale. Hugh Williams, the master-distiller for Gordon's Gin, comments that the recipe used by his company is over 150 years old.

TECHNIQUE:
The domestic method requires sloes mixed with gin and sugar – some recipes also call for a few bitter almonds. It is often recommended that the sloes be left on the trees until after the first frosts, which damage the skin slightly, helping release the flavour. The mixture is steeped for about 3 months, stirred occasionally and strained; the gin is bottled and allowed to mature. Damsons can be used in the same way.

Sloe gin is made commercially by Gordon's to a method developed from this: the sloes are frozen and the gin poured over them. They are left to macerate for about 4 weeks before the liquid is drawn off. Demineralized water is added to the residue to extract alcohol absorbed by the sloes, as well as a little more colour and flavour. This is also strained off, and the liquids are mixed and left for 10 days for sediment to precipitate. The batch is filtered and bottled.

Two other brands of sloe gin available are 'Hawkers' and 'Lamplight'. At least one is made by a method requiring the addition of essences.

REGION OF PRODUCTION:
SOUTH EAST ENGLAND.

Anchovy Sauce

HISTORY:
This is a store sauce, a long-keeping concoction of various flavourings. Anchovies have always been used to enrich gravies and sauces. The origin of the modern sauce may lie in 'cullis' (French *coulis*), a strong broth of meat or fish (often anchovy), herbs, spices, vinegars or wines for thickening and flavouring all sorts of ragouts and soups.

It was a logical step to develop a compound based on anchovy which kept well and could be added to food as required. It is probably more correct to call them ketchups or essences; they should not be confused with fresh sauces flavoured with anchovy sent to table. These essences were first commercialized in the late eighteenth or early nineteenth centuries. An early success was 'Lazenbys Anchovy Essence' (Wilson, 1973). Dr Kitchiner (1817) gives recipes, comments on adulteration and imitation of these products, and quotes prices for them. Bottled anchovy essences have been in production ever since. Although anchovies are occasionally caught off the British coast, the salted fish have been imported from the Mediterranean since the sixteenth century and, because of the quantities required, must always have been used for making essences.

TECHNIQUE:
Modern ingredients are listed as anchovies, salt, xanthan gum, spices, and colouring (E162). The method is a trade secret but is no more complex than pounding the fish in water, simmering with seasonings (including cayenne and mace) and rubbing through a sieve (*Law's Grocer's Manual, c.* 1895). Colouring has long been used: bole Armeniac (a reddish, astringent clay formerly imported from Armenia) in the past, now replaced by extract of beetroot. Early recipes show the essence was usually thickened with flour; gum now has this function.

REGION OF PRODUCTION:
SOUTH EAST ENGLAND

Chelsea Physic Garden Honey

DESCRIPTION:
THIS IS A MEDIUM-COLOURED, AROMATIC, POLYFLORAL HONEY WHICH REMAINS LIQUID FOR ABOUT 5 MONTHS AFTER REMOVAL FROM THE COMB.

HISTORY:
The honey owes its characteristics to its site. The Chelsea Physic Garden was established in the late seventeenth century on about 4 acres (2 hectares) of land beside the River Thames in Chelsea to grow herbs for medical purposes and teach their identification and use to physicians and apothecaries. It flourished through the eighteenth century under the direction of some very distinguished gardeners but was neglected by the early 1900s. It was rescued from

decline and used until the 1980s for teaching purposes; it then became an independent charity and was opened to the public. Still functioning as a research centre, it is a rare example of an urban garden which exists for more than ornamental purposes and is an ideal place in which to uphold the tradition of urban beekeeping which has existed for many years in Britain. Amateur beekeepers (of which there are a large number in the UK) recognize that bees kept in towns produce good yields of honey, because they can exploit the wide range of ornamental flowering plants cultivated by city gardeners to give colour through the year.

TECHNIQUE:
The garden occupies a well-drained, sheltered, south-facing site in central London. About 6,000 species are represented. The area immediately round is also rich in mixed flowers and shrubs, some of which inevitably are worked by the bees. A number of hives are kept in the garden all year; they remain in one place, carefully sited to keep the main flight-lines out of the paths of the visiting public. Swarms are prevented by removing extra queens so that only one remains in each hive. The honey is removed in late July, extracted from the comb by conventional methods, and bottled.

REGION OF PRODUCTION:
SOUTH EAST ENGLAND, LONDON.

Cumberland Sauce

DESCRIPTION:
CUMBERLAND SAUCE IS DARK RED AND TRANSLUCENT; SOME TYPES HAVE MUSTARD GRAINS VISIBLE. THE FLAVOUR IS SWEET-SOUR, REDOLENT OF SPICED FRUIT.

HISTORY:
The history of this sauce is obscure. It appears to have little to do with Cumberland. 'Oxford Sauce' is a similar recipe but has not been commercialized. The ingredients point towards origins in British cookery after 1700, when each of them was popular as accompaniment or flavouring for meat dishes. The sauce is eaten with ham, tongue, game or other cold meats.

Elizabeth David (1970) quoted a legend that the sauce was named for Ernest, Duke of Cumberland, brother of George IV. She suggests that it may have been German in origin, and observes that, 'it is odd that no recipe for Cumberland sauce as such appears in any of the nineteenth-century standard cookery books'. The first recipe for a sauce of this type is given by chef Alexis Soyer in 1853, and the first one specifically named Cumberland was given by Suzanne in *La Cuisine Anglaise* early in the 1900s. The earliest use of the name in a literary context is 1878, mentioning its use with game (*OED*). The recipe was confined to the home kitchen until after 1939–45 when the development of a market in speciality foods and the availability of affordable technology combined to see it manufactured and bottled by several small companies.

TECHNIQUE:
Recipes all contain red currant jelly, port wine, mustard and orange, which should be in the form of zest. It is extremely simple to make: the ingredients are gently heated together to form a smooth mixture, then bottled. A gelling agent is usually included in commercial varieties; this may be pectin, or, in cheaper types, cornstarch, which must be gelatinized before the sauce is bottled.

REGION OF PRODUCTION:
SOUTH EAST ENGLAND.

Mushroom Ketchup

DESCRIPTION:

MUSHROOM KETCHUP IS A DARK BROWN, THIN, CLEAR LIQUID. ITS FLAVOUR IS SALTY (SALT CONTENT IS ABOUT 12 PER CENT), WITH MUSHROOM AND SPICES.

HISTORY:

The word ketchup is thought to derive from a word in the Amoy dialect of Chinese denoting a brine of pickled fish. It began to appear in English cookery books in the mid-eighteenth century. Whether the recipes were influenced by Chinese methods or whether a fashionable new word was used for pre-existing recipes for spiced pickles is not clear. Mrs Glasse (1747) recognizes two things about ketchup: keeping qualities and foreign connections. One recipe, in a section addressed to 'Captains of Ships' is entitled 'To make Ketchup to keep Twenty Years'. In another, she observes that if a pint of ketchup is added to a pint of mum (a type of ale) 'it will taste like foreign ketchup'. An early recipe from Mrs Harrison (1748) entitled 'Kitchup or Mushroom Juice' suggests the word still needed explanation.

By the early nineteenth century ketchups were well-known, some based on elderberries, walnuts, lemons, or cockles but the most common was mushroom. Mrs Rundell (1806) gave 2 recipes using mushrooms. One requires the mushrooms to be salted and fermented, the liquid produced boiled with spices, bottled and sealed for 3 months, then strained and re-boiled with fresh spices, and bottled for keeping. What was often a domestic production (in the same way as anchovy sauce, above) was soon commercialized. The company of Geo. Watkins, under which brand mushroom ketchup is still made today, claims to have been established in 1830. The sauce is even now presented in a bottle of characteristically Victorian shape. Eliza Acton (1845) wrote that sauces of the ketchup kind could be bought and some of them were excellent. She also gives a recipe for 'tomata catsup', the first known reference to this sauce in English yet which has now almost annexed the word to itself alone.

TECHNIQUE:

Mushrooms are brined (5 parts mushrooms to 1 part salt) for several days. They are simmered for about 2 hours. Soy sauce, spices (typically ginger, cloves, pimento and black pepper) are added; the mixture is strained and bottled.

REGION OF PRODUCTION:

SOUTH EAST ENGLAND.

***

Also produced in South East England
GINGER WINE (P. 324)

East Anglia

Bramley's Seedling Apple

DESCRIPTION:

A LATE-SEASON COOKING APPLE, DESCRIBED BY MORGAN & RICHARDS (1993) AS LARGE TO VERY LARGE (OVER 7.5–8CM DIAMETER), THE SHAPE FLAT-ROUND, OFTEN LOPSIDED, WITH A BROAD BASIN OF MEDIUM DEPTH, WHICH IS RIBBED AND PUCKERED; THE EYE LARGE, CLOSED OR PARTIALLY OPEN; THE SEPALS BROAD AND DOWNY; THE CAVITY QUITE BROAD AND DEEP, LINED WITH RUSSET, AND THE STALK SHORT AND THICK; THE COLOUR OF THE SKIN CHARACTERISTICALLY GREEN OR GREENISH YELLOW, WITH BROWNISH ORANGE FLUSH, BROAD RED STRIPES AND LENTICELS AS RUSSET DOTS; THE FLESH WHITE TINGED WITH GREEN; THE FLAVOUR IS ACID, WITH A SHARP APPLE TASTE RETAINED EVEN WHEN COOKED AND SWEETENED.

HISTORY:

In Britain, apples are divided into those used for dessert and those used for cooking. Bramley's Seedling is the foremost example of the latter. The original was raised in the early nineteenth century by Mary Anne Brailsford in Nottinghamshire. The tree attracted attention in the 1850s, and was commercialized thereafter. It remains very important and can only be grown successfully in Britain. It is an apple of the type known as a codlin. Originally this seems to have denoted an immature apple, unsuitable for eating raw; this was the sense the word carried in the seventeenth century (OED). Later, it had come to mean a hard apple intended for coddling or cooking. A characteristic of these is that they collapse in a froth when cooked.

These cooking apples were very much to British taste and British climate. The Bramley displaced the earlier Victorian favourite, Dumelow's Seedling. This last was the apple that may have sired Newton Wonder, a famous breed that was first located as a seedling growing in the thatch of a Derbyshire inn – considered by some to be a cross of Blenheim Orange and Dumelow's. A further cross-breeding, early last century, between Newton Wonder and Blenheim Orange was the start of an apple called Howgate Wonder. Both this and the Newgate Wonder are still sometimes found on sale. All these breeds are old-fashioned codlins of the British sort.

Bramleys were first cultivated on a large scale in the 1880s, particularly in East Anglia – above all around Wisbech (Cambridgeshire) where orchards of tall old trees underplanted with gooseberries survived until the 1980s, although now much diminished in area. This pattern of planting is very old, 'similar to that advised by Austen in 1657' (Roach, 1985).

Bramley apples are much used by the food processing industry for sauces, purées and pie fillings; for juicing, when they are usually included in blends; and also as part of blends for cider, especially in East Anglia.

TECHNIQUE:

Since the 1920s, rootstocks for grafting apple trees have been standardized in Britain, using stock developed at East Malling Research Station in Kent, a major centre of apple growing. Dwarf stock is now favoured. Intensive modern orchards now grow about 3,000 trees per hectare, renewed every 10–15 years. In old orchards, it was about 110 per hectare, renewed every 50 years, but few of these now survive. The trees are trained into a pyramid, with low horizontal branches bearing the burden of crop. The old orchards planted in the Wisbech area used vigorous M12 or M13 rootstocks, planted 13 metres square, inteplanted with gooseberries. Bramleys are a fairly hardy variety, relatively tolerant of a wide range of soils. Optimum pollination time is early to mid-May, and the variety is partly triploid, requiring 2 pollinators (Worcester Pearmain is a variety used for this); it is a heavy cropper, but prone to bitter pit. For commercial apple production, the fruit is chemically analysed to determine storage potential; picking is then carried out by hand. Bramleys are picked in early October. Grading is by diameter (sizes are set according to variety) and by quality (EU standards, for appearance) into Grade 1 or Grade 2. Storage is in controlled atmosphere (low in oxygen, high in carbon dioxide) and temperature. Bramleys have benefited greatly from the development of controlled-atmosphere storage techniques, which now allow for 10 months' storage.

REGION OF PRODUCTION:
EAST ANGLIA.

Cambridge Gage

DESCRIPTION:
A SMALL-MEDIUM ROUND PLUM, WITH FLESH THAT CLINGS TO THE STONE. COLOUR: MOST GAGES ARE GREEN RIPENING TO AMBER; TRANSPARENT GAGES HAVE SEMI-TRANSPARENT SKINS. FLAVOUR: JUICY TENDER FLESH, WITH WELL-BALANCED SHARP-SWEET FLAVOUR.

HISTORY:
The plum has had a long history in Britain. The sloe (*Prunus spinosa*) is found in the wild; there have been archaeological finds of bullace (*Prunus institia*) stones – the antecedent of the damson; and the domestic plum (*Prunus domestica*), which is a hybridization of the wild cherry plum or Myrobalan and the sloe, seems also to have existed in Roman Britain (Roach, 1985). Further varieties were known and cultivated in the Middle Ages and improved breeds were encouraged and imported during the Tudor and Stuart period. Among these were plums of the Reine Claude group, so called after its introduction into France from Italy in the reign of François I (d. 1547). This type was described by writers in England during the seventeenth century. They were probably known earlier, as their stones were found in the wreck of the *Mary Rose*, which sank off Southampton in 1545. If the French called this 'sweet, tender and juicy' (Roach, 1985) variety after their Queen, the English took even longer to think up a name. Some time before 1724, plum trees of the Reine Claude type were sent to Sir Thomas Gage at Hengrave Hall in Suffolk from his brother who was a Catholic priest in France. The saplings lost their labels in transit and Sir Thomas's gardener simply called them 'Green Gages'. Not much time was lost before they were being listed under this name by London nurserymen. The garden writer Philip Miller described them in 1731 as 'one of the best plums in England'.

Most high-quality English plum varieties were of foreign origin until the end of George III's reign. One East Anglian cultivar, the Fotheringham, is mentioned in 1665, and the Bury St Edmunds (Suffolk) gardener, Jervaise Coe, developed Coe's Golden Drop at the end of the eighteenth century. The real work of breeding and expansion of the English plum list was by

Thomas Rivers, a nurseryman working in East Anglia in the years after 1834.

The plum is a fruit that often produces chance seedlings that prove to be of great worth. They are almost invariably propagated by suckers taken from the original *trouvaille*, and they are usually taken up by farmers, gardeners and growers in the district immediately local to their discovery. Kea plums (Cornwall), Purple Pershore (Worcestershire) and Dittisham plums (Devon) are examples of this process. Another was the Cambridge Gage. Its origin is unknown, but it is indubitably a seedling of a Green Gage (Smith, 1978), though showing 'greater vigour and better cropping'. It is grown much around Cambridge, was received at the National Fruit Trials in 1927, and was thought 'the best of all the old English gages' by the gourmet André Simon (1960).

TECHNIQUE:

Cambridge Gages form large, vigorous trees, but these can be kept relatively compact by appropriate pruning in summer. For large-scale commercial growing, St Julien A is the favoured rootstock. This makes an earlier-cropping and smaller tree than some. Cambridge Gages are self-pollinating under good conditions, but ideally a pollinator of another mid-season flowering plum variety should be planted close by. The variety is less demanding than some gages, fairly hardy and resistant to pests and diseases, but the fruit has a tendency to split if there is heavy rainfall at the point of ripening. It is also an erratic cropper. Nevertheless, the flavour is considered so good that one company, Wilkin of Tiptree in Essex, use only this variety for greengage-based preserves and jams.

REGION OF PRODUCTION:

EAST ANGLIA.

Careless Gooseberry

DESCRIPTION:

CARELESS HAS LARGE, YELLOW, SLIGHTLY SWEET FRUIT USED FOR COOKING.

HISTORY:

The gooseberry, *Ribes grossularia*, a plant native to Europe, has been cultivated since at least the fifteenth century in Britain. It is a very popular fruit in early summer. It has been used in a tradition of cooked, sweetened desserts which extends back at least to the early seventeenth century. These include gooseberry fool, pies and tarts, all important today. 'One of the servants partook too plentifully last night of gooseberry-fool after a rout his lordship gave … and she is dead this morning of cholera morbus,' quipped George Augustus Sala (1859), reflecting the perennial attraction of the fruit. The bush is easy to cultivate and takes up little space. It was much grown by poor people and many gardens and allotments contain at least one example.

The earliest cultivated varieties that receive literary and botanical notice seem to have been imported into this country during the sixteenth century from Flanders and northern Germany, where it was also much valued. In France, and countries further south, it was little esteemed, or even known. The French called it *groseille à maquereau*, recognizing its cardinal virtue as a sauce for mackerel (appreciated in the province of Normandy). The English, too, may have called it after its culinary use – the berry to be served as sauce for goose. The name was not at all fixed throughout the nation – there were alternative names of feaberry (North Country), feabes (pronounced fapes, in Norfolk), carberry and wineberry.

During the eighteenth century, a custom of competitive growing for the finest and biggest fruit arose in various parts of the country, especially the Midlands and the North; at one time, there were 170 clubs or societies devoted to this. The enthusiasm was such that many people held the opinion that the gooseberry was 'the English fruit' (Roach, 1985). Shows are still held in Cheshire and at Egton Bridge, Yorkshire. The berries are exhibited and assessed, using very old-fashioned units of weight, with a prize going to the heaviest. These clubs were instrumental in developing many of the varieties still grown. Careless was one, raised by a Mr Crompton before 1860. Roach remarks that demand for culinary gooseberries (which are very acid) was stimulated by the abolition of sugar tax in 1874. Shortly after this, a pattern of underplanting top-fruit orchards of plums or apples with gooseberries became important in the Vale of Evesham, Kent and East Anglia. Orchards on this plan, of Bramley apple trees with gooseberries (mostly Careless, but also other British varieties) were established in the Wisbech area of East Anglia. When growers discovered the Careless at a horticultural show in Lancashire in 1897, they brought it home for wholesale adoption. Commercial cultivation of gooseberries has almost died out in the West Midlands, but carries on in East Anglia, where some orchards arranged in the customary manner can still be found.

TECHNIQUE:
Gooseberry bushes are propagated by cuttings; they are cultivated outdoors and the bushes are grown to have a distinct stem so the branches clear the ground. Careless is a variety which requires little specialized pruning, although the bushes are generally encouraged to grow with an open centre, and it is trimmed to control the spreading growth characteristic of this variety. It is moderately vigorous and a heavy cropper, but susceptible to mildew, which is controlled by spraying from April onwards. Protection from birds is required. The fruit is picked by hand in late May and early June.

REGION OF PRODUCTION:
EAST ANGLIA, WISBECH (CAMBRIDGESHIRE); SOUTH EAST ENGLAND.

Conference Pear

DESCRIPTION:
A DESSERT AND COOKING PEAR; MEDIUM SIZED, LONG AND TAPERING SHAPE, YELLOWISH GREEN SKIN, EXTENSIVE RUSSETTING (ROUGH AREAS), FIRM TENDER-COARSE FLESH, JUICY, VERY SWEET WHEN RIPE.

HISTORY:
The work of breeding and improvement of pears was really undertaken in continental Europe. With a few exceptions, English varieties have not proved of lasting value.

Two Victorian nurseries which proved exceptions to that rule were Rivers of Sawbridgeworth and Laxton Brothers of Bedford. Thomas Rivers' Conference pear was their most successful creation. It was bred out of a Belgian cooking pear, the Léon le Clare de Laval, and the first orchard was planted at Allington in Kent in 1895 (Roach, 1985). It was exhibited at the International Pear Conference in Chiswick, where it was awarded the only first-class certificate; the judges asked for it to be named in honour of the occasion. A hundred years later, it is still very important in the British market. Conference pears are often cooked, but are also very good dessert pears when ripe.

TECHNIQUE:

The cultivation of pears is similar in principle to that of apples, although the trees can stand less favourable soils but are more temperature-sensitive. They are grafted on quince rootstocks to give dwarf trees and allow for closer planting. Under the old system, trees were planted 4.6m apart each way, with replacement about every 40 years. Developments in orcharding techniques now allow for a distance of 4m one way and 1.8m the other, and replacement every 25 years. Temperature affects the fruit shape of Conference, giving elongated 'naturals' if this is not favourable at flowering time.

REGION OF PRODUCTION:

EAST ANGLIA; SOUTH EAST ENGLAND.

'Serenely full, the epicure would say, Fate cannot harm me; I have dined to-day.'
SYDNEY SMITH, 'RECIPE FOR SALAD'

D'Arcy Spice Apple

DESCRIPTION:

A LATE-SEASON DESSERT APPLE, MEDIUM-SIZED, OBLONG, RIBBED, YELLOWISH GREEN TO GOLD WITH BRICK RED FLUSH; OCHRE RUSSETING. FLAVOUR: HOT, SPICY, REMINISCENT OF NUTMEG.

HISTORY:

The first D'Arcy Spice tree was found in the gardens of Tolleshunt d'Arcy Hall (Essex) in the late 1700s. As with many English late-season dessert apples, it has a complex flavour. Though it does not seem to have enjoyed the commercial success of some others, it is locally popular (Morgan & Richards, 1993). It is traditionally picked on Guy Fawkes Day.

TECHNIQUE:

See entry on Cox's Orange Pippin (p. 60) for more details of apple growing.

REGION OF PRODUCTION:

EAST ANGLIA, ESSEX.

Norfolk Beefing Apple

DESCRIPTION:

A LATE COOKING AND DESSERT APPLE; DIMENSIONS, MEDIUM TO LARGE. FORM IS FLAT-ROUND. THE SKIN, WHICH IS QUITE TOUGH, HAS A DARK PURPLISH FLUSH AND SHORT RED STRIPES OVER GREEN, RIPENING TO CRIMSON OVER GOLD; FLESH IS WHITE, TINGED WITH GREEN. NORFOLK BEEFINGS HAVE A RICH FLAVOUR WHICH, WHEN PRESERVED BY DRYING, IS DESCRIBED AS BEING 'ALMOST OF RAISINS AND CINNAMON'.

HISTORY:

This apple was apparently known in Norfolk by the late eighteenth century, although Beefings are mentioned in correspondence a hundred years earlier. It was a popular variety in the nineteenth century, planted both commercially and in gardens, but had fallen out of favour by 1900. Trees are still to be found in Norfolk (Morgan & Richards, 1993).

Beefings were apples much favoured for drying. They have tough, rather dry flesh and a resilient skin which allows the fruit to be baked without bursting. If they were placed in bread ovens after baking and allowed to dry in the residual heat, they were known as biffins. Throughout the Victorian period, they were dried by Norwich bakers, packed in boxes, and dispatched as presents (mail-order *avant la lettre*) or to London fruiterers (Dickens mentions a window display including biffins in *A Christmas Carol*) – a Christmas delicacy rather in the same style as tangerines were invariable components of the Christmas stockings of our youth.

Their popularity declined, presumably because of changes in technology in the baking industry – gas and electric steel ovens do not have the same good-natured falling heat and availability of the old brick monsters. Even so, they could certainly be found on sale up until the 1950s and may still be produced by private households. Biffins are described by Hartley (1954) as being red, round, and wrinkled, packed down flat in layers. Norwak (1988) recommended that biffins be coated with sugar which had been melted without colouring. 'Black caps' are biffins which have been baked with candied peel, sugar and wine.

Early in the season, the Norfolk Beefing is a cooking apple; after storage until spring, it is sweet enough to eat fresh.

TECHNIQUE:

Cultivation of Norfolk Beefings on a commercial scale has died out, but the trees are still found in gardens. The apples are picked in mid-October and are stored in trays if they are to be eaten fresh. A modern method for making biffins requires whole, unblemished, unpeeled Beefings. They are placed on racks and allowed to dry at a low temperature (about 105°C) for approximately 5 hours. They are removed from the oven and pressed a little to flatten; then returned to the oven for another hour, after which they are removed and allowed to cool. If desired, they can be coated lightly with uncoloured caramel made by melting sugar very gently. The traditional method required them to be left packed in straw layers with a weight on top in the residual heat of a cooling oven.

REGION OF PRODUCTION:

EAST ANGLIA.

Parsnip

DESCRIPTION:

A ROOT WEIGHING BETWEEN 150–300G. COLOUR: PALE CREAM SKIN, WHITE FLESH. FLAVOUR: SWEETISH.

HISTORY:

Parsnips are native to Britain. There are many references to them in Anglo-Saxon documents (they were also marked on the garden plan of the Swiss abbey of St Gall in contemporary Europe) and they continue to be mentioned throughout the Middle Ages, although skirret (*Sium sisarum*), a species of water parsnip and very sweet-tasting, was also a popular culinary root. Parsnips were valued for their own natural sweetness at a time when sugar was expensive. They were used in sweet pies during the sixteenth and seventeenth centuries. They were also more important as a root vegetable before potatoes were widely cultivated. Thomas Cogan wrote at the end of Elizabeth's reign, 'they are common meate among the common people all the time of Autumne, and chiefly upon fish daies'. The cultivation of parsnips and other roots increased enormously to feed the growing population of London during years of bad grain harvests (Thick, 1998).

They never quite shook off their character of food for the poor, and the less intrusive potato was an easier staple and provider of dietary bulk, so that although their use continued: stewed or mashed, roasted, in soups and stocks, in pies, or as a basis for fermented drinks – beer in Northern Ireland, wine in the rest of the country (Cassell's, 1896) – they have not the cachet of the young turnip or the celeriac, to name 2 other roots (Riley, 1995). They are, however, easy to grow and tolerant of frost. Simon (1960) repeats a bizarre idea that if cooked and cooled and sliced then mixed with mayonnaise, they make a 'Poor Man's Lobster'.

There is a long-standing tradition of cultivating root vegetables in East Anglia, which probably originated with an influx of Dutch religious immigrants who plied their trade as gardeners (those who dug intensively rather than ploughed extensively, a new skill to Tudor Britain) in the sixteenth century. They began to grow roots in the area around Norwich before moving on to the London market and the South-East. Since the eighteenth century, farmers and gardeners in East Anglia and have cultivated turnips, swedes, beets, parsnips and carrots for both local and national consumption, and vegetables are much used in the diet of local people. There is a certain symmetry between the East Anglian supply of human needs and the development of an animal husbandry based on winter-feeding with roots.

TECHNIQUE:

East Anglia includes large areas of free-draining, sandy soils. Easy to work, and allowing the growth of long, straight roots, they are ideal for parsnips and carrots. As a field crop, parsnips are grown from seed planted in November–January. The roots are left in the soil until required; they are now harvested as early as mid-July in response to demand from supermarkets. It is always said that parsnips should not be harvested until they have been exposed to frost. Whilst this is not technically necessary, frost does affect the roots, improving the flavour and making them significantly sweeter. East Anglia has a micro-climate which tends to cold winter weather. As long as the roots are left in the soil until winter, the combination of sandy soil (which reacts quickly to changes in ambient temperature, thus cooling rapidly as the season progresses) and local climate produces well-flavoured parsnips. Several varieties are grown. Some farmers use organic farming techniques; in order to avoid carrot root fly, they drill their parsnips later in the season, and therefore the roots are not ready for harvesting until winter when they have been affected by frost.

REGION OF PRODUCTION:
EAST ANGLIA.

Buckling

DESCRIPTION:
HOT-SMOKED, UNGUTTED HERRING, HEADS REMOVED, ABOUT 18–20CM LONG. WEIGHT: 80–100G. COLOUR: GOLDEN BROWN SKIN, PALE PINK OPAQUE FLESH. FLAVOUR: MILDLY SMOKED.

HISTORY:
Buckling is the name of a cure for herring, *Clupea harengus*. It was first mentioned in English in the early 1900s (*OED*). Grigson (1975) states that it was only after World War II that the cure became familiar in England. Even by 1957, it was possible to write that the cure was not as well known as it should be (Hodgson, 1957). It was German in origin and has been applied to some of the vast quantities of herring processed on the coast of East Anglia, but never seems to have been widely popular (Davidson, 1980).

TECHNIQUE:
The fish are washed and knobbed (gutted and decapitated). Any roe or milt is left in place. Brining is about 45 minutes. They are spitted and assembled on wooden frames, then smoked over hot smoke in small ovens or kilns lined with fire brick. The first part of the cure is to dry the fish in a warm temperature with plenty of draught; then a higher temperature, over a bright fire, is used until they are cooked; finally, they are given the requisite amount of dense smoke, using hardwood sawdust and water, until they are 'an attractive golden colour'.

REGION OF PRODUCTION:
EAST ANGLIA.

Cockle (Stiffkey Blues)

DESCRIPTION:
STIFFKEY BLUES ARE COCKLES, *CARDIUM EDULE*; COLLECTED WHEN THE SHELL IS 25–30MM DIAMETER; THEY ARE SOLD BY WEIGHT OR BY VOLUME, USING THE BRITISH IMPERIAL PINT (APPROXIMATELY 500ML). COLOUR: THE SHELLS VARY FROM PALE LAVENDER TO A DARK GREY-BLUE. FLAVOUR: A RICH SHELLFISH FLAVOUR, REFRESHING AND SLIGHTLY SALTY.

HISTORY:
Cockles were popular beyond Wales; they were much used in British cookery, sent from many coastal towns to industrial cities including London, where they were regarded as a delicacy in the East End. The very cold winter of 1898 killed many cockles and this more general, national, trade seems never to have completely revived. Many of the recipes then current have fallen out of use (Ayrton, 1982). Cockles are gathered at other sites in the British Isles, for example the Thames estuary and the Wash. Processing takes place in several towns, including

A Culinary Celebration of Norfolk
Menu devised by Delia Smith

25th August 2000

When we began to plan this menu for Canary Catering at the Norwich City Football Club, we had no idea if we could actually have everything produced in Norfolk. But we did and all ingredients were sourced locally, including the coffee, which was our trump card. There was actually a special coffee produced in Norfolk, blended with Norfolk wheat!

Canapés of Norfolk Smoked Eel, Bloater Paste and Smoked Salmon with fresh Norfolk Horeseradish

Wild Mushroom Tartlet with Poached Quails' Eggs and Foaming Hollandaise

Potted Crab from Cromer and home-made wholemeal bread (made from locally milled flour)

Confit of Norfolk Duckling with a marmalade of Discovery apples, shallots and Norfolk Cider, runner beans (chosen because the menu was designed for the Olympics!) and gratin of Norfolk Potatoes

Norfolk White Lady and Wissington Ewe's Milk Cheeses with home-made Oat and Raisin Biscuits

Blackcurrant and Oatmeal Torte with blackcurrant ice cream

Coffee with Mini Norfolk Treacle Tarts

Leigh on Sea (Essex), Kings Lynn (Norfolk), and Liverpool. An account of the shellfish trade of the Thames estuary makes clear how badly it was affected at the beginning of the last century by a combination of circumstances. Aflalo (1904) wrote, 'Anyone standing beside the heaps of cockle-shells at Leigh and looking forth upon the fishing-boats that lie idle on the mud banks, may easily realise the ruin brought upon once flourishing communities by the inexorable mandates of modern hygiene.'

In 1736, Richard Bradley thought the best cockles he had ever seen were in Torbay, 'as large as a good Oyster'. Two centuries later, Alan Davidson (1989) pronounced, 'the best British cockles are generally held to be the Stiffkey blues'. Stiffkey is a small village on the north Norfolk coast. In fact the written name of this particular cockle is usually spelled as pronounced – stewkey or stookey.

In the 1800s, the women of Stiffkey supplemented their income by gathering from the cockle beds some miles from their homes. This participation of women in the exploitation of the foreshore is a common feature, met in northern France (the flat sands of the Cotentin), the shallows of the River Exe (searching for mussels and oysters), or the deeper, freer-flowing water of the River Dart. The same gender distinction is encountered in the catching and marketing of sea-fish. The men took to the boats, but fishwives carried it inland to sell. As a free food, Stiffkey cockles must have been used for as long as the area has been inhabited, but no records survive. A local government report (1911), commenting on public hygiene, was happy to exclude the cockle beds of Stiffkey from its strictures, so averting the decline experienced in other parts of the estuary. At this time, there were 20–30 women gathering the cockles.

The blue colour has always been thought noteworthy. An alternative, obsolete, name was bluestones. The colour is derived from the anaerobic mud the cockles inhabit.

Domestic cooks steam stewkey blues and use them in soups and pies. They are also boiled and sold from seaside stalls, with pepper and vinegar to taste. Local restaurants serve them with marsh samphire in the season.

TECHNIQUE:
The cockle beds are located several kilometres from Stiffkey, on the seaward side of a salt marsh. The shellfish are gathered from the mud by raking them out; they are then washed and packed in sacks for carriage back to the village. For cleaning, they are immersed in sea water; some people add flour or oatmeal to assist this process. They are opened by steaming. In the Wash, cockles are fished by suction dredging. Locally, worries are expressed about declining numbers and pollution. It is also recognized that the cockle beds unaccountably vanish every few years; possible reasons include the action of the tides washing away the beds or exposing them to seabirds.

REGION OF PRODUCTION:
EAST ANGLIA, NORFOLK.

COMPARE WITH:
Cockle (Penclawdd), South Wales (p. 187)

Crab (Cromer)

DESCRIPTION:

FOR CRABS LANDED ON THE NORFOLK COAST THE MINIMUM CARAPACE WIDTH IS 115MM. IT IS CLAIMED BY INHABITANTS THAT CROMER CRABS ARE NOTICEABLY SWEETER THAN THOSE FISHED ELSEWHERE.

HISTORY:

Oral tradition states that crabs, *Cancer pagurus*, have been fished in the area for centuries; material relating to this was collected by Sally Festing (1977). The reason why the crabs in this area are better than others is not clear, beyond the fact that it lies close to the spawning grounds and the crabs are probably younger than most of those fished in Britain. It is also possible the underwater geography of the area, notably a chalk shelf with runs offshore, influences the feeding of the crabs.

Fishermen on the South coast, parts of the West Country, Wales, the West of Scotland and the North-East all land crabs at local ports and many fishing towns claim them as a speciality. However, special qualities are claimed for those landed in Norfolk. The minimum landing size is smaller than that elsewhere except Cumbria.

TECHNIQUE:

The crabs are caught in pots, brought ashore, measured, and put into fresh water to make them drowsy, before scrubbing and boiling. They may be sold whole, or dressed by picking the body and claws, cleaning the shell, and packing the meat back into it.

REGION OF PRODUCTION:

EAST ANGLIA, CROMER (NORFOLK)

COMPARE WITH:

Crab, Scotland (p. 364)

Mussel (England)

DESCRIPTION:

MINIMUM LENGTH IS 50MM; THE CULTIVATED MUSSELS ARE RELIABLY FATTENED AND WELL-FLAVOURED.

HISTORY:

Fisheries for mussels are found on the East, South and West coasts of Britain. In East Anglia, Harwich was an important eighteenth-century centre of the trade (Cutting, 1955). Although some sophisticated recipes appear in early cookery books, mussels were generally considered food of the poor. At Brancaster (Norfolk), oral tradition states the fishery has been there for as long as anyone can remember, and in the late nineteenth century, local fishermen leased beds for mussel and oyster cultivation from the lord of the manor. A committee to regulate the Norfolk mussel fishery was formed in the late nineteenth century, as local farmers had started to exploit the beds as a source of fertilizer, threatening stocks. Recently, there has been a shortage of mussels in the Wash, possibly due to a drop in fertility as a consequence of a reduction in the minimum size allowed to be fished.

TECHNIQUE:

In East Anglia, the 'mussel seed' (mussels about 1 year old) are collected by hand from sandbanks in the Wash and taken to Brancaster. Here, the fishermen put them in the lays – short stretches of foreshore along tidal creeks – to fatten in the nutrient-rich water. The lays are small and are carefully maintained by cleaning the mussel beds of mud, which accumulates as the shellfish grow, before new stocks are laid. They are harvested by hand at 2–3 years and purified under ultra-violet light, graded, and sold fresh.

REGION OF PRODUCTION:
EAST ANGLIA, BRANCASTER (NORFOLK)

COMPARE WITH:
Mussel, Scotland (p. 334); Mussel, North Wales (p. 189)

Potted Crab

DESCRIPTION:
CRAB PASTE, PRESERVED IN BUTTER, SOLD BY WEIGHT IN SMALL POTS OR TUBS OF 100–200G. COLOUR: A LIGHT REDDISH BROWN. FLAVOUR: CRAB, WITH SPICES AND BUTTER.

HISTORY:
This falls into the long tradition of preserving meat and fish under a layer of melted butter in a shallow container. Small game birds and some types of fish were preserved whole or in large pieces, but usually the flesh was cooked, picked from the bones and pounded to a paste. This was common practice in eighteenth-century households. Peggy Gates, housekeeper to the Northumberland gentleman Henry Ellison in the 1720s, 'had a reputation for potted charrs, goose-pie, potted woodcock and grouse, and bottled mushrooms' (Hughes, 1952).

These preserves were commercialized from an early date (see Windermere char, p. 214), but during the nineteenth century, the process entered a semi-industrial phase as fish or meat pastes, sealed in small jars, became part of a grocer's stock in trade and reached an ever broader public as sandwiches became a staple at midday and at teatime. The entry given to them in *Law's Grocer's Manual* (*c.* 1895) suggests they were not highly regarded and they have continued to suffer from a poor image. However, they remained popular, and were widely available.

The development of commodities such as potted crab or potted shrimps has avoided some of the odium cast upon meat and fish pastes. The latter were wholly industrial, often using the detritus of more wholesome commerce, offering pungent flavour at minimal cost. Potting crab or shrimps, like potting char, was a means of preserving a coastal delicacy for sale inland. There is a long tradition of potting crab on the East coast of Britain, as indeed can be found in other regions.

The popularity of such stratagems in our day has been stimulated by the advance of domestic food processors, delivering a texture suitable for potting without the grim labour. It has enabled small companies to enter the field, while other technologies have eased distribution and storage.

TECHNIQUE:
The crabs are cooked, cooled, and all edible meat is removed and carefully separated from shell and cartilage. The meat is mixed with butter and spices – black pepper, mace and cayenne are customary – then blended in a processor. Similar products are made, based on other fish, especially herring roes, smoked mackerel, and fresh or smoked salmon or trout.

Smoked salmon is usually potted without being cooked first, often blended with cream cheese. The deep layer of butter that used to be essential no longer is.

REGION OF PRODUCTION:
EAST ANGLIA.

Red Herring

DESCRIPTION:
RED HERRING ARE LEFT UNSPLIT, WITH THEIR HEADS ON, AND WEIGH ABOUT 300–350G. THE COLOUR IS A BRIGHT PINK-RED. THEY HAVE A HARD, DRY TEXTURE, VERY CONCEN-TRATED FLAVOUR.

HISTORY:
Herring curing has a long history in East Anglia. The fish were landed in the ports along the coast in vast quantities – in 1902–3 over 500 million herring were caught by Yarmouth boats – and subjected to curing processes intended to preserve them for many months under conditions of uncertain hygiene. Of these cures, that used for red herring is one of the older and more rigorous.

Great Yarmouth (Norfolk) has always been an important fishery. There were 24 fishermen recorded living there in the Domesday Book. Excavations have revealed a tremendous range of fish bones – of all the species caught there today – from the Anglo-Saxon period, mute witness of many fishy feasts. Investigations elsewhere in East Anglia have revealed an apparent increase in the presence of herring at about the time of the Norman conquest – the fish has always been subject to notorious shifts and migrations (Hagen, 1995). Doubtless, the town's pre-eminence in the trade dates from the same period. The household of Katherine de Norwich, a Norfolk widow in the 1330s, was buying great numbers of herrings – red, white (bloaters) and fresh – from Yarmouth (Woolgar, 1992) and this pattern was repeated across the country. The connection was celebrated by a town fair, already going in the Middle Ages, which ran through the month of October (Mabey, 1978).

The poet Thomas Nashe, a native of Lowestoft, wrote 'Lenten Stuffe, or the Praise of the Red Herring' recounting the legend that a Yarmouth man discovered red herring accidentally when he hung his excess catch from the rafters where, in the smoke of the fire, they turned from white to red. While the first customers for red herrings may have been English folk needing to eat fish on fast days, trade never fell away with a change in religion or politics because new buyers were continually appearing. First there were the Catholics of mainland Europe; then the fish was found a convenient food for the slave traders to offer their captives in transit (thus entering into the African and Afro-Caribbean culinary repertoire); then it carved out a market for its particular flavour in Asia.

Modern refrigeration means that the heavy cures used for red herring are unnecessary for the British, and only a few are produced for those who still have a taste for such strong, salty food. However, exports continue, although even these cures tend to be lighter than formerly. Variant names reflect the nature of the cure: 'high dries' on the one hand, 'golden herring' for something lighter. They were also called 'militiamen' (referring to the red coats) in Yarmouth. Their Scottish sobriquet was 'Glasgow Magistrates' – reference perhaps to a match of facial hue and herring skin.

Autumn fish with a fat content of about 15 per cent are required: this is important – not enough and they dry out, too much and they go rancid. These are fish landed in October–November. The fish are left whole. The closest cure to the traditional red herring made today is: dry salt for about 2 days, then over cold smoke for 4–6 weeks, after which the fish are removed from the kiln and packed. For lighter cures, brined fish are smoked for 3–7 days, depending on the market for which they are destined.

REGION OF PRODUCTION:
EAST ANGLIA.

Smoked Sprats

DESCRIPTION:
WHOLE, UNGUTTED HOT-SMOKED FISH. A KILO OF SMOKED SPRATS CONTAINS APPROXIMATELY 40 FISH. COLOUR: GOLDEN. FLAVOUR: RICH, OILY, SMOKED.

HISTORY:
Sprats, *Sprattus sprattus*, are caught in waters beyond the Thames estuary. The fish were once caught in stow-nets, wide-necked traps held stationary against the tide. It was a technique at least as old as the Tudor period. The catches were at times enormous. In the 1870s there were 600 boats working the Thames estuary; they were landing anything up to 130 tons a day at Billingsgate in the 1860s (Dyson, 1977).

For centuries the fishing towns of the Suffolk coast have been preserving their catch. An early reference in Defoe (1724–6) speaks of sprats being cured in Southwold and Dunwich by being made red, as herrings were at Yarmouth. The author of *The Art and Mystery of Curing, Preserving and Potting* (1864) gives 2 methods for curing sprats, including a method for 'redding' which he called Aldeburgh smoked sprats (Aldeburgh being one of the towns at which the fish were landed). Later, *Law's Grocer's Manual* remarked that sprats 'are found in immense shoals on many parts of our coasts during the latter part of the year … often remarkably abundant, especially off the coast of Suffolk, Essex and Kent. They are often cleaned and cured by being soaked in brine and finally dried, or smoked, for sale in small bundles of 30, or put in small wood boxes.' The men at Brightlingsea (Essex) both smoked the sprats for the home market and packed them in barrels with salt and spices for export to Holland (Dyson, 1977).

Sprats have long been a particular delicacy in England, much as sardines in more southerly countries, or whitebait – a taste that was at its height in the Victorian period. Sala (1859) wrote, 'I don't think there is … a more charming red-letter night in the calendar of gastronomy, than a sprat supper. You must have three pennyworth of sprats, a large tablecloth is indispensable for finger-wiping purposes – for he who would eat sprats with a knife and fork is unworthy the name of epicure – and after the banquet I should recommend … the absorption of a petit verre of the best Hollands.'

TECHNIQUE:
Sprats are landed in the small fishing ports of the Suffolk coast in late autumn, the season beginning in November. The fish are picked over and given a short brining before they are threaded by hand on hooks and suspended in cold smoke for a short time. As with other

smoked fish, the exact length of time depends on the oil content of the fish and ambient temperature. The temperature of the smoke is then increased and the fish smoked briefly in hot smoke to cook through. After cooling, the smoked sprats keep for about a week.

Some fresh sprats are frozen, to be thawed and smoked later in the year, when fresh fish of the correct oil content are not available.

A now outmoded method called for 4 hours of brining, a period of draining and the fishes to be smoked until they were 'the colour of Spanish mahogany', after which they were packed for export.

REGION OF PRODUCTION:
EAST ANGLIA, SOUTHWOLD AND ALDEBURGH (SUFFOLK).

Yarmouth Bloater

DESCRIPTION:
COLD-SMOKED UNGUTTED HERRING, ABOUT 30CM LONG. WEIGHT: 350–400G. COLOUR: SILVERY GOLD SKIN, DARK PINK TRANSLUCENT FLESH. FLAVOUR: MILDLY SMOKED, FISHY, SLIGHTLY GAMEY.

HISTORY:
Bloater indicates a specific type of cure used for herring, *Clupea harengus*. Yarmouth bloaters were first noted in the early nineteenth century, but 'bloat herring' are mentioned 2 centuries earlier. The description bloat or bloater is conjectured to have links with Scandinavian languages, indicating either fish that had a soft texture, or fish which had undergone a steeping process (*OED*).

Yarmouth legend has it that the process was discovered by accident when a fish curer threw salt over fresh herrings to preserve them temporarily. But the date given for this supposed event is later than the date of the first quotation in the *Oxford English Dictionary*. Although the evolution of the process is a matter for conjecture, the fame of the product is not. *Law's Grocer's Manual* (*c.* 1895) was firm in its praise. Bloater paste, a favourite Victorian spread for toast, was made by skinning, cleaning and mincing the fish, mixing with lard and spices, and pressing into fancy pots, patent jars or tins, which were hermetically sealed. Because the mild cure results in fish that will not keep for very long, paste was a convenient means of extending the range of the trade. None the less, manufacture remains the preserve of the immediate area round Yarmouth. Refrigeration allows wider distribution.

TECHNIQUE:
Bloaters are only made at a time of the year when the herring have the correct oil content, commonly the autumn. Fish landed at East Anglian ports are preferred. The time spent in the salt brine varies, but about 2 hours is typical. The fish are suspended on spits of wood pushed through the gills and hung in cool smoke from hardwood sawdust for 12–18 hours.

REGION OF PRODUCTION:
EAST ANGLIA, GREAT YARMOUTH (NORFOLK).

Newmarket Sausages

DESCRIPTION:

FRESH PORK SAUSAGE (65–70 PER CENT PORK); EACH 10CM LONG, AND 8 SAUSAGES TO THE LB (450G). COLOUR: DEEP PINK-BEIGE WITH A FEW FLECKS OF HERB. FLAVOUR: MODERATELY SPICY, WITH A FAIRLY DRY TEXTURE.

HISTORY:

Newmarket, east of Cambridge, is best known for horse racing. It appears its sausage developed as a souvenir. No doubt fresh sausages have been made in the area for centuries, but the Newmarket sausage as known today appears to have a shorter history. It was first made in the 1880s. There are 3 butchers in the town who sell 'Newmarket' sausages, each one producing a slightly different version. This much is certain.

There are various claims to the original coarse-cut, pork-based sausage with a secret spicing mix. One maker, Grant Powter, uses a recipe invented by his great-grandfather, William Harper, who was apprenticed to a butcher in Newmarket in the 1880s. The company of Musk's say that their recipe was evolved by James Musk in 1884. Whatever the truth, the sausages are now firmly established.

TECHNIQUE:

Powter's selects heavier-grade pigs from local sources; the carcass is hand-boned and meat from all parts used in the sausages. It is minced coarsely, mixed with rusk and a fairly spicy, piquant seasoning made to a secret family formula, plus salt, and then filled into natural casings and hand-linked.

Musk's use a 'heavy' old-fashioned bread, made for them by a baker in a neighbouring village, in place of the rusk; they too use meat from the whole pig in their sausages. Neither uses preservatives or artificial colourings.

REGION OF PRODUCTION:

EAST ANGLIA, NEWMARKET (SUFFOLK).

Norfolk Black Turkey

DESCRIPTION:

NORFOLK BLACKS HAVE BLACK FEATHERS AND MATURE SLOWLY TO GIVE HENS WEIGHING ABOUT 4.5–6.8KG AND STAGS OF 7.2–10.5KG. THE SKIN HAS A DISTINCTIVE BLACK PITTING OF DARK FEATHER STUMPS. FLAVOUR IS MEATIER AND MORE INTENSE THAN THAT OF COMMERCIAL HYBRIDS.

HISTORY:

East Anglia has always been important for its cereal crops. After the harvest was gathered, poultry were fattened on the stubble. 'In the seventeenth century, great flocks of turkeys (often five hundred or more) were driven more than a hundred miles down the rough roads to the London markets. Their feet were bound in rags and dipped in tar to prevent damage, and each night they would be penned in fields by the roadside where they could feast on the remains of the corn in the autumn stubble' (Norwak, 1988).

Turkeys are not indigenous but were brought back from Mexico in the sixteenth century. The fact their name suggests they came from the East not the West is all of a piece with the confusion of new consumers, who were faced at the same time with the guinea fowl – also called turkey in the first instance. Another introduction, maize, was called Turkey corn in a similar muddle about origin. The historian Sir Richard Baker (1643) claimed the bird came into the country in 1524, citing a rhyme that went, 'Turkeys, carps, hoppes, piccarell, and beer, Came into England all in one year.' The fact that this is quite wrong about the fishes need not make it completely mistaken about the turkey. In the 50 years from their probable introduction, they had penetrated as far as the East Anglian table of Thomas Tusser (1573) who wrote of the Christmas board laden with 'pig, veale, goose and capon, and turkey well drest'. The progressive ousting of the goose had begun and the replacement of the bustard, the peacock and other 'great birds' of medieval feasts was assured.

As Kent was the garden and orchard, so Suffolk and Norfolk were the grain and meat larder of London. The Norfolk Black was the historic race of turkeys fattened by East Anglian farmers, but there have always been two principal strains of turkey in this country. The Norfolk is the smaller, perhaps the less hardy. The other is the Cambridge, which has a more varied plumage. The Cambridge has been crossed many times with the American Bronze, the largest of the turkey kind, giving rise to the present breed of Cambridge Bronze. In recent years, Cambridge and Norfolks have been crossed themselves. The result is the Kelly Bronze, which combines slow maturation, good flavour and more breast meat than is usual in Norfolk Blacks. It is sometimes held the two English strains represent a double introduction. The Cambridge represents the turkey of Mexico, brought over by the Spaniards; the Norfolk that of north-east America, now the United States and Canada, which may have been carried in English or French boats.

The pure-bred Norfolk Black's rarity in modern Britain has been caused by constant hybridization: growers sought greater productivity and a different conformation once turkey entered the mass-market food supply. The Norfolk Black grows slowly, and supermarkets insist on a bird with a white skin. Consumers also favour a plump breast. However, one large flock of Norfolk Blacks was maintained by the Peel family, farmers in East Anglia, when the breed was virtually forgotten for commercial purposes. It is now raised on a small scale by farmers and smallholders in the area.

TECHNIQUE:
There is no particular method attached to rearing Norfolk Blacks, but the small scale on which they are farmed means that many are free-range, feeding in the fields, their diet supplemented with grain. They are killed at 25 weeks and dry-plucked. The Traditional Farm Fresh Turkey Association recommends hanging for a minimum of 7 days; in practice, many producers give up to 14 days.

REGION OF PRODUCTION:
EAST ANGLIA.

Suffolk Ham

DESCRIPTION:
A CURED SMOKED HAM. WHOLE HAMS WEIGH 6.3–8KG. THE BEER CURE YIELDS A DEEP BLACKISH-BROWN SKIN, THE CIDER CURE A PALER, MOTTLED COLOUR. THEY HAVE A STRONG, SWEET HAM FLAVOUR, LIGHTER WHEN THE CIDER CURE IS USED.

In 1838 Suffolk hams were spoken of with approval by a contributor to the *Magazine of Domestic Economy*, who considered this county made the best in England. The cure was similar to that used today. First the hams were rubbed with plain salt and left for a short time; then a pickle was composed of salt, saltpetre, coarse brown sugar, strong old beer and spices. These were boiled together until thick and syrupy and rubbed into the hams which then lay for 5 weeks, after which they were dried and smoked. Although Mrs Beeton (1861) gave a 'Suffolk Recipe' for pickling hams, hers was a dry-salt cure, including sugar and vinegar, unlike others quoted. In the early twentieth century a wet pickle using stout was being used by various manufacturers, including the Jerrey family, now into the third generation using the recipe – with the original smokehouse as well. In the past, several farms and companies in the Suffolk area made hams by this cure but their number has diminished since the Second World War.

TECHNIQUE:

The pork legs are selected for a specified level of fat. They are brined in salt, saltpetre and water, then pickled in a mixture of black treacle, sugar, salt and stout or cider for 3–4 weeks. Smoking takes place for 5 days over oak sawdust. They are matured for at least one month. Farmhouse methods involved 3 days' dry-salting before the hams were immersed in the sweet pickle; the hams were considered to be at their best when between 1 and 2 years old.

REGION OF PRODUCTION:

EAST ANGLIA, SUFFOLK.

Suffolk Sweet-Cured Bacon

DESCRIPTION:

SMOKED CURED PORK FOR COOKING. COLOUR: THE PICKLE MAKES THE OUTSIDE VERY DARK; THE FAT HAS A VERY SLIGHT BROWN CAST AND THE LEAN IS A DEEP PINK-RED. FLAVOUR: DISTINCTLY SWEET, WITH HINT OF MOLASSES, BUT ALSO VERY SALTY, UNDERPINNED WITH A SLIGHT ACID NOTE.

HISTORY:

The word 'bacon' meant back. It was only transferred to its exclusive application to the cured backs of pigs in mute recognition of a constant of British food culture. A similar transference may be seen in the word 'brawn', which once applied to the flesh of any animal (or human), but in culinary terms was progressively restricted to that of the wild boar and then of the pig.

It is the use of a sweet cure, similar to that used for hams, which distinguishes this from other artisanal bacon. How long it has been used is unknown. Suffolk bacon was discussed in 1838 by a contributor to the *Magazine of Domestic Economy*, who obviously thought highly of it, but considered Buckinghamshire made finer. The use of a similar pickle is a tradition in the family of Nigel Jerrey, one of the present makers, dating back at least 75 years. The bacon should be grilled rather than fried.

TECHNIQUE:

The cure of the 1840s was similar to today's: salt and coarse brown sugar applied hot to the flitches. This is just as for Suffolk ham, but bacon is cut from the back and belly. As the joints are thinner, the meat is not pickled as long as the hams. It is smoked after curing.

EAST ANGLIA, SUFFOLK.

COMPARE WITH:

Ayshire Bacon, Scotland (p. 306); Welsh Bacon, Wales (p. 190); Wiltshire Bacon, South-West England (p. 28).

Pressed Tongue (Suffolk Cure)

DESCRIPTION:

CURED AND COOKED OX TONGUES CURLED TO FIT A CYLINDRICAL MOULD 18–20CM DIAMETER. CUT IN THIN SLICES. COLOUR: DEEP PINK WITH SMALL WHITE FLECKS, SURROUNDED BY AMBER JELLY; DARK EXTERIOR. FLAVOUR: HIGHLY SALTED, WITH A RICH TEXTURE.

HISTORY:

Tongue has long been a valued part of the offal from cattle, although the fact that it is generally referred to as coming from the ox (the Anglo-Saxon word for cattle) as opposed to beef (from the Norman French *boeuf*, which was adopted into English to mean ox-flesh once it became meat on the overlord's table) indicates that it may not have been considered amongst the choicest parts of the animal. Early recipes show tongues cured in much the same way as salt beef or bacon, using dry salt and saltpetre and spices or herbs. After the meat had been pickled 7–10 days, it was dried and smoked (David, 1970).

Acton (1845) gave 'A Suffolk Receipt' for curing tongue which included coarse sugar and was similar to that still used for curing bacon. This early confirmation of a regional particularity was endorsed by Webb (c. 1930) in her study of the curing of meat, including tongue, in East Anglia.

Processed tongues were sold in various forms: straight from the cure, dried and smoked, or cooked and pressed by the butcher. The latter is now by far the most common. Suffolk-cured tongues can be obtained today from specialist suppliers. 'Lunch tongues' are a name for pigs' or sheep's tongues, brined, cooked and moulded in similar fashion. The name perhaps reveals the favoured time for eating these meats, often with salad or in sandwiches. When hot, a Cumberland or cherry sauce is a recognized accompaniment.

TECHNIQUE:

Initial preparation requires tongues to be washed thoroughly and trimmed at the root. They are brined in a salt, saltpetre and brown sugar pickle for 3 weeks, then simmered in fresh water for about 4 hours. As soon as they are cool enough to handle, any remaining bone and gristle is trimmed from the root and the skin carefully removed. The tongue is curled to fit a circular mould with a little aspic jelly. A cover is placed on top and the meat pressed until absolutely cold, then it is unmoulded and cut in very thin slices. A butcher may prepare several tongues at once in a mould deep enough to accommodate them.

Brines or pickles for tongue are basically the same as those for bacon and ham, with small regional variations in salt and sugar content. It seems that producers do not smoke tongues now; this was a preservation method of the past which canning and freezing have made unnecessary. Consumers have lost the taste for heavily salted and smoked meat.

REGION OF PRODUCTION:

EAST ANGLIA, SUFFOLK

I n Norfolk, dumplings were originally called 'floaters' because they were traditionally made with bread dough (containing yeast) rather than suet, and thus they float rather than sink. Many people now mix suet with flour when making dumplings, although the suet variety used to be derided by Norfolk men as 'sinkers' and dumplings when properly cooked the Norfolk way should be as light as a feather.

It is traditional to have dumplings with stews or with boiled beef or boiled bacon. When meat used to be an expensive luxury, many families ate dumplings (much as others ate Yorkshire puddings) before the main meat course, the idea being that the dumplings would blunt the appetite and so less meat would be needed.

When making Norfolk dumplings, the traditional methods should be followed. Wives of Norfolk farmers used to make them to weigh exactly four ounces each. Today, they are still made from proved bread dough (dough left to rise in a warm place) rolled into balls and then left to prove again before being slipped into a large saucepan of fast-boiling water and boiled with the lid on for twenty minutes. The lid should never be lifted during the cooking time and the dumplings should then be served immediately with gravy. Traditionally, dumplings should not be cut with a knife, but torn apart with two forks at once so that they do not become too heavy. As I said earlier, many people now use suet when making dumplings and instead of cooking them separately in boiling water steam them over a pan of boiling water or over the top of a casserole, or even throw them into the casserole for the last twenty minutes of cooking, but this results in a much heavier dumpling.

Galton Blackiston

CHEF AND PROPRIETOR, MORSTON HALL, MORSTON

Norfolk Dumplings

450G (1 LB) PLAIN FLOUR

1 TSP SALT

4 TBSP CHOPPED PARSLEY

15G (½ OZ) FRESH YEAST

1 TSP CASTER SUGAR

150ML (¼ PINT) WARM WATER

2 TBSP WARM MILK

Place the flour, salt and chopped parsley into the bowl of a food mixer and, using the mixer's dough hook, mix thoroughly. Combine the yeast and sugar in a bowl and mix with your fingertips so that the yeast breaks down and becomes smooth and almost liquid. Add the water and milk to the yeast, and mix this together well.

With the food mixer still running, slowly add the yeast mixture to the flour. Allow the machine to knead the dough for five to eight minutes, or until it comes away from the sides of the bowl.

Remove the bowl from the mixer and cover the dough with a clean, damp tea towel, then leave it in a warm place for about one hour or until the dough has doubled in volume.

Turn the dough out onto a lightly floured surface, knead well with the palm of your hand and then form into eight dumplings. Place the dumplings on a tray and leave them to prove again in a warm place.

Bring a large saucepan of water to a rolling boil and, once the dumplings have proved again, slip them quickly into the boiling water. Place the lid on the saucepan and boil for exactly twenty minutes.

Using a slotted spoon, remove the dumplings from the boiling water. Serve immediately either on their own with some gravy or to accompany boiled beef, boiled bacon or a casserole.

Norfolk Knob

DESCRIPTION:

ROUND RUSKS WITH A HOLLOW CENTRE, 40MM DIAMETER, 30MM DEEP. WEIGHT: 12G. COLOUR: PALE GOLD TOP AND BOTTOM, WITH A DISTINCT PALE BAND AROUND THE MIDDLE. FLAVOUR AND TEXTURE: SLIGHTLY SWEET, LIGHT, VERY CRISP AND FRIABLE.

HISTORY:

These little rolls, also known as hollow cakes, are biscuits in the true sense of being twice baked (Latin *bis coctum*, French *bis cuit*). Norwak (1988) mentions the connections East Anglia has had with the Netherlands, suggesting they influenced the development of rusk-like breads in this area; similar biscuits, but smaller and richer, are made in Suffolk. James Woodforde, a Norfolk parson, records a gift of hollow cakes in 1788. Grigson (1984) quotes a recipe from 1821. According to Mr Ashworth, the baker best known for the product, the name 'Norfolk Knob' was the invention of a bakery company called Stannard, who traded in Norwich for about a century until the 1970s. The local name is 'hollow biscuits'; this use of the word biscuit in its original sense suggests a long history. It is always said that King George VI, when staying on his estate at Sandringham, would order a supply. To eat, the knobs are first broken in half by twisting, then spread with butter, jam or cheese.

TECHNIQUE:

A yeast-leavened dough of flour and water with a little fat and sugar is used. Cold water is preferred, as it stops the mixture rising too quickly. The dough is rolled, folded once, docked, then rolled by hand into 20mm circles. Once proved, they are baked for 15 minutes at 190°C. The knobs are cooled then dried out in a low oven for about 2 hours. Some domestic recipes are chemically leavened.

REGION OF PRODUCTION:

EAST ANGLIA, WYMONDHAM (NORFOLK).

COMPARE WITH:

Dorset Knob, South West England (p. 38).

Custard Tart

DESCRIPTION:

AN OPEN ROUND TART WITH SLOPING SIDES AND CRIMPED EDGES; 70MM ACROSS THE TOP, 45MM ACROSS BASE, 20–30MM DEEP; LARGER SIZES ARE MADE, USUALLY STRAIGHT-SIDED AND SHALLOWER. WEIGHT: 100G. COLOUR: YELLOW SPECKLED WITH BROWN. FLAVOUR AND TEXTURE: RICH, EGGY AND SWEET, SMOOTH TEXTURED, SPICED WITH NUTMEG.

HISTORY:

From medieval times, pastry cases containing spiced custard (a mixture of eggs and milk or cream) have been baked in Britain. A *crustarde lumbarde*, or open pie containing spices, sugar and dried fruit, appeared in one of the earliest cookery manuscripts dating from *c.* 1390. Such sweet custards have been flavoured with bay leaves, cinnamon or lemon, made into puddings to be boiled in a cloth, or baked in moulds or cooked in pastry. A group of rich custard recipes appears to belong to the Cambridge and Norfolk area. An example is 'the Charter', a baked custard of cream and eggs served with apricots, traced by Jane Grigson (1984) to a Norwich recipe of the 1820s. Burnt cream, another rich custard served under a layer of caramelized sugar, is claimed by various Cambridge colleges. White (1932) gives a recipe for tartlets of pastry made with ground almonds filled with cream custard, remarking that these were favourites with Cambridge undergraduates in the 1890s; they were called cream darioles. Dariole originally meant a small pastry case with various fine fillings. It has come to refer to the small tin moulds, rather deep with steeply flared sides, similar in shape to the foil dishes used by commercial bakers to hold custard tarts even now.

TECHNIQUE:

An unsweetened short-crust pastry is generally used with flour and fat (lard) in the proportions 2:1. A mould is lined, a custard (the richer ones use cream rather than milk) is poured to the top, and nutmeg is sprinkled over the surface. Richer custards contain more egg yolks; plainer ones may include cornflour.

REGION OF PRODUCTION:

EAST ANGLIA.

Cider (Eastern Tradition)

DESCRIPTION:

CIDER FROM EASTERN ENGLAND TENDS TO BE LESS PERFUMED THAN THAT FROM THE WEST, WITH A NUTTY DRYNESS AND MARKED ACIDITY. IT IS 7.5–8 PER CENT ALCOHOL BY VOLUME (6 PER CENT IN THE WEST).

HISTORY:

Some of the earliest records of cider in Britain come from the East. Wilson (1973) mentions Sussex and Kent as cider-making areas in the twelfth century, and Norfolk in the early thirteenth century. Its history was affected by factors similar to those which influenced the drink in the West Country, with one important difference. The interest in apples specifically for making cider which developed in Herefordshire during the 1600s never really penetrated east. Consequently, the tradition is to use whatever apples are available. The industry is smaller than in the South West.

TECHNIQUE:

The method used is the same as that in the West; the significant difference being the apple varieties. Bramleys provide the bulk.

REGION OF PRODUCTION:

SOUTH AND EAST ENGLAND.

'I hate a man who swallows it, affecting not to know what he is eating. I suspect his taste in higher matters.'

CHARLES LAMB, *ESSAYS OF ELIA*

Old Ale (East Anglia): Strong Suffolk

DESCRIPTION:
DARK, RICH RED-BROWN IN COLOUR; A TOASTY, WINY, BITTER FLAVOUR. IT IS 6 PER CENT ALCOHOL BY VOLUME.

HISTORY:
The brewery producing Strong Suffolk is in Bury St Edmunds. Barley has long been a major crop here, and malting is a local industry. The Greene King brewery dates from the late 1700s, although the town has a history of brewing stretching back over a thousand years. Strong Suffolk has been produced since the early twentieth century. It is regarded as a type of old ale, but it differs from most beers in this style because it is produced by an early, but now very unusual technique of blending 2 beers together, one of which is aged in wooden vats.

TECHNIQUE:
Strong Suffolk is a blend of 2 beers, neither of which is sold on its own. The brewery uses water from its own wells, and makes most of its own malt from East Anglian barley; English hops are used exclusively. One of the beers used in the blend is known as 5X: this is brewed to an original gravity of 105, fermented, then transferred to oak vats which are sealed and covered with a layer of Suffolk marl (a local clay containing carbonate of lime, once used as a soil improver and fertilizer). This acts as a filter, against contamination by wild yeasts and other harmful microflora. The beer matures in these vats for 1–3 years, developing a spicy flavour and gradually increasing in alcoholic content. 5X is blended with a full-bodied malty beer called BPA, which is brewed as required and used after a short period of warm conditioning.

REGION OF PRODUCTION:
EAST ANGLIA.

COMPARE WITH:
Old Peculier, Yorkshire (p. 272).

Cider Vinegar

DESCRIPTION:
CIDER VINEGAR IS CLEAR AND ORANGE-YELLOW. THE FLAVOUR IS ACID WITH DISTINCT CIDER OVERTONES. IT IS NORMALLY ABOUT 5-5.5 PER CENT ACID.

HISTORY:
Formerly, almost every town would support at least one vinegar brewer and regional differences were more marked, reflecting local methods of making beer or cider. Cider-makers found vinegar all too easy to make accidentally, since apple juice left to ferment alone can easily develop into vinegar. In the mid-nineteenth century one comment was that much vinegar was 'made in Devonshire and America from refuse cider'. Although many cidermen still make a little vinegar in this casual way, since the 1950s, large-scale production is controlled by using an acetator.

The 2 largest cider-makers producing vinegar are in East Anglia and the South-East. One is Aspall's, founded in 1728 when a member of the Chevallier-Guilders family moved to Suffolk from Jersey, bringing cider-apple trees with him.

TECHNIQUE:

Cider is fermented by the English method. After resting, it undergoes acetous fermentation in which cultured bacteria are introduced under controlled conditions. Aspall's, which produces an organic vinegar, uses a Green Shield acetator; Merrydown uses a Fring. The vinegar is matured for several weeks before filtering, dilution to specified acid content and bottling.

REGION OF PRODUCTION:
EAST AND SOUTH ENGLAND.

Colman's Mustard

DESCRIPTION:
MUSTARD POWDER IS LIGHT YELLOW IN COLOUR AND, FRESHLY MIXED, HOT AND PUNGENT TO TASTE, MELLOWING ON STORAGE. THE INGREDIENTS ARE MUSTARD FLOUR, WHEAT FLOUR, SALT AND TURMERIC.

HISTORY:
The manufacture of mustard powder has, for about a century, been almost synonymous with the firm of Colman's in Norwich, which has developed a product based on particular strains of mustard seed. Colman's has forged close relationships with specified growers to ensure continuity of quality and supply.

The original creation of dry mustard powder by Mrs Clements of Durham (see Taylor's, below, p.240) did not long remain her sole monopoly. Producers sprang up all over the country during the 1700s, one of the most important being the London firm of Keen & Company – hence the phrase 'keen as mustard'. Manufacture in Durham eventually ceased.

The fact that mustard began one segment of its history in Durham was no coincidence: that county grew a lot of the plant and therefore had an industry to process or grind its seeds. Likewise, the rise of Colman's of Norwich was a reflection of agricultural reality. Jeremiah Colman acquired a flour mill which also ground mustard seed. The business grew, enhanced by clever advertising and careful quality control. By the end of the century, *Law's Grocer's Manual* observed that no other country in the world carried on the preparation of mustard as energetically as England. Colman's bought Keen's and several other mustard companies in the early twentieth century and now dominates the market.

TECHNIQUE:
Mustard has been grown in East Anglia for a long time but, after World War II, Colman's developed strains of brown and white mustard for their own use, and improved agricultural methods associated with the crop. Much of the skill in producing mustard lies in blending the correct proportions of various types of seed.

Colman's formula is closely guarded. Brown and white seeds come from specified growers, their entire crop acquired by Colman's. It is cleaned, dried, crushed with steel rollers and sifted to remove the husks. The flours are blended, wheat flour and turmeric added, the mixture packed in tins. The pungency is enhanced by the product not being heat-treated.

REGION OF PRODUCTION:
EAST ANGLIA.

Maldon Sea Salt

DESCRIPTION:

MALDON SALT IS WHITE, WITH A SOFT, FLAKY TEXTURE. ITS FLAVOUR IS CLEAN, SHARP AND FREE FROM BITTERNESS. THE MALDON PROCESS RESULTS IN A PYRAMID-SHAPED CRYSTAL. ONLY THE MALDON CRYSTAL SALT COMPANY PRODUCES THIS PARTICULAR TYPE.

HISTORY:

Sea salt has been extracted at various sites around the British coasts for thousands of years. The southern coast of East Anglia is flat, with salt marshes and tidal inlets well-suited to salt extraction. In the Domesday Book (1086), 45 salt pans are listed in the Maldon area. In the Middle Ages, salt was extracted by boiling sea-water in 'leddes' (lead pans). References to these are found in wills of the sixteenth century. In the eighteenth century, Mrs Glasse (1747) mentioned salt from 'Malding' in Essex as a large, clear salt which gave meat a fine flavour.

The present company grew from a salt works established in 1823; it became the Maldon Crystal Salt Company in the 1880s.

TECHNIQUE:

Sea water is collected from salt marshes when the salt content is at its maximum, after a period of dry weather at the spring tides. It is kept in holding tanks and allowed to settle before being filtered and pumped into storage tanks. It is then drawn off into pans about 3 metres square, mounted on a system of brick flues. The water is brought to a rapid boil and skimmed. The heat is reduced to just below boiling point and the water allowed to evaporate, concentrating the salt in minute, pyramid-like structures. When the quantity of crystals in the remaining water reaches the surface of the liquid, heating is stopped. The pans are cooled and the salt harvested by raking it to one side with wooden hoes. It is then drained in special bins for 48 hours and drying is completed in a salt store. Before packing, the humidity of the crystals is adjusted by drying in a low-temperature oven.

REGION OF PRODUCTION:

EAST ANGLIA.

Medlar Jelly

DESCRIPTION:

FRUIT JELLIES ARE TRANSLUCENT, THEIR COLOURS VARY: MEDLARS YIELD A BRIGHT RED-BROWN, RED CURRANTS A RICH RUBY, QUINCES A RED-ORANGE, AND CHERRIES A DEEP DARK RED. MEDLAR IS A RELATIVELY ACID JELLY, WITH A SLIGHTLY WOODY AROMA. MOST MAKERS OF JELLIES NOW AIM FOR A HIGH FRUIT CONTENT WITH A SUGAR CONCENTRATION OF ABOUT 66 PER CENT.

HISTORY:

Recipes for medlar jelly, very similar to that now used, appear sporadically in British cookery texts from the early eighteenth century. Jellies based on fruit juices have always been popular with the British, if only as a means of preserving the crop; red currants, cherries, quinces and japonica (Japanese quince) are some of their favourite candidates. They owe their origin to European recipes such as that for quince paste (*marmelo*, the first stage of marmalade), popular in Renaissance Spain and Portugal (Wilson, 1973). They were made from many different

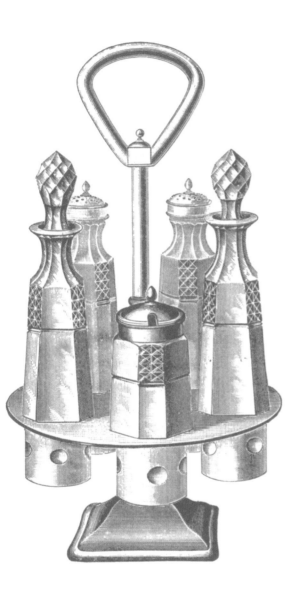

'They dined on mince, and slices of quince,
Which they ate with a runcible spoon;
And hand in hand, on the edge of the sand,
They danced by the light of the moon.'

EDWARD LEAR, 'THE OWL AND THE PUSSYCAT'

types of fruit juice, boiled until concentrated enough to produce long-keeping, solid confections, stored in boxes and cut into slices for use. During the nineteenth century, different forms developed: one was the solid fruit jelly used as a sweetmeat, from which originated various children's sweets – the jellies, gums and pastilles now made on a vast scale – and the jellies made by housewives and jam companies as preserves. It is in the latter sector that one can still find artisan production of jellies based on unusual fruits. The southern part of East Anglia appears to be particularly rich in these products. It has relatively low rainfall and high summer temperatures, and is a good area for orchard and soft fruits of many types. Two of the country's largest jam companies, Tiptree (established by Wilkin & Sons in 1885) and Elsenham (1890) are located here, taking their names from their home towns in Essex.

TECHNIQUE:
Medlars need first to be chopped roughly. They are simmered with water and lemon juice until they become a pulp; the juice is extracted by draining it through a cloth without any pressure. The juice is measured and the appropriate amount of sugar added (normally reckoned to be about 675g per litre of juice). Once boiled to setting point, the jelly is potted, cooled and packed. Added pectin is not required.

REGION OF PRODUCTION:
EAST ANGLIA.

Sea Lavender Honey

DESCRIPTION:
THIS HONEY IS A PALE YELLOW-GREEN WHEN RUNNY, BUT GRANULATES RAPIDLY TO A HARD SET WITH A VERY SMOOTH TEXTURE. ITS FLAVOUR IS MILD BUT DISTINCT.

HISTORY:
Sea lavender is *Limonium vulgare*, a plant of the Statice family. This and several closely related species are natives, growing on mudflats around the coast of England and parts of southern Scotland. In places, especially Norfolk, it is a dominant species. According to F.N. Howes (1979), sea lavender was recognized in the 1930s or before as a bee-plant, producing light, good-quality honey.

The history of sea-lavender honey in East Anglia is essentially the effect on its habitat of man's attempts to protect the land. Much of the coast is made up of low-lying salt marshes, tidal creeks and mudflats. As long as records have been kept, there have been problems of erosion. A system of channels, dykes and sea walls has evolved to control the water levels which creates a larger area of suitable habitat for sea lavender than would naturally occur. Consequently, honey can be collected in economic quantities.

Bees have been kept for centuries in Britain, and sea-lavender honey has probably been collected, either alone or as part of a mixed flower honey, for as long as they have been present in East Anglia. The honey is not widely known, as the crop is small and almost all the production is consumed locally.

TECHNIQUE:
The hives are moved to the appropriate area at the start of the flowering season. Growing along tidal river channels between the high and low water marks, sea lavender flowers in

August and good autumn weather promotes a large honey crop. The plant is a useful source of nectar at a time when the flowering season of most other species is over. Bees actively seek the plant, flying up to 1 km to work it. A few beekeepers collect the honey separately, have it analysed to establish the principal source and bottle it apart.

REGION OF PRODUCTION:
EAST ANGLIA.

COMPARE WITH:
Heather Honey, Scotland (p. 395) and Chelsea Physic Garden Honey, South East England (p. 106).

***

Also produced in East Anglia
OYSTER (P. 88)
SMOKED MACKEREL (P. 16)
WHELK (P. 91)

East Midlands

Good King Henry

DESCRIPTION:

GOOD KING HENRY IS A PLANT WHICH GROWS ABOUT 75CM HIGH, AND HAS LONG-STALKED, ARROW-SHAPED LEAVES. THE FLAVOUR IS LIKE SPINACH, ALTHOUGH IT BECOMES BITTER AS THE SEASON PROGRESSES.

HISTORY:

The plant *Chenopodium bonus-henricus* is known by many names: Blite, Lincolnshire Spinach, Wild Spinach, Allgood, Goosefoot and Mercury among them. This suggests that it has been known in Britain for a long time. There are plenty of archaeological remains that show it to have been part of Anglo-Saxon diet (Hagen, 1995). The name Good King Henry is derived originally from the German, *Guter Henrick*, a connection discussed by the herbalist John Gerard in 1636. John Evelyn (1699) said of English Mercury, 'or (as our country house-wives call it) all-good', that the young shoots could be eaten like asparagus, or it could later (i.e. the leaves) be boiled in a pottage.

With improved garden varieties of beet or spinach available at every turn, these semi-wild plants received scant notice in later works of kitchen wisdom. It was food for the poor, the gatherers of the countryside – in historical times, Scottish crofters turned to it for nourishment after the Clearances (MacNeill, 1929). However, the French gardener Vilmorin-Andrieux (1885) noticed that it was extensively grown by Lincolnshire farmers, 'almost every garden having its bed … Some say they like it better than asparagus,' and this comment has been echoed in general, without the Lincolnshire label, by subsequent authors (Rohde, 1943; Simon, 1960), who give the same culinary advice as John Evelyn.

In modern Britain, the use of Good King Henry for food is highly localized and does indeed occur principally in Lincolnshire. It is grown on a small scale by a few market gardeners, and sold on local produce stalls in central and north Lincolnshire. Local food specialist, Eileen Elder, says that it is boiled in plain water, or enclosed in a net and suspended in the broth whilst cooking bacon.

TECHNIQUE:

For the cultivation of Good King Henry, deep rich soil is best. Well-manured trenches about 60cm deep and 40cm apart are required; the plants are grown at intervals of about 30cm. The plant is a perennial and can also be found growing wild.

REGION OF PRODUCTION:

EAST MIDLANDS, LINCOLNSHIRE.

Seakale

DESCRIPTION:

SEAKALE HAS IVORY-COLOURED STALKS, SOMETIMES WITH A PURPLE TINGE; IN APPEAR-
ANCE THEY LOOK A LITTLE LIKE CELERY. THEY ARE PICKED WHEN ABOUT 23CM LONG. THE
DIAMETER IS VARIABLE, RANGING FROM A FEW MILLIMETRES UP TO ABOUT 16MM. FLAVOUR:
NUTTY, REMINISCENT OF CELERY BUT GENTLER.

HISTORY:

Wild sea kale, *Crambe maritima*, is native to the sea coasts of western Europe; as a garden
plant, the English claim major responsibility for developing. It has been used as food in
Britain since at least the seventeenth century, when John Evelyn (1699) wrote, 'our sea-keele
… growing on our coast [is] very delicate'. The precise moment at which the vegetable
entered the mainstream of British cookery is uncertain, but around this time the inhabitants
of Kent, Sussex and Hampshire started to bleach the stems by banking them up with sand
before cutting and taking them to market (Grigson, 1977). The plant was taken into cultivation at the end of the eighteenth century, and 'the popularity that it achieved in the eighteenth
century is attributed to Dr Lettsom of Camberwell, London' (MacCarthy, 1989). It was
forced in beds of manure and straw to provide a fresh winter vegetable. Tall, bell-shaped ter-
racotta pots were used to cover the plants and blanch the stalks. This was an expensive method
of growing and led to a decline in the popularity of seakale towards the end of the century. Its
cultivation was described in great detail by Vilmorin-Andrieux (1885), noting that it was very
little used in France but much in England. Seakale can still be found growing wild in East
Anglia but few plants are left because the passion for it during Victorian times stripped the
coast almost bare when they were transported to gardens (Mabey, 1978).

Although seakale was widely cultivated at its height, it was always a luxury except in the
areas to which it was native. In the first half of the twentieth century, a little seakale continued to be grown, mostly in private gardens, and the wild plants were harvested from the
seashore.

TECHNIQUE:

The harvesting of wild seakale is now illegal on environmental grounds. About 30 years ago
commercial production was recommenced by the Paske family in Lincolnshire. Because of the
difficulty in obtaining plants, a strain was developed using seed collected from the Sussex
coast. Propagation is continued by the use of thongs or root cuttings which are planted out in
January. Deep, sandy, well-drained soil prepared by digging and manuring is best; the soils of
Lincolnshire are well suited to this plant. They are allowed to grow for a season and then die
back. Seakale is now grown in forcing sheds as a summer vegetable: the roots or crowns are
lifted and stored in refrigerated conditions for a few weeks, then planted in heated sheds to
produce the stems for cutting. Seakale must be blanched or it develops an acrid flavour,
although Simon (1960) considered the taste of unblanched stalks to be much better developed.

REGION OF PRODUCTION:

EAST MIDLANDS, LINCOLNSHIRE.

Derby Cheese

DESCRIPTION:

HARD, PRESSED, PASTEURIZED COW'S MILK CHEESE MADE IN SMALL WHEELS 30–34CM ACROSS AND 8–10CM DEEP, WEIGHING 14KG. COLOUR: WHITE; SAGE DERBY IS MARBLED WITH GREEN JUICE. FLAVOUR AND TEXTURE: CLEAN, MILD, SMOOTH.

HISTORY:

The history of Derby cheese is obscure. There are records as early as 1750 of its being carted to London for sale, but more precise documentation is lacking (Black, 1989). It belongs to the same family as Cheshire, and 'is one of the oldest British cheeses to become distinct from the ancient widespread type once common to all the Midlands' (Rance, 1982). The recipes were kept secret and many forgotten. Derby cheese was the first to be made in a creamery, in 1870. Some farmhouse cheese-making survived in South Derbyshire until 1930s. The local agricultural college at Sutton Bonnington was responsible for introducing standards.

Historically, the sage-flavoured cheeses were produced in spring to be eaten in the autumn. Sage juice was used for flavour, and the juices of some other leaf, such as spinach, for colour. White and coloured curd were made separately and used for alternate layers in the mould.

TECHNIQUE:

The milk is heated to a temperature of 21°C and 1.5 per cent starter added. The temperature is raised to about 28°C and the acidity allowed to develop to the correct level, at which point rennet is added and the surface of the milk gently stirred until it begins to coagulate. About 45 minutes after coagulation the curd is cut into 1cm cubes, and allowed to settle for a few minutes. The curd (which is rather fragile) is stirred carefully whilst the temperature is raised to 34°C over a period of about 50 minutes. The curd is allowed to settle until the acidity is correct, after which it is drained quickly, cut into blocks, and piled down the sides of the vat. The process of cutting and turning continues until the correct acidity is achieved. The curd is put though a coarse mill, mixed with the salt, and then packed into moulds lined with coarse cloths. The cheeses are pressed until the whey runs freely; pressing continues for 24 hours, the cheeses being removed and turned once. They are capped and bandaged or waxed. Ripening is at 12°C. The cheeses are turned daily. The technique for making Sage Derby is identical until moulding when colouring and flavouring are added to the curd.

REGION OF PRODUCTION:

EAST MIDLANDS.

Leicester Cheese

DESCRIPTION:

A PRESSED COW'S MILK CHEESE IN LARGE, SHALLOW WHEELS 40CM ACROSS AND 8CM DEEP; OR IN RECTANGULAR BLOCKS. COLOUR: DEEP ORANGE-RED. FLAVOUR AND TEXTURE: SWEETISH, SLIGHTLY CARAMEL; FLAKY.

HISTORY:

Leicestershire has contributed 2 great cheeses to the British repertoire. One, Stilton, is famous; the other, Leicester, is less well known yet probably has as long a history. Both owe their celebrity to the rich pasture lands around Melton Mowbray.

Leicester had become a distinct variety before the eighteenth century. The southern half of the county was known for its large, hard, red cheeses. Rance (1982) speculates the makers were influenced by Gloucestershire methods, citing similarities in technique. Much of the production was consumed in towns nearby. This remained true until 1939–45 for, Burdett (1935) says, Leicester was not well known in London.

Wartime circumstances affected production through the banning of annatto – used in large amounts to produce the deep red considered a part of the character (it is often called Red Leicester). Although the cheese continued to be made through the war, the pale, undyed version upset many consumers. Experts of today would have agreed with their distress. Rance states that the dye contributes to the visual assessment of quality as it is mottled in a badly-produced cheese. He also claims it enhances flavour. Most Leicester is now factory made.

TECHNIQUE:

Craft and creamery methods are similar. The milk is heated to 21°C and the starter (about 2 per cent) mixed through; annatto is added and the milk stirred thoroughly. The temperature is raised to 29°C and rennet added when the correct acidity is reached; the surface is stirred to prevent the cream separating. The curd is cut several times until the particles are the size of wheat grains. The curd is stirred and the heat raised to 33–34°C over 40 minutes; then it is allowed to settle until the correct acidity is reached. The whey is drained by pressing the curd under weighted wooden racks, after which it is cut into blocks and stacked at either side of the vat. The blocks are cut and repiled until the acidity is correct. The curd is finely ground in a Cheshire-type mill, and salt is added (about 1kg to 45kg curd). Moulding is into the characteristic shallow hoop, lined with a much lighter cheese-cloth than generally used in Britain. It is pressed for 2 days, the cheeses turned twice into clean cloths. Maturing takes 6–9 months. Traditionally, the cloth was removed for the last 2 weeks of ripening to allow the crust to blue.

REGION OF PRODUCTION:

EAST MIDLANDS.

Stilton Cheese

DESCRIPTION:

PASTEURIZED COW'S MILK CHEESE. WEIGHTS ARE 2.5–5.7KG; SMALL STILTONS, ABOUT 500G, ARE ALSO PRODUCED. THE SHAPE IS A TALL CYLINDER. A BLUE STILTON SHOULD HAVE AN UNCRACKED, TOUGH, HARD CRUST, SLIGHTLY IRREGULAR, PALE BROWN-GREY IN COLOUR, WITH POWDERY WHITE PATCHES. THE INTERIOR VARIES FROM CREAM TO PALE YELLOW, DEPENDING ON THE MAKER, SHADING DARKER TOWARDS THE RIND, WITH EXTENSIVE, WELL-SPREAD, GREEN-BLUE VEINING; TEXTURES RANGE FROM CRUMBLING TO SMOOTH, SOFT TO FIRM. WHITE STILTON IS VERY PALE. THE CHEESE SOFTENS AS IT BLUES, AND BLUE STILTON IS CREAMY AND MELLOW. THE BEST EXAMPLES HAVE AN INTENSE, WINY FLAVOUR. WHITE STILTON HAS A SHARP FLAVOUR.

HISTORY:

Unlike other British territorial cheeses, it was named for the place where it was sold, rather than the area where it was made. It originated around Melton Mowbray, on the borders of Leicester, Rutland and Nottingham. Quality cheese was known in the district at least as early as the reign of Queen Anne (d. 1714). The first Stilton was probably white and high-fat, but with a natural tendency to blue. The excellent flavour produced when this happened meant it became famous as a blue-vein cheese. It gained its reputation when it was sold at the Bell Inn in Stilton, Huntingdonshire, in the first quarter of the eighteenth century. This was a coaching house on the main route north from London. By the time Daniel Defoe passed through in 1722, he was able to write that Stilton was a town 'famous for cheese, which is called our English Parmesan, and is brought to the table with the mites or maggots around it, so thick, that they bring a spoon with them for you to eat the mites with, as you do the cheese'. Another enthusiast of Stilton, though with reservations, was the botanist Richard Bradley (1736). He claimed that its rennet was flavoured with plenty of mace, and that 'without the people of Stilton keep up the antient way of making it, agreeable to the old Receipt, they must of necessity lose the Reputation they have gained ... I shall not pretend to affirm why the Cheeses now in that town are not generally so good as they were formerly; but perhaps it is because the Cheese-sellers there ... now buy Cheeses from other parts, where nothing of the true Receipt is known.' By the end of that century, the cheese was widely made round Melton Mowbray, and in many villages of Rutland. It was supplied to nearby innkeepers, who sold it to their often well-heeled customers who were in the country to hunt (see Melton Mowbray pork pie, below, p. 151).

Creamery Stilton was first produced in the 1870s, but it remained quite different from the farmhouse cheese. The makers were very secretive and it was not until early in the 1900s, when they formed an association, that recipes came into the public domain. (Although one had in fact been published several times in the 1720s by Richard Bradley.) The making of Stilton extended by that time as far as Hartington in Dovedale (Derbyshire) but never any further. The makers, aware of the damage done to other British cheeses by copies made outside the area of origin, sought legal protection for their product. Stilton was defined by them in 1910, and given a protected name under a High Court judgement of 1969 which stated: 'Stilton is a blue or white cheese made from full cream milk, with no applied pressure, forming its own crust or coat and made in cylindrical form, the milk coming from English dairy herds in the district of Melton Mowbray and the surrounding areas falling within the counties of Leicestershire (now including Rutland), Derbyshire and Nottinghamshire.' This has prevented the development of block cheeses and imitations. Both blue and white Stilton have been awarded Protected Designations of Origin.

TECHNIQUE:

All Stilton is manufactured in creameries using pasteurized milk. The methods vary in detail. After pasteurization, the milk is cooled to a temperature of about 30°C and starter is added, followed by rennet. After 60–90 minutes, the curd is cut and allowed to settle. The whey is drawn off over 1–4 hours until the curd has shrunk by half. When the correct acidity is achieved, the curd is scooped on to a long, perforated metal tray or 'Stilton sink'. Providing the acidity develops correctly, the curd is cut into blocks 4.5cm square after the first hour and then turned. Cutting and turning continue until the correct acidity is reached. The curd is milled coarsely to give pieces the size of walnuts. The curd is divided into batches sufficient for each cheese and salt mixed through (30g to 1.5kg curd). It is then scooped into a Stilton hoop (a perforated metal cylinder 30cm deep and 18cm diameter). These are drained 4–10 days at

15°C, turned daily. They are injected with mould spores. On removal of the hoop, the cheeses are scraped, the scrapings used to seal any cracks or holes. The cheeses are stored in a cool, damp room until a coat is formed. They are ripened at 10°C in a relative humidity of 94–98 per cent. After 4 weeks the cheese is pierced with skewers to admit air and speed the growth of mould. Each cheese is turned daily and brushed to prevent mite infestation.

White Stilton is based on a drier, less acid curd, and is eaten at about the age of 20 days.

REGION OF PRODUCTION:
EAST MIDLANDS.

Faggot

DESCRIPTION:
ROUGHLY SPHERICAL RISSOLES OF COOKED PORK AND OFFAL WRAPPED IN CAUL FAT OR COATED IN CRUMBS, 6–8CM DIAMETER, WEIGHING 100–150G. COLOUR: GREYISH-BROWN, WITH A PALE LACE PATTERN FROM A WRAPPING OF CAUL FAT; ALTERNATIVELY, THEY MAY BE SPRINKLED WITH BREAD CRUMBS (ESPECIALLY THE NORTHERN VERSIONS). FLAVOUR: MEATY, TENDING TOWARDS LIVER, WITH ONIONS, SPICES AND HERBS, SAGE THE MOST COMMON.

HISTORY:
Faggots (the word means a bundle) are really a primitive type of sausage, collections of finely chopped pork offal held together by squares of caul fat as opposed to skins. Originally, they provided a way for using the less attractive parts of a pig such as the pluck. An early use of the word is found in Mayhew (1851) and, a few years later, the faggot is dismissed as a product of 'cheap pork butchery' (*OED*), but such dishes must have been known long before that and have been quite widespread. Sometimes, they also seem to be called haslet, see below. Wright (1896–1905) cites mentions from counties in the East and West Midlands and the South from Sussex to Somerset. Versions are also known in Wales as Welsh faggots, where the recipe diverges from that of the Midlands by using oats instead of bread crumbs, and sometimes the addition of apple pieces, alongside the chopped or minced offal and pork. Bog myrtle (*Myrica Gale*) was a seasoning in Wales, although now little used (Mabey, 1978).

In Yorkshire and Lancashire a similar dish is known as savoury duck. This is sometimes presented as a loaf from which chunks are cut, rather than as rissoles. It tends to have a higher cereal content and is blander in flavour. It sounds very like a method of getting rid of all the scraps in a pork-butcher's. Instructions for making savoury ducks (Finney, 1915) read: 'To make Savoury Ducks (sometimes called Spice Balls), take all the odds and ends, such as Puddings, Sausages, Brawn, Ends of Bacon, or whatever may be left over, boil for a short time, chop fine and season … Pack into roasting tins, and place in a good sharp oven until the fat commences to boil out of them. If not allowed to boil as stated, they invariably turn sour in a short time.'

In all areas where such items are popular, they can be seen displayed on trays in the windows of butchers' shops, especially those who specialize in pork products. In some places, butchers sell a mixture of raw faggot meat for home cooks to use in their own versions. Faggots can be eaten cold but are more usually heated. They are often served with peas: opinions vary as to whether this should be a dish of green peas or a purée of dried ones. As faggots would originally have been a winter dish made at pig-killing time, dried peas are probably what was expected. Savoury duck is sometimes sliced and fried.

TECHNIQUE:
A mixture of pork offal – liver, lungs, spleen – and fat, bread crumbs, onions and flavourings is chopped or minced finely and then parcelled in squares of caul (the fatty membrane which wraps and suspends the various organs in the abdomen). Odds and ends of lean pork and meat products such as ham are added by some butchers. In some places, the mixture is simply pressed into a tray and baked. The parcels are packed into a tin and baked at 180°C for 40–60 minutes. They are reheated at home.

REGION OF PRODUCTION:
MIDLANDS; SOUTH ENGLAND; WALES.

Haslet

DESCRIPTION:
COOKED, BRINED PORK AND OFFAL IN LONG OBLONG LOAVES 10–15CM WIDE, 6–8CM DEEP; IT IS CUT THINLY TO GIVE SLICES 3–4 MM THICK, WEIGHING ABOUT 30G. COLOUR: BEIGE-PINK WITH SPECKS OF WHITE AND DEEPER PINK; SOMETIMES SPECKLED WITH HERBS; WITH A DARK BROWN EDGE ON THE SIDE EXPOSED TO HEAT IN COOKING. FLAVOUR: BRINED PORK, SEASONINGS (USUALLY BLACK PEPPER AND SOMETIMES SAGE).

HISTORY:
Haslet is often treated as a dialect word, although Wright (1896–1905) places it in Lincolnshire and Cheshire and most counties directly south, as far as the Isle of Wight, which makes it quite a non-regional dialect. The food, however, does have a regional ring – Lincolnshire is the county linked most closely. The word itself (found as harslet, hazelet or acelet) is derived from an Old French root that relates both to spits and the meat roasted on them. By the time Cotgrave wrote his French–English dictionary in 1611, the French had particularized some of the original meaning onto offal and innards that might be spitted and roasted (*OED*). So, too, had the English, connecting it especially (but not invariably) to the pig, rather as they had the once more general words bacon and brawn. This was the sense in which Pepys and Hannah Glasse used haslet, as it was the farmers' wives of Northamptonshire who sent pies filled with haslet as presents to neighbours at pig-killing time. Eliza Acton (1845) describes 'harslet' pudding, containing 'the heart, liver, kidneys &c of the pig', which she says was held in much esteem in certain counties. By transference, it came to describe the very dish itself, made from the pluck by chopping and roasting or boiling the pieces. In Lincolnshire, haslet was closely related to faggots or sausages, and Maria Rundell (1807) seems also to describe a faggot, but she calls it haslet, when she instructs her readers to enclose a mixture of offal, scraps of lean pork and some onion in caul, sew it up and roast it.

Haslet nowadays means a kind of meat loaf, made of finely chopped odds and ends of lean and cured pork, highly seasoned, and baked until brown on top. It is usually sliced and eaten cold with salad for dinner or high tea. It is widely produced by craft butchers, particularly in

Lincolnshire but also throughout southern England.

TECHNIQUE:

The meat is minced or finely ground and mixed with seasonings, often with a proportion of cereal; the mixture is packed into dishes then baked at about 180°C for 60 minutes.

REGION OF PRODUCTION:

EAST MIDLANDS, LINCOLNSHIRE; SOUTH ENGLAND.

Lincoln Red Cattle

DESCRIPTION:

A YOUNG HEIFER YIELDS 220–250KG; A 2-YEAR-OLD ANIMAL GIVES 300–350KG; GOOD CONFORMATION WITH LONG HINDQUARTERS. FLAVOUR EXCELLENT, ESPECIALLY OLDER ANIMALS; WHEN FATTENED, THE FLESH IS WELL MARBLED.

HISTORY:

Lincoln Red cattle (so-called because of their dark, ginger-maroon pelts) were developed in the nineteenth century out of the classic Victorian beef breed, the Shorthorn. This was interbred with the local red cattle to give a slow-growing, hardy animal which could live on the poor grasslands of the Wolds, an area of rolling country which stretches from the Humber southwards to East Anglia. In fact, in the seventeenth century, Gervase Markham had praised Lincolnshire 'pied' cattle – not red – but had none the less thought the county top-notch for fine bloodstock. Early this century, Lincoln Reds were reckoned the largest of the British beef breeds. Modern imperatives demand lean, fast-maturing beef animals: they have done no favours to the slower Lincoln, with a tendency to put on fat when generously fed. Extensively farmed cattle are leaner. Polled Lincoln Reds are a variant, bred from bloodlines without horns.

TECHNIQUE:

Lincoln Reds were developed to be docile and good mothers. They can thrive on sparse vegetation; they grazed the marginal grassland on the dry, chalky soils of the Wolds. A few herds still exist in this way. In the past, they were kept for several years for breeding before being slaughtered for beef, a custom which produced very well-flavoured meat. However, many are now raised on mixed farms which grow barley for winter fodder. The herds calve in spring or autumn; spring is currently more favoured. The calves are suckled until weaning, then finished for market. They are killed rather young, at 12–18 months. For commercial herds, continental European breeds are now much favoured for crossing, particularly the Limousin and the Belgian Blue. However, pure-bred Lincoln beef still has its supporters, and some butchers in their home region specialize in it.

REGION OF PRODUCTION:

EAST ENGLAND, LINCOLNSHIRE.

Lincolnshire Sausages

DESCRIPTION:

AN UNCOOKED, FRESH PORK SAUSAGE 12CM LONG, 2–2.5CM DIAMETER. WEIGHT: USUALLY 8 TO THE POUND (450G). COLOUR: PALE PINK, MOTTLED WITH DEEPER RED, AND GREEN

W ho would think that an Australian would consider the Lincoln Red as one of the best types of beef cattle in the world? Worryingly, it is now on the endangered list distributed by the Rare Breed Society Trust, the guardians of pure-breed British cattle, sheep, pork and poultry.

Rich in flavour with well-formed textural meat, these cattle are hard to come by but deliver at the highest order. Beef with heritage has always been my personal choice, as I wholly believe in true provenance. Traceability is just a made-up word to cover intensive farming and shortcuts in farming practices.

The Lincoln is quality beef that should be served with reverence, the loin left on the bone to mature for at least twenty-four days and as long as sixty days. (At sixty days the flavour changes from a rich butter to a mature cheese with veins of blue.) It should be butchered into thick steak, the fore-rib left on the bone, seasoned well and brushed with the smallest amount of oil. Place the steak over glowing coals, cook it rare and set it to one side to rest for five minutes before serving it with fresh horseradish spiced with a squeeze of lemon and bound with the smallest amount of fresh cream.

John Torode

Chef, Smiths of Smithfield, London

HISTORY:

Lincolnshire has relied on the pig more than most for meat and fat. A famous nineteenth-century breed (now sadly extinct), the Lincolnshire Curly Coat, developed here. Country people kept pigs and preserved their meat for the family. Sausages in the British tradition (fresh lean and fat pork, bread or rusk, and seasonings) were made by everyone at pig-killing time. The breed of pig used has been affected, as have all other pork products, by the development of modern hybrids and the demand for lean meat.

It is not clear how long Lincolnshire sausages have been thought noteworthy; only that the tradition of pork butchery has been in existence for centuries. Neil Curtis, whose family have been pork butchers in the city of Lincoln since 1828, remarks that the sausages are made with meat more coarsely chopped than that used elsewhere. Dalton (*c.* 1930) noted in his compilation of butchers' recipes that use of coarsely chopped meat is a distinctly northern preference. The addition of sage is essential to the modern Lincoln sausage seasoning. This is paralleled by the Lincolnshire pork pie seasoning, recorded as demanding sage (Finney, 1915).

A strong base of small butchers, plus a handful of larger firms, still produce good Lincolnshire sausages throughout the county and surrounding areas. Elsewhere, the designation 'Lincolnshire' is sometimes used for a premium quality, herb-seasoned sausage.

TECHNIQUE:

The pork is selected in the correct proportions of fat and lean; it is coarsely chopped or ground, combined with bread crumbs or rusk, plus a little iced water, and seasoned – always with sage and salt, other spices to taste. Some makers add preservative. The meat is filled into casings; natural casings made from the small intestines of the hog (bacon pig) are the usual choice, although sheep's small intestines may be used for chipolatas.

REGION OF PRODUCTION:

EAST MIDLANDS, LINCOLNSHIRE.

Lincolnshire Stuffed Chine

DESCRIPTION:

STUFFED CHINE IS MADE FROM THE UNSPLIT BACKBONE OF A BACON PIG; THE SMALLEST PIECE WHICH IS PRACTICABLE WEIGHS ABOUT 2.5KG. WHOLE CHINES AVERAGE 7–8KG, AND MAY WEIGH UP TO 15KG. THE JOINT IS SQUARISH-OBLONG IN SHAPE. COLOUR: THE MEAT IS A DEEP PINK-RED WITH WHITE FAT ON THE SKIN SIDE; THE STUFFING IS DARK GREEN, AND WHEN CORRECTLY CARVED, THE SLICES ARE STRIPED RED AND GREEN IN NARROW BARS. FLAVOUR: THE MEAT RESEMBLES BACON; THE STUFFING HAS A MILD PARSLEY FLAVOUR, WITH A HAY-LIKE AROMA.

HISTORY:

Chine is an old English word for backbone, derived from Norman French. It was in general culinary use to indicate the backbone, with some attached flesh, of any animal, both fish and meat, until the eighteenth century. It continued to be used in connection with bacon pigs – from which the sides are normally removed without splitting the backbone. This progressive narrowing of a word's meaning from all species to the pig alone is a tendency already noticed with bacon, brawn and haslet.

It is not apparent when the Lincolnshire version of stuffed chine developed, but it is a county in which pig rearing has always been important, and oral tradition states the dish has a long history. When the French poet Verlaine was schoolmastering in the south Lincolnshire town of Boston, he fell in love with chine – so much so that he tried, and failed, to find it elsewhere in Britain (Grigson, 1984). The chine is preserved by salting until required, and then made up by slashing the meat and stuffing it with chopped herbs. Webb (c. 1930) noted that the stuffings varied, some households using only chopped parsley, and others relying on a mixture of herbs including lettuce leaves, young nettles, thyme, marjoram, sage and black currant leaves.

Customarily, the chine was reserved for special occasions, including christenings and May hiring fairs (at which farm workers returned to their homes). It is still more popular at certain times of the year, in May and at Christmas, and at the local agricultural shows.

TECHNIQUE:

The pig forequarter is butchered to give the spine with some muscle still attached on either side. The meat is wet-cured in a mixture of salt, saltpetre, sugar, black treacle, beer and spices for 2 weeks, followed by 1 week's dry cure in salt. The meat is slashed at right angles to the spine and stuffed with chopped parsley or a mixture of herbs. At this stage the joint is ready to be cooked. It is immersed in simmering water for up to 7 hours (depending on size); the meat should be enclosed in a huff paste, a cloth, or, more commonly today, a roasting bag. Once removed from the pot, the meat is drained, cooled and carved in thin slices, parallel to the bone.

REGION OF PRODUCTION:

EAST MIDLANDS, CENTRAL LINCOLNSHIRE.

Melton Mowbray Pork Pie

DESCRIPTION:

A COOKED, RAISED PIE FILLED WITH PORK. COLOUR: DEEP GOLD BROWN PASTRY CRUST; A FILLING OF COARSELY CHOPPED UNCURED PORK, MARBLED GREYISH-PINK AND WHITE, WITH A THIN LAYER OF PALE OPAQUE JELLY BETWEEN THE MEAT AND PASTRY. FLAVOUR: PORK FLAVOUR, HIGHLY SEASONED WITH PEPPER; CRUNCHY PASTRY.

HISTORY:

The raised or standing pie, of which this is an example, developed from the medieval and Elizabethan habit of making pastry cases, or coffins, from a very robust paste. These could be filled and baked without any support from a mould. Originally they were made simply from water and flour and were only intended to contain and protect the meat during baking: they were thrown away, not eaten. It is from this tradition, not from simple dish pies covered with pastry, that modern pork pies descend.

There are 2 reasons why those of Melton Mowbray in Leicestershire probably achieved fame, says Stephen Hallam, who makes them. Firstly, from at least the 1700s, the area supported a substantial cheese-making industry, producing surplus whey to feed large herds of pigs. Secondly, the town was headquarters of aristocratic hunts. Pork pies were the ideal pic - nic for hungry sportsmen who came to follow the fox hounds.

How long the pies have been recognized is not clear, perhaps no longer than 150 years (Mabey, 1978). The firm of Dickinson and Morris was founded in the mid-nineteenth century and it is now only Dickinson and Morris's Ye Olde Pork Pie Shoppe that claims to make pies to the original specification. At the end of the 1800s, the pies were available by post from Tebutt's, another local manufacturer, who had 'an unsullied reputation extending over thirty years' (Law, *c.* 1895).

Consumer perception of Melton Mowbray pork pies is nowadays confused. People from outside the area perceive them as a premium pie of the standard English type. They certainly fit the bill, having particular qualities that aficionados desire: the 'baggy' shape, rich crunchy pastry, and coarsely chopped fresh pork (not brined as are generic pork pies – see below), with a good seasoning of black pepper.

TECHNIQUE:

A hot-water crust is used. Lard, water and salt are boiled and mixed into flour. Whilst still hot, the crust is moulded by hand around a 'dolly', or cylindrical wooden block later removed to leave space for the filling. This is hand-chopped, lean, uncured pork with salt and a little fat. A circle of pastry is placed over the top of the filled pie, sealed and egg-washed. Pies are baked at 210°C for 30 minutes, then at 160°C for 1–2 hours. Once baked, a stock from pigs' feet and bones is poured in through a hole in the top. This must be at the right temperature: too hot and the crust absorbs the stock and softens. The whole is cooled; the stock jellies.

REGION OF PRODUCTION:

EAST MIDLANDS, MELTON MOWBRAY (LEICESTERSHIRE).

'Let the stoics say what they please, we do not eat for the good of living, but because the meat is savory and the appetite is keen.'

RALPH WALDO EMERSON

Pork Pie

DESCRIPTION:

COOKED RAISED PIES OF BRINED PORK; INDIVIDUAL ONES WEIGHING ABOUT 150G ARE APPROXIMATELY 7CM DIAMETER, 4–5CM DEEP; LARGER PIES ARE MADE IN WEIGHTS OF 250–1000G. FORM: CIRCULAR, WITH CRIMPED EDGES, OFTEN DECORATED WITH PASTRY LEAVES. THE PIES ARE ALWAYS DEEP IN PROPORTION TO THEIR HEIGHT, AND MAY BE STRAIGHT-SIDED (IF MADE IN A MOULD) OR SLIGHTLY IRREGULAR AND BAGGY IF HAND-RAISED. COLOUR: EXTERIOR IS A DEEP GOLD-BROWN PASTRY WITH A SHINY TOP; WHEN CUT, THE PASTRY IS WHITE INSIDE, WITH A LAYER OF CLEAR JELLY BETWEEN IT AND A FILLING OF PORK, WHICH IS USUALLY BRINED AND A DEEP ROSE-PINK. FLAVOUR: RICH SALTED PORK FLAVOUR, OFTEN HIGHLY SEASONED WITH PEPPER, PLUS VERY CRISP PASTRY.

The stronghold of the pork pie is the Midlands, although they are popular, widely marketed and made, to a lesser extent, in other parts. There is a noticeable trend away from pork as one progresses through the far north of England into Scotland, where beef and lamb are more common in meat products, including pies.

Farmers and yeomen, or even cottagers, might make them at pig-killing time, after putting the main joints down to bacon and ham. Great lords might eat them at any time: Henry de Lacy, Earl of Lincoln, had his kitchen buy a shilling's worth of pork 'pro pastillis' – for pies – in 1299 (Woolgar, 1992). Today, however, they are more likely part of the special range of products associated with pork butchers. Until recently, most large towns had at least one of these. From this base of artisanal knowledge several large companies have developed. In the view of many, pork pies were a useful way of using up scraps left over after the pig had been butchered for fresh meat, hams or bacon. The bones contributed the savoury jelly and the flesh was an economical by-product.

It is curious that both pork pies and pork butchers have little detectable history before the nineteenth century. The social historian Robert Roberts who wrote an account of his early life in Salford at the beginning of the last century (Roberts, 1971), makes the observation that one consequence of the introduction of compulsory military service in a united Germany after 1871 was emigration, particularly of Bavarians. Many of them settled in Britain, often in the wake of richer settlers involved in the cotton and wool trades of Manchester and Bradford. Among this second wave were many pork butchers – themselves well versed in their trade and anxious to extend the meagre British range compared to the variety and ingenuity of German products. 'By the outbreak of the First World War it is doubtful if there was a single Northern town, large or small, that did not have its German pork butchers. Each one … introduced a range of new tastes to the British working class.'

They did not need to invent the pork pie, for pies in general were well-known. This included large raised 'standing pies' composed of meat fillings in a hot-water crust. Pork pies share a common heritage with other English raised pies such as the Melton Mowbray (filled with unbrined pork, see above) and game pies, in that the pastry probably originated as a simple flour and water mixture intended to contain and protect the meat. Dorothy Hartley (1954) gives a fourteenth-century recipe for a 'pig pye' (probably indicating a sucking pig at this date). She discusses variants on seasonings, fillings and decorations used in the Midland counties of England, most of which are now rarely encountered outside domestic kitchens. Many have disappeared as the country habit of killing pigs on farms has been eroded by advances in food preservation, changes in shopping habits, and the tightening of regulations relating to slaughter and meat handling.

Few literary paeans to the pork pie can be as eloquent as Rebecca West's in her novel *The Fountain Overflows* (1957): 'Aunt Lily … paused to tell us that whereas there were a great many good butchers, ordinary butchers, a good pork butcher was as rare as an archbishop.' This is preface to an account of buying the ingredients (including the best black peppercorns and the whitest lard), magically raising the crust (to use a mould was 'a mug's game'), and producing the finished article. 'Queenie would never let the children eat anything vulgar,' is the epilogue, 'Harry liked it, when he went out in his boat.'

Aunt Lily's pork pie contained hard-boiled egg – by no means an invariable component, but long, loaf-shaped pork pies with hard-boiled eggs running through the middle are also made. This arrangement is also seen in the veal-and-ham pie.

TECHNIQUE:

Pork pies differ over minor points to do with shape and seasoning between makers and regions. For the pastry, they require a hot-water crust, made by heating water and lard to boiling point, stirring it into the flour and kneading; this produces a dough that is malleable whilst hot but which sets firm when cold. This is important when the pies are raised by hand: the warm pastry is shaped over a wooden dolly or cylindrical mould which is removed to leave a deep case which holds the shape without support. However, many butchers and large pie companies use tin moulds in which the pies remain during baking. For very special occasions, elaborately moulded and fluted tins may be used. The filling is always composed of a mixture of lean and fat pork, usually (but not invariably) brined, turning the meat a characteristic pink. The texture of the filling is generally fairly solid, the pork being minced coarsely. Pepper is the favoured seasoning; other spices, such as ginger and nutmeg, may also be added. The pork butcher Thomas Finney (1915) listed seasonings for Nottingham, Liverpool, Yorkshire, Manchester and Lincolnshire: distinguished by the inclusion of mace, cinnamon, nutmeg, coriander, and ginger respectively. A portion of meat is placed in the case, covered with a pastry lid, and the edges crimped together; a small hole is cut in the centre of the lid; in the past, this was often covered with a pastry rose, and the top of the pies decorated with pastry leaves and flowers. Pies are baked at 230°C for 45 minutes or longer, depending on size. After baking, the hot pies are filled with a strong gelatinous stock which sets to become a clear jelly on cooling.

The best pies are generally made by pork butchers, and hand-raising shows care and attention to detail, although perfectly good pies are made in tins. In Lincolnshire, the pie was a customary treat for breakfast at Christmas. They are found in all regions, even if their epicentre is the Midlands, and are consumed by the million as a snack or as part of a summer salad meal.

REGION OF PRODUCTION:

MIDLANDS.

Spiced Beef

DESCRIPTION:

COOKED, SPICED AND CURED BEEF, SOLD SLICED OR IN JOINTS OF 2.5–3KG. COLOUR: THE OUTSIDE IS DEEP BROWN, THE INSIDE BROWNISH PINK. FLAVOUR: A GOOD BEEF TASTE, SALTY, WITH PEPPER AND SPICES.

HISTORY:

For many centuries, beef was preserved by salting. Spiced beef is a development of this. In most surviving recipes it is dry-salted, the meat being kept in pickle for 10–21 days and then smoked or cooked. The beef kept well after cooking; up to 3 weeks is generally quoted. This was a virtue, especially when numbers at table were unpredictable. Kitchiner (1817) remarked that the dish deserved 'the particular attention of those families who frequently have Accidental Customers dropping in at Luncheon or Supper'. David (1970) remarks that it was a regular Christmas dish in many English country houses and farms, and that it has been known for at least 300 years under various names. There is a persistent association between this dish and hunting; it is often called hunting or huntsman's beef and would have sat well on the sideboard at a hunt breakfast. Melton Hunt beef, made in huge pieces up to 15kg at a time, was one of the best-known recipes. It is now more likely to be centrepiece of a buffet and is mostly made at Christmas.

TECHNIQUE:

Although numerous recipes for spiced beef, huntsman's beef and variations with regional names attached can be found, the principles and ingredients are all similar. The cuts are round or topside; brisket can also be used. The piece should weigh about 3kg; it can be larger, in which case curing time will be longer, but it should not be smaller. The beef is rubbed with the curing mixture – the producer located for this study includes black treacle, mace, allspice and garlic in the mix; other recipes require salt, saltpetre, and brown sugar and crushed spices – black peppercorns, allspice, juniper berries and bay leaves are often used. Nutmeg and cloves are sometimes used instead of the allspice and juniper; shallots and garlic were used in Melton Hunt beef. The meat marinates in this, being turned and rubbed every day for up to 2 weeks, depending on the size of the joint. Once removed from the pickle, the meat is cooked on a very low heat for about 5 hours in a close-fitting pot half-filled with water, sealed with grease-proof paper or a flour and water crust. The joint is removed from the cooking liquor, wrapped in greaseproof paper and pressed under a small weight until absolutely cold.

REGION OF PRODUCTION:

MIDLANDS; SOUTH-WEST ENGLAND.

Ashbourne Gingerbread

DESCRIPTION:

EACH PIECE HAS A DOMED PROFILE; THE BASE IS AN ELONGATED HEXAGON. ON THE TOP, THE MARK RESULTING FROM SLICING THE DOUGH, WHICH HAS THEN RISEN A LITTLE, GIVES A SIMPLE BUT DECORATIVE PATTERN OF LINES. THEY MEASURE APPROXIMATELY 65MM BY 55MM BY 15MM HIGH. WEIGHT: 25G. COLOUR: PALE GOLD TO DEEP CREAM ON OUTSIDE, CREAMY YELLOW OPEN CRUMB INSIDE, WITH SMALL LENGTHWAYS CRACKS. FLAVOUR AND TEXTURE: SWEET, MILD GINGER FLAVOUR, WITH CANDIED PEEL GIVING A BITTER ORANGE NOTE; CRISP, BISCUIT TEXTURE.

HISTORY:

So many of the cakes and pies that have survived in British towns and villages are in some sense or other fairings, made for a high day or holiday. Presumably, 'Ashbourne' was a fairing too, fixed for perpetuity by the town being a centre for tourism in the Peak district (tourism seems to act as stimulus and preservative for local foods) as well as by the existence of a long-lasting commercial baker – in this case the firm of Spencer. Spencer's claims that this gingerbread dates from at least the 1820s. The estimate seems conservative. Since then, several other companies have been started by members of the Spencer family or people who have worked for them.

Ashbourne gingerbread always seems to have been pale in colour but, unlike that once known in Grantham (Lincolnshire), never to have contained eggs. The recipes which are available show it to be similar to shortbread. The texture and the addition of candied peel (also found in some other British gingerbreads) indicate a long history, perhaps with an origin in the buttery, unleavened shortcakes of the seventeenth century rather than the stiff, dark, spiced confections of flour and treacle then known as gingerbread.

TECHNIQUE:
The exact method is a trade secret. The ingredients are given as flour, sugar, margarine, eggs, butter, ground ginger, citrus peel, raising agents, salt. Published recipes call for flour, butter and caster sugar in the approximate proportions 4:3:2. The butter and sugar are creamed together and mixed to a dough with flour, powdered ginger and chopped candied lemon peel. It is fashioned into a roll about 20mm thick which is cut into 40mm lengths. It is baked at 180°C for 20 minutes. The gingerbread should remain very pale. ,

REGION OF PRODUCTION:
NORTH MIDLANDS, ASHBOURNE (DERBYSHIRE).

Grantham Gingerbread

DESCRIPTION:
HOLLOW, SLIGHTLY DOME-SHAPED BISCUITS, ABOUT 50MM DIAMETER. COLOUR: PALE GOLD. FLAVOUR AND TEXTURE: SWEET AND GINGERY, WITH AN OPEN HONEYCOMB CENTRE WHICH IS CRISP BUT DISSOLVES EASILY IN THE MOUTH.

HISTORY:

This belongs to a family of hard, pale gingerbread biscuits made in the East Midlands. An early reference to a Grantham biscuit is in the diary of the seventeenth-century antiquary Ralph Thoresby who noted a peculiar sort of thin cake known as Grantham whetstones (Pointer, 1980). No-one knows exactly what these were; an eighteenth-century recipe for whetstone cakes from neighbouring Leicestershire shows a flour, sugar and egg biscuit spiced with caraway and rose water. The relationship between these and Grantham gingerbreads is not clear. The 'invention' of the gingerbread is said to have been an accident, possibly in the early 1800s but, as usual, there is no contemporary documentation. Lightness and hollowness have long been accepted features of the gingerbread. These attributes may have come from early use of chemical raising agents. Several formulae include bicarbonate of ammonia, used in the first half of the nineteenth century before the development of modern baking powders. George Mercer, a confectioner in the town in the early nineteenth century, is said to have evolved the recipe. It passed through several families and became famous as Caitlin's Grantham Gingerbreads. Although Caitlin's recipe is not made commercially at present, the gingerbread is still being produced in Southwell, Nottinghamshire. Florence White (1932) notes a record of Grantham gingerbread being sold as fairings. White gingerbreads, known also as Lincolnshire white gingerbreads, and Norfolk fair buttons were similar confections.

TECHNIQUE:
Published recipes vary slightly; they call for equal quantities of flour and sugar; the proportion of butter is variable, but falls between one-third to two-thirds the weight of flour. They were mixed by either creaming or by rubbing in. Eggs are sometimes, but not always, added to

make a soft dough; milk was an alternative. Volatile salts (ammonium bicarbonate) are the raising agent in most recipes. Commercial recipes state the dough should rest overnight before it is made into a rope then cut into slices to form the biscuits.

REGION OF PRODUCTION:
EAST MIDLANDS, GRANTHAM (LINCOLNSHIRE).

Bakewell Pudding

DESCRIPTION:
DIMENSIONS: A LARGE EXAMPLE IS AN OVAL 140MM BY 170MM, 50MM DEEP. WEIGHT: ABOUT 550G. FORM: A PUFF PASTRY CASE WITH A SMOOTH SEMI-TRANSPARENT FILLING WITH A THIN LAYER OF JAM BETWEEN THE PASTRY AND THE FILLING; THE PASTRY EXTENDS WELL ABOVE THE FILLING. COLOUR: THE PASTRY IS GOLDEN BROWN; THE FILLING IS BROWNED ON THE SURFACE BUT A DEEP YELLOW WHEN CUT. FLAVOUR: RICH, WITH EGGS AND ALMONDS.

HISTORY:
Bakewell pudding as it is now understood consists of a pastry case baked with a layer of jam (strawberry or raspberry) covered by a filling of eggs, sugar, butter and ground almonds. In Bakewell there is a story that the pudding originated as a result of a mistake by a cook at a local inn. This is almost certainly a legend. The earliest recipe, given by Eliza Acton (1845), is essentially an inch-thick, rich custard of egg yolks, butter, sugar and flavouring – ratafia (almond liqueur) is suggested – poured over a layer of mixed jams and candied citron or orange peel. There is no pastry lining. Miss Acton noted, 'This pudding is famous not only in Derbyshire, but in several of our northern counties, where it is usually served on all holiday-occasions.' In this form, it bears some resemblance to various cheesecake recipes of the preceding century, or, in its omission of milk curds, the 'transparent' puddings popular in the same era (Grigson, 1984). Acton drew parallels between her recipe and one 'known in the south' as Alderman's pudding. Her preference was for the latter; Bakewell pudding was not, in her opinion, 'very refined'. Mrs Beeton (1861) gave a recipe much closer to the one we know. It included ground almonds in the custard, omitted the candied peel, reduced the quantity of jam and added a lining of puff pastry (or a layer of breadcrumbs instead of paste for a plainer pudding). Since then, there has been a tendency to less jam and more almonds.

PRODUCTION:
There are 3 producers in Bakewell but it is now manufactured throughout the country. The Bakewell recipes are trade secrets.

REGION OF PRODUCTION:
NORTH MIDLANDS, BAKEWELL (DERBYSHIRE).

Lincolnshire Plum Bread

DESCRIPTION:

A BATCH LOAF OF LOW, ROUNDED SHAPE, 120MM LONG, 80MM WIDE, 35MM DEEP, WEIGHING ABOUT 300G. COLOUR: DEPENDS PARTLY ON THE INGREDIENTS, ESPECIALLY THE TYPE OF SUGAR USED; GENERALLY A DEEP GOLD OUTSIDE WITH THE DRIED FRUIT SHOWING PROMINENTLY; THE CRUMB BEIGE, SPECKLED WITH FRUIT; SOME EXAMPLES ARE A DEEPER BROWN. FLAVOUR AND TEXTURE: SWEET, LIGHTLY SPICED; THE VERSIONS WHICH USE LARD AS SHORTENING HAVE CLOSER TEXTURE AND CAN BE GREASY.

HISTORY:

Plum in this context refers to the dried fruit in the bread. This usage was once common (e.g. plum pudding) suggesting the form has a long history. No early references have yet been found in the area; the earliest date which has been established is that of a recipe used by one of the bakers who make the bread, Derek Myers and Sons, which is some 100 years old. Although this is especially associated with Lincolnshire, it probably shares a common history with other spiced, sweetened and fruited breads. Plum bread is rich and heavy and distinguished by the use of lard as a shortening, reflecting the region's strong emphasis on pork products. It is often eaten with cheese. Although available all the year round, it is more popular at Christmas.

TECHNIQUE:

Ingredients include plain flour, lard, sultanas, currants, mixed peel, spices, sugar, eggs, yeast, salt and water. Recipes vary in detail, and the lard may be replaced with other fats. There is a short bulk fermentation, but final proof after shaping is up to 3 hours. It is baked for about 75 minutes at 160°C.

REGION OF PRODUCTION:

EAST MIDLANDS, LINCOLNSHIRE.

Melton Hunt Cake

DESCRIPTION:

A CAKE, 140MM DIAMETER, 40MM DEEP. WEIGHT: 1KG. COLOUR: DARK BROWN, FLECKED WITH DARK FRUIT, THE TOP DECORATED WITH ALMONDS AND GLACÉ CHERRIES IN CONCENTRIC CIRCLES; THE CUT SURFACES SHOW PLENTIFUL CURRANTS, RAISINS, FLAKED ALMONDS AND A FEW CHERRIES. FLAVOUR AND TEXTURE: RICH, WITH SLIGHT TOFFEE-CARAMEL NOTE, CLOSE TEXTURE.

HISTORY:

The Melton Hunt cake is in the tradition of the enriched, fruited and spiced cakes of earlier centuries. By the mid-nineteenth century the modern cake raised with beaten egg and baking powder had evolved and the Melton Hunt cake is of this type. The exact recipe was created in 1854 by John Dickinson. He started making it for the members of the Melton Hunt (the town has been famous as a centre for fox-hunting for over 200 years). It was originally intended to be eaten with the stirrup cup as the huntsmen assemble at the meet. The modern recipe has not changed and great effort is made to ensure the finest ingredients. It is the sole property of one company in Melton Mowbray.

REGION OF PRODUCTION:

MIDLANDS, MELTON MOWBRAY (LEICESTERSHIRE).

Marmite

DESCRIPTION:

MARMITE IS A STICKY, SHINY SUBSTANCE, SO DARK BROWN AS TO BE ALMOST BLACK. THE FLAVOUR IS SALTY, REMINISCENT OF BROWN FRIED ONIONS OR CONCENTRATED MEAT JUICES.

HISTORY:

Marmite is prepared from the yeast generated as a by-product of the brewing industry in Burton-upon-Trent. The Marmite Food Co. was formed in 1902 to exploit some of the nutritive qualities of yeast discovered during the nineteenth century. The original process, which had been developed on the Continent, was adjusted to yeast produced by British methods of fermentation. The discovery of vitamins boosted the popularity of Marmite. It was shown to be a good source of B vitamins. Output has grown steadily through the twentieth century. There is no other producer. Marmite is a registered trademark.

TECHNIQUE:

After the fresh yeast arrives at the factory, the main process it undergoes is autolysis: this takes place in large tanks. The yeast breaks down and releases its nutrients into solution. The fluid is centrifuged and filtered to remove the cell walls which are not required in the finished product. It is then condensed under vacuum until the correct consistency is reached. Finally, it is blended and flavoured with vegetable extracts and spices.

REGION OF PRODUCTION:

EAST MIDLANDS.

West Midlands

Asparagus (Evesham)

DESCRIPTION:

IN ENGLAND ASPARAGUS IS USUALLY CUT IN SPEARS ABOUT 20CM LONG, 10–15MM DIAMETER. IT IS SOLD IN BUNDLES OF 250G OR 500G. IT IS BRIGHT MID-GREEN, PURPLISH OR WHITE TOWARDS THE BASE.

HISTORY:

Gerard recognized in 1636 that asparagus grew wild; he identified several sites on the eastern side of the country. But it was the garden plant, heavily manured and intensively cultivated, that was especially valued. The Romans appreciated it too. Cato, in the first Roman agricultural handbook, gave instructions for creating an asparagus bed that were not so different from those broadcast today. He also drew the distinction between the wild and the garden plants. It continued as a serious delicacy on the Roman table; even Anthimus, the sixth-century Gothic ambassador to a Frankish king in the barbarian North, could discourse on its culinary and medicinal virtues. While the Anglo-Saxons made reference to it in their leechdoms or medical treatises, the plant appears to have dropped from the cook's provisions throughout the Middle Ages, only being reintroduced to British shores at the end of Henry VIII's reign.

It was still an unimproved oddity in England in 1614, the year Giacomo Castelvetro wrote his submission on vegetables and fruit to Lucy, Countess of Bedford (1989). 'When I see the weedy specimens of this noble plant for sale in London I never cease to wonder why no one has yet taken the trouble to improve its cultivation,' he wrote, happy that matters were better managed in his native Italy. London gardeners were soon to take up the cudgels. The playwright Philip Massinger mentions an asparagus garden in *The City Madam* (1632), and 30 years later Pepys goes to buy his spears from another. Soon the whole city was ringed by growers, especially in Mortlake and Deptford. As the market developed, so did the production of early, forced spears, grown on hotbeds to peak in January rather than from March to May (Thick, 1998).

By the eighteenth century, cultivation was general. Martha Bradley (1756) wrote, 'We are now advanced into the middle of March, a season at which he is but an indifferent gardener … who has not good asparagus for the table.' Generally, the British seem to have preferred long, thin green spears, of more intense flavour than the fleshy, pale stems that were esteemed on the Continent.

Where London went, the rest of the country followed, and soon other districts had market gardens producing asparagus for local towns. The Vale of Evesham, running south-west from Stratford on Avon in Warwickshire to the River Severn, developed as an area producing early fruit and vegetables. Horticultural expansion was helped by the presence of the large manufacturing towns close by, and the early development of canal and railway transport through the region, linking it with wider markets in Bristol and London. Evesham and asparagus, particularly in the first decades of this century, became identified. More recently, the industry here has declined relative to that of Lincolnshire and East Anglia.

There is a second apparent regional connection in respect of this plant, Bath asparagus. In fact, it is a counterfeit asparagus, the wood star of Bethlehem (*Ornithogalum pyrenaicum*), that grows in the woods and waste around the cities of Bath and Bristol. 'Eaten by the common people,' was one dismissive remark, although in living memory it has been gathered in sufficient quantity to be sold in local markets. It resembles sprue, the very thin spears of true asparagus that are gathered from young plants or as a by-product of a healthy bed.

TECHNIQUE:

Local climatic conditions allow crops in the Vale of Evesham to ripen 10–14 days ahead of the main growing regions in the east of Britain. Asparagus used to be a crop to utilize the ground between trees in plum orchards. The soils are heavy clay, and the long-established variety, still much used, is Connover's Colossal, although heavy cropping F1 hybrids are also now grown. After preparation of the ground into ridges, young plants are transplanted in peat nodules. The first picking takes place after 2–3 years, and the plants are left on site for up to 20 years. The shoots may be left entirely green, or partially earthed up and picked 'green-white', that is, with the lower parts blanched. In the past, asparagus was presented for market in bundles of 60 or 120 spears, bound with osier twigs tied in traditional patterns. This craft is now in decline, but can still be seen at the annual asparagus auction held at the Fleece Inn, Bretforton, in the latter part of May, when large bundles of very high quality asparagus are sold.

REGION OF PRODUCTION:

WEST MIDLANDS, THE VALE OF EVESHAM.

Black Currant

DESCRIPTION:

DEEP PURPLE-BLACK BERRIES ABOUT 1CM DIAMETER, STRIPPED FROM THE BRANCHES. FLAVOUR: SWEET, WITH DISTINCTIVE MUSKY AROMA. VERY RICH IN VITAMIN C.

HISTORY:

The black currant, *Ribes nigrum*, appears to have been introduced as a garden plant by John Tradescant in 1611. MacCarthy (1989) says they were taken to be the fruit from which currants (which are actually dried grapes) were produced, hence the name. Black currants were at first disliked because the leaves and berries have a strong smell; red and white currants were preferred (Roach, 1985). During the eighteenth century the fruit slowly gained acceptance, and was used in puddings, tarts and jellies, but its chief attraction has always been medicinal, as a base for drinks and potions. It was, indeed, only after it had been discovered to contain abnormally high quantities of vitamin C that the black currant became a plant universally adopted by English gardeners.

The black currant is native to northern climates. It has never, therefore, figured in cuisines of Mediterranean countries, and is only grown in France (principally in Bordeaux and Burgundy) as a base for a cordial. Britain is its culinary stronghold and there are several historic cultivars, particularly Black Naples and Baldwin, that are important here.

Black currants have their longest history as a dessert crop in Herefordshire. According to Keith Worsley, as early as 1643 they were exported to London, packed in ice, carried by boat down the River Wye and thence round the coast. Commercial considerations to do with picking and productiveness have affected the production of black currants for processing, but Baldwin remains an outstanding variety, sought for its flavour, and still cultivated in Herefordshire for the dessert market.

Ninety per cent of black currants grown in Britain are used for processing, mostly to make cordial. It is said that a proportion of fruit from the variety Baldwin is essential to the flavour of 'Ribena', the best-known brand of black currant drink in Britain. Dessert black currants, of which Baldwin is the principal representative, are also used for summer pudding, pies, sauces, jams, jellies and to flavour fools and yoghurt. Black currant tea, made with jam and hot water, is a soothing drink for children with a cold; black currants are also made into pastilles.

TECHNIQUE:

Black currants are grown on bushes out of doors. Soil type is not of primary importance, but water supply is. Herefordshire, an area in which these are an accepted crop, is bounded to the west by the Black Mountains and the Brecon Beacons, high ground which creates a rain shadow area. Just enough rain spills across from these hills to give the right conditions for successful black currant cultivation. The climate is also relatively frost-free, but cold enough to provide the necessary vernalization required for British cultivars of black currants. Fruit for the dessert market is usually harvested by hand from bushes in their first year of growth; mechanical harvesting can be used for older bushes. Replanting takes place every 12–15 years. Baldwin is relatively low yielding, and the cultivation of it and other old varieties is diminishing. New cultivars such as Ben Alder, Ben Tiron and Ben Lomond developed at the Scottish Crop Research Institute yield almost three times as much, with increased disease resistance, but are not considered to have such a fine flavour. As harvesting by hand is labour intensive, the pick-your-own market is increasingly important.

REGION OF PRODUCTION:

WEST MIDLANDS.

Black Worcester Pear

DESCRIPTION:

A COOKING PEAR; LARGE AND ROUNDED; DARK MAHOGANY SKIN WITH RUSSET FRECKLES; SMALL AREAS OF ROUGH SKIN; SHARP, BITTER AND HARD WHEN RAW, SOFTENS ON COOKING.

HISTORY:

Although the wild pear is found growing in Britain, it is doubted that it is indigenous. In any event, its fruit is hardly palatable and we benefited from centuries of breeding by the Greeks and Romans, then the French and Belgians (above all other nations) to create the range of fruit we have grown with enthusiasm from the Middle Ages (more specifically, from the Norman Conquest) until today.

The pear does not grow true from seed. It is best grafted. However, seedlings often arise and give us new cultivars. The pear, like the apple, is a species of infinite variety. Like the apple, again, there is a broad distinction between those suitable for eating and those for cooking alone. Cooking pears were termed wardens or wardons in later medieval England, taking their name from the abbey of Wardon in Bedfordshire – no one knows the reason why. There was also a third category of pear, not really recognized until the sixteenth century, which was suitable for making perry.

All these pears proliferated as a multitude of varieties – comparable to the multiplication of apples and plums. Often the breeds were local, sometimes not spreading beyond the village or valley of their discovery. John Gerard expressed this nicely in 1597 when he denied himself the pleasure of listing all the varieties 'as it would fill a whole volume, each county having its own'. John Parkinson mentioned 'the Norwich, the Worcester, the Warwicke, the Arundel and the Petworth' in his *Paradisi in Sole* of 1629.

The Worcester was a warden or baking pear. The West Midlands region had begun to take its pears seriously with the development of perry, the cider made from pears. Many early references to perry have been gathered by Davies (1993): they emphasize its strong links with the county of Worcester, especially in Tudor and Stuart times. One writer noted it as a product of Kent, Sussex and Worcestershire; another made a distinction – perhaps reflecting commonly accepted reality – cider in Kent but perry in Worcestershire. Perry was at first, it seems, made from wild hedgerow pears, but as production increased, so did the requirement for raw material.

A preoccupation with pears, therefore, may be the reason for Queen Elizabeth I permitting the inclusion of 'three pears sable' in the coat of arms of the city of Worcester when she visited in 1575. The heraldry may also be the explanation why the Worcester is now the Black Worcester. What is certain is that this variety has been recorded, and linked to the city, for many centuries.

The tree grows very tall, and was planted in hedgerows or in orchards as a windbreak tree: 'Worcestershire is a pleasant, fruitful, and rich county abounding in corn, woods, pastures, hills, and valleys, every hedge and highway beset with fruit, but especially with pears, whereof they make a pleasant drink called perry which they sell for a penny a quart, though better than ever you tasted in London,' wrote the Roundhead Nehemiah Wharton during the Civil War (Davies, 1993). More lyrically, the poet John Phillips carolled,

'...the sturdy pear-tree here
Will rise luxuriant, and with toughest root
Pierce the obstructing grit, and restive marle.
Thus nought is useless made...'

The Black Worcester is disease resistant, and the fruit keeps without being given any special attention for several months. Today, interest is as much for the emblematic significance and the genetic material it holds as stomachic delight. A scheme to encourage the planting of the Black Worcester Pear, together with other local apple and pear cultivars, is being run by the County Council in conjunction with the local agricultural college.

TECHNIQUE:

No particular method of cultivation is attached to this tree; at present it survives as a curiosity, growing untended in hedges and parks.

REGION OF PRODUCTION:

WEST MIDLANDS, WORCESTERSHIRE.

Pershore Plum

DESCRIPTION:

A MEDIUM TO LARGE PLUM, OVAL IN SHAPE AND YELLOW IN COLOUR; A CULINARY PLUM, THE FLAVOUR OF THE RAW FRUIT IS NOT PARTICULARLY GOOD.

HISTORY:

This plum was discovered by George Crooke growing as a seedling in Tiddesley Woods near the town of Pershore in 1827 (Smith, 1978). It is part of a similar sequence of events as noticed already under the Cambridge Gage (p. 112) – a chance seedling, thereafter propagated by sucker and extremely popular in the district of its discovery. In the Pershore example, the timing was also fortunate. By the 1840s, Worcestershire (in which Pershore and most of the Vale of Evesham lie) was important for supplying plums to the markets in the Midland towns immediately to the north (Roach, 1985). A combination of other factors, including the expansion of market gardening on smallholdings, led to an increase in plum growing; the availability of a local variety, easily propagated from suckers, encouraged this. There was also greater demand for plums for processing, especially jam manufacture and canning, for which Pershore is a suitable variety.

This variety also had a substantial effect on British plum cultivation in general, as it provided strong rootstock for grafting, and has been important in the development of new cultivars. This plum is also called the Yellow Egg – for its colour – and there is a Purple Pershore, too, which has the same season and is also useful in canning and jam making. The Purple is a cross of Early Rivers and Diamond made by a local grower in the 1870s.

TECHNIQUE:

The Vale of Evesham runs south-west towards the river Severn. It has a slightly milder climate than the surrounding area, and has long been known for the production of fruit and vegetables, especially early asparagus and plums. Provided the soil is correct and the land sheltered from frost, plums do well. A band of clay outcropping along the Vale sides is well-suited to plum cultivation: it holds moisture well and escapes the frosts to which the valley floor is susceptible. Most of the orchards are located where the ground begins to rise at the edges and occupy poorer soils than other crops grown locally (such as salads). Old orchards are on strong rootstocks, giving large trees. Pershore Yellow Egg can be propagated from suckers. After the first 2 years, little maintenance beyond light pruning is carried out.

REGION OF PRODUCTION:

WEST MIDLANDS, PERSHORE (WORCESTERSHIRE).

Worcester Pearmain Apple

DESCRIPTION:

AN EARLY DESSERT APPLE. DESCRIBED BY MORGAN & RICHARDS (1993) AS A MEDIUM-SIZED APPLE (5–7CM DIAMETER), OF ROUND-CONICAL SHAPE, SOMETIMES SLIGHTLY LOPSIDED, AND SLIGHTLY RIBBED; THE BASIN IS NARROW, OF MEDIUM DEPTH TO SHALLOW, AND SLIGHTLY RIBBED, OFTEN WITH FIVE BEADS; THE EYE SMALL AND CLOSED, THE SEPALS SMALL AND QUITE DOWNY, THE CAVITY OF MEDIUM WIDTH AND DEPTH, AND RUSSET LINED; THE STALK IS SMALL AND QUITE THICK; THE COLOUR OF THE SKIN IS CHARACTERIZED BY A

'Fame is at best an unperforming cheat;
But 'tis substantial happiness, to eat.'

ALEXANDER POPE, 'PROLOGUE FOR MR D'URFEY'S LAST PLAY'

BRIGHT RED FLUSH WITH SOME FAINT RED STRIPES ON A ON A GREENISH YELLOW OR PALE YELLOW BACKGROUND, WITH LENTICELS QUITE CONSPICUOUS AS RUSSET DOTS; THE FLESH IS WHITE. THE FLAVOUR IS VERY SWEET, WITH AN INTENSE STRAWBERRY NOTE AND FIRM JUICY FLESH.

HISTORY:

The word pearmain to denote apple varieties has been in use in English since the late twelfth century. Early pearmains were primarily for cider. Both Winter and Summer Pearmains were known. A variety known as Old Pearmain is in the collection at Brogdale, but it is not certain if this is the true medieval pearmain.

The Worcester Pearmain is a relative newcomer, having arisen in the 1870s. It was commercialized shortly afterwards, and has been important ever since. It is believed to have been a seedling of a much older variety, the Devonshire Quarrenden, first mentioned in the late seventeenth century. The strawberry flavour seems characteristic of several early dessert apples, including Ben's Red, also sometimes known as Quarrenden, and the true Devonshire Quarrenden.

Several other varieties fall into the category of early dessert apples, including Discovery, raised just after the Second World War. This, too, has a detectable element of strawberry in its flavour. It claims the Worcester Pearmain as a parent but has eclipsed it commercially. The other apple which probably played a role in the ancestry of Discovery, the Beauty of Bath, is no longer grown commercially. Tydeman's Early, another apple with the Worcester in its ancestry, also has a strawberry flavour. Other early dessert apples which are still available are Epicure (Bedfordshire), Norfolk Royal (Norfolk), and James Grieve (raised in Scotland, but now widely grown commercially in Europe).

Worcester Pearmain is high in tannin and can be used effectively to produce a cider in the style of the West Country. It is also used as a pollinator for Bramley's Seedling.

TECHNIQUE:

See Bramley's Seedling (East Anglia) for more information about rootstocks. Optimum pollination time for Worcester Pearmain is early to mid-May; the tree is of medium vigour and is a heavy cropper, and produces fruit buds partially at the tips of new growth. Picking is by hand in early to mid-September. Grading is by diameter (sizes are set according to variety) and by quality into Grade 1 or Grade 2. Early dessert apples are not expected to keep for long; Worcester Pearmain is no exception, and is only available for about 6 weeks.

REGION OF PRODUCTION:

WEST MIDLANDS; SOUTH ENGLAND.

Hereford Hops Cheese

DESCRIPTION:

PRESSED, UNPASTEURIZED COW'S MILK CHEESE WITH COATING OF HOPS, IN 3 SIZES: 7CM DIAMETER, 7CM HIGH; 12CM DIAMETER, 8CM HIGH; 16CM DIAMETER, 4CM HIGH. WEIGHT: APPROXIMATELY 400G, 1.2KG, AND 2KG. COLOUR: PALE SMOOTH CURD WITH COATING OF DRIED HOPS. FLAVOUR: RICH, CREAMY, DELICATE LEMON TASTE, CONTRASTING WITH SAVOURY HOP FLAVOUR.

The Hereford area has no great tradition of cheese-making, save probably on a small scale by farmers' wives (Rance, 1982). However, in this century various people have experimented with the craft, including Ellen Yeld who evolved 'Little Hereford', for small dairies, shortly before 1920. Oral tradition collected by Nicholas Hogetts, the maker of Hereford Hops, states that local farmers used once to have a habit of placing cheeses in barrels of hops to preserve them, and that local tastes in cheese varied, tending towards a higher cream content in the west of the area. Hereford Hops cheese evolved from these traditions, making use of local ingredients (hops) and skills. The name 'Hereford Hops' is protected.

TECHNIQUE:

Unpasteurized milk from a designated herd of British Friesian cattle is used. A small quantity of starter is added, followed by vegetarian rennet. The curd is cut into cubes of about 1cm and left to settle for 20 minutes. It is scalded at 32.5°C, after which the cheese is drained, the curd broken by hand, salted (2 per cent) and filled into hoops. It is pressed for 2 days under gradually increasing pressure. On removal from the hoops, the cheese is allowed to dry for about 5 days then coated with hops and matured a further 10 weeks.

REGION OF PRODUCTION:

WEST MIDLANDS, HEREFORD AND WORCESTERSHIRE.

Fidget Pie

DESCRIPTION:

A COOKED PORK, HAM OR BACON, VEGETABLE AND APPLE RAISED PIE; ABOUT 18CM DIAMETER, 5.5CM DEEP, WEIGHING 1500G. DEEP GOLD PASTRY CASE WITH CRIMPED EDGES; FILLINGS VARY A LITTLE, BUT ARE USUALLY COMPOSED OF LAYERS OF PINK HAM, GAMMON OR CURED PORK, WITH PALER LAYERS OF POTATO, APPLE AND ONION. THE FLAVOUR OF THE HAM OR PORK PREDOMINATES, WITH APPLE AND VEGETABLES AS A BLAND, SWEET COUNTER-BALANCE. SEASONING SOMETIMES INCLUDES SAGE.

HISTORY:

Fidget (or fitchett) pie has a persistent association with harvest time and was made in much of the Midlands, though apparently especially popular in Shropshire.

Early pork pies, for instance Nott (1726), included apples with the meat. Regional affiliation for the combination is proposed by Hannah Glasse (1747) who gives 2 recipes for Cheshire pork pies. One is a raised pie with fresh pork, pippins (sweet apples) and white wine; the other, 'for the sea', consists of fat, salt pork and potatoes. Joseph Wright (1896–1905) records that fitchett pie, in Cheshire, was a pie given to the reapers at harvest home, and was composed of apples, onions and bacon fat in equal quantities. Apparently cheese was sometimes substituted for the bacon in the West Midlands, but this was a departure from the old usage. The pie was reputed to smell foully during baking (perhaps it was thought to smell like a polecat; 'fitchett' was a dialect name for these animals). However, Lizzie Boyd (1988) suggests that the name comes from the term 'fitched', meaning five-sided, referring to the original shape of the pie.

Recipes for fidget pie appear in many books on English country cooking published during the twentieth century. Hartley (1954) states that the area around Market Harborough made especially good ones; White (1932) describes one from Shropshire; and a recipe from Huntingdon appears in a collection issued by the magazine *Farmer's Weekly* in 1963.

The mixture of meat and apples – mutton, pork or beef, in this case – is also found in another regional dish, Devonshire squab pie. This is identified as a speciality late in the seventeenth century, although it is no longer commercially produced. Bradley (1756) wrote of it: 'This is a particular dish, some are very fond of it; a right Devonshireman will prefer it to the best and nicest of all …'

TECHNIQUE:

A filling of pork, fresh or cured, and apples is essential; onions, potatoes, stock, wine and seasoning are usual. The pie could be made in a dish topped with pastry and eaten hot; or it could be a raised pie produced for carrying away and eating hot or cold. The former was made for domestic consumption only; the latter is sometimes seen on sale. The meat is diced, and apples and vegetables prepared. They are placed in the crust in layers. Seasoning, wine or stock is added. The pie is covered with a pastry top, the edges crimped, the centre decorated and glazed with egg. It is baked at 160–170°C for up to 90 minutes.

REGION OF PRODUCTION:

MIDLANDS.

Old Horned Hereford Cattle

DESCRIPTION:

THE DRESSED WEIGHT FOR A CARCASS FROM A 20-MONTH STEER IS ABOUT 275KG. OLD HORNED HEREFORDS HAVE SHORT LEGS, HEAVY DEWLAPS AND DEEP BODIES. THOSE WITH IMPORTED BLOOD ARE TALLER AND LONGER-BODIED. THE MEAT IS VERY WELL MARBLED, WITH DEPTH OF FLAVOUR AND VERY TENDER.

HISTORY:

The Old Horned Hereford, now designated a rare breed, represents the genetic line from which the millions of Hereford cattle found in the New World originally sprang. According to Peter Symonds, a breeder, the origins of all Herefords go back to the late eighteenth and early nineteenth centuries. At this time, various breeders in the Herefordshire area, which lies on the Welsh Marches and was, at that time, relatively isolated, began to improve local cattle. Benjamin Tompkins (1745–1815) did much to lay the foundations. In the 1840s, John Hewer, deciding that it would benefit the stock to have distinctive markings, deliberately bred Hereford cattle to have a white face and a red-brown body, the pattern which persists today. At the same period, a stud book was started. All Hereford cattle were once horned (the polled variety was developed through interbreeding with the naturally polled Galloway or with North American stock). In the late nineteenth century, Hereford bulls were much exported to the New World to upgrade the existing cattle. During the 1950s, restrictions on the importing of breeding cattle into Britain were relaxed and Horned Hereford bulls from North America were used to give extra height to the domestic strain. The vast majority of Hereford cattle now in Britain are of mixed British-North American blood: these are defined as Horned Hereford and Polled Hereford. Recently, an initiative by the Rare Breeds Survival Trust to protect genetic material in the original English Hereford has resulted in the naming of the indigenous, uncrossed cattle as Old Horned Hereford to distinguish them from the modern variants.

TECHNIQUE:

The agriculture of Herefordshire and environs is traditionally mixed, with some arable land, apple and pear orchards and good pasture, plus rougher grazing on higher ground. Hereford cattle were originally three-purpose, used for draught oxen (this continued up until 1939 on one estate), for milking, and for beef. The latter has been latterly the most important. In common with all British breeds, the cattle are hardy and flourish on grass alone; 'kings in grass castles' was one description of them earlier this century. The majority of breeders keep their cattle outdoors, except in late winter when they may be housed to prevent the pastures being damaged by the heavy animals trampling wet grassland. Supplementary feeding may be given to the breeding cows, in the form of hay or silage according to the individual farmer; some feed grain, although it is regarded as a virtue of the breed that this is unnecessary. Calves are born in spring or autumn, and remain with their mothers until naturally weaned. They are killed for beef at about 18–20 months.

One butcher, Andrew Sebire, runs an initiative to provide beef from Hereford cattle which is reared, slaughtered and butchered to tight specifications, and hung in the traditional way for 3–6 weeks. A large number of the modern breed reach the market, and the breed is also used commercially for crossing. There is one major herd of Old Horned Herefords in the native area and a handful of pedigree Horned or Polled herds. There are a couple of other large herds of Old Horned Herefords in the country at large, and several breeders with a few pedigree animals.

REGION OF PRODUCTION:

WEST MIDLANDS.

Scratchings

DESCRIPTION:

SALTED, CRISP, COOKED PIG SKIN; INDIVIDUAL PIECES MEASURE 2–10CM LONG, 1–2CM WIDE. SOLD LOOSE OR IN BAGS OF 100G. COLOUR: DEEP GOLD, POWDERY. FLAVOUR: SALTY, CRISP, SOMETIMES TOUGH.

HISTORY:

Originally the word referred to the crisp, cooked membrane left after pig fat had been rendered. As scratchings are an inevitable by-product of lard-making, they must have been available for centuries, but they are little mentioned before the 1800s. Presumably, they were considered inconsequential. It cannot be said that anyone set out with the intention of making scratchings; they were there for whoever cared to eat them at pig-killing time.

Wright (1896–1905) gives instances of the word from an area stretching through the whole of middle England as far south as Devon. This is still the broad region in which they are most found. They were sometimes baked into a cake – mixed with flour – or they were spread and eaten on bread. In the country round Birmingham, the word could mean a specific dish of diced, fried leaf-lard eaten with pepper and salt. The word has been extended to cover pieces of crackling (crisply cooked pig skin), and the old types of scratchings are now uncommon.

Scratchings are salted and sealed in plastic bags for sale as a snack; they are widely available

I t's a bit of a mystery what has happened to British food in the last century and how
it lost its way… There was the move from rural areas to cities, the Second World War,
the frozen Chicken Kiev school of thought, but none of them fairly can be blamed for
a nation which likes its meat anonymous, pink and in plastic. Especially if, as a nation, we
enjoy the rigours of British seasons, which will write a glorious menu for you.

To start the year, native oysters are in season, then sea kale, St George's mushrooms,
gulls eggs, English asparagus, jersey royals and spring lamb. The summer brings strawberries and raspberries – my favourite season is around June, when broad beans are small,
Berkswell Cheese is in fantastic condition, there are suckling kids around and I've got
about a month and a half to fantasize about my first grouse. Before you know it, it's 12
August and delicious birds are falling from the sky – grouse, grey-legged partridge,
pheasants and woodcock – and root vegetables are ready for harvesting. Undeniable
goodness. How we've ignored this is a rum old do.

Fergus Henderson

Founder, St. John Restaurant, London

in pubs in the West Midlands and south-west England where they are a popular and thirst-provoking accompaniment to beer.

TECHNIQUE:

The method for rendering lard involved cutting the fat small or mincing it, soaking and then melting it over very low heat. The residue of cooked connective tissue left after the fat had been poured off was the scratchings. Modern, factory-produced scratchings are made from pig skin with its underlying fat, baked until crisp.

REGION OF PRODUCTION:

MIDLANDS.

Tamworth Pig

DESCRIPTION:

A DRESSED CARCASS DESTINED FOR BACON WEIGHS AT LEAST 64KG. THEY MAY ALSO BE USED FOR FRESH PORK. THEY HAVE GOOD BACON CONFORMATION: LONG IN THE SIDES, LIGHT SHOULDERS AND WELL-FILLED HAMS. THEIR SANDY-RED BRISTLES DO NOT AFFECT THE SKIN, WHICH DRESSES WHITE. THE COLOUR OF THE MEAT DEPENDS TO AN EXTENT ON AGE AND FEEDING; IT IS SUCCULENT, WELL-FLAVOURED AND FINE-GRAINED.

HISTORY:

The Tamworth is sometimes known as the original English pig and is thought a descendant of the feral woodland pig. It is believed it was not cross-bred with animals of Chinese origin – a ploy much favoured for improving pigs in the early nineteenth century.

It has long been famous beyond the boundaries of Staffordshire and was the traditional British bacon pig, producing carcasses with long sides and fine hams. In the 1800s it was used for crossing with the Berkshire to produce bacon pigs (Samuel, 1860). Tamworths began to decline in popularity when, like many other old breeds, they were supplanted by leaner animals which matured in less time.

TECHNIQUE:

The Tamworth is exceptionally hardy, surviving on a minimal diet, foraging on grass and rough ground. It may be used to clear old pasture or scrub, can tolerate extremes of temperature and does not suffer from sunburn. Outdoor sows are generally kept in hard conditions except at far-rowing, or if conditions are very muddy. They do not require special feeding, although many get supplementary dry rations and vegetable scraps. Tamworths are well suited to the present movement towards extensive agriculture. They can yield a lean carcass if required, although breeders prefer a degree of fat. In recent years a renewed interest in the breed has inspired work on the improvement of litter sizes, the number of pigs reared and their weaning weight.

The animals destined for bacon are killed at 8–9 months. After slaughter, the carcasses are dressed to yield sides suitable for bacon; there are regional and personal preferences in the exact shape of these. Until the mid-nineteenth century, a dry-salt cure was always used for bacon. It persists in some places, but modern light-brine cures work well with Tamworths, as their meat has an excellent flavour.

REGION OF PRODUCTION:

WEST MIDLANDS.

Banbury Cake

DESCRIPTION:

A POINTED OVAL SHAPE OF PASTRY WRAPPING A FRUIT FILLING; THE COLOUR IS PALE, WITH
A CRISP, BUBBLED SUGAR COATING. DIMENSIONS: 150MM LONG, 60MM WIDE, 10–20MM DEEP.
WEIGHT: 50–75G. FLAVOUR: RICH, DRIED FRUIT AND SPICES.

HISTORY:

In Ben Jonson's play *Bartholomew Fair* (1614) there is a character, Zeal-of-the-Land Busy, a Banbury baker whose cakes 'were served to bridals, may-poles, morrises and such profane feasts and meetings'. As Addison said in *the Tatler*, 'Banbury is a town known for cakes and zeal.' The first known recipe is given by Markham (1615), although the apparent form has changed over the years. A recipe book in 1655 contains complicated instructions headed, 'The Countess of Rutland's Receipt of making the rare Banbury Cake, which was so much admired at her Daughters (the Right Honourable the Lady Chaworths) Wedding.' It described a rich, sweet, spiced, yeast-leavened dough divided into 2 portions. One was left plain, the other mixed with currants. That with currants was sandwiched between thin layers of the plain paste. Size was left to the cook's discretion, but if the quantities given were used for one cake, it would have weighed about 4kg. Similar cakes were known elsewhere, one example being the Shrewsbury Simnel. Another was the now extinct Coventry Godcake which was triangular. A third is the black bun, made in Scotland at New Year; Eccles and Chorley cakes are yet other relations (see below, p. 228–9). By the 1800s, Banbury cakes had become as small as we know them to-day. Dr Kitchiner (1822) cites a filling like that known in the seventeenth century but enclosed in puff pastry.

A shop in Parsons Street, already known in 1833 as 'The Original Cake Shop', was said to have been started by one Betty White in 1638. Subsequent owners are documented through the 1800s and Banbury cakes were exported in considerable numbers to India. They were also found in refreshment rooms on stations up and down the Great Western Railway, which ran through the town (Grigson, 1984).

An earlier method of packaging the cakes was preserved as an exhibit in the shop: a spherical basket with a domed lid on a rope handle. Baking ceased at the shop and attached tearoom in 1969 and the building was partially demolished. Recipes still in use in the town exhibit many variations, for example using cake crumbs in the middle layer of currants. Recently, supermarkets have started to sell items called Banbury cakes, but they make them square or round, not in the usual shape.

TECHNIQUE:

Puff pastry is cut into rounds. A filling of currants, candied peel, flour, butter, brown sugar, rose water, lemon essence, rum essence and nutmeg is sandwiched between the puff pastry. The edges are folded over to form a little roll. Then the cake is rolled out to elongate it, and given final shape by pressing to flatten, with the seam underneath. The tops are brushed with egg white and sprinkled with a pulverized sugar. They are baked for 20 minutes at 220°C.

REGION OF PRODUCTION:

MIDLANDS, BANBURY (OXFORDSHIRE).

Market Drayton Gingerbread

DESCRIPTION:

OBLONG FINGERS WITH LENGTHWISE RIDGES; SOLD IN BLOCKS OF 7, EACH 80MM LONG, 12MM WIDE, 10MM DEEP. WEIGHT: EACH FINGER APPROXIMATELY 20G. COLOUR: MID-BROWN. FLAVOUR AND TEXTURE: SWEET, SPICY WITH GINGER AND LEMON; HARD, WITH SHORT, CRISP TEXTURE.

HISTORY:

In the early 1800s, a baker named Thomas sold gingerbread similar to that made today in this small Shropshire town. A chain of named people have held the formula since Mr Thomas. By 1900 there were 4 gingerbread bakers and a flourishing postal export trade to the colonies. Billington, the family name now associated with the speciality, held the recipe for about 100 years to 1939–45. Wartime rationing limited the quantities which could be made; afterwards, it remained a little-known curiosity until the 1980s when it was revived.

A domestic recipe is given in a manuscript from the 1850s. The commercial recipes (of which there appear to have been at least 4 in existence at the time of its heyday) are kept secret. The characteristic ridged shape has been linked with the gingerbread as long as the Billingtons were involved in its manufacture. A hand-cranked machine for extruding ribbons of dough through a star-shaped nozzle – which imparts the ribs – was made for the firm and is still in use.

TECHNIQUE:

The ingredients are given as wheat flour, sugar, margarine, Golden Syrup, eggs, ground ginger, rum, spices, sodium bicarbonate and cream of tartar. The exact recipe and method are a trade secret. Ginger from both Cochin and Jamaica are quoted in connection with the recipe.

REGION OF PRODUCTION:

WEST MIDLANDS, MARKET DRAYTON (SHROPSHIRE).

Pikelet

DESCRIPTION:

A CIRCULAR FLAT BREAD, WITH A PATTERN OF SMALL HOLES COVERING THE UPPER SUR-FACE, EDGES THINNER THAN THE CENTRE, AND A SLIGHTLY IRREGULAR SHAPE; 90–110MM DIAMETER, ABOUT 5MM DEEP. WEIGHT: ABOUT 30–35G. COLOUR: VERY PALE, ALMOST WHITE, WITH A LITTLE BROWN SPECKLING ON TOP; SMOOTH BROWN SURFACE UNDER-NEATH. FLAVOUR AND TEXTURE: MILDLY SWEET, SPONGY; ALWAYS EATEN TOASTED.

A WELSH PIKELET, BOUGHT IN SWANSEA MARKET, IS THE SAME DIAMETER BUT THICKER (10–15MM) AND HEAVIER (75G).

HISTORY:

The word belongs to the dialects of the English Midlands, and indicates a small, rather thick, yeast-leavened griddle-bread, characterized by a spongy, holey surface. They are like crumpets, which are better known and usually thought a thicker, more regular bread baked in ring-shaped moulds. In some regions there is much confusion between the terms, not helped by the fact that the size of crumpets was more variable in the past. They ranged from 'large brownish dinner-plate size made with an admixture of brown flour ... to small, rather thick, very holey [ones] made in the Midlands' (Hartley, 1954).

The origin of the words pikelet and crumpet is problematic and derivations from Welsh are postulated. Joseph Wright (1896–1905) offers bara picklet, obsolete Welsh for yeast-leavened cakes of fine wheat flour, and crumpet may have derived from crempog, which meant a pancake or fritter (David, 1977). The proposed derivation of the Scottish crumpet should, however, be noted (see below, p. 385). The first known recipe for pikelet and crumpet-type products is 'tea crumpets' given by Mrs Raffald (1769). These were made from a thick batter with milk and water, flour, yeast, eggs, which was cooked on a bakestone; the baker was instructed to 'let it run to the size of a tea saucer' and, 'when you want to use them roast them very crisp, and butter them'. The recipe suggests she is describing something which would now be regarded by most people as a pikelet.

While it is possible that both products have a common region of origin, the pikelet has remained a Northern and Welsh speciality, while the crumpet is universal through Britain. The chief difference is that pikelets may be irregular in shape if the batter is not contained on the bakestone by hoops or rings (as were invariably used for crumpets). However, many earlier writers claimed simply that pikelet was the Northern name for crumpet. The holes in the tops of both breads were caused by the batter being liquid enough to allow the yeast fermentation (sometimes reinforced by chemicals) to manifest itself. A griddle-cooked scone, which was not fermented, was smooth on both sides; a muffin, which was fermented but made with a stiffer dough, was also smooth, the fermentation acting upon the texture of the crumb, not forcing its way to the outside.

TECHNIQUE:
The flour used for pikelets and crumpets is usually softer than that used for the more bread-like muffin. Bicarbonate of soda is sometimes added to help the characteristic holey appearance on the top surface. A yeast-leavened batter of flour and water with a little sugar and cream of tartar is left to work for 45 minutes; extra water plus a little salt and bicarbonate of soda are added. The batter is deposited in small pools on a hot-plate, and the network of holes allowed to set. The industrial method is a scaled-up version of this process.

REGION OF PRODUCTION:
MIDLANDS; NORTH ENGLAND; SOUTH WALES.

COMPARE WITH:
Scottish Crumpet, Scotland (p. 385)

Shrewsbury Cake

DESCRIPTION:
A ROUND BISCUIT WITH FLUTED EDGE, 70–80MM DIAMETER, 8MM THICK. WEIGHT: ABOUT 30G. COLOUR: PALE GOLD, SPECKLED WITH CURRANTS. FLAVOUR AND TEXTURE: SWEET, WITH SLIGHT LEMON PERFUME, CRISP.

HISTORY:
Doubt surrounds the first mentions of these cakes, also called biscuits (Lloyd, 1931). Cakes are often mentioned in the bailiffs' accounts for the town during the 1500s and in contemporary correspondence. Their ingredients may be unknown, but they were already famous for their crisp, brittle texture. Lord Herbert of Cherbury sent his guardian in 1602, 'a kind

of cake which our countrey people use and made in no place in England but in Shrewsbury… Measure not my love by substance of it, which is brittle, but by the form of it which is circular.'

Just this brittleness was celebrated by the playwright Congreve in *The Way of The World* (1700) when he used the expression 'as short as a Shrewsbury cake'. The earliest recipe, in Eliza Smith (1728), is for a sweet biscuit spiced with cinnamon and nutmeg. A hundred years later the Reverend Hugh Oven noted that Shrewsbury had always been distinguished for 'a kind of sweet, flat cake' and that great quantities were sold in the town. A reference to them in *The Ingoldsby Legends* (1840) ensured their fame, for the poem mentions a maker of Shrewsbury cakes named Pailin. Whether he was a historical figure has never been quite established. It is possible that a Miss Hill, daughter of one of the town's confectioners, married a Mr Palin, but no satisfactory link with Shrewsbury cakes has been demonstrated. Inspired by the poem, the trademark 'Pailin's Original Shrewsbury Cakes' originated in the late nineteenth century. They were made to a secret recipe by Phillip's Stores Ltd until the outbreak of the Second World War. During the war and the years of rationing which followed, the firm gave it all up because of shortage of ingredients, especially butter. Today, though Shrewsbury cakes are known, little curiosity about them is expressed by the inhabitants themselves. A recent enquiry to a local bakery producing 'Shrewsbury Biscuits' yielded only a few uninterested comments and it seems this once famous speciality has lost its identity and is ripe for a revival.

TECHNIQUE:

The present whereabouts of the recipe used by Phillip's is unknown, but many others are extant. They are for a shortbread. Simon (1960) mixes equal parts of flour, butter and sugar into a paste with one egg white per 250g of mixture. This is baked at about 160°C for 20 minutes. Earlier instructions, such as Hannah Glasse (1747), have twice as much flour which makes something crisper. Rose water is often mentioned as a flavouring, as well as spices such as cinnamon, nutmeg and caraway.

REGION OF PRODUCTION:

WEST MIDLANDS, SHREWSBURY (SHROPSHIRE).

Simnel Cake

DESCRIPTION:

A ROUND CAKE WITH A HORIZONTAL LAYER OF ALMOND PASTE THROUGH THE MIDDLE, AND ANOTHER ON TOP WITH A CHARACTERISTIC DECORATION OF 11 BALLS OF ALMOND PASTE; SOMETIMES THIS IS REPLACED BY SUGAR ICING WITH DECORATIONS CONSIDERED SUITABLE FOR THE SEASON. IT MEASURES 160–300MM ACROSS, ABOUT 80MM HIGH. COLOUR: REDDISH, GOLDEN-BROWN OR CREAMY-YELLOW CRUMB, SPECKLED WITH DRIED FRUIT. FLAVOUR: SWEET, RICH, WITH ALMONDS AND DRIED FRUIT.

HISTORY:

The cake was originally associated with Mid-Lent Sunday, a time when the Lenten fast was relaxed to allow consumption of richer foods, adding variety to an otherwise monotonous diet. This day was also known as Mothering Sunday: pilgrimages were made to the mother

cathedral of a diocese. Later, the holiday developed into the secular festival of Mother's Day. During the nineteenth century it was said that servant girls were allowed to bake simnel cakes to take as presents for their mothers when they visited their families.

The development of the simnel cake had 3 overlapping phases (Wilson, 1985). In its early medieval form, simnel was classified as a type of bread, made from fine white flour (the word is derived from Latin *simila*, the whitest, most finely ground flour). It may have been lightly enriched, and was said to have been 'twice baked'. By the seventeenth century, the recipes had been greatly enriched with dried fruit (especially currants), almonds and spices, including saffron. The dough was enclosed in a pastry crust and the whole was boiled before being painted with egg yolk and baked, giving a very hard exterior. This form, illustrated in a fifteenth-century dictionary, survived into the mid-nineteenth century as the Shrewsbury simnel. Several other localities made simnels to their own specification. The Bury simnel, from Lancashire, was one of the better known and was sent by post all over the country, a trade only stopped by the imposition of rationing during the Second World War. This was a yeast-leavened fruit cake containing high proportions of dried fruit and ground almonds. The pastry crust disappeared from most simnel recipes during the late nineteenth century and they evolved into their present form, related to the rich fruit cakes characteristic of English cookery. The almond paste layers and decoration are of twentieth-century origin, replacing an earlier tradition of preserved fruits and sugar flowers. In its present form, the cake is eaten at Easter, and the 11 balls of almond paste are said to represent the 11 loyal disciples. Its connection with Mothering Sunday is defunct and the apparent regional affiliations mentioned above have been severed.

TECHNIQUE:
Many small bakeries make simnel cakes using craft methods. Two types are recognized: yeast-leavened, and a conventional rich fruit cake.

REGION OF PRODUCTION:
WEST MIDLANDS; NORTH WEST ENGLAND.

Staffordshire Oatcake

DESCRIPTION:
CIRCULAR FLATBREAD, SIMILAR TO A THICK PANCAKE; ABOUT 200MM DIAMETER, 4MM THICK. WEIGHT: ABOUT 110G. COLOUR: PALE BROWN, SPECKLED, SMOOTH ON UNDERSIDE AND FULL OF SMALL HOLES ON TOP. FLAVOUR AND TEXTURE: OATY, SLIGHTLY SOUR, SOFT.

HISTORY:
Staffordshire oatcakes are the main representatives of batter pancakes made in the southern Pennines and North Midlands. This area has a long tradition of oatcake making. Murray (*c.* 1974) cites reports of oatcakes and oatbread from the late eighteenth century in Staffordshire and Derbyshire. The batter was apparently mixed in a tub kept especially for the purpose, giving the cakes a sour flavour. In 1813, Sir Humphry Davy observed, 'The Derbyshire miners in winter prefer oatcakes to wheaten bread; finding that this kind of nourishment enables them to support their strength and perform their labour better.' The people of the Staffordshire pottery towns have kept the habit of eating thick oatmeal pancakes. The tradi-

tion flourishes and many oatcake makers are working in the area. Derbyshire oatcakes are similar but almost extinct.

TECHNIQUE:

The recipes used by professional oatcake makers are kept secret. This is a domestic recipe: equal quantities of flour and fine oatmeal are mixed with salt, water, yeast and a little melted bacon fat. It is left to ferment for about 30 minutes, poured in small amounts on a hot griddle and allowed to cook until bubbles appear on the surface, then turned to cook the other side.

REGION OF PRODUCTION:

NORTH MIDLANDS, STAFFORDSHIRE.

Toffee Apples

DESCRIPTION:

A WHOLE FRESH APPLE DIPPED IN HIGH-BOILED SUGAR SYRUP, 130–150G WEIGHT. COLOUR: DEEP, BRIGHT CHERRY RED WITH A LITTLE OF THE NATURAL APPLE COLOUR SHOWING WHERE THE SUGAR HAS COATED INCOMPLETELY. FLAVOUR: SWEET SUGAR, TART APPLE. COMPOSITION: APPLES, SUGAR, CREAM OF TARTAR, COLOURING.

HISTORY:

The earliest recorded allusion to toffee apples dates from early last century. However, the use of the term as soldiers' slang for a type of bomb used in the First World War suggests that they were well known and probably have a much longer history than that. The apparent use of the word 'toffee' in a specialized sugar-boilers' sense (i.e. to mean simple boiled sugar as opposed to the mixture of sugar and dairy produce which this word denotes in common English) may also indicate an older origin. Possibly toffee apples were a crude, more widespread version of the Norfolk Biffin, described by Mary Norwak as a dried apple of the Beefing variety, crusted with melted sugar. Biffins seem to have disappeared, but ordinary toffee apples are easily available for a few weeks in the autumn. There is a strong association with funfairs. They were once made on a small scale by showmen at fairgrounds, but this habit appears to have died. One company now seems to supply the market from a base at Solihull in the Midlands, coincidentally the region in which many of the largest autumn fairs are held.

TECHNIQUE:

A pan of 'toffee' made from sugar and water plus a little cream of tartar or vinegar and a dash of red food colouring is boiled to hard crack (149–154°C). The apples are obtained from local farmers in the Midlands. Each apple is speared on a stick and dipped into coloured molten sugar, allowed to set and wrapped in Cellophane.

REGION OF PRODUCTION:

WEST MIDLANDS.

'I saw him even now going the way of all flesh, that is to say towards the kitchen.'

JOHN WEBSTER, *WESTWARD HOE*

Banks's Mild

DESCRIPTION:

BANKS'S MILD IS SOLD FROM THE BARREL, IN BOTTLES AND IN CANS. IT IS A CLEAR COPPER BROWN WITH A CREAM HEAD. MILD IS GENERALLY LIGHTLY FLAVOURED, SLIGHTLY SWEET, WITH A WINY NOTE. THE HOPS ARE NOT SO PRONOUNCED AS IN BITTER, HENCE THE NAME. IT IS ABOUT 3.5 PER CENT ALCOHOL BY VOLUME.

HISTORY:

Mild originally denoted beer that was neither acid nor stale; later it came to mean one that was mildly hopped. Dark milds may have developed from the porters which were well known in parts of England (Jackson, 1993). Mild was used at harvest as a long drink for field workers; it retained identity as a thirst quencher and is now associated with areas of heavy industry in the West Midlands and, to a lesser extent, Manchester. Similar beers are known as dark in Wales; a mild type made in Newcastle is called Scotch ale; and in Scotland this is called light ale or 60/- (sixty shilling) ale. The word hock, of unknown derivation, is an old name for mild in some places. Banks, a brewery in Wolverhampton which produces large quantities of mild, is owned by Wolverhampton and Dudley Breweries, founded in 1890. At least a dozen other brewers market milds.

TECHNIQUE:

Banks prepares its own malt from Maris Otter barley, grown by specified farms, and has its own borehole for water. The wort is strained off into a brew kettle and boiled with a mixture of hop varieties, including Goldings (from Kent), Fuggles (from Worcestershire), Progress and Bramling Cross, for 60–90 minutes. The wort is strained and cooled and yeast added. Fermentation lasts about 7 days after which the beer is fined with leaf isinglass, primed and put in casks (95 per cent of the total production), or pasteurized for bottling and canning.

REGION OF PRODUCTION:

WEST MIDLANDS.

Bitter Beer (Burton-Upon-Trent): Marston's Pedigree

DESCRIPTION:

THE COLOUR IS BRIGHT COPPER-GOLD; THE FLAVOUR SHARP, FRUITY WITH A SULPHURY NOTE; LIGHT-BODIED. PEDIGREE IS 4.5 PER CENT ALCOHOL BY VOLUME.

HISTORY:

The main factor in the development of a particular beer style is the water supply. Here, it is rich in gypsum. A tradition of brewing on a large scale has existed in the town since at least the thirteenth century. Wilson (1973) notes that Burton ale was being sold in London by 1630. The town has given its name to a process called 'burtonizing', i.e. adding mineral salts to water to give a beer similar to that of Burton.

Marston's Pedigree is an example of the type of beer known as bitter. It is distinguished by its employment of the 'Burton Union' system, a method which was fully developed by the early nineteenth century. It is based on a complex, linked series of casks and troughs through which the fermenting beer flows. It has been in use so long that strains of yeast unique to the system have developed. Jackson (1993) considers the process may have originated from a habit of catching the overflow from casks which fermented too vigorously. Two of the largest brewers in Burton abandoned the method as too cumbersome and costly; it is now unique to Marston's, who have been brewing for almost 100 years. Bass Charrington use yeast derived from the Union system in some of their beers.

The expressions 'pale ale' and 'bitter' are not well defined and overlap to some extent. Pale ale is the older, used in the 1800s to distinguish newly fashionable, light beers from older, darker brews; the word bitter came into common use around the time of World War II. Many people associate pale ale with bottled beer and bitter with draught.

TECHNIQUE:

Brewing begins with a mash of crushed pale ale malt mixed with liquor (water) at about 70°C for several hours; the wort (liquid) is strained off into a brew kettle and boiled with Fuggles and Goldings hops for 60–90 minutes; the mixture is strained and cooled and the yeast favoured by Marston's is added. All the yeast used in the brewery is derived from the Union system, which has evolved to give a powdery strain that remains in suspension. Fermentation begins in open square tanks. With Union fermentation, after 2 days the wort is dropped to the sets of unions below; it first arrives in a long trough whence it is fed by pipe into casks below; it returns from cask to trough via swan-neck pipes, and then feeds back into the cask. This circulation continues for 3–4 days. The brewery has the capacity to produce about 40 per cent of their beer by the Union system. It is racked into conventional casks to stand for 3–4 days before distribution. If it is to be bottled, it is first filtered and pasteurized.

REGION OF PRODUCTION:

MIDLANDS, BURTON-UPON-TRENT (STAFFORDSHIRE).

COMPARE WITH:

Bitter Beer (Kent), South East England (p. 103); Samuel Smith's Old Brewery Strong Pale Ale, Yorkshire (p. 269)

Cider Brandy

DESCRIPTION:

THIS IS A PALE STRAW YELLOW; IT HAS A PRONOUNCED APPLE BOUQUET AND IS RICH AND SPICY ON THE PALATE. IT IS 42 PER CENT ALCOHOL BY VOLUME.

HISTORY:

Cider spirits were being distilled in England by the second half of the seventeenth century, and royal cider, which was cider fortified with cider brandy, was also made at this time. During the eighteenth century, the local spirit was eclipsed by imported brandy (for the rich) and home-produced gin (for the poor). The tradition of distilling almost vanished. Both the companies now involved cite evidence for its continuance but it is extremely difficult to find documentation, as it was illegal and covert. The first licence granted by Customs & Excise for distillation of cider brandy in this country went to the King Offa Distillery at Hereford Cider Museum in the early 1980s. Since then, one other has been granted, to the Somerset Cider Brandy Company, Kingsbury Episcopi. Cider brandy is also blended with either apple juice or cider to make aperitifs, liqueurs and a product similar to the royal cider referred to above.

TECHNIQUE:

Somerset Royal Cider Brandy comes from apples grown by the company on their own land. They are picked and pressed late in the year, the juice fermented in December and January, the spirit distilled January–May. Ageing is still subject to experiment; barrels from various sources are used.

Hereford Cider Brandy is distilled slowly, twice, in a small copper pot still. The spirit is matured for 5 years in casks of English oak.

REGION OF PRODUCTION:
WEST MIDLANDS; SOUTH WEST ENGLAND.

Indian Pale Ales (I.P.A.): Worthington White Shield

DESCRIPTION:

WHITE SHIELD IS SOLD IN BOTTLES; ITS COLOUR IS LIGHT, BRIGHT COPPER-GOLD. THE FLAVOUR IS DRY, WITH MARKED BITTERNESS. IT IS CHARACTERIZED BY A HIGHER ORIGINAL GRAVITY THAN MANY ORDINARY ALES AND BITTERS, BEING 5.6 PER CENT ALCOHOL BY VOLUME. WHITE SHIELD IS ONE OF FEW BEERS PRODUCED IN BRITAIN TO UNDERGO SECONDARY FERMENTATION IN THE BOTTLE. IPAS IN GENERAL ARE STRONGLY HOPPED, WITH FLOWERY AROMAS. BECAUSE OF THE SECONDARY FERMENTATION, THERE IS A YEAST SEDIMENT.

HISTORY:

In the nineteenth century, Burton-upon-Trent, already an important centre of brewing, had good links by river and canal to sea-ports, allowing transport of such heavy and fragile cargo as bottled beer. The beer in the local style, known as pale ale, was exported to various parts of the British Empire, including India. A particular type evolved for this market, distinguished by a high original gravity (which allowed for a secondary fermentation in the bottle during the voyage) and a heavy flavouring of hops, which acted as a preservative protecting the beer from infection by wild yeasts. 2–2.5kg of hops per barrel (about 80 litres) was typical (Jackson, 1993). The style became popular in Britain, although modern IPAs have a lower gravity and are less heavily hopped. Few are now bottle-conditioned. There has been a new interest in IPAs, with several breweries reviving them.

White Shield was originally brewed by Worthington in Burton. This company was founded in the mid-eighteenth century and remained independent until acquisition by Bass in 1927. The original brewery was closed in the 1960s, but Bass still produces White Shield.

TECHNIQUE:

A conventional British brewing process is followed. Northdown and Challenger hops are added and Bass yeast used. After fermentation, the beer is filtered, primed with sucrose and a different yeast strain and bottled. It is warm-conditioned for 2–3 weeks, then released on the market. Ideally, it is stored for 6–18 months in a cool cellar while flavour develops further.

REGION OF PRODUCTION:
EAST MIDLANDS, BURTON-UPON-TRENT (STAFFORDSHIRE).

Perry

DESCRIPTION:

THE FERMENTED DRINK FROM THE JUICE OF PEARS IS PALE STRAW-GOLD. THE FLAVOUR OF FARM-MADE PERRIES IS VARIABLE; THEY MAY BE FERMENTED TO DRYNESS, BUT WILL RETAIN A DISTINCT PEAR BOUQUET. THEY ARE 6–8 PER CENT ALCOHOL BY VOLUME.

HISTORY:

It is probable that few people know much about perry although most are almost certainly aware of its most famous manifestation, Babycham. Yet perry has been made in southern England for centuries. The name originally applied to wild pear trees, and later was transferred to the drink produced from their fruit. As with cider and cider apples, particular varieties of pear are grown expressly for making perry.

Less attention has been paid to the history of perry than of cider. It seems to have been less well known outside its native region. That said, there are many references to production in Worcestershire and other Western counties in the medieval and early modern periods (Davies, 1993) and it shared in cider's popularity and esteem during the seventeenth century. It was even, said the poet Southey, sold in Georgian London as champagne. However, the fame did not last. By the end of the nineteenth century, *Law's Grocer's Manual* observed that it was chiefly prepared in the counties of Devon, Gloucester, Hereford and Worcester, that it was still popular in those districts, but that 'elsewhere it seems to have declined in public favour'. At this time the best perry was quite strong, about 9 per cent alcohol and sometimes bottled by the Champagne method.

The drink might have remained as obscure as the word had it not been for developments shortly after World War II. An especially good sparkling perry was exhibited at local agricultural shows by the Showering family of Shepton Mallet, Somerset. It won many prizes and was nicknamed 'baby champion' or 'baby-champ', later contracted to the brand name Babycham. The fact that perry did not have a clear place in the hierarchy of drinks worked to its advantage: 'clever use of a brand name, coupled with a reminder of the drink's claim to be a wine, brilliantly did the rest' (Dunkling, 1992). Gloucester, Herefordshire and Worcestershire perry have all been awarded Protected Gepgraphical Indication (PGI).

TECHNIQUE:

The method for producing perry is essentially the same as that for cider. The fruit is harvested, milled to a pulp and pressed to extract the juice, which is treated with sulphur dioxide and fermented. The difference lies in the treatment towards the end of fermentation. Much perry is bottled and allowed to undergo a secondary fermentation to give a sparkling drink. Commercially, the carbonation is required to be uniform and a little carbon dioxide may be added to ensure the correct level of 'sparkle'.

REGION OF PRODUCTION:

WEST MIDLANDS; SOUTH WEST ENGLAND.

Worcestershire Sauce

DESCRIPTION:

OPAQUE, DARK BROWN COLOUR, WITH A SWEET-SOUR TASTE INFUSED WITH AROMATICS AND PEPPERY SPICES.

HISTORY:

Lea & Perrins Original and Genuine Worcestershire Sauce is a trademark and each bottle bears a characteristic orange label. It is one of the longest-lived and most celebrated store sauces, admired and appreciated by British cooks and diners. On the one hand it imparts taste and flavour to a cookery that may have lacked those qualities, on the other it imparts zest and strong taste to palates that need them.

The recipe is said (by Lea & Perrins Ltd) to have been brought to Britain from India by Marcus, Lord Sandys. In 1835 he commissioned a Worcester pharmacy owned by John Lea and William Perrins to make it up. The mixture was considered inedible and the jars were placed on one side and forgotten. On their rediscovery a year or so later, the sauce was tasted and discovered to have matured, with a very beneficial effect on flavour. The company bought the recipe from Lord Sandys and the sauce was first manufactured and sold in 1837. It was being advertised by 1843 in the *Naval and Military Gazette* as 'Lea & Perrin's Worcestershire Sauce, prepared from a recipe of a nobleman in that county'.

TECHNIQUE:

The precise recipe and process are trade secrets. Raw materials are vinegar, molasses, sugar, salt, tamarinds, shallots, garlic and unspecified spices and flavourings. The vegetables are matured in vinegar, and the anchovies in brine for 3 years. The ingredients are mixed together and infused for 3 months. The mixture is filtered, other ingredients are added and the sauce is bottled.

'Original and genuine' Worcestershire sauce is unique to one company, Lea & Perrins Ltd, whose market share is 98.2 per cent; 55 per cent of this is exported. Several other firms produce similar sauces under the name Worcester or Worcestershire.

REGION OF PRODUCTION:

WEST MIDLANDS.

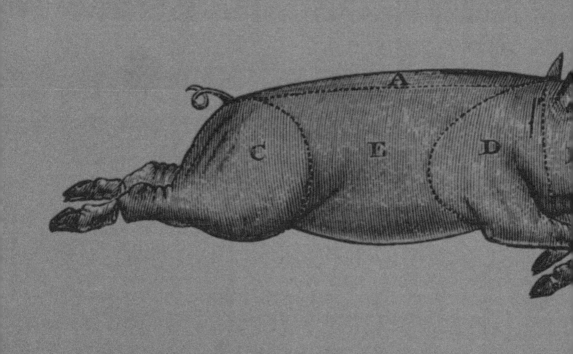

Wales

Glamorgan Sausage

DESCRIPTION:

Weight: about 50g. Form: made in rissoles or sausage shapes. Colour: pale cream-brown, with white and green flecks. Flavour: cheese and mild onion predominate.

HISTORY:

Glamorgan sausage is not a meat sausage but a kind of savoury rissole made of cheese, leek or onion, eggs and bread crumbs. The origin is mysterious. George Borrow (1862) mentioned eating them for breakfast, and remarked that he thought them 'not a whit inferior to those of Epping', which could indicate either that he ate a meat sausage comparable with those of Epping, near London, or that he ate a meatless sausage and was pleasantly surprised by it. Epping sausages were skinless, like those from Oxford (p. 69), and coated with egg and crumbs (Freeman, 1996).

Perhaps the use of cheese in savouries such as 'rabbits', made by melting cheese with flavourings, was a habit inherent in Welsh cookery – speedily transferred to this meatless sausage. Glamorgan sausages were probably a dish of domestic cookery until recently, if they existed at all. One theory scouted is that they were developed in response to the meat shortages of the Second World War. After their moment of Victorian fame, they are little recorded until the mid-twentieth century, when Dorothy Hartley (1954) gave the recipe which is essentially that still used.

TECHNIQUE:

The main ingredients are bread crumbs and cheese, in the ratio of approximately 2:1; a little finely chopped leek or onion, a pinch of mixed herbs, a little mustard powder, plus salt and pepper are bound with egg yolk; the mixture is divided into portions and rolled on a floured board before frying.

REGION OF PRODUCTION:

South Wales.

Laverbread

DESCRIPTION:

Laverbread is a dark greenish-brown purée. For sale it is wrapped in clear Cellophane to make packs of about 200–250g; the fresh seaweed from which it is produced has purplish fronds and is attached to rocks on the seashore below the high tide mark. Flavour: gelatinous texture, faint iodine-sea taste.

HISTORY:

Laverbread is the common name for *Porphyra umbilicalis*, a type of seaweed common on the shores of western Britain. It is associated with the food habits of South Wales and is eaten to a lesser extent in north Devon and Scotland.

Florence White (1932) discussed laver as a speciality of Devonshire, Somerset and Wales. She noted that it was well known in London 'before the invasion of French chefs in 1848', although consumption had declined by the end of the century. She mentions it was packed in earthenware pots for transport from Watchet in Somerset in 1797, and that it 'is prepared at the place where it is gathered, Braunton in particular is one'. Theodora Fitzgibbon (1965) observed that it was also known in Bath during the eighteenth century, where it was sold in little china pots.

The Welsh have the most persistent tradition of laver gathering and eating. It is known there as *bara lawr, llafan, menyn y môr*. 'In the eighteenth and nineteenth centuries, women living in the coastal regions of Anglesey, Glamorgan and Pembrokeshire were ardent gatherers of laver,' it was a trade pursued strictly by low-income families (Tibbot, 1986). Mabey (1978) also commented on this well-organized trade, 'with large drying houses built along the shore, where the weed was cured so that it would keep well'. Glamorgan and Pembroke are now the most important areas of production. In fact the supplies of the raw material are becoming scanty in South Wales and Scottish seaweed is brought down for processing (Davidson, 1979). A little gathering is still carried on for consumption in Scotland where the Gaelic words *slouk* and *sloke* describe the same plant. There is some evidence (Evans, 1995) that it is still gathered between Clovelly and Westward Ho! on the north Devon coast.

In Wales, laver is mixed with oatmeal and fried in bacon fat for breakfast. Laver heated with butter and the juice of Seville oranges was a classic Victorian sauce for roast mutton.

TECHNIQUE:
Laverbread is gathered from the rocks at low tide. It is gathered at any time of the year, but storms and changes in the level of sand around the rocks can make the harvest difficult. It is washed many times – in 7 lots of water – to remove any sand and grit, then steeped in fresh water to reduce saltiness, with a little bicarbonate of soda added to counteract any bitterness. The fronds are stewed in their own moisture for up to 7 hours until they become a soft purée. The excess water is drained off; the laverbread is now ready for sale and finishing at home as required. According to Welsh food expert Gilli Davies, it is collected daily and boiled in small, family-run factories; it is sold from market stalls and travelling fish vans. A small quantity is canned, principally for export.

REGION OF PRODUCTION:
SOUTH WALES.

Caerphilly Cheese

DESCRIPTION:
PRESSED COW'S MILK CHEESE. CAERPHILLY CHEESES ARE MADE IN A WHEEL OR MILLSTONE SHAPE, A FLAT CYLINDER WHICH IS SHALLOW IN PROPORTION TO ITS DIAMETER. THIS WAS ABOUT 18CM DIAMETER AND 6CM HIGH; SIZES ARE NOW VARIABLE ACCORDING TO WEIGHT, WHICH IS GENERALLY IN THE RANGE 400G–4KG. COLOUR: WHITE. FLAVOUR AND TEXTURE: ACIDIC, WITH SLIGHT LEMON NOTE AND A FLAKY TEXTURE.

HISTORY:
Caerphilly is a town which has given its name to the only Welsh cheese which has become well known outside the Principality. Other cheeses were made in Wales in the past. Rance (1982) speculated that Caerphilly cheese supplanted an earlier type from a region known as Eppynt, which was a similar shape but was kept for 2–6 months before being eaten. He states

that Caerphilly cheese, 'was widely available for Welsh miners from the farms of Glamorgan and Monmouth between the early 1800s and 1914', and that small-scale farm cheese production seems to have been common. Demand began to exceed supply with the growth of cities during the 1800s.

Since that time, the cheese has also been associated with Somerset. Caerphilly, a small cheese intended to be eaten young, offered commercial advantages over Cheddar, which requires months to mature. Somerset Caerphilly was sold at Highbridge market, whence much was exported to Wales.

Under terms imposed by the Ministry of Food during 1939–45, production ceased as it was not long-keeping. When it resumed, in Wales it was concentrated in creameries. Some farm production continued in Somerset, where it is made to this day. Traditional farmhouse methods at about the time of the First World War were recalled by Arthur Jones in an article written in the 1950s. Recently, Caerphilly has been revived in South Wales, where it is now produced on several farms. Occasionally, an aged Caerphilly is available from cheese shops.

TECHNIQUE:

Craft method: 1–2 per cent starter is added and the temperature gradually raised from 21 to 31°C; then it is renneted and cut into 5mm cubes. It is stirred for 15 minutes. Stirring continues as the temperature of the curd is raised to about 33°C and the particles break cleanly without being soft in the centres. Then the curd is allowed to settle in the whey for 10–15 minutes before the vat is drained. After the whey has run off, the curd is cut and piled into half-cone-shaped masses, then cut in wedges and piled at the back of the vat. The curd is cut into 2.5cm cubes, salted, and put into moulds. It is lightly pressed for about 18 hours, then brined for 24 hours and kept 4–5 days.

Creamery production is a similar process up to the stage at which the whey is drained; then the curd is cut and piled along the sides of the vat in a smooth bank, gradually draining the whey and allowing the acidity to develop for the next stage. The curd is passed through the mill once, salted, and packed into moulds. Pressing, brining and ripening are carried out in a similar manner to craft production. Caerphilly is available all the year.

REGION OF PRODUCTION:

SOUTH WALES; SOUTH WEST ENGLAND.

Cockle (Penclawdd)

DESCRIPTION:

THE LEGAL MINIMUM SIZE WAS REGULATED IN 1959 TO 20MM ACROSS. THEY ARE SOLD RAW IN THEIR SHELLS OR COOKED AND SHELLED, BY WEIGHT OR VOLUME MEASURE. COLOUR: THE SHELLS VARY FROM YELLOW (FROM THE LOW TIDE MARK), THROUGH GREY, TO ORANGE AND GREY WITH BLACK PATCHES (FROM THE HIGH TIDE MARK). FLAVOUR: CONSIDERED TO BE AMONGST THE BEST-FLAVOURED COCKLES FISHED AROUND THE BRITISH COAST; WHEN FRESH, THEY ARE VERY SWEET AND SUCCULENT.

HISTORY:

Cockles (*Cardium edule*) were important in the Welsh diet. The gathering of shellfish developed into a commercial enterprise as the population of South Wales increased during the industrial revolution (Jenkins, 1977). The Victorians appreciated fully the value of the cockle fisheries in South Wales, including Penclawdd, a village on the Burry estuary on the north side of the Gower Peninsula. The freshly dredged cockles were boiled in the open air, placed over the fire in large pans with a little water. The liquor was reserved and used for washing the batches, after riddling to remove the shells from the flesh. Finally they were washed in fresh spring water and placed in baskets or wooden tubs. Women took the cockles to market in Swansea on the train, carrying the containers on their heads. Jenkins cites living memories of them waiting at the station, dressed in Welsh costume, their baskets covered with white cloths. Until the 1920s, donkeys were used for transport on the beach, the sacks of cockles hung like panniers. Horse-drawn carts with a higher carrying capacity replaced them about the time of the World War II. Horse transport ceased in 1987, replaced by tractors and Landrovers.

In the post-war years, the fishery has been strictly regulated as a conservation measure. The number of people involved has declined from over 200 in 1900–10 to less than 50 in 1970–77. Several reasons are postulated, including pollution, natural variations in the course of rivers, over-fishing and changes in foreshore vegetation. Cocklers also believe that oyster-catchers eat many of the shellfish, and that cockles migrate. A cockle fair takes place in Swansea Market every September.

Today cockles are eaten freshly cooked and seasoned with white pepper and vinegar, made into pies with bacon, dipped in batter and deep-fried, or used in soup. The form in which most landlocked British consumers encounter them is pickled in vinegar.

TECHNIQUE:
Penclawdd is on a river estuary known as Burry inlet. It is the best known of several villages whose inhabitants collect shellfish from wide sands on either side of the estuary; the relative importance of these beaches varies according to changes in the course of the river. The cocklers observe and test the beds carefully for years before deciding which ones to work. They work with the ebbing tide, using a small knife with a curved blade to scrape the sand and expose the cockles, which are drawn together with a rake, and then riddled to separate those which are too small. After washing in pools on the beach, the shellfish are loaded into sacks. The best cockles are considered to come from sandy stretches of beach. They may be sold uncooked in their shells, or boiled and shelled. The method of cooking is to steam the shellfish in perforated baskets for 6–7 minutes, sieve them, and wash the meats in fresh water. Hygiene regulations now being introduced demand that the cockles be cooked for a specified time at a temperature no lower than 98°C; the process is recorded on a continuous read-out. Two methods are being experimented with to achieve this: the use of a steam-jacketed cooking pan; and the use of a continuous belt which carries the washed, shell-on cockles through hot water for 4 minutes, before shaking the cooked meats free into a salt bath (which allows for separation of grit), after which they are washed in cold water.

REGION OF PRODUCTION:
SOUTH WALES.

COMPARE WITH:
Cockle (Stiffkey Blues), East Anglia (p. 119)

Mussel (Wales)

DESCRIPTION:

Minimum length is 50mm; the cultivated mussels are reliably fattened and well-flavoured.

HISTORY:

Fisheries for mussels are found on the East, South and West coasts of Britain. In North Wales, a mussel fishery was recorded in the River Conway in the eleventh century. Mussels are still fished there today from naturally-occurring beds, and a much bigger fishery has developed in the Menai Straits, to the South-West.

TECHNIQUE:

In North Wales, a small-scale fishery is pursued by hand methods using rakes and small boats to harvest the natural mussel bed of the Conway estuary. Larger-scale mussel farming, using mussel seed collected from the Irish Sea littoral is centred on Bangor. The mussels are fattened in lays, and harvested by dredging.

REGION OF PRODUCTION:

North Wales, Conway (Gwynedd).

COMPARE WITH:

Mussel, East Anglia (p.121); Mussel, Scotland (p. 334)

Sewin

DESCRIPTION:

Sewin weigh 750g–9kg. In Wales, fishermen divide the sizes into 3 categories: under 900g, they are known as a shinglin; 900–1400g, they are twlpyn; and from 1400g up to 9kg, they are called gwencyn. The skin of sewin is grey on the back, silver-white on the belly and an evenly distributed pattern of black flecks over the sides and back; the flesh is a light pink. It has a delicate, rich flavour. Sewin taken in nets are always in excellent condition, with firm flesh.

HISTORY:

Sewin, sea trout or salmon trout, is *Salmo trutta*, a member of the brown trout family. It is a freshwater fish which spends part of its life cycle at sea. Wales is not the only part of the British Isles in which it is caught, but certain rivers there have a reputation for being rich in these fish. The rivers Teifi, Dyfi and Conway have long been important for catching sewin, the Teifi in particular. The river Taff was noted for its abundance of sewin in the early 1800s.

It is probable that sewin have been taken from Welsh rivers for as long as there have been human inhabitants. A few fishermen carry on interesting methods of catching them. J. Geraint Jenkins (1971) discussed these in detail, noting that they are of ancient origin. Most notable is the net held between 2 coracles, a craft thought to have been used for thousands of years in Britain. Coracle fishing is fast disappearing; the craft requires skilful handling and they have been discouraged by those responsible for fishing rights. Coracle men once had a reputation for poaching: the boats were noiseless, difficult to see at night and easily portable to the pools where salmon congregate. Fishing licences are also expensive for coracle operators. There is now much competition from leisure anglers – a growing breed. The fish population has also been affected by the building of hydro-electric dams and by fungal disease. Further restrictions are proposed on the season the coracles are allowed to fish and the number of licences issued. Sewin are caught between the beginning of May and the second week in June and coracle fishing in general is limited to 1 March to 1 September. Despite all this, the tradition survives, although the men express doubts about the future.

The fish, of course, is caught in other rivers in Britain and Europe. The link to this region of Wales is in the manner of fishing. There is a recipe that has been christened after the river of origin: Teifi sauce, made from fish stock, port, anchovy, mushroom ketchup and butter, reduced to a strong liquor. This is a frequent accompaniment, although trout are often eaten with nothing more complicated than boiled new potatoes and fresh peas.

TECHNIQUE:
Coracles and nets are used either at night or when the rivers are in spate. The fishermen operate in pairs, each one in his own coracle. Boats move downstream with the current, to catch the fish as they swim upstream. One man is recognized as the senior; he gives orders, hauls in the net, and kills any sewin or salmon caught by clubbing the fish. The partner is usually a son or younger brother; he always occupies the coracle on the right-hand side of the river as the boats move downstream. They continue for a mile or more; once the end of the trawl is reached, the boats are carried on the fishermen's backs to the start once more, for as many passes as are deemed suitable.

Formerly, the rivers were divided into sections, each corresponding to the fishing rights of a particular village. Apart from coracles and nets, hand nets are also used in estuaries, and weirs and basket traps in the rivers. The details of construction vary from river to river.

REGION OF PRODUCTION:
SOUTH WALES, DYFED.

Welsh Bacon

DESCRIPTION:
UNSMOKED CURED PORK FOR COOKING. SIDES MEASURE 50–60CM LONG, 30–40CM WIDE, 3–5CM THICK; A MEDIUM SIDE WEIGHS ABOUT 7KG. COLOUR: THIN, DARK RED STREAKS OF LEAN, IN A WHITE FAT LAYER 3–4CM DEEP; THE OUTSIDES ARE POWDERED WITH DRY SALT. FLAVOUR: VERY SALTY, WITH GOOD CURED PORK FLAVOUR.

HISTORY:
Archaeological sites in Wales yield a higher proportion of pig bones than of any other domestic animal, but improved breeds are not identifiable until the 1800s. The Welsh pig, known in the 1920s as Old Glamorgan, has indeed become a useful commercial strain. There was much keeping of house pigs – in both town and country – fed on waste and whey or buttermilk and fattened on barley. Home-cured bacon was common until the 1950s. The distinctive features of Welsh bacon, the fat and salt, would not have been so remarkable in the past. It was generally considered desirable for pigs to be very fat, and a heavy salt cure was employed to ensure preservation when control of hygiene and temperature were less than certain. The development of lighter cures, demands for leaner meat, worries about the consumption of saturated fat and the death of the tradition of home curing have led to the disappearance of this type of

bacon except in West Wales, where it is still much favoured. The meatier back bacon, cut from the loin, can be grilled or fried, or used in cawl (Welsh broth). The fattier part is better employed as a source of fat, salt and flavour for cooking vegetables, especially leeks and potatoes. Several examples of this type of dish are known in Welsh cookery. Bacon fat is the customary medium for heating laverbread.

TECHNIQUE:

Pigs are selected for weight; the largest are favoured. Specific breeds are not sought. After slaughter, the sides are cut: for Welsh bacon, these do not include either the shoulder or the leg, they consist of the loin and attached belly only. They are placed in a bed of dry salt plus a very small proportion of saltpetre. The mixture is rubbed in by hand once every 1 or 2 days for 3 weeks. The sides are hung to dry for about 14 days. Before sale, they are divided longitudinally into a short back piece containing the lean and a longer streaky portion, which is very fatty. These can be further cut into rashers if required. Some makers roll the sides, in which case they are boned before salting and rolled afterwards.

REGION OF PRODUCTION:

SOUTH WALES, DYFED.

COMPARE WITH:

Suffolk Sweet-Cured Bacon, East Englia (p. 128); Ayrshire Bacon, Scotland (p. 306); Wiltshire Bacon, South West England (p. 28).

Welsh Black Cattle

DESCRIPTION:

A DEEP, RICH RED LEAN, WITH WHITE FAT. TENDER, WELL-MARBLED BUT OTHERWISE RELATIVELY LEAN; EXCELLENT FLAVOUR.

HISTORY:

The forerunners of the Welsh Black were known to the graziers and butchers attending the cattle fairs of the Midlands and London as 'Welsh Runts' and were admired for their hardiness. As a mountain breed, they were small and thin to begin with; during the long journey to the English fairs (including, for the animals reared on the island of Anglesey, a swim across the Menai Straits) they became even more emaciated. However, as early as 1695, the ability of Welsh runts to do well on good pasture – for instance Romney Marsh, in Kent – was noted. The beef from such animals was much admired; in 1747 Hannah Glasse recommended Scotch or Welsh beef for making beef hams, a recipe which required 'the leg of a fat but small beef'. Youatt (1834) described Welsh cattle as very fair milkers with a propensity to fatten. He thought the beef equal to that of Scottish cattle, that they would live where others starved, and that they found a ready sale with London graziers and butchers who were rarely disappointed, despite the apparently poor appearance of the animals on arrival.

Two breed societies were established at first but they amalgamated in 1904. The cattle were recognized as a dual-purpose breed up to the 1970s, popular as milk animals with those who require a small supply for the family. Today they are recognised primarily as Wales' only native Beef Breed. About 700 pedigree herds are now registered in the United Kingdom and the breed is also strong in Canada, New Zealand, Australia and Europe.

The emphasis in commercial herds has been on beef production and consequently the animals have become larger and their conformation has altered in favour of this use. They are grass-fed for much of the year, but housed in late winter and fed on silage, hay and, in some cases, locally produced barley. Those cattle destined for beef are killed at 18–24 months.

REGION OF PRODUCTION:
WALES.

Welsh Ham

DESCRIPTION:
A CURED, UNCOOKED HAM WEIGHING UP TO 22KG. THE EXTERIOR OF A WHOLE RAW HAM DISPLAYS DARK BROWN-RED LEAN AND YELLOW FAT, COVERED BY GOLD-BROWN SKIN. WHEN SLICED, THE LEAN IS A DEEP TRANSLUCENT ROSE-PINK TO DARK RED, WITH WHITE FAT; ON COOKING IT BECOMES AN OPAQUE, PALER PINK. FLAVOUR: A WELL-SALTED HAM, WITH DISTINCT SWEET PORK FLAVOUR.

HISTORY:
Ham curing in Wales is largely undocumented but the importance of pig meat in the Welsh diet is long established (Wilson, 1973). In the seventeenth and eighteenth centuries, Welsh hams were often made from sheep meat, but no survivals of this can now be found. Like the English, Welsh farmers killed their own pigs and cured the meat for ham and bacon (Webb, c. 1930). Albert Rees, the company now producing Welsh hams and Carmarthen hams, evolved from the country habit of selling produce such as butter and hams in the local markets. The founder's mother took home-cured bacon and hams to the local towns and the present company was founded in 1962 to sell Welsh hams and dry-cure bacon in the markets of South Wales. The dry-cure Welsh hams were always eaten cooked; from these, the uncooked Carmarthen hams have evolved to suit modern taste for something designed to be cut into very thin slices to eat raw.

TECHNIQUE:
Hams from large pigs are preferred; they are selected by weight rather than breed. The hams are removed from the carcass and left square-cut. They are placed in a bed of dry salt with a very small proportion of saltpetre; this is rubbed in several times a week for 6 weeks. Welsh hams are dried and matured for 3 months. Carmarthen hams are kept and matured for another 3–6 months.

REGION OF PRODUCTION:
SOUTH WALES, CARMARTHEN.

O ver the past year I've been busy travelling around the British Isles to search out the best of British produce and producers with a view to restoring our culinary heritage and as part of my new book, *British Regional Food*. In fact, *The Taste of Britain* was a part of my inspiration. For me, Wales held lots of delicious surprises and although laverbread wasn't one of them as I'd had it before, I had forgotten just how good it was. Laverbread has lots of possibilities – it can even be spread on toast! – but I think one of my favourites is when it's served simply with rashers of cured bacon.

BACON CHOP WITH LAVERBREAD

4 THICK BACON CHOPS (EACH WEIGHING ABOUT 120-150G – ON THE BONE,
 THEY WILL BE HEAVIER), CURED OR SMOKED ON THE BONE OR 4 THICK RASHERS
 OF BACON
200-250G LAVERBREAD
SALT

Preheat grill or griddle pan and cook the bacon chops for four-five minutes on each side. Meanwhile, put the laverbread into a pan with a knob of butter and gently reheat. Spoon the laverbread on to four serving plates, with a bacon chop on each.

Mark Hix

COLUMNIST, AUTHOR, AND CHEF DIRECTOR OF LE CAPRICE,
THE IVY AND J. SHEEKEY, LONDON

Welsh Mountain Sheep

DESCRIPTION:

DRESSED CARCASS WEIGHT VARIES FROM 10KG (FOR VERY SMALL, MOUNTAIN-BRED LAMB) TO ABOUT 19KG (FOR THE LARGEST LAMBS OF THESE BREEDS, GROWN AT A LOWER ALTITUDE). AN EXCELLENT SWEET, NUTTY FLAVOUR, VERY TENDER AND RELATIVELY LEAN.

HISTORY:

The various Welsh Mountain and Hill sheep breeds evolved in a harsh environment whose climate is cold and wet. Don Thomas of Welsh Lamb Enterprise remarks that, from the late seventeenth century, the excellent flavour of the lamb was praised and attributed to the mixture of heather, herbs and grass that formed their diet. In the mid-nineteenth century, George Borrow wrote ecstatic lines about the small, tender, aromatic leg of Welsh mutton on which he dined, celebrating the herb-rich pastures of the area where the sheep were reared. The reputation of Welsh Mountain breeds for tender, sweet meat has grown since then. The inclusion of the word Mountain in the titles of the various breeds indicates the animals have been selected over the years to tolerate a difficult climate and poor pastures. Other characteristics, such as speckled or striped faces and the colour of the wool, have been dictated by a desire to breed more ornamental animals. The meat from the various breeds shares general elements of size, flavour and tenderness. There are a number of breeds recognized as Welsh Mountain: Black Welsh Mountain; South Wales Mountain; Welsh Mountain Badger Face; Welsh Mountain Hill Flock; Welsh Mountain Pedigree. They are each represented by their breed societies. At slightly lower levels, the hill breeds Kerry Hill, Hill Radnor, Beulah Speckled Face, and Welsh Hill Speckled Face all produce lamb which has a good flavour but on somewhat larger carcasses.

TECHNIQUE:

Welsh Mountain breeds are reared on old-established pastures at altitudes of 200 metres or more. These are herb-rich, and receive little fertilizer; some production also takes place on ley pasture at lower levels. The sheep are tough, hardy and self-reliant. Several breeds have exceptional resistance to health problems. Lambing is between mid-February and late April, depending on the altitude. Lambs remain with their mothers until fully weaned and then are finished slowly on mountain grazing. The short lambing season and the lack of winter grazing mean that most of the pure-bred lambs are killed in early and mid-autumn.

Welsh Mountain sheep are also much used in the stratified system of lamb production. The ewes produce cross-bred lambs with lowland sires (often one of the Leicester breeds); the progeny are known as Welsh Halfbreds or Mules, depending on the exact parentage. In turn, the ewes from this generation, pastured in the valleys, produce lambs destined entirely for the meat trade, using meat breeds (traditionally Suffolks) as sires. This system, typical of all highland regions of Britain, utilizing breeds traditional to those areas, produces various sizes and flavours of lamb, destined for specific markets within the country.

REGION OF PRODUCTION:

WALES.

Aberffraw Cake

DESCRIPTION:

A THIN, SHELL-SHAPED BISCUIT, 70MM DIAMETER, 3–4MM THICK. WEIGHT: ABOUT 14G. COLOUR: PALE GOLD. FLAVOUR: RICH, BUTTERY, SWEET.

HISTORY:

Aberffraw or Aberfrau, from which these cakes take their name (they are called, in Welsh, *teisen Berffro*), is a village on an estuary in the south of Anglesey. It was once upon a time (in the twelfth century) the seat of the Eisteddfod. Another name for these biscuits is *cacen* [cakes] *Jago*, i.e. St James's cakes, recalling their distinctive shape of a scallop shell, the emblem of pilgrims to Santiago de Compostela in Spain (Freeman, 1980). The shape was obtained from shells of the small queen scallops readily found on the shore near Aberfrau.

The earliest known reference is Cassell's (1896). They have since appeared from time to time in collections of regional recipes. Recipes are of 2 types: a shortbread composed of flour, butter and sugar; or one based on a Victoria sponge which includes these ingredients plus eggs. Until recently they were made occasionally by local bakers, but are now a rarity. Joan Griffiths, who still makes them in North Wales, uses a recipe inherited from her mother-in-law, who came from the Aberffraw area.

TECHNIQUE:

The recipe most frequently cited is a shortbread of flour, butter and caster sugar in the proportions 4:3:2. The butter is rubbed into the flour until fine crumbs, then the sugar stirred in. The method of shaping is to take a knob of the mixture and press it over the underside of a sugar-sprinkled scallop shell to give a thin, fan-shaped biscuit. Alternatively, the mixture can be shaped into a long roll, chilled, and sliced; lines are marked on top to imitate the shell markings. The cake-type recipes state that the mixture should be spooned into a greased shell as if into a patty tin. They are baked at 190°C for 5–10 minutes. The cakes should not brown; they become crisp as they cool.

REGION OF PRODUCTION:

NORTH WALES, ANGLESEY.

Bara Brith

DESCRIPTION:

BARA BRITH IS GENERALLY BAKED IN A LOAF SHAPE. ONE WEIGHING 400G MEASURES APPROXIMATELY 70MM WIDE, 140MM LONG, 90MM DEEP. THE CRUST IS GOLDEN BROWN. COMMERCIAL VERSIONS OFTEN USE WHITE FLOUR AND SUGAR, GIVING A PALE GOLD-BEIGE CRUMB SPECKLED WITH FRUIT. SOFT BROWN SUGAR GIVES A DARKER CRUMB. THE OUTSIDE OF THE LOAF IS STICKY WITH A TRANSPARENT SUGAR GLAZE. FLAVOUR: SLIGHTLY SWEET AND SPICED.

HISTORY:

The name in Welsh means speckled bread. It shares a common origin with other British spiced and fruited loaves. No early references have been located; oral tradition shows that such breads, known as *teisen dorth* in South Wales and *bara brith* in the north have been known since the early twentieth century (Tibbott, 1976). Originally they were based on leftover

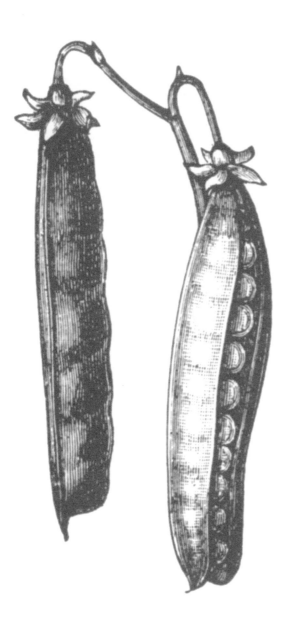

'Part of the secret of success in life is to eat what you like and let the food fight it out inside.'

Mark Twain

bread dough, but eventually a separate recipe evolved. The North Wales name became more general in the middle of the century, and is now used almost exclusively.

TECHNIQUE:
There are many recipes for this bread, which should be yeast-raised, although chemical agents are frequently substituted. At first, lard was the accepted shortening and whey the liquid. Butter or margarine and milk are now used. Otherwise, the essentials are a light enrichment of butter and sugar, dried fruit and candied peel, and a flavouring of mixed sweet spices. Eggs are sometimes, but not always, included. After fermentation, shaping and proof, it is baked at 210°C for 60 minutes. Most commercial bakers produce the bread.

REGION OF PRODUCTION:
WALES.

Bara Planc

DESCRIPTION:
A THICK, GRIDDLE-BAKED DISC, FLATTENED TOP AND BOTTOM, SLIGHTLY BOWED AT THE SIDES, IN 2 SIZES, 100MM DIAMETER, 40MM THICK OR 140MM DIAMETER, 60MM THICK. WEIGHT: 300G (SMALL), 450G (LARGE). COLOUR AND TEXTURE: BROWN ON TOP AND BOTTOM, DARKER IN IRREGULAR PATCHES, DEEP CREASES SHOWING WHERE THE DOUGH HAS BEEN ROUGHLY PRESSED TOGETHER, A WHITE BAND AROUND THE MIDDLE; WHEN CUT, THE SECTION SHOWS A CRUMB WHICH IS RELATIVELY OPEN IMMEDIATELY INSIDE THE CRUST, BUT BECOMES PROGRESSIVELY CLOSER TOWARDS THE MIDDLE; DENSE-TEXTURED BREAD, CONTAINING VERY LITTLE SALT; THE CRUST IS CHEWY.

HISTORY:
The Welsh means griddle-bread. How long these thick, round loaves have been made in the industrial towns along the Glamorgan coast is unknown. This is an area of heavy industry, which had a large and impoverished working population. Enclosed ovens were uncommon in the houses of the poor until the mid-twentieth century. Griddle baking was the usual method for cooking all sorts of breads, cakes and pastries. It is impossible to say if they are an evolution of an older, rural bread (possibly including barley or oats), or a type which developed separately when cheap roller-milled wheat flour became available. Recipes are often quoted in collections, such as *Farmhouse Fare* (1963). Jan Whitehouse, whose family have been bakers in Swansea for more than 100 years, states they have been made for as long as any present-day inhabitants can remember.

TECHNIQUE:
The recipe is very plain, using white flour, a little lard, milk and water. The raising agent is yeast. Once mixed and risen, the dough is knocked back and moulded roughly into a large cake. The thickness should be no more than 40–60mm. After a final proof of 15 minutes, the dough is placed on a 'planc' (round cast-iron griddle) over a clear fire. The planc should not be too hot or the bread will scorch. It is cooked for 20 minutes on each side, then turned, and cooked for another 20 minutes. Fixed gas-fired or electric griddles are now used.

REGION OF PRODUCTION:
SOUTH WALES.

Crusty Swansea

DESCRIPTION:

A LARGE ROUND OR OVAL LOAF, SLASHED ACROSS THE TOP WITH 3 DIAGONAL CUTS; 200MM DIAMETER, 120–130MM HIGH. WEIGHT: ABOUT 800G. COLOUR AND TEXTURE: A THICK, SLIGHTLY TOUGH, WELL-BAKED CRUST, GOLD TO DARK BROWN, WITH A ROUGH, IRREGULAR SURFACE; WHITE CRUMB, FAIRLY CLOSE TEXTURED WITH A FEW IRREGULAR LARGE HOLES.

HISTORY:

According to Christine Gough, who bakes bread in a wood-fired bakehouse at the National Folk Museum, the name 'Swansea' is recognized generally in South Wales for this type of bread. Jan Whitehouse, whose family have been bakers in South Wales for 100 years, states they are simply called 'crusty' loaves in nearby Llanelli. Little is known about their history beyond an oral tradition of long usage. Their shape is closely related to the bloomer loaf, a similar but more elongated crusty, oven-bottom loaf with about eight diagonal cuts on top made in much of southern England. Even the history of this is not well documented. The word may derive from the 'bloom' on the surface or the sheen or lustre of very good quality crumb, or it may relate to the Old English word for ingot (which shape it resembles).

TECHNIQUE:

Although one baker at the Welsh National Folk Museum makes Swanseas according to old-fashioned methods of setting a yeast sponge, the majority are made from conventional white bread dough. After fermentation, the loaves are shaped into ovals, the joins of any folds left on the underside. The cuts in the top crust are made after final proof.

REGION OF PRODUCTION:

SOUTH WALES.

Welsh Cake

DESCRIPTION:

A GRIDDLE-BREAD, CIRCULAR, WITH DECKLE EDGES; ABOUT 50–70MM DIAMETER, 10–15MM DEEP. WEIGHT: 40–50G. COLOUR: MOTTLED GOLD BROWN AND CREAM IN LARGE PATCHES, WITH DRIED FRUIT SHOWING THROUGH THE CRUST. FLAVOUR AND TEXTURE: CLOSE SOFT TEXTURE, RICH FLAVOUR.

HISTORY:

Pice ar y maen (Welsh for 'cakes on the stone', where they are also known as *cacennau cri*) have become so well known outside their native area that they are simply termed Welsh cakes. They are a Welsh variant on the theme of flat griddle-breads and scones found throughout western and northern Britain. The recipe now used, leavened with baking powder, cannot date much before the mid-nineteenth century when this ingredient was first introduced. They were known in Glamorgan at the end of that century and they were baked either on a griddle or in a Dutch oven, a three-sided tin oven that was placed directly before the flames of the kitchen fire (Tibbott, 1976). They are still very popular and widely made in their native area. They are cooked on special griddles every day, in full view of the public, by many stallholders in the urban markets of South Wales.

Commercial cakes that use only lard are not as good as those using butter (Freeman, 1980).

Cooking on a griddle makes the cakes drier than if they are cooked under a grill or in a Dutch oven. Welsh cakes are very like a Glamorgan variety known as round cakes, and they are not unlike scones, more widely known in the British Isles. They are best eaten hot from the griddle, sprinkled with sugar, or toasted and spread with butter, jam or honey. They are popular for afternoon tea.

TECHNIQUE:

Recipes generally call for flour and fat in the proportions 2:1, with a slightly lower ratio of sugar than fat. A combination of lard and butter or lard and margarine is used. A little sweet spice (cinnamon, allspice and nutmeg) or lemon may be used as a flavouring. The dry ingredients (including leavening) are mixed together, the fat is rubbed in and the mixture is made into a soft dough with egg. Some recipes call for milk. The dough is rolled 5mm thick and cut into rounds with a biscuit cutter. They are cooked on a heated griddle, lightly greased, for 4 minutes each side.

REGION OF PRODUCTION:
WALES, SOUTH WALES.

Welsh Pancake

DESCRIPTION:

THERE ARE MANY VARIETIES; IN SWANSEA, CIRCULAR PANCAKES ARE ROLLED INTO A LONG CIGAR SHAPE; ELSEWHERE, THEY ARE LEFT FLAT; THE EDGES ARE IRREGULAR. PANCAKES MADE IN SWANSEA ARE 120MM DIAMETER AND 7–8MM THICK IN THE MIDDLE, THINNING SLIGHTLY TOWARDS THE EDGES. FLAT PANCAKES ARE 120–170MM DIAMETER. A PANCAKE OF 120MM DIAMETER WEIGHS ABOUT 50G; ONE OF 170MM IS 100–125G. COLOUR: THE PROPORTION OF WHITE, VERY LIGHTLY COOKED BATTER TO PALE GOLD PATCHES, WHERE THE PANCAKE HAS TOUCHED THE GRIDDLE, IS VARIABLE. IN SWANSEA, WHITE PREDOMINATES, AND THE PANCAKES LOOK SMOOTH; FURTHER WEST THEY ARE AN EVEN BROWN AND THE SURFACE IS FULL OF TINY HOLES. WHEN CURRANTS ARE ADDED, THEY ARE INVARIABLY IN A TIGHT CLUSTER IN THE CENTRE OF THE PANCAKE. FLAVOUR AND TEXTURE: VERY LIGHTLY SWEETENED, WITH A SLIGHTLY EGGY FLAVOUR. SOMETIMES LEMON IS ADDED.

HISTORY:

The Celtic cultures of Brittany and Wales have the pancake in common. Wales has long been a stronghold of pancakes – offered for sale in bakeries or on market stalls. Minwel Tibbott (1986) writes that at the beginning of twentieth century, 'the most common luxury item offered for afternoon tea throughout the country would be pancakes or drop scones. The hostess would proceed to bake them after the arrival of an unexpected guest, and they would be served warm, spread liberally with farm butter and homemade jam.' Pancakes were easily made and could be quickly produced. The use of buttermilk for the batter is characteristic, as is a leavening of bicarbonate of soda and vinegar. In this form, the recipe cannot date back beyond the first half of the nineteenth century, when baking soda was first introduced. However, the concept is probably much older. Early recipes contain a high proportion of eggs, although in urban industrial areas, this would have made pancakes into a luxury food.

Each district has its own particular name for the pancake, including: *cramwythen*

(Carmarthen/Glamorgan); *crempog* (North Wales); *ffroesen* (Glamorgan); *poncagen* (Pembrokeshire); *pancoesen* (Carmarthen/Cardiganshire). The habit of rolling them up now found in Swansea is a revival of an old custom, other bakers leave pancakes flat. There are many recipes, varying in richness. Welsh pancakes have long been used for savoury foods as well as sweet. For serving, plain pancakes are stacked in layers with a filling of fish or cheese in between, and heated. The stack is cut in quarters to give 4 helpings. Pancakes containing currants are often served with butter and sugar.

TECHNIQUE:

Recipes vary greatly. Milk is the most popular liquid for mixing; buttermilk was traditional. Cream is sometimes cited for special occasions, but it is unlikely that pancakes made with this would be found on sale. One maker, Enfys Marks, uses her grandmother's recipe and finds the use of very fresh milk makes a great difference to the finished result. Margarine often replaces butter in pancakes made for commercial sale. Flour and salt are mixed together in a suitable bowl, melted butter is added, followed by eggs and milk or buttermilk. The mixture is well beaten to make a thin batter, and then left to stand an hour. Some recipes call for a leavening of a little bicarbonate of soda, plus lemon juice or vinegar to be added just before the pancakes are cooked. The batter is beaten again before use. It is cooked in a frying pan or on a griddle until lightly browned on one side, then turned. If currants are added, they are sprinkled on the upper side before turning.

REGION OF PRODUCTION:

WALES.

Welsh Plate Cake

DESCRIPTION:

A FLAT CAKE 120MM DIAMETER, 20–30MM THICK. OBLONG CAKES HAVE ALSO BEEN RECORDED. WEIGHT: ABOUT 450G. COLOUR: PALE GOLD EXTERIOR, PALE YELLOW INTERIOR, SPECKLED WITH DRIED FRUIT. FLAVOUR AND TEXTURE: SWEET, WITH A CRUNCHY SURFACE, A MOIST TEXTURE.

HISTORY:

Teisen lap is a Welsh fruit cake. The name means moist cake. Since it was neither friable nor thirst-provoking, it was useful as work-food for coalminers in South Wales (Tibbott, 1976). The recipes must have originally developed from the same sources as other British fruit cakes but there is one very important difference which influenced the final form. It was baked in front of an open fire rather than in an enclosed oven. Until quite recently, *teisen lap* made in Welsh homes was baked in the bottom of a Dutch oven (a 3-sided tin oven that was placed directly before the flames of the kitchen fire), the mixture being either spread on a plate or placed in the shallow oblong pan which forms the base of this utensil. The cake cooked slowly, producing a crunchy surface, now mimicked by sprinkling with sugar and baking in a hot oven. It is possible that 'slab cakes' – wide, shallow, oblong cakes based on a plain sponge mixture containing fat and dried fruit – had their origins in this habit.

TECHNIQUE:

Several recipes exist. They are generally plain with dried fruit. Older versions were mixed with buttermilk; a recipe based on sour cream is also cited by Minwel Tibbott (1976). The version now commonly made calls for flour, butter and sugar in the proportions 4:1:1. Where spices are added, nutmeg is a favourite. The cake is leavened with baking powder.

REGION OF PRODUCTION:
SOUTH WALES.

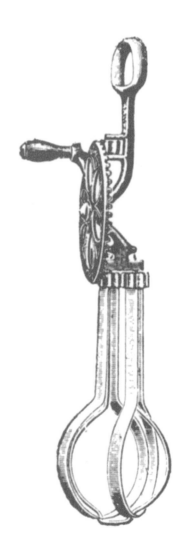

***

Also produced in Wales
CHEVIOT SHEEP (P. 308)
FAGGOT (P. 146)
PIKELET (P. 174)

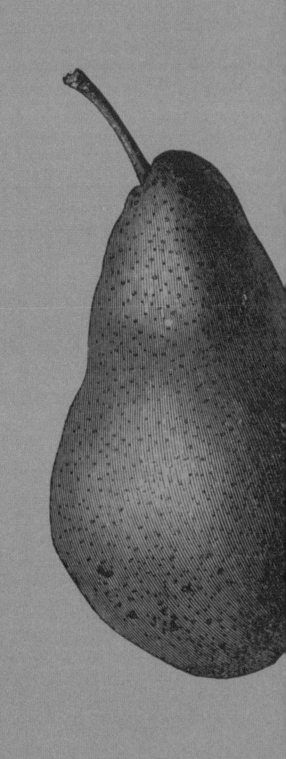

Isle of Man

Kipper (Manx)

DESCRIPTION:

COLD-SMOKED MANX KIPPERS ARE ABOUT 22CM INCLUDING HEAD AND TAIL, WEIGHING APPROXIMATELY 120G. COLOUR: THE SKIN IS DARK GREY BROWN ON THE BACK, FADING TO SILVER ON THE BELLY, WITH A DISTINCTLY GOLD TINGE; THE FLESH IS DARK GOLDEN BROWN. FLAVOUR: MILDLY FISHY, MELLOW, WITH SALT MORE DOMINANT THAN SMOKE; QUITE OILY.

HISTORY:

The Isle of Man is a good base from which to catch herrings. There is an island tradition of salting and curing them to make either barrelled salt herring, or red herrings. These were much exported in the past. Kippered herring, made to the cure developed by John Woodger from Northumberland, first became popular in the 1840s and the process must have spread rapidly to other parts of the country. Certainly, it was well known by the time the company of George Devereaux was established in 1884. John Curtis, the other company producing Manx kippers, has also been in existence for about 100 years. Manx kippers are the traditional product. Isle of Man kippers, whilst made on the island, are not the same. They use dyes, illegal on Manx kippers.

TECHNIQUE:

The cure used for kippers on the Isle of Man is similar to that used elsewhere; the herring are prepared by splitting and cleaning; they are then brined for a short time, hung on tenterhooks and smoked.

There are several points which make Manx kippers unique. Firstly, they are always undyed. Secondly, the excellence of the herring, which have a fat content and composition which render them highly suitable for this type of cure; fish caught early in the season – the Manx season is from June to August – are best, and those from Irish boats, which fish in pairs with 1 net between 2 boats, are preferred, as the fish landed by these are in excellent condition with no bruising. Finally, there is the skill and attention given to them during the smoking. Peter Canipa, who smokes fish for Devereaux and Son, uses a smoke temperature higher than that used elsewhere and remarks that timing is crucial to quality. This depends on the fishes' size and oil content and ambient temperature.

REGION OF PRODUCTION:

ISLE OF MAN.

COMPARE WITH:

Kipper (Craster) and Kipper (Whitby), North-East England (pp. 277–9); Kipper (Scottish Cure), Scotland (p. 333).

Scallop (Isle Of Man)

DESCRIPTION:

GREAT OR KING SCALLOP (PECTEN MAXIMUS): FLAT BOTTOM SHELL AND A CONCAVE UPPER SHELL; MUSCLE DIAMETER APPROXIMATELY 50MM; MINIMUM LEGAL CARAPACE SIZE

100MM. QUEEN SCALLOP (*CHLAMYS OPERCULARIA*): TOP AND BOTTOM SHELLS BOTH CON-
CAVE; MUSCLE DIAMETER APPROXIMATELY 30MM. PRINCESS SCALLOP (AN IMMATURE
QUEEN): MUSCLE DIAMETER APPROXIMATELY 10MM. THE GREAT SCALLOP AND THE QUEEN
HAVE BEIGE SHELLS, AND A CREAM OR WHITE MUSCLE SURROUNDED BY AN ORANGE ROE.
THE PRINCESS SCALLOP HAS A REDDISH-PINK SHELL AND A CREAM OR WHITE MUSCLE BUT
THE ROE, BECAUSE OF ITS AGE, HAS NOT DEVELOPED. THEY HAVE A DISTINCTIVE AND SUB-
TLE SEA-FLAVOUR FROM RICH FEEDING IN UNPOLLUTED NORTHERN WATERS.

HISTORY:

Dr Larch Garrad, of Manx National Heritage, observes that scallop shells have been
found on the Isle of Man in archaeological deposits 2–3,000 years old, as well as in early
medieval contexts. The extent to which they were used for food in the past is unknown, as
they are difficult to fish without the aid of modern equipment. However, local people have
a long-standing tradition of gathering food from the shore after storms, and certain pools
are known for sometimes yielding scallops after high seas. The smaller queenies are also
exposed at the ebb of very low spring tides and can be taken from boats. By the end of the
nineteenth century, dredges from the Isle of Man capable of fishing scallops were being
exhibited at international fishing exhibitions.

According to Dr A.R. Brand at the Port Erin Marine Laboratory, a fishery intended pure-
ly for scallops was founded on the Isle of Man in the 1930s. This rapidly became the most
valuable fishery on the island and, with the exception of a few years in the 1970s when the
herring yielded some excellent catches, has remained so.

An important dredged- and dived-scallop industry arose in the 1950s and 1960s, harvesting from natural West-coast beds. The scallops were exported to the British mainland and
sold in Billingsgate. Research into scallop farming began on the Isle of Man in the early 1970s
and, although no farming takes place there, the methods developed have been successfully
applied off the West coast of Scotland, where the popularity of the farmed scallop has grown,
partly due to its guarantee of quality. Scallops from natural beds can live for up to 20 years,
when the texture of their muscle becomes tough.

TECHNIQUE:

In the wild, scallops spend most of their life on the sea bed and spawn many millions of eggs
each year. These go through a free-swimming stage, during which time they are carried
around on currents and tidal streams. After 3 or 4 weeks they settle on a suitable substrate
such as seaweed. The muddy gravel sea bed round the Isle of Man provides suitable conditions
and contains substantial natural scallop beds. The shellfish feed on phyto-plankton, and tidal
currents provide some water movement, a necessity for scallops. They are harvested by dredging. The daily catch is processed on the island by shelling and cleaning; a small proportion is
frozen, but most are exported, fresh and chilled, by air.

REGION OF PRODUCTION:
ISLE OF MAN.

COMPARE WITH:
Scallop, Scotland on p. 336.

Manx Loghtan Sheep

DESCRIPTION:

DRESSED CARCASS WEIGHT FOR A 6-MONTH LOWLAND LAMB: ABOUT 18KG. THE LEAN MEAT IS DARK, CLOSE-GRAINED, WITH A VERY GOOD FLAVOUR.

HISTORY:

Manx Loghtans are visually arresting: they have a mouse brown coat (*loaghton* in Manx) and, whilst some are 2-horned, they are noted for the fact that many grow 4 horns. The latter characteristic is shared with Hebridean (St Kilda) sheep from Scotland, and Jacob's sheep, an ornamental parkland breed widely distributed in Britain. Manx Loghtans have close affinities with Icelandic and Scandinavian strains and may originate from stock brought to Britain by the Vikings (Hall & Clutton-Brock, 1989). For centuries they were the only sheep on the Isle of Man, providing both meat and wool. They went into decline with the arrival of improved breeds from the British mainland in the early nineteenth century.

Together with the other 4-horned and so-called primitive sheep, the Manx Loghtans really came to public attention in 1913 when a display was organized for an agricultural show by John Elwes. At this time, the breed was almost extinct, but a few people on the Isle of Man were sufficiently enthusiastic to conserve flocks. The formation of the Rare Breeds Survival Trust about 35 years ago led to a renewed interest. Several flocks were established on the mainland, and one was established on the Calf of Man, an almost uninhabited island at the southern end of the Isle, as a conservation measure against outbreak of disease amongst the main flocks.

TECHNIQUE:

The rolling hills of the Isle of Man are in a mild maritime climate with no great extremes of temperature, though very windy. The native flora is grass and heather, and the land generally well drained. The breed has developed to be hardy, grazing the unimproved grass of the higher land. It requires little or no supplementary feeding except before lambing. The ewes are good mothers and prolific milkers. Lambs are raised outdoors with little human intervention. The breed is slow maturing and does not run to fat. As a meat sheep, there is some interest in crossing it with lowland terminal sires to give commercial lamb for the mass market. There is also interest in marketing it as a distinct breed, both on the Island and the mainland. However, in the past, there has been some prejudice against the sheep on the Isle of Man, which still works against effective marketing. Older people display an irrational distaste for the meat; abattoirs dislike the carcasses because they do not conform to official grading and, due to legislation from last century, butchers on the Isle of Man are not allowed to identify the meat as coming from Manx Loghtans. The breed society is working to overcome these problems and there is now some interest in the sheep as a local speciality.

PRODUCTION:

Some pure-bred Manx Loghtan meat reaches the market every year, but the quantity is not great, perhaps a few hundred lambs on the Isle of Man. Since the inauguration of a pedigree registration scheme, numbers have started to recover, and there are a few large flocks kept on the Isle of Man, including 3 owned by the Manx Museum. About 80 breeders in mainland Britain keep examples of the sheep.

REGION OF PRODUCTION:

ISLE OF MAN.

North West England

Damson

DESCRIPTION:

DIMENSIONS: 3CM LONG. WEIGHT: 6–8G. FORM: SMALL TEAR-SHAPED FRUIT. COLOUR: PURPLE-BLACK SKIN WITH POWDER BLUE BLOOM, YELLOW-GREEN FLESH. FLAVOUR: SWEET-SHARP, AROMATIC.

HISTORY:

The name damson indicates the fruit of *Prunus institia*, native to Britain (Roach, 1985). The tree occurs in a wild form known as the bullace; the cultivated form, or damson, may have taken its name from Damascus, in Syria. There are English literary references to damsons from the fifteenth century onwards; they have always been popular in this country.

They are valued in the West Midlands and the North-West. In both they were grown partly as a fruit crop and partly for use as a dye in the woollen industry. In the North-West, the southern Lake District, especially the Lythe Valley, contains many old orchards of the trees. They were first planted here in large numbers in the 1850s. For a while they flourished, and much of the crop was sent to the cloth-weaving towns of Yorkshire, but picking became uneconomic, and the orchards were neglected or grubbed up. A few were replanted in the 1950s.

The *Catalogue of Plums at the National Fruit Trials* (1978) records that a variety of damson known as Blue Violet, local to Westmoreland, was received in 1932. Westmoreland Damson is also a local name for another variety, more widespread in Britain, the prune damson, itself recorded at the Trials in 1950. Damsons from the southern Lake District are sometimes called Witherslack damsons after the village of that name (Mabey, 1978). Other names that have been recorded are Kendal Damsons, Westmoreland Prunes, and Lythe Valley Damsons. Recipes for damsons include jams and cheeses; the fruit is also used to flavour beer and gin.

TECHNIQUE:

Cumbria contains several sub-regions, including the Lake District; the Lythe Valley drains the south-eastern part of this. Climate is moderated by proximity to the sea to give high rainfall and relative warmth at sea-level. The valleys provide shelter for the trees, many of which are planted in alkaline soils, on steep marginal farmland, with south-eastern aspect.

Little systematic attention has been given in recent years to the orcharding of damsons in this area and many trees are now very old. The habit of planting them as hedgerow trees, or in orchards on hillsides, makes them difficult and time-consuming to harvest. As the orchards have become neglected, trees have weakened and blown down, leaving those still standing more exposed. For replanting, stock is usually obtained by taking suckers from old trees. Recently, at the instance of the Countryside Commission, interest in damsons as a crop in the area has revived and some orchards have been replanted with appropriate varieties, both for the sake of the crop and for their value as a feature of the landscape, especially in spring when the trees are in blossom. The fruit are sold by the 'score' (20 lb, 9.1kg) in local markets and from the roadside during the season.

REGION OF PRODUCTION:

NORTH WEST ENGLAND, CUMBRIA.

Black Peas

DESCRIPTION:

SOLD DRIED, LOOSE FROM ANIMAL FEED VENDORS, OR IN PACKS FROM GROCERS AND SUPER-
MARKETS; OR OFFERED COOKED IN PORTIONS OF ABOUT 75–100G. COLOUR: DEEP GREY-
BLACK. FLAVOUR: EARTHY, COOKED-BEANS, USUALLY EATEN HEAVILY SEASONED WITH VINE-
GAR.

HISTORY:

Pulses, formerly a staple of the British diet, have lingered on, especially in Lancashire where black peas, *Cajanus cajan*, are sold in the markets of the industrial towns to the north and east of Manchester. Oral tradition states that this has been the case for as long as anyone can remember; the dish is well-known locally, but is unknown in southern Britain.

A similar custom was recorded in the North East until the early years of the last century. It now appears extinct. The habit of consuming pigeon peas on Carling Sunday (the fifth in Lent) has been reported for many years, at least since the Tudor period (*OED*). Some link name and custom to Northumberland alone, but it was known throughout northern England. The peas were par-cooked in water and finished in lard.

Everywhere the peas are eaten, they are said to have first arrived as cargo on a ship driven ashore in a storm. Peter Brears (1987), in a discussion of Carling peas, remarks that this is probably apocryphal, as the peas are known far inland and the legend is recounted in several places. However, the pigeon peas used for this dish are a tropical crop, from Africa or the West Indies. There may be other, more tenuous links with seafaring, as brown beans seasoned with vinegar and syrup and served with fried salt pork are known as a Lenten dish in Sweden (ICA, 1971). The late Roy Shipperbottom, an expert on Lancashire food, remarks that black peas were served at fairs, and that Mrs Abbott's 'Black Pea Saloon (Quality, Cleanliness and Civility)' was a feature of Bolton New Year Fair.

Their consumption seems to be most persistent in areas where the pattern of urban working-class life led to a demand for ready-cooked food. Eunice Schofield (1975) mentions cooked peas as takeaway food in Jarrow, and black peas in Blackburn. According to Julia Smith (1989), Carling peas were placed on the bar in pubs in Driffield (East Yorkshire) during the early part of Lent. They were prepared with extra salt to encourage thirst. As is perhaps apt for a foodstuff with so regional a pattern of affection, it goes under several names: parched peas (north Lancashire), pigeon peas, grey peas, and carlins or carlings (Northumberland, Durham, North Yorkshire).

TECHNIQUE:

Grey peas is a misnomer; what is actually required is the small brown pigeon pea. These can be found pre-packed in the markets and supermarkets of Lancashire as 'Black Peas', complete with a small tablet of bicarbonate of soda. They are bought, either by housewives to cook at home, or by vendors who sell them as a hot dish in the market halls. They are soaked for 24 hours in cold water with bicarbonate of soda added. The peas are boiled in the soaking water until they are deemed cooked. According to Samantha Saunders, a vendor of black peas, this judgement varies from area to area. In some towns, they are preferred whole, just soft when the skins have started to loosen, and are eaten cold. In others, they are cooked to a mush. Vendors keep the peas hot in the liquor or water in which they are cooked and sell them as portions in disposables, which have replaced the thick pottery cup once used. The customer adds vinegar. Carling peas were made by draining the cooked peas and finished by 'parching' them in large tins of lard seasoned with salt and pepper.

REGION OF PRODUCTION:
NORTH WEST ENGLAND.

Cheshire Cheese

DESCRIPTION:

PRESSED COW'S MILK CHEESE. WHITE CHESHIRE AND RED CHESHIRE ARE ESSENTIALLY THE SAME CHEESE, EXCEPT THAT ANNATTO IS ADDED TO THE LATTER. SOME IS ALLOWED TO DEVELOP BLUE MOULD, IN WHICH CASE IT IS KNOWN AS BLUE CHESHIRE. BLUE SHROPSHIRE, A CHEESE CREATED IN THE LATE 1970S, IS OF THE SAME TYPE. CHESHIRE CHEESE IS PRODUCED IN CYLINDERS; THE TRADITIONAL SIZE WAS ABOUT 22CM DIAMETER BY 26CM HIGH, BUT WEIGHTS NOW RANGE FROM 500G TO 25KG. BLOCK CHESHIRE IS ALSO EXTENSIVELY PRODUCED. COLOUR: WHITE CHESHIRE IS A VERY PALE CREAM COLOUR; THE 'RED' IS A PALE PINKY-ORANGE; THE BLUE IS A PALE CREAMY ORANGE WITH HEAVY BLUE-GREY VEINING. FLAVOUR: BOTH WHITE AND RED ARE SALTY, CRUMBLY AND MOIST; THE BLUE DEVELOPS A SHARPER FLAVOUR, WITH A NUTTY AFTERTASTE.

HISTORY:

Cheshire is one of a family of cheeses from west Cheshire and the bordering parts of Wales and Shropshire. One factor which contributed to its distinctiveness is that the area is located on salt-bearing rock strata. This is said to lend a special flavour to the milk of the cattle which graze there. The mild, damp climate is ideal for pasture, in turn promoting high milk yields.

Cheese-making in this area has a long history. Rance (1982) speculates that cheese was made in the North-West prior to the Roman conquest, and that cow's milk was used from an early date. He also notes that it is mentioned in the Domesday Book (1087). There are many early references, from the late sixteenth and early seventeenth centuries, to cheese from this specific region (*OED*).

The basic craft method used for making Cheshire was established by the eighteenth century. A complex finishing process was followed, including repeated skewerings, pressings, turnings, and rebandaging in progressively finer grades of cloth, plus external salting. Finally, the cheeses were stored in a room designed to maintain a high ambient temperature with a carpeting of sedge, hay or straw. Production of Cheshire flourished. Some farmers used a cooperative system, contributing milk to a communal dairy, a custom which continued until the 1950s. Cheese fairs were held in several major towns. Construction of canals encouraged the export of Cheshire to other parts of the country, notably the Midlands and Yorkshire as well as the large cities closer to home, Liverpool and Manchester.

During the late 1800s, competition for farmhouse cheeses came from industrial producers. The supply of expanding markets with raw milk also diverted their attention away from cheese. Farmhouse production continued, but fell throughout the first half of the last century. During 1939–45 the Ministry of Food encouraged a harder, drier version of the cheese, and the number of farmhouse makers declined still further. However, the modern method for making cylindrical farmhouse Cheshire is essentially that used in the eighteenth century. Only the finishing has changed, many now dipping their cheeses in wax after bandaging. Block versions are also now available.

The phenomenon of blue veining in Cheshire was known locally as 'green fade'. It was discouraged in previous centuries, although Rance (1982) observes that the moist, loose-textured curd and the finishing process must both have promoted mould growth. However, green-fade cheeses were thrown away, or kept for medicinal use, to be applied externally to wounds and sores. In the late nineteenth and early twentieth centuries, green fades became more widely appreciated. Research was undertaken to investigate which cheeses blued the best. In the 1960s a recipe was developed with the explicit aim of producing blue Cheshire.

TECHNIQUE:
Craft method: details vary a little depending on the fat content of the milk, and whether a young or long-keeping cheese is desired. The milk is brought to 30°C. Specially cultured starter is added, typically 1.5–2 per cent, although up to 5 per cent may be added by some. If a red Cheshire is wanted, annatto is added. After 60–90 minutes rennet is added, and the surface stirred gently to prevent the fat rising. The curd is cut 3 ways to give particles the size of haricot beans. The temperature is raised gradually to 32°C, whilst the curd is stirred; this takes about 45 minutes. The curd is allowed to settle and the whey drained off. The curd is cut into blocks which are turned to the edge of the vat, leaving a central draining channel. When the acidity reaches the correct level, the blocks are broken in half and turned by hand; this process is repeated several times over a period of about 90 minutes. Salt is sprinkled over (about 1kg salt to 45kg curd). The curd becomes firm and dry and is milled when the acidity level is deemed correct; this depends on the final use of the cheese; an early-ripening cheese is milled at a higher acidity than one intended for long keeping. It is filled into moulds and pressed well down to consolidate, turned out again into coarse cloths, returned to the mould, and removed to a draining floor. The cheeses remain overnight, at 18°C, without any pressure being applied. Next day they are turned into clean smooth cloths. The cheeses are put under gradually increasing pressure for about 24 hours, then they are capped, bandaged and coated – traditionally with a flour paste, but now with either an edible cellulose paste or wax. They are ripened at 12°C, at a humidity of 85 per cent, turned every day. They are matured for 6–10 weeks.

Block farmhouse Cheshire is made from unpasteurized milk by the same method, but differences are imposed by the shape and the fact that the cheese will be matured and stored in plastic film. A drier curd is required, the cheese is pressed immediately after moulding, at a higher and more constant pressure than that used for farmhouse cheeses. Maturing is carried out at a lower temperature.

Blue Cheshire is now deliberately produced using a slightly more acid curd which is cut less finely and given a lighter pressure.

REGION OF PRODUCTION:
NORTH WEST ENGLAND.

Cumberland Rum Butter

DESCRIPTION:

A FLAVOURED BUTTER, SOLD IN QUANTITIES OF 110 OR 220G. COLOUR: A CREAM-YELLOW BROWN, DEPENDING ON THE TYPE OF SUGAR USED. FLAVOUR: SPICY, SWEET, ALCOHOLIC.

HISTORY:

Rum butter has been associated with Cumberland since at least the late nineteenth century, when Joseph Wright, collecting information for his *Dialect Dictionary*, noted the association of the dish with this region and several customs linked with it. Rum butter was 'eaten by wives during their confinement; and is offered to, and is expected to be partaken of, by visitors. The lady who first cuts into the bowl is predicted to require a similar compliment.' Coins for the baby were collected in the empty bowl. The *Oxford English Dictionary* gives the first instance of rum butter in print as Mrs A.B. Marshall's *Cookery Book* (1887). The recipe probably pre-dates this, as the ingredients are all traditional to Lake District cookery. It is also known in Cumbria as hard sauce. Today a brandy-flavoured version is also made.

TECHNIQUE:

Recipe and method are simple and vary only in the scale of operation from domestic kitchen to commercial confectioners. Unsalted butter is whipped to a cream, mixed with soft brown sugar and rum, and spiced to taste. The mixture is chilled until required. Light-brown or muscovado sugar can be used as taste dictates. The proportions are 1 part butter to 2 parts sugar.

REGION OF PRODUCTION:

NORTH WEST ENGLAND, CUMBRIA.

Lancashire Cheese

DESCRIPTION:

PRESSED COW'S MILK CHEESE, MADE IN 2 SIZES, EITHER WITH A DIAMETER OF ABOUT 30CM, WEIGHING ABOUT 23KG; OR A DIAMETER OF 16CM, ABOUT 12CM HIGH, WEIGHING APPROXIMATELY 5.5KG. THE TRADITIONAL SHAPE IS A TALL CYLINDER. COLOUR: A CLEAR PALE CREAMY YELLOW. FLAVOUR AND TEXTURE: CREAMY IN TEXTURE; THE FLAVOUR VARIES FROM MILD TO STRONG DEPENDING ON AGE.

HISTORY:

Lancashire cheese had become a distinct style, made in the centre of the county, by the eighteenth century. The traditional method is complex and time-consuming, requiring curd made on one day to be divided and mixed with that made the day before or the day after. This allows sufficient acidity to develop. According to *Law's Grocer's Manual* (*c*.1895), portions of curd were sometimes kept for 4 or 5 days. Starter cultures were not introduced until the twentieth century, and were only used in very small proportions.

The first creamery Lancashire appeared early last century. Farmhouse cheese-making survived until 1939–45 but ceased because of regulations about use of milk for specific cheeses. It was revived on a limited scale in the late 1940s. By the early 1970s, a handful of farms were producing in the area traditionally associated with the craft. Lancashire is fragile. Almost all is produced around Preston, Chipping, and Garstang. It does not travel well and there is a strong preference for it on its home ground. The slowness and complexity of the method have

Having long been a devoted fan of Kirkham's excellent Lancashire cheese, I was finally able to arrange a visit to the farm by combining it with an opportunity to see an Albert Irvin exhibition in Lancaster. It therefore didn't take too much persuasion before I was blasting out of London on my motorcycle early one clear but cold spring morning a few years ago.

I pulled up in the farmyard at about 10.30 a.m. having ridden fairly briskly and was met by Graham, the cheesemaker and son of the much-heralded Mrs. Ruth Kirkham. As I removed my helmet, the conversation went something like this:

G: *(in very strong north Lancashire accent)* 'So where did you stop over last night?'
B: 'What do you mean?'
G: 'Where did you sleep last night?'
B: 'At home in London – I left this morning.'
G: 'But where did you *stop over*?'
B: 'I didn't; I came up this morning on the bike!'
G: *(calling excitedly and loudly into the farmhouse)* 'Mum, Mum come out here – Bruce is here' – she rushes out – '...look, I can't believe you're standing here in front of us now and you were in London this morning. How on earth did you get up here – did you fly? It normally takes us best part of a day to get down to London in the wagon.'

There ensued a tour of the farm and the dairy, followed by bacon sandwiches in the farmhouse kitchen and afterwards huge mugs of tea in front of the coal fire in the parlour. Ruth and Graham are naturally warm and convivial folk who would not dream of receiving guests without offering generous helpings of proper Lancashire hospitality.

Truly wonderful people and truly a world-class cheese.

Bruce Poole

CHEF AND PROPRIETOR, CHEZ BRUCE, LONDON

inhibited creamery production. A block version was criticized by Patrick Rance (1982) who commented on the 'recent abuse' of the name: 'The real Lancashire was and remains a semi-soft, loose textured, crumbly, buttery cheese, unlike any other in flavour and resembling only the softer dales cheeses in consistency.' It retains a strong regional identity. It can be eaten alone but is excellent for cooking, especially toasting. 'Leigh Toaster' is an old name. In the past, a sage-flavoured Lancashire was made for Christmas. Beacon Fell Traditional Lancashire Cheese has been awarded PDO status.

TECHNIQUE:

Craft method: starter is used in very small proportions in the evening milk; then morning milk is mixed in and brought to 29°C. The vat is covered and the milk left to ripen for 45 minutes; rennet is added and stirred (to prevent the cream from separating) until coagulation. The vat is covered again and the curd left to firm for 45 minutes. It is cut into pieces the size of small beans and the whey drawn off. Then the curd is cut into blocks and scooped into a drainer in which it is pressed hard enough to release the whey but not so hard that the fat is lost. During this process the curd is broken by hand at intervals and the pressure gradually increased over about 90 minutes. At this stage, the curd can either be stored in the vat to add to the next day's curd or added to that from the previous day; the batch is usually divided in half to preserve continuity. This process, known as the 'two-day curd' method, helps to give Lancashire cheese its unique identity. Occasionally, a three-day curd method is used on the same principles. The curd which is destined for cheese that day is salted (750g to 45kg curd) and milled twice. After the second milling, the curd is put into cloth-lined moulds and left to drain overnight. It is left under light pressure for 2 days, during which the cloths are changed twice, then the cheese is bandaged and returned to the press for another 12 hours. The cheeses are ripened at 13°C, turned daily. Then they are kept for varying lengths of time, according to the strength of flavour desired. These are mild (1–4 weeks), creamy (4–8), tasty (8–16), and strong (16 and over).

An industrial version is sold under the name of Lancashire. However, the step of keeping some curd back, essential to the flavour and texture of the cheese, is omitted. The result is sharp and crumbly and is called 'acid Lancashire'; it dominates the market in volume.

REGION OF PRODUCTION:
NORTH WEST ENGLAND, LANCASHIRE.

Ribblesdale Cheese

DESCRIPTION:
PRESSED, PASTEURIZED-MILK CHEESE. COW'S, GOAT'S AND SHEEP'S VERSIONS ARE MADE – PLAIN, SMOKED, OR WITH GARLIC. WEIGHT (APPROXI-MATE): SHEEP: 1.25KG; GOAT: 1.7KG; COW: 2KG. FORM: FLAT WHEELS. COLOUR: ALMOST WHITE CURD; WAXED. FLAVOUR: FIRM, NUTTY AND MILD.

HISTORY:
Ribblesdale, on the west of the Pennines, probably shared the general cheese-making tradition of the dales. The area has long been known for mild pressed cheeses. Both sheep and cow milk types are recorded.

No documentary evidence for cheese-making in the dale has been found, but artefacts such as a stone weight from a press at Ashes farm (where Ribblesdale cheese is now made) indicate that it was made there in the past. The modern cheese was evolved by the Hill family, using Wensleydale recipes, during the early 1980s.

TECHNIQUE:

The milk for the goat and cow cheeses comes from local suppliers; the sheep's is from further afield. It is curdled with starter, followed by vegetable rennet. The curd is always cut, but the particle size depends on the qualities of the milk from season to season; the curd is then scalded and salted before milling. The curd is filled into a mould and pressed for 48–72 hours. Maturation is 3–12 weeks; the cheeses are wax-dipped early in the maturing process.

REGION OF PRODUCTION:

NORTH WEST ENGLAND, RIBBLESDALE (YORKSHIRE).

Char (Windermere)

DESCRIPTION:

CHAR ARE A FISH SIMILAR TO TROUT, WITH REDDISH SKIN ON THE UNDERSIDE; THEY ARE NOTED FOR THEIR DELICATE FLAVOUR.

HISTORY:

The char, *Salvinus alpinus*, is popularly associated in Britain with Windermere. The salt-water fish is known as the Arctic char, but land-locked populations survive in lakes throughout Europe (left behind as the waters receded after the Ice Age). Its range is limited to deep lakes whose waters maintain a temperature well below 20°C in summer. The *omble chevalier* of Lake Geneva is the most celebrated of these relics. There are few such lakes in England, all in the North-West, but it is also found in some places in Wales, where it is known as *torgoch*, and Scotland. Mrs Beeton (1861) said the 'largest and the best kind is found in the lakes of Westmoreland, and, as it is considered a rarity, it is often potted and preserved.' There are many early references to char as a delicacy: it was sent in barrels to the royal court in the fifteenth century and mentioned in the form of pies in the seventeenth. The pie seems to have been the first method of preserving the food. Surviving correspondence from the Restoration period indicates that giant pies were sent down to London to give exiled Cumbrians a taste of home, or to persuade politicians of the worth of an applicant's cause. However, some time between 1670 and 1680, the experiment was made of substituting pottery for pastry, and the potted char was born. Not many years later, the intrepid traveller, Celia Fiennes, appreciated char potted with sweet spices by an innkeeper in Kendal in 1698 (Wondrausch, 1995).

It is to the custom of potting that the fish probably owe their fame. Potted fish was a store-room constant before rapid transport and refrigeration permitted distribution to all classes in all places. To be stable in any climate, fish needed to be either salted, dried, smoked, pickled or potted. All these methods were pursued in early British kitchens, if for no other reason than to avoid monotony of flavour.

There was a whole industry for potting char. The fish were cleaned, spiced and packed in attractive dishes made especially for the purpose, then covered with butter and cooked. In this form they kept well and were exported to the rest of Britain. The fishery was in decline by

1860, due to overfishing by netsmen. Stocks recovered slightly as a result of official restrictions (ultimately all netting was forbidden), but they have never reached their former heights. Some fish are still taken. Char are now usually grilled for lunch or dinner. Potted char is made only at home or in restaurants and is rarely seen for sale.

TECHNIQUE:
On Windermere, a distinctive method of fishing is employed. It requires a rowing boat to support 2 rods, each of which bears a vertical line weighted with 750g lead weights. At intervals from each vertical line, 6 horizontal lines are trailed, each bearing 6–10 spinners or lures, the theory being that fish swimming at different depths can be caught. The boat has to be kept in constant motion so that the lines trail correctly and do not become tangled.

REGION OF PRODUCTION:
NORTH WEST ENGLAND, WINDERMERE.

Potted Shrimps

DESCRIPTION:
POTTED SHRIMPS ARE COMPOSED OF SHELLED, COOKED SHRIMPS COVERED WITH SPICED BUTTER. THE SHRIMPS HAVE A SALTY, SWEET, SHELLFISH FLAVOUR; THE BUTTER IS FLAVOURED WITH SPICES TO TASTE. MACE IS CUSTOMARY. BENZOIC ACID, OF NEUTRAL FLAVOUR, IS SOMETIMES ADDED AS A PRESERVATIVE.

HISTORY:
The general remarks on potting food given under Potted Crab, East Anglia (p. 122) refer also to potted shrimp. This has been a speciality of Morecambe Bay since at least 1799, the date of foundation of Baxter's, one of the producers of potted shrimps today. There is also a smaller trade in potted shrimps based on East Anglian ports.

TECHNIQUE:
Boiled shelled shrimps are added to spiced butter, allowed to cook briefly, chilled and packed into tubs which are then sealed with a little more butter.

REGION OF PRODUCTION:
NORTH WEST ENGLAND, MORECAMBE (LANCASHIRE).

Shrimp (Morecambe Bay)

DESCRIPTION:
MAXIMUM LENGTH 6CM. COLOUR: TRANSLUCENT REDDISH BROWN WHEN ALIVE, OPAQUE PINK-BROWN WHEN COOKED. FLAVOUR: SALTY, WITH A MILD, FISHY SWEETNESS AND CLOSE TEXTURE.

HISTORY:
Shrimps, *Crangon crangon*, are abundant and easily caught in the shallow waters found on various parts of the British coast. Morecambe Bay is famous for them. David Stocker (1988) notes the existence of a subsistence fishery in the Morecambe Bay area since at least the late eighteenth century. This developed rapidly after the mid-nineteenth century, when a railway was built connecting the town to a wider market for sale of produce and reception of visitors.

Shrimps were a fashionable food at this time, much in demand for afternoon tea. Michael Marshall (1987) observes that distinctive boats, known since the time of the First World War as 'nobbies', are associated with this fishery. There is also a substantial shrimp fishery in parts of the bay which relies on tractors (replacing the horses and carts used in earlier decades). Cedric Robinson is guide to the estuary sands; he is also one of a family which used horses to fish for shrimps. He remarks that the quality of catch has declined in recent years, which he attributes to over-fishing in the 1950s when tractors were first used.

Other important grounds for shrimps are the Solway Firth, the Wash (East Anglia) and the Thames. The shrimps are often known by the name of the town where they are landed, for instance Flookburgh, Parkgate.

At Leigh on Sea (Essex) and in the Thames estuary generally, the shrimp fishery was carried on in boats rather than off the beach. There, too, the ground was treacherous: 'I once worked aboard a shrimper which went on a mud bank and broke up. Every man knew there was only one thing left for him this side of death, and that was to sink slowly in the black ooze of the bank till it covered his head,' reported one old fisherman (Dyson, 1977). The fishermen of Leigh had a secret weapon in their exploitation of the shrimp. Early in Victoria's reign one of their number fitted a boiler in his boat so the catch was cooked on board without the need to set up a shore-based process. Marketing was the more direct and rapid. By 1850, there were 100 boats out of Leigh. The fishery declined thereafter (Dyson, 1977).

TECHNIQUE:

At low tide, well over 200 square kilometres of sand and mud are exposed in Morecambe Bay, deposited by 2 large rivers and several smaller streams which empty into the Irish Sea at this point. Extremely dangerous for those without local knowledge, they include areas of quicksand which change unpredictably, and the tide comes in fast, trapping the unwary. The village of Flookburgh is the centre of shrimp fishing from tractors; the fishermen set out as the tide ebbs, as soon as the water becomes shallow enough to ford the channels and creeks that cross the sands. For shrimping, long nets with a float at the cod end (the closed end which holds the catch) are hung from outriggers on a bogey or wheeled trailer. The whole arrangement is aligned so that the bogey and net are several metres beyond the water-line, even submerged under the water, attached by a long line to the tractor, which is driven slowly along the water-line. Periodically the net is emptied, the catch riddled or sieved and small and immature fish returned to the sea. On return to the shore, the shrimps (or prawns, also caught in this area) are boiled in sea water, riddled again, shelled if necessary, and packed.

REGION OF PRODUCTION:

NORTH WEST ENGLAND, MORECAMBE (LANCASHIRE).

Herdwick Sheep

DESCRIPTION:

NEW-SEASON HERDWICK LAMB HAS A DRESSED CARCASS WEIGHT OF ABOUT 16KG; THE WETHERS (CASTRATED MALES OVER 1 YEAR OLD) YIELD 20–21KG. THE MEAT IS DARK, FINE-GRAINED, TENDER AND VERY LEAN. FLAVOUR IS SLIGHTLY GAMY.

HISTORY:

Herdwick sheep are the traditional breed of the Lake District. They have distinctive white heads and legs; the lambs are born with black wool which greys with age. Their origins are unknown; a link with Scandinavian breeds has been suggested on genetic grounds. Their hardiness was noted in the late eighteenth century. The defining characteristics of the breed were established in the 1840s, but the Herdwick Breeders Association was only founded in 1916. Then, Herdwicks were found over a wide area of Cumbria, but they are now reduced to the central and western parts of the Lake District. The breed was kept alive by the efforts of the writer Beatrix Potter. She bequeathed the farms and flocks she owned in the region to the National Trust, on condition this breed was kept on the land in perpetuity.

TECHNIQUE:

Herdwick sheep are exceptionally hardy. They spend their lives outdoors in the harsh climate of the hill tops, living on the native vegetation which includes lichens, heather and bilberries. It is to this diet that the good flavour is attributed. Little or no supplementary feed is given. The lambs are born in April and May, and reared outdoors by their mothers. The sheep are noted for their homing ability, and have a tendency to return to the patch of land on which they were reared. Although many Herdwicks are killed in the autumn of their first year to produce lamb, a proportion of wethers are over-wintered and slaughtered at 18–24 months to give meat with a stronger, more distinctive flavour. These older sheep are kept on the hill tops until late summer, and then brought to lower levels and finished on grass. The new season's lamb becomes available in September, and continues until about May; the wether mutton is available from late summer until May or June.

REGION OF PRODUCTION:

NORTH WEST ENGLAND, LAKE DISTRICT.

Black Pudding

DESCRIPTION:

BLOOD PUDDING, USUALLY SAUSAGES 35–60MM DIAMETER, 60–150 MM LONG, BUT SOME-TIMES BAKED IN TRAYS 60MM DEEP, OR A SLICING SAUSAGE ABOUT 70MM DIAMETER AND 400MM LONG. THE SMALLER SAUSAGES WEIGH 115–200G. FORM: OPPOSITE ENDS OF THE PUDDING ARE SOMETIMES TIED TOGETHER WITH STRING TO FORM SMALL 'BERRIES', LONGER ONES ARE SHAPED TO FORM HORSESHOES OR LOOPS. COLOUR: THE OUTSIDE IS BLACK-BROWN, AND MAY BE RUBBED WITH VEGETABLE OIL TO GIVE IT A SHEEN; THE CUT PUDDING IS A DARK RED-BROWN, STUDDED WITH SMALL PIECES OF WHITE FAT. FLAVOUR: RICH, SAVOURY AND SPICY.

HISTORY:

The word pudding is of uncertain derivation and its relationship to the French word *boudin* unclear. It seems always to have carried a meaning of a mixture enclosed in a casing of animal gut. The English black pudding and the French *boudin noir* are obviously related but have developed along different lines.

Blood, especially pig's blood, was recorded in combination with cereals by both Homer and Apicius in classical times. It is safe to assume the inhabitants of the British Isles followed similar practices although no direct evidence has survived. Blood puddings are described in cookery books and manuscripts in Britain in the Middle Ages and an explicitly 'black' pudding crops up in the 1500s (*OED*).

They were made all over the country and were certainly consumed by people in all walks of life. The courtesan Harriette Wilson writes in her memoirs (1825) of 2 sisters visiting in Mayfair. 'Oh! by-the-bye, I forgot to order any dinner, and my maid and man are both out … However I can soon manage to get a black pudding broiled. You will not mind running to South Audley-street for a pound of black pudding? Shall you, my dear?'

As blood puddings were universal in Britain, it is not clear why the products of Lancashire should now be so pre-eminent. Stretford and Bury both developed reputations for the excellence of their puddings. There is plenty of evidence for them being made in Bury from at least the 1820s, and the presumption must be that manufacture long antedated that. The Thompson family, who still sell puddings in Bury market, trace their recipe back to 1865, and a shop called Casewell's, demolished in 1968, also claimed a very old recipe, never wittingly changed (Pollard, 1991). The concentration of large numbers of urban poor in the North-West evidently increased the demand for cheap meat products and offal – see the entries for tripe (pp. 221, 225-6). The many Irish immigrants, who had a tradition of such delicacies in their birthplace, must also have acted as stimulus. The difference between Lancashire puddings and those elsewhere revolved round variations in seasoning. *Law's Grocer's Manual* (*c*. 1895) listed seasonings for Cheshire, Shropshire, Staffordshire, Yorkshire and Stretford. Finney's manual for pork butchers (1915) listed the 'far-famed' Bury, Stretford, North Staffordshire, Cheshire and Yorkshire. Stretford and Bury mixtures each contained marjoram, thyme, pennyroyal and mint. Bury added celery seed. Staffordshire enjoyed the taste of pimento and coriander, as did Cheshire – with the extra zing of caraway. Yorkshire's cocktail consisted of thyme, marjoram, savoury and lemon thyme.

Regional distinctions have now lessened or been masked by brand names. Modern black puddings have also been affected by developments in pig breeds and by the requirements of public hygiene. Pigs are now bred to be lean and this has resulted in a diminution of the preferred leaf fat and increased the use of back fat. Considerations of hygiene have affected the use of fresh blood. Pig blood, which has good setting qualities, is now excluded because the pig has been found to urinate on slaughter, contaminating the blood. Tube-handled knives have been developed to overcome this problem, but butchers and health inspectors are suspicious of the technique. Fresh blood used in black puddings is now almost invariably ox blood. Dried blood is commonly used, and is approved by health officials.

Black puddings are eaten at breakfast, and widely served in hotels as part of an English fried breakfast. They are less commonly available at other meals except in the North. They are also popular street food in some places; the Black Pudding Stall sells hot puddings, eaten as people walk around Bury market, and they are also available at fairs and shows in Lancashire. When served as takeaways, they are split and served with mustard.

'Salads and eggs, and lighter fare,
Tune the Italian spark's guitar.
And, if I take Dan Congreve right,
Pudding and beef make Britons fight.'

Matthew Prior, *Alma*

A typical black pudding mixture is 2.8kg groats or pearl barley, 2kg leaf or back fat, 1.5kg barley flour or fine oatmeal, 750g onions, 750g farina or rusk, 90 litres blood, 300g salt, 100g pepper. Seasonings vary according to the locality and are the only real distinguishing feature, beyond the care and skill of individual makers. Seasonings are added as ground or rubbed dried herbs. The barley is tied in a bag and boiled until cooked; whilst it is still hot the seasoning, flour and onion are added. The diced fat (which may be lightly sautéed) is mixed in, the blood added and the mixture thickened with oatmeal. The casings are filled, shaped and tied. Skins made from ox intestines are preferred, as the finished puddings fold into more elegant loops than those made from collagen or synthetic materials. The puddings are simmered in water at a temperature near boiling for 25 minutes; in some districts, a dye is added to give a more intense black. The puddings are then cooled and ready for sale. Although they are already cooked, puddings are always reheated at home by boiling gently, grilling, frying or baking.

REGION OF PRODUCTION:
NORTH WEST ENGLAND.

Cowheel

DESCRIPTION:
COOKED COWHEELS ARE INELEGANT, LONG RAGS OF PALE CREAMY-WHITE SKIN AND GRISTLE, USUALLY WITH THE BONES SHOWING. FLAVOUR: BLAND; IT IS THE GELATINOUS TEXTURE WHICH IS VALUED.

HISTORY:
Calves' feet were delicacies – treated like pigs' trotters or made into a delectable jelly – or they were useful reinforcements to fine cookery, in stews or stocks or sauces. Cowheel was altogether more substantial: strongly gelatinous and containing much gristle, it took a long time to become tender. An early mention in a work by the seventeenth-century physician Thomas Moufet shows it was considered a valuable restorative, but generally it did not figure in dainty cookery books. Martha Bradley (1756) was one of the few who proposed using cowheel at genteel tables, 'though it may have an ordinary sound, [it makes] a very rich and fine soup, few exceeding it'. Apart from occasional appearances in standard Victorian works such as Mrs Beeton (1861), it was probably mostly left to the poor.

It is usually boned before eating; cowheel can be eaten cold with vinegar and salt; or cut up and made into a stew with a white sauce, or added to a richer mixture with beef and vegetables. The historian Robert Roberts (1971) was brought up in a corner shop in the working-class district of Salford (Lancashire). He recalled how 'relishes', or tasty little morsels that were for the father's tea alone, were part of their stock-in-trade: 'brawn, corned beef, boiled mutton … saveloys, tripe, pig's trotters, sausage, cow heels …' The French, by contrast, must sometimes have seemed to have used all their cowheels in *tripes à la mode de Caen*. However, the account in Charles Dickens' *The Old Curiosity Shop* of a supper cooked at the Jolly Sandboys inn may dispel the view that such dishes were French alone: "It's a stew of tripe," said the landlord, smacking his lips, "and cowheel," smacking them again, "and bacon," smacking them once more, "and steak," smacking them for the fourth time, "and peas, cauliflowers, new potatoes, and sparrow-grass, all working together in one delicious gravy."

By the 1940s and 1950s, cowheel was associated with the North Country, where Hartley (1954) remarked it was a favourite stand-by in cattle-market towns, and was made into a jellied brawn. Cowheels were prepared by tripe dressers; Roger Taulbman, president of the National Association of Tripe Dressers says this is because, in the past, a 'tripe set' of offals from a cow consisted of the tripe, feet, reed and weazand or windpipe. Already, in 1762, the advice was, 'take a cowheel from the Tripe House ready drest.' (*OED*)

TECHNIQUE:

Cowheels come from animals over about 8 months old (any younger, and they are classed as calves and have smaller, more delicate feet). After washing, scalding and removal of the hair and hooves, they are cooked by boiling for 3–4 hours, then cooled, drained and bleached.

REGION OF PRODUCTION:

NORTH WEST ENGLAND, LANCASHIRE.

Cumberland Ham

DESCRIPTION:

AN UNSMOKED, CURED HAM FOR COOKING. THE SKIN IS A PALE CREAM-GOLD, THE LEAN A DEEP, TRANSLUCENT RED WHEN RAW AND MID-RED TO PALE PINK WHEN COOKED, THE FAT IS WHITE. THOSE PRODUCED TODAY WEIGH IN THE REGION OF 7.5KG. FLAVOUR AND TEXTURE: A DEEP, PRONOUNCED HAM FLAVOUR, SLIGHTLY SPICY, HEAVILY SALTED, WITH A CLOSE, RELATIVELY DRY TEXTURE.

HISTORY:

Lake District ham has had a good reputation for 200 years. The county of Westmoreland appears to have been noted for it when Nicholson and Burn (1777) wrote of it being cured in the smoke of a peat fire. Mrs Beeton (1861) gave a recipe, 'to cure sweet hams in the Westmoreland way', using a mixture of salt, sugar, bay salt and beer; the ham was to be pickled 1 month and smoked 1 month. Fifty years later, in *Law's Grocer's Manual*, it was Cumberland, not Westmoreland, which was recognized as the regional name associated with hams. Douglas's *Encyclopaedia* also observed that Cumberland was an area noted for ham curing. These hams owed some of their special character to the local pigs. An unimproved breed, they were kept by farmers and cottagers and allowed to scavenge the farmyard and woodland. Their diet was supplemented with household waste, often with plenty of potato peelings. Towards the end of their lives, they were fed on oats and became extremely fat. Killed in winter, the meat was divided up and parts of it, including the hams, reserved for curing at home. The modern Cumberland ham is not well known outside its native region.

TECHNIQUE:

After being separated from the carcass, the hams are dry-salted for 1 month with salt and salt-petre; they are then dried and matured at ambient temperature for 3 months before sale. They are no longer smoked.

REGION OF PRODUCTION:

NORTH WEST ENGLAND, THE LAKE DISTRICT.

Cumberland Sausage

DESCRIPTION:

A LONG, UNLINKED, UNCOOKED FRESH PORK SAUSAGE OF LEAN AND FAT PORK (TYPICALLY 85–95 PER CENT OF THE FILLING), 2–3CM DIAMETER, 2–3 METRES LONG. COLOUR: WHEN UNCOOKED, A PALE GREY-PINK. FLAVOUR: RICH PORK TASTE, GENERALLY HIGHLY SPICED WITH BLACK PEPPER, SPICES AND HERBS.

HISTORY:

Cumberland sausage, whilst belonging to the tradition of British fresh meat sausages, is recognized as a distinct type. Its history is largely undocumented. English fresh sausages are usually divided into links about 12cm long, a habit which has been followed ever since the early seventeenth century (Wilson, 1973). For some reason, this tradition was not pursued in the North West and the sausage was measured and sold by the yard. Until the turn of the twentieth century, Richard Woodall's shop in Waberthwaite had had two drawing pins on the counter for measuring the sausage. All that can be said from information available at present is that this sausage has been made in the region for the last 100 years and is thought typical of the area. Correspondence in *Cumbria Magazine* (1957) mentions Cumberland sausages 'about 30 years ago' and remarks that they were 'bigger and better … with a flavour entirely different to any others'. James Cranston, whose family set up a butcher's business in the area before the First World War, remarks that sausages are invariably made with a high meat content.

TECHNIQUE:

A Cumberland breed of pig did exist but is now extinct. Small butchers in the area use locally reared commercial breeds. The meat is coarsely chopped, originally by hand but now mechanically. The method is similar to other British fresh sausages: a simple mixture of raw chopped pork, seasoning and rusk is used to fill sausage skins, but the meat content is typically very high, up to 98 per cent of the filling and, once filled, the sausage is left as a long piece, not twisted into links. Black and white pepper, marjoram, nutmeg and mace are perhaps the major seasonings (Poulson, 1979); sage is used by many butchers.

REGION OF PRODUCTION:

NORTH WEST ENGLAND, CUMBRIA.

Cumbria Air Dried Ham

DESCRIPTION:

AN UNSMOKED CURED HAM FOR EATING RAW. THE SKIN IS PALE CREAM-GOLD, THE LEAN DEEP, TRANSLUCENT RED. WEIGHT: ABOUT 6KG. FLAVOUR: INTENSE SALT HAM WITH SLIGHT SWEETNESS.

HISTORY:

Hams made in Britain are usually cooked before eating. However, the continental raw hams have long been well known and highly regarded and there has always been a market for them. During the twentieth century, legal status aimed at preventing the spread of notifiable diseases amongst farm animals meant that imports of raw ham from abroad were limited, so the development of home-produced types was a logical step.

Cumbria air-dried ham is an emergent regional food. In this particular case, Woodall's, the company which created the ham, has a history stretching back to the early 1800s when they began as bacon-curers. Cumbria air-dried ham is firmly rooted in a long tradition of taking foreign ideas and techniques and turning them into a distinctively British affair.

Cumbria Mature Royal Ham, made by the same company, is another emergent product, based on a mid-nineteenth century recipe from Suffolk. This was brought to Cumberland in the 1920s by the mother of the present chairman. It is based on a brine cure containing molasses, which fits in well with the food traditions of the Lake District where the use of unrefined sugar is typical. It is also smoked, recalling the Westmoreland hams of the 1700s.

TECHNIQUE:

A dry cure is used. Carcasses from selected pigs are hung for at least a week, then butchered. The hams are laid on a slab for about a month with salt and saltpetre, then dried and hung to mature for 12 months.

REGION OF PRODUCTION:

NORTH WEST ENGLAND, CUMBRIA.

Herdwick Macon Ham

DESCRIPTION:

WHOLE, SMOKED, CURED HAMS MADE FROM SHEEP MEAT WEIGHING AROUND 3KG (BONE IN) OR 1.8KG (BONED). COLOUR: VERY DARK RED, TRANSLUCENT LEAN WITH STREAKS OF PALE, CREAMY GOLD FAT; DARK GOLD OUTSIDE. FLAVOUR: PRONOUNCED GAMY LAMB FLAVOUR WITH HERB UNDERTONES AND MILD SMOKE.

HISTORY:

The word ham is used in connection with cured pig meat in modern Britain, but it has a broader meaning of the hind leg of any animal, especially those killed for meat. Goat hams were cured in Wales and other regions until the late eighteenth century (Wilson, 1973) and badger hams were not unknown. The use of mutton (meat from a sheep over one year old) to make hams is also a long British tradition, which lingered in the more remote uplands.

The word macon was a hybrid (m[utton + b]acon) of the Second World War to describe mutton cured as bacon – an innovation that took advantage of an excess of highland sheep at a time when pigs were an increasing rarity. Another solution, adopted with enthusiasm by both the Ministry of Food and the population as a whole, was urban backyard pig-keeping, a skill that had fallen into desuetude since the industrial revolution.

Hannah Glasse (1747) gives instructions for dry-curing mutton hams with salt and sugar, followed by smoking and boiling. Recipes were also to be found in nineteenth-century books on curing meat (David, 1970). In the modern era, mutton hams were a rarity although the idea was preserved in some parts, notably the Lake District. Poulson (1978) collected an old recipe for brining a mutton ham in a mixture which included molasses and spices, before drying and smoking. Until recent years, they were produced by only a few families for their own use. Modern interest in unusual foods has led to a revival of commercial production by a company based at Corney (Cumbria). The preserved ham would once have been soaked and boiled, then eaten with bread at ordinary meals. Those made today are eaten raw – the manufacturer suggests with fruit in the manner of Italian air-dried hams.

TECHNIQUE

A local sheep breed, the Herdwick, provides the meat. They are killed at 2–3 years. Cross-bred sheep are used to provide larger hams. The hams remain in a dry cure of spiced salt for about 3 weeks. They are cold-smoked over oak and juniper, then matured for 8 months.

REGION OF PRODUCTION:

NORTH WEST ENGLAND, CUMBRIA.

Pressed Beef

DESCRIPTION:

PIECES OF COOKED BEEF SET IN DARK BROWN JELLY, THINLY SLICED (ABOUT 5MM THICK) AND SOLD BY WEIGHT.

HISTORY:

This foodstuff is similar in concept to brawn. Like brawn, it probably began as something larger, more elaborate and more esteemed. The origins may lie in collaring, a way of preserving large, boned joints by brining and spicing, then rolling tightly in a cloth (collar) tied with tape or string, before boiling slowly. The meat could be preserved still longer if it were then potted under a layer of melted suet (Hartley, 1954). Early recipes for fine dishes of well-seasoned beef joints in jelly may also have influenced the development of this dish (David, 1970).

By the mid-nineteenth century, collaring was no longer fashionable, but jellied meats pressed into moulds and served cold (much as pressed tongue, another English favourite) had entered the repertoire of the cooked-meat counter as a way of using some of the less saleable cuts. *Dalton's Meat Recipes*, published in the 1930s, describes several products of the pressed-beef type, of varying degrees of sophistication. Mabey (1978) found the quantity and variety of cooked meats available in the industrial towns of Lancashire remarkable, mentioning amongst other items, 'various types of pressed meat in slices or moulds: beef, pork, lamb, chicken ...They are put into sandwiches, wedged into rolls, baps and barmcakes, or set out on plates for high tea.'

TECHNIQUE:

Pressed beef may use cheaper cuts from the forequarter, especially the brisket, which have excellent flavour but are not prime roasting material. The meat is covered with water and sea-soned; old recipes call for the addition of cowheels. The whole is cooked gently for up to 3 hours, any bones removed and the meat put into a pudding basin. At this stage, if no cowheel was used, some butchers add gelatine to the stock poured over the meat. It is cooled, then pressed and the stock sets to a jelly.

REGION OF PRODUCTION:

NORTH WEST ENGLAND, TODMORDEN (LANCASHIRE).

Tripe

DESCRIPTION:

TRIPE IS SOLD BY WEIGHT. IN APPEARANCE, ON THE SLAB, IT IS SHEETS OF PALE, CREAM-COLOURED TISSUE, IN ROUGHLY-CUT PIECES 15–20CM SQUARE. THE MOST DISTINCTIVE TYPE IS HONEYCOMB, WHICH HAS A PATTERN OF RAISED LINES CROSSING THE SURFACE

HISTORY:

Internal organs were no doubt more important foods when meat was a luxury and all parts of a slaughtered animal were carefully utilized. The name tripe derives from Norman French, but some of the dialect words associated with it are of Teutonic origin. This would suggest that, even in the early Middle Ages, it was not thought of as utterly dainty or high-status (on the analogy of Norman French being the root language of aristocratic culinary usage, while Anglo-Saxon implies something more popular). It is mentioned in numerous texts from the fifteenth century onwards, and appears in Shakespeare's *Taming of the Shrew* in the line, 'How say you to a fat tripe finely broiled?'

There were plenty of ways to deal with it: boiled, with onion; broiled, with saffron fricassees; or dipped in batter and fried (Glasse, 1747; Bradley, 1756; Raffald, 1769). Samuel Pepys enjoyed it in the company of his wife in 1662, 'a most excellent dish of tripes of my own directing, covered with mustard, as I have here-to-fore seen them done at my Lord Crews.' It was held in some esteem, considered easily digested and thought to be good for invalids. As late as the 1950s, the British Medical Association publicized it as a nourishing dish.

Nourishing perhaps, but it was not often encountered on the tables of gentlefolk. Its presence usually indicates some form of dearth – it cropped up a lot during wartime rationing. In recent years it has suffered a drop in popularity along with most other sorts of offal and is now a minority taste.

Tripe's recent history, however, is most eloquent in the northern districts of Lancashire and Yorkshire. Here, the immense increase in an urban proletariat that needed cheap and easy feeding meant the survival of a number of otherwise unmentionable parts of cows, pigs and sheep. Tripe was one of the most popular. There were 260 specialist tripe shops in Manchester in 1906 and 76 shops in Bolton in 1911 (Shipperbottom, 1995). Like the fish fryers, they produced cheap, nourishing food.

Faced with a great increase in purveyors, the industrial towns speedily enforced the 1875 Public Health Act which designated tripe-boiling amongst the offensive trades and regulated the cleaning of premises in which it was carried on. This was stimulus to a concentration of businesses. In Lancashire, during the early 1900s, there were amalgamations of tripe dressers and agreements to improve and enhance the trade. Every Lancashire town had tripe shops, and some of these had restaurants. The Tripe de Luxe Restaurant in Wigan had a female musical trio, and seating for 300 in an oak-panelled room with chandeliers. Marjory Houlihan, in her pamphlet on the Lancashire tripe trade, notes that such establishments were flourishing as late as the 1960s, and describes a magnificent banqueting suite in one of them.

Tripe-boiling is now less important, partly due to the decline in the Lancashire cotton trade and the way of life associated with it; and partly because of competition from other foods. The large company, United Cattle Products, found their premises had a higher property value than the tripe business could justify and sold their sites. The declining

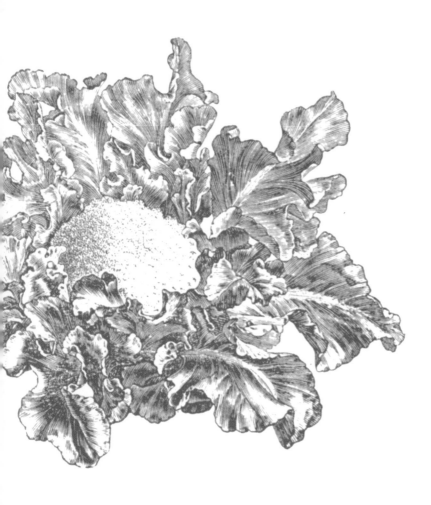

'A smiling face is half the meal.'

LATVIAN PROVERB

number of outlets has had its effect on the trade, and there are far fewer tripe dressers. The requirements of public health regulations, which insist on expensive improvements to premises, has caused some to close and forced the price of tripe to rise.

Tripe is the English term for the stomach bags of animals, especially cattle. The various parts of the tripe are given names which are often very localized. Some examples are: for the first stomach (*rumen*), thick seam, blanket; for the second (*reticulum*), honeycomb tripe; for the third (*omasum*), bible tripe, monkshood, psalterium, book, manifold, many-plies; for the fourth (*abomasum*), black or raggy tripe. The oesophagus is also treated as part of the tripe, and is known as weasand or bellrope. Pig's stomach is also eaten, but has only one chamber, similar to *abomasum* tripe.

Tripe in the north of England is cooked and ready to eat at point of sale. That sold in the South requires further cooking. Bleached tripe is the norm. Unbleached tripe is sometimes sold, but is now almost impossible to obtain. Tripe is consumed cold with vinegar and salt. Tripe and salad is a popular meal in hot weather, or it can be heated up in milk flavoured with onions, or made into more elaborate dishes to individual taste.

TECHNIQUE:
Preliminary cleaning is done at the abattoir, where the tripes are washed. They are then taken to specialist tripe dressers. The tripes are tumbled in a hot lime and soda solution which cleans, bleaches, and removes some of the fat and membranes. Removal of the outer skin (a process which was originally by hand with a scrubbing brush) is now done in a machine called a 'Parmentière', fitted with an abrasive drum. Boiling takes 2 hours or longer. Some areas only par-boil the tripe. The tripes are steeped in a mild peroxide solution to whiten them further; then they are thoroughly washed. In the final dressing, the tripe is trimmed and made ready for sale.

REGION OF PRODUCTION:
NORTH WEST ENGLAND, LANCASHIRE.

COMPARE TO:
Jellied Tripe, Scotland (p. 374)

Borrowdale Tea Bread

DESCRIPTION:
BAKED IN A LOAF SHAPE, A SMALL DEEP OBLONG. COLOUR: DARK BROWN, WITH PALER CRUMB AND DRIED FRUIT. FLAVOUR AND TEXTURE: SWEET AND AROMATIC, WITH A FAIRLY DENSE, CHEWY TEXTURE.

HISTORY:
There are 2 reasons why this might be called tea bread: one is because the dried fruit used for making it is soaked in tea prior to mixing; the other is that it is suitable for eating with tea. Both are equally plausible. The reason for the persistent association of this type of fruited bread with the North-West is unknown. The most likely is the existence of commercial tourism from an early date. Tea-time specialities have been developed in most areas of Britain with a substantial tourist industry. In the Lake District tourism has been important since the early 1800s. Bakeries in the area also produce very plain fruit loaves using bread dough and dried fruit, without the pre-liminary step of soaking the fruit in tea. Domestic cooks of Borrowdale and district frown on this,

saying the result is not as well flavoured and does not keep as well. However, plain breads may represent earlier types of this product, as tea cannot have been used as an ingredient for more than 200 years at the most, and this type of spiced and fruit dough has a much longer history.

TECHNIQUE:
Modern recipes for the loaf show it to be rather plain; it is leavened with baking powder. Flour, brown sugar, currants and raisins in the proportions 2:1:1:1 are used. The fruit, plus some candied peel and sugar are soaked overnight in cold tea. It is baked at 180°C for 60–90 minutes. Commercial bakers tend to produce a yeast-leavened version.

REGION OF PRODUCTION:
NORTH WEST ENGLAND, THE LAKE DISTRICT.

Chorley Cake

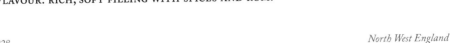

DESCRIPTION:
DIMENSIONS: APPROXIMATELY 80MM DIAMETER, JUST OVER 10MM DEEP. WEIGHT: ABOUT 75G. COLOUR: PALE BROWN PASTRY, DARKER TOWARDS THE EDGES, DARK CURRANT FILLING. FLAVOUR: PREDOMINANTLY SWEET CURRANTS, WITH CRISP PASTRY.

HISTORY:
Chorley cakes are regarded by some as a poor relation of Eccles cakes. There are distinct similarities; both involve a filling of currants in a pastry crust. It is probable that they spring from a common tradition, although Eccles cakes are the more famous and better documented. The earliest known reference to Chorley cakes dates from the 1920s when a local newspaper editor reminisced about the 1880s. He recalled 2 sisters, the Misses Corbitt, who made Chorley cakes and sold them for 2d (1p) each, a high price at a time when a working man could expect to be paid about 15p a day. A trade directory in the town records a Miss Corbitt keeping a confectionery shop from at least 1874. The tradition of Chorley cakes has continued to the present day. Similar confections are made in nearby towns, using pastry left over from pie-making. One firm, Hall's, still makes the cakes in the town itself.

TECHNIQUE:
The cakes are made using short-crust pastry rolled to 50mm thick, and cut into rounds about 200mm across. A layer of currants is placed in the centre of each, the edges of the pastry brought together, and sealed. These are rolled lightly until the currants show through the pastry and the shape is a flattened round. They are baked at 180°C for 30 minutes.

REGION OF PRODUCTION:
NORTH WEST ENGLAND, CHORLEY (LANCASHIRE).

Cumberland Rum Nicky

DESCRIPTION:
A CIRCULAR TART, NOW ALSO BAKED IN LONG OBLONGS, WITH A DECORATIVE PASTRY LATTICE ON TOP. COLOUR: A GOLDEN CRUST WITH DARK, RICH BROWN FILLING. FLAVOUR: RICH, SOFT FILLING WITH SPICES AND RUM.

Rum Nicky contains elements present in British cookery for many centuries. Rum, the vital ingredient, has been imported from the West Indies into ports on the Cumbrian coast for at least 200 years. The filling contains dates and preserved ginger. It bears some resemblance to the combination of spice and dried fruit known as mincemeat, but also to mixtures proposed in sixteenth-century cookery books, such as one from 1587, of prunes with breadcrumbs, claret, ginger, and sugar.

Earlier last century, it was the form of the dish rather than the filling which distinguished it. In the 1930s, Mrs Arthur Webb recorded visiting a Lake District farmhouse on a day when nickies were being baked. She recorded that they were of several sorts (including some sounding very like mince pies or Eccles cakes), some were made with dough and some with shortcrust. The local method was to leave the edge plain, but make cuts or nicks to and fro across the top. As the present-day tart always involves a decoration of pastry trellis, it would seem that this, rather than the rum filling, is what gave the dish its identity. Several small bakeries continue to manufacture it; one at least has a large mail-order business at Christmastide.

TECHNIQUE:

Examples collected recently used either short-crust or puff pastry rolled to fill a shallow dish. The filling is chopped dates, preserved ginger, butter, sugar and rum. It is baked at 220°C for 10–15 minutes, followed by 30 minutes at 180°C.

REGION OF PRODUCTION:

NORTH WEST ENGLAND, CUMBRIA.

Eccles Cake

DESCRIPTION:

A FRUIT-FILLED PASTRY, 60–80MM DIAMETER, 20MM DEEP. WEIGHT: 30–40G. COLOUR: LIGHT BROWN PUFF OR FLAKY PASTRY OFTEN WITH GLIMPSES OF DARK CURRANTS; IN SOME VARIATIONS THE CURRANTS ARE CLEARLY VISIBLE THROUGH SLASHED CUTS ON THE TOP; THE SURFACE IS OFTEN GLAZED AND SPRINKLED WITH SUGAR. FLAVOUR: SWEET, WITH CRISP PASTRY AND RICH CURRANTS; A TYPICAL CAKE IS ABOUT 40 PER CENT CURRANTS TO 60 PERCENT PASTRY.

HISTORY:

Similar affairs of puff pastry with currant fillings exist in other parts of England but they are of different shapes and their historical relationship to the Eccles cake is unclear.

There is a myth that this particular recipe was given to a girl as she left the employ of Mrs Raffald, whose *English Housekeeper* was an important Georgian kitchen vade-mecum and who was a noted confectioner in Manchester nearby. It is certainly true that Raffald's book contains plenty of patties – some of which have currants in the filling – and that by a stretch of imagination an Eccles cake could be termed a patty (in fact those were much smaller), but the connection is exiguous. It is perhaps more germane to note that cakes were recorded before this time (the 1770s) as being sold at Eccles but that nobody wrote down their composition. They were a feature of the town wakes, a religious festival commemorating the foundation of the local church. Wakes Week used to be in September, but is now in July.

There has long been dispute about which family in the area produced the originals but the arguments settle no facts about antecedents or early history. By the early 1800s, however, there is evidence of an established pattern of wholesaling well beyond the town boundaries. By then, there were several makers and some were producing large numbers for sale. Surviving details from auctioneers' records mention that Birch's shop was making 5,000 cakes every day; and evidently the principal shop, Bradburns, baked 8,000. The cakes were popular at public events, especially sports meetings and at racecourses. There are also claims of a large export trade to America during this period.

A recipe from the first half of the nineteenth century calls for a spicy currant filling in a puff pastry case although other early recipes called for the currants to be mixed through the dough. *Law's Grocer's Manual* (*c*.1895) noted 'the great guiding principle' in Eccles cakes is currants, sweetness and lightness. It went on to say that cakes made in south Lancashire were often baked in a very hot oven, caramelizing the sugar on the outside. Recipes from professional manuals of the same date seem to treat Eccles and Banbury cakes as nearly identical, the main difference being shape: an Eccles cake is always round. No-one can deny a basic similarity, but comparison reveals very different products.

TECHNIQUE:
The essential characteristic of pastry for Eccles cakes is that it does not have as much 'lift' as other puff pastry products. Care is taken to avoid waxy, palate-clinging pastry. The better cakes are made with butter and only a small amount of scrap pastry (offcuts from earlier batches) is incorporated. The filling always includes currants (the best local maker uses Vostizza) and brown sugar; some add cake crumbs, chopped peel, spice and Golden Syrup. The pastry is cut into 100–120mm discs. The filling is placed centrally and the edges folded in to cover it. The pastry is turned over, slightly flattened, brushed with egg white or milk, sprinkled with sugar and 2 or 3 parallel cuts made on top. After resting for 40 minutes, it is baked at 225°C for 20–25 minutes.

REGION OF PRODUCTION:
NORTH WEST ENGLAND, ECCLES (LANCASHIRE).

Goosnargh Cake

DESCRIPTION:
A CIRCULAR BISCUIT, 80MM DIAMETER, 10MM DEEP. WEIGHT: 50G. COLOUR: OFF-WHITE, DARKER TOWARDS THE EDGE, WITH DARK SPECKLES AND A THICK COATING OF FINE SUGAR. FLAVOUR AND TEXTURE: BUTTERY, CARAWAY SEEDS; A FINE, SHORT TEXTURE.

HISTORY:
Goosnargh is a village north of Preston. Butter, the essential ingredient of Goosnargh cakes, is a product of the region. The origin of the cakes is unknown. Their texture is close to shortbread, the ancestors of which were popular all over Britain in the sixteenth and seventeenth centuries. Caraway, in the form of whole seeds, was a common ingredient in contemporary biscuit and cake recipes. Beyond these general observations, these cakes cannot be traced other than from local historian Richard Cookson's observation in 1888 that 'Goosnargh has almost world-wide fame for making of penny cakes of a peculiar pastry, and great as the

depression of trade at present is, about 4,000 dozens are disposed of annually about Whitsuntide.' This implies the cakes had been well known for years. The connection with the religious festival also speaks of a long usage: the area was conservative, preserving remnants of traditions associated with Catholicism long after they had vanished in other parts. Similar cakes were known in other towns in the region, baked at other times, often as fairings.

As with so many other British specialities requiring dairy produce, the cakes suffered from wartime rationing. Spicer (1948) remarked that Goosnargh (the name was often used without further qualification) had been almost impossible to make since the war, because of the large quantities of butter required. In recent years they have been made again and the old preference for caraway spicing – often jettisoned by modern bakers – has been continued. However, the link with Whitsuntide has vanished.

TECHNIQUE:

The ingredients are flour, butter, sugar, in the proportions 6:4:1. Flavourings are ground coriander and whole caraway seeds. The butter, sugar and spices are creamed, the flour is rubbed in and the mixture pressed into a coherent dough without any liquid. This is rolled out and cut into rounds with a plain cutter. The surface is sprinkled thickly with caster sugar. The raw biscuits are left to stand for at least 2 hours. They are baked at 140°C for 30–40 minutes. The cakes should be firm, but remain very pale. In airtight tins, they keep for several months.

REGION OF PRODUCTION:

NORTH WEST ENGLAND, PRESTON (LANCASHIRE).

Grasmere Gingerbread

DESCRIPTION:

OBLONG OR SQUARE PIECES OF GINGERBREAD; SARAH NELSON'S GRASMERE GINGERBREAD IS THINNER THAN OTHER ENGLISH GINGERBREADS AND IS MADE IN PIECES 80MM BY 50MM, 8MM DEEP; OTHER TYPES ARE CUT IN SQUARES OR BARS OF VARYING SIZE, ABOUT 15MM THICK. WEIGHT: SARAH NELSON'S IS CUT IN PIECES OF ABOUT 35G; OTHER TYPES ARE SOLD IN PIECES OF AROUND 50G. COLOUR: RICH MID-BROWN; SARAH NELSON'S HAS A SANDY APPEARANCE. FLAVOUR AND TEXTURE: SWEET, SPICY, WITH HARD, CHEWY TEXTURE; SARAH NELSON'S HAS EXCEPTIONAL FLAVOUR OF STRONG GINGER WITH A BITTER FRUIT NOTE.

HISTORY:

Grasmere is a small town in the centre of the English Lake District. The nearby coast has several important harbours and formerly traded with the West Indian colonies and the port of Liverpool. Local cookery has an emphasis on rum, unrefined sugar and spices, especially ginger, which may derive from this trade. The grain used in the area until the nineteenth century was oats. Some types of gingerbread made in the north of England, including ones quoted in domestic cookery books under the title Grasmere, still call for it.

However, the earliest form of gingerbread in Grasmere may have been quite different. Brears (1991) refers to an entry in the church-wardens' accounts for 1819, recording payment for 'rushbearers' gingerbread'. This refers to the custom of carrying rushes to St Oswald's church, originally as floor covering but more recently as decoration. A succession of bakers in the town are recorded as providing gingerbread to the church as payment to the rushbearers.

This confection, still made for the rushbearing on the feast of St Oswald (6 August), is not the type now associated with the town. The vicar says that it is thick and soft and is stamped with a rushbearing motif.

Dorothy Wordsworth writes in her Grasmere journal for 1803 (Clark 1960): 'W[illia]m had a fancy for some ginger bread ... and we walked towards Matthew Newton's. I went into the house. The blind man and his wife and sister were sitting by the fire, all dressed very clean in their Sunday clothes, the sister reading. They took their little stock of gingerbread out of the cupboard, and I bought 6 pennyworth. They were so grateful when I paid them for it that I could not find it in my heart to tell them we were going to make gingerbread ourselves. I had asked them if they had no thick – "No," answered Matthew, "there was none on Friday, but we'll endeavour to get some." The next day the woman came just when we were baking and we bought 2 pennyworth.' This account seems to confirm both sorts of gingerbread, thin and thick, that are available today.

Grasmere gingerbread developed its current identity with the development of the tourist trade. In the 1850s, Sarah Nelson, a Lancashire woman, began to bake a Lancashire type of gingerbread for sale to locals and visitors. The present business which bears her name was established in 1854 in a small building formerly the village school. Her recipe has been the sole property of 3 families during the intervening years. Other recipes have been published in various cookery texts: they are generally for a type of shortbread, flavoured with ginger, and may or may not involve a portion of oatmeal. 'Sarah Nelson's Grasmere Gingerbread', the most famous variety, is a trademark. Others are sold simply as Grasmere gingerbread and, while they may share a common origin, are not exactly the same.

TECHNIQUE:

The method of making Sarah Nelson's Gingerbread is a trade secret and it is company policy to withhold information. Other recipes are for a simple shortbread mixture, using flour, butter and moist brown sugar in proportions of 8:5:4, ginger and baking powder. Some call for oatmeal in place of flour, and rub the butter into the mixture rather than melt it. This type of recipe and method is used by local bakers.

REGION OF PRODUCTION:

NORTH WEST ENGLAND, GRASMERE (CUMBRIA).

Hawkshead Wig

DESCRIPTION:

AN OVAL BREAD ROLL 70MM LONG, 40MM WIDE, 40MM DEEP. WEIGHT: ABOUT 40G. COLOUR: GOLDEN WITH A SHINY TOP. FLAVOUR: A PLAIN BREAD, LIGHTLY SPICED WITH CARAWAY.

HISTORY:

Wigs (sometimes spelled whigs or wiggs) were light-textured, white bread, raised with yeast. The origin of the name is not clear. It is possibly derived from a Teutonic word meaning wedge. In some later recipes the wigs are formed into rounds quartered by a cross, allowing them to be broken into wedges after baking. Both buns and wigs are fine white breads connected with Lent (for instance hot cross buns, see below, p. 417). Samuel Pepys wrote that he had a Lenten supper of wigs and ale in 1664. Buns were early defined as Lenten bread. The word possibly derives from the Old French *bugne*, later *beignet* – a small something which puffs up, as fine white bread leavened with yeast would do. Wigs were thought of in the same terms. They were obviously made with fine white flour, and a fifteenth-century reference equates them with buns. The Restoration herald Randle Holme defined wigs as white bread moulded longways and thick in the middle.

By the time we have recipes, they were sweetened, enriched with butter and usually spiced – with coriander (Nott, 1726) or caraway (the most common). *The Magazine of Domestic Economy* (1840) requires cream, butter, sugar and spices, including caraway seeds. Irrespective of the connection with Lent, wigs do crop up as a festive food eaten at particular times. Spicer (1948) recorded several special days at which wigs were eaten at different locations, including Christmas (Shrewsbury), St Catherine's (Buckinghamshire, where the wigs were an oblong shape) and St Andrew's (Bedfordshire).

From the 1850s they seem to be mentioned much less frequently. It is possible that the name simply went out of current use. A Victorian comment was that there were so many 'common buns' around that the word wig had been forgotten (David, 1977). Minwel Tibbott (1976) observes that in North Wales, the word wig was applied to the long narrow iced currant bun, made from a lightly sweetened dough known in the rest of the country as iced bun.

Florence White (1932) found that rolls known as wigs were still made and sold in the small town of Hawkshead. According to Phyllis Graham, a native, they are still known and occasionally made in the locality although little interest is taken in them. Only one commercial producer has so far been located.

TECHNIQUE:

Hawkshead wigs are plain and include lard – none of the sugar, butter and milk of many early recipes. An ordinary dough is set to rise; it is knocked back and softened lard (8 parts dough to 1 part lard) is kneaded in, together with a small quantity of caraway seeds. The mixture is scaled off into portions of about 40g, shaped into ovals, and allowed to rise again; the tops are brushed with milk and sugar. The buns are baked for 20–30 minutes at about 220°C.

REGION OF PRODUCTION:

NORTH WEST ENGLAND, HAWKSHEAD (CUMBRIA).

Kendal Pepper Cake

DESCRIPTION:

CIRCULAR CAKES, 30–40MM DEEP. COLOUR: DARK, RICH BROWN SURFACE, SPECKLED WITH CURRANTS, SUGAR AND CANDIED PEEL; INTERIOR PALER, WITH A DRY CRUMB; FLAVOUR: SWEET, BITTER NOTE FROM PEEL DOMINATING, DISTINCT SPICY-PEPPER FLAVOUR.

HISTORY:

Pepper cakes belong to the general tradition of spiced, fruited cakes. This was originally a Christmas recipe and the connection of extravagant spices with festivities is hallowed. The use of pepper in this context is curious. There are 2 possible explanations. According to Wright (1896–1905), pepper originally meant a spicing of ginger in Northern counties. A similar usage is found in Sweden, where ginger biscuits are called *pepparkaker*. Alternatively, the name may have come from the use of allspice (*Pimenta officinalis*), which was known as Jamaica pepper in the eighteenth century. Brears gives a recipe for 'pepper cake' dating from 1792 which includes both allspice and ginger. Otherwise, the history of this speciality of the Lake District remains obscure. The present-day version contains black pepper, and this is given in 2 recipes from the 1970s. There is no evidence of a long-standing tradition of the use of this spice in sweet dishes in Cumbria, and it seems probable that modern practice is due to confusion over meanings.

TECHNIQUE:
The ingredients of a commercial pepper cake are listed as wheat flour, raisins, vegetable margarine, eggs, sugar syrup, sugar, mixed candied peel, milk, honey, glucose, oranges, raising agents E334 & E500, black pepper, cloves, and ground ginger. Domestic recipes show flour, treacle, sugar and butter used in the proportions 4:2:2:1. The cake is kept for at least a week before cutting.

REGION OF PRODUCTION:
NORTH WEST ENGLAND, CUMBRIA.

Ormskirk Gingerbread

DESCRIPTION:
A CIRCULAR BISCUIT, ABOUT 60MM DIAMETER, 5MM THICK. WEIGHT: ABOUT 14G. COLOUR: RICH, EVEN BROWN. FLAVOUR AND TEXTURE: SWEET, STRONGLY SPICED WITH GINGER AND OTHER SPICES; CRISP.

HISTORY:
Ormskirk has been noted for gingerbread for at least 200 years. Travellers recorded how the vendors descended upon arriving stage coaches; later, they congregated on the railway station and sold gingerbread to passengers (Hallam, 1979). The only commercial recipe which survived into the late twentieth century is the property of the Mawdsley family who started making the gingerbread in 1800 (Spicer, 1949). For a few years during the 1980s, it went out of commercial production, but has recently been revived and is now made under licence for a grocer in the town.

TECHNIQUE:
The commercial recipe is a trade secret. Several recipes have been published before. They call for flour, butter and soft brown sugar in the proportions 5:2:2. The butter and sugar are creamed, mixed with molasses/Golden Syrup, lemon zest, ginger, cinnamon and flour. This is rolled and cut in rounds. The biscuits are baked at 170°C for 25–30 minutes in falling heat.

REGION OF PRODUCTION:
NORTH WEST ENGLAND, ORMSKIRK (LANCASHIRE).

Blackpool Rock

DESCRIPTION:
CYLINDERS OF PULLED SUGAR, 2–5CM DIAMETER, 20–40CM LONG. COLOUR: A WHITE CENTRE SURROUNDED BY A THIN, PINK OUTER LAYER, WITH LETTERS FORMED OF RED SUGAR RUNNING

THE INTERNAL LENGTH OF THE STICK IS TRADITIONAL, BUT YELLOW, ORANGE OR GREEN ARE SOMETIMES USED IN PLACE OF THIS. VARIETIES WITH A STRIPED OUTSIDE LAYER ARE ALSO MADE. FLAVOUR: USUALLY MINT. COMPOSITION: SUGAR, GLUCOSE, FLAVOURING, COLOUR.

HISTORY:

Seaside rock developed from the art of boiling and pulling sugar. The technique of pulling sugar is used to make other types of rock, with lettering, abstract patterns or pictures of fruit running through it. Some have flavourings of fruit, aniseed or liquorice instead of the old standby, mint. Many miniatures and novelties are also made from pulled sugar, often imitating foods such as fruits, cakes, fish and chips, or bacon and eggs. This visual tradition descends from the delight in sugary imitations made for the sweet banquets of the sixteenth and seventeenth centuries.

The craft of pulled sugar developed into a complex art during the nineteenth century, when confectioners worked out how to recombine batches of differently coloured boiled and pulled sugars into stripes, letters and patterns. A recipe given in the 1830s for striping pulled sugar comes from a Nottingham confectioner, S.W. Stavely, who gave instructions for making Paradise Twist to be streaked red and white. In the middle of the century, Henry Mayhew noted a vendor on the streets of London who had found a method for inserting mottoes into sugar sticks. This is doubtless the precursor of seaside rock – the perfect edible souvenir. The making of rock goes hand in hand with the growth of mass transport and holidays for the working population of industrial England. Blackpool, one of the first beneficiaries of the process, is a natural candidate for particular association with the sweetmeat.

Two people have claims to be the first to market the novelty. One, 'Dynamite Dan', is said to have worked in Morecambe, near Blackpool, in the 1890s. The other, Ben Bullock, was a confectioner from Dewsbury in South Yorkshire. Margaret Race (1990) claims that Bullock began making rock in Dewsbury for sale at Blackpool in the late 1880s, though rock was not made in Blackpool itself until the early twentieth century.

TECHNIQUE:

Sugar, glucose and water are mixed, brought to the boil and allowed to cook to 138°C. The sugar is then poured on to a greased, water-cooled steel table. As it begins to cool, the batch is turned sides-to-middle several times before division into 3. One piece is left plain and the other 2 are coloured: red for the sugar to be used for letters, and pink for that destined for the outer layer. The uncoloured part of the batch is pulled by machine until opaque and white; flavouring is added during this process. Pulling may be done by hand: hanging the cooling sugar on a fixed hook and working it by repeated stretching and folding. This converts the batch into an opaque white mass.

The letters that are destined to run through each stick of rock are formed by making long strips of red sugar, and packing the spaces between them with white. For instance, an 'O' is made from a long cylinder of white sugar, wrapped in a thin layer of red. The form of the letter is only apparent in cross-section. The letters are assembled in the correct order, separated by strips of white. Then a large piece of white sugar is prepared to become the core, and 2 thinner 'flaps'. The rock is assembled by covering the letters reading BLACKPOOL with one flap, and those reading ROCK with the other; the flaps, carrying the letters, are then wrapped around the central core. Then the whole is enclosed in a layer of pink. The entire assemblage is very large at this stage, about 1.5 metres long, 300mm diameter at one end, tapering to about 120mm at the other. The confection is transferred to a batch roller, a machine which maintains it at the correct heat. It rolls it first in one direction and then the other (so that the letters do not twist). Then it is spun, by leading the thinner end of the rock through a narrow aperture and pulling it out in a 'string' on a long table. Once the end of the table is reached, the string is cut and another one begun. As soon as the strings of rock are spun, they must be rolled back and forth by hand until they are completely cool, otherwise, the side closest to the table flattens. The rock is cut into lengths and wrapped in Cellophane.

REGION OF PRODUCTION:
NORTH WEST ENGLAND.

Cough Candy

DESCRIPTION:
COUGH CANDY IS BROKEN INTO CUBES OF ROUGHLY 10MM AND SOLD BY WEIGHT. COLOUR: LIGHT BROWN, USUALLY WITH SOME SUGAR CRYSTALS SHOWING. FLAVOUR: SWEET, POWERFULLY HERBAL, WITH ANISEED, LIQUORICE AND HOREHOUND. COMPOSITION: SUGAR, HERBAL ESSENCES.

HISTORY:
Cough candy is a survivor of a long tradition of herbal cures. These remedies were made by adding decoctions of herbs to sugar syrups. The latter acted as preservatives and helped to make the bitter flavours more palatable. They were made at home or by apothecaries and sweet-sellers. Stavely (1830) gave a recipe for horehound cake, a mixture of candied sugar and horehound (*Marrubium vulgare*). Mayhew (1851) mentions the vendors of cough drops in the streets of London. According to Skuse (*c.* 1892), cough candy was made from grained sugar, horehound and oil of aniseed. The London product was unlike that in the rest of the country. It was not a candy but a boiled sweet which was pulled and twisted. This type has disappeared.

As a consequence of advances in medicine and drugs, many formulae went out of use or developed into confectionery with a medicinal emphasis. A few herbalists and confectionery companies still make products which might be regarded as sweets. They are mostly to be found in the north of England, and the products are seen as a local taste, notably consumed by the elderly. Fisherman's Friends (see below) may be considered as part of the same tradition.

TECHNIQUE:
Sugar is dissolved in water and boiled to 121°C; the syrup is rubbed against the side of the pan until it begins to cloud; the required herbs, essences and flavourings are stirred in; the mixture is poured on to a warm, oiled slab and allowed to set, after which it is broken up.

REGION OF PRODUCTION:
NORTH WEST ENGLAND.

'Tell me what you eat and I will tell you what you are.'

ANTHELME BRILLAT-SAVARIN

Fisherman's Friends

DESCRIPTION:

AN OVAL LOZENGE 19 X 14 X 4MM. WEIGHT: 1G. FLAVOUR: 3 FLAVOURS ARE MADE – ORIGI-
NAL, ANISEED, AND MENTHOL – EACH PRODUCED IN A SUGAR-BASED OR A SUGAR-FREE VER-
SION. COMPOSITION: SUGAR, DEXTRIN, GLUCOSE SYRUP, PEPPERMINT OIL (1 PER CENT), EDI-
BLE GUM, MENTHOL (0.3 PER CENT), COLOURING, CHLOROPHYLLIN.

HISTORY:

Fisherman's Friends are a survival of the patent medicines which flourished in nineteenth-
century Britain. The formula was compounded by a pharmacist in the town of Fleetwood,
James Lofthouse, and first sold as a liquid medicine in 1865. It was specifically intended to ease
the throat ailments suffered by trawlermen working for the local fishing industry. Lofthouse of
Fleetwood remains the sole manufacturer and the sweet is a registered trademark. The product
remained localized until the 1960s, when the company sought new markets, at first in northern England, then throughout the world. Though first intended for coughs or colds, today it is
popular as sugar confectionery. In excess of a billion lozenges are produced per annum.

TECHNIQUE:

The tablets are made by a paste method, mixing sugar and other ingredients with a gum base.
The paste is rolled, cut, dried and packed. In the sugar-free varieties, sorbitol replaces the
sugar, and the tablets are made by mixing the ingredients as a dry powder which is compressed
into small lozenges.

REGION OF PRODUCTION:

NORTH WEST ENGLAND, FLEETWOOD (LANCASHIRE).

Kendal Mint Cake

DESCRIPTION:

AN OBLONG MINT CANDY, 150MM LONG, 90MM WIDE, 8MM THICK. WEIGHT: 170G. COLOUR:
WHITE OR PALE BROWN, DEPENDING ON SUGAR USED. THE SURFACE IS MARKED INTO
SQUARES AND HAS A SPARKLING APPEARANCE. FLAVOUR: VERY SWEET, WITH A POWERFUL
MINT FLAVOUR; A HARD, FRIABLE TEXTURE. COMPOSITION: SUGAR, MINT OIL. VERSIONS ARE
MADE WITH WHITE OR BROWN SUGAR; MINT CAKE COATED WITH CHOCOLATE IS ALSO SOLD.

HISTORY:

Mint cake is a survival of older sweetmeats which were boiled to set in a crystalline mass. They
are described in many texts of the 1700s. In 1868, W. Bowness noted that Barbara Gray's shop
in Kendal sold gingerbread and mint cake. In the following year, Joseph Wiper established the
first of the 4 companies still making mint cake today. Each is based in the town.

Mint cake was popular with Victorian tourists and, in 1914, was supplied to Shackleton's
Polar Expedition. This set its character, still used as a marketing ploy, of an energy-giving
food, suitable for mountaineers. Each manufacturer has packaging detailing the various expe-
ditions that have used their particular brand.

TECHNIQUE:

Commercial methods used are secret but cannot be much different to that made at home.
Sugar, glucose and water are heated in a copper pan until the sugar dissolves. The mixture is

cooked to 116°C. The heat is turned off and peppermint oil added. While hot, the mixture is rubbed against the side of the pan until it grains. An alternative method of encouraging sugar crystals to form is to add a small amount of prepared fondant containing crystals of the right size. The mixture is poured into moulds, then cooled and left overnight to crystallize evenly before unmoulding and packing in parchment or plastic wrappers.

REGION OF PRODUCTION:
NORTH WEST ENGLAND, KENDAL (CUMBRIA).

Tizer

DESCRIPTION:
THIS IS A CARBONATED DRINK OF BOLD ORANGE HUE WITH A SWEET CITRUS FLAVOUR.

HISTORY:
At the beginning of the last century, there was a general push towards the commercialization of bottled drinks that combined both pleasure and health-giving properties. Dandelion and Burdock, Sarsaparilla, and 'black beers' (combined with raisin or lemon flavours) belong to this tradition. When healthcare had to be paid for by the recipient, such tonics and pick-me-ups seemed cheap and alluring preventatives. A number of these soft drinks were developed in the Manchester area in the 1920s. 'Tizer' (a trademark coined from the word 'appetizer') was first made in Manchester in 1924 by the company F. Pickup. The brand was extremely popular in the 1920s and 1930s, and the company controlled a large business empire from their Manchester base.

During the Second World War the formula for Tizer was altered. On the death of the original manufacturer in the early 1970s, the company was acquired by A.G. Barr (see Irn-Bru, p. 327). The new owners researched the original formula intensively and reinstated it.

TECHNIQUE:
Ingredients are water, sugar, carbon dioxide, citric acid, flavourings, preservative, colours. The flavouring and colouring ingredients are mixed to make a syrup, which is combined with water and sugar, carbonated and bottled.

REGION OF PRODUCTION:
NORTH WEST ENGLAND, MANCHESTER.

Vimto

DESCRIPTION:
THE CORDIAL IS THE ORIGINAL FORM OF THIS DRINK AND IS SOLD IN BOTTLES OF CHARAC-TERISTIC SHAPE. IT IS DEEP RUBY RED AND TASTES OF BERRY FRUITS WITH VANILLA AND SPICE UNDERTONES. IT IS FORTIFIED WITH VITAMIN C.

HISTORY:
The history of this cordial is similar to that of Tizer. It, too, was Manchester-based and originated in the early 1900s. The inventor was Noel Nichols, a wholesale druggist and herb importer. The name is short for Vimtonic, to reflect an image of health and vigour. Originally made as a cordial, it was swiftly adapted to become a carbonated drink, and the company appointed agents to bottle it in various towns.

I don't really care about the history of Scouse – maybe it was the Vikings, maybe a nomadic, non-violent Norwegian tribe looking for the Beatles, or maybe aliens – all I know is I love it. It reminds me of childhood and makes me want to hug my mum. Now, for those of you who've never had the good fortune to scoff down a pan of Scouse, here's the basics: lamb (shoulder these days, but a bit of neck is still a fine thing), spuds, carrots, onion and water or stock. So far all Scousers are happy… But like with all good regional recipes, nobody just does that. For me, I like to add celery, red wine or beer, a splash of tabasco, butter on the spuds, a handful of herbs and sometimes (but please don't tell anyone) a dash of Worcestershire sauce. Oh, and pickled beetroot on the side.

The heady smell of Scouse when my mum makes it each time the prodigal returns is enough to make me want to put on my jim-jams, watch Blue Peter and look through my football cards, learning everything about all the Liverpool players. Scouse is the best dish in the world – it warms like nothing else, it should feel like a hug going in and like a lovely duvet once it settles. 'You'll never walk alone.'

Simon Rimmer

BROADCASTER, CHEF AND PROPRIETOR, GREEN'S RESTAURANT, MANCHESTER

During World War II the formula was altered temporarily, although the original has now been reinstated. The Nichols family still retains a substantial interest. Cordials like this, and flavoured black beers can still be bought from Fitzpatrick's Herbal Health, a herbalist and temperance bar in Lancashire, either to take away or mixed on the premises with hot water, or with soda to make a sparkling drink. Vimto is a trademark.

TECHNIQUE:
The flavouring ingredients are a closely guarded secret. They include raspberry, black currant and grape juices, vanilla, capsicum and horehound. It is available sweetened either with sugar or artificial sweeteners. For the cordial, the flavouring and colouring ingredients are mixed into a syrup. If a long drink is required, this is combined with water, carbonated and bottled.

REGION OF PRODUCTION:
NORTH WEST ENGLAND, MANCHESTER.

Pickled Damson

DESCRIPTION:
THIS PICKLE IS DARK RED WITH WHOLE FRUIT VISIBLE. THE FLAVOUR IS SWEET-SOUR, WITH A DISTINCT, RICH PLUM TASTE, LIGHTLY SPICED.

HISTORY:
Damsons, *Prunus institia*, are grown throughout Britain and are especially valued in North-West England, where the Lythe Valley in particular contains many old orchards. It is not clear when the plums were first planted there, but they have been associated with Westmoreland for over 150 years. The *Catalogue of Plums at the National Fruit Trials* (1978) records that a variety known as Blue Violet, local to Westmoreland, was received in 1932. There were several methods for preserving them, including jams and fruit pastes. Another was a pickle in vinegar and sugar. They were the only locally-produced fruit available in sufficient quantity for this type of product, as the area does not support the large orchards and market gardens found in the South-East. Total annual production is probably in the order of hundreds of kilos. It is most likely found on market stalls, for instance those run by the Women's Institute.

TECHNIQUE:
A mixture of spirit or malt vinegar, sugar and spices (cloves and cinnamon) is boiled to make a syrup. Each damson is pricked several times and added to this. They are cooked in the pickle for 10 minutes then potted. Some cooks crack the stones and add the kernels.

REGION OF PRODUCTION:
NORTH WEST ENGLAND, LAKE DISTRICT.

Taylor's Original Prepared English Mustard

DESCRIPTION:
TAYLOR'S ORIGINAL IS A SMOOTH PASTE, THE COLOUR YELLOW WITH AN OCHRE TONE, VERY SALTY, AROMATIC, MILDLY PUNGENT, WITH A SLIGHT BITTER UNDERTONE.

HISTORY:

Mustard in Britain has a long history (Man and Weir, 1988). The plant was probably introduced by the Romans and it is often mentioned in English texts about food from the Middle Ages onwards. Over the centuries, methods for making mustard evolved and the location of the industry moved several times. In the sixteenth and seventeenth centuries, Tewkesbury mustard from Gloucestershire was the most famous. It was coarse and included much horseradish. It was compacted into balls which were dried and sent round the country. Users could reconstitute it with wine, vinegar or water. Sir Hugh Plat (1602) noticed that in Venice the mustard seed was ground much more finely, as if it were wheat flour. It could be sold ready to be mixed into a condiment. He suggested the idea be adopted in Britain. Eventually, this happened, although it took another hundred years. The invention is attributed to one Mrs Clements of Durham, who began to grind and sift the seed as Plat advised. She sold the powder all over the country in the early eighteenth century.

In 1830, William Taylor, an apothecary in Newport Pagnell, Buckinghamshire, devised a method for making a ready-mixed mustard paste which had excellent flavour and keeping qualities. Taylor never milled mustard flour. He bought his supplies and the product relies on a specific blend of flours, a unique method of mixing and the use of salt as a preservative. The formula was preserved in his recipe book, and is the first known example of a ready-prepared smooth English mustard. Originally stoneware jars, corked and sealed with wax, were used as containers, but now they are glass. The present owner of Taylor's, Ross Southwell, speculates the product's success may have stemmed from its keeping qualities. It was popular with naval officers, who included it in their private stores; the salty paste, well sealed, resisted damage from sea-water and damp conditions.

The company founded by William Taylor diversified into soft drinks – as did many former apothecaries – and this side became the most important. However, by the 1970s it was unable to resist competition from larger businesses and forced again to rely on mustard. In the late 1980s the firm very nearly went out of business but was rescued as a result of a greater public awareness of characterful British food produce and greater vigour imparted by a new owner.

TECHNIQUE:

The formula and method are trade secrets. Mustard flours are purchased, blended and mixed with water, wheat flour, salt and turmeric. This releases an enzyme and a glycoside, giving pungency. The mixture is heated, using a temperature-gradient sufficient to partly destroy the enzyme, or the flavour is too harsh, but leaving enough undamaged to give character.

REGION OF PRODUCTION:

NORTH WEST ENGLAND.

North England

Dock Pudding

DESCRIPTION:

DOCK PUDDING IS A BROWNISH-GREEN PURÉE. ITS FLAVOUR IS SALTY AND SPINACH-LIKE.

HISTORY:

This spring dish, regarded as a blood purifier, is associated with south Yorkshire and the Lake District, where it is known as Easterledge. It is made from common plants which appear early in the year, and probably aided the health of the population by providing necessary vitamins after a long winter diet of preserved and salted foods. In composition it amounts to a vegetable porridge. Essentially, it is now a poverty food, based on groats (husked, crushed oats) with wild greenery. It is better documented in the Lake District, as early-nineteenth-century tourists to the area found it interesting. Peter Brears (1991) discusses some of these reports. He notes that the herbs used include bistort (*Polygonum bistorta*) nettles, lady's mantle, black currant and raspberry leaves, dandelion, plus onions, chives, cabbage and lettuce. Victorians realised its value for the poorer classes: a recipe for sweet docks with oatmeal was included in Alexis Soyer's *Shilling Cookery for the People* (1856 edition).

Production is now limited and mostly domestic, but it is still made for sale in Calderdale, a valley in the southern Pennines. A dock pudding competition is held in the village of Mytholmroyd (West Yorkshire) every May.

TECHNIQUE:

The vegetable ingredients, principally bistort and nettles, plus other herbs as desired, are assembled, washed and stripped from their stems. The greenery, chopped onion and some seasoning are cooked in water for 20 minutes, then oatmeal is added and the mixture cooked for 20 minutes more. The mixture is strained. At this point, it can be put into a jar or deep frozen. To reheat, it is cut in slices and fried in bacon fat for breakfast. It was used to accompany veal in the Lake District.

REGION OF PRODUCTION:

NORTH ENGLAND, CALDERDALE (SOUTH YORKSHIRE).

Rhubarb (Forced)

DESCRIPTION:

FORCED RHUBARB PLANT STEMS ARE USED WHEN ABOUT 45CM LONG AND 1–2CM ACROSS. THEIR COLOUR IS A FINE, BRIGHT PINK SKIN COVERING A WHITE INTERIOR, TERMINATING IN SMALL LEMON YELLOW LEAVES. WHEN EATEN UNACCOMPANIED, IT IS ACID AND ASTRINGENT; HOWEVER, RHUBARB IS ALWAYS EATEN COOKED AND SWEETENED. OUTDOOR RHUBARB HAS LARGER, THICKER STEMS OF A DEEPER RED OR PALE GREEN MOTTLED WITH DEEP RED; THE INTERIOR OF THE STEM IS GREEN, AND THE LEAVES, WHICH GROW VERY LARGE AND DARK GREEN, ARE CUT OFF BEFORE THE RHUBARB IS SOLD.

HISTORY:

Rhubarb, of Siberian origin, has been known in Britain since the fifteenth century, when its root was imported and used principally in medicine. The first recipe for the kitchen is dated 1783 and even as late as Mrs Beeton (1861), it was 'comparatively little known till within the last twenty or thirty years, but is now cultivated in almost every British garden'. Two decades later, Vilmorin-Andrieux remarked that its cultivation was 'as yet unpractised on the continent', but was of much importance in Great Britain and North America, drawing attention to the rhubarb beds he had seen in the Surrey area. Garden accounts from Viscount Courtenay's estate at Powderham Castle in Devon in 1819 show rhubarb being grown for Exeter market, thus confirming part of Mrs Beeton's statement; further reinforcement comes from gardeners' manuals. In Thomas Mawe and John Abercrombie's *Every Man his Own Gardener* (1805 edition) there is no mention of the plant. A century later, in Beeton's *Everyday Gardening*, a dozen varieties are listed, all with names of the time like Prince Albert and Victoria.

Although at first rhubarb recipes made no distinction between forced, early-season rhubarb and the main crop grown in the open air, it was that which was raised under cover with extra heat that captured the imagination and was taken up in West Yorkshire. There was a gap in the calendar of dessert fruit that could usefully be filled by the elegant, forced stalks. 'The first rhubarb of the season is to the digestive tract of winter-logged inner man what a good hot bath with plenty of healing soap is to the outer after a bout with plough and harrow,' wrote the American farmer's daughter Della Lutes (1938).

Rhubarb-growing became important in West Yorkshire as the plant was accepted into the English kitchen. Several factors combined to make it a prime crop in an otherwise agriculturally unpromising area. These include heavy clay soils; a climate which tends to cold early in the autumn providing the necessary conditions for early 'vernalization' (the growers' term for dormancy induced by winter temperatures, essential for forced rhubarb); a suitable annual pattern of rainfall which was also of a low pH (because of pollution from neighbouring industrial towns); the availability of suitable fertilizers; a nearby supply of cheap coal to heat forcing sheds; and excellent transport links to the rest of the country, initially through the railways and subsequently by the road network.

Forced rhubarb production has recently declined. It is labour-intensive with low profit margins. It suffers from an old-fashioned image associated with wartime rationing. It has to compete in a market flooded by imported exotic fruit. It remains important in West Yorkshire because the land is unsuitable for most other crops.

TECHNIQUE:

Most farmers grow their own rootstocks. Rhubarb sets (a major segment of root plus one crown bud) are produced by splitting unforced roots aged at least 2 years old. They are grown at a density of about 24,000 per hectare in ground treated heavily with organic material. In West Yorkshire this was farmyard manure, sewage sludge or 'shoddy' (waste woollen rags provided by the local textile industry). Flower stalks are removed in the summer before forcing. To ensure successful forcing, the roots must be vernalized. Practice had developed to accommodate this requirement; growers now keep temperature charts to deduce the correct time. The roots are lifted from mid-November onwards. They are removed to forcing sheds, stacked into beds on the shed floor, then earth is scattered on top and washed down into the roots with water. The plants are then forced in complete darkness at a constant temperature of 26°C for 4–6 weeks, after which the buds produce long sticks of pink rhubarb. As natural light spoils the colour of the leaves, which is a prime determinant of quality, harvesting is carried out by candlelight which illuminates only the area being worked on at a given time. The stalks are carefully picked by hand. The rhubarb is graded into 'Class 1' or 'seconds' (short, thin or poorly-coloured) and packed into 7kg boxes for sale. The exhausted rootstock is ploughed back into the soil.

REGION OF PRODUCTION:
NORTH ENGLAND, WEST YORKSHIRE, BETWEEN LEEDS, WAKEFIELD AND MORLEY.

Ribston Pippin

DESCRIPTION:
A LATE-SEASON DESSERT APPLE, MEDIUM SIZE, ROUND- TO OBLONG-CONICAL. COLOUR: WHEN RIPE, HAS REDDISH STRIPES OVER GOLD SKIN, DEEP CREAM FLESH. FLAVOUR: RICH, AROMATIC FLAVOUR, QUITE ACID.

HISTORY:
The apple takes its name from Ribston Hall, Knaresborough (Yorkshire). It is believed to have been raised in the early 1700s from a pip brought from France by Sir Henry Goodricke. It was esteemed by the Victorians: Dallas (1877) described it as 'the favourite apple of England'. It was grown in gardens and orchards all over the country, and is thought a parent of the Cox's Orange Pippin, now the most important British dessert apple. The Ribston Pippin lost commercial popularity in the early 1900s, but continued to be grown in gardens.

TECHNIQUE:
See entry on Cox's Orange Pippin (p. 60) for more details of apple growing.

REGION OF PRODUCTION:
NORTH ENGLAND, YORKSHIRE.

Coverdale Cheese

DESCRIPTION:
PRESSED, PASTEURIZED COW'S MILK CHEESE IN TALL, WAXED TRUCKLES SIZED 10CM ROUND, 6.5CM TALL; 12.5CM BY 14CM; 12.5CM BY 15CM; 23CM BY 15CM. WEIGHT: 500G–6KG. THE CHIVE-FLAVOURED VARIANT IS MADE IN WHEELS (3KG ONLY). COLOUR: ALMOST WHITE. FLAVOUR AND TEXTURE: MILD, CREAMY WITH SHARP OVERTONES; A CLOSE TEXTURE.

HISTORY:
Coverdale is on the east side of the Pennines. This is a dales cheese; the common heritage of the group is touched upon on p. 282. The recipe for Coverdale was recorded in 1912 by Alfred Rowntree. Local historian Kate Mason recalls his stating that milk collected from farms in Coverdale behaved differently to that from other dales, and that he found that if he wished to make Wensleydale he had to modify the recipe. He established a small dairy at Coverham in Coverdale. Production declined during the 1930s and it was not made for some decades after

World War II. It has been revived by a nearby creamery who use the 1912 recipe.

TECHNIQUE:

Coverdale is a dales cheese. Differences in micro-climate and flora give the various cheeses distinctive characteristics which are enhanced by variations in recipe and method. The method for Coverdale is not disclosed by the maker but it is broadly similar to Wensleydale. Vegetable rennet is used.

REGION OF PRODUCTION:

NORTH ENGLAND, NORTH YORKSHIRE.

Swaledale Cheese

DESCRIPTION:

PRESSED, PASTEURIZED EWE'S AND COW'S MILK CHEESES, SOLD IN WEIGHTS OF 250G, 500G (FOR BOTH SHEEP'S MILK AND COW'S MILK), 2KG (LARGE SHEEP'S MILK), 3KG (LARGE COW'S MILK), AND 1.5KG (FOR THE FLAVOURED COW'S MILK CHEESES). FORM: SMALL TRUCKLES. COLOUR: VERY PALE CREAM. FLAVOUR: FRESH, LEMONY, BUTTERY. THE COW'S MILK CHEESES ARE AVAILABLE SMOKED, OR FLAVOURED WITH CHIVES AND GARLIC, APPLEMINT, OR SOAKED IN OLD PECULIER ALE (P. 272).

HISTORY:

Swaledale belongs to the dales group of small, sharp-flavoured, softish cheeses. When most of the land about there was owned by the Cistercian monastery of Jervaulx, the valleys were farmed from granges – outlying cells that managed vast flocks of sheep (England's wool was the best in Europe) and herds of cows. Cheeses were made in great number. A monastery could get through tons a year. Many were of sheep's milk. The skills first refined by the monks and their labourers spread to the community at large. We are their inheritors.

Swaledale cheese pursued much the same course as Wensleydale (see below) and suffered as badly as its neighbours in the years 1939–45, when cheese-making was centralized and reduced to 2 basic types. Rance (1982) remarks that some on-farm production survived in the area – several are documented – but the makers were convinced their activity was illegal, so little got to the market-place until interest revived in the 1970s. This encouraged some who had learnt to make cheese from their parents, such as Mrs Longstaff who grew up on one of the most noted farms, to begin once more (Mitchell, 1986). On-farm cheese, however, has not taken root and Swaledale is now produced in moderately large quantities by a creamery in the valley. The cow's milk cheeses are available all year. Those made with sheep's milk tend to be seasonal, from January until late autumn. Protected Designations of Origin have been granted to both sheep's milk and cow's milk versions.

TECHNIQUE:

Much of Swaledale is now thinly populated; sheep and cattle form the mainstay of the local economy, pastured on the herb-rich grassland which flourishes on the underlying limestone and millstone grit.

A recipe for Swaledale cheese, still used in the 1980s, was recorded by Patrick Rance. The milk was taken straight from the cow and renneted without the addition of starter at 32°C and left for an hour. The curd was broken into fine pieces and left for an hour, then the whey was poured off. The curd was put into muslin and hung up to drip for 12 hours. The curd was crumbled fine by hand, salted, and mixed, and turned into fine muslin; it was then moulded and pressed for at least 12 hours. On removal from the press, the cheese was unmoulded, the cloth removed and the cheeses stored in a cool place, turned daily for 3 weeks (soft) or up to several months (for a drier, crumbly cheese).

The milk comes from specified herds and flocks in Swaledale. It is pasteurized before use. Exact details of the method are not disclosed. Swaledale is based on a similar recipe to Wensleydale and both use cow's milk and sheep's milk. The cheeses are lightly pressed, and salted by brining after removal from the moulds.

REGION OF PRODUCTION:
NORTH ENGLAND, NORTH YORKSHIRE.

Wensleydale Cheese

DESCRIPTION:
HARD, PRESSED COW'S MILK CHEESE ONCE INVARIABLY MADE IN SMALL TRUCKLES 16CM DIAMETER AND 18CM HIGH. SIZE NOW DEPENDS ON WEIGHT, WHICH IS 450G–2.3KG. BLOCK VERSIONS ARE ALSO MADE. COLOUR: WHITE; THE BLUE BECOMES A PALE CREAM WITH BLUE VEINS. FLAVOUR AND TEXTURE: A GOOD WENSLEYDALE HAS A MILD SHARP FLAVOUR AND A CRUMBLY, MOIST CURD. A SOFT EWE'S MILK CHEESE IS ALSO MADE UNDER THE NAME WENSLEYDALE.

HISTORY:
Wensleydale cheese has suffered much from being poorly copied. This is unfortunate, as it has a long and interesting history and is the only British territorial cheese which can clearly be demonstrated to have its origin in a sheep's milk cheese. In the past, it was usually blue-veined, with a moist, spreadable consistency.

Wensleydale is just one of several river valleys cut into the Pennine hills. The predominant rock is limestone. The economy has always been based on pastoral farming; cheese-making may have been carried on from a very early date. Cistercian monks are always claimed to have brought recipes and methods which naturalized to become the true Wensleydale. Cheeses are mentioned in monastic inventories from the twelfth century. The monks may have instructed tenant farmers on their surplus land in the art of cheese-making, the cheese later being used to pay the rent. After the dissolution of the monasteries, the lay population continued to make cheese using a mixture of cow's and sheep's milk. The use of sheep's milk gradually disappeared in Wensleydale although it survived in neighbouring areas.

In the nineteenth century, cheese-making was a seasonal activity, commencing in mid-May. Two shapes were made, those from spring and late autumn being flat millstones and from mid-season being tall truckles. Everything stopped with the first frost. The method used until late in the nineteenth century was based on the use of full-cream milk, with that from the evening's milking being ripened to start the next morning's. The cheeses were usually salted externally, in a brine bath or by brine washing. Much of the cheese blued naturally. The use of the name Wensleydale for the cheese is relatively recent. The first firm date is the first half of the nineteenth century, when cheese fairs began in the local market town of Leyburn.

Factory production commenced in the early 1900s, when farmhouse production was already in decline. Standardization of the recipe, particularly shifting to salting the curd in preference to brine washing, altered the consistency, and a higher proportion was eaten young, reducing the number of blue cheeses. By the 1930s, a local man, Kit Calvert, realizing that Wensleydale made by the old methods was under threat, formed the Wensleydale Cheesemakers Association to aid those farmers still following the practices of their ancestors. In the end, the struggle was too much for them and such cheeses died out in the late 1950s. Attempts at revival after wartime rationing had failed because of inflexible rules imposed by the Milk Marketing Board. It was not until renewed interest in small-scale cheesemaking during the 1980s that farmhouse Wensleydale was seen once more.

Since 1939–45, most Wensleydale has been sold young and only a very limited quantity of blue is available. In Yorkshire, it is traditionally served with fruit cake or apple pie, or eaten with oatcakes. Formerly it was a summer-only cheese, but now is made throughout the year.

TECHNIQUE:
Craft method: the milk is heated to 21°C and a small proportion of starter added. Then the morning milk is mixed in and the temperature raised to 28°C for the addition of rennet. The surface is stirred gently to prevent the cream from rising. The curd is cut into 3mm cubes and then settled for 10 minutes before cutting again; then it is settled for 20 minutes, followed by 20 minutes' stirring as the temperature rises to 30°C; the curd is then left in the whey for up to an hour. It is drained and milled into walnut-sized pieces. Salt may be added before or after this process. The cheese is packed into cloth-lined moulds; the following day they are turned, lightly weighted for 24 hours, then turned again. They are washed in salt water and bandaged. Wensleydale cheese is eaten after maturing for between 2 weeks and 3 months.

In the creamery method the temperatures are slightly higher. Blue Wensleydale requires a less acid, softer curd, more coarsely milled and lightly pressed. An even temperature of 12°C and a humidity of 95 per cent is needed during the ripening; the cheese may be inoculated with the mould spores and pierced with needles during ripening to encourage blueing.

REGION OF PRODUCTION:
NORTH ENGLAND, NORTH YORKSHIRE.

Denby Dale Pie

DESCRIPTION:
AN OBLONG, COOKED MEAT AND POTATO PIE. SMALL PIES MADE IN THE VILLAGE ARE 9CM LONG, 5CM WIDE, 3CM DEEP, WEIGHING 175G. COLOUR: PALE GOLD PASTRY COVERING PALE POTATO LAYER WITH BROWNED BEEF FILLING. FLAVOUR: SAVOURY BEEF.

HISTORY:
The Denby Dale is a special-occasion pie baked in the West Riding village of that name once in about every 25 years; the last making took place in 2000. Large celebration pies have been recorded elsewhere in England, but it is its huge size which distinguishes the Denby Dale (Bostwick, 1987). Custom has it that each time the pie is baked, it should be larger than the last. That baked in 2000 weighed 12 tonnes and measured 40 foot long.

'Nothing would be more tiresome than eating and drinking if God had not
made them a pleasure as well as a necessity.'

VOLTAIRE

The first to be documented was in 1788 to celebrate the return to health of King George III. This was followed by: the Victory Pie (1815, to commemorate the Battle of Waterloo); the Repeal of the Corn Laws Pie (1846, to celebrate the removal of unpopular legislation which kept the price of corn artificially high); the Golden Jubilee Pie (27 August 1887, intended to celebrate Queen Victoria's Golden Jubilee); the Resurrection Pie (3 September 1887, to replace the Golden Jubilee Pie which went bad and had to be buried in quicklime); the Repeal of the Corn Laws Jubilee Pie (1896, commemorating that from 50 years earlier); the Infirmary Pie (1928, to raise funds for the local hospital); the Would-Be Coronation Pie (1953, planned but never made, because meat was still rationed in the aftermath of the Second World War); the Village Hall Pie (1964, to raise funds for a community hall); the Bicentenary Pie (1988, to recall the beginning of the tradition); and, most recently, the Millennium Pie (2000, to celebrate the new Millennium and the Queen Mother's 100th birthday). A local butcher holds the formula for a special seasoning mixture which has been used in the last 2 pies and is also put into small pies made from day to day.

The pie was originally filled with meat and game, but after the débâcle of 1887, the recipe was changed to one similar to that now used. This is a gigantic version of the common meat and potato pie, a stew of beef covered with sliced potato, topped with shortcrust pastry and baked. These pies are well known in Yorkshire and Lancashire. Fresh beef is always used, distinguishing them from cottage pies, which are leftover meat, and demonstrating a relationship with Lancashire hotpot, a mutton stew covered with sliced potatoes. Small meat and potato pies are popular for dinner in the industrial areas of West Yorkshire and South Lancashire. Only the village of Denby Dale makes the huge pies.

TECHNIQUE:
The last Denby Dale Pie to be baked entire was in 1928. To satisfy hygiene regulations, large pies are now made by producing a stew of beef and potato using the special seasoning, cooking the crust separately and assembling on site.

Small pies are made as follows. The meat is always fresh beef, cut into pieces of 1–2cm and partially cooked with seasoning and liquid (usually water) to produce plenty of gravy. The beef is first covered with a layer of sliced, lightly seasoned raw potato, then with a sheet of shortcrust and baked for 45 minutes, at 190°C.

REGION OF PRODUCTION:
NORTH ENGLAND, WEST YORKSHIRE AND SOUTH LANCASHIRE.

Elder

DESCRIPTION:
COOKED COW'S UDDER. COLOUR: PINK, MOTTLED WITH CREAMY-YELLOW. FLAVOUR: A LITTLE LIKE TONGUE, BUT BLANDER, WITH A CHEWY TEXTURE.

HISTORY:
Elder is a dialect word for cow's udder known in much of the north and west of Britain, but now archaic except in parts of Yorkshire and Lancashire. The use of udder as food is not well-documented, but was formerly widespread. When the pig-cook Ursula was bantering with her friend Knockem in Jonson's *Bartholomew Fair* (1614), she denies reports of her demise of a surfeit of

bottle-ale and tripes. 'No,' replied Knockem, 'it was better meat, it was cow's udders.' Today, its sale is limited to the industrial towns of South-West Yorkshire and East Lancashire (Brown, 1987). The first recorded use of the word elder appears to be in a collection of North-Country dialect published in the late 1600s. Presented as thick slices, arranged on trays in the windows of cooked meat shops and takeaway food shops, elder has a very distinctive appearance, mostly due to the colour. The texture is also particular, resembling coarse-textured, chewy tongue. Martha Bradley (1756) counselled that it should treated in exactly the same way as tongue. In northern towns and villages, it is customarily eaten cold with salt and malt vinegar, but there are many more interesting ways of dealing with it should this food ever return to popularity.

TECHNIQUE:

The udder is skinned and drained of any remaining milk. It is boiled for about 6 hours (sometimes more) until tender; the elder is left to cool in the liquid, and may be given a second boiling for another 2 hours the next day, then rapidly cooled. It is given a final dressing to remove excess fat and scraps of skin, then trimmed neatly.

REGION OF PRODUCTION:

NORTH ENGLAND, SOUTH WEST YORKSHIRE, EAST LANCASHIRE.

Middle White Pig

DESCRIPTION:

A DRESSED CARCASS OF 50KG AT 12–16 WEEKS. A SHORT, DEEP BODY, ROUNDED HAMS AND DISTINCTIVE SNUB NOSE. A TRADITIONALLY-REARED MIDDLE WHITE YIELDS DARKER LEAN THAN COMMERCIAL BREEDS; IT IS WELL-MARBLED, TENDER, JUICY, WITH EXCELLENT FLAVOUR; A BREED WHICH IS GOOD AS SUCKING PIG.

HISTORY:

As the name suggests, there are other white pigs: the Large White is still important commercially and it is thought there was also a Small White, now vanished. They flourished in Yorkshire during the late eighteenth and early nineteenth centuries when, as detailed by William Youatt, the breeding of prize pigs on a small scale was both a hobby and a source of meat and income for craftsmen and cottagers (Samuel, 1860). The Middle White may have originated in a cross between the Small White and an imported Chinese pig, to give the characteristic snub profile and rounded shape. An early name was the Yorkshire. Until World War II, they were a popular pork breed but subsequently declined in numbers because tastes in meat changed.

TECHNIQUE:

Middle Whites can be kept outdoors, at least in the summer, but do not forage as efficiently as other breeds because of their short noses. Most people keep them as sty pigs, with food entirely provided. This was the method used by cottagers and small farmers, who had limited space but none the less access to domestic and garden waste or edible by-products such as spent grain from brewing. For sucking pig, they are killed at 7–8 weeks; for pork they are grown on to 12–16 weeks. To obtain pork suitable for the current market this breed should be slaughtered before it accumulates large amounts of fat.

REGION OF PRODUCTION:

NORTH ENGLAND.

Polony

DESCRIPTION:

A COOKED PORK SAUSAGE SOLD IN LOOPS 40–50CM LONG; ABOUT 4CM DIAMETER. COLOUR:
THE SKIN IS BRIGHT RED, ENCLOSING PALE PINK MEAT. FLAVOUR: MILD CURED-PORK
FLAVOUR, LIGHTLY SPICED AND SMOKED.

HISTORY:

The name may be a corruption of Polonia (Poland) or Bologna, the Italian town. Opinion tends towards the latter. Whichever, polony has had over 300 years to develop a British identity, for Bologna or Polony sausage was popular in the seventeenth century (Wilson, 1973). A recipe for 'Bolonia' sausages in John Nott (1726) displays several characteristics still associated with polony, including a flour paste to bind, large size, and the fact that they were precooked. Polony has always been red; red sage, saltpetre, red wine or cochineal were all used as colourings.

The spa town of Bath, close to an important pig-raising area, was famous for polony in the past. Smith (1951) mentions Bath polonies, which, 'have been given a high place amongst those eatables for which the city has become famous'. and mentions Dill's Polonies, Cheap Street, in existence since 1784 (they have now vanished). The second area linked with them was Yorkshire. Douglas's *Encyclopaedia* gave a Yorkshire recipe including pork and rice or rusk plus salt, white pepper, cayenne, nutmeg and mace. *Law's Grocer's Manual* (*c.* 1895) stated that 'Sheffield is more celebrated for these cooked sausages than any other town in England.' Finney's instructions for pork butchers included 2 named polony mixtures – Yorkshire and Bath – but all the others were identified only by number (1915). In the 1930s, Sheffield polony was among butcher's recipes published by Percy Dalton. It included lean pork, mutton or corned beef, ham or beef fat, flour and rusk, salt, pepper, mace, coriander and ginger. It is difficult to escape the conclusion that individual butchers used whatever ingredients they felt would achieve the correct texture.

Polonies still flourish and many butchers make their own. Highly commercialized polony in a red plastic skin is sold in supermarkets, but bears little resemblance to good artisan versions.

TECHNIQUE:

A mixture of lean and fat raw pork is chopped fine, mixed with flour paste or rusk and seasonings according to individual recipes (salt, pepper, mace, coriander and ginger are all cited), then filled into wide casings. They are boiled for about 45 minutes with red food colouring in the water. They are chilled in iced water, drained and displayed for sale and are sold by weight.

REGION OF PRODUCTION:

NORTH ENGLAND, YORKSHIRE.

York Ham

DESCRIPTION:

A CURED HAM. WEIGHT: ABOUT 14KG. COLOUR: PALE GOLD OR BROWN RIND, WHITE FAT AND DEEP RED LEAN WHEN UNCOOKED; ROSE-PINK LEAN AFTER COOKING. FLAVOUR: RICH SALTY HAM, WITH DISTINCT PORK FLAVOUR, DRY TEXTURE.

HISTORY:

York hams are esteemed far beyond English shores. There are countless foreign references to them. Take Flaubert's *Education Sentimentale* (1869), describing a dinner given by the dandified Vicomte de Cisy: 'For the first course alone, there was a sturgeon's head drenched in champagne, a York ham cooked in tokay, thrushes *au gratin*, roast quail, a *vol-au-vent Béchamel*, a *sauté* of red-legged partridges, and, flanking all this, stringed potatoes mixed with truffles.' York ham kept high-falutin' company. But curiously little attention was ever paid to the delicacy in the place whence it takes its name. There are several reasons why this might be. Firstly, it would probably be more accurate to regard them as hams from the county rather than the city of York. In 1747, the earliest mention found so far, Hannah Glasse wrote 'Yorkshire is famous for Hams'. She thought it was the quality of the salt used in their manufacture which made the difference. William Ellis, at about the same time, noticed the London market being flooded by cheap Yorkshire ham. By 1817 they had become known as 'York Hams'; Kitchiner said that 'real' York hams were preferable to any, but gave no reasons. The word suggests that imitations were known and the term was becoming generic, implying a particular cure not a place of birth.

Douglas's *Encyclopaedia* (*c.* 1905) described hams cured in Ireland for export to France as 'York' hams: they were small, 12lb (6kg) in weight, mildly cured and lightly smoked, whereas Yorkshire-produced hams were large, up to 50lb (25kg), and were very salty.

Opinions vary as to whether York (or Yorkshire) hams should be smoked. The *Magazine of Domestic Economy* (1838) said they were smoked over wood shavings with aromatic herbs. It has been claimed by various twentieth-century authors (for instance Hartley, 1954) that York hams were made in the Middle Ages, and smoked over sawdust generated from building the cathedral in the town. There is no evidence for this. Scott's, the butchers in York who produce them today, do not smoke them. In the past, the quality of the pigs – Yorkshire was the home of the Large White, an important commercial breed – may well have contributed to the excellence of hams from Yorkshire, just as did the availability of feed, which included spent brewers' grain. The growth of river and canal transport links may also have been a factor in the low price of York ham in the eighteenth century. Modern York hams are smaller, about 14kg, and less salty.

TECHNIQUE:

The pork legs, cut from bacon pigs, must carry a specified level of fat, otherwise they become dry; they are long-cut, giving a rounded shape. They are cured in dry salt with saltpetre and sugar for 1 month, then drained for 3 days and matured for 4–24 months, depending on the manufacturer. Temperature and humidity are controlled, leading to a shorter maturing time as well as production all year round. W. Hogan (1978) remarked that long and careful maturing, over 6 months, was the true secret of a modern York ham.

REGION OF PRODUCTION:

NORTH ENGLAND, YORKSHIRE.

Fat Rascal

DESCRIPTION:

A ROUND, DOMED TEACAKE ABOUT 100MM DIAMETER, 30–40MM DEEP. WEIGHT: ABOUT 170G. COLOUR AND TEXTURE: RICH BROWN CRUST, CRACKED IN PLACES WITH PALER, LESS HIGHLY BAKED INSIDE SHOWING THROUGH; CLOSE-TEXTURED, PALE YELLOW INSIDE, WITH CURRANTS AND CANDIED PEEL. FLAVOUR: SWEETISH WITH CITRUS NOTE.

HISTORY:

The origin of the name for these teacakes is unknown, but has been in use since at least the mid-nineteenth century; a reference from the 1860s makes clear that the cake was composed of flour, currants and butter or cream, and that it was closely associated with the Cleveland area, on the borders of Durham and Yorkshire. It was not a complex dough. It was raised with baking soda and was easy for domestic cooks to bake in a 'yetling' or pot oven, a cast iron, deep, lidded pot raised on short legs which could be placed in hot ashes in the fireplace. There are several North-Country cakes of this nature with more or less evocative names such as girdle cake, flap cake or turf cake. Singin' hinnies, made in Durham and Northumberland, are based on a similar recipe, as are rock buns. White (1932) and Brears (1987) cite variations, for example using lard instead of butter.

Fat rascals from bakers' shops are larger and richer than those which are made at home; they are baked in an oven, and have an added decoration of a face made from halved glacé cherries and almonds which is not associated with the cakes of the past. Modern versions are usually leavened with baking powder.

TECHNIQUE:

The ratio of flour to fat is 2:1. The dough is rolled out to a sheet a little over a centimetre thick and cut into rounds of about 60mm across. They are baked for 10–15 minutes at about 200°C.

REGION OF PRODUCTION:

NORTH ENGLAND, YORKSHIRE.

Muffin

DESCRIPTION:

CIRCULAR FLAT BREAD, 80–90MM DIAMETER, 30MM DEEP. WEIGHT: ABOUT 70G. COLOUR: PALE GOLD OR WHITE; ALMOST WHITE AROUND THE SIDES. SOFT TEXTURE, ALWAYS EATEN TOASTED.

HISTORY:

Muffins are food for English tea. Their history, and that of crumpets which are closely related, is confusing. The term is first recorded in English during the early eighteenth century. The *OED* suggests it is 'a word connected with old French *moufflet*, soft, said of bread'. The characteristics of softness and a flat shape, usually baked on a hot stone or griddle, are essential points. However, a firm definition of early muffins or crumpets is elusive (David, 1977). Peter Brears (1984) cites a seventeenth-century Yorkshire recipe for oatcakes which in fact contains no oats and would have turned out like a muffin. A recipe for muffins from Hannah Glasse (1747) is for soft flat cakes of plain yeast-leavened dough. (She instructed the consumer to pull, not cut the muffin: a *sine qua non* of muffin consumption in the years since her book.)

Recipes over the following 150 years varied in terms of relative richness, some included eggs, butter or milk. The results were always cooked on hearthstones or iron plates and, according to *Law's Grocer's Manual*, bakers had special stones set in brick for the purpose.

The chief distinction between muffins and crumpets is the consistency of the raw mixture. A muffin is made with a soft dough while crumpets use a pouring batter. The flour preferred for muffins was usually stronger (with more protein) than that for crumpets.

For years muffins were cried through the streets of cities by vendors who bought their stock from bakers. The breads were folded in flannel to keep hot. They appear to have been eaten for tea by almost everyone. Housewives bought them from the muffin men, gentlemen's clubs served them for tea in silver dishes, and famous writers made observations about them. Early in the twentieth century, their popularity declined, the muffin man vanished, the breads themselves a rarity. The one area where they survived was Lancashire and West Yorkshire. This is a stronghold of griddle-baking, and Joseph Wright (1896–1905) recorded the word muffin as Lancashire and Yorkshire dialect. Whether this represents some deeper tradition is not clear, but David Mabey (1978) commented that muffins were rarely seen except in Lancashire, where they were still being made and sold by bakers when he was writing.

Matters have changed much since then. The muffin has been adopted by supermarkets and plant bakers, who fill it with dried fruit or spices for variation's sake. The modern muffin has come to be (mostly because of these extra ingredients) a rather close-textured bread cake, but some craft bakers make very good muffins of the old type; one company in Lancashire uses a local recipe which dates back at least 70 years.

The English muffin is quite different from the American, which is a chemically-leavened bun or cake with or without added flavouring. English muffins are eaten by toasting on the outside, split by pulling apart, and buttered by laying on a piece of butter. The halves are then put back together and kept warm until the butter has melted. They are eaten for tea, but now often for breakfast as well.

TECHNIQUE:
For muffin making, the texture of the dough and the heat of the griddle are vital. These can only be learnt through experience. The craft method needs a soft dough made from warmed flour, water, yeast, salt, and small quantities of sugar and butter. The butter is rubbed through the dry ingredients; the yeast is dispersed in the water, and used to mix the dough. It is left to rise for 1 hour, then knocked back, scaled off and shaped into rounds. These are placed on trays dusted with rice flour and proved. The rounds are placed in hoops on a hot-plate; halfway through cooking they are turned over.

REGION OF PRODUCTION:
NORTH ENGLAND, LANCASHIRE, WEST YORKSHIRE.

Ripon Spice Cake

DESCRIPTION:
A LOAF 140MM LONG, 70MM WIDE, 90MM HIGH. WEIGHT: ABOUT 450G. COLOUR: RICH BROWN CRUST, BEIGE CRUMB WITH PROMINENT FRUIT. FLAVOUR: SWEET, AROMATIC, HEAVILY SPICED.

No early references have been found to substantiate a long association of this cake with Ripon. Spice cakes, however, were known in the region and made frequently until at least 1939–45. They were a Christmas speciality and known as Yule spice cakes. Recipes show them containing sugar, dried fruit, and candied peel, enriched with butter and lard and flavoured with nutmeg and lemon. Cassell's *Dictionary of Cookery* (1896) includes an entry under the heading 'Yorkshire Spice Cake (sometimes called Yule Cake)'. It points to several other recipes which it would classify together, including 'Aunt Edward's Christmas Cake', remarking that the Yorkshire cake was 'freely offered to strangers and presented to friends, and frequently eaten with cheese instead of bread'.

Today's recipe belongs to the Ripon business which produces the cake. It was bought with the shop 20 years ago. It deserves attention because it contains elements which are old – the use of lard as a shortening and yeast as a leavening agent – alongside candied cherries and walnuts which are both relatively new to the British cake-baking tradition. If the Yule spice cakes used to be made for Christmas, the present maker ignores that feast, leaves Yule out of the name altogether and concentrates production on the Ripon festival of St Wilfrid's (see Wilfra cakes, below). This is an innovation. There is but the one maker of Ripon spice cakes but Yule spice cakes can still sometimes be bought from bakeries in North Yorkshire.

TECHNIQUE:

The cake is a lightly sweetened, yeast-leavened cake. Once enriched with lard, changes in taste have led to its replacement by margarine. Some recipes also called for eggs. Dried fruit, candied cherries, walnuts and spices, including cinnamon and nutmeg, are added and kneaded through. The mixture is scaled off, placed in tins and proved. They are baked at 150–160°C for 60–90 minutes. The cakes are dusted with icing sugar before going on sale.

REGION OF PRODUCTION:

NORTH ENGLAND, RIPON (NORTH YORKSHIRE).

Suet Cake

DESCRIPTION:

CIRCULAR BISCUITS OR CAKES, 80MM DIAMETER, 10MM THICK. WEIGHT: 75G. COLOUR: PALE GOLD, FLECKED WITH DRIED FRUIT. FLAVOUR AND TEXTURE: BLAND AND PLAIN.

HISTORY:

Suet cakes are one representative of a group of bland, close-textured, pastry-type biscuits made in West Yorkshire and East Lancashire. They are now considered old-fashioned and production is limited but the spread of recipes and names suggests they were formerly common. Variants include hard cakes, fatty cakes (West Riding of Yorkshire), sad cakes (West Riding of Yorkshire, Rossendale area of Lancashire) and cracknells (Blackburn). The descriptor 'sad' indicates a baked item which does not rise very much, while 'hard cakes' suggests the texture. Brears (1987) gives some details: fatty cake is a short cake of flour with butter, dripping or lard; sad cakes are made from a flour and lard dough leavened with baking powder and filled with currants and a little sugar; suet cakes are made from flour shortened with lard, suet, currants and yeast. These were cooked on a bakstone, the regional term and spelling for griddle.

Boyd (1988) shows Blackburn cracknells to be biscuits of the same type but without the fruit. Cracknell is a word descended from the French *craquelin*, which described 2 sorts of dry cake or biscuit. The first was a dough poached then dried in the oven, described by Dawson (1596), the second was a plain, sugared biscuit for which recipes abound. Citations of the other names have not been found before 1850, but this is not conclusive. They are probably ancient in origin. The use of the word cake to indicate pastry or biscuits is very old (see Shrewsbury cakes, p. 176). The use of currants in the mixture relates them to other pastries popular in the area, such as Eccles cakes and Chorley cakes. So far, one baker has been located making suet cakes (a family-owned business, founded about a century ago), and one other which bakes Blackburn cracknells. Several early references relate these cakes specifically to breakfast. They are usually spread with butter.

TECHNIQUE:
Suet cakes were originally leavened with yeast. The lard was rubbed into the flour, the other ingredients added and some yeast, mixed with milk and water, used to form a dough. This was shaped into small cakes, proved and baked. Those made now are leavened with baking powder. They require flour, suet, lard and currants in the proportions 4:1:1:1. A firm dough is rolled to 10mm thick, cut into cakes and baked at 170°C until pale gold.

Sad cakes are a short pastry (flour and fat in the proportions 2:1), mixed with currants and rolled out. According to Mabey (1978) they varied from a type of pasty in which the currants were kept in the middle of a pastry envelope, to something more like a biscuit, with the currants thoroughly incorporated into thin pastry. Spicer (1949) mentions these, and directs the cook to cut them into fancy shapes.

A Yorkshire recipe for hard cakes is for plain biscuits with no currants, raised with volatile salts – ammonium carbonate (White, 1932).

REGION OF PRODUCTION:
NORTH ENGLAND, YORKSHIRE–LANCASHIRE BORDER.

Wilfra Tart

DESCRIPTION:
A DOUBLE-CRUST PIE WITH A DECORATION OF 3 PASTRY LEAVES AROUND A CENTRAL VENT, 120–130MM DIAMETER, 20MM DEEP. WEIGHT: ABOUT 350G. COLOUR: PALE GOLD PASTRY, WITH YELLOW MELTED CHEESE SHOWING THROUGH THE CENTRAL HOLE. FLAVOUR: CRISP UNSWEETENED PASTRY, WITH A FILLING OF SWEETENED APPLE AND A LAYER OF CHEESE.

HISTORY:
Various tarts have been known by this name in the past, with fillings such as sweet mincemeat, curd cheese, and jam. That described here is the one commercially available today.

Wilfra tarts are made in the town of Ripon in North Yorkshire. The name is a corruption of St Wilfrid (634–709, bishop of York and monk at Ripon), the patron of the town's cathedral. The tarts are made for a procession held in his honour on the Saturday before the first Monday in August. This procession has a history which stretches back at least to the late Middle Ages. Earlier evidence about the tarts themselves is not forthcoming. Hence the first description is in White (1932) who noted them as small jam tarts or cheesecakes. Later sources comment that the tarts were handed out to passers-by or left on plates by house door-ways for people to help themselves.

At least 2 versions now seem to be known; the apple and cheese version made for sale, and another recipe which calls for a filling of butter, ground almonds, sugar, lemon rind, soaked breadcrumbs and egg. This last is similar to early almond cheesecake recipes, for instance Eliza Smith's (1758). The origin of the apple and cheese combination is less obvious. English cooks were rather indiscriminate about the basis of their cheesecakes, which quite often contained no cheese or curded milk but were based on eggs and almonds instead; later, ground rice or desiccated coconut were substituted for the almonds, and sometimes mashed potato was added. It is possible that the current recipe is an evolution of a formerly more complex 'cheesecake' which included apples amongst its ingredients. The baker who now bakes it uses a recipe which belonged to the business which he acquired some 25 years ago. He is the only producer.

TECHNIQUE:

An English shortcrust is used to line a deep pie dish, and a portion is rolled out for the top. A layer of sliced apples is placed in the bottom, brown sugar sprinkled over, and some grated cheese placed on top. This should traditionally be Wensleydale but Cheddar, which is a deeper yellow, is used in preference. The pie is covered and decorated. It is baked at 180°C for about 40 minutes. It may be eaten hot or cold.

REGION OF PRODUCTION:

NORTH ENGLAND, RIPON (NORTH YORKSHIRE).

Whitby Gingerbread

DESCRIPTION:

A LOAF, WITH A PATTERN OF LOZENGES IMPRINTED ON THE SURFACE, 140MM LONG, 90MM WIDE, 60MM DEEP. WEIGHT: ABOUT 500G. COLOUR: CHESTNUT BROWN. FLAVOUR AND TEXTURE: MILDLY SPICED, DRY.

HISTORY:

Whitby is a small port on the Yorkshire coast. Tradition has it that gingerbread has been made there since the 1700s. It was certainly known by the time the company which now makes it, Elizabeth Botham & Sons, was established in 1865. According to Joe Botham, who now runs the company, references are found in the *Whitby Gazette* for 'gingerbread for ships' during the 1850s. He speculates that this trade was the reason for the characteristically dry texture and excellent keeping-qualities of the cake. Recipe and method show links with the oatmeal-based parkin known further west. Originally the gingerbread was baked in blocks of 4lb (1.8kg) which were then quartered. The loaves are now cut into thin slices, spread with butter, and eaten with the mild cheeses produced in the Yorkshire Dales. It was a customary food at Christmas.

TECHNIQUE:

The exact method is a trade secret but the gingerbread uses lard which is melted with a dark syrup. Flour, spices, a powder raising agent, water and other ingredients are mixed to make a very sticky dough. After a period of resting, this is scaled off, shaped, placed in tins, marked with a mould, and given a long bake in gentle heat. The gingerbread is then matured for several weeks before sale.

REGION OF PRODUCTION:
NORTH-EAST ENGLAND, WHITBY (NORTH YORKSHIRE).

Whitby Lemon Bun

DESCRIPTION:
A SQUARE OR ROUND BUN, DEEP IN PROPORTION TO HEIGHT, WITH A THICKLY ICED TOP; ABOUT 100MM DIAMETER, 50MM HIGH. WEIGHT: 70–80G. COLOUR: GOLD-BROWN CRUST ON TOP, PALE UNDERSIDE, TORN APPEARANCE ON SIDES, WHERE BUNS ARE TORN APART AFTER BAKING; WHITE ICING; CREAM-YELLOW CRUMB WHEN CUT, WITH DRIED FRUIT. FLAVOUR: SLIGHTLY SWEETENED AND ENRICHED BREAD, LIGHT, SOFT OPEN TEXTURE, LEMON-FLAVOURED ICING.

HISTORY:
According to Joe Botham, who makes these buns in Whitby, no one is sure why they became a speciality of the town, except that they appear to have been one of the original lines made by Mrs Elizabeth Botham, who founded the bakery that bears her name in 1864. The dough is similar in taste to that used for other nineteenth-century enriched breads; this is a local version. It is richer than the small teacakes commonly made in Yorkshire, yet not as rich as the 'twopenny buns' recorded in a late eighteenth-century manuscript from the hills to the west of Whitby.

Whitby is a fishing port and developed as a popular tourist resort in the 1800s. Perhaps this had something to do with the success of the buns. It would inevitably bring a demand for foods that visitors found interesting and acceptable. The same imperative governing local specialities is seen in Bath buns, Bath Olivers and Sally Lunns. In the 1940s, the former manager of Botham's in Whitby (a descendant of the founder) moved to the city of Leeds and began to make his own version. It is slightly drier, less sweet, and baked as an individual bun (rather than in a batch torn asunder after baking). Only these 2 companies have been identified as making the buns.

TECHNIQUE:
The exact recipe is a trade secret. The buns are based on a soft, rich dough similar to that used for the Sally Lunn. The mixture is yeast-leavened, and sultanas are kneaded in; the dough is scaled off, shaped, placed close together on trays and 'batch baked': as the dough rises, the individual buns are so close together that they touch and have to be pulled apart on removal from the oven. When cooled, they are given a thick cap of lemon-flavoured glacé icing.

REGION OF PRODUCTION:
NORTH ENGLAND, YORKSHIRE.

Yorkshire Curd Tart

DESCRIPTION:

A CIRCULAR OPEN TART, A COMMON SIZE IS 140MM WIDE, 20MM DEEP; INDIVIDUAL CURD TARTS ARE NOT CUSTOMARY. WEIGHT: ONE OF THE SIZE QUOTED WEIGHS APPROXIMATELY 220G. COLOUR: THE PASTRY SHELL BAKES TO A PALE GOLD; THE FILLING HAS A GRANULAR APPEARANCE WHICH COLOURS UNEVENLY FROM CREAM TO GOLDEN BROWN; IT IS SPECKLED WITH CURRANTS. FLAVOUR AND TEXTURE: MILD, CREAMY AND SWEET, WITH GRANULATED TEXTURE.

HISTORY:

A curd tart is also known as a cheesecake. Baked cheesecakes have been known in England since at least the thirteenth century (Wilson, 1973), when household accounts record 'cheese for tarts' – perhaps referring to hard cheese rather than the fresh cheese used in later recipes. An early recipe, essentially the same as that used today, including both currants and nutmeg, is found in Lady Elinor Fettiplace's manuscript (Spurling, 1987). Subsequently, there is an infinity of instructions for curd cheesecakes in published manuals. Similar dishes, which were colloquially called cheesecakes but which contained ground almonds or other ingredients instead of curd to thicken the custard, were also made. What is not clear is the point at which these dishes were given up by the majority of the population and became local specialities. The evidence available suggests this took place some time between 1750 (when both Mrs Raffald and Mrs Smith included recipes for cheesecakes in their books, which were known throughout the country) and 1860 (when neither Miss Acton nor Mrs Beeton did). Nor is it clear why certain areas maintained a habit of making them. Today, curd tarts are now very much local specialities and their stronghold is Yorkshire – specifically for festive times, notably Whitsuntide and Christmas – where once they were gathered from housewives for communal feasts. This tradition is recorded in the towns of Muker and Redmire and in Fulford, now a suburb of York (Brears, 1987). Today, they have few associations with particular events and they are baked commercially by most bakeries in Yorkshire. Curd tarts have also been identified in Lincolnshire.

TECHNIQUE:

The curd is based on cow's milk. Traditionally, colostrum is used; this is simply brought to the boil, at which point it curdles naturally. Modern dairy practice now makes colostrum difficult to obtain. There are several other methods for making curd, including heating milk to just below boiling then stirring in Epsom salts, adding vinegar, adding rennet to warm milk, and stirring fresh, cold buttermilk into ordinary milk heated almost to boiling. The curd is then cooled and strained. Few make their own curd, but those who do have individual recipes which vary in their cream content; some give a very rich result.

The strained curd is mixed with sugar, eggs, margarine or butter and currants. Flavourings include nutmeg, lemon zest or rum. The mixture is beaten to break the curd into small particles. The mixture can be used immediately but it is thought better kept 1–3 days. An unsweetened short-crust pastry using lard is used. The curd mixture is poured on to the uncooked pastry to the desired depth. The tarts are baked at 180°C for about 30 minutes.

REGION OF PRODUCTION:

NORTH ENGLAND, YORKSHIRE.

Yorkshire Mint Pasty

DESCRIPTION:

A FLAT PASTRY MADE IN LARGE SQUARE TRAYS ABOUT 20MM DEEP. WHEN OFFERED FOR SALE, IT IS CUT INTO PIECES 8MM WIDE, 80MM LONG. WEIGHT: ABOUT 100G PER PIECE. COLOUR: PALE GOLD PASTRY, WITH A DARK LAYER OF CURRANTS. FLAVOUR: SWEET, WITH DRIED FRUIT AND MINT.

HISTORY:

The large size of a mint pasty relates it to the 'currant slice', made in a similar shape but omitting the mint, which is relatively common in British bakers' shops. The form, consisting of a layer of currants and other ingredients sandwiched between pastry, points to a relationship with regional specialities such as Chorley and Eccles cakes. A 'mint cake' of mint-flavoured pastry is mentioned from the beginning of the nineteenth century in Wright (1896–1905), and Florence White (1932) gives a recipe 'To make Old Yorkshire Mint Pasty', attributed to an inhabitant of Leeds. It is more complex than the recipe used by the present maker but similar to those pasties made in Yorkshire farmhouses until about 30 years ago, according to local historian Kate Mason. Mint pasties have been revived by at least one commercial baker after a gap of about 20 years in production.

TECHNIQUE:

The recipe given by Florence White requires shortcrust pastry (flour and fat in the ratio 2:1) to be rolled out thinly and cut into large rounds or squares. A thick filling of currants, raisins and candied peel layered with chopped fresh spearmint and brown sugar, topped with dabs of butter, grated nutmeg or other sweet spice is laid over one half of the pastry, the other is folded over the top, the edges dampened and pinched together. The pasty is baked at 220°C for about 30 minutes. Pasties produced commercially are simpler, based on currants only; white sugar and dried mint are substituted for the brown sugar and fresh mint.

REGION OF PRODUCTION:

NORTH ENGLAND, WEST YORKSHIRE.

Yorkshire Oatcake

DESCRIPTION:

AN ELONGATED OVAL, ABOUT 300MM LONG, 70MM WIDE, 2MM THICK. WEIGHT: APPROXIMATELY 45G. COLOUR: UNDERSIDE (CLOSEST TO THE BAKSTONE WHEN BAKED) IS SMOOTH GOLD-BROWN WITH A FEW UNEVENLY SCATTERED SMALL HOLES AND A PALER LINE AROUND THE EDGE; THE SIDE WHICH IS UPPERMOST DURING BAKING IS ROUGH, GREYISH AND DUSTED WITH CREAM-COLOURED OATMEAL. FLAVOUR AND TEXTURE: NUTTY, OATY, SLIGHTLY SOUR; SUPPLE AND SOFT WHEN FRESH, BUT CRISP AND HARD ONCE DRY.

HISTORY:

The type of oatcake associated with Yorkshire and Lancashire during the past century has a long history and a highly evolved method attached to it. The climate of this region is cool and wet, and oats were the main cereal crop until the nineteenth century. The alternative name havercake is thought to be derived from Old Norse *hafre*, meaning oats.

Many travellers from the South of England commented on oatcakes and noted the distinct northern preference for them over wheat bread. Although consumption is now limited to parts of Yorkshire and Lancashire, with a second type finding favour in Staffordshire, the oatcake was once a staple of the entire region. Two distinct types existed: one made of dough, the other of batter. The stiffer dough was driven out thin by 'clapping' it with the hand on a special board. This is now extinct. The second was oatcake made with a pouring or runny batter. This might be spread by the complex 'throwing' method found in parts of Yorkshire and Lancashire, or could be poured on to the griddle as if a simple pancake – as found in the Midland counties of Stafford and Derby.

Yorkshire oatcakes are made from finely ground meal, mixed to a thin batter and leavened either by sourdough fermentation or yeast or, more recently, bicarbonate of soda. A complex method developed for shaking the batter until it became as thin as possible. It was riddled or shaken on a special wooden board scored with criss-cross lines, then slipped onto a hot bakstone (heated stone slab). This process is the origin of the variant name riddle cake or riddlebread. Later, an even more complex method evolved. Described by Frederic Montagu (1938), it began with riddling, but then the batter was slid on to a cloth and thence flicked on to the bakstone in a long, narrow and very thin trail. After 30 seconds or so on the bakstone, the cake was skimmed off with a spatula. Those not required straightaway were hung on a special rack to dry, after which they would keep indefinitely. Thin, light oatcakes were the most valued and a mechanical process, developed in the mid-nineteenth century, which required the batter to be scraped across the bakstone, was not considered to give good results. Several skilled oatcake bakers are recorded during the nineteenth century. Eventually, a machine for throwing oatcake batter was patented that met the specifications of oatcake aficionados. This was still in use in 1999.

Oatcakes were eaten fresh or dried with butter or treacle, or with cheese and beer in the fields. They were also dried and served soaked in gravy, or crumbled into broth, a mixture which was known as 'stew and hard'. Today, they are most likely to be eaten with cheese.

TECHNIQUE:
Fine oatmeal and water or buttermilk are mixed to a thin batter and left overnight to sour. The batter is placed in a wooden tub which is not cleaned between batches. More meal is stirred in next morning to give the right consistency. A riddling board is sprinkled with oatmeal and a ladleful of batter poured on top. The board is shaken with a rotary motion, and then the batter is slid on to a linen band, mounted on a trolley over the hot-plate. Using a handle, the trolley is moved rapidly across the hottest part of the hot-plate: the cloth band moves round, depositing the batter in a long trail over the plate. The oatcake remains over high heat for about 30 seconds and is then removed with a spatula to a cooler part of the plate to finish cooking. If soft oatcakes are required, they are removed at this point and allowed to cool. Hard oatcakes are dried off under the hot-plate.

REGION OF PRODUCTION:
NORTH ENGLAND, WEST YORKSHIRE, LANCASHIRE.

Yorkshire Parkin

DESCRIPTION:

A GINGER CAKE, CUSTOMARILY SQUARE, ALTHOUGH NOW SOMETIMES BAKED IN ROUND CONTAINERS; 300MM SQUARE AND 40–50MM DEEP IS A TYPICAL SIZE, USUALLY SOLD IN SMALLER PORTIONS. WEIGHT: THE SIZE QUOTED WOULD WEIGH ABOUT 2KG. COLOUR: DARK CHESTNUT, A SHINY, STICKY SURFACE. FLAVOUR AND TEXTURE: VERY SWEET, WITH DISTINCT GINGER FLAVOUR; STICKY, CLINGING TEXTURE.

HISTORY:

Parkin goes under a variety of names or qualifications. Often, it is called after the county in which it is made: Yorkshire, Lancashire, and so on. Then there are the archaic names, for instance those found in South Yorkshire and Derbyshire of thar, thor or tharf cake. Moggy is the name for a wheat-flour parkin which is very sticky in texture.

The entry for parkin biscuit, below (p. 319), discusses the origin and types of parkin. Stead (1991) suggests the name thar cake is Middle English, associated with the pre-Christmas Martinmas fast and, possibly, with pagan bonfire ceremonies which took place at the end of October (later christianized into All Souls). Parkin is still a customary food for the end of October and beginning of November, especially Bonfire Night (5 November). The name parkin or perkin (related to a diminutive of the Christian name Piers) is inexplicable but may denote affectionate disdain.

Parkin and thar cake were originally made on a griddle or bakestone. Suet, dripping, lard or butter were used depending on availability. The presence of spice would class it as a typical cake eaten on feast days and holidays, those moments in the year which justify extravagant ingredients. Some of the oatmeal was replaced by wheat flour in the 1800s, and the cake was further lightened by the addition of baking powder. The molasses was partly replaced by Golden Syrup when this product came on the market after 1880. Parkin is produced by al-most every craft baker in the North Country.

TECHNIQUE:

Ingredients are equal quantities of oatmeal and wheat flour. Golden Syrup, sugar, and butter are used – each about a third the amount of the total flour. Molasses or black treacle may be substituted for part of the syrup. Additions are ginger, to flavour; a little baking powder to leaven; and milk to mix. Some people add an egg. The syrup or treacle, sugar and butter are heated gently together and stirred; in a separate container, the dry ingredients are blended. The mixtures are amalgamated; milk and egg (if required) are mixed for a soft, runny dough; this is poured into a well-lined tin. It is baked at 180°C for 60–90 minutes. The cooled parkin is wrapped in paper or foil and left for a few days before eating.

REGION OF PRODUCTION:

NORTH ENGLAND, YORKSHIRE AND LANCASHIRE.

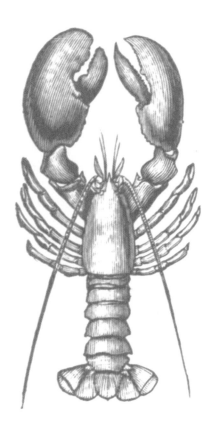

'I sacrifice to no god save myself – And to my belly, greatest of deities.'

Euripides

Yorkshire Teacake

DESCRIPTION:

A CIRCULAR BUN ABOUT 30MM DEEP, 100–110MM ACROSS, SOMETIMES LARGER. WEIGHT: ABOUT 75G FOR THE SIZE GIVEN. COLOUR AND TEXTURE: GOLDEN CRUST, SPECKLED WITH FRUIT, FADING TO WHITE AT THE BASE, PALER BROWN UNDERNEATH; CRUMB SOFT BUT NOT OPEN, OFF-WHITE, WITH WELL-DISTRIBUTED CURRANTS. FLAVOUR: FRESH BREAD SMELL, WITH FRUITY SWEETNESS FROM CURRANTS; CANDIED PEEL IS SOMETIMES ADDED, ALTHOUGH IT IS UNCOMMON; SWEET MIXED SPICE (CINNAMON, CLOVES, NUTMEG) IS THE TYPICAL AROMA.

HISTORY:

The compound word tea-cake is listed from the 1830s in the *OED*. Who is to say what precisely was being denoted? Was it that the drink needed a solid companion? Or was it that a new meal, tea, was a moment in the day celebrated by the production of sweet breads?

Yorkshire teacakes were at first just Yorkshire cakes. That is the name given them in 1817, in the earliest recipe so far located (David, 1977). It is a lightly enriched dough with milk, eggs and a little butter, similar to that still used, but with no fruit. They had become teacakes by the time of Cassell (1896) who wrote, 'a hospitable Yorkshire housewife would consider her tea-table was barely spread if it were not liberally supplied with these delicious cakes, constant relays of which should be served steaming hot.' If the transformation of cakes into teacakes is a mark of one small social revolution, the firm association of Yorkshire with these buns must also be indication of some reality of social geography. We are reduced to speculating that the county was a place with a reputation for good baking and a tradition of high tea, a large early-evening meal involving many baked items.

That regional affiliation has long vanished, although the cakes are still valued in Yorkshire. Industrial production has meant their spread throughout the country.

TECHNIQUE:

Teacakes are made with an enriched bread dough. Kirkland (1907) wrote that they were on the borderline between bread and buns. By this he meant that the fermentation was usually a two-stage affair – a yeast, flour and water sponge followed by mixing in the fat, fruit, sugar and eggs (if used) – and that they were only lightly enriched. The ratio of fat to flour is about 1:3. The fat is either lard or butter. They are baked at 240–250°C for 15–20 minutes.

REGION OF PRODUCTION:

NORTH ENGLAND.

Coltsfoot Rock

DESCRIPTION:

HEXAGONAL STICKS 10CM LONG, 1CM DIAMETER. WEIGHT: 10G. COLOUR: LIGHT BROWN. FLAVOUR: SWEET, HERBAL, ANISEED. COMPOSITION: SUGAR, LIQUORICE, GELATINE, PAREGORIC, CAPSICUM, OIL OF ANISEED, COLTSFOOT EXTRACT (.0012 PER CENT).

HISTORY:

Coltsfoot, *Tussilargo farfara*, was long used as a remedy for chest infections. Culpeper's *Herbal* gives coughwort as an alternative name. It was also used to bolster meagre supplies of tobacco, much as boys would once smoke old man's beard. When a medicine, it was used as juice or made into syrup. From an early date, it was probably used for flavouring boiled sugar or sugar paste, but Mayhew's (1851) description of a street-vendor with coltsfoot sticks amongst his wares is the first known reference. A recipe in Skuse's *Confectioner's Handbook* (*c.* 1892) shows them to have been a paste of gum tragacanth, liquorice, aniseed, lemon essence and sugar extruded as sticks. The modern version appears essentially unchanged. It now has a strong regional identity, particularly with West Yorkshire and Lancashire. Until the 1950s, several companies produced it, now but one manufacturer survives, Stockley Sweets Ltd of Oswaldtwistle, Accrington, Lancashire.

TECHNIQUE:

The rock is made from sugar paste by a simple mixing of sugar, gums, water and coltsfoot essence to the correct consistency; this is extruded in sticks, allowed to dry for 2 days and packaged.

REGION OF PRODUCTION:

NORTH ENGLAND, WEST YORKSHIRE, LANCASHIRE.

Lily Of The Valley Creams

DESCRIPTION:

CHOCOLATES FILLED WITH FIRM, WHITE-SUGAR FONDANT, 25MM DIAMETER, 20MM DEEP. WEIGHT: 12G. COMPOSITION: CHOCOLATE, SUGAR, FLAVOURING. OTHER FLOWER FLAVOUR-INGS USED FOR FONDANT-FILLED CHOCOLATES IN ENGLAND ARE ROSE AND VIOLET. FRUIT, MINT AND COFFEE FLAVOURS ARE MORE COMMON.

HISTORY:

England has a long tradition of using flowers to flavour sugar syrups. It can be seen in some of the earliest confectionery texts, such as Sir Hugh Plat's *Delightes for Ladies*, in which roses, violets, borage, cowslips, gillyflowers (carnation pinks), marigolds and rosemary are mentioned. This continued into the eighteenth century when they were made into little 'cakes' of sugar. It is not clear if these were high-boiled, clear drops or similar to the modern grained-sugar Kendal mint cake. Mary Eales (1733) called one of her flower-flavoured recipes 'honeycomb cakes'. This sort of sweet was probably made wherever suitable flowers grew, but the skill and expense involved limited production to professional confectioners and the still-rooms of the wealthy. Their audience was only enlarged once confectioners adopted industrial techniques. Thereafter, grained-sugar fondant became a popular filling for chocolates, often with floral perfumes. Old-fashioned rose and violet flavours are still used by some companies.

One is Bonnet's of Scarborough, founded by a Swiss immigrant in 1880. It has always used flower essences in a range of confectionery much coveted as souvenir of this elegant resort. The firm was almost certainly responsible for the wallflower creams remembered from his youth by Compton Mackenzie (1954). The range has become ever more limited as the necessary essences are difficult to obtain, but it still makes one perfumed with lily of the valley.

TECHNIQUE:

Few, if any, chocolatiers make their own fondant any longer. Instead it is bought in blocks and mixed with ingredients such as glycerine and flavouring essences. Some, like Bonnet's, use starch-moulding to produce the fondant centres: the fondant is melted and poured into impressions made in trays of fine starch and then allowed to set. Once the pieces are firm enough to handle, they are carefully removed, rid of excess starch, then coated with chocolate, either by hand-dipping (in a few companies) or enrobing. The chocolates are decorated, left to set, then displayed or packed for distribution.

REGION OF PRODUCTION:
NORTH ENGLAND, YORKSHIRE.

Pontefract Cakes

DESCRIPTION:
TABLETS OF LIQUORICE, 30MM DIAMETER, 4MM THICK, A DESIGN STAMPED ON ONE FACE. WEIGHT: 4–6G. COLOUR: SHINY BLACK. FLAVOUR: SWEET LIQUORICE AND ANISEED; TOUGH, CHEWY TEXTURE.

HISTORY:
The town of Pontefract in south Yorkshire was first noted for liquorice cultivation in the mid-1600s, although the plant had probably grown there for longer. The juice from its roots was used to treat colds and chest complaints. Though there is no written evidence, it is likely that from a very early date the juice was also boiled into a compound that could be chewed or sucked. A seal dated 1614 found in the town bears a design similar to that used on the face of modern Pontefract cakes. (The owl that forms part of the crest belongs to the heraldic device of the Savile family, local landowners.)

The first cakes that were recognizable as those of today are dated to 1760, when a local apothecary, George Dunhill, is said to have added sugar to the recipe. Thereafter, the industry prospered, first using locally-produced liquorice, later relying on imported block juice. In 1893, 11 manufacturers were listed, all of whom made Pontefract cakes.

An industry based on imported juice still flourishes even though cultivation of the plant has ceased. Two manufacturers of Pontefract cakes and other confectionery remain.

TECHNIQUE:
The ingredients are listed as treacle, wheat flour, sugar, water, caramel, liquorice extract, salt, invertase, artificial flavours. The exact process is a trade secret. A batch method for producing li-quorice is as follows. Water and flour are blended and heated to boiling. Water, sugar and block juice are mixed separately, then treacle and glucose syrup added and brought to the boil. The mixtures are amalgamated, and cooked. Caramel, aniseed, gelatine, colours and flavours are added and mixed through. The mixture is extruded to give the desired shape. After moulding, liquorice is stoved at 40–50°C for 12–24 hours. It is conditioned for 1 day at 20°C and 50 per cent relative humidity. It may then be packed for sale.

REGION OF PRODUCTION:
NORTH ENGLAND, PONTEFRACT (SOUTH YORKSHIRE).

Treacle Toffee

DESCRIPTION:

A HARD, CRUNCHY CONFECTION SOLD FROM OPEN TRAYS 400MM WIDE, 200MM LONG, 10MM DEEP. COLOUR: CHESTNUT TO DEEP BROWN. FLAVOUR AND TEXTURE: SWEET WITH BUTTERY OVERTONES, SLIGHT BITTER NOTE IF BLACK TREACLE OR MOLASSES IS USED; HARD, SLIGHTLY TOUGH. COMPOSITION: SUGAR, GOLDEN SYRUP OR TREACLE, BUTTER.

HISTORY:

The origin of the word toffee is obscure. It has been used since at least the early 1800s. Sometimes spelt taffy, it may be derived from tough or toughy, describing the texture of toffee made to early recipes (*OED*). These often involved pulling the sugar, which made it harder. There is a possible link with the word tafia, a rum-like drink made from molasses. The persistent use of molasses, black treacle and, later, Golden Syrup in toffee supports this idea. Toffee is also used by sugar-boilers as a general term to indicate high-boiled sugar, and some early toffee recipes (such as that for Everton toffee, once very famous) are closer to the modern concept of butterscotch.

Nor are the beginnings of toffee well documented. Only the recipe for Everton toffee (p. 425) appears to have been thought worth recording. But, during the 1800s, toffee of many types was obviously known and loved, and 'toffee-pulls' were social gatherings for young people. Presumably the variants were so well known to cooks and back-street confectioners that no-one thought any more of them. The first published recipe for treacle toffee so far discovered is from the first decades of the twentieth century. By this time, one of the best known names in toffee, John Mackintosh, had established his factory in Halifax, West Yorkshire, where he produced treacle toffee and the newly fashionable soft American caramels. Many other companies, large and small, produced toffee in these same years, but among those who survive today, the old treacle toffee accounts for a fraction of their output; softer, more chewy toffees are now favoured. In the North country this hard treacle toffee was often called Bonfire toffee or Plot toffee in recognition of the fact that it was made as part of the celebrations surrounding the night of 5 November, Bonfire Night.

TECHNIQUE:

An old recipe used by toffee-boilers calls for black treacle, soft light brown sugar and butter in the proportions 2:2:1; these are brought to the boil, with the addition of a little water and tartaric acid or vinegar, and cooked to 125°C. The mixture is poured into buttered tins and cooled. In the past, it was then then distributed to shops and newsagents where a special little hammer is used to break the hard toffee into irregular pieces, weighed out as the customer requires. Less traditionally, perhaps more hygienically, it is now broken and pre-packed in Cellophane.

The sugar – white, pale or dark brown, fine or coarse – and the treacle – golden, black or molasses – are variable. Some recipes call for milk or, in commerce, condensed milk; the quantity of butter may be reduced accordingly. Glucose is now usually added, rather than relying on the action of tartaric acid or vinegar to achieve the correct texture. Modern recipes show a tendency to a lower proportion of black treacle and more brown sugar or Golden Syrup. Modern versions of toffee are rarely pulled.

REGION OF PRODUCTION:

NORTH ENGLAND.

Bitter Beer (Tadcaster):
Samuel Smith's Old Brewery Strong Pale Ale

DESCRIPTION:

THIS BEER IS DARK COPPER IN COLOUR, SWEETISH, HOPPY AND RELATIVELY FULL-BODIED. IT IS 5 PER CENT ALCOHOL BY VOLUME. THE COMPANY ALSO PRODUCES A STRONGER BEER CALLED MUSEUM ALE. THESE ARE BREWED BY THE 'YORKSHIRE SQUARES' METHOD, USED BY OTHERS IN THE AREA, NOTABLY THE BLACK SHEEP (MASHAM, USING STONE SQUARES), AND TETLEY'S (LEEDS, USING STAINLESS STEEL). TADCASTER HAS 3 BREWERIES BUT THE OTHERS (BASS CHARRINGTON AND JOHN SMITH'S) DO NOT USE THE METHOD. BITTERS FROM TADCASTER ARE SOMETIMES CALLED PALE ALES.

HISTORY:

Tadcaster's association with good brewing goes back to the Middle Ages, due in part to the water, drawn from wells which penetrate limestone strata. Samuel Smith's brewery was founded in 1758. In the 1840s, 2 brothers divided the business between them, one branch continuing at Samuel Smith's, the other as John Smith's, now subsumed into a larger group. The Yorkshire squares system is known in other towns in the area and its use has been recorded to the south, on the border with Nottingham. Its origin is unknown. Jackson (1993) notes a suggestion that its development was linked with a scientific paper on the absorption of gases in liquids, published in the late eighteenth century by a Leeds chemist. It is associated with strains of yeast which lend distinctive characteristics to beers produced by the method.

TECHNIQUE:

Brewing commences with a mash of malt and liquor drawn from the brewery's own wells; the wort is strained off into a brew kettle and boiled with Goldings and Fuggles hops for 60–90 minutes; the wort is strained and cooled and the yeast strain favoured by Smith's added. Fermentation begins in the lower half of large, covered, slate-lined square tanks. As the yeast begins to work, the wort rises through an opening in the top of the tank and overflows into a second tank above; then the beer settles and sinks back, leaving a yeast residue behind. This cycle is repeated several times in the 4–5 days it takes for fermentation to complete. About halfway through, the beer is 'roused' by pumping it from the lower to the upper tank through a pipe, encouraging the yeast to work more. When the beer rises for the final time, it is skimmed and led into settling tanks. It is racked into wooden casks, allowed to stand for 3-4 days and primed and fined. If it is bottled, it is first filtered and pasteurized.

REGION OF PRODUCTION:

NORTH ENGLAND, TADCASTER (YORKSHIRE).

Black Beer

DESCRIPTION:

BLACK BEER IS VERY DARK BROWN; ITS FLAVOUR IS SWEET-BITTER WITH MALTY, MOLASSES OVERTONES. IT IS 8.5 PER CENT ALCOHOL BY VOLUME.

HISTORY:

The drink originated as a prophylactic against scurvy. It was carried as part of ships' stores and was drunk mixed with rum. Jackson (1993) notes possible relationships with spruce beer, which included the tips of spruce branches in the mash and must have had a distinctly resinous flavour. This was known in the Baltic states and is also drunk on the eastern seaboard of Canada. Beers like this, used primarily as mixers and dietary supplements, were extensively made in the north of England. There were about 6 companies involved at the end of the nineteenth century, but by the 1970s only one survived. The beer is still made in Yorkshire, where various folk traditions have grown up around it: one often met is that a pregnant woman who drinks it will give birth to twins. It is not clear if it is the same black beer that was served in the temperance bars of neighbouring Lancashire up to the 1920s.

The remaining company which makes black beer is owned by a larger group producing ciders, perries and other English drinks. Unlike other alcoholic drinks, black beer, because it is used as a mixer and has a high original gravity in relation to alcoholic content, is exempt from duty under UK and EU laws. It may be mixed with milk, lemonade or rum (in which case it is known as 'rum and black'); it also added to fruit cakes and Christmas puddings.

TECHNIQUE:

For black beer, the malt is mashed and the wort concentrated; this step was once carried out by the manufacturer, but the original equipment proved too costly and it is now prepared by the Association of British Maltsters. This is blended with barley syrup and raw cane sugar and fermented with a specialized yeast. It is allowed to settle before pasteurization and bottling.

REGION OF PRODUCTION:

NORTH ENGLAND, LEEDS (YORKSHIRE).

Dandelion And Burdock

DESCRIPTION:

AVAILABLE AS A CORDIAL OR READY-DILUTED WITH SODA WATER. IT IS DARK COPPER-BROWN IN COLOUR AND SLIGHTLY ANISEED, MILDLY BITTER IN FLAVOUR.

HISTORY:

Dandelion, *Taraxacum officinale*, and burdock, *Arctium Lappa*, were both recognized for their medicinal qualities in Britain from early times, in particular as blood purifiers, useful in early spring. Burdock was also used to flavour ale before hops became the most common addition (Dunkling, 1992). During the latter half of the nineteenth century, herbal drinks were promoted as an alternative to beer and spirits. Apart from dandelion and burdock, perhaps sarsaparilla is the best known. The companies which now manufacture this drink have their origins in the temperance movement. One, Ben Shaw's of Huddersfield, West Yorkshire, began in 1871, when Ben Shaw set up in partnership with his brother, as Shaw Brothers, Manufacturers of Non-alcoholic Beverages. The company manufactured various drinks including Horehound Beer, Dandelion Stout and Botanic Porter. Some of the early 'non-alcoholic' drinks were brewed. The company's first registered trademark was a dandelion plant. Another much smaller company still making the drink is Herbal Health, based in Lancashire; their premises include the last-known temperance bar in Britain. There are 3 known producers.

TECHNIQUE:
A mixture of herbal extracts, flavourings and sugar syrup is used; either sold as a cordial or diluted with carbonated water and bottled.

REGION OF PRODUCTION:
NORTH ENGLAND, WEST YORKSHIRE AND EAST LANCASHIRE.

Oatmeal Stout

DESCRIPTION:
ALMOST BLACK WITH DEEP RED LIGHTS AND A BEIGE HEAD. IT HAS A FRUITY AROMA, ROUNDED NUTTY FLAVOUR AND A SMOOTH, SILKY, ALMOST OILY TEXTURE. IT IS 5 PER CENT ALCOHOL BY VOLUME.

HISTORY:
Oats were malted for beer in parts of northern and western Britain in the late medieval period. However, it is a difficult grain for brewers to work with as it gelatinizes at mashing temperatures. Mostly, it is used mixed in small proportions with other grains. Oatmeal stout as known today owes much to the fashion for brewing 'nutritious' beers current during the late nineteenth and early twentieth centuries. Oatmeal stouts have been produced in small quantities ever since. Eldridge Pope (Dorset) brewed one until 1975, and Samuel Smith's revived the style in 1980. Several breweries now produce them. Such dark, heavy beers are generally more favoured as winter drinks.

TECHNIQUE:
In Britain, oats are typically northern. Production of oatmeal stout is like that of other British beers save that a proportion of oats is added to the brewing grain; in some cases these are rolled oats. Samuel Smith's uses pale ale, crystal and roasted barley malts to make its oatmeal stout, and the beer is fermented for about 12 hours longer than ordinary bitter beers.

REGION OF PRODUCTION:
NORTH ENGLAND, YORKSHIRE.

Old Peculier

DESCRIPTION:
OLD PECULIER IS DARK BROWN; ITS FLAVOUR IS HEAVY, RICH AND SWEET. THIS SORT OF BEER HAS A HIGH ORIGINAL GRAVITY BECAUSE IT CONTAINS MUCH SUGAR; ALCOHOL CONTENT IS VARIABLE, USUALLY 5.5–8.5 PER CENT.

HISTORY:
The concept of old ale as a beer evoking nostalgia for the good things of the past dates back at least a century in Britain and is primarily an English style (Jackson, 1993). The brews are

generally sweetish and rich, supposedly recalling dark beers from the 1700s. It is, however, a field in which brewers are very idiosyncratic, and there are no hard rules. Wilson (1983) notes that very strong ales were being brewed by the sixteenth century, and that in the seventeenth century, Yorkshire ale was drunk stale old and strong. The best was said to come from Northallerton. There is a seventeenth-century poem in praise of the ales of Northallerton and Thirsk. These towns are near Masham, where Old Peculier originated. The brewery, T. & R. Theakston, was founded in 1827. It is claimed that Old Peculier has been made from the early days and has been known under this name since the 1890s. It derives from the town having its own peculiar, or separate ecclesiastical jurisdiction. The seal is used as a trademark by the brewery.

During the 1980s, Theakston's was bought by Scottish & Newcastle Breweries and now only that part of the production of the beer intended for the North Yorkshire market is brewed in Masham. Many other brewers make strong, dark, sweetish beers – known as old, winter or strong ales, but often given fanciful names. They are more popular in cold weather and some only brew in mid-winter.

TECHNIQUE:
Brewing begins with a mash of crushed pale ale and crystal malts and torrefied wheat mixed with liquor (water heated to 70°C), brewer's caramel and 3 types of sugar. The wort is strained into a brew kettle and boiled with English hops; Fuggles (for aroma) are added towards the end of boiling; then the wort is strained, cooled and Theakston's yeast added. Fermentation is in vessels of the Yorkshire squares type for 4–5 days after which the beer is either fined and dry-hopped with more Fuggles and put into casks, or brewery-conditioned in large tanks before filtering, fining, pasteurizing and bottling.

REGION OF PRODUCTION:
NORTH ENGLAND, MASHAM (NORTH YORKSHIRE).

Raspberry Vinegar

DESCRIPTION:
RASPBERRY VINEGAR IS A DEEP, CLEAR RED, WITH A SWEET-ACID FLAVOUR AND DISTINCT RASPBERRY TASTE.

HISTORY:
Recipes for flavoured vinegars were common, often using herbs but also fruit. Those for raspberry usually required wine or cider vinegar to be flavoured with the fruit and sweetened with sugar. It was recommended, diluted, as a soothing drink for sore throats and fevers, and in hot weather. Recipes for a version based on malt vinegar appear in local collections in the north of England in the late nineteenth and early twentieth centuries. It is not clear when malt was substituted for wine vinegar. As the former was cheap and commonly available, it is possible that it had always been used by poorer people. *Law's Grocer's Manual* (*c*. 1895) mentions it could easily be made at home with raspberries and ordinary (malt) vinegar, and gives the addresses of 2 London manufacturers.

As drinks, flavoured vinegars went out of fashion before 1939–45. Raspberry vinegar lingered in the north and east of England because of a strong tradition of using it as a

condiment for Yorkshire pudding.

During the 1970s and 1980s, flavoured vinegars were rediscovered by cooks and have again become popular.

TECHNIQUE:

For a raspberry vinegar of the type used as a condiment for Yorkshire pudding, the proportions are 500g fresh fruit: 700ml malt vinegar: 500g sugar. The fruit is washed and soaked in the vinegar in a cool place for 4 days. The liquid is strained off, then sugar dissolved in it and boiled for 15 minutes. It is cooled, strained and bottled.

Other flavourings were once common: red currants, blackberries, gooseberries, roses and elderflowers were all used to make drinks and condiments; herbs, spices, horseradish, shallots or garlic and chillies were steeped in vinegar for pickling or as a store sauce to be added to meat. Many are enjoying a revival. Some manufacturers import wine vinegar, but many use cider or spirit (distilled malt) vinegar, plus fruit, flowers and herbs available in their locality.

REGION OF PRODUCTION:
NORTH ENGLAND.

Yorkshire Relish

DESCRIPTION:

EACH VARIETY OF YORKSHIRE RELISH HAS ITS OWN APPEARANCE: 'THIN' IS DARK BROWN; 'SPICY' AND 'FRUITY' ARE THICKER AND REDDISH-BROWN. THE FLAVOUR IS FRUITY (DATES, TAMARIND) AND ACIDIC.

HISTORY:

This is one of a group of patent sauces manufactured under trademarks to secret recipes in Britain for over a hundred years. Yorkshire Relish was registered in 1877.

The use of relish in the sense of a sharp substance which provided a contrast, making something else taste sweeter, is old. It was well enough known for an author to use it in the early 1600s as a metaphor when writing about life not being unmingled happiness, but 'having some sour sauce to relish it'. Though the word had wider currency – to do with pleasure and strong flavours in eating and drinking generally – the mention of 'sour sauce' is interesting. Modern Yorkshire Relish could still be described thus.

The sauce known today originated in 1837, when Robert Goodall, a Leeds chemist, started to bottle the thin type, which was made by his wife. It is mentioned in the *Trademarks Journal* in 1877, when the firm had expanded to become Goodall, Backhouse & Co. There was a vigorous advertising campaign in the 1880s. The production of Thick Yorkshire Relish commenced in 1932. Like other English brown sauces it is based on tamarinds and secret spice mixtures. They were imitations of Indian sauces and chutneys. The methods and spices were Indian, buttressed by vinegar and home-grown fruit and vegetables. Eliza Acton's 'Bengal Receipt' for 'Chatney sauce', based on unripe plums or crab apples, spices, sugar and vinegar, would probably give a result quite similar to modern brown sauces.

In 1959 Hammond's, another sauce company based in Yorkshire, already making the relishes under licence, acquired Goodall's. Although there have been 3 subsequent mergers, the name Yorkshire Relish survives and it is still produced in the Leeds area.

The ingredients of Thick Yorkshire Relish are tomatoes, date purée, sugar, apple purée, malt vinegar, flour, soy sauce concentrate, salt, molasses, spirit vinegar, acetic acid, onions, spices, tamarind concentrate, colour (caramel), garlic, stabilizer (Karaya gum), hydrolyzed vegetable protein, flavouring.

The method is a trade secret but is essentially a simple process of mixing and cooking in open pans. The sauce can be used as soon as it is made but benefits from a short maturation.

REGION OF PRODUCTION:
WEST YORKSHIRE.

***

Also produced in North England
PARKIN BISCUIT (SEE SOUTH SCOTLAND P. 319)
SAVOURY DUCK (SEE FAGGOT, P. 146)

North East England

Pease Pudding

DESCRIPTION:

PEASE PUDDING IS A SOLID PURÉE, SOLD BY WEIGHT. COLOUR: PALE ORANGE-YELLOW. FLAVOUR: DISTINCT, EARTHY, PULSE FLAVOUR; OFTEN SALTY.

HISTORY:

Every British child used to learn the rhyme, 'Pease pudding hot, pease pudding cold, pease pudding in the pot, nine days old,' which asserted the pulse's ubiquity, longevity, as well as monotony, when diet was limited by primitive transport and preservation methods.

Dishes made from dried peas were associated with Lent and fasting, 'Pease pudding developed from the old pottages of dried peas which were a national dish in England during the sixteenth and seventeenth centuries, known in French recipe books as "pottage in the English style"' (Wilson, 1973). Popularity declined during the eighteenth century and the pudding gradually became regionalized to North-East England. Because it is an accompaniment for salted pork, as in pease pudding and boiled bacon – there are medieval instructions for the identical combination (Hieatt, 1986) – it is made and sold by pork butchers.

Mushy peas, sold throughout Britain in fish-and-chips shops or pie shops, are also a purée based on dried peas.

TECHNIQUE:

Split yellow peas are soaked and cooked in water until they disintegrate to a purée. They are seasoned to taste, usually just with salt, poured into a bowl and left to cool. Alternatively, salty stock from cooking bacon can be used to cook the peas. The housewife seasons and enriches it with butter and egg as desired, and reheats the mixture.

REGION OF PRODUCTION:

NORTH EAST ENGLAND.

Cotherstone Cheese

DESCRIPTION:

PRESSED, PASTEURIZED COW'S MILK CHEESE. DIMENSIONS VARY ACCORDING TO WEIGHT; ONE WEIGHING 1KG IS APPROXIMATELY 12CM DIAMETER AND 8CM HIGH. WEIGHT: MADE IN SIZES OF ABOUT 500G–3KG. FORM: A SMALL MILLSTONE. COLOUR: PALE CREAMY YELLOW WITH A FEW SMALL, IRREGULAR HOLES. WHEN MATURED IN A HUMID ATMOSPHERE IT DEVELOPS A PINKY-GOLD COLOUR ON THE RIND. FLAVOUR AND TEXTURE: MILD, ACID FLAVOUR, BUTTERY LACTIC AFTERTASTE; A SMOOTH CREAMY TEXTURE.

HISTORY:

Cotherstone takes its name from a village in Teesdale, on the Durham–Yorkshire border. It was mentioned as early as 1911, when it was noted in the *Encyclopaedia Britannica* (Rance, 1982). It shares the same general history as the Swaledale, Wensleydale and Coverdale made just to the south, inheriting a common tradition of cheese-making from medieval monasteries. However, Cotherstone thinks itself proudly individual. Manufacture suffered, as did all other British cheeses, from centralization of cheese-making during 1939–45 and its after-effects. One of these was a deep conviction held by many that farm-made cheese was not allowed by the Milk Marketing Board, the body set up to control the fresh milk supply. Consequently, on-farm cheese-making in the area survived on a very small scale. In 1956, Simon recorded it as 'a double-cream cheese which repaid keeping and watching: it was similar to Stilton both as to shape and size. It was farm-made, very good, but never made in large quantities.' In the past, some of these cheeses are reported to have blued naturally, although the present maker does not achieve this. This type of mild cheese is often eaten with fruit cake and apple pie in Yorkshire.

TECHNIQUE:

Pasteurized milk from Friesian cattle grazed in Teesdale is used. The maker remarks that its distinctive nature is probably derived from the local flora. A basic recipe commences by leaving the evening milk to set and, in the morning, skimming the cream, heating it, and returning it to the milk together with the morning's milk. The milk is brought to 21°C and starter added; the temperature raised to 27°C, and rennet added once the correct acidity is reached. It is stirred until setting begins. It is then left for an hour. The curd is cubed gently and the temperature raised gradually to 30°C whilst stirring gently; then it is allowed to settle until the acidity is correct. The whey is drained. The curd is cut into large cubes, milled and salted (12g salt to 1kg curd), then lightly packed into lined moulds and pressed for about 12 hours. After removing the binding, the cheeses are ripened for 2–3 weeks before selling, but can be matured successfully for up to 2 months, given suitable temperature and humidity.

Cotherstone was once made from spring until the first frost but is now available all year.

REGION OF PRODUCTION:
NORTH EAST ENGLAND.

Kipper (Craster)

DESCRIPTION:

A WHOLE HERRING SPLIT FROM MOUTH TO TAIL, WITH GILLS AND INTERNAL ORGANS REMOVED BUT BACKBONE INTACT, COLD SMOKED. KIPPERS FROM THIS AREA ARE GENERALLY SMALL, 22–23CM FROM HEAD TO TAIL, WEIGHING 140–150G EACH. COLOUR: THE SKIN IS GREY-BROWN, DARK ON THE BACK, FADING GRADUALLY TO SILVER ON THE BELLY; THE FLESH IS PALE GOLD-BROWN. FLAVOUR: A GOOD BALANCE OF SALT AND SMOKE, WITH NEITHER PREDOMINATING; OILY FLESH.

HISTORY:

Some discussion of the meaning of the word kipper is to be found in the entry relating to smoked salmon of Scotland (p. 369). The *Oxford English Dictionary* itself is not sure about the transition from a word describing a spent salmon to a definition of a type of cure. All that can be said is that a fish cure which consisted of brining followed by drying and smoking was known as kippering; that it was applied to both salmon and herring treated this way; and that it has links with the north-eastern coast around the Scottish Borders and with Scotland itself.

The origin of the kipper in a modern sense, referring exclusively to cured smoked herring, is usually attributed to John Woodger who worked at Seahouses on the Northumbrian coast in the 1840s. The 'Newcastle Kipper', as it was first called, was deliberately invented after several years of experiment, and was first sent to London in 1846, based on the 'kippered salmon' of the area; 'Woodger transferred the epithet to the herring smoked overnight after splitting down the back, removing the guts and gills, and lightly salting, originally in solid salt' (Cutting, 1955). According to Alan Robson, whose family have made kippers in Craster for at least 3 generations, the smokehouse currently used was built in 1856.

The production of kippers in spring and summer meant that they did not compete with the cured herring produced in Yarmouth, which came from the autumn catch. The East-coast herring fishery was a migratory affair, progressing southwards as the year advanced. The work at sea was supported on land by a mobile labour force, principally Scottish and female, who followed the herring down the coast gutting, filleting and processing. Craster's kipper season fitted nicely into this seashore transhumance.

TECHNIQUE:

Herrings landed from May to late August are used for kippers. These are now difficult to obtain as the decline in herring stocks, the introduction of freezing at sea, and patterns in marketing fish have affected ports in the North-East. It is quite possible that fish caught in the area may now be taken north and landed at Fraserburgh on the Scottish coast, where the catch is certain to find a good market.

Kippers from the North-East are small, selected with size and oil content (12–20 per cent) in mind. On arrival at the smokehouse, the fish are split and gutted mechanically. They are brined for about 20 minutes. The fish are stretched open on tenterhooks or wooden pegs and hung in rows on frames; these are suspended in the smokehouses. Fires of oak sawdust are burnt for 12–16 hours, depending on size and weather. A properly smoked kipper will keep for about a week.

REGION OF PRODUCTION:

NORTH EAST ENGLAND, CRASTER (NORTHUMBRIA).

COMPARE WITH:

Kipper (Manx), Isle of Man (p. 203); Kipper (Whitby) below; Kipper (Scottish Cure), Scotland (p. 333).

Kipper (Whitby)

DESCRIPTION:

A WHOLE COLD-SMOKED HERRING, SPLIT FROM MOUTH TO TAIL, WITH GILLS AND INTERNAL ORGANS REMOVED, BUT BACKBONE LEFT INTACT; THOSE FROM WHITBY ARE SPLIT THROUGH THE BACK RATHER THAN THE BELLY, WHICH IS THE NORMAL PRACTICE. EXAMPLES OF KIPPERS RECENTLY OBTAINED FROM WHITBY ARE LARGE, ABOUT 27–30CM FROM HEAD TO TAIL, WEIGHING ABOUT 270–300G. COLOUR: WHITBY KIPPERS ARE RELATIVELY DARK GOLD BROWN, WITH DARK SKIN ON THE BACKS AND SILVERY BELOW; THE SKIN OF A NORFOLK KIPPER IS GREY-SILVER ON THE BACK, SILVER-WHITE ON THE BELLY, WITH PALE, PINK-BROWN FLESH. FLAVOUR: WHITBY KIPPERS HAVE A POWERFUL SMOKE FLAVOUR.

T
he brown crab fishery on South Wight is managed by just a few longshoremen from families who, according to island interpretation, make a living from the beach. This can mean anything from keeping the beach clean and putting out deck chairs to helping a sailor with a heavy dinghy. Among the families, who go back up to 400 years, are the Wheelers and the Blakes. The Blakes sell their fish in Ventnor and the Wheelers are a few minutes' walk away on Steephill Cove. Recently, the ministry responsible for fisheries (DEFRA) contributed to the building of a small 'haven' harbour in Ventnor, a safe place for boats to come in and out in all weather. Previously, the fishermen could only fish when the weather was good enough to drag returning boats onto the beach, so this commonsense policy has done much to preserve a way of life. The longshoremen families in South Wight manage their fishery carefully, but this is not the only element that will ensure a future for the Isle of Wight crab: Cheryl Blake's cheerful shop on Ventnor's esplanade sells the freshest picked crab to nibble on the beach and the Wheelers run an excellent restaurant – the Boathouse – at Steephill Cove. Crab pasties, steaming hot from the oven of a neighbouring fisherman's cottage, are offered for sale to grateful walkers.

Rose Prince

AUTHOR OF THE NEW ENGLISH KITCHEN

280

Isle of Wight Crab Pasties

Makes 5

1 SLICE OF WHOLEMEAL BREAD
240G (8OZ) CRABMEAT, BROWN AND WHITE
120G (4OZ) LEEKS, CHOPPED
2 TSP LEMON JUICE
WALNUT-SIZED PIECE OF BUTTER, MELTED
1/4 TEASPOON SALT
A PINCH OF TURMERIC
480G (1LB) PUFF PASTRY
A LITTLE MILK
FRESHLY GROUND BLACK PEPPER

Preheat the oven to 200°C/400°F/Gas Mark 6. Chop the bread in a food processor, transfer to a bowl and stir in the crabmeat, leeks, lemon juice, melted butter, salt, turmeric and some pepper. Roll out the puff pastry thinly and cut out five circles about 15cm (6 inches) each in diameter. Place a heap of the crab mixture in the centre of each one. Brush the edges with milk and then fold over and pinch them together to form a pasty. Brush the tops of the pasties with milk, place them on a baking tray and bake for about thirty minutes, until golden. Serve straight from the oven.

After the kipper cure for herrings was invented in the 1840s on the Northumbrian coast, it spread rapidly southwards. John Woodger, the inventor, set up a kipper processing works in Yarmouth, capitalizing on the locally landed fish and the skilled labour provided by the migrant Scottish 'herring lassies' who followed the shoals south through the summer to work in the towns where herrings were landed at different times of the season. The words of the Gaelic poet Iain Crichton Smith, born on the Isle of Lewis, in *To My Mother* are apposite: 'You were gutting herring in distant Yarmouth and the salt sun in the morning rising out of the sea, the blood on the edge of your knife, and that salt so coarse that it stopped you from speaking and made your lips bitter ...'

The same process was also adopted in Whitby, where kippers have also been made for over a hundred years; one maker, Fortune's, is in the fourth generation. The industry, as everywhere else, has been affected by the decline in herring catches since the 1950s.

TECHNIQUE:

No herring have been landed in Whitby since the 1970s. By the time the herring have travelled further south, and arrived off the East Anglian coast, they are often too low in oil content to make successful kippers. Therefore, kipper curers in both locations buy fish from wherever a suitable size and oil content can be obtained, usually from Icelandic or Norwegian waters. Cures vary slightly between makers. Fortune's, in Whitby, salt the fish for about 40 minutes and smoke them for 16–30 hours, depending on the weather. The kippers are always sold in pairs (presented with the split sides together). The selection of wood for smoking herrings is, to some extent, down to the personal preference of the maker, but most favour oak.

REGION OF PRODUCTION:

NORTH EAST ENGLAND, WHITBY (NORTH YORKSHIRE); EAST ANGLIA, GREAT YARMOUTH, (NORFOLK).

COMPARE WITH:

Kipper (Craster), above, and Kipper (Scottish Cure), Scotland (p. 333).

Pig's Trotters

DESCRIPTION:

PIGS' FEET, CLEANED AND SOMETIMES BRINED, DISPLAYED READY-COOKED ON TRAYS. TROTTERS CAN BE SEEN FOR SALE IN OLD-FASHIONED BUTCHER'S SHOPS.

HISTORY:

Animal feet were once more used in the British kitchen than they are today. They were valued both as a source of gelatine and as meat in their own right. They were available to any householder who killed a beast, or could be cheaply purchased from butchers. Since at least the sixteenth century, the word for animal feet when used as food has been trotters; however, some regions still refer to pig's trotters as pig's feet. They were not considered elegant, and are now mostly a food of the urban poor or of the gormandizing, probably francophile, middle classes. Like many kinds of offal in Britain, they now have a strong association with the food habits of South Lancashire. There has always been a good market for pre-prepared food in this area, as many women still worked after marriage, and both pig's feet and sheep's feet were popular here until quite recently.

Sheep's feet have almost disappeared from the menu, due to changing tastes and the prolonged handiwork required to prepare them for the market, but pig's feet are still easily available.

TECHNIQUE:

Pigs' trotters are cleaned thoroughly, cooked in brine and cooled before being sold.

REGION OF PRODUCTION:

PIGS' FEET ARE AVAILABLE NATIONALLY; SHEEP'S FEET ARE RARELY SEEN FOR SALE OUTSIDE LANCASHIRE.

Stotty Cake

DESCRIPTION:

AN IRREGULAR, THICK DISC, SOMETIMES WITH A SMALL HOLE ROUGHLY IN THE CENTRE; 200MM DIAMETER, 30MM DEEP. WEIGHT: ABOUT 270G. COLOUR AND TEXTURE: WHITE AROUND THE EDGES, AND AROUND THE HOLE IN THE MIDDLE; BROWN IN IRREGULAR PATCHES OVER THE REST OF THE SURFACE; DUSTED WITH FLOUR; CRUSTY TEXTURE.

HISTORY:

The origin of the name stottie, or stotty, is unknown and little notice seems to have been taken of it until well into the twentieth century. The word stot in North-Eastern dialect has several meanings, one of which is to bounce or rebound. Lillian Patterson, of Gregg's Bakers in Newcastle-upon-Tyne, says this name is given to the cakes because the dough was stotted or thrown on to the floor of the oven. The Yorkshire name for the same item, oven-bottom cake, simply reflects the baking method. Another name, scuffler, is current in Yorkshire, perhaps referring to the process of cleaning the oven bottom of ash before baking commences – the tool used was a scuffle. Brears (1987) and Spicer (1948) show the bread was made before the Second World War. Stotties were made from ordinary bread dough. They may be likened to Italian or French hearth-breads that were made from the main batch of dough and baked as a preliminary before the oven was fully charged. Stotties were also an economical way with leftovers from the main batch of dough: knead them all together and roll them out. They are popular for making sandwiches, cut or pulled apart horizontally and filled with ham or bacon. Instead of spreading with butter before filling the bread, people in the North-East sometimes prefer pease pudding.

TECHNIQUE:

After bulk fermentation, the dough is knocked back and divided into pieces which are patted into large discs. These are pricked, or a hole is made in the centre, and then proved. They are baked on the oven floor at about 200°C for 15 minutes. They are then turned and allowed to bake another 15 minutes at a slightly reduced temperature.

REGION OF PRODUCTION:

NORTH EAST ENGLAND, YORKSHIRE, DURHAM, SOUTHERN NORTHUMBERLAND.

Berwick Cockles

DESCRIPTION:

OVAL SWEETS, 25MM LONG, 15MM WIDE, 10MM DEEP. COWE'S OF BERWICK PACK THEIR SWEETS IN TINS OF 227G WITH A RED AND GREEN DESIGN ON THE FRONT. COLOUR: PALE FAWN WITH PINK STRIPES. FLAVOUR: MILDLY PEPPERMINT. COMPOSITION: SUGAR, WATER, GLUCOSE, MINT AND COLOURING.

HISTORY:

Berwick cockles take their name from the east-coast town of Berwick-upon-Tweed. They belong to a tradition of 'boilings' – a collective term for the boiled-sugar sweets popular in this region and north into Scotland. McNeill (1963) states they have been made in Berwick for nearly 200 years, suggesting a mid-eighteenth century origin but giving no evidence in support. Sweets of this general type, striped with red, have certainly been known in Britain since the early nineteenth century, when Stavely (1830) gave a recipe for Paradise Twist.

Wm. Cowe and Sons claims to be the originator of Berwick cockles. The sweets are packed in a tin which carries the legend, 'This tin contains Cowe's Genuine Original Celebrated Berwick Cockles; Delicious and Wholesome Sweetmeats. Entirely Different from Imitations; Purveyors to HRH the late Princess Mary Adelaide of Teck.' Similar confections are made by other companies in the Borders and south-eastern Scotland.

TECHNIQUE:

Cowe's recipe and method are trade secrets. A general method for producing this type of sweet requires a mixture of glucose and white and brown sugar made into a syrup and boiled to a temperature of about 145°C ('hard crack' in sugar-boilers' terms). This is stirred to induce graining (crystal formation by the sugar) and poured on a slab of marble or water-cooled steel. Peppermint flavouring is added. (Alternatively, the mass can be worked on a 'stretcher' – a machine which pulls the sugar mass, aerating it and lightening the colour.) A portion of the mixture is cut off from the main lump and coloured red; this is made into long narrow pieces and used to stripe the main batch. This is made into cockles either by spinning through a rock roller into long narrow pieces, which are then cut into short lengths, or putting through a drop roller which moulds the batch into small round shapes. After the sweets have cooled, they are allowed to mature for 7–10 days, during which time they reabsorb moisture and the texture softens.

REGION OF PRODUCTION:

BORDERS, BERWICK-UPON-TWEED (NORTHUMBERLAND).

Black Bullets

DESCRIPTION:

SPHERICAL SWEETS OF 20MM DIAMETER. WEIGHT: 6G. COLOUR: GOLDEN, TRANSLUCENT. FLAVOUR: MINT, BROWN SUGAR. COMPOSITION: SUGAR, GLUCOSE, OIL OF PEPPERMINT.

HISTORY:

In the dialect of the North-East, the word bullet indicates a hard, sugar sweet. It has had this meaning for at least 100 years and probably much longer. It derives from a diminutive of the French *boule*, used in English in the seventeenth century for small round objects made of various substances, for example, wax or wood. Apart from the fact that black bullets are small and round, there may be a more direct link with sugar boiling, as *petit boulé* (little ball or, more commonly now, soft ball) and *gros boulé* (large ball, or hard ball) are terms belonging to the special knowledge of the sugar confectioner. These are names for sugar solutions at 109–116°C and 120–126°C respectively.

Black bullets are in the general tradition of British high-boiled confectionery; the use of brown, unrefined sugar suggests an origin before the mid-nineteenth century when white sugar became cheap and widely available. There are several similar sweets made in other parts of the country, including Uncle Joe's Mint Balls (Lancashire). One brand, 'Jesmona', is a trademark belonging to Maxon's Ltd of Sheffield.

TECHNIQUE:
Black bullets are made from a syrup based on brown sugar, boiled to the 'hard crack' stage (145–150°C). The syrup is poured on a slab, and mint flavouring kneaded through it. It is formed into a rope, spun out and cut on a ball-spinning machine. The sweets break apart as they cool, giving smooth, round balls which are wrapped individually or packed in airtight tins.

REGION OF PRODUCTION:
NORTH EAST ENGLAND, YORKSHIRE.

*'We may live without friends; we may live without books
But civilized men cannot live without cooks.'*

OWEN MEREDITH

Brown Ale (North East): Newcastle Brown Ale

DESCRIPTION:
BROWN ALES IN THE NEWCASTLE STYLE ARE DRIER AND MORE ALCOHOLIC THAN OTHERS IN ENGLAND. NEWCASTLE BROWN IS MALTY, DRY, WITH NUTTY AND FRUITY OVERTONES. IT IS 4.7 PER CENT ALCOHOL BY VOLUME.

HISTORY:
Brown ales are sweeter and less hoppy than bitters and pale ales, but a particular style has developed in the North-East – in between the sweet, old-fashioned browns still found in the South and the pale ales known in the Midlands.

The history of brewing in Newcastle-upon-Tyne goes back at least to the 1300s, when there are records of a brewers' guild. Scottish & Newcastle Breweries, the company which produces Newcastle Brown, was created by a merger of several smaller businesses. The ale was developed over a period of 3 years by a brewer named Colonel Porter and was launched in Newcastle in 1927. It is still brewed there.

This is a blend of 2 beers; one, the lighter, is marketed separately as Newcastle Amber. The other, stronger and darker, is just for blending. Both are made by the standard British brewing method. The malts used are pale ale and crystal (which is a slightly darker, fuller roast) and there is less emphasis on hops than in bitters. Newcastle Brown Ale has been awarded Protected Geographical Indication (PGI).

REGION OF PRODUCTION:
NORTH EAST ENGLAND.

Fentiman's Ginger Brew

DESCRIPTION:
A PALE STRAW YELLOW; CLOUDY. IT IS SWEET, WITH A STRONG GINGER FLAVOUR AND SPICY, BITTER HERBAL NOTES. THERE IS A SLIGHT CHILLI 'KICK', AND MILD CARBONATION. IT IS NOT MORE THAN 0.05 PER CENT ALCOHOL BY VOLUME.

HISTORY:
The use of herbs and spices to flavour brewed drinks can be traced back to the late medieval period when long pepper, nutmeg and cinnamon were all recorded as being added to ale. The spices added flavour and probably had a preservative effect at a time when hops were unknown in Britain (Wilson, 1973). A tradition of flavoured ales continued well into the nineteenth century; one, known as 'Covent Garden Purl', was drunk as a hot, morning pick-me-up by Londoners. Some sizeable brewers used ginger and liquorice in beer into the 1960s (Jackson, 1993).

During the 1800s, fermented ginger drinks with a low alcohol content became popular. An early recipe occurs under the name 'pop' in S.W. Stavely (1830); it is composed of water, lemons, cream of tartar, sugar and ginger, fermented for a few days. Fentiman's Ginger Brew, a cloudy drink made by a process of fermentation, but with a very low alcohol level, belongs to this tradition. The company originated before World War I, as 'Botanical Brewers', making soft drinks for a temperance and herbal tradition strong in the north of England. These drinks were eclipsed by fruit squashes and carbonated soft drinks but new interest has led to a revival of Fentiman's by a descendant of the original maker after a few years' absence from the market.

TECHNIQUE:
'Botanical brewing' means the drink is brewed from bruised roots and herbs. The bruised-root component, which gives the drink its character, comes from dried ginger root which is milled, boiled and mixed with essences derived from other herbs and sugar. The mixture is fermented with yeast until the alcohol content is 0.5 per cent, then pasteurized before bottling to guarantee that no more fermentation takes place. The alcohol content is strictly controlled so that this drink falls within the category of soft drinks. The drink is not strained and the ginger remains as a sediment; the bottle should be shaken before pouring.

Ingredients include fermented ginger root extract, carbonated water, sugar, glucose syrup, natural flavourings (ginger, capsicum, lemon, speedwell, juniper, yarrow), mono-potassium L tartrate, and citric acid. Only the one manufacturer makes Fentiman's Ginger Brew, but several others make a non-alcoholic carbonated ginger ale or strongly alcoholic ginger beer. These are based on conventional techniques, using malt sugar. Some are mixed with ginger essences, others use root ginger, added after the wort has been strained through the hop-back, and left immersed during fermentation.

REGION OF PRODUCTION:

NORTH EAST ENGLAND, NEWCASTLE-UPON-TYNE.

Mead: Lindisfarne Mead

DESCRIPTION:

LINDISFARNE MEAD IS PALE STRAW-GOLD, ITS FLAVOUR SWEET AND MILDLY SPICY WITH A HONEYED BOUQUET. IT IS 14.5 PER CENT ALCOHOL BY VOLUME.

HISTORY:

The word mead reaches back to the Indo-European root word for honey and exists in all Celtic and Teutonic languages of the British Isles. Fermented honey drinks have been made here from early times. The ancient geographer Strabo recorded that a honey drink was made in Ireland and other northern lands. It was one of the principal sources of alcoholic cheer in Anglo-Saxon England, referred to in heroic poems, chronicles and folk riddles. Mead was probably made by anyone who harvested honey; this included monasteries, whose monks kept bees to produce wax. In the simplest form, mead is a mixture of honey and water left to ferment under the action of wild yeasts. It existed in Britain in parallel with beer and ale: an Anglo-Saxon mead-seller is recorded in an early document, much like an alehouse-keeper. However, it was easier to make large quantities of beer than it was a honey-based drink. And wine, whether imported or home-produced, had a higher social standing.

A tradition of elaborate honey drinks mixed with ingredients such as apple or grape juice, and flavourings of herbs and spices, culminated in the seventeenth century, codified in many recipe collections. They were known as hydromel, melomel or metheglin. They were very dry and wine-like. The taste for such concoctions did not vanish immediately: Mrs Raffald (1769) gave a recipe for a fortified mead, mixed with sack (a sherry-like wine). However, these drinks were not produced commercially after the Middle Ages, being rather the preserve of the domestic still-room.

Imports of cheap sugar led to a decline in beekeeping and mead became a curiosity made by a few beekeepers for their own consumption. A revival of interest in traditional foods led to the experimental production of mead on a commercial scale in the late twentieth century. Lindisfarne Ltd was established in 1962 on Holy Island off the coast of Northumberland. The company emphasizes the historic connections of mead and the traditions of the Celtic monks who established the monastery.

TECHNIQUE:

This mead is based on an old English recipe evolved to suit modern tastes and preconceptions of honey drinks. A fermented grape base is mixed with honey, herbs and water.

REGION OF PRODUCTION:

HOLY ISLAND, NORTHUMBRIA.

***

Also produced in North East England
CHEVIOT SHEEP (P. 308)

South Scotland: East, South, Central & Borders

Kale

DESCRIPTION:

KALE HAS NO HEART BUT GROWS ON A LONG STEM WITH CURLED FINELY DENTED LEAVES. COLOUR: DARK GREEN. FLAVOUR: CHANGES FROM MILD TO MORE INTENSELY SPICY AFTER IT HAS BEEN FROSTED.

HISTORY:

Kale was originally a staple, surviving well in a harsh winter, consumed throughout northern Europe. The word cole, i.e. kale, used generically for members of the brassica family, stems first from the Latin, *caulis*. Similar derivations are widespread in European languages, from the Welsh *cawl*, to the German *Kohl*. Borecole is curly kale, an improved variety taken from the Dutch, where it was called *boerenkool*, 'peasant's cabbage'. In the same way, hearted cabbage was sometimes called cabbage-cole (from the French *caboche*, head).

The kail-yard (kitchen garden) was to the Scots (particularly in the Lowlands) what the potato-plot was to the Irish peasant. Kail was so inextricably linked with eating, that the mid-day meal became known as 'kail'. The bells of St Giles Cathedral in Edinburgh which chimed at dinner-time (in the eighteenth century at 2 o'clock) were known as the 'Kail-bells'. In Meg Dods (1826), Scotland is referred to as 'The Land o' Kail'. So attached is the word to a particular vision of the country that 'kail-yaird' has been applied to a school of fiction which depicts Scottish village life. Two practitioners were Sir James Barrie and S.R. Crockett.

While the Scots used the spelling kail, the northern English called it cale. Today, it is known in Scotland and the rest of Britain as kale and the Scots continue to use it in broths, or as a vegetable, while in England it has largely remained winter feed for cattle.

TECHNIQUE:

The advantage of kale for Scottish growers is that it is hardy. Also, it has the rare quality in a vegetable of benefiting from periods of frost. In a normal Scottish winter, several frosts, the duration and number depending on altitude, aspect and the general weather, can be expected, so any vegetable resistant to these is useful.

Traditional varieties such as Green Curled and Thousand Headed Kale are little grown, although efforts to preserve their genetic material is carried on by a dedicated band. F1 hybrids, which crop uniformly and reliably, are now favoured. Commercially, kale is grown from seed in mid-May to early July for winter use. It is less hardy in rich soils. Older methods of growing survived in the Orkneys into the 1970s, the seed being sown in plantie crubs – specially constructed enclosures of turf or stone in the common grazings. In April, the growing plants were transferred to kaleyards near the houses to grow on to maturity (Fenton, 1973).

REGION OF PRODUCTION:
GENERAL SCOTLAND, SOUTH EAST SCOTLAND, FIFE AND LOTHIAN.

Leek (Scotland)

DESCRIPTION:
COLOUR: WHITE STEM, DARK GREEN LEAVES. FLAVOUR: SWEET, LESS PUNGENT THAN ONIONS. A SCOTTISH LEEK WILL HAVE ALMOST AS MUCH GREEN AS WHITE, WHILE 'LONG BLANCHED' LEEKS WITH ONLY A VERY SHORT GREEN FLAG ARE MORE TYPICALLY ENGLISH.

HISTORY:
Leeks are the dominant vegetable in cock-a-leekie, a Scottish national dish. It is broth made with fowl and leeks, first developed in the Lowlands. The earliest known reference is in the Ochtertyre House book (*c.* 1737). Success depends to a large extent on the quality of leeks. The dish flourished, certainly in Edinburgh taverns, as a direct result of the market gardens on the fertile soils along the Lothian coast which supplied the city with vegetables and fruits and were renowned for the fine quality of their leeks. A variety of the Common Long Winter Leek, raised near Edinburgh and possessing a longer, thicker stem and broad leaves, is described as a 'Poireau de Musselbourgh' [Musselburgh, Lothian] by William Robinson in *The Vegetable Garden* (1885): 'The fine qualities of this vegetable are much better known to the Welsh, Scotch and French than to the English or Irish.'

Scots leeks are distinguished from others by their long leaf (green flag) and short blanch (white). The large amount of green is necessary to give broths a good colour. Because it is sweeter and more delicate than the onion, it is often described as the 'king of the soup onions'.

TECHNIQUE:
Leeks are grown from seed in rich, well-drained soils. Fife and Lothian, lowland areas with fertile, light soils, continue to be important. Small- to medium-sized leeks have the sweetest flavour. The Musselburgh is grown by some amateurs though no longer commercially.

REGION OF PRODUCTION:
CENTRAL AND EAST SCOTLAND.

Raspberry (Scottish)

DESCRIPTION:
VISUAL AND TASTE DIFFERENCES BETWEEN THE 3 MAIN VARIETIES OF SCOTTISH RASPBERRY ARE MINIMAL: CLOVA IS A MEDIUM-SIZED, LIGHT- TO MEDIUM-COLOURED FRUIT WITH A SWEETISH-SHARP FLAVOUR; PROSEN IS A LARGER FRUIT, MEDIUM RED-COLOURED AND IS GENERALLY REGARDED TO HAVE A SOURER FLAVOUR BUT IS FIRMER AND MORE EASILY TRANSPORTABLE; MOY IS A LARGE BERRY, MEDIUM RED COLOUR, GENERALLY REGARDED AS THE BEST FLAVOURED, BUT THE MOST DIFFICULT TO GROW.

HISTORY:
The English name comes from the Old English *raspis*, a word of obscure origin, probably

connected with the slightly hairy, rasping surface of the fruit. Grown in Europe for centuries, it was not until the seventeenth that British horticulturists began to take the fruit seriously and cookery books started including recipes for raspberry wine and vinegar. Though also grown commercially in England, it was a group of Scottish market gardeners in Angus at the beginning of the twentieth century who decided, because of the damp climate, to move out of strawberry production. They joined together as a co-operative growing raspberries commercially and eventually made the Scottish crop the dominant British supply.

In 1946 the Scottish Raspberry Investigation was set up at University College, Dundee, transferring to Mylnefield Farm at Invergowrie in 1951 when the Scottish Crop Research Institute was set up as a horticultural research station in the heart of raspberry-growing country. Over the years it has supported the industry and been largely instrumental in its success by developing varieties with a view to increasing yields, producing disease-resistant plants, improving flavour and retaining quality. All of this has made this the major raspberry growing area in Britain and the SCRI the lead centre for British research on soft fruits.

The very successful raspberry breeding programme at SCRI is best known for the 'Glen' series of cultivars which are now grown throughout the world. The first of the series was Glen Clova (1970) and was a mainstay of the raspberry industry. Glen Moy (1981) was the first spine-free raspberry. Glen Prosen was also released in 1981, and Glen Ample in 1996. Other minor varieties are Glen Garry (1990); Glen Lyon (1991); and Glencoe (1989), a purple raspberry. Autumn-fruiting Autumn Bliss is also grown, serving a niche consumer market. SCRI cultivars occupy 96 per cent of the raspberry market in Scotland.

The distribution of the crop is between the various sectors of the market: fresh; punnet-frozen; quick-frozen in bulk; canned; puréed. Recently, the allocation to canned and puréed production has declined while there has been an increase in fresh and frozen.

TECHNIQUE:

Scottish growers turned to their advantage a cooler climate and shorter growing season, combined with the fertile soils of the East coast, in an area favoured for farming ever since it was cultivated by monks in the Middle Ages. Raspberries are grown outdoors on rows of posts at 10-metre spacing; these are joined by double wires running parallel and clipped together with small metal clips; individual fruiting canes are tied with twine to a single wire further up the posts, about 1.4 metres above the ground. Canes are propagated by suckers from the parent plant. The fruit matures slowly, benefiting from the dryish summers and long periods of mid-summer daylight rather than any great heat. Mid-season varieties crop on two-year-old canes. They may be harvested mechanically or by hand.

REGION OF PRODUCTION:

EAST SCOTLAND, TAYSIDE; NORTH EAST SCOTLAND, MORAYSHIRE; SOUTH SCOTLAND, BORDERS.

Swede-Turnip

DESCRIPTION:

A ROOT VEGETABLE WITH A WOODY OUTER SKIN, USUALLY SOLD FOR DOMESTIC CONSUMPTION AT 1–2KG WEIGHT. FOR CATTLE AND SHEEP FEEDING IN WINTER, THEY ARE GROWN MUCH LARGER, WHEN THEY BECOME TOUGH AND COARSE-FLAVOURED. COLOUR: DARK BROWN TO PURPLE ON OUTER SKIN, PALE YELLOW TO ORANGE INSIDE. FLAVOUR: SWEETISH, MILD SPICINESS WHEN YOUNG AND SMALL, THE FLAVOUR DETERIORATES IN LARGE SPECIMENS.

HISTORY:

While the Romans were responsible for introducing the English white turnip, *Brassica rapa*, the yellow turnip, *Brassica campestris*, came to Scotland in the late 1700s. English farming experiments had led to the development of root crops for feeding to cattle during the winter, among them the yellow turnip or swede from Bohemia (rather than Sweden [Stobart, 1980]). The Scots took to the yellow turnip as a vegetable for human consumption more enthusiastically than the English. In Scotland it is known as neeps (a shortening of turnip); rutabaga is its American name, deriving from the Swedish dialect name *rotbagga*; and in England it is known as Swedish turnip or swede. The turnip is generally used in England for the white turnip (French *navet*). 'Our club,' said Meg Dods (1826), 'put powdered gineger [sic] to their mashed turnips, which were studiously chosen of the yellow, sweet, juicy sort, for which Scotland is celebrated.' This appreciation was otherwise only shared by some in northern England.

Mashed turnips, or bashed neeps, became the accepted accompaniment to haggis at Burns' suppers, along with mashed potatoes (champit tatties). In the Islands and parts of the Highlands where both potatoes and turnips are grown they were often mixed together as the main dish of the day in an eating tradition largely devoid of meat. In Orkney mixed potato and turnip was called clapshot, a word whose origin is unknown. It is now common throughout the country, frequently eaten with haggis.

TECHNIQUE:

The plants withstand cold winters and are hardier than English white turnips, making them a useful vegetable in the northern chill before the development of modern transport and distribution systems for fresh vegetables. They grow well in light, rich soils; they are grown from seed, normally sown in May for production mid-August to April. A relatively early sowing date is necessary in the north as it gives a longer growing season. Magres is the dominant variety grown in Scotland, other established varieties are Acme, Doon Major and Ruta Otofte. Newer varieties include Ruby and Joan. For processing, some Laurentian (pale-fleshed) and Merrick (white-fleshed) are grown. The main growing districts are on the eastern side of the country, from East Aberdeenshire to the Lothians.

REGION OF PRODUCTION:

SCOTLAND.

'*Cabbage: A familiar kitchen-garden vegetable about as large and wise as a man's head.*'

Ambrose Bierce, *The Devil's Dictionary*

Tomato (Clyde Valley)

DESCRIPTION:

A TOMATO WITH RED SKIN AND FLESH AND A WELL-BALANCED TART SWEETNESS WITH A PLEASING BITE.

HISTORY:

A sheltered valley with fertile soils and a mild West-coast climate, with easy access to the largest and densest area of population in Scotland, provided the right conditions for the development of fruit and vegetable growing in the Clyde Valley. Once markets were assured, with the growth of population in the late nineteenth century, horticultural crops flourished, among them tomatoes. Though not traditionally a crop grown in northern climates, those from the Clyde were widely acclaimed for their intense, pleasing flavour and commanded a premium price as 'Scotch Tomatoes'.

Since tomato growing had depended largely on the use of cheap fuel to heat the glasshouses, the increase in the price of oil at the beginning of the 1970s meant that the growers could no longer produce economically. For the next couple of decades tomato growing practically died out. Its revival in the 1990s was largely due to the development of the marketing consortium 'Scotland's Tomatoes', a group of 5 of the largest growers who invested in new and more efficient nurseries, combined with a promotional effort to re-establish Clyde Valley tomatoes as a high-quality product.

Part of the success of this venture is due to enhanced flavour because the fruit can be left on the vine until much later than most other tomatoes which must be picked under-ripe to allow the time necessary for transportation. The Clyde Valley tomato is fresher, better-tasting, and more naturally ripened.

The variety which was largely responsible for the early 'Scotch Tomatoes', known as Ailsa Craig, is no longer grown since it was not disease resistant. Growers have developed others to suit the climate and growing season. The most widely cultivated is Spectra.

TECHNIQUE:

Mostly grown in a hydroponic system in bags of perlite or in long narrow channels containing a stream of nutrients, the plants rely solely on a liquid solution for nourishment. Air temperature and humidity are carefully controlled. Bumble bees are used to pollinate.

REGION OF PRODUCTION:

CENTRAL SCOTLAND.

Vegetarian Haggis

DESCRIPTION:

FORM: AN OVAL BALL SHAPE. WEIGHT: 75G–2KG. COLOUR: GREYISH CREAM. FLAVOUR: NUTTY-MEALY, SAVOURY, NOT HIGHLY SPICED.

HISTORY:

Haggis is now considered an exclusively Scottish dish based on sheep offal though recipes were once plentiful in English cookery texts (see Haggis p. 370). These show that the ingredients have varied over the years. In the seventeenth century a meatless 'Haggas Pudding in a Sheep's Paunch' requires parsley, savoury, thyme, onions, beef suet, oatmeal, cloves, mace, pepper and salt while a 'sweet' meatless haggis recipe has been handed down through the writer's family for 4 generations. Something akin to the Hebridean 'Marag', it is made with flour, oatmeal, beef suet, dried fruit, and a little sugar, and steamed in a cloth (cloot) like a clootie dumpling (p. 366, 379). Though the marag ingredients are the same, the sweet haggis is less solid, more crumbly in texture and arguably more palatable. Another mention of a similar meatless Scottish haggis is in Hartley (1954) under the description of 'Gold Belly' which she describes as a version of an 'English oatmeal pudding, Scotch mountain recipe'.

In 1984 Edinburgh butcher John MacSween was challenged by a vegetarian poet, Tessa Ransford, to make a haggis for the Burns' Supper held to open the Scottish Poetry Library. After a number of experiments, he developed a recipe based on lentils, beans, oatmeal and vegetables. The enthusiastic response from guests and press encouraged him to make the haggis commercially, taking the old idea of the meatless haggis but using a plastic casing rather than a sheep's stomach bag. Output increased steadily every year. The haggis needs reheating only and is eaten, as customary, with tatties and neeps or with clapshot. 'Haggis meat,' said Meg Dods (1826), 'for those who do not admire the natural shape, may be poured out of the bag, and served in a deep dish.' It may also be sliced and fried or grilled and eaten with bacon and eggs for breakfast.

TECHNIQUE:

Lentils, black beans, onions and oatmeal are soaked in water overnight. Mushrooms, turnips and carrots are prepared and put through a fine mincer with the black beans. The mixture then goes through a coarser mincer with the lentils; oatmeal and onions, seasoning and melted margarine are added and mixed. The mixture is then fed into the skins which are sealed and boiled in water.

REGION OF PRODUCTION:
SCOTLAND, EDINBURGH.

Ayrshire Milk

HISTORY:

The Ayrshire breed of milk cow is thought to have developed during the seventeenth century. There are few early records of any sort of milk production. Cattle were kept as draught animals, for tallow and for fresh and salt beef. The dairy cow was first noted in the Cunningham district of north Ayrshire in a report of 1794 for the Board of Agriculture: 'In Cunningham, a breed of cattle has for more than a century been established, remarkable for the quantity and quality of their milk in proportion to their size. They have long been denominated the Dunlop breed, from family and place of that name, where great attention was paid to milk yields and quality.'

Though the qualities of the native stock were the foundation of the breed, it is likely that there was some crossing with blood from elsewhere. The first Ayrshire Herd Book was set up in 1877. Though some early portraits of Ayrshires depict oxen and other fatstock, it has been a dairy breed for most of its history and certainly established itself as such throughout the nineteenth century when most cattle husbandry in Britain was oriented towards beef.

A vital factor in its development was the butter and cheese industry of South-West

Scotland. When the cheese industry slowed down in the 1880s, the response of the dairy farmers within easy distance of the big cities of central Scotland was to switch to liquid milk supply. Managed and distributed by the Milk Marketing Board from 1933, the distinctive character of milk from Ayrshire herds was lost and has only been revived with the disbandment of controls in 1994, giving renewed opportunity for milk from specific herds to be marketed separately.

Ayrshire milk has a minimum butterfat content of 4 per cent. It is bought by those with a preference for a deeper-flavoured milk; it has a higher protein and lactose content which gives it a richer, sweeter taste. The fat globules are also smaller and more uniform which is known to make the milk more digestible that some other milks.

REGION OF PRODUCTION:
SCOTLAND, AYRSHIRE (STRATHCLYDE).

Dunlop Cheese

DESCRIPTION:
PASTEURIZED, HARD, COW'S MILK CHEESE, DISTINGUISHED FROM SCOTTISH CHEDDAR AS 'MEATIER', WITH A MORE MELLOW, NUTTY FLAVOUR AND SOFTER, CREAMIER TEXTURE. COLOUR: PALE YELLOW. FORM: ROUNDS FROM 2KG.

HISTORY:
The lowlands of Ayrshire form a crescent along 70 miles of the Firth of Clyde. The warm, wet winds, and the clay and heavy loam soil have combined to grow the most succulent pasture, making this the largest dairying area in the country and the home of Ayrshire cattle, first known as Dunlops or Cunninghams.

Until the late seventeenth century, cheese had been essentially a short-keeping by-product of butter-making, made from the skimmed milk of both cow and sheep. Around 1690, however, a farmer's daughter and Covenanter from Ayrshire, Barbara Gilmour, is said to have returned home after a period of exile in Ulster fleeing religious persecution. She brought with her a recipe for making cheese which revolutionized the product. Instead of using skimmed milk, she used full-cream cow's milk, pressing the cheese until it was quite hard and improving both the keeping quality and the flavour. While the old cheese was described as 'common cheese', the new cheese became known as a 'sweet-milk cheese' or 'new milk cheese'. By the 1790s, when parish accounts were compiled for the Statistical Account of Scotland, it had become a Dunlop cheese, identified as being manufactured in 5 Ayrshire and 2 Lanarkshire parishes.

The rise of Dunlop to more than local significance relates to the growth of the cities of central Scotland, particularly Glasgow and Paisley. The cheese was further improved in 1885 when the Ayrshire Agricultural Association brought a Somerset farmer and his wife to the country to teach the Cheddar method. Original Dunlop was still being made by at least 300 farms in the South-West of Scotland in 1930: 'Each farm had a fully matured cheese open for cooking, and a softer one for eating. At breakfast, porridge was followed on alternate days by bacon and eggs or toasted cheese on a scone made of home-ground flour eaten in front of the fire' (Rance, 1982).

The subsequent decline – though not extinction – of Dunlop was a result of developments during and after World War II: milk was bought in bulk from farms by Milk Marketing Boards

(MMB) and trucked to large creameries to make factory Cheddar. Its position was further undermined when the MMB took Cheddar rather than Dunlop as the name for their creamery cheeses, believing that Dunlop presented the wrong image, since it happened to have the same name as a leading rubber tyre company of the day, now defunct. Only in some creameries, notably on some of the islands, particularly on Arran, did they retain the Dunlop name and tradition. Elsewhere, Scottish cheese took the Cheddar tag though there have been moves recently to restore Dunlop to its traditional role as a Scottish cheese of distinguished ancestry.

TECHNIQUE:

Made from pasteurized cow's milk. Commercially, it follows the basic Cheddar method but is pressed for a shorter time and matured 4–12 months (average 6 months). An historical recipe is given by McNeill (1929): 'As soon as the milk is taken from the cows it is poured into a large pail, or pails, and before it is quite cold the substance called the steep, i.e. rennet, is mixed with it. When it is sufficiently coagulated it is cut transversely with a broad knife made for the purpose, or a broad three-toed instrument, in order to let the curd subside and to procure the separation of the whey from it. When this separation is observed to have taken place, the curd is lifted with a ladle, or something similar, into the chessel where it remains a few hours, till it has acquired something of a hardness or consistency. It is then taken out of the cheese press and cut into small pieces with the instrument above mentioned, of the size of one or 2 cubic inches, after which it receives the due proportion of salt, and is again replaced in the chessel and put into the press, where it remains a few hours again. Then it is taken out a second time, cut as before and mixed thoroughly, so that every part may receive the benefit of the salt; and for the last time it is put into the cheese press where it remains till replaced by its successor. After this is done it must be laid in a clean and cool place till sufficiently dried and fit to be carried to market; great care is to be used in frequent turning and rubbing, both to keep the cheese dry and clean and to preserve it from swelling and bursting with the heat, vulgarly "fire-fanging". When these cheeses are properly made and dried as they ought to be, they have a rich and delicious flavour.'

REGION OF PRODUCTION:
SCOTLAND, AYRSHIRE, SOUTH WEST AND SOME ISLANDS.

Dunsyre Blue Cheese

DESCRIPTION:
A ROUND, UNPASTEURIZED, BLUE-VEINED COW'S MILK CHEESE. WEIGHT: 3KG. COLOUR: CREAM OR WHITE WITH BLUE VEINS. FLAVOUR: CREAMY, SHARP WITH LONG AFTERTASTE.

HISTORY:
A tradition of artisan farmhouse cheeses, dating back at least to the 1600s, flourished in the dairying areas of the south of Scotland until World War II. Other entries (see Dunlop, above) touch on the reasons for its decline.

Dunsyre Blue is an artisan-made cheese which has gained a considerable reputation. It is made by Humphrey Errington in Lanarkshire. In the 1990s he set up a group of artisan cheese-makers as a marketing co-op called the Hand-made Cheeses of Scotland Group, taking cheeses to trade fairs and other promotional occasions.

Made from unpasteurized milk from a herd of Ayrshire cows. The milk is started with an inoculation of bacteria and penicillin followed by vegetarian rennet which sets the curd. The curd is cut and drained. 4–4.5kg of curd is packed into moulds and left to settle without pressure for 4 days. The cheeses are dipped in brine, rubbed with salt and, after 6 days, pierced to develop the mould. Maturing is over about 3 months during which time they are turned every day and, when necessary, will be wrapped in foil to prevent surface mould developing.

REGION OF PRODUCTION:
SCOTLAND, LANARKSHIRE.

Kelsae Cheese

DESCRIPTION:
HARD, PRESSED, UNPASTEURIZED COW'S MILK CHEESE. THERE ARE 2 TYPES, KELSAE AND STITCHILL; THEY COME IN SEVERAL SIZES, 500G–6.5KG. FLAVOUR: BOTH HAVE A RICHNESS DERIVED FROM THE JERSEY MILK; KELSAE HAS A SHARP NOTE; STITCHILL IS MILD AND CREAMY.

HISTORY:
See the entry for Bonchester, above, for the fall and rise of farmhouse cheese-making in Scotland. Brenda Leddy is a Yorkshire dairy-woman who moved to Kelso (Borders). In approximately 1988, she began making the cheeses Stitchill and Kelsae (the old name for Kelso) from a herd of 25–32 Jersey cows. Both recipes were given to her by artisan cheese-makers in the Highlands (their origin and history is unknown) but she has altered and developed them to suit the Jersey milk, while retaining the characteristics of the originals. A cream cheese, known as Stitchill Soft, is made by the same farm.

TECHNIQUE:
Kelsae and Stitchill are made from unpasteurized milk from a herd of Jersey cows. The method for both is similar but varies in detail. Curdling: with bacterial starter (Stitchill), with yoghurt (Kelsae), followed by rennet which sets the curd in about an hour. Cutting: the curd is cut and heated in a hot-water bath to the correct acidity. (Kelsae is only just warmed, Stitchill is heated to hand-hot.) It is cooled and drained, left overnight, milled, salted and mixed. The curd is poured into cheesecloth-lined moulds and pressed for 3–4 days. It is matured for 5–7 months. The season runs from spring to autumn.

REGION OF PRODUCTION:
SCOTLAND, BORDERS.

Lanark Blue Cheese

DESCRIPTION:
A ROUND, UNPASTEURIZED, BLUE-VEINED EWE'S MILK CHEESE. WEIGHT: 3KG. COLOUR: CREAM TO WHITE, MOTTLED WITH BLUE VEINS. FLAVOUR: SHARP YET CREAMY, WITH A LONG AFTERTASTE.

The original stronghold of ewe's milk cheese appears to have been the Border counties. Here it survived at least into the early nineteenth century: 'the much deforested Forest of Ettrick in Selkirkshire was one of the areas in which ewe's milk cheese was still of importance. The parish of Ettrick, to which no reliably passable roads then led, exported mutton and cheese to the market fifteen miles off from its flocks of 30,000 sheep, whose fleece was too coarse for wool buyers' (Rance, 1982). Better-keeping and better-tasting cheese from cow's milk was the main reason for its decline. (See Dunlop, above.)

The entry for Bonchester, above, describes the revival of Scottish hand-made cheese. Lanark Blue and its maker, Humphrey Errington, have been of the first importance in guiding the course of events. Lanark Blue has become recognized as a gourmet cheese, classed for quality and type beside Roquefort.

TECHNIQUE:

Milk from a Friesland-cross dairy flock is used. It is started with an inoculation of bacteria and penicillin followed by vegetarian rennet which sets the curd. This is cut and drained; 4–4.5kg is packed into moulds and left to settle without pressure for 4 days. The cheese is dipped in brine, rubbed with salt and, after 6 days, pierced to develop the mould. Maturing takes place over about 3 months. The cheeses are turned every day and, when necessary, will be wrapped in foil to prevent surface mould developing.

REGION OF PRODUCTION:

SCOTLAND, LANARKSHIRE.

Italian (Tally's) Ice-Cream

DESCRIPTION:

CLASSIC SCOTTISH 'ITALIAN' VANILLA ICE-CREAM IS USUALLY MADE ENTIRELY OF MILK AND IS THEREFORE LESS CREAMY THAN THOSE ICES A RICHER CREAM CONTENT. IT IS ALSO SLIGHTLY COLDER AND MORE ICY, TAKING LONGER TO FREEZE. THIS GIVES IT AN INCREASED DENSITY, WHICH HAS THE EFFECT OF INTENSIFYING THE FLAVOUR TO SOMETHING WHICH IS CLEAR, CLEAN, LIGHT AND WHOLLY MILKY.

HISTORY:

This is the product of the 'Tallys', Italian cafés which are a feature of Scottish high streets. The first Italians came to Britain in the 1850s but, by the end of the century, as economic conditions worsened in Italy, the trickle of immigrants became a flood. Recruited by agents of masters in London, they were hired as cheap labour. In winter they worked as hurdy-gurdy men, but in summer they cranked and froze the ice-cream mix they had made the previous night.

According to Bruno Sereni in *They Took the Low Road* (1973), the first Italians to arrive in Glasgow were from the Ciociana district, and they were responsible for laying the foundations of what was to become a flourishing ice-cream (and fish-and-chip) industry in Scotland. 'With great courage and initiative, in the space of about seventy years (1850–1920), they had graduated from itinerant begging … to itinerant ice-cream salesmen … to owners of shops in slum quarters … to proprietors of luxurious ice-cream parlours in Sauchiehall Street with mirrors on the walls and wooden partitions between the leather-covered seats.'

As the Italian ice-cream trade developed, a hierarchy was established with the most prosperous playing a major role in the training and careers of many of the young immigrants. They started at the bottom of the ladder and worked up to the ownership of a shop. Itinerant ice-cream selling continued (as it still does) but many more Italian cafés were opened, often as part of a chain. Then the individual shops were sold off to employees when they showed that they could make a profit.

This large community of quality Italian ice-cream makers spread themselves about Scotland to such an extent that every town had at least one, if not two, Italian cafés (nicknamed Tallys). Robert McKee (1991) gave figures which reflect their growing importance: in 1903 there were 89 in Glasgow, a year later 184, and by 1905, 336. Italian ice-cream had become one of the great pleasures of the working classes, and was soon to become socially acceptable to the prissy middle classes as well. Young men like Denis in A.J. Cronin's novel about Glasgow, *Hatter's Castle*, started taking their girlfriends to the forbidden territory of the Tally. Cronin's Mary had expected to find a 'sordid den', but instead there were clean marble-topped tables, shining mirrors, plush stalls and, best of all, seductive ice-cream.

A range of ices became popular, with some borrowing from the American sundae tradition, but most distinctive and persistent was the habit of pouring a raspberry sauce over the ice-cream. One legend has it that it was invented in Glasgow when a supporter of Clyde football club, whose colours are red and white, persuaded his Tally to make a red and white ice-cream. The ice-cream was named 'Macallum' after the supporter. Special 'Macallum Saucers' are remembered, though the raspberry sauce (commonly known as Tally's Blood) is now mostly poured over cones.

The extent to which Scottish tastes have been influenced by this quality ice-cream can be seen in its continued popularity. Before the discovery of soft-scoop ice-cream – made with the maximum amount of air which can be beaten in to increase the volume because it is sold by volume not weight – a post-war generation of Scottish children had tasted the real thing. They had queued at their local Tallys, if not with the family milk-jug for a fill-up of ice-cream in the days when no one had a refrigerator, then certainly for a penny-cone dripping with bright red Tally's blood. The soft-scoop 'whippy' ices were no match for the Tally's ice-cream.

TECHNIQUE:

The ingredients are first pasteurized, i.e. heated at varying temperatures from 60°C upwards. They are then homogenized under pressure, the degree of pressure depending on the percentage of solids in the mix. The mixture is cooled quickly through chilled coils, it is then put into an 'ageing' vat where, again depending on the percentage of solids, the mixture is left to mature. It is then put into the freezer, which may be a batch-type taking about 25 litres at a time, or a continuous freezer. In the batch-type, 40 per cent (and upwards) of air is beaten into the ice-cream; in the continuous freezer it is pumped in. If the amount of air added exceeds 100 per cent, the subsequent amount is known as 'overrun'. Italian ice-cream manufacturers are reluctant to declare the exact percentage of air added, but maintain it is much less than 100 per cent but not quite as low as 40 per cent.

REGION OF PRODUCTION:

CENTRAL SCOTLAND.

Arbroath Smokie

DESCRIPTION:

A HOT-SMOKED, HEADED, GUTTED, UNFILLETED HADDOCK. WEIGHT: 250G–300G. COLOUR:
COPPER-BROWN ON OUTSIDE, FLESH INSIDE CREAMY WHITE. FLAVOUR: MELLOW OVERTONES
OF SALT AND SMOKE.

HISTORY:

First developed in Auchmithie, a fishing village a little north of Arbroath, this was originally known as an Auchmithie lucken or close fish or pinwiddie. Auchmithie was largely populated by families of Norse origin. Their names still bear the evidence. The Norse-descended Spink family owns the largest traditional smokie-curing company in Arbroath. Auchmithie was also unusual amongst other fishing villages of that coast in its setting of the fisher-houses high on the edge of a cliff above the harbour several hundred feet below.

The fish were originally smoked over domestic fires, but the need for more smoking facilities caused numerous 'smoke-pits' to be set up in half whisky barrels tucked into ledges on the cliff face. Making good use of the natural upward draught to keep the fires going, the fish, after being salted and dried, were hung in pairs on poles across the top of the barrels. The whole contraption was then covered with several layers of hessian sacking which was used to regulate the heat: on dry days with a brisk wind, more layers would be piled on to prevent the fire getting too hot, on wet, windless days the layers would be fewer. Originally, all kinds of surplus fish were smoked in this way but haddock became the most popular. In the early 1800s, a number of Auchmithie fisher-folk settled in Arbroath nearby. They built square, brick smoke-pits in their back gardens, continuing to make the smokie cure. By the end of the century, output from Arbroath greatly exceeded that from Auchmithie and the name of the smokie was changed to reflect this.

Today, the people of Arbroath continue to smoke in their backyards, selling smokies from small shop counters. When the pits are in use, the smell wafting through the streets is overwhelming. Though some prefer to remain small with a single smoke-pit, selling to loyal and regular customers, others have developed a more commercial operation in large plants. They have not, however, managed to reproduce the genuine smokie in computer-operated, high-tech kilns. Those who produce the original continue to work with the old method of small pits covered with sacking. Undoubtedly the best flavour is when the fish is 'hot off the barrel'. Otherwise, it may be split open and the bone removed, the centre filled with butter, and heated in the oven or under a grill. It has been granted Protected Geographical Indication (PGI).

TECHNIQUE:

The fish are gutted, beheaded and dry-salted for about 2 hours, depending on size, to draw excess moisture from the skin and impart a mild salty flavour. They are tied in pairs and hung over wooden rods; the salt is washed off and they are left to dry for about 5 hours to harden the skins. The rods are placed in the smoke-pit and hot-smoked over oak or beech, covered with layers of hessian. Smoking time is approximately 45 minutes.

REGION OF PRODUCTION:

EAST SCOTLAND, ARBROATH (TAYSIDE).

Finnan Haddock

DESCRIPTION:

A WHOLE HADDOCK, WITH THE HEAD REMOVED BUT THE BONE LEFT IN, SPLIT, BRINED AND SMOKED. COLOUR: PALE STRAW THROUGH TO GOLDEN BROWN; NO ARTIFICIAL DYE IS USED. FLAVOUR: LIGHTLY SALTED, DELICATELY SMOKED.

HISTORY:

A salt-cured haddock, known as a spelding, can be traced back to the sixteenth century when they are mentioned in the household book of King James V. They are also mentioned by Robert Fergusson in his poem *The Leith Races* (1773), 'Guid speldins, fa will buy'. In the same year, James Boswell describes them in his diary as, 'salted and dried in a particular manner, being dipped in the sea and dried in the sun, and eaten by the Scots by way of a relish'. He also says they were available in London. Speldings, however, were heavily salted and the subsequent move towards a lightly salted, smoked haddock began as communications improved and fish which might otherwise spoil could be delivered with enough dispatch. Due to the reputation of curers who smoked, as well as salted, fish in the village of Findon a few miles south of Aberdeen, the cured fish became known as a Finnan. It is also said that their reputation spread quickly through the country because they were transported to a dealer in Edinburgh by a relation who was guard on the Aberdeen to Edinburgh stage-coach at the beginning of the nineteenth century (Dyson, 1977).

They are mentioned by Robert Southey in his *Journal of a Tour in Scotland* (1819): 'A good breakfast as usual in Scotland, with Findon Haddocks, eggs, sweetmeats, and honey.' Included in the fishwife's creel of smoked and fresh fish, they were hawked about the country during the heyday of the East-coast fisheries and became common fare, cooked simply in milk and butter or made into the fishwife's soup-stew, admired throughout the country as a Cullen Skink. The reputation of Finnan haddock suffered in the 1870s when the cure was spoiled by the use of bad peat and a resinous, soft-wood sawdust, making the fillets acrid. It recovered its celebrity and quality, though not without competition from alternative modern cures using artificial dyes, 'painted ladies'. Sometimes described as a 'Golden' fillet, the lightly brined and lightly smoked skinless haddock or whiting should not be confused with the Finnan. A variation with more integrity is the undyed Aberdeen fillet, or smoked fillet, which can be used in the same way as the bone-in Finnan.

TECHNIQUE:

The original Finnans were split with the bone on the left-hand side of the fish, looking at the cut surface with the tail downwards. They were dry-salted overnight and smoked over soft 'grey' peat for 8–9 hours then cooled and washed in warm salted water. Other original Finnan cures around the country included Eyemouth and Glasgow 'Pale' which was a much milder paler cure, smoked for only 30 minutes to 2 hours and split with the bone on the right-hand side. A Moray Firth Finnan was split like a 'Pale' but smoked for about 12 hours making it a much darker, more heavily smoked fish. Methods today vary from commercially produced large-scale smoking in Torry kilns to small independent smokers, using simpler equipment.

REGION OF PRODUCTION:

NORTH EAST AND CENTRAL SCOTLAND.

Smelt

DESCRIPTION:
A FISH WITH A LIGHT OLIVE-GREEN BACK, SILVER STRIPE ALONG THE SIDE, AND A CREAMY
WHITE BELLY; IT GROWS UP TO 20CM LONG, AND THE SOFT-TEXTURED FLESH IS SAID TO
SMELL OF CUCUMBER OR VIOLETS – REASON FOR THE ALTERNATE NAMES OF CUCUMBER FISH
AND CHERRY OF THE TAY.

HISTORY:
Smelts (*Osmerus eperlanus*) have always been considered a delicacy, and there are records of
their fishery in various British rivers. Relatively little is known about the species, but they
are an inshore fish, associated with specific rivers and estuaries which they enter to spawn.
The River Tay has been noted for a reliable population of smelts for as long as people can
remember and supports a very small commercial fishery.

According to the *Dundee Courier and Advertiser*, smelts were 'once a very popular meal in
towns and villages around the Tay, dating back to medieval times when the fish was caught by
the monks from the monastery at Newburgh'. Oral tradition, recounted by Sandy Doig, the
person who currently exploits this fishery, states that around 1939–45, 17 yawls fished regularly for smelts. The number declined progressively in the intervening years until only one was
left. This belonged to Charlie Johnston of Newburgh, who began fishing after the war, and
continued up until his death in the early 1990s. The work is now continued by one boat from
Newburgh; recently, others have shown an interest.

Smelts are usually fried, although they can be poached or pickled. They are also excellent
smoked. In French, the fish is known as *éperlan*, translated by francophile Scots into sparling.

TECHNIQUE:
Smelts tolerate water of low salinity and, in the River Tay, the fishing ground is a 30km stretch
of brackish water between Newburgh and Dundee. The fish travel up the tideway in autumn
to spawn at the highest point reached by the tide and then return to the sea in April or May.
They are caught on incoming, strong spring tides, from boats anchored in the stream. Boom
nets are used, held open just below the surface: these are conical, tapering from about 22cm at
the open end down to 2cm. They are lowered into the water so the strong current washes the
fish in and holds them there. Once the net is full, the fisherman winches the lower boom up
to close it and bring the catch in.

REGION OF PRODUCTION:
EAST SCOTLAND, RIVER TAY.

Ayrshire Bacon

DESCRIPTION:
SMOKED OR UNSMOKED CURED PORK FOR COOKING. COLOUR: CREAM FAT, DARK PINK FLESH.
FLAVOUR: MILDLY CURED, VERY LIGHTLY SALTED; DEPENDS FOR ITS FLAVOUR ON THE BREED
AND QUALITY OF PIG AS WELL AS THE CURE. AYRSHIRE BACON IS MADE FROM GREAT
WHITE PREMIUM-GRADE PIGS. BOTH SKIN AND BONES ARE REMOVED BEFORE CURING. THE
BACK OR CUTLET PART AND THE STREAKY OR FLANK ARE NOT SEPARATED. ONCE CURED,
THE MIDDLE IS ROLLED TIGHTLY, THE FAT SIDE OUTERMOST. THE GIGOT (LEG) IS ROLLED

AND TIED AND THE SHOULDER CUT INTO BOILING JOINTS. THESE ARE KNOWN AS AN AYRSHIRE ROLL.

HISTORY:

This is the only distinctive bacon cure in Scotland. It is thought to have arisen in the South-West, which has a history of dairying going back at least to the 1600s. In Britain, by-products from the cheese and butter industries have always been used to feed pigs. Potatoes too, grown in south-west Scotland, contributed much to their diet (Mabey, 1978). Demand may have been stimulated by the presence of many large, wealthy households in the Upper Clyde. Ramsay's of Carluke has been making Ayrshire bacon since 1857 and is now the largest producer.

The bacon was always skinned, boned and rolled. Rolling is necessary because the flank is left attached to the side, giving a very long rasher: the only sensible method for dealing with it is to roll the meat. In contrast to other cures in Britain, the carcasses are not scalded after slaughter. This is because the bristles, normally scraped away with hot water, are removed with the skin. The end product has a finer colour and firmer texture than meat which has been scalded.

The rolled back-bacon is usually cut thinly into rashers and grilled or fried. The round shape of the cut is convenient as a filling for a roll. In the cities of central Scotland, bacon rolls are a popular fast-food – eaten at any time of the day. The gigot is usually cut into steaks for grilling or frying. Both the gigot and the shoulder may be cut into joints for boiling. The term ham in Scotland loosely refers to any kind of bacon and not just the cured leg joint which is the usual English interpretation. In Scotland, this is called cooked ham or gammon.

TECHNIQUE:

Only gilts (young female pigs) of a specified weight are used by Ramsay's. The whole side is boned out and the skin removed. It is wet-brined for 2 days with a small proportion of nitrates for preservation. It is dried for 2–3 weeks before it is cut up and rolled. Some of the production is lightly smoked over oak chips. Some bacon with the back and streaky still in one piece, which has been cured with the skin on and the bone still in, is subsequently skinned, boned and rolled into the Ayrshire cylindrical shape. It is described as Ayrshire-style bacon but is not true Ayrshire. Some Ayrshire bacon curers also cure whole legs on the bone but because the skin and bones have not been removed, neither is this regarded as an authentic Ayrshire cure. The demand for smoked or unsmoked is a local preference. A special spiced cure is made for festive occasions, in small quantities to order.

REGION OF PRODUCTION:

SOUTH-WEST SCOTLAND.

COMPARE WITH:

Suffolk Sweet-Cured Bacon, East Anglia (p. 128); Welsh Bacon, Wales (p. 190); Wiltshire Bacon, South West England (p. 28).

Cheviot Sheep

DESCRIPTION:

As well as the original Cheviot, two distinct strains are recognized: the North Country (in North England and West Scotland) and the Brecknock Hill or Sennybridge (in central Wales). Carcasses (dressed weight, in late winter) are 17–22kg (Cheviots), 25–30kg (North Country Cheviots). Good meat conformation with strong shoulders and broad backs; Cheviots are smaller and blockier than the large North Country Cheviot. Large, meaty sheep which yield well-flavoured lamb.

HISTORY:

The breed takes its name from the hills that run along the Scottish border. The primitive 'dun faced' sheep of the Highlands, noticed in the seventeenth century, was probably an ancestor. The breed we know today developed in the Northumberland-Berwick region (Hall & Clutton-Brock, 1989). Lincoln rams were used to improve the strain in the mid-eighteenth century, and some Leicester blood at the start of the nineteenth. Cheviots had some reputation by the time Mrs Beeton (1861) commented on them as providers of wool and meat. The breed society was founded at the end of the 1800s.

Not long before that, Cheviots were taken south and were found to do well on the high ground and in the exposed climate of central Wales. They were also taken north to graze the great tracts of land available after the Highland Clearances. With some Merino blood, these developed into a breed known as North Country Cheviots, or 'Northies'. A breed society for these was established in 1912.

Cheviot breeds are used for the production of quality lamb. A first cross is made with Leicester rams, and the female progeny is put to Suffolk, Downland or continental rams to breed large, lean, fast-maturing lambs. Much of this reaches the market as 'Scottish Lamb'.

TECHNIQUE:

All Cheviot breeds are hardy; the original is still the best for the bleak hills themselves, which rise to 1,000 metres, with short grass and little cover for sheep. They live out all year. Extra feed, usually hay, is only given during the severest conditions and to pregnant ewes in the 6 weeks before lambing in mid-April. Hill lambs are late-maturing; they are killed for meat from August onwards but many are kept as stores on low ground, fed on arable crops and slaughtered in late winter.

The North Country Cheviot has two further strains. One is the Caithness, which, while living further north than the original Cheviot, is not as hardy; it grazes the low ground and rich grass of Caithness. The second is the 'Heather' or Sutherland, an exceptionally hardy, but somewhat smaller, sheep which does well in the harsh climate of western Scotland on unimproved native hill pasture and heather. Cheviot and North Country ewes are much sought by breeders for their excellent mothering qualities. Hill ewes are often sold at about 6 years to lowland farms, where they can be used productively for several more years in a gentler climate.

REGION OF PRODUCTION:

Scotland; North East England.

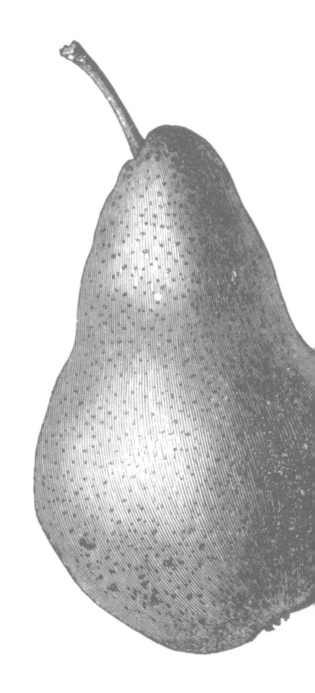

Forfar Bridie

DESCRIPTION:

A HORSESHOE-SHAPED, BAKED BEEF AND ONION PASTY, WEIGHING 200–750G. COLOUR: PALE
BROWN. FLAVOUR: SAVOURY BEEF AND ONIONS.

HISTORY:

Third-generation bridie-baker in Forfar, William McLaren, believes that his family's account
of the origins of the bridie is more credible than the much-quoted story of Margaret Bridie of
Glamis, renowned for her meat pasties which she sold in the Buttermarket in Forfar.
According to McLaren, the bridie was a speciality of Jolly's bakery where his grandfather,
James McLaren, served his time and learned to make them. This was in the late 1890s and
meat was not commonly eaten by the majority of the population: the staple diet was based on
porridge and brose, 3 times a day, Sundays and holidays included. Bridies were for special
occasions, the horseshoe shape a lucky symbol eaten at the bride's meal, or wedding feast. The
lucky bridie continues to be eaten at weddings, also christenings, but has now become a convenient everyday food.

Bridies in Forfar, made to the traditional method, have a high meat content which makes
them more expensive than others made elsewhere. In the heart of Aberdeen-Angus country,
people reckon lots of meat is essential to eating quality and are critical of any compromises.
With a sausage-type filling and without onions, bridie has also become a generic name across
Scotland for a crescent-shaped item made with puff pastry. This is not recognized in Forfar as
authentic. They are eaten hot, for high tea or lunch with beans and bread and butter.

TECHNIQUE:

Jolly's nineteenth-century recipe (McNeill, 1929): 'Take a pound of the best steak. Beat it
with the paste roller, then cut it into narrow strips, and again cut these into one-inch lengths
and season with salt and pepper. Divide into three portions. Mince finely three ounces of suet.
Make a stiff dough with flour, water and a seasoning of salt, and roll out thin into three ovals.
Cover the half of each oval with meat; sprinkle with the suet and a little minced onion if
desired. Wet the edges, fold over, and crimp with the finger and thumb. Nip a small hole on
top of each. Bake for a about half an hour in a quick oven and they will come out golden
brown dappled beauties, fit for a king's supper.'

The modern recipe includes mincing the beef through a large plate to give a coarser texture than for pies, mixing with the other ingredients, then following the Jolly method of shaping the pastry and filling. Modern pastry recipes include a fat. Bridies are baked in a hot oven
for about 40 minutes depending on size.

REGION OF PRODUCTION:

EAST SCOTLAND, FORFAR (TAYSIDE).

COMPARE WITH:

Bedforshire Clanger, South England (p. 67); Cornish Pasty, South West England (p. 20)

Galloway Cattle

DESCRIPTION:

AVERAGE LIVE WEIGHT FOR 16-MONTH STEER, 470KG. FLESH DEEPLY RED WITH LIGHT MAR-
BLING OF INTRA-MUSCULAR CREAM FAT. FLAVOUR AT ITS BEST WHEN IT HAS BEEN HUNG 2–3
WEEKS.

HISTORY:

Though their subsequent bloodlines followed very different paths, the two modern Scottish
breeds of black, hornless beef cattle – the Aberdeen-Angus and the Galloway – have
superficial similarities which reflect descent from the same primitive stock. But while the first
has responded to intensive feeding, resulting in a rapidly maturing animal, the Galloway has
made the most of marginal and hill lands in the South-West of Scotland by producing a more
slowly maturing breed.

During the eighteenth century, Galloway was a major source of store cattle which were
taken by drovers to be fattened in Norfolk or Suffolk for the London market. By the mid-
nineteenth, however, the droving trade had ended as beef breeds were developed for supplying Smithfield direct with carcass meat (see Aberdeen-Angus, p. 341). South-Western cattle
farmers, therefore, turned to dairying, and the beef cattle were forced to live in the hills.

The Galloway Cattle Society was formed in 1877 in Castle Douglas, still the headquarters
of the breed. Until its inception, the polled Angus or Aberdeen cattle and the Galloways were
entered in the same herd book, but with the founding of the society the copyright of the
Galloway portion was purchased.

During World War II the value of the pure-bred Galloway for hill grazing was recognized
and numbers were expanded with Government encouragement. While the breed has maintained its position, despite subsequent changes in Government policy, its most recent history
has been significantly affected, once again, by its ability to forage on rough ground without
too much expense, making it attractive at a time of rising costs. A variant is the Belted
Galloway, so called for the vertical white stripe on its body.

Most Galloways are in southern Scotland with a concentration in the South-West; there
are some in Cumbria and other parts of the North of England and a few elsewhere in England
and Ireland.

TECHNIQUE:

The cattle are out-wintered and maintained on exposed hill and marginal land. They thrive
and produce on low-cost rations in winter and in summer on unimproved rough grazing.
They are particularly suited to extensive husbandry.

REGION OF PRODUCTION:

SOUTH-WEST SCOTLAND.

Dundee Cake

DESCRIPTION:

A ROUND FRUIT CAKE, 180–230MM DIAMETER, 100MM DEEP (SOMETIMES OBLONG).
COLOUR: DARK BROWN EXTERIOR, THE TOP COVERED WITH WHOLE ALMONDS, GOLDEN
INSIDE, WITH SULTANAS. FLAVOUR: RICH, BUTTERY, FRUITY.

'…*bannocks and a share of cheese*
Will make a breakfast that a laird might please.'

ALLAN RAMSAY, 'THE GENTLE SHEPHERD'

South Scotland

It is claimed this cake originated as a by-product of the Keiller marmalade industry (see below p. 328). The firm was already working with Spanish and Mediterranean produce for orange marmalade; therefore the extra ingredients for the cake were not difficult to obtain. The habit of industrial food production was easily transferred from jam to cake. Until Keiller's was absorbed by a larger business in the 1980s, a gentlemen's agreement existed among the bakers of Dundee that only Keiller's should make the cake. However, this recipe, which appears indeed to have been developed sometime during 1850–1900, was widely copied by people beyond the city walls.

David Goodfellow, of the Dundee bakers, Goodfellow and Steven (established 1897), claims a direct connection with the early days of the Keiller version through a craftsman with first-hand knowledge from working in their bakery. He was reputed to have written down the specification before he went off to the First World War. This genuine Keiller item, as Goodfellow understands it, was a rich, buttery sultana cake, with no other fruits, no spices and certainly no cherries. The chief flavourings were the orange peel and almonds from Spain.

Recipes for Dundee cake have appeared in professional manuals for the last century or more. They have suggested variations (more often economies) on the simple richness of the original: topping with flaked, not whole, almonds, or adding black-jack colouring. Though more authentic cakes are now being produced in Scotland, the industry has not invariably maintained either the quality or the original concept.

TECHNIQUE:

Ingredients are slightly salted butter, muscovado sugar, eggs, plain cake flour, ground almonds, candied orange peel, sultanas, whole blanched almonds. These are mixed in the order given, save the whole almonds arranged on the top of the cake. It is baked at 180°C for 120–160 minutes.

REGION OF PRODUCTION:

SCOTLAND.

Glasgow Roll

DESCRIPTION:

A SQUARISH MORNING ROLL WITH HARD OUTER SURFACE, 100MM LONG, 50MM HIGH. WEIGHT: 40G. COLOUR AND TEXTURE: FROM LIGHT BROWN THROUGH TO ALMOST BLACK ON THE SURFACE OF A BURNT ROLL; A LIGHT, OPEN, WELL-AERATED TEXTURE WHICH IS NONE THE LESS CHEWY. FLAVOUR: SALTY.

HISTORY:

This is a local form of the morning roll which developed its hard outer crust and airy, non-doughy, centre for the special purpose of holding bacon or a fried egg (or both at once) as a worker's breakfast. They were eaten in large quantities by men in places such as the Clydeside shipyards, as well as other local industries, as the mid-morning snack. The roll was popular because of its robust quality. Alternative names were hard rolls and burnt rolls – so requested by those who liked their bread very well fired. Glasgow rolls are torn open rather than cut.

TECHNIQUE:

The dough is made with 100 per cent Canadian high-protein flour, mixed with water, liquid malt, yeast, and salt, and bulk fermented for 4–5 hours. Shaping is still done by hand, even in some large bakeries; final proving is also relatively extended. The rolls are baked for 14 minutes at 240°C.

REGION OF PRODUCTION:
CENTRAL SCOTLAND, GLASGOW.

Puggie Bun

DESCRIPTION:
AN OVAL BUN COMPOSED OF A FILLING OF GINGER DOUGH ENCLOSED IN A PALE CREAMY-GOLD PASTRY CASE WHICH IS SLASHED 4 TIMES ACROSS THE TOP; ABOUT 90MM LONG, 70MM WIDE, 15–25MM DEEP. FLAVOUR AND TEXTURE: DOUGHY, PASTRY DRY-TEXTURED; CRUMBLY, GINGER-FLAVOURED FILLING.

HISTORY:
The name is of unknown origin. The word 'puggie' or 'puggy', has several meanings in English and Scots dialects, including one relating to mixing operations and another (obsolete) a term of endearment. Whether either of these has anything to do with this bun is unclear. The alternative name of Gowrie bun, remembered by some older inhabitants in the south-eastern Scottish Highlands, suggests a strong connection with the lowlands along the north side of the River Tay, a fertile corn-growing area known as the Carse of Gowrie, close to which these buns are still produced.

The puggy bun is an outer wrapping of plain pastry which hides a spiced and sweet filling which is almost equal quantities of treacle or syrup and flour. There are strong precedents for pastry-wrapped goods of this type in the baking traditions of the British Isles; the one which is most relevant in this context is probably the Scottish black bun, a large cake of dried fruit wrapped in pastry (see below). The filling for puggie buns is a substance called gundy dough by the bakers who make it (gundy is an old Scottish word for a spiced sweetmeat). It is a very similar mixture to one used for an old Scottish speciality, no longer made, which was a type of gingerbread called parleys, or parliament cakes. Kirkland (1907) comments that the dough for these 'was invariably made up in large quantities, and stocked in barrels, to be worked up afterwards as required'. Although these buns were apparently well known in central Scotland in the past, only one baker (in Cupar, Fife) has been located who produces them. He remarks that they are most popular with older people, who eat them as a snack or for tea, cut in half and spread with butter.

TECHNIQUE:
A gundy dough is made up from flour, syrup and spices and stored for use as needed. Pastry is made up fresh using a hot-water method and beef dripping as the fat. When required, the gundy dough is scaled off and shaped into balls; the pastry is wrapped around and sealed. The bun is turned so the join in the pastry is underneath and pinned or rolled further until the correct oval shape is achieved. The top is slashed. During baking the bun rises and the slashes open to reveal the filling; they are deliberately baked until rather dry. The gundy dough used to be raised with a mixture of pearlash and alum. At the turn of the century, bakers converted to bicarbonate of soda.

REGION OF PRODUCTION:
EAST CENTRAL SCOTLAND.

Selkirk Bannock

DESCRIPTION:

A WEIGHTY, ROUNDED BUN, FLAT ON THE BOTTOM AND CURVED ON TOP, 150–200MM DIAMETER, MADE IN SMALL AND LARGE SIZES. WEIGHT: 450G (SMALL)–800G (LARGE). COLOUR: GOLD. FLAVOUR: RICH BUTTERY YEAST BREAD FLAVOURED WITH SULTANAS.

HISTORY:

The word bannock referred originally to a round, unleavened dough the size of a meat plate which was baked on the girdle and used by the oven-less Scots in place of yeast-raised, oven-baked bread. The word in Old Scots, *bannok,* is thought to come from Latin, probably through the influence of the Church and may have originally referred to Communion bread. It is now generally used to described any baked item which is large and round.

A Selkirk baker, Robbie Douglas, opened a shop on the Market Place in 1859 and so impressed his customers with the quality of his rich yeasted bannocks that in time they took the name of Selkirk. He discovered that the finished flavour was greatly influenced by the quality of the butter and, after some experimenting, found the best came from cows grazing on neighbouring pastures. He used only the best sultanas from Turkey and together with his baking skills produced the legendary bannock. On her visit to Sir Walter Scott's granddaughter at Abbotsford in 1867, Queen Victoria refused all else of the sumptuous baking save a slice of the Douglas bannock.

While a number of bakers now make the bannock, the original Douglas recipe is said to have come down from Alex Dalgetty, one of the bakers who worked with Douglas. Dalgetty's descendants continue to make the 'original' at their bakery in Galashiels, though Houston's in Hawick now owns the actual bakery where Douglas worked. Hossack's in Kelso has recently developed the Tweed Bannock using wholemeal flour.

Once an everyday bread dough, bakers now make up a special bannock dough. Some, but not all, continue to follow the original method of a 'sponge' which leaves the dough overnight for slower fermentation and development of a finer, more mature flavour.

TECHNIQUE:

Yeast dough is made up with about 4 parts flour to 1 part butter and lard. It is left to rise and then knocked back with 1 part sugar and 2 parts sultanas added.

REGION OF PRODUCTION:

SOUTH SCOTLAND, BORDERS.

Softie

DESCRIPTION:

A ROUNDED BUN 100MM DIAMETER, 40MM HIGH. WEIGHT: 50–60G. COLOUR: GOLDEN. FLAVOUR: SLIGHTLY SWEET.

HISTORY:

This bun appears to have taken its name mainly to distinguish it from the Aberdeen butterie or rowie (see p. 350) and is also sold as a morning roll. The fact that the rowie is a harder, crisper product gave rise to the term softie. This, at least, is one interpretation. An alternative name was soft biscuit: a literal description of their quality and the word biscuit describing a small roll or cake – a similar usage may be found in Guernsey (David 1977) and in North America. Though there is no written evidence, an Aberdeenshire baker of over 50 years' experience has established that softies and rowies have been common since the early 1900s. Production has spread beyond Aberdeen, down the east coast and Fife to Edinburgh. Because they contain more sugar than baps or rowies, and less fat than rowies, they are most commonly eaten at tea or supper with preserves, but may also be used as an envelope for savoury fillings. Simon (1960) records their being toasted for rusks.

TECHNIQUE:
Softies contain double the sugar used in a bap. Otherwise, the doughs are similar.

REGION OF PRODUCTION:
EAST SCOTLAND.

Black Bun

DESCRIPTION:
COLOUR: VERY DARK CENTRE, ALMOST BLACK WITH SPICES, DRIED FRUITS AND BLACK TREACLE, ENCLOSED IN A SHORT-CRUST PASTRY. FLAVOUR: INTENSE FRUIT, SPICE AND ALCOHOL.

HISTORY:
Though inextricably linked with the Scots and Hogmanay, not all Scots regard this cake as an essential element of the festivities. It has no real following in the Highlands and Islands, nor in the North-East. Their spiced, fruited speciality is a clootie dumpling (see p. 379). According to Meg Dods (1826), the bun, which was originally made with bread dough enriched with spices, dried fruit, eggs and brandy and then wrapped in a plain layer of bread dough, was made by all the leading Edinburgh bakers in the run-up to Christmas. She says that it was exported in sizes of 'four, eight, ten, twelve, sixteen and more pounds' to the rest of Britain.

Although this item was originally described as a 'Plum Cake' in eighteenth-century recipes, it is claimed by McNeill (1929) to have been the original Scottish Twelfth Cake used at Twelfth Night celebrations. Around the first half of the nineteenth century, it seems to have been rechristened a 'Scotch Christmas Bun', retaining its style as an enriched and yeasted bread dough wrapped in an thin outer casing of plain dough. The description 'bun' may have been introduced to avoid confusion with the meaning which the Scots had for 'cake' as a hard biscuit, as in oat 'cakes'. The use of 'Christmas' as a further qualifier is also confusing since, post Reformation, the Protestant church in Scotland actually banned Christmas as a Catholic aberration. A possible explanation for the name and subsequent development may lie in its success as an export product to neighbours who delighted in richly spiced foods. It could almost be described as an English Christmas pudding in a crust. Another clue to its English, rather than Scottish, popularity, is its inclusion by Meg Dods among the English baking specialities rather than in the chapter on Scottish national dishes. Eventually, it had become so intensely spicy and fruity that the bread dough was abandoned, very little flour was added to the spice and fruit mixture, and the whole mixture was wrapped in a short pastry crust. It was described by Robert Louis Stevenson as 'a black substance inimical to life'. The last mention of a 'Scotch Christmas Bun' appears to be around 1914; by 1929 it is described as 'Black Bun', the name it has retained ever since.

The main spices used in the eighteenth century were cinnamon, nutmeg, cloves, and caraway, along with currants, lemon and orange peel and almonds, with French brandy for good measure. In the nineteenth century, raisins are included and ginger used instead of caraway. McNeill's recipe in 1929 omits nutmeg, uses ginger and adds Jamaica pepper (allspice) and black pepper. All Scottish bakers who make the bun have their own spice mix and flavours vary from strongly peppery to mildly cinnamony. Black treacle is a modern addition. Today, it is almost invariably served with a dram of whisky.

TECHNIQUE:

Spices and fruit are steeped in brandy for several days, mixed with flour and sometimes grated apple and black treacle. These are pressed into a cake or loaf tin which has been lined with short-crust pastry. It is baked slowly until the pastry is crisp and the filling set firm. It may be stored for months in an airtight container.

REGION OF PRODUCTION:

CENTRAL AND SOUTH SCOTLAND.

Border Tart

DESCRIPTION:

A ROUND OPEN TART 150MM DIAMETER, 20–30MM DEEP; SOMETIMES ICED WITH WHITE GLACÉ ICING, WITH A DARK, DRIED-FRUIT FILLING; ALTERNATIVELY, A RICH SPONGE WITHOUT THE ICING. FLAVOUR: SWEET, RICH WITH DRIED FRUIT, BUTTERY.

HISTORY:

The modern Border tart is different from the original casing of yeast dough filled with a rich egg custard and flavoured with marzipan, almonds, lemon and orange peel and sultanas. Border bakers have developed their own, more economical versions. It is now also known as Eymouth tart and Ecclefechan butter tart.

Sophisticated tarts are thought to have developed in this part of Scotland as a result of the French connection before and immediately after the Act of Union in 1707. Contemporary recipe books show the degree of refinement of Scottish tarts (often described as 'flans') from which the modern Border tart appears to descend. Interpretation by modern bakers has meant styles vary widely. No two are identical. They range from something akin to a Bakewell tart with a rich almond sponge, but which usually includes dried fruit and nuts, to an intensely sweet sponge-less filling of fruit, sugar, butter and egg.

TECHNIQUE:

Made with a short-crust pastry case, filled with dried fruit, sugar, melted butter and egg. Alternatively, a sponge-cake filling, including a proportion of ground nuts. When baked and cooled, it is often coated with white glacé icing.

REGION OF PRODUCTION:

SOUTH SCOTLAND, BORDERS.

Cumnock Tart

DESCRIPTION:

A DOUBLE-CRUST, INDIVIDUAL, SWEET, FRUIT TART 130MM LONG, 100MM WIDE, 30MM DEEP. WEIGHT: ABOUT 110G. COLOUR: SHINY, BROWNED-SUGAR SURFACE WITH LIGHTLY BURNT EDGES. FLAVOUR: FRUITY, SWEET WITH SAVOURY LARD PASTRY.

HISTORY:

This is a regional variation and development of the Scotch pie (a raised pie filled with mutton or beef). The sweet version, using apple or rhubarb, was created by an Ayrshire baker named Stoddart around 1920, using the same savoury lard pastry as the meat pies. The tart was made first in Cumnock (Strathclyde). The second-generation owner of Bradford's bakery in Glasgow, Hugh Bradford, learned to make it from his father who had been apprenticed to Mr Stoddart. The tart is made to the original recipe for the chain of bakery shops owned by Bradford's.

TECHNIQUE:

Each tart is made from an individual piece of dough which is pinned out by hand to form an oval bottom or base. This is filled with apple or rhubarb. Sugar is added and a thin oval lid placed on top. An edge or rim is formed using the thumb and forefinger while sealing the lid to the base. They are baked for 20–25 minutes. During baking, they are glazed twice with sugar syrup to produce a rich colour and sticky, shiny top.

REGION OF PRODUCTION:
CENTRAL SCOTLAND, GLASGOW.

Kirriemuir Gingerbread

DESCRIPTION:

LIGHT-TEXTURED, CAKE OR DUMPLING GINGERBREAD, 120MM SQUARE. WEIGHT: 320G. COLOUR: DARK BROWN. FLAVOUR: SWEET-MALTED, LIGHTLY SPICED.

HISTORY:

The style of what is known today as gingerbread has changed from the original biscuit form, made with bread crumbs mixed with honey and ginger, rolled out flat, often stuck with whole cloves and baked until very hard. This had developed from the popularity of ginger through-out the country. No annual fair was complete without its gingerbread booth, the hard biscuit appearing in many novel shapes. It was the start of a tradition which survives in the wide variety of ginger-flavoured delights, both hard biscuits and soft cakes, such as parkin biscuits, wigs, ginger nuts, ginger snaps, coburg cakes, cracknels, fairings, honey cakes, Grasmere gingerbread and Yorkshire parkin.

The old hard gingerbread was known in Edinburgh as Parliament cake, described in Chambers' *Traditions of Edinburgh* (1868). The judges, lawyers and the men of Parliament Square would meet for their midday break of whisky, rum or brandy, accompanied by a salver of ginger biscuits or parlies. Very strongly ginger-flavoured, to match the strong drink, the recipe appears in Meg Dods (1826): 'With two pounds of the best flour dried, mix thoroughly one pound of good brown sugar and a quarter-pound of ground ginger. Melt a pound of fresh butter, add to it one of treacle, boil this, and pour it on the flour; work up the paste as hot as your hands will bear it, and roll it out in very large cakes, the sixth of an inch thick or less; mark it in squares with a knife or paper-cutter, and fire in a slow oven. Separate the squares while soft, and they will soon get crisp.'

While parlies are no longer made, Scottish bakers continue the gingerbread tradition with a number of other items, among them the soft cake known as a Kirriemuir gingerbread. It was first made by Walter Burnett, a Kirriemuir baker who sold the recipe to a plant bakery in East Kilbride in the early 1940s. It was made there until 1977 when the recipe was bought by the present owners of the recipe, Bell's of Shotts.

TECHNIQUE:

Like many British gingerbreads, the Kirriemuir involves syrup, an ingredient which probably replaced the honey of earlier recipes and has a similar humectant effect. The commercial product lists as its ingredients wheat flour, sugar, syrup, vegetable and animal fats, currants, malt extract, baking powder, spices, colour caramel, honey, preservative (E200). These are mixed with milk, and beaten to aerate (although chemical leavening is also added). They are baked at 160°C for 55 minutes.

REGION OF PRODUCTION:

CENTRAL SCOTLAND, LANARKSHIRE.

Parkin Biscuit

DESCRIPTION:

PARKIN BISCUITS ARE CIRCULAR, THEIR FORM RANGES FROM THICK, BISCUIT-LIKE CAKES ABOUT 140MM DIAMETER, 30MM THICK, TO THIN, HARD BISCUITS ABOUT 60MM DIAMETER, 5MM THICK. COLOUR: LIGHT GINGER-BROWN. FLAVOUR: SWEET, WITH GINGER.

HISTORY:

Parkin, known as perkin in Northumberland and southern Scotland, is the northern form of gingerbread. It is based on oatmeal, the grain of the region, mixed with flour and syrup and flavoured with ginger. Two distinct types exist: a soft sponge, found mostly in Yorkshire, south Lancashire and neighbouring areas; and a harder biscuit which is made mostly in counties either side of the Scottish border, although it is also found in isolated pockets further south. Stead (1991) speculates that it is derived from an older, honey-sweetened oatbread. The name was in use some time before the 1730s, when it was cited in a Halifax (West Yorkshire) court case about stolen oatmeal.

Parkin and the related 'thar' cake (see Yorkshire Parkin, p. 263) were originally made on a griddle. The biscuits may be modern representatives of this older form, though now baked in conventional ovens. Like sponge parkins, the recipes have been altered to include white flour and Golden Syrup or molasses. Although best known in the Borders, they are to be found as far south as Haworth in Yorkshire where a hard, bannock-like shortbread has been made in the town for as long as any one can remember. Biscuit parkins made further south are usually softer and thicker, and the dough is moulded by hand into a large round which is rolled out to the correct thickness before baking.

Parkin is traditionally a food for the end of October and beginning of November, especially Bonfire Night (5 November). Biscuit parkin is sometimes rolled very thin and cut into human or animal shapes, pigs above all.

TECHNIQUE:

All parkin biscuits are based on oatmeal, wheat flour, ginger, Golden Syrup and fat, often lard or beef dripping. Cake crumbs are required by one recipe. The exact proportions are variable. A recipe from Westmoreland requires flour and medium oatmeal, fat, black treacle and sugar in the proportions 3:3:2:2:2. The fat and treacle are melted together, flour, ginger and bicarbonate of soda mixed in, oatmeal and sugar added. The dough is rolled out, cut into rounds and baked at 170°C for 30–40 minutes.

REGION OF PRODUCTION:
SCOTTISH BORDERS; NORTH ENGLAND.

COMPARE WITH:
Yorkshire Parkin, North East England (p. 263)

Paving Stone

DESCRIPTION:
A LONG, NARROW BISCUIT, LIKE A CYLINDER CUT IN HALF LENGTHWAYS, ABOUT 70MM LONG, AND 20MM HIGH AT THE THICKEST POINT, TAPERING TOWARDS THE ENDS. COLOUR: MID-BROWN, CONTAINING CURRANTS, WITH SUGARY WHITE OUTER COATING. FLAVOUR AND TEXTURE: SPICY, QUITE SWEET, WITH AN AERATED, HARD TEXTURE WHICH SOFTENS A LITTLE ON KEEPING.

HISTORY:
The origin of these biscuits, a type of gingerbread, is unknown. Made in eastern Central Scotland, they appear to be the speciality of one company, which was founded in 1919, which has been making them ever since. Many recipes for crisp gingerbreads are to be found in Scotland. Edinburgh, not far to the south of Fife, was famous for its Parliament cakes (see Kirriemuir gingerbread, above). Parkins, hard gingerbread biscuits which soften on keeping, are also known in the South and East of Scotland. The coating of grained sugar given to Paving Stones seems to be unique in British cookery.

TECHNIQUE:
The exact method is a trade secret, but the biscuits call for a dough based on creamed fat and sugar, mixed with flour, spices, baking powder, currants and milk. After baking, boiled sugar is poured on to an oiled slab; the biscuits are placed on top and tossed, using wooden bats, until the sugar grains and forms a white coating on the biscuit surface. The biscuits are separated, cooled and dried.

REGION OF PRODUCTION:
EAST SCOTLAND, FIFE.

Raggy Biscuit

DESCRIPTION:
A CIRCULAR BISCUIT WITH AN IRREGULAR EDGE, 70MM DIAMETER, 5MM DEEP. COLOUR: CREAM TO LIGHT GOLD SURFACE, DARKER EDGES; IRREGULAR DOCKING IN A BAND ACROSS THE CENTRE OF THE BISCUIT. FLAVOUR AND TEXTURE: CRUNCHY, LIGHTLY SWEETENED.

These are a type of plain biscuit, slightly shortened and sweetened, formerly popular in Scotland and related to numerous others once made in the British Isles. Eric Milne of Cupar (Fife), the only baker traced who now makes them, comments that at least one other town in the area, Brechin, made a similar product, known as heckle biscuits, which were plainer. Heckle is a local dialect word meaning to dock or to puncture the surface of the uncooked biscuit with a pattern of small holes to prevent blistering during cooking. He also remarks that they show similarities to Abernethy biscuits, another Scottish speciality with a history stretching back 200 years.

It seems possible that raggies represent the plain, hand-made biscuits from which the modern Abernethy developed: Kirkland (1931) commented on the popularity of hand-made Abernethies in Scotland and said that (although the recipe is different) they 'have the quality of eating very short – in fact, not unlike ordinary shortbread'. He also notes the dough had to stand for a long time before it was moulded into biscuits, otherwise they cracked all round the edges – an effect which is encouraged in raggy biscuits and has given them their name. Raggies are nowadays eaten with cheese.

TECHNIQUE:

The exact recipe and method are trade secrets. Ingredients are flour, a relatively low proportion of fat (lard is used for many plain biscuits in Scottish baking) and sugar. Recipes for old-fashioned biscuits of this type also call for water to mix, and some involve raising agents. After mixing, the dough is scaled off and pinned out by hand to give the characteristic rough, 'raggy' appearance, docked several times in the centre, and baked in a hot oven until golden and crisp.

REGION OF PRODUCTION:

EAST CENTRAL SCOTLAND.

Edinburgh Rock

DESCRIPTION:

STICKS 10–15MM DIAMETER, 120–140MM LONG. COLOURS AND FLAVOURS: THERE ARE 7 CUSTOMARY TYPES, WHITE (VANILLA), PINK (RASPBERRY, STRAWBERRY), GREEN (LIME), FAWN (GINGER), LEMON (YELLOW) AND ORANGE. COMPOSITION: SUGAR, WATER, COLOUR AND FLAVOURINGS. IT HAS A POWDERY, CRYSTALLIZED TEXTURE.

HISTORY:

Edinburgh rock is said to have been discovered accidentally by a nineteenth-century Edinburgh confectioner, Alexander Ferguson, popularly known as 'Sweetie Sandy'. He found some rock which had been left uncovered in the warm atmosphere of the sweet factory for several months. The rock had crystallized to a brittle texture and its pleasant crunch and delicate flavour became so popular that it was the foundation of Ferguson's business. He became one of Edinburgh's most successful confectioners.

However, the technique of pulling sugar and then allowing it to grain has been known for many centuries, and a mid-fifteenth-century sugar-boiling text of northern provenance, in archives held in the City of York, gives instructions for making 'penides', or sugar sticks. At the end of the recipe, the confectioner is told to leave them in a warm place to take the toughness off them (i.e. to allow them to soften by graining). Whether Ferguson rediscovered this or built on an older tradition is not clear. This rock is now made by many confectioners and is sold throughout the country.

TECHNIQUE:

In many sweets, the confectioner makes strenuous efforts to avoid 'graining' (recrystallization of the sugar once manufacture is complete). In Edinburgh rock, the reverse is true and graining is positively encouraged by omitting ingredients such as acids and adding seed crystals in the form of powdered sugar to the boiled mixture. A batch commences by mixing sugar and water, and boiling it to 130°C (hard ball); it is then poured on to a slab. The flavourings are added and the sugar is dusted with icing sugar and 'pulled' until it hardens, when it is set in the rock shape. The pieces of rock are coated in icing sugar and left in a warm atmosphere until the rock becomes powdery. This takes 1–7 days. Rock with added glucose is made by some but is not regarded as authentic as it produces a 'claggie' (sticky) texture.

REGION OF PRODUCTION:
SOUTH SCOTLAND.

Hawick Balls

DESCRIPTION:
ROUND BALLS, 20MM ACROSS. COLOUR: DARK BROWN. FLAVOUR: PEPPERMINT. COMPOSITION: SUGAR, GLUCOSE, BUTTER, MINT ESSENCE, BURNT (CARAMELIZED) SUGAR.

HISTORY:

The remnants of a strong tradition of sugar-boiling by home confectioners, street hawkers and grocers in small towns in Lowland Scotland survive in a number of distinctive local and national sweets. Hawick balls, locally known as Taffy [toffy] Rock Bools [balls], are one of these. The area in which they are made, the Scottish Borders, has a particularly rich selection of local sweet specialities, many of which are flavoured with mint.

Notable sweetie-makers Jessie McVitie and Aggie Lamb made them in their shop in Drumlanrig Square in Hawick around the 1850s. Another local maker was grocer John Hill, who put out a sign in the early 1900s advertising his 'Home Made Hawick Balls'. John Hill's son, David, carried on making them in the back shop until he died in 1978. The business was bought by a firm of local bakers who continued the name of the firm and its tradition, until they passed it on to a larger sweet manufacturer. Hawick balls are not toffee as it is now generally understood: a mixture of sugar cooked with dairy produce. Earlier use of the word taffy suggests they may once have been pulled sweets; or it may simply be applied to denote a high-boiled mixture of sugar, the sense of the word as used by modern confectioners.

TECHNIQUE:

A mixture of sugar, water, butter and glucose is boiled to 160°C (hard crack), then poured on an oiled slab. Peppermint flavouring is folded into the hot sugar, then a moulding machine shapes the round balls. They are packed in air-tight containers as soon as they have cooled.

REGION OF PRODUCTION:
SOUTH SCOTLAND, HAWICK (BORDERS).

Jeddart Snails

DESCRIPTION:

BOILED SWEETS, 20MM ACROSS, TWISTED ON CUTTING TO MAKE AN UNEVEN SNAIL-LIKE SHAPE. COLOUR: DARK BROWN. FLAVOUR: BUTTERY, MILDLY PEPPER-MINT. COMPOSITION: SUGAR, BUTTER, CREAM OF TARTAR, OIL OF PEPPERMINT.

HISTORY:

Sweet confectionery in Scotland dates back to the first shiploads of sugar from the West Indies which came up the Clyde in the late 1600s, giving rise to an important refining and sweet-boiling industry. While at one time a large range of sweeties was made by small confectioners and itinerant sugar-boilers, only a few have survived. The Borders region is particularly rich in local specialities.

'Jeddart' is the colloquial name for the town of Jedburgh, where the Snails are made. The recipe is said to have been brought to the Borders by a prisoner of war during the Napoleonic wars. Released to work for local people, he is reputed to have made the sweets for a family named Curl. The original recipe has been handed down from one generation to the next to the present owner, Bill Millar, who runs a greengrocer's in Jedburgh. Demand currently outstrips supply but the family is reluctant to expand, feeling that a larger factory-type operation would destroy the character of the sweetie.

TECHNIQUE:

These sweets are hand-made in back-of-shop, sweetie-boiling fashion; the family boils up 6–15lb (6kg) batches of sugar on 3 afternoons a week. The ingredients are boiled to hard crack (154°C), poured on to the table and worked by hand, that is, pulled into long sticks which are twisted and cut into the snail shape.

REGION OF PRODUCTION:

SOUTH SCOTLAND, JEDBURGH (BORDERS).

Moffat Toffee

DESCRIPTION:

A DARK BROWN SWEET WITH AN ASTRINGENT, SHERBET-LIKE CENTRE, MEASURING 125MM ACROSS.

HISTORY:

The enthusiasm for sugar confectionery in Scotland developed to a peak in the Victorian period as ships loaded with sugar from the West Indies sailed up the Clyde to be refined in Greenock, popularly known as 'Sugaropolis'.

Making a living from sweetie-boiling became a common occupation for many small traders. They would boil up a few pans of sugar in the back shop. Janet Keiller – of marmalade fame – is reputed to have used her sweetie-boiling pans to make her first marmalade. Though many of the colourful and unusual sweets hawked round the streets and markets have not survived the passing of their original makers, remnants of this tradition exist in a number of distinctive local confections.

The recipe for Moffat Toffee has been in Blair Blacklock's family for at least 3 generations. Its origins, however, have been lost and no more can be said than that Mr Blacklock remebers his great-grandmother making sweets. The toffee is largely sold in the family sweet shop in the centre of Moffat.

TECHNIQUE:
The sugar is boiled to 148°C (hard crack). Some of the mixture is poured on to a slab and worked or pulled on a pulling machine to aerate it and lighten the colour. It would appear that it is at this point that the 'secret' ingredient is added. This flavoured and lighter mixture is then encased in the original, and pulled into thin sticks which are cut into sweets.

REGION OF PRODUCTION:
SOUTH WEST SCOTLAND, MOFFAT (DUMFRIES AND GALLOWAY).

Starry Rock

DESCRIPTION:
STICKS, 120MM LONG, 70–100MM DIAMETER. WEIGHT: 15G. COLOUR: PALE YELLOW-GOLD. FLAVOUR: SWEET, SLIGHTLY LEMON.

HISTORY:
Starry Rock is an old-fashioned sweet of the same type as barley sugar. Recipes appear in many early manuals and it was probably widespread during the 1800s. In the small Scottish town of Kirriemuir, this sweet has been known as starry rock since 1833, when the shop which still sells it was established. The present owner says the recipe is always sold with the shop. Older people in the town remember with great affection 'Starry Annie', who could be seen making the rock in the front of the shop early last century.

TECHNIQUE:
A mixture of sugar, Golden Syrup, water and a little fat is boiled to a very high temperature; secret flavouring essence is added. The mixture is poured on a marble slab and worked a little, then pulled out by hand to make sticks and cut into appropriate lengths.

REGION OF PRODUCTION:
EASTERN SCOTLAND, KIRRIEMUIR (TAYSIDE).

Ginger Wine

DESCRIPTION:
LIGHT GREEN IN COLOUR, CLEAR TO THE EYE, SWEET AND DISTINCTLY GINGERY IN TASTE.

HISTORY:
In the late nineteenth century, *Law's Grocer's Manual* defined this as 'a British wine or liquor, generally made with water, sugar, lemon rinds, ginger, yeast, raisins, and frequently fortified with added spirit and a little capsicin'. Alcohols based on raisins, sugar and lemons fermented together had been known since the early 1700s. An early recipe for ginger wine appears in Mrs Raffald (1769); it is a sugar syrup flavoured with lemon and ginger, in which raisins were infused. Mrs Beeton (1861) gave a similar recipe, fortified with brandy after 2 weeks' fermentation. Among manufacturers, Stone's of London was especially famous. At the outset, the wine was made in the Finsbury distillery in North London (established 1740). It was sold by the cask, which shop-keepers bought and sold in parcels to their customers. One, Mr Stone,

'Dost thou think, because thou art virtuous, there shall be no more cakes and ale?'

WILLIAM SHAKESPEARE, *TWELFTH NIGHT*

sold so much his name became identified with the product (Grigson, 1984). Though once there were many brands, only Stone's and Crabbie's now remain. Crabbie's, still working in Edinburgh, make 'green ginger wine'.

TECHNIQUE:

The recipes are trade secrets, but ginger wine is made from dried grapes steeped in water and fermented; powdered root ginger is added; the wine is filtered and matured for at least 9 months in large oak vats.

,REGION OF PRODUCTION:

LOWLAND SCOTLAND, LONDON.

Scottish Cask-Conditioned Beer Or Ale

DESCRIPTION:

SCOTTISH BEER IS GENERALLY REGARDED AS SWEETER THAN ENGLISH. COLOUR VARIES FROM LIGHT GOLDEN TO DARK BROWN. TRAQUAIR BREWERY IS THE ONLY BRITISH BREWERY TO FERMENT ITS TOTAL PRODUCTION IN OAK CASKS.

HISTORY:

The German method of brewing is thought to have been introduced to Scotland during the twelfth or thirteenth centuries. Ale derived from malted barley gradually superseded the original heather ale.

At this time, it was made in the monasteries all over the country until private citizens began to take over the monks' role as brewsters. For example, in 1495 the abbot and monks of Cupar granted the right of brewing to certain tenants. Ale remained the common beverage of Lowland and North-Eastern Scotland, including Orkney and Shetland, where (known as home-brew) it was brewed in every village tavern, as well as in the farmhouses, usually by the wives of publicans and farmers. The subject of Burns' poem, 'Scotch Drink', is not whisky but ale. These aproned brewers apparently thrived on their occupation, for the term brewster-wife was commonly used to describe any extremely stout woman. There is a story that, in 1661, 'twelve brewster-wives, all of portly condition, ran a race to the top of Arthur's Seat for the prize of a cheese weighing one hundred pounds'.

A well which the monks of Holyrood in Edinburgh had sunk in the twelfth century was the source of water to brew their ale. It initiated what was destined to become one of the city's major industries. In 1600, the abbey had been abandoned and Holyrood was a royal residence. John Blair, an enterprising Edinburgh brewer, took over the monks' maltings at the foot of the Royal Mile, and started selling his beer to the palace.

As brewing was increasingly commercialized so the businesses and companies with which we are familiar today were established, centred on Edinburgh, Alloa and Glasgow. Some had won such a high reputation that exiled French royalists who took refuge in Edinburgh in 1831 called their liquor 'Scottish Burgundy'.

Edinburgh brewing owes much to a freak of nature in the form of a structural trough – a sort of underground lake – which runs beneath and beyond the Royal Mile from Fountainbridge to Arthur's Seat. It is this water that feeds the breweries along the line of the trough. It contains a high percentage of gypsum which is thought to constitute the flavour which has given Edinburgh ales their distinctive quality.

Brewing in Scotland has changed greatly since the Campaign for Real Ale (CAMRA) drew attention to the quality of those smaller breweries producing cask-conditioned ales and stouts. This includes a new version of the ancient Heather Ale, made using fresh shoots of wild heather and sold as 'Fraoch' (pronounced fruich, p. 354), as well as the oldest ale made at Traquair House at Innerleithen in the Borders, where ale was being brewed when Bonnie Prince Charlie sheltered during his stay in 1745. The twentieth-century laird, the late Peter Maxwell Stuart, set about renovating the brewery and revived the brewhouse using the original vessels. His heir, Catherine Maxwell Stuart, continues the tradition. Brewing now takes place twice a week to make the Traquair Ale. There is also a weaker brew known as Bear Ale. This was named after the famous Bear Gates at the entrance to the house. They were closed in 1745 after the Prince's visit. The family vowed never to re-open them until a Stuart king returned to the throne.

TECHNIQUE:

Hot water plus crushed malt is mixed in a mash tun, left for an hour, then drained through a sieve. It is transferred to a copper (hot-liquor tank), and brought to the boil. Some hops are added and the mixture boiled for 2 hours to reduce the gravity strength. The final hops are now added and the mixture boiled for 10–15 minutes. This is left to settle for 30 minutes, then transferred from the copper to a filter through a cooling system into the fermenting vessel. Yeast is added and left to ferment 2–4 days. The beer is cooled to 16°C, transferred to storage tanks and matures for 4–8 weeks after which it is bottled.

REGION OF PRODUCTION:
SOUTH SCOTLAND.

Irn-Bru

DESCRIPTION:
IRN-BRU IS ORANGE-GOLDEN IN COLOUR, ITS FLAVOUR SWEET-SPICY WITH A CITRUS TANG, RATHER LIKE BOILED SWEETS. IT CONTAINS AMMONIUM FERRIC CITRATE (0.002 PER CENT). THIS FORTIFICATION WITH IRON DISTINGUISHES IT FROM OTHER SOFT DRINKS.

HISTORY:
Prior to the development of twentieth-century medicines, herbalists made cordials and tonics, giving rise to a number of 'health' drinks. This tradition, combined with a strong temperance movement in the early decades of the twentieth century was a source of many patent bottled drinks made under brand names by various companies. 'Iron-Brew' was a common mixed-flavour drink developed in Scotland during the early 1900s and was made by several manufacturers, each with a different recipe. Few actually contained iron.

All these drinks were affected by changes brought about by World War II. Iron brews disappeared as the industry was rationalized and companies became numbered production units. After the war, legislation was passed which made it compulsory to add 0.125g of iron per fluid ounce (30ml) to any beverage named iron-brew. There was also a rumour that the Government was planning to ban the misuse of terms like brew which did not actually apply to a brewing process. Because of this, and the fact that Barr's recipe did not contain the necessary amount of iron, in 1946 the then Chairman of A.G. Barr decided to overcome the problem by registering the phonetic 'Irn-Bru' as a trade name. At the same time, a major advertising campaign with a cartoon strip depicting the adventures of 'Ba-Bru and Sandy' was inserted in one of Glasgow's main newspapers, the *Bulletin*, and ran until the 1970s. Other companies producing iron brews did not survive but Barr's Irn-Bru became so successful that it has now taken the title 'Scotland's other drink'. It is carried around the world by nostalgic Scots – particularly to football matches where Scotland's other drink is not allowed.

TECHNIQUE:

The flavourings that give these drinks their distinctive character are closely-guarded trade secrets. The ingredients for Irn-Bru are water, sugar, carbon dioxide, citric acid, flavourings, preservative (E211), caffeine, colours (E110, E124), ammonium ferric citrate (0.002 per cent). Manufacture follows the standard method for all carbonated drinks: the flavouring and colouring ingredients are mixed to make a syrup which is combined with water and sugar, carbonated and bottled.

REGION OF PRODUCTION:
CENTRAL SCOTLAND, GLASGOW.

Dundee Marmalade

DESCRIPTION:
COLOUR: BRIGHT ORANGE THROUGH TO DARK BROWN. COMPOSITION: SEVILLE ORANGES AND SUGAR, SOMETIMES BLACK TREACLE OR BROWN SUGAR. DUNDEE MARMALADE HAS SHREDDED PEEL (SEE ALSO OXFORD (THICK CUT) MARMALADE, P. 75). WHILE ONCE PRESUMED TO BE MADE WITH ORANGES, MARMALADE IS NOW APPLIED TO ANY CITRUS PRESERVE SUCH AS LIME, GRAPEFRUIT, SWEET ORANGE OR TANGERINE. IT MAY BE FLAVOURED WITH BRANDY, WHISKY, GINGER OR BLACK TREACLE.

HISTORY:

Today, nearly all bitter Seville oranges grown in southern Spain are destined for marmalade for the British market. Pots of marmalade have followed the British around the world for more than a century. In the early 1900s, the Empress of Russia and the Queen of Greece, granddaughters of Queen Victoria, had supplies sent regularly from Wilkins of Tiptree. The firm of Frank Cooper of Oxford still has a tin which was taken on Scott's expedition to the South Pole in 1911, discovered in perfect condition in 1980. Marmalade has also been taken by the British up Mount Everest.

In the course of its history, marmalade has generated at least a couple of myths for which the Scots must accept some responsibility. One involves the belief that it gets its name from Mary, Queen of Scots. Another is that it was an invention of Janet Keiller, whose Dundee family built the first marmalade factory in 1797. Marmalade made its first appearance in both Scotland and England in wooden boxes: a solid, sugary mass of *marmelos* (quinces), exported from Portugal, and first mentioned as 'marmelada' in port records at the end of the fifteenth century. This is what travelled with Mary Queen of Scots when she became seasick on the crossing from Calais to Scotland in 1561 and which may – or may not – have helped restore her equilibrium. Quinces were regarded at the time as healing fruits. Her request, 'Marmelade pour Marie malade,' was no more than a medicinal pun.

The medicinal properties of oranges were also highly regarded. Candied orange peel was eaten during a fast, so it was a natural thing to pulp and sweeten oranges into a 'marmelade'. It first appears in seventeenth-century English cookery books when it was eaten as a sweetmeat to aid digestion. Now enter the Scots. Until about 1700, a bowl of ale with some toast floating in it had been regarded as the most warming way to start the day. Then came the tea revolution and thereafter tea and crisp toast was the meal *de rigueur*. If it was not to be floated or dunked, this toast required an accompaniment. A solution came in a bargain-load of bitter oranges from Spain, bought by Janet Keiller's husband from a boat in Dundee harbour. This she made into a preserve. According to her English recipe, you pounded and pulped, with much patience, with a pestle and mortar. Instead, she decided to use a French way which was quicker and which chopped the peel into shreds. With a shrewd eye to economy, she decided not to reduce this 'marmelade' to a concentrated paste but to make it less solid, which produced many more pots per pound. It was cooked for a shorter time, improving the flavour and making it easier to spread on toast.

The epicurean traveller, Bishop Richard Pococke (1704–65), indicates the use of what appears to have been marmalade for spreading on toast at breakfast: 'They always bring toasted bread, and besides, butter, honey and jelly of currants and preserved orange peel.'

TECHNIQUE:

In Mrs E. Cleland (1755) a recipe appears for shredded orange marmalade: 'To make a Marmalade of Oranges – Take your Oranges, grate them, cut them in quarters, take the skins off them, and take the pulp from the strings and seeds; put the skins in a pan of spring-water, boil them till they are very tender, then take them out of the water, and cut them and leave the thin slices to boil by themselves. To every pound of oranges put a pound of fine sugar, first wet the sugar in water, boil it a good while then put in half of the pulp, keep the other half for the sliced orange; to every mutchkin of the pulp you must put in a pound of sugar likeways, then put in the grated rind, boil till it is very clear, then put in Gallypots; when cold paper them.'

The fruit is softened by boiling on its own. It may be left whole or chopped before boiling. The pulp and water is measured and for every 500ml of pulp, 500g sugar is added. The pips are usually kept separate, but included in the boiling to aid setting, before the fruit is finely chopped. The marmalade is boiled until it sets. Seville oranges are harvested in January, and much marmalade is made at this time.

REGION OF PRODUCTION:
EASTERN SCOTLAND.

***

Also produced in South Scotland	MUSSEL (P. 334)
BERWICK COCKLES (P. 285)	OATCAKE (P. 353)
TAYBERRY, TUMMELBERRY (P. 362)	OYSTER (P. 335)
BERWICK COCKLES (P. 285)	SCALLOP (P. 336)
HEATHER ALE (P. 354)	SPOOT (P. 340)
MEALIE PUDDING (P. 344)	TAYBERRY, TUMMELBERRY (P. 362)

North Scotland:
North, West, & Highlands
& Islands

Dulse

DESCRIPTION:

A BROAD-LEAVED SEAWEED WHICH GROWS TO ABOUT 30CM. THE YOUNG FRONDS ARE THIN AND PAPERY.; WEIGHT: SOLD IN 50G PACKS. COLOUR: A DEEP REDDISH PURPLE. FLAVOUR: STRONG, SALTY, IODINE AROMA AND FLAVOUR.

HISTORY:

In the Scottish Highlands and Islands, sea vegetables were originally a regular part of the diet; there are 22 Gaelic names for varieties of seaweed: that for dulse is *duileasg*. Gathered from the foreshore, dulse (*Rhodymenia palmata*) was used in broths, deepening the flavour with the seaweed's high content of strongly flavoured amino acids. Dulse was fed raw to children as an impor-tant source of vitamins in a harsh climate with limited resources. It was also sold in the nineteenth century along with tangle (*Laminaria digitata* or *saccherina*), in city markets by itinerant street-sellers to the cry of 'Dulse and Tangel'. Oral tradition states that seaweeds of various types were dried to preserve them. In recent years, there has been a revival of sea veg-etables for their nutritional qualities and the unpolluted shores around the north of Scotland have begun to be exploited for their abundant seaweeds.

There are 2 variations on dulse: Autumn Dulse is harvested at that season, when the plant is more vibrant, the colour is deeper and the flavour more astringent; there is also Pepper Dulse (*Laurencia pinnatifida*) which is a variety of colours from red-brown to yellow-green and whose fronds measure up to 18cm. Long stems are chewed for their pungent flavour. Other harvested Scottish sea vegetables include dabberlocks, grockle, sugar ware, finger ware, and *sloke* (wild nori), which is laver in Wales.

TECHNIQUE:

Picking is direct from the sea bed by divers, who take particular care not to damage new growth. It is harvested just before it becomes fertile and builds up the bitter content which gives an unpleasant taste. It is air-dried in a recirculating drying oven at a low heat to preserve the flavour.

REGION OF PRODUCTION:

NORTH SCOTLAND.

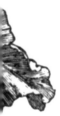

Caboc Cheese

DESCRIPTION:
SOFT, DOUBLE-CREAM CHEESE ROLLED IN TOASTED PINHEAD OATMEAL TO MAKE LOGS ABOUT 10CM LONG, 4CM DIAMETER. WEIGHT: 125G. COLOUR: CREAM INSIDE, GREY OATMEAL OUTSIDE. FLAVOUR: RICH CREAM, BUTTERY WITH A MILD TANG.

HISTORY:
In the period prior to the Highland Clearances the native soft cheese of Viking and Pictish ancestry was made by every crofter with surplus milk. Its demise came with the increase in sheep farming and shooting estates, putting an end to the crofter's system of taking his cattle, sheep and goats to the mountain grazings in summer where the women and children made the peasant cheese known as crowdie (see p. 362-3).

A recipe for a richer cheese, made for the clan chiefs, is reputed to be the oldest historical record of a traditional Scottish cheese and was passed down through the female line of the descendants of Mariota de Ile, a daughter of a fifteenth-century Macdonald of the Isles. The present descendant, and owner of the recipe, Susanna Stone, has revived the cheese, making it in her creamery in Tain where she began by making the crofters' cheese, crowdie, in the early 1960s (see below, p. 362).

A pioneer of the post-war farmhouse cheese-making revival, she called the oatmeal-coated chieftain's cheese Caboc, a derivation from the Scots word for any round cheese 'kebbuck'. Others cheese-makers have copied the recipe with varying degrees of success and the cheese is now established in the Scottish speciality cheese market.

TECHNIQUE:
The recipe uses pasteurized milk from cattle on 3 designated farms. This soft, double-cream cheese is made with lactic acid but no rennet and the logs are finished by rolling in toasted pinhead oatmeal before packing. The exact method is a trade secret.

REGION OF PRODUCTION:
SCOTLAND, HIGHLANDS.

Orkney Farmhouse Cheese

DESCRIPTION:
A YOUNG, LIGHTLY PRESSED, UNPASTEURIZED COW'S MILK CHEESE. WEIGHT: 1–2KG. COLOUR: CREAM OR WHITE, YELLOWER WITH SUMMER MILK. FLAVOUR: BUTTERY, MELLOW. TEXTURE: CRUMBLING, SOMETIMES LIKENED TO SCRAMBLED EGGS.

HISTORY:
Because of their remoteness, farms on the islands of Orkney have continued the tradition of artisan cheese-making without interruption. Made on a very small scale, often with milk from only one cow, it continues for both family use and for selling locally. Only a small amount is exported to the mainland.

TECHNIQUE:
The milk is heated with rennet for about 15 minutes until it separates. The curdled milk is hung in a muslin bag to drip for a day. It is mixed with salt and packed into muslin-lined moulds and pressed for 2–3 days, then unmoulded and matured in a cool draught for a few

weeks, though it may be kept longer. The best cheese is made from May to October.

REGION OF PRODUCTION:
SCOTLAND, ORKNEY.

Air-Dried Salted Fish

DESCRIPTION:
HARD, DRY FISH, WHOLE OR SPLIT, WITH CREAM OR WHITE FLESH. FLAVOUR: SALTY, MATURE.

HISTORY:
Drying and salting the abundant fish from the seas off the North of Scotland was an important preservation process before refrigeration and rail transport. Various methods of curing white fish, for instance sillocks, cuiths, ling, cod and saith, gave distinctive flavours and 'our fisher-folk rely mainly upon the use of the elements to give them *goût*, such as sun drying, wind drying, exposure on the rocks within reach of sea-spray, and brief storage under turf' (McNeill, 1929). For long storage, excess landings were salted and dried on flat pebbles on beaches and hung up and air-dried on rows of hooks outside the houses until quite hard. This was especially true in the Shetlands where it was a staple of the winter and spring diet and where dried ling was a major export to Germany and Spain in the late 1700s (Hope, 1987). The export has continued and, in the 1950s, it was still being sent to the West Indies and Africa.

The habit of drying fish persists on both a domestic and commercial scale in some of the remoter parts of the mainland and on the Islands. Air-dried fish is also produced on the Orkney Islands and sometimes can be observed hanging outside on dry and breezy summer days. Air-drying is practised on a larger scale in Aberdeen, and some fishmongers in urban areas of central Scotland produce small quantities of the cure.

In Scotland, cooking preserved fish normally meant boiling with potatoes, using the highly flavoured fish as a seasoning. Or the flaked fish was mixed with mashed potatoes to make a dish called hairy tatties, which was also formed into fish cakes and fried.

TECHNIQUE:
The fish are gutted and beheaded, then split if large, left whole if small. If large, the top part of the backbone is removed, then they are layered in coarse salt and completely covered. They may be left for a few days, or up to a fortnight, when they are removed from the salt. They may be washed and pressed (in some cases, between stones) to remove as much moisture as possible or simply hung up by the tails to dry, usually in pairs if they are small, in a cold place with a good draught until very hard.

REGION OF PRODUCTION:
NORTH SCOTLAND.

Kipper (Scottish Cure)

DESCRIPTION:
WEIGHT: UP TO 250G. COLOUR: PALE GOLDEN SKIN, LIGHT TO DARK BROWN FLESH. FLAVOUR: MILD SMOKE AND SALT.

Though kippering herring was first developed in Northumberland in the 1840s, the Scots have a history of kippering salmon (see smoked salmon, p. 369). The kippered herring's greatest misfortune was during the First World War, when food was in short supply. Some enterprising fish-smokers had the idea of feigning the kippering process. Reducing the smoking times and, therefore, reducing the amount of moisture lost, they dyed the fish a smoky colour, inventing the commercial coal tar dye Brown FK (for kippers).

Though generally regarded at the time as a good war effort, the habit persisted and it is only a small (but now growing) band of dedicated independent smokers who have kept true to the original concept of an undyed kipper. And now the large curers, who always resisted the move back to undyed fish, have taken to producing the original pale kipper as public concern about unnecessary additives and colourings in food has gathered momentum.

In Scotland independent smokers are concentrated around the West-coast grounds where plump herring, particularly from the Minch and Loch Fyne, have a history of quality. Undyed kippers were smoked in large sheds on the pier at Mallaig and the Mallaig kipper is classed, along with the Loch Fyne, as one of the best cures. The undyed Loch Fyne kipper is described by McNeill (1929): 'Some years ago, when staying at a fishing port on Lochfyneside, I used to watch the herring-boats sail in at dawn and unload their cargo, which was run straight up to the kippering sheds. Here the fish were plunged into a brine bath and thereafter hung up to smoke over smouldering oak chips, while their colour changed slowly from silver to burnished copper.'

TECHNIQUE:

Usually brined in salt for about 30 minutes to provide a shine rather than to impart a strong salt taste, they are then cold-smoked for 18–24 hours over oak chips (sometimes from whisky barrels). Individual curers have their own brining recipes with 'secret' flavourings.

REGION OF PRODUCTION:

WEST SCOTLAND.

COMPARE WITH:

Kipper (Craster) and Kipper (Whitby), North East England (pp. 277–9) and Kipper (Manx), Isle of Man (p. 203).

Mussel (Scotland)

DESCRIPTION:

COMMON MUSSEL: 50–80MM LONG; HORSE MUSSEL: 150–200MM LONG. COLOUR: BLUE-BLACK SHELLS, BRIGHT ORANGE FLESH.

HISTORY:

As part of the general foraging for seafood, both common mussels, *Mytilus edulis*, and the large horse mussel, *Modiolus modiolus*, were eaten by Scottish peasants living in coastal areas. Mussel brose was a common dish, mentioned in a poem by Robert Fergusson (1750–74), and according to a traditional recipe (McNeill, 1929), it was made with cooked mussels and their liquor, fish stock and milk. These were poured on top of a handful of oatmeal in a bowl, as you do for a brose, and returned to the pan for a few minutes to cook through.

Mussels were also a common street food; fishwives are recorded setting up market stalls selling mussels in saucers, plus condiments. The tradition survives in The Barras street-market in Glasgow (the name deriving from a common stall, originally a simple barrow) where several shops sell plates of freshly cooked shellfish, mostly mussels, horse mussels and whelks. They may be sold either on the premises at a simple bench and table, when they are served with a cup of the bre (cooking liquor), or they may be sold as a takeaway in a paper bag.

TECHNIQUE:

While some mussels are collected wild, cultivation has been practised throughout Europe. First recorded in Scotland in the 1890s, several experiments took place on the east coast growing mussels on ropes but the idea was abandoned following a series of disasters. In 1966, however, experiments were resumed cultivating again on ropes and commercial ventures started in the early 1970s using ropes attached to both longlines and rafts. Both methods continue, with each farmer developing a system which suits his particular site. Once harvested they are washed and graded. Horse mussels are harvested from natural beds lying at extreme low water mark.

REGION OF PRODUCTION:

NORTH SCOTLAND AND GENERAL SCOTLAND.

COMPARE WITH:

Mussel (England), East Anglia (p. 121); Mussel (Wales), North Wales (p. 189)

Oyster (Scotland)

DESCRIPTION:

NATIVE OYSTERS ARE FAN-SHAPED, ALMOST CIRCULAR, ONE HALF OF THE SHELL IS FLAT, THE OTHER CUPPED. THE SHELL OF THE PACIFIC OYSTER IS MORE DEEPLY CUPPED, ROUGHER AND MORE ELONGATED. MOST WEST-COAST OYSTERS ARE PACIFIC. DIMENSIONS: GRADED BY SIZE 70–80G; 80–95G; 95G AND UPWARDS. COLOUR: A WIDE VARIETY OF COLOUR AND TEXTURE ACCORDING TO THEIR ORIGIN. FLAVOUR: SEA-TASTING, DETERMINED BY THE FEEDING AND VARIES FROM LOCH TO LOCH. IN TERMS OF THE QUALITY OF THE FLAVOUR, ALL SCOTTISH OYSTERS ARE GRADE A, THAT IS, THEY HAVE NOT BEEN PURIFIED BY PASSING THROUGH PURIFICATION TANKS OR HELD IN AERATED HOLDING TANKS BEFORE SALE.

HISTORY:

Eaten with great relish, oysters were celebrated during the heyday of the oyster cellars of Georgian and Victorian Edinburgh. They were consumed, nightly, by the thousand. The poet James Hogg (1770–1835), an enthusiast, complained that 'a month without an R has nae right being in the year'. So cheap and plentiful was the supply, that recipes for soups and stews often demanded 60 oysters. These were the large European native oysters which are mentioned by Martin Martin in his *Description of the Western Islands of Scotland* (1709) as growing on rocks and 'so big that they are cut in four pieces before they are ate'.

The beds of native oysters fell victim to pollution and over-fishing and by around 1950 were almost totally wiped out. Revival, which has occurred over the last 30 years, has depended entirely on farming gigas (*Crassostrea gigas*) – though some farms are experimenting with natives – in sheltered sea-lochs on the West coast, the Islands and in Orkney. The gigas has

been used since cold water inhibits breeding. This means they do not retain their eggs and can therefore be sold all year without tasting unpleasant.

TECHNIQUE:

Lochs chosen for oyster farming must have shelter, total lack of pollution and a rich supply of nutrients. The most common methods are to put the young seed (brought from hatcheries at about 12–15mm) into mesh bags on metal or wooden trestles at low-water mark, or into plastic trays which are stacked on the sea bed or suspended from a headline. The first gives access to sort and grade during the spring tides and the second, weather permitting, allows work at any time. Allowing the oysters to be uncovered is considered important since it allows them to close tightly and survive in air, essential when they are eventually transported for sale. They are usually harvested after 2 summers' feeding.

REGION OF PRODUCTION:

WEST SCOTLAND AND GENERAL SCOTLAND.

COMPARE WITH:

Oyster, South-East England (p. 88)

Scallop (Scotland)

DESCRIPTION:

GREAT OR KING SCALLOP (*PECTEN MAXIMUS*): FLAT BOTTOM SHELL AND A CONCAVE UPPER SHELL; MUSCLE DIAMETER APPROXIMATELY 50MM; MINIMUM LEGAL CARAPACE SIZE 100MM. QUEEN SCALLOP (*CHLAMYS OPERCULARIA*): TOP AND BOTTOM SHELLS BOTH CONCAVE; MUSCLE DIAMETER APPROXIMATELY 30MM. PRINCESS SCALLOP (AN IMMATURE QUEEN): MUSCLE DIAMETER APPROXIMATELY 10MM. THE GREAT SCALLOP AND THE QUEEN HAVE BEIGE SHELLS, AND A CREAM OR WHITE MUSCLE SURROUNDED BY AN ORANGE ROE. THE PRINCESS SCALLOP HAS A REDDISH-PINK SHELL AND A CREAM OR WHITE MUSCLE BUT THE ROE, BECAUSE OF ITS AGE, HAS NOT DEVELOPED. THEY HAVE A DISTINCTIVE AND SUBTLE SEA-FLAVOUR FROM RICH FEEDING IN UNPOLLUTED NORTHERN WATERS.

HISTORY:

The food culture of the Western Highlands and Islands of Scotland was, among the impoverished peasantry, one of subsistence. It was not until the nineteenth century that commercial fisheries began to develop on this coast, under the influence of the British Fisheries Society who established ports for processing and collection. The expansion of the railway network meant the catch could reach markets hitherto unattainable.

An important dredged and dived scallop industry arose in the 1950s and 1960s, harvesting from natural West-coast beds. Research into scallop farming began on the Isle of Man in the early 1970s and, although no farming takes place in that location, the methods developed have been successfully applied off the West coast of Scotland. The development of the farmed scallop began here in the 1974 and its popularity has grown, partly due to its guarantee of quality. The age of the farmed scallop is controlled to around 5 years, yielding tender muscle and regular size, encouraging wider use of farmed scallops in the catering industry.

TECHNIQUE:

Scallop farming produces a more uniform supply than wild scallops. The young spat are put into collectors where they attach themselves to the sides of the nets. As their shells begin to grow they fall off the nets and are gathered and put into free-floating 'lantern' nets suspended in the sea water where they feed and grow (queen scallops for 18 months to 2 years; king scallops for 4–5 years). Princess scallops are harvested when they are about 12 months old. Aquaculture is still a developing industry and methods are constantly undergoing change. Ranching, or bottom culture, is seen by some farmers as the way forward. This has always been a risky business because it was not possible to protect stocks from dredgers or divers. Recently, however, the first Several Fishery Order has been recommended to be granted to stocks of farmed scallops giving them legal protection.

REGION OF PRODUCTION:
WEST SCOTLAND AND GENERAL SCOTLAND.

COMPARE WITH:
Scallop, Isle of Man (p. 203).

'He was a very valiant man who first ventured on eating of oysters.'

THOMAS FULLER, *THE HISTORY OF THE WORTHIES OF ENGLAND*

Scotland suffers poor press when it comes to its eating habits, which is a real pity when you consider what incredible produce it has. I have always looked upon Scotland as a very rich larder of ingredients, from the most amazing beef and venison, to salmon, scallops and lobster. This was one of my signature dishes at Royal Hospital Road. Our customers protested every time we changed the menu so we've been offering it off-and-on for years. We insist on using diver-caught scallops (mostly from Western Scotland) at the restaurants – the dredged alternatives often end up terribly muddy or damaged and are simply not an option. For this dish, we generally use large king scallops, which we dust with a little bit of curry powder to enhance their natural sweetness.

Gordon Ramsay

Chef, restauranteur, broadcaster and author

Pan-roasted Scallops with Cauliflower Purée

Serves 4

12 LARGE SCALLOPS
1 TSP MILD CURRY POWDER
SEA SALT AND FRESHLY GROUND BLACK PEPPER
1 TBSP OLIVE OIL
A HANDFUL OF SALAD LEAVES (SUCH AS FRISÉE AND LAMBS LETTUCE), TO GARNISH

Vinaigrette:
1 TBSP SHERRY VINEGAR
3 TBSP OLIVE OIL
SEA SALT AND FRESHLY GROUND BLACK PEPPER

Cauliflower purée:
$^1/_2$ HEAD OF CAULIFLOWER (ABOUT 350G), TRIMMED AND CUT INTO FLORÊTS
30G BUTTER
1-2 TBSP MILK
100ML SINGLE CREAM
SEA SALT AND FRESHLY GROUND BLACK PEPPEr

Shell, trim and clean the scallops, then pat dry with kitchen paper and chill them until ready to cook. Combine the curry powder with a teaspoon of salt and a grating of pepper and set aside. Mix together the ingredients for the vinaigrette and season to taste.

Trim the cauliflower and cut into florêts. Melt the butter in a saucepan and add the cauliflower. Sauté for about three-four minutes, add the milk and cream and partially cover the pan with a lid. Cook for another three-four minutes over gentle heat until the florêts are soft. Season well to taste. While still hot, tip the cauliflower and cream into a food processor and blend for a few minutes until really smooth, scraping the sides of the processor a few times.

Lightly sprinkle the curry powder mixture on both sides of the scallops. Heat a little oil in a large non-stick frying pan. Cook for just a minute on each side and turn them in the order they were put in. They should be nicely brown on both sides and feel springy when pressed. Remove from the pan and leave to rest for a minute. Slice each in half horizontally and lightly season again.

Place the six scallop halves on little spoonfuls of the cauliflower purée around each plate. Garnish with the salad leaves and drizzle with the vinaigrette to serve.

Spoot

DESCRIPTION:

A BIVALVE; THE NARROW SHELL CAN BE UP TO I2CM LONG BUT IS ONLY I.5–2CM WIDE; IT IS STRAIGHT, AND SLIGHTLY GREEN-BROWN IN COLOUR. THE MEAT IS TRANSLUCENT WHITE, COARSELY TEXTURED, WITH AN EXCELLENT SEA FLAVOUR. IF OVERCOOKED, IT BECOMES CHEWY AND INEDIBLE.

HISTORY:

Spoots is the name in Orcadian dialect for *Ensis ensis*, the razor-shell clam. These are not eaten in the British Isles except by the inhabitants of some Scottish islands, who regard them as a delicacy. They form part of an ancient gathering tradition in an area in which food was often in short supply and all available edible items found use sooner or later. The Orkney Islands exhibit the strongest appetite for these fish. It is not clear for how many centuries they have been considered a local delicacy: the name spoots was noted by the beginning of the 1800s (*OED*).

The Moray Firth, a little further south, also yields spoots. Dived and dredged spoots are available October–May; hand-fishing takes place principally in March and September, when the equinox produces low ebb tides.

In the Orkneys, spoots are eaten for any main meal. They are taken plain, straight from the opened shell, or turned briefly in melted butter.

TECHNIQUE:

Spoots are renowned for being difficult to catch. They are found in wet sand, and are only exposed at very low ebb tides. The method for spooting is to walk backwards along the beach, watching for the little spoot (spout) of water ejected by these creatures, which lie concealed just below the surface. If one is located, the spooter inserts a knife into the sand to locate the shell and then twists it round very quickly to bring it to the surface. This requires practice and skill for if the spoots sense danger they burrow quickly downwards beyond reach. On some beaches, it is claimed that they can be brought to the surface by pouring a small quantity of dry salt into the hole on the surface, but mixed reports about the effectiveness of the technique are given by those who have tried. Modern methods in commercial use are diving (which also requires skill, as it too involves problems locating and catching the fish) and suction dredging, which is the easiest but the most capital-intensive method.

If desired, the fish can be left in sea water overnight to cleanse them. As spoots have shells which are permanently open at both ends, the risk of contamination is too great to allow them to be marketed alive like other bivalves; this may account for their localized popularity. Spoots are opened just before eating by placing the shellfish on a hot griddle and removing the meat as soon as the shells open. Or they can be placed in boiling water. The stomach bag can be cut away before consumption.

Although these clams are found on English beaches, they have not been gathered with any great gastronomic enthusiasm. An episode on the beaches of south Devon in 1998 left 200 holiday-makers lacerated on the feet by the (razor) sharp shells (hence the English name) that were unexpectedly exposed on the surface by abnormally low tides. No mention in news reports was made of their palatability, only their capacity to wound.

REGION OF PRODUCTION:

THROUGHOUT GENERAL SCOTLAND, HIGHLANDS AND ORKNEYS.

Aberdeen-Angus Cattle

DESCRIPTION:

AVERAGE CARCASS WEIGHT OF STEER AT 18–19 MONTHS, 275KG. FLESH DEEPLY RED, FAT CREAM-WHITE, MARBLED WITH INTRA-MUSCULAR FAT.

HISTORY:

Though the most widely known Scottish breed, Aberdeen-Angus is also the most recently established. Pioneer breeder Hugh Watson (1780–1865), from Keillor near Dundee, first showed his black, polled cattle in 1820 and by 1829 was sending some of his stock from the Highland Show in Perth to Smithfield. Hitherto, cattle had been exported on the hoof for fattening in East Anglia. Now, the trade to London of prime beef in carcass (sending only the most expensive cuts) developed with the success of Watson's herd. This new method became the norm with the completion of the railway to London in 1850. Watson is regarded as having fixed the type of the new breed and by the time his herd was dispersed, in 1861, it had been highly selected within itself. For the 50 years of its existence, it seems he never bought a bull. He sold stock to William McCombie (1805–1880), of Tillyfour near Aberdeen, who carried on the programme, attaching the same importance to meeting the requirements of the London trade. The breed's main rival was Amos Cruickshank's Scotch Shorthorn, established in the 1830s when he and his brother became tenants of an Aberdeenshire farm. It could be fattened more rapidly, but did not milk so well and was less hardy than the Watson stock. To overcome its problems and to induce more rapid fattening in the Aberdeen-Angus, the characteristics of the breeds were combined. The Aberdeen-Angus cross Shorthorn became the source of most prime beef in Scotland.

The Polled Cattle Herd Book was started in 1862; the Aberdeen-Angus Cattle Society inaugurated in 1879. In 1891, a separate class at the Smithfield Show was provided for the breed and it has never lost its pre-eminence. At the Perth sales in 1963 a single bull made history with a world-record price of 60,000 guineas.

Changes have occurred in the last 30 years. A demand developed in the 1960s for a small, thick bull with a lot of meat. The trend reversed with entry to the EU, since when the preference has been for taller, leaner animals with a minimum of fat. 'But this meat,' said the breed society president, 'does not have the succulence and flavour that the consumer requires. Thus the aim now is to have meat that has a marbling of fat through it, to give a healthy product that is succulent and tasty.' This has stimulated a new departure, as retailers themselves support the identification of beef as Aberdeen-Angus as a guarantee of quality. A Certification Trade Mark has been registered.

TECHNIQUE:

The breed thrives on low-quality pasture and rations such as silage and arable by-products. It converts these more effectively than most others into high-quality, early-maturing beef with marbled fat, making it both economically and environmentally desirable.

REGION OF PRODUCTION:

NORTH-EAST SCOTLAND.

This salt–sugar pickle is the old method for adding character to more mature mutton from native breeds such as the Blackface (Blackie). Reestit Mutton is a variation using native Shetland Sheep which is available from Shetland butchers where the joints are both pickled and then dried. Just as fish smokers in the early nineteenth century modified their smoking cures to produce a more lightly preserved fish, so an early method for mutton is modifed with shorter pickling times.

Catherine Brown

FROM *A YEAR IN A SCOTS KITCHEN*

PICKLE FOR 2–3KG/4LB 8OZ–6LB 12OZ LEG OF MUTTON

2L/3PT 10FLOZ WATER
600G/1LB 5OZ COARSE SEA SALT
250G/9OZ BROWN MUSCOVADO SUGAR
1 SPRIG OF BAY LEAVES
1 SPRIG THYME
5 CRUSHED JUNIPER BERRIES
5 CRUSHED PEPPERCORNS

to pickle:
Put the ingredients into a pan and bring to the boil. Stir to dissolve the salt and sugar and leave to simmer for about ten minutes. Leave to cool.

Put the cold pickle into an earthenware crock or plastic bucket with a lid. Immerse the meat and keep below the surface by laying a heavy plate on top. Cover and keep in a cool place.

Pickle time should be shorter if meat is thin and without bone, longer if it is thick and with bone. For a 3kg/6lb 12oz leg of mutton between twelve and twenty-four hours will produce a well-flavoured result. The longer it is left in the pickle the stronger it becomes.

If kept in a cool dark place, the pickle mixture will keep for several months and can be used again.

to cook the meat:
Rinse under cold water; put into a large pot with three medium onions stuck with three cloves; a sprig of bay leaves; eight peppercorns; three carrots peeled and chopped in two; a small turnip, peeled and chopped roughly in large pieces. Cover with cold water and simmer very gently till the meat is tender. Remove and serve hot with boiled floury potatoes or cold with oatcakes and butter. Use the cooking liquor to make broth. Check first for saltiness and adjust by adding water if necessary. Some of the less choice cuts of meat can be chopped and added to the broth.

Note: This pickle can also be used for pork, duck and chicken.

Mealie Pudding

DESCRIPTION:

A COOKED SUET AND CEREAL SAUSAGE IN SEVERAL SHAPES: A SINGLE LINK SAUSAGE, A SLIC-ING SAUSAGE, A LARGE LINK SAUSAGE CURVED AND THE ENDS JOINED TO MAKE A LOOP, A BALL-LIKE HAGGIS SHAPE. WEIGHT: 125–250G. COLOUR: GREY. FLAVOUR: OATMEAL AND ONION, BUT DEPENDS LARGELY ON THE FLAVOUR OF THE SUET OR FAT.

HISTORY:

In the days before the turnip was used as winter feed for animals, Martinmas (11 November) was the time for killing the animals which could not be kept through the winter. 'Mairt' was an incredibly busy time and several families would join together to do the work. Every scrap of the beast was used – the meat salted and puddings made from the innards. Mealie puddings (black and white) were made when beef cattle were killed. In the original communal system, oatmeal, onions and beef suet were mixed with salt and pepper in a large basin. Then blood was added to some of the mixture to make the 'bleedy' ones (black puddings). The intestines were thoroughly washed, usually in a burn, and then stuffed loosely with the mixture. They were tied up and boiled in a large pot.

The operation has now become almost completely commercial, carried out by either a butcher or meat-processing plant, though there are a few individuals who still make their own at home. They are consumed throughout the country. The pudding is sliced and fried with bacon and eggs; a whole pudding is cooked on top of a beef stew, or served as an accompani-ment to meat or boiled potatoes; or they can be deep-fried and eaten with chips. They are also known as white pudding and, in Aberdeenshire as Jimmys while black puddings are known as Jocks. Without their skins, the mixture of oatmeal and onions is fried in a pan with fat and is known as 'skirlie' from the term 'skirl in the pan' meaning making a loud noise.

TECHNIQUE:

The 'Traditional Method' (McNeill, 1929): 'Toast two pounds of oatmeal in the oven, mix with it from a pound to a pound and a half of good beef suet and three or four fair-sized onions, all finely chopped. Add about a tablespoonful of salt and half that quantity of Jamaica pepper. Prepare your tripe skins as for Black Puddings and fill, not too full with the oatmeal mixture in the manner there indicated. Boil for an hour, pricking them occasionally with a fork to prevent them from bursting. These puddings will keep good for months if hung up and kept dry, or better, if kept buried in oatmeal in the girnel or meal chest.'

REGION OF PRODUCTION:
THROUGHOUT GENERAL SCOTLAND.

North Ronaldsay Sheep

DESCRIPTION:

SMALL, FINE-BONED ANIMALS, WITH DARK, TENDER, FINE-GRAINED, WELL-FLAVOURED AND SLIGHTLY GAMY FLESH. PRIMITIVE SHEEP HAVE A LOWER PROPORTION OF SATURATED FATTY ACIDS THAN COMMERCIAL BREEDS.

HISTORY:

North Ronaldsay sheep evolved in an oceanic climate, windy and wet but mild, thanks to the

Gulf Stream. The Orkneys are flat and low-lying; the soil is good and much is cultivated or used as pasture for cattle and sheep, which are part of a subsistence economy known as crofting. This incorporates small-scale farming and cultivation of crops like potatoes and kale, backed up by fishing and cottage industries such as weaving or knitting. All the good land is used for crops and cattle; sheep are expected to live on the common, less fertile land, which in the Orkneys often means the foreshore surrounding habitable land.

The first recorded comments on the native sheep were in the early nineteenth century (*OED*). In 1861, Mrs Beeton remarked they were 'restless and unprofitable'. They may be considered as ancestors of the Shetlands which, together with other primitive breeds found on the Scottish islands, probably owe many of their characteristics to introductions by the Vikings. The sheep now survive only on a single inhabited island, North Ronaldsay, and on several small holms or uninhabited islands the most notable of which is Linga Holm – hence their other names of Holme sheep or Holmies. In the early nineteenth century, a wall was built around North Ronaldsay's agricultural acreage to exclude these near-feral sheep from more conventional grazing. They have since lived on the foreshore, surviving largely on seaweed. They are physiologically adapted to this diet, utilizing dietary copper very efficiently, even developing copper poisoning on richer grazing. The ewes are brought into grass fields for a few weeks around lambing in May.

After long decline, the primitive breeds are now valuable for both genetic and commercial reasons. In the 1970s, fears for the health of this small population in so restricted an area led to the purchase of Linga Holm by the Rare Breeds Survival Trust who established and manage a flock there. There is a demand for their meat. However, the potential market is very distant, adding to difficulties and cost. Lamb from North Ronaldsay is available on the Orkneys and in a few specialist butchers on the mainland in late August and early September. Other lambs are raised on the Orkneys to a more settled agricultural pattern: these are Cheviots (p. 308).

TECHNIQUE:

North Ronaldsay sheep are recognized to be exceptionally hardy and prolific. Meat from all the primitive breeds requires hanging for 7 days to develop optimum flavour and tenderness.

REGION OF PRODUCTION:

ORKNEY ISLANDS.

Red Deer Venison

DESCRIPTION:

A STAG WEIGHS APPROXIMATELY 105KG, HIND 70KG (CLEANED). THE MEAT IS DARK CRIMSON RED, CLOSE-GRAINED, WITH FIRM, WHITE FAT.

HISTORY:

The word venison formerly referred to the flesh of game in general. Now it is restricted to that of the various species of deer found in Britain. There is much early evidence for its use as food by the whole population. After 1066, first in England and later in Scotland, landowners became increasingly restrictive about hunting. In the Scottish Highlands, venison was caught and distributed through the clan, which shared equitably the produce of the land among its people. The deer were hunted by a method known as the tinchel (Hope, 1987). This involved a large number of men moving herds from the hills over days, or weeks, into a funnel-like enclosure at the head of a glen. The deer were killed as they attempted to escape. The animals concerned would be red deer, as the woodland species live on lower ground. This method was used into the 1700s. Thereafter, as landowners claimed the Highlands for themselves, the meat only entered the diet of the poor when it was poached.

By the nineteenth century the range of red deer had become restricted to very specific areas of Britain, by far the most important was the Scottish Highlands. At this time, the art of stalking, still practised today, became important. The factors which led to its development were the retreat of the deer to remote and inaccessible areas; the depopulation of the Highlands, reducing the manpower available; the availability of improved firearms; and the need for Scottish landowners to earn money – which they did by creating shooting estates. In 1811 there were 6 of these in the Scottish Highlands; by 1842, there were 40.

The pattern thus set has never been completely reversed and venison remains a luxury meat. For a long period in the second half of the twentieth century a large percentage of Highland venison was exported, principally to Germany. But largely due to several companies' efforts to reverse this trend, as well as the production of a small amount of farmed venison's unique flavour and high-quality, lean meat is now gaining more local customers.

The history of English venison is not so very different from the experience of Scotland. The meat of the roe deer and other species has always been jealously reserved to those groups who have had the privilege of hunting it: at first the king, then his noble vassals, then land-owners whoever they may be. Venison entered the general diet through gift, not sale, unless it was poached (Thompson, 1975). Culinary treatment of the meat has been conservative, but with better hanging and butchering techniques, as well as more available information, it is being used in a more adventurous fashion.

TECHNIQUE:

The season in Scotland is 21 October–15 February for hinds; 1 July–20 October for stags. After shooting, the deer are gralloched (innards removed) imme-diately. They are transport-ed on hill-ponies to a collection point to be trucked in refrigerated vehicles to a production unit. Here they are skinned, inspected by a veterinary surgeon, hung for approximately 2–3 days and then butchered into prime cuts and other products such as sausages and mince.

REGION OF PRODUCTION:

SCOTLAND, HIGHLANDS.

Reestit Mutton

DESCRIPTION:

CURED MUTTON FROM VARIOUS CUTS. COLOUR: PALE CREAM FAT, DEEP RED LEAN. FLAVOUR: SALTY, MATURE MUTTON. TEXTURE: HARD, DRY.

HISTORY:

Reestit mutton originated in the need to preserve a surplus through the winter. It was salted and dried by hanging from the rafter (reestit) in a croft house with an open peat fire; photographs from the early 1900s show the reestit mutton still hanging from the roof frame though the fire has been transferred to a range with a chimney. While Shetlanders continue to reest mutton at home, some Lerwick butchers also cure the meat. An explanatory notice for visitors in a butcher's window is headed: 'Reestit Mutton What is it? Traditionally, it was salted lamb or mutton dried above a peat fire. It will keep for years if you keep it dry. Reestit mutton soup is an acquired taste that you acquire at the first taste. A small piece is enough to flavour a pot of soup which should include cabbage, carrots, neeps and tatties.'

The meat is first used to make stock for broths, then taken out and eaten separately with potatoes, or chopped finely and returned to the broth. Alternatively, it can be eaten cold in a Shetland bannock (made from wheat, not barley or oats), or chopped finely and mixed into 'milgrew', a colloquial term for milk gruel (porridge made with milk). Reestit mutton is an important feature of the festive food at the Up-Helly-Aa celebrations in January when platters of the best cuts are served with bannocks, oatcakes and butter at *ceilidhs* after the ritual burning of the Viking longboat.

TECHNIQUE:

The meat is cut up and put into a 'secret' brine recipe which one butcher describes as approximately 80 per cent salt to 20 per cent sugar. It is left for 10–21 days, then hung on hooks to dry. The recipe in *A Shetland Cookbook* (1968) requires 'three and a half pounds (1.5kg) of salt; four quarts (4.5 litres) of water; six ounces (150g) of sugar; two to three ounces (50–75g) of saltpetre; about sixteen pounds (7.25kg) of mutton'.

REGION OF PRODUCTION:

SHETLAND.

Shetland Sassermeat

DESCRIPTION:

A MIXTURE OF RAW, SALTED AND SPICED BEEF, EITHER MOULDED INTO 'SQUARE' SAUSAGES (IN A TIN OF THE TYPE USED FOR LORNE SAUSAGES) WHICH PRODUCES A SLICE APPROXIMATELY IOCM SQUARE AND ICM THICK, OR SOLD UNSHAPED BY WEIGHT.

HISTORY:

Links with Scandinavia (Shetland was once part of Norway) and the need for a method of preservation that would last through lengthy northern winters have created a number of original Shetland cures for meat and fish. Unlike reestit mutton (which retains its original form), sassermeat, also known as saucermeat, has been modified and is not now intended to last the winter through.

It used to be heavily salted and spiced. Crofters would make a winter's supply all at once, stored in an earthenware crock for use as required. It would be mixed with onions and either fresh meat or bread crumbs, then bound with egg or milk to make fried patties ('bronies') or a baked loaf. Though some traditionalists continue to make their own, most sassermeat is now made by butchers in a milder form.

TECHNIQUE:

Beef and fat are minced together and mixed with rusk, water, salt and a spicing mixture. Each butcher uses a different seasoning and regards his particular formula as a trade secret. Proportions quoted in *A Shetland Cookbook* are 3kg meat and 100g salt mixed with 1 teaspoon each of allspice, black pepper, white pepper, and ground cloves, and half a teaspoon of cinnamon. This can be pressed by hand into a Lorne sausage tin to make a loaf 38cm by 10cm, with sloping sides, weighing about 2kg. The sausage is turned out of this mould and left to set and harden in the refrigerator for several hours before slicing to order.

REGION OF PRODUCTION:
SHETLAND.

Shetland Sheep

DESCRIPTION:
SHETLANDS ARE SMALL AND FINE-BONED; THE NATIONAL SHEEP ASSOCIATION COMMENTS THAT THE HILL-BRED WETHER MUTTON 'IS CLAIMED TO BE UNSURPASSABLE'. MEAT IS GENERALLY TENDER, FINE-GRAINED, WELL-FLAVOURED AND SLIGHTLY GAMY, A WELL-FATTENED PRIME LAMB YIELDING A CARCASS OF 11–12KG, ALTHOUGH SOME AS LITTLE AS 8KG. THEY HAVE A LOW PERCENTAGE OF SATURATED FATTY ACIDS.

HISTORY:
Shetlands have long been valued both for meat and for their very fine wool, coloured from white to dark brown. They are the foundation of an important textile industry on the islands. The wool is comparable in fineness to the Merino's and its worth was early recognized by those anxious to encourage domestic resources and manufacture. Shetlands are one of the Scottish primitives. Several are known on the islands, such as the North Ronaldsay (p. 344-5). At first, they were spread through the whole of northern Scotland, only dying out on the mainland in the 1880s due to constant cross-breeding, especially with the Cheviot, to develop a more meaty conformation while retaining something of the quality of the wool.

The Shetland Flock Book Society was founded in 1927. After a long period of decline, the primitives are now thought valuable for genetic and commercial reasons. It was never in doubt that it would survive on the islands themselves, but its worth as a grazer of marginal lands has made it among the most popular of British rare breeds. The pure-bred stock remains for breeding but is still muchcrossed with Cheviots for meat, and has now been awarded Protected Designation of Origin (PDO).

TECHNIQUE:
Shetland sheep are kept on common grazings, where they take care of themselves for much of the year. The breed is hardy and easy to lamb; it is also naturally short-tailed and resistant to foot-rot. Although these breeds are shorn in conventional husbandry systems, they will shed their fleeces naturally in summer if left alone. Excess lambs culled from these flocks in the late summer are used for meat, but some breeding according to the stratified system of production also goes on, in which a first-cross generation is produced using Cheviots. In turn, these are crossed with Suffolks, to give lambs intended solely as meat for the mainland. These crossbred animals are kept on the inbye land. The National Sheep Association remarks, 'It is unlikely that it will ever be supplanted in its native area where the breed will remain as a pure bred stock under the harsher hill conditions, or as a parent stock for the production of cross ewes and lambs under more kindly conditions.'

REGION OF PRODUCTION:
SCOTLAND, SHETLAND ISLANDS.

Smoked Game

HISTORY:

SMOKING WAS A COMMON HIGHLAND METHOD OF PRESERVING SURPLUS GAME FOR USE THROUGHOUT THE WINTER. ORIGINAL METHODS INVOLVED SALTING AND DRYING THE MEAT UNTIL IT WAS QUITE HARD AND THEN HANGING IT FROM RAFTERS ABOVE THE PEAT 'REEK' FROM THE FIRE WHERE IT TOOK ON A STRONG, PEATY FLAVOUR. IT WAS THEN STORED IN COLD, DARK CELLARS, CAVES OR BARNS. AS THE NEED FOR A LESS HIGHLY PRESERVED ITEM DEVELOPED, LIGHTER CURES HAVE BEEN USED AND A SMALL BUT SPECIALIST INDUSTRY IS NOW PRODUCING A CHARACTERFUL PRODUCT WHICH SOME REGARD AS EQUAL TO, IF NOT A BETTER, THAN SMOKED SALMON.

TECHNIQUE:

A venison cure is likely to involve the haunch meat: usually hung for just over a week, depending on temperature and humidity. The individual muscles (topside, silverside and thick flank), with sinew and fat removed, are brined at a controlled temperature in a mixture, usually containing sugar and salt along with other ingredients, for up to 3–4 days. They are dried for 2 days, then cold-smoked over oak-chips from whisky barrels. The meat is packed in slices, sometimes moistened and flavoured further with olive oil and herbs.

REGION OF PRODUCTION:
SCOTLAND, HIGHLANDS.

Soay Sheep

DESCRIPTION:

SOAYS KILL AT 8KG (DRESSED WEIGHT) FOR A LAMB; THE ANIMALS ARE FINE-BONED WITH A SLENDER CONFORMATION, MORE LIKE GOAT OR DEER THAN ORDINARY SHEEP. THE MEAT IS GENERALLY TENDER, FINELY GRAINED, WELL-FLAVOURED AND SLIGHTLY GAMY. PRIMITIVE SHEEP HAVE A LOWER PROPORTION OF SATURATED FATTY ACIDS THAN COMMERCIAL BREEDS.

HISTORY:

Soays are a good example of a primitive sheep; these are small, coloured, with short tails and a single pair of horns. They are, 'relics of unimproved breeds that have probably remained much as they were when first introduced to the British Isles between the Neolithic and the Iron Age periods, some 4,000 to 2,000 years ago' (Hall & Clutton-Brock, 1989). Soays take their name from an island in the St Kilda group, about 200 kilometres west of the mainland. The word means 'sheep island' in Old Norse. The breed was once part of a subsistence economy and feral flocks still inhabit the islands. They were first described by a traveller to western Scotland, Martin Martin, in the late seventeenth century. They remained a little-known curiosity until the twentieth, when several ornamental flocks were started in parks, including one by the Duke of Bedford in 1910; these animals are the strain now recognized as Park Soays – they have been used to found flocks on at least 2 other islands. The Hirta Soay strain is derived from animals used to stock the island of Hirta in the St Kilda group when the human population was evacuated in 1930. Some of these sheep were brought to the mainland in 1968 and have been kept separate from other flocks.

See the remarks about Shetlands, above, for general agricultural matters. Soay are sometimes considered difficult to shepherd, but benefit from frequent handling. Apart from their ornamental value and in situations where high stocking rates are required, Soays are used in reclmation schemes, especially in the South-West of England where wasteland, worked for china clay and then re-seeded, provides a fragile environment on which small, light animals are necessary. Conditions are similar to, if less extreme than, their original home. Meat, from pure-bred animals and from crosses with breeds like Ryelands or Southdowns, is much prized by consumers and is available from specialists.

REGION OF PRODUCTION:

SCOTLAND, ST KILDA GROUP OF ISLANDS.

Aberdeen Rowie

DESCRIPTION:

A MISSHAPEN, UNEVEN, VAGUELY ROUND, FLAKY, FLAT BUN ABOUT 10–20MM DEEP, 80MM DIAMETER AND WEIGHING ABOUT 75G. IT IS SOMETIMES LIKENED TO A CROISSANT WITHOUT THE SHAPE. THERE ARE SEVERAL VARIATIONS ON THE ORIGINAL FORM, FOR EXAMPLE WEE ROWIES (TWO-THIRDS THE NORMAL SIZE), DOUBLE ROWIES (STUCK BACK-TO-BACK WITH BUTTER) AND LOAFIES (MADE WITH ROWIE DOUGH, BUT BAKED IN A BATCH PRODUCING A SQUARE, DEEPER ROWIE). IN SOME PARTS THE DOUGH IS THICKER AND MORE BREAD-LIKE THAN THE ABERDEENSHIRE FLAKY, LAYERED, YEASTED PASTRY. COLOUR: DEEP GOLDEN BROWN FOR WELL-FIRED, 'CREMATED' ROWIES TO PALER GOLDEN FOR LESS WELL-FIRED 'PALES'. FLAVOUR: A BURNT SALTINESS WHICH IS LARGELY DETERMINED BY THE DEGREE OF FIRING AND THE FLAVOUR OF THE FAT.

HISTORY:

These are thought to have developed as a result of the boom in the fishing industry in Aberdeen around the turn of the last century when an enterprising baker (origin unknown) was asked to make the fishermen a roll which would not go stale during their 2–3 week trips to the fishing grounds. The first literary mention of them is of a street-seller in Arbroath in 1899: 'Between butteries, Rob Roys [a kind of Bath bun], and turnovers, her basket was weel filled.'

Although Aberdeen still has more bakers producing their own distinctive and, they would claim, 'authentic' rowies, others, from Caithness to Edinburgh, sell what they describe as Aberdeen butteries. A rowie, or roll, is how they are commonly referred to in Aberdeen. The term butterie is odd since they are not made with butter. The name seems to have been given to them by non-Aberdonians, aware that they are fatty but not realising that the fat used is not butter. Most bakers use vegetable shortening or lard, though the original fishermen's rowies were made with butcher's dripping.

TECHNIQUE:

Two doughs are made. One very soft and sticky with very little fat and the other stiffer with most of the fat. In large bakeries the 2 batches are mixed by machine for a few seconds only, to preserve the layers. In smaller bakeries they are folded and rolled by hand in the same way

'A Book of Verses underneath the Bough,
A Jug of Wine, a Loaf of Bread – and Thou
Beside me singing in the Wilderness –
Oh, Wilderness were Paradise enow!'

Edward Fitzgerald, 'The Rubaiyat of Omar Khayyam'

as puff pastry, using the sticky dough as if it were the butter. Shaping is invariably by hand. Mechanical devices have been tried: none has been satisfactory. The dough it is divided into approximately 50g pieces which are pressed out first with 4 outstretched, floured fingers, then knocked into their uneven shape with the floured backs of 4 fingers of the left hand and the floured clenched knuckles of the right. Proved in a warm, steamy atmosphere for 20 minutes they are baked for 18–20 minutes in a fairly hot oven. They are left on the tray until stacked on their sides.

REGION OF PRODUCTION:
EAST SCOTLAND.

Beremeal Bannock

DESCRIPTION:
DISCS 150MM DIAMETER, 12MM THICK. COLOUR: LIGHT GREY-BROWN CRUMB, ROUGH, MEALIE CRUST. FLAVOUR: STRONGER THAN PEARL BARLEY FLOUR, THEY HAVE AN ASTRINGENT, EARTHY TANG, UNSWEETENED.

HISTORY:
Barley was the staple cereal crop in Scotland from Neolithic times until it was progressively displaced by oats (introduced by the Romans) and then by wheat, from the seventeenth century. Barley remained the vital ingredient for beer, whisky distilling, barley broth and barley bannocks; in the Highlands and Islands and among the lower classes in the Lowlands, it continued to be used for making bread. The practice has persisted to this day in the Highland region, particularly in Orkney.

The distinctive form of barley used for bannocks is the variety known as bigg or big (the four-rowed barley, *Hordeum vulgare*). Bigg is called bere or bear (pronounced bare). While the modern bannock is leavened with buttermilk and baking soda, the original was made by cooking the meal first in milk and butter to make a paste. This was then rolled out into thin chapati-like pancakes which were cooked on the girdle or flat iron baking plate. When cooked, they were spread with butter, rolled up tightly and eaten hot. They are still eaten as a savoury part of evening supper in Orkney, accompanied by butter and a slice of fresh, young cheese.

TECHNIQUE:
Modern recipes vary the proportion of beremeal to wheat flour. Most printed Orkney recipes suggest about half and half but some Orcadians make their bannocks with very little wheat flour, preferring the stronger flavour of the beremeal. The flour is mixed with baking soda and buttermilk to make a moist dough which is rolled out and baked on a floured girdle or hot-plate, turning once.

REGION OF PRODUCTION:
NORTH SCOTLAND, ORKNEY.

Scottish Oatcake

DESCRIPTION:

OATCAKES PRODUCED COMMERCIALLY ARE FLAT BISCUITS CONTAINING FLOUR TO BIND THE OATMEAL TO PREVENT BREAKAGE. NON-COMMERCIAL OATCAKES, WITHOUT THE FLOUR AND BAKED IN TRIANGLES ON A GIRDLE, CURL UP AT THE EDGES AS THEY DRY OUT. THE MAIN SHAPES ARE ROUNDS AND FARLS (TRIANGLES) OR CORTERS (QUARTER-CIRCLES OF A LARGE 200MM DISC). OATCAKES ARE 30–100MM DIAMETER, 3–10MM THICK. COLOUR: GREYISH TO LIGHT BROWN. FLAVOUR AND TEXTURE: MEALY, NUTTY.

HISTORY:

These developed in the seventeenth century as oats took over from barley as the staple food grain. The oatcake took its form from the primitive hearthstone cake of meal and water mixed to a paste and spread out to cook on hot stones. At the start, the grains were mixed. 'They make a kind of bread, not unpleasant to the taster of oats and barley, the only grain cultivated in these regions, and from long practice, they have attained considerable skill in moulding the cakes. Of this they eat a little in the morning, and then contentedly go out a hunting, or engage in some other occupation, frequently remaining without any other food till evening' (Buchanan, 1629).

By the early 1800s, however, oatcakes and barley cakes had taken on a separate existence: 'For breakfast the cheese was set out as before, with plenty of butter and barley cakes, and fresh baked oaten cake, which no doubt were made for us; they were kneaded with cream and were excellent' (Dorothy Wordsworth, 1803). Though the habit of mixing with cream is not common today, a recipe, dated 1893, appears in Lady Clark of Tillypronie (1909): '8 oz [250g] of fine oatmeal freshly ground and kept from the air, a pinch of salt, half a teaspoon of baking powder, and as little cream as possible – only just enough to make it into a dough. Too thick cream does not do. Roll it out as thin as possible, and cut it into three-cornered pieces. Put it on the girdle to set. It must not be turned over or it will be tough, but put it on a toaster in front of the fire to brown the top side, toaster sloping towards the fire. To use again it must be re-toasted and sent to table warm. If baked in an oven oatcake will be hard. If without cream, use water with a bit of butter previously melted into it; milk would make flinty cakes. It has no merit if it does not eat short and crisp, but it must not be buttery.'

Despite the attractions of soft white bread, oatcakes have retained their popularity in Scotland where the population continues to consume a higher percentage of hard biscuits than the English. Oatcakes have proved as versatile an accompaniment as bread, since they can be eaten with oily fish like herrings and sardines, cheese of all kinds, jams, jellies, marmalade and honey, or eaten with broth, with a slice of unsalted butter laid – not spread – on top (spread the butter and you break the brittle oatcakes).

TECHNIQUE:

Oatcakes are made with various cuts of ground oatmeal, salt, a little dripping, and water to mix. *Bonnach Imeach* (Hebridean oatcake) is usually made with a fine oatmeal and is rolled out more thickly (5–10mm) than other oatcakes. A thinner, crisper cake (about 3mm thick) is more common. Wheat flour may be added which makes them less brittle. A slightly coarser oatmeal makes them crunchier and rougher.

The dough or paste is rolled out while still hot and cut into shapes which are dried off on a girdle or hot-plate or in the oven. Only hand-made oatcakes made on a girdle will curl at the edges.

REGION OF PRODUCTION:
NORTH SCOTLAND AND GENERAL SCOTLAND.

Water Biscuit

DESCRIPTION:
A THICK CIRCULAR BISCUIT ABOUT 85–90MM DIAMETER, 5–8MM THICK. WEIGHT: ABOUT 20G. COLOUR: IRREGULAR CREAM TO PALE GOLD, BLISTERED IN PLACES WITH GOLD-BROWN BUBBLES, DOCKED WITH SMALL HOLES. FLAVOUR AND TEXTURE: RICH, NUTTY FLAVOUR, EXTREMELY CRISP, WITH FLAKY TEXTURE.

HISTORY:
Water biscuits are the principal survivors of a class developed from ship's biscuits, formerly of great importance in the British Isles. These hard biscuits which, as the name suggests, originated as bread substitutes for provisioning ships, developed into more palatable forms in the late 1800s, evolving, with a little enrichment, through 'Captain's Biscuits' into water biscuits. The latter were well known when a recipe given by Harris and Borella (c. 1900) instructs soft flour, a little salt and sufficient water to make a tight dough; this was then folded and worked intensively through the rollers of a biscuit-brake. The recipes developed further with small enrichments of fat and sugar.

Although a number of companies still make water biscuits in different parts of the UK, there is good evidence for various regional types in Scotland. *Law's Grocer's Manual*, roughly contemporary with the recipe above, remarks on the use of different flours by manufacturers, the English typically using moderately soft flour (giving a hard, crisp biscuit which offered some resistance to the teeth), and strong flour being favoured in western Scotland, resulting in a more coloured, flaky appearance and biscuits which were more easily broken. Gardens and Stockans Water Biscuits and Black's Water Biscuits, both trademarks, are examples of this type. They contrast strongly both in thickness and texture with Carr's Table Water Biscuits and Jacob's Cream Crackers, the varieties made and best known in England.

REGION OF PRODUCTION:
SCOTLAND, ORKNEY ISLANDS.

Heather Ale

DESCRIPTION:
HEATHER ALE IS AMBER-GOLD AND HAS A FLOWERY, AROMATIC FLAVOUR, WITH A BITTER NOTE. IT IS 4 PER CENT ALCOHOL BY VOLUME (CASK ALE), 5 PER CENT ALCOHOL BY VOLUME (BOTTLED VERSION). PICTISH ALE IS 5.4 PER CENT ALCOHOL BY VOLUME.

HISTORY:
Neolithic remains from the Inner Hebrides include pottery with residues indicating it had held a fermented beverage containing heather. There are many references from the Middle

Ages onwards to beers brewed with heather and other herbs, especially bog myrtle. Such drinks survived the introduction of brewing methods from continental Europe in some areas of the west and north of Scotland, especially Galloway and the remoter parts of the Highlands and Islands. The traveller Pennant encountered heather ale in Islay in the eighteenth century, and McNeill, writing in 1956, recalls a woman on Orkney who made it. The Islands were remote from mainstream brewing practices, with no major commercial brewers until the twentieth century; consequently, the habit of brewing with local herbs, rather than hops, survived and remains as a tradition of home-brewing. Recently, heather ale has been revived as a commercial product by a Glasgow company, Heather Ale Ltd, who began to develop a recipe translated from Gaelic in the mid-1980s. It is marketed as 'Fraoch' (pronounced fruich); *leann fraoch* is Gaelic for heather ale.

TECHNIQUE:

Heather for this beer is gathered from bell heather (*Erica cinerea*) and ling (*Calluna vulgaris*), 2 species native to the British Isles. It is cut during the flowering season, in shoots 8–10cm long, including the young leaves and flowers. To make the beer, Scotch ale malt is sparged (sprayed with hot water) to extract the malt sugars, giving a solution called wort. The wort is boiled in a brew kettle, to which heather and a small quantity of hops are added; after boiling, the mixture is run through a hop-back (sieve) in which fresh heather is placed. Brewer's yeast is added, and the wort allowed to ferment for several days, depending on the alcoholic strength desired; more heather flowers are laid on the top during this time. The beer is conditioned in bulk for about 10 days until the appropriate carbon dioxide level is reached; during this process it is fined and then filtered into casks or bottles as appropriate. The bottles are capped and pasteurized, the casks stoppered and distributed with no further treatment. Heather ale is produced in early June–early December; the cask-conditioned ale is available July–October; the bottled ale from July until early spring; the stronger Pictish Ale is made as a Christmas or New Year drink.

REGION OF PRODUCTION:

WEST SCOTLAND AND GENERAL SCOTLAND.

Silver Birch Wine

DESCRIPTION:

THE WINE IS A PALE STRAW COLOUR, WITH A LIGHT, DRY, CLEAN, REFRESHING FLAVOUR.

HISTORY:

Records of the use of birch sap to make alcoholic drinks go back at least 200 years in Scotland. 'Quantities of excellent wine,' says Thomas Pennant, writing of the Highlands (1796), 'are extracted from the live tree (silver birch) by tapping.' Mrs Dalgairns (1829) instructed, 'Bore a hole in a tree and put in a faucet, and it will run for 2 or 3 days together without hurting the tree; then put in a pin to stop it, and next year you may draw as much from the same hole.' The same drink was called 'Birk' wine by Meg Dods in 1826; her recipe was, 'To every gallon of the sap of the birch tree, boiled, put four pounds of white sugar, and the thin paring of a lemon. Boil and skim this well. When cool, put fresh yeast to it. Let it ferment for four or five days; then close it up. Keep the bung very close, and in four months rack it off and bottle it.'

This wine is noted by Queen Victoria in her journals as being one of Prince Albert's

favourite drinks. It is also mentioned in the annals of Moniack Castle and it was the evidence of this tradition which encouraged the present owner Phillipa Fraser to start making Silver Birch wine commercially at her ancestral home in 1982. The wine-making business has developed well and they now also make elderflower, meadowsweet, raspberry and bramble wines as well as sloe gin and mead.

The wine was also known in other parts of Britain, *vide* the recipes in John Evelyn's MS cookery book (*c.* 1700), Richard Bradley (1736), Hannah Glasse (1747) and Mrs Raffald (1769) – who also suggests sycamore wine by the same process. A 'traditional birch wine' is made today in Cawston, Norfolk using birch sap and grape juice. It should be noted in this context that the word 'wine' has been used colloquially in English for centuries to denote drinks of 8–14 per cent alcohol fermented from fruit, flowers and vegetables.

TECHNIQUE:
Sap for birch wine made in Scotland is collected from trees in the area around the winery. In the spring when the sap is rising, holes are bored 1m up the tree and 2.5cm into the wood, a cork is put in and attached to a plastic tube running into a 5-gallon drum, which fills up with sap. Once the sap has been collected, the hole is stopped. The sap is mixed with yeast, sugar and water, and allowed to ferment. It matures for 9 months before bottling.

REGION OF PRODUCTION:
NORTH SCOTLAND, EAST ANGLIA.

Beremeal

DESCRIPTION:
COLOUR: GREY-BROWN. FLAVOUR: STRONGER THAN PEARL BARLEY FLOUR, AN ASTRINGENT EARTHY TANG.

HISTORY:
Despite the fact that today barley is mainly malted and used for whisky, it was the main cereal crop in Scotland from Neolithic times until the introduction of oats. Oats were used increasingly as the grain staple for human consumption, although they only consolidated their position after the seventeenth century. For most Scots, barley then became the grain for beer and whisky and was marginalized as a foodstuff. But barley breads continued to be eaten by poorer people in the Lowlands until improvements in agricultural practice and import of foreign grain brought wheaten bread to a wider public. This change did not, however, reach as far as the Scottish Highlands and Islands, where barley continued to be an important staple used for bread in the form of a flat, girdle-baked bannock. Most of the bere grown today comes from Orkney and it is the Orcadians who preserve the tradition of making the beremeal bannock. The distinctive form of barley used is the Northern variety known as bigg or big (the four-rowed barley, *Hordeum vulgare*). Bigg is called bere or bear (pronounced bare). Most of the beremeal comes from a mill on Orkney and another at Golspie (Sutherland).

TECHNIQUE:
Beremeal is kiln-dried and stone-ground into fine flour.

REGION OF PRODUCTION:
NORTH SCOTLAND.

'Beautiful Soup, so rich and green,
Waiting in a hot tureen!
Who for such dainties would not stoop?
Soup of the evening, beautiful Soup!'

LEWIS CARROLL, *ALICE'S ADVENTURES IN WONDERLAND*

Rowan Jelly

DESCRIPTION:

THIS IS CRIMSON RED WITH A SWEET-ASTRINGENT FLAVOUR. OTHER FRUIT PRODUCE DIFFERENT COLOURS: SLOE, DARK PURPLE; HAWTHORN, PALE RUBY RED; WILD CHERRY, DARK RUBY RED; BRAMBLE, BLACKISH-PURPLE.

HISTORY:

The jelly from wild Highland berries was originally used as a reviving drink – a spoonful mixed with boiling water, whisky or rum – or as a sweet pudding with cream. The drink is mentioned by St Fond (1784) in his account of travels in the Hebrides. A description of jellies with cream as a dessert appears in an account by young Elizabeth Grant of Rothimurchus when visiting a relative in 1812. Inside her hostess's deep-shelved pantry, beside the butter, honey, sweetmeats and spiced whisky, were pots of preserved jellies. The cook skimmed some cream off the milk, emptied the whole pot of jelly on a plate and poured over the cream. The dish, she explains, was known as 'bainne briste' meaning broken milk.

Several companies make rowan jelly but the pioneer of preserves from wild fruits has been Phillipa Fraser, of Moniack Wineries, who started collecting berries as a consequence of country wine-making.

TECHNIQUE:

The berries are gathered, beginning in late summer with wild cherries and running through to late autumn for rowan and sloes. After cleaning, they are boiled with apples (which contribute pectin) in water to produce a juice; this is strained and boiled with sugar until setting point is reached. Commonly there are 60g berries per 100g of jelly. Total sugar content 60g per 100g.

REGION OF PRODUCTION:

NORTH SCOTLAND.

Peasemeal

DESCRIPTION:

ROASTED, MILLED PEAS, A BROWN-YELLOW POWDER WHOSE TEXTURE VARIES A LITTLE ACCORDING TO HUMIDITY, FROM FINE AND SMOOTH TO VERY SLIGHTLY GRITTY; THE FLAVOUR IS QUITE STRONG AND EARTHY.

HISTORY:

Flour ground from peas and foods made from it, notably brose (a soup or porridge) and bannocks, have a long history in Scotland, especially as food for the common people. McNeill (1929) mentions pease bannocks, instructing that they were made in the same manner as barley bannocks – that is, the flour was mixed with water, milk or whey, rolled thinly and baked on a girdle. She quotes a much earlier reference to pease scones (a similar type of bread) from the early eighteenth century. Macleod, in her foreword to McLintock (1736), remarks that pease and bean meal were baked into bread and that pease meal has survived in the Orkneys and North-East Scotland. In the twentieth century it was a food associated with poverty and is now mostly consumed by the elderly.

Peasemeal is considered very digestible. For brose it is mixed with boiling liquid, usually water, and consumed straight away. This is a form of convenience food, made quickly, and

eaten with butter and pepper or salt, or with sugar and raisins. Uses in the modern kitchen include adding it to soups and stews and as a vegetarian food, especially for pastes flavoured with herbs and garlic.

TECHNIQUE:

Yellow field peas imported from eastern England are used for this product. They are roasted gently, a process which caramelizes some of the sugar, makes more starch and protein available for digestion and darkens the colour. They are ground through 3 pairs of water-powered millstones, becoming successively finer with each set. There is one miller of peasemeal at Golspie (Sutherland).

REGION OF PRODUCTION:

NORTH EAST SCOTLAND.

***

Also produced in North Scotland
CROWDIE CHEESE (P. 362-363)
DUNLOP CHEESE (P. 299)
FINNIAN HADDOCK (P. 306)
KALE (P. 291)

Scotland: Countrywide

'Floury' Potatoes

DESCRIPTION:

ROUND OR OVAL-SHAPED, FIRM TUBERS OF VARYING SIZES AND WEIGHTS. THE 2 MOST COMMON VARIETIES ARE: GOLDEN WONDER, WITH A RUSSET SKIN AND WHITE FLESH, A STRONG FLAVOUR AND ELONGATED PEAR-SHAPE; KERR'S PINK, WHICH HAS A PARTLY PINK SKIN, CREAM FLESH, A DISTINCTIVE FLAVOUR, AND IS A ROUND SHAPE.

HISTORY:

By the nineteenth century, farm carts selling 'mealy tatties' (dry floury potatoes boiled in salted water) had become a common sight on the streets of Scottish cities. This type of potato, favoured by the Scots, has a dry, powdery surface when cooked, and a stronger, more dominant flavour than most available in the British market. Potatoes had been gradually accepted in Scotland during the late eighteenth and early nineteenth centuries, especially in areas of impoverished peasantry. The crop became very important in the West and the Islands. *An Account of the Economic History of the Hebrides and Highlands* (1808) states that by about 1763 the people were subsisting on potatoes for 9 months of the year. Potatoes also combined well with the northern Scots' staple diet of milk and fish. 'Fish with oat bread or potatoes, without any accompaniment at all, forms the three daily meals of the Shetland cottager,' said E. Edmondston, in *Sketches and Tales of the Shetland Isles* (1856). Annette Hope (1987) cites numerous references to illustrate the importance of potatoes to the inhabitants of western and northern Scotland. Both she and Jeremy Cherfas (1995) comment on regional preferences for floury varieties which exist in western Scotland down to the present day.

Many floury varieties have been raised, including Dunbar Rover, Arran Victory, Duke of York and Champion as well as Golden Wonder and Kerr's Pink. Golden Wonder was raised in 1906 by John Brown near Arbroath; it remains one of the varieties with the highest amount of dry matter. Kerr's Pink was raised by James Henry in 1907 and was originally known as Henry's Seedling until it won the Lord Derby Gold Medal at the Ormskirk Trials in 1916. Its merits were recognized by a seedsman (Mr Kerr) who bought the seed and renamed it in 1917.

TECHNIQUE:

Growing underground, potatoes have an advantage over grain crops in a climate which tends towards high rainfall and strong winds; and the rain and cool temperatures also suit the crop. Potatoes flourish in the poor soils of the Scottish Highlands, although for commercial growth, areas of flatter land are favoured – in Ayrshire, on the West coast, and in the fertile soils of East and Central Scotland from Aberdeenshire to the Borders. In the nineteenth century, potatoes were cultivated on a system of hand-dug furrows known as 'lazy beds', whose remains can be seen in many remote parts of the West Highlands. Cultivation is now mechanized. The Scots have particular expertise in the development of new potato varieties, originally derived from the realisation that potato blight would otherwise seriously affect the crop.

March is the main month for early potato planting, April for maincrop. Disease-free seed potatoes are planted in drills in clod-free soils. Harvesting starts in September and is mostly mechanized. All potatoes are lifted by the end of October. They may be sold immediately or treated with sprout-suppressants and fungicides and stored in cool conditions excluding light. Though neither Golden Wonder nor Kerr's Pink are grown on a large scale, the demand remains. Recently, increased interest in potato varieties has led to more attention to their qualities.

REGION OF PRODUCTION:
SCOTLAND.

Tayberry, Tummelberry

DESCRIPTION:
TAYBERRY: A LONG FRUIT (ABOUT 4CM), DEEP PURPLE-RED WHEN FULLY RIPE, WITH A SWEET AND AROMATIC FLAVOUR. TUMMELBERRY: DEEPER RED WITH A SLIGHTLY ROUNDER FRUIT AND SHARPER, LESS AROMATIC FLAVOUR.

HISTORY:
Tayberries and Tummelberries (named for rivers whose valleys disgorge on the Strathmore area, the main berry-producing region of eastern Scotland) are derived from a long tradition of fruit cross-breeding which began in America in the 1860s with Judge Logan's berry when he set about crossing a cultivated (and too bland for his liking) blackberry with a wild variety with more flavour.

The Tayberry is a hybrid of an unnamed raspberry bred at the Scottish Crop Research Institute at Invergowrie (1978) and the blackberry cultivar Aurora from Oregon. The Tummelberry is a newer hybrid, obtained by crossing the Tayberry with one of its sister hybrids (1984). The Scottish contribution, particularly the Tayberry, is now grown widely in the USA as a commercial crop with a plant patent, also in France, Germany, Holland and Scandinavia, while at home it has established itself most successfully on farms which have a pick-your-own facility.

TECHNIQUE:
Tayberries and Tummelberries are commercially cultivated in the open, on a post and wire support system. Like blackberries, they grow best in well-drained, medium loam with a pH of about 6.5 and do best on sites with a sheltered, sunny aspect.

REGION OF PRODUCTION:
SOUTH SCOTLAND AND GENERAL SCOTLAND.

Crowdie Cheese

DESCRIPTION:
PASTEURIZED, SOFT COW'S MILK CHEESE. THERE ARE SOME VARIANTS. GRUTH DHU (BLACK CROWDIE): CROWDIE MIXED WITH DOUBLE CREAM AND ROLLED IN TOASTED OATMEAL AND BLACK PEPPER. HRAMSA: CROWDIE MIXED WITH WILD GARLIC AND WHITE AND RED PEPPER. GALIC HRAMSA: ROLLED IN CRUMBLED FLAKED HAZELNUTS AND ALMONDS. CROWDIE IS SOLD IN PLASTIC TUBS OF APPROXIMATELY 150G; GRUTH DHU IN CYLINDRICAL ROLLS OF APPROXIMATELY 125G, UP TO 1KG; HRAMSA AND GALIC IN ROLLS OF 125G; HIGHLAND SOFT IN TUBS OF 150G. COLOUR: CREAM OR WHITE. FLAVOUR: SHARP, ACIDIC, REFRESHING.

HISTORY:

HISTORY:

Crowdie was at one time the universal breakfast dish of Scotland. In the seventeenth century the name was applied to foods akin to porridge – mixtures of oatmeal and water which had a slightly curdled texture (*OED*). There were various developments of this in the Lowlands but in the Highlands, by the nineteenth century, the word had come to denote a species of milk curd.

Today, the Lowland meaning has been replaced entirely and crowdie has become known solely as the Highlanders' soft cheese. It is of ancient origin, probably having roots in Pictish or Viking practices, and linked to a system of transhumance, in which cattle, sheep and goats were taken to mountain pastures and the milk made into butter and cheese. Surplus crowdie was mixed with butter, packed in earthenware crocks, then covered with a sealing layer of melted butter. These were kept in a cool barn for use through the winter. This was known as crowdie-butter.

This butter and the way of life that engendered it were stopped by the Highland Clearances. The commercial revival of the soft crowdie is almost entirely due to the pioneering efforts of Susanna Stone and her late husband Reggie, who started making it for sale in the early 1960s. They were post-war revivalist farmhouse cheese-makers who in the early days battled against bureaucracy to produce the native cheese. 'The great treat,' said G.W. Lockhart in *The Scot and his Oats* (1983), 'was to have crowdie mixed with fresh cream and piled on an oatcake with fresh salted butter. Then you had a royal feast of flavours – acid, sweet and salt, and better perhaps, a royal mixture of textures, soft, crisp and crunchy.'

TECHNIQUE:

The traditional croft method, described by Susanna Stone as made by her mother, was to leave the bowl of milk at the fireside in winter or in a warm place in summer. It soured naturally and formed a curd. The curds were cooked lightly, until they scrambled (the curd and whey separated). The curds were poured into a muslin-lined bowl and the ends of the muslin were drawn together and tied with string. The bag was hung from a branch of a tree for a few days to drip, or over the tap in the sink, until most of the whey drained out.

The modern method, made by Susanna Stone, follows the old by souring the milk with a starter and allowing it to curd without rennet. The scrambling procedure is followed and the curd is hung in muslin bags to drain. Others now make crowdie, though not all in the old way without rennet. Flavourings are added by some brands to suit the modern palate.

REGION OF PRODUCTION:

NORTH SCOTLAND AND GENERAL SCOTLAND.

Scottish Cheddar Cheese

DESCRIPTION:

MOSTLY PASTEURIZED, HARD, COW'S MILK CHEESE; A FEW SMALL FARMHOUSE CHEDDARS FROM UNPASTEURIZED MILK. COLOUR: PALE YELLOW, OR ARTIFICIALLY COLOURED ORANGE-YELLOW. FORM: ROUNDS, PLASTIC-WRAPPED, WAX-DIPPED AND CLOTHBOUND; ALSO RIND-LESS BLOCKS. FLAVOUR: 12–14-MONTH-OLD WILL HAVE A SHARP BITE TO IT, WHILE A 4–5-MONTH-OLD WILL BE MORE MELLOW AND ROUNDED. MATURITY CLASSIFICATION: MILD; MEDIUM MATURE; MATURE; EXTRA MATURE; VINTAGE.

The rise of Scottish Cheddar occurred with the growth of the cities of central Scotland, particularly Glasgow and Paisley, in the late nineteenth century. It developed from the Ayrshire Dunlop, which was significantly improved after the Ayrshire Agricultural Association brought a Somerset farmer and his wife to teach the Cheddar method in 1885.

The subsequent decline – though not extinction – of Dunlop came about during World War II. Milk was bought in bulk by Milk Marketing Boards and trucked to large creameries to make a cheese by the cheddaring method which they subsequently described as Cheddar. Though it might just as easily have retained the name of the old Ayrshire cheese, the MMBs believed at that time that Dunlop presented the wrong marketing image, having the same name as a leading tyre company of the day. Only in some creameries, notably on Arran and Islay, was the name preserved. Elsewhere, Scottish cheddared cheese of Dunlop ancestry took the Cheddar tag. There are now several variants, such as Orkney, Arran, Rothsay, Islay, Campbeltown, Galloway, Lockerbie.

TECHNIQUE:
Made from pasteurized cow's milk following the basic Cheddar method (p. 4).

REGION OF PRODUCTION:
SCOTLAND.

Crab (Scotland)

DESCRIPTION:
WIDTH ACROSS THE SHELL UP TO 300MM; MINIMUM LEGAL SIZE 125MM. COLOUR: REDDISH, PINK-BROWN TINTED WITH PURPLE, LEGS REDDISH AND CLAWS BLACK. FLAVOUR: STRONG DARK (LIVER) MEAT, WHITE MEAT IS MORE DELICATE THAN LOBSTER.

HISTORY:
There is archaeological evidence for the use of shellfish of all types in the West of Scotland from at least 5,000 BC. It appears likely that the crab was a common item of food for coastal communities eking out a living from a meagre environment. Crabs were more easily caught than lobsters and became more integrated into the daily diet, providing a useful supply of high-quality protein. In Scotland the brown crab was known in the dialect as a partan; under this name they were cried through the streets of Georgian Edinburgh, and 'partan's taes', or toes, i.e. crab claws, were counted amongst the delicacies served in taverns.

The extensive East-coast fishery for crabs must have developed after the building of railheads at the ports during the nineteenth century. This allowed it to tap an expanding market among the middle classes in large towns of Scotland and England (Hope, 1987).

As if to celebrate their place in the national diet, Scottish recipes for crab abound. For instance, they flavoured soups, the most famous being the creamy broth Partan Bree; a Victorian recipe for this was recorded by Lady Clark of Tillypronie (1909).

Although many other British districts have a long connection with crab fishing, for instance Cromer, or Dartmouth and Kingswear in Devon, it is argued that the crab landed from Scottish waters has a finer and more intense flavour from rich feeding in unpolluted, cold northern waters.

Caught in deep-water lobster pots (creels) with fresh fish bait. May be sold live, frozen or processed. At centres of intensive crab fishing, plants have been set up to boil the crabs in large tanks and to remove the meat (mostly by hand) before packing and freezing.

REGION OF PRODUCTION:
SCOTLAND.

COMPARE WITH:
Crab (Cromer), East Anglia (p. 121).

Lobster (Scotland)

DESCRIPTION:
CARAPACE LENGTH UP TO 45CM; IT IS ILLEGAL TO LAND LOBSTERS WITH A CARAPACE SHELL OF UNDER 85MM.

HISTORY:
As part of the general foraging for seafood, to eke out a meagre diet from the produce of the land, the European lobster, *Homarus gammarus*, was eaten by those living in coastal areas of Scotland. By the nineteenth century, however, there is evidence that it had been taken up by Scottish gourmets, notably in the gathering of gastronomes known as the Cleikum Club where their recipe for 'Lobster Haut Gout' tells the cook: 'Pick the firm meat from a parboiled lobster or two and take also the inside, if not thin and watery. Season highly with white pepper, cayenne, pounded mace, and cloves, nutmeg and salt. Take a little well-flavoured gravy – for example the jelly of roast veal – a few tiny bits of butter, a spoonful of soy or walnut catsup, or of any favourite flavoured vinegar, and a spoonful of red wine. Stew the cut lobster in this sauce for a few minutes.'

The association of Scotland with lobster, over and above any other shellfishery in Britain, has much to do with its plentiful supply and the distinctive and intense flavour produced by rich feeding in clear, cold, unpolluted waters. After commercial creel fishing began in the mid-eighteenth century, catches of live lobsters in Orkney were put into floating chests or 'keep boxes' and collected each week by large fishing boats which took them to the London market. In the 1970s around 60 boats were creel fishing for lobsters in the Orkneys.

TECHNIQUE:
Caught live in baited lobster pots (creels) in rocky areas.

REGION OF PRODUCTION:
SCOTLAND.

Salmon (Scotland)

DESCRIPTION:
ADULT SALMON ARE LIKELY TO BE 80CM–1M LONG. WEIGHT: 4–30KG. COLOUR: SILVER ALONG BELLY TURNING TO BLUE-BLACK ALONG BACK, INTERNAL COLOUR VARYING SHADES OF REDDISH-PINK ACCORDING TO FEEDING AND CONDITION.

The clootie dumpling has been made in the glen for generations, and is still commonly produced in Scotland to this day. It is a wonderful winter pudding, though it can also be served for afternoon tea and is often eaten sliced and fried for breakfast.

The clootie dumpling is made of flour, baking soda, currants, raisins, suet, ginger, cinnamon, syrup and treacle, brown sugar, bread crumbs, grated carrot, milk and – traditionally – a silver sixpence. The word 'clootie' comes from the cloth (or 'clootie') bag in which flour was bought and in which the dumpling is cooked.

To cook the dumpling, put the cloth bag into boiling water for five minutes, then take it out and wring it dry with a wooden spurtle or spoon (though be warned, there's a knack involved). Dust the outside of the bag with flour to stop the water penetrating it, then pour the combined ingredients into the bag and draw it up tightly with a string. The end result should resemble a cannonball. Boil the bag for two to three hours, and serve the dumpling hot with cream. *(See recipe for Clootie Dumpling, p. 379)*

Tom Lewis

CHEF, MONACHYLE MHOR, HIGHLAND PERTHSHIRE

Early salmon fisheries on the rivers Tay, Spey, Tweed, Don and Dee produced large catches which were eaten fresh in summer and kippered (smoked and dried) in winter. The quantity caught each year was such that it was one of the most common foods of the people and became so firmly fixed in the minds of the upper classes in Scotland as a cheap, working-man's food that a Highland gentleman, on visiting London, made the mistake of choosing beef for himself and salmon for his servant: 'The Cook, who attended him humoured the Jest, and the Master's eating was Eight Pence and Duncan's came to almost as many Shillings' (Burt, Letters from the North of Scotland, 1730).

While supplies of wild salmon remained plentiful for the best part of the last century, there has since been a gradual decline. Over-fishing and netting have been just two of the problems; research is being undertaken to discover the reasons.

Salmon have, of course, been caught in many other rivers as long as they have been prey to Scottish fishermen. There is no simple difference between a Scottish and an English salmon. However, the number and wealth of Scottish streams and their lack of pollution has meant that Scottish Salmon is a regional descriptor of some force and meaning. It has become more distinct and valid with the growth of salmon farming in the last 30 years. As demand for fresh fish increased around the world – and the means to deliver matched the possibilities of sale – so stocks in the wild came under pressure. The expansion of salmon farming, almost exclusively in Scottish waters, was therefore timely. Common standards among producers will allow the existence of rigid quality markers. This is regional food in the making.

Farming began on the West Coast in 1969 and has spread to the Islands, above all the Shetlands, where they market their salmon separately from the rest of Scotland. There have been problems with farmed salmon, but aquaculture has brought employment to a remote and declining population whose traditions have always been based on harvesting from the sea. Many problems have been solved and much research undertaken to farm more efficiently and with less damage to the environment. Skilled farming can produce a high-quality fish which has made its name in the markets of Europe, gaining a French Label Rouge accolade of prime quality.

TECHNIQUE:

During their life-span salmon go through various stages: in the wild, very young fish, or fry, are at risk from predators and starvation. But after about 3 months in river water, if they survive, they change into parr and then, 1–4 years later, when they are large and strong enough, they change into smolts. They have silvery skins and are, in effect, miniature salmon. Smolts go to sea and feed extensively. Their feeding grounds are thought to be off Greenland and the Faroe Islands. Migration from river and sea generally takes place in early summer, which is another time of high mortality for wild fish.

After only a year at sea, some of the smolts return to the river to spawn; they weigh about 2.25kg, and are known as grilse. The remaining fish stay at sea, growing by about 2.25kg a year. When they return as salmon to fresh water to spawn, it is to their home river where they were hatched. The best quality are caught early in the season when still fat and flavoursome from the rich sea feeding grounds. They are likely to weigh from 8lb to about 60lb. When, and if, they reach their place of hatching and the female spawns and the male ejects his milt on top of the spawn, they become either spent kelts and die from exhaustion and lack of food, or mended kelts and make it back to the sea. Around 5 per cent return to spawn again. They will usually spend 2–3 winters in the sea, sometimes up to 5. The oldest recorded salmon, caught on Loch Maree in Wester Ross, was 13 years old and had spawned 4 times.

Salmon farming depends on breeding stocks which are milked for their eggs in November. The eggs are checked to ensure they are free from disease and they are kept in controlled conditions until they hatch in March. The young fish are very tiny and are carefully monitored. They are reared in special tanks, and as they grow in size are transferred to larger tanks in freshwater lochs, where they grow until they are large enough to be transferred to the sea farms in lochs fed by sea water.

The main practical difference between farmed and wild salmon is that the first is available all year. The debate about the difference in eating quality will long continue. The best farmed fish approach the wild in texture and taste.

REGION OF PRODUCTION:
SCOTLAND.

Smoked Eel

DESCRIPTION:
EELS FOR SMOKING ARE 45–50CM LONG. WEIGHT: MAXIMUM 4KG, BUT EELS FOR SMOKING ARE USUALLY AROUND 500G. THEY MAY BE SOLD WHOLE, UNFILLETED OR FILLETED, IN VACUUM PACKS FROM 115G UPWARDS. COLOUR: ADULT FISH ARE USUALLY BLACK, GREEN-BLACK OR GREY-BROWN ON BACK AND SIDES AND YELLOWISH BELOW; INTERNAL FLESH, DARK CREAM. FLAVOUR: WOODY-OILY, SUCCULENT, SALTY.

HISTORY:
Recently, a number of small Scottish smokers have made use of the abundant supplies of common eels (*Anguilla anguilla*) in some rivers, most notably the Tweed. The Tweed Salmon Fishers Association has given exclusive eel-catching rights to a local smoker who has been trusted not to catch salmon.

There is also a certain amount of farming of eels, one farm claims production of 100,000 eels per annum.

TECHNIQUE:
The eel-catcher/smoker takes his supply of eels in the autumn as they return to the sea after feeding. A fyke net is used for catching them; this is strung across the river, deflecting the eels left or right into closed ends where they are trapped. The fish are first starved in the river for about 2 weeks. After killing, they are immersed in brine then cold-smoked over oak chips for 6–7 hours. They are finished over hot smoke, which cooks them through, for about 3 hours.

REGION OF PRODUCTION:
SCOTLAND.

Smoked Salmon (Scotland)

DESCRIPTION:

Sold in whole, trimmed sides weighing 675g–2kg, or in smaller packs. Colour and flavour vary according to the cure and the quality of the fish – from the intense peatiness of a wild fish which has been slowly smoked over peat, to very lightly salted and delicately smoked farmed salmon. 'All smoked salmon is not created equal. Most aficionados give the nod to smoked Scotch salmon as the best. It is, as a rule, the least oily, the most subtly flavoured, has the firmest and most pleasing texture and the least amount of salt.'

HISTORY:

Preservation of salmon began with a method known as kippering, recorded early, in a document dated 1479, when a fishery was obliged to deliver 3 dozen salmon a year, either 'fresh or kippered', to a monastery in Fife.

The salmon sent for kippering had spawned and were therefore no longer in their prime. They were 'spent', lacking fat and moisture, hence easier to pickle and smoke. The Dutch word *kuppen*, meaning to spawn, was applied originally to a spent fish. By association, it was also applied to a kippered or spent salmon which had been cured. Kippered salmon is mentioned in the household book of King James V (d. 1542).

From an expedient way to deal with less-than-prime fish, a smoked salmon industry has developed with a variety of cures, for both wild and farmed fish, to suit all tastes, but with a jealously guarded reputation of quality. To safeguard this, a quality approval specification has now been drawn up covering all aspects of production. There is a Certified Quality Mark governing smoked salmon.

TECHNIQUE:

There was a time when kippering salmon was a job for the domestic cook – like the Scandinavians who continue to cure gravlax at home. McNeill (1929) describes 'To Kipper Salmon: A Modern Method', involving salt, demerara sugar, olive oil, rum or whisky. She suggests that the best flavour will be achieved if the fish is smoked in an outside shed without windows, used as a kiln, over a mixture of peat, oak chips and juniper wood.

Today, cures are all commercial and recipes closely guarded secrets. The basic method involves filleted sides. Salting may be dry or wet, the intention is to stabilize salt content to a minimum of approximately 3.5 per cent. The most common method is to lay the fish on trays of salt and sprinkle more salt over them by hand, how much extra depends on the taste of the customer. They are left for 12–24 hours. Smokehouses may add their own ingredients – sugar, juniper berries, herbs, molasses, rum or whisky – at the salting stage. Fillets are washed and left overnight to dry, laid out on wire mesh trays then wheeled on trolleys into electronically controlled smoking kilns. They are cold-smoked at 20–30°C, usually over smouldering oak chips, though some smokers continue to use peat. During the process, the temperature and moisture content are monitored and controlled. Some curers rest, or mature, the fish for 3–4 days at a low temperature.

REGION OF PRODUCTION:

Scotland.

COMPARE WITH:

Smoked Salmon (London Cure), South East England (p. 90)

Beef Shorthorn

DESCRIPTION:

Average live-weight of bull aged 16 months, 622kg. Flesh deeply red, well-marbled with intra-muscular cream fat. Flavour at its best when it has been hung 2–3 weeks.

HISTORY:

The Beef Shorthorn, or 'The Great Improver' as it has often been called, has a recorded history of over 200 years and has played a major part in the beef industry throughout the world. It is generally thought the pure Shorthorn was developed in Yorkshire in the late eighteenth century. The distinct yet related Scotch Shorthorn (later described as the Beef Shorthorn) was the consequence of work begun in the 1830s when Amos Cruickshank of Sittyton and his brother became tenants of an Aberdeenshire farm. By the 1870s, Cruickshank's bull calves were being sold to his neighbours for breeding. New herds were being built up and it was from this source of beef cattle that the breed was born. The beefy type of Shorthorn was eventually treated as a separate breed from the Dairy Shorthorn.

By the 1940s and 1950s, Beef Shorthorns were numbered in thousands and emphasis was put on the export market. The fashion was for early maturing 'baby beef', short and dumpy by today's standards. Fat animals were the order of the day and in the following decades the breed suffered a decline. As a result of some dedicated supporters, however, who have modernized the breed to ensure it meets the requirements of height and smooth fleshing, while still retaining the other qualities of flavour and character in the meat, it has experienced substantial revival. Because modern beef consumption requires a higher quality and taste, there has been a return to native breeds such as the Shorthorn. The bulk of the national herd is in Scotland, the remainder principally in North Yorkshire.

TECHNIQUE:

Beef Shorthorn are used in regions where there is a need for extensive farming, where ease of calving and hardiness are essential. Their eyes, skin pigment and coat texture ensure a greater tolerance of extreme weather conditions and their excellent feet and legs make them ideal for ranching. Carcasses are hung for 2–3 weeks.

REGION OF PRODUCTION:

Scotland.

Haggis

DESCRIPTION:

A cooked pudding of sheep's pluck in a sheep's stomach bag: the shape an oval misshapen ball. Weight: from 75–100g (individual size) to 4–5kg ('Chieftain' haggis to feed 20); the mean is 250–500g. Colour: greyish-cream. Flavour: peppery, sometimes with a strong liver taste.

HISTORY:

Though the habit of cooking the entrails of an animal stuffed into the stomach bag has an ancient ancestry, at least as far back as Roman cookery, the haggis's development in Britain has taken some curious twists. The word itself is English, not exclusively Scottish, its derivation unknown. There are plenty of medieval and early-modern English references to establish it was a dish eaten throughout Britain – especially in the highland zones where oatmeal was an acceptable grain. It was not always made with sheep's pluck. Calf and pig are mentioned by Gervase Markham (1615). Robert May (1660) devotes a section to 'Sheeps Haggas Puddings', and includes a fast-day version as well as one made with calf's paunch and innards. The dish also figures in much later English dialect glossaries, for example from Northumberland and Gloucestershire, but at some point in the eighteenth century, it begins to be perceived as specifically Caledonian. Hannah Glasse (1747) refers to 'Scotch haggass' (although suggesting it be made with calf's pluck) and Smollett writes in *Humphrey Clinker* (1771), 'I am not yet Scotchman enough to relish their singed sheep's-head and haggice.'

Around this time, Scotland's poet Robert Burns wrote his 'Address to a Haggis'. Drawing attention to the charms and usefulness of bringing together the odds and ends of offal in an economical 'Great Chieftain o' the Puddin race', he turned the humble haggis into a symbol of Scottish sense of worth. After his death in 1796, the Edinburgh literati honoured his memory with a supper where the haggis was piped in by a piper and addressed with Burns' poem in a ritual procedure. Burns' Suppers have continued to be celebrated every year around 25 January, the poet's birthday, and the haggis has become inextricably linked with Scotland and Burns. Today it is made by all Scottish butchers and several meat-processing companies to meet a year-round demand.

The ingredients have varied over the years. Fifteenth-century recipes use the liver and blood of the sheep, while later, in the 1600s, a meatless 'Haggas Pudding in a Sheep's Paunch' requires a highly seasoned mixture of oatmeal, beef suet, and onions; it was sewn up and boiled, and served after cutting a hole in the top to be filled with butter melted with two eggs. Another recipe uses a calf's paunch and entrails, minced with bread, egg yolks, cream, spices, dried fruits and herbs, served as a sweet with sugar and almonds. Meg Dods (1826) has what she calls a finer haggis, 'made by parboiling and skinning sheep's tongues and kidneys, and substituting these minced, for most of the lights [lungs], and soaked bread or crisped crumbs for the toasted meal [oatmeal]'.

Among professional haggis-makers there is some controversy about the correct ingredients, since not all use a sheep's pluck of liver, heart and lights (lungs) but add other meats, or pig or ox liver – deemed by purists to produce a haggis without the real 'haggis-flavour'. These recipes are closely guarded secrets. The recent winner of a competition remarked that his had come from an old butcher he had worked for who had only relinquished his recipe under pressure when on the point of retirement.

Haggis may be served in its skin with mashed potatoes and mashed turnip ('tatties and neeps'), or with clapshot (mashed potatoes and turnip mixed together). To reheat, it should be wrapped in foil and baked in the oven. 'Haggis meat,' said Meg Dods, 'for those who do not admire the natural shape, may be poured out of the bag, and served in a deep dish.' It may also be made in a long sausage shape, sliced and fried or grilled.

Haggis is made by many craft butchers and several larger companies. It is sent through the mails to expatriate Scots throughout the world.

TECHNIQUE:

The pluck or innards (liver, heart and lungs) are washed and put to boil until tender. When cool, the meat is chopped or minced finely and mixed with oatmeal (which may be pinhead, coarse or medium), onions, salt, pepper and spices. It is again put through a coarser mincer. The mixture is moistened, usually with meat gravy, and pumped into prepared natural or artificial casings which are then sealed. The haggis is boiled in water for about an hour, depending on size. The filling is always rather loose as it swells up to fill the skins during boiling.

REGION OF PRODUCTION:
SCOTLAND.

Highland Cattle

DESCRIPTION:
AVERAGE DRESSED CARCASS WEIGHT FOR 26-MONTH STEER, 280KG. FLESH DARK RED, MARBLED WITH INTRA-MUSCULAR CREAM FAT; LEAN EXTERNAL FAT. DEEP-FLAVOURED MEAT BECAUSE OF MATURITY; AT ITS BEST WHEN IT HAS BEEN HUNG 2–3 WEEKS.

HISTORY:
Before the Jacobite Rebellion of 1745, native Highland cattle were an important part of the clan-based economy. Used as a supply of milk, cheese and butter, the dairy cows were driven in the summer months to the mountain pastures. The women and children of the clan moved with them to live in sheilings (dwellings in the hills). While the women made cheese and butter, men herded the surplus cattle south along ancient drove roads to markets in Falkirk and Crieff where they were bought by graziers for finishing on more lush lowland pastures.

By the mid-nineteenth century the trade had reduced, partly on the break-up of the clan system following the Highland Clearances, partly because of demand for better quality beef. Those early cattle were often 4–5 years old, their carcasses did not provide the same tender meat as young beasts reared and fattened nearer the market on the new fodder crops.

Although in commercial decline, the breed was encouraged by certain lairds, notably the Stewart brothers of Harris, McNeil of Bara, and the Dukes of Hamilton and Argyll. Stock was selected from island and Highland populations, with no evidence of lowland blood. The breed society was founded in 1884 with 516 bulls listed in the first herd book. Most were black or dun. Some exports went to Canada in 1882 and, in the 1920s, more were made to the USA and South America. Now there has been a revival of interest, particularly for the quality of the lean meat. Butchers who specialize in pure Highland beef attract a loyal following.

TECHNIQUE:
Hardiness has remained a key characteristic of this breed. Like the Aberdeen-Angus, it is related to the Galloway. There is a common ancestry of primitive native stock. The Highland can survive well on rough mountain pasture with some additional feeding in winter. Because of their hardiness and very long, thick coats they withstand extreme cold and thrive outside during the winter.

REGION OF PRODUCTION:
SCOTLAND.

'*Better is a dinner of herbs where love is, than a stalled ox and hatred therewith.*'

PROVERBS, 15:17

Jellied Tripe

DESCRIPTION:

TRIPE, ONIONS, MILK, FLOUR AND SEASONINGS SET IN VARYING SIZES OF PLASTIC POT. COLOUR: CREAMY-WHITE IF MADE WITH BLEACHED TRIPE. FLAVOUR: A STRONG ONION TASTE, USUALLY WELL PEPPERED. MAY ALSO BE SET IN JELLIED COOKING LIQUOR WITHOUT THICKENING OR ONIONS.

HISTORY:

Tripe suppers were a feature of Edinburgh taverns through the eighteenth and well into the nineteenth centuries, supplied with plentiful quantities of cleaned tripe from the flesh-market. It was put in cutlet-sized pieces into a huge earthenware jar along with a knuckle bone or cowheel. The jar was covered and put into a cauldron of hot water and left at the side of the fire, just simmering, for about a day. The bone was removed, the contents left to set to a firm jelly then kept in a cool larder for future use. Scots were adventurous with their tripe, described in Meg Dods (1826) as evidence of 'good old French cookery', when the tripe was stewed in its liquor with herbs, onions, chives, wine, tarragon and mustard, the sauce thickened with flour.

During the twentieth century, their sense of adventure perhaps moderated. Included in the diet of the urban working classes as a cheap, sustaining meal, tripe's image deteriorated as it became associated with poverty and deprivation and a method of cooking which did not always enhance its qualities. It survives because of *aficionados* who have not only the cooking skills to make the most of its plebeian qualities, but also the sense not to be snobbish about its origins. Jellied tripe is brought home from the butcher's, then is reheated and eaten with boiled floury potatoes.

TECHNIQUE:

For the flour-thickened version, a white sauce is made with onions and the pre-cooked tripe, cut into small pieces, is added. It is poured into moulds and left to set. For the jellied version: the pre-cooked tripe is set in jellied stock without added gelatine or aspic. The tripe was originally unbleached.

REGION OF PRODUCTION:

SCOTLAND.

COMPARE WITH:

Tripe, North West England (p. 225)

Lorne Sausage

DESCRIPTION:

AN UNCASED, UNCOOKED, FRESH BEEF SAUSAGE WITH A SQUARE SECTION. CUT FROM A LARGE BLOCK AND SOLD IN SLICES APPROXIMATELY 10CM SQUARE, 1CM THICK. COLOUR: PINK. FLAVOUR: BEEF.

HISTORY:

This became associated in Glasgow with the comedian Tommy Lorne, a popular music-hall performer of the decades between the world wars who often made rude jokes about the Glasgow square sausage describing it as a 'doormat'. It was an important part of the urban eating habits of industrialized Scotland but remains popular. Known only in Glasgow as a Lorne sausage, the rest of the country refers to it as a square or sliced sausage. Its square, flat shape is a convenient fit for a morning roll along with a fried egg. The use of beef reflects the less prominent place that pig meat has in Scottish food habits.

TECHNIQUE:
Beef and fat in equal quantities are minced together and mixed with binder, seasonings and water. The mixture is then pressed into a Lorne tin (38cm long by 10cm at the top edge, tapering to 8cm at the base and holding 2kg of mixture). The surface is pressed by hand and the tin inverted on a tray immediately and the sausage turned out. It is left to set and harden in the refrigerator for several hours before slicing to order.

REGION OF PRODUCTION:
SCOTLAND.

Potted Hough

DESCRIPTION:
JELLIED MEAT (USUALLY BEEF) SET IN A POT, 125–250G. COLOUR: GREYISH BROWN. FLAVOUR: STRONGLY BEEF, SOMETIMES HIGHLY PEPPERED AND SPICED.

HISTORY:
This is a useful by-product for butchers, using tough and sinewy meat by boiling it with bones to a jelly. It was an economy food that took advantage of household scraps and was once made in domestic kitchens, but is now almost exclusively commercially produced. Recipes from the late 1800s (McNeill, 1929) show Scottish potted meats as closer to the English brawn of jellied pig's head than to those meat pastes ground in a mortar once made in the country-house kitchens of the wealthy.

The word hough (-gh pronounce as the -ch in Bach) means shin. The dish has extended its purview to take in similar bits of the animal such as head meat, knuckle and other bones. Some of this, although not all, is first pickled in brine. An alternative name in some butchers' shops is potted heid (head).

Hough became especially popular among the city poor, where it made a cheap meal with toast and tea. Today, in large housing schemes on the outskirts of towns, an independent butcher might make 15kg a week. Primarily a summer food, it is always eaten cold, often with pickled beetroot or salad.

TECHNIQUE:
Hough (shin of beef), head meat and bones are boiled for 6–12 hours. Mace and cloves are sometimes added. The pot is left to set overnight and fat which has risen and hardened can be removed. The meat is minced finely and the stock strained. They are mixed, seasoned and poured into wetted moulds.

REGION OF PRODUCTION:
SCOTLAND.

Scotch Pies

A ROUND, RAISED PIE OF COOKED BEEF OR MUTTON, GENERALLY 9CM DIAMETER, BUT SMALL-
ER ONES (5CM ACROSS) ARE ALSO MADE. THE HEIGHT IS 3.5–4CM TO THE TOP EDGE, WHICH
EXTENDS (BY ABOUT 1CM) BEYOND THE ROUND OF PASTRY WHICH COVERS THE FILLING, MAK-
ING A CENTRAL SPACE FOR HOLDING 'FILLINGS' OR GRAVY. COLOUR: PALE GOLD, THE TOP EDGE
USUALLY DARKER GOLD TO DARK BROWN. FLAVOUR: SOMETIMES QUITE PEPPERY.

HISTORY:

The pie (which is an English word of no certain derivation) was not indigenous to Scotland.
At one critical juncture, it was identified as a luxurious, immoral introduction from dissolute
England. In 1430, some years after the return of King James I from exile south of the border,
his subjects were upbraided by the Bishop of St Andrews for their 'wicked usage' and adoption of the manners of the sophisticated English. The consequence was a self-denying ordinance – a reduction in the elaboration of meals in the country at large. Only the gentry, henceforth, and only on feast days, would be served pies: 'this use of them not being knowne in
Scotland till that season' (Allen, 1994).

Scotch pies, once also commonly known as mutton pies, are descendants of these fifteenth-
century villains: a raised pie made with hot-water paste coaxed up the side of a mould, then left
to set and harden before the filling, is added. It is manufactured in a size suitable for a single serving.
Its popularity appears to have developed in the latter part of the nineteenth century as industrialization brought large numbers of people into cities, where wages were low and living (and cooking)
conditions poor. Made by local bakers, itinerant pie-men or -women or by tavern cooks, the 'hot-
pie' ('het-pey' in Dundee) became a sustaining convenience food for workers. They had to be
eaten hot: either hot from the bakers, or reheated at home. Some bakers who provided the 'hot-
pie' service also kept a jug of hot gravy for pouring into the centre of the pie. Tinned beans and
mashed potatoes became popular 'fillers' piled up in the space above the meat.

At first, the pie was always minced mutton, making use of tough, mature meat unsuitable
for other purposes. This has largely been superseded today by beef. McNeill (1929) quotes a
St Andrews professor describing the pies of his childhood which were made by the pie-wife:
'Delightful as were her pigeon and apple pies, her chef-d'oeuvre … was a certain kind of mut-
ton-pie. The mutton was minced to the smallest consistency, and was made up in standing
crust, which was strong enough to contain the most delicious gravy … There were no lumps
of fat or grease in them at all … They always arrived piping hot … It makes my mouth water
still when I think of those pies.'

On the West Coast, the most renowned pie-maker was also a woman, known as 'Granny
Black', whose tavern in the Candleriggs in Glasgow became Mecca for pie-lovers around the
early 1900s.

Though sold today from all bakeries on a daily basis, the hot-pie trade moves into mass-
production on Saturdays as they are delivered to football grounds for eating at half-time –
with a cup of hot Bovril. An average-sized baker's, with a football ground to supply on a
Saturday, could make 35,000 pies each week.

Smaller, half-size pies are made by a few bakers. The range of fillings has now extended
beyond plain and simple minced beef. Some are made with onion; others are still filled with

mutton as of old; some have chopped beef steak rather than mince, when they are described as steak pies; more adventurous concoctions may be suitable for vegetarians, perhaps a custard of cheese and tomato, macaroni cheese, or vegetables in a savoury custard. These last are mostly baked without the pastry lids.

TECHNIQUE:

A hot-water paste is made, but using beef dripping instead of the lard – rendered pig fat – used in England. The proportion of flour to fat is relatively high, about 4:1; this is shaped in the pie-moulding machine before it cools. The pie shells are left overnight to harden. The meat is prepared and seasoned with salt, pepper and other spices such as mace or nutmeg; this is used to fill the cases about half-full. The lids are placed on top and the pies baked in a very hot oven for 15–20 minutes.

REGION OF PRODUCTION:
SCOTLAND.

Abernethy Biscuit

DESCRIPTION:

A THIN, ROUND, FLAT BISCUIT PRICKED ON TOP, 65–85MM DIAMETER. WEIGHT: 15G. COLOUR: PALE GOLD. FLAVOUR AND TEXTURE: A SEMI-SWEET, CRISP BISCUIT BUT CONTAIN-ING LESS BUTTER AND SUGAR THAN SHORTBREAD, ORIGINALLY FLAVOURED WITH CARAWAY.

HISTORY:

Before the Norse invasions Abernethy (Tayside) was the seat of Pictish kings. The banal explanation of these biscuits' name is that they emanated from the eponymous burgh (Simon, 1960). A more fanciful tale suggests they are named for a surgeon, Dr John Abernethy (d. 1831), an ornament of St Bartholomew's Hospital in London. He had the habit of taking a lunchtime snack at the nearby baker's of hard captain's or ship's biscuits. Abernethy is reput-ed to have suggested to the baker, John Caldwell, that the biscuits might be more palatable with the addition of some sugar and caraway. As a result the new biscuit became very popular and Caldwell named them after his customer. How the recipe made the jump from London to Scotland is not explained. Abernethy himself was educated at Wolverhampton Grammar School and died at his home in Enfield, not a Scot at all.

Early recipes, for example Cassell (1896), Bond (1923) and Simon (1960), are for a dry biscuit with no more than an ounce of butter and sugar to a pound of flour. Modern recipes call for more fat and sugar and no flavouring with the caraway which was once universal.

TECHNIQUE:

Domestic recipes are based on 250g flour to 75g of both sugar and butter to 1 teaspoon bak-ing powder, 1 egg, 1 tablespoon milk and 1 teaspoon caraway seeds. The method involves mixing the dry ingredients, rubbing in the butter and mixing with the egg and milk to make a stiff dough. When rolled out, the centres are pricked with a fork and they are baked in a moderately hot oven for about 10 minutes. Commercial recipes are simpler, using only flour, sugar, fat, baking powder, salt and water, without caraway seeds.

REGION OF PRODUCTION:
SCOTLAND.

Bap

DESCRIPTION:

A SOFT ROLL, USUALLY ROUND, SOMETIMES OVAL OR TRIANGULAR; AN ABERDEEN BAP IS SQUARISH; FLAT-TOPPED AND FLOURY, SOMETIMES WITH A SINGLE INDENTATION IN THE MIDDLE TO PREVENT IT RISING TO A DOME. COLOUR: WHITE OR LIGHT BROWN UNDER A DUSTING OF FLOUR. FLAVOUR: SALTY.

HISTORY:

Bap is the Scots word for a soft morning roll. It is also known as floury bap, a simple reference to its dusting of flour. The origin of the word is obscure. McNeill (1929) suggests an analogy with pap, the Scots word for the mammary gland, because of its shape and size. Their first identified mention is in account rolls of the sixteenth century, and there are several references in later printed sources, for example Alan Ramsay's *Tea-table Miscellany* (1724-7). The word was a generic description (much as loaf is of bread), therefore the size and shape of baps has been extremely varied. A shearer's or harvester's bap, taken out into the fields at midday, was the size of a large meat plate (McNeill, 1929). Dean Ramsay's *Reminiscences of Scottish Life and Character* (1858) includes the question, 'Are ye for our burial baps round or square?' Another source confirms the truth: 'The grandfather of the late Prime Minister of Great Britain [W.E. Gladstone] kept a shop in Leith Walk in Edinburgh, where he sold "baps", flour, oatmeal, peas, etc., and where he was popularly known to the boys of the neighbour-hood as "Sma' Baps", because his baps were reputed to be smaller than those of his brother tradesmen' (Mackay, 1888).

Although softer in texture and crust, the bap fulfilled the same function for many Scots as the Glasgow roll (see above, p. 313): it was used as an envelope for a filling. Baps are split in half through the middle and buttered rather than broken up to eat. MacClure (1955) describes his earliest (and best) recollection: 'having it stuffed with Ayrshire bacon and a fried egg to eat while hastening to beat the bell for morning school … On these occasions it was still warm from the baker's oven.'

TECHNIQUE:

MacClure (1955) gives instructions for a bap: 'sift a pound of flour into a warmed bowl with a teaspoonful of salt, and you lightly rub in two ounces of lard. On the side in another bowl, you mix an ounce of yeast with a teaspoon of sugar until they become liquid, then you add half-a-pint of tepid water-and-milk mixed in equal proportions. This warmish liquid you strain into the flour, obtaining a soft dough. You cover this dough with a cloth, and leave it in a warm place for about an hour so that it will rise. Then you lightly knead your dough, which you divide into oval pieces, say about four-and-a-half inches long by about three wide. This makes a man-size bap. One hears of glazed baps, but they are unorthodox. 'Floury baps' are the thing. You brush the tops with milk, as if to give a glaze, but you immediately dust them with flour, which you repeat just before you place them in the oven. But before doing this last, you place the baps on a greased and floured oven-tray, and leave them for quarter-of-an-hour or so to prove. To stop the baps from blistering, you press a finger in their centres just before they go into the oven. This last should be fairly hot, and about twenty minutes should bake the man-size bap. The bap should go warm to the breakfast table.'

REGION OF PRODUCTION:

SCOTLAND.

Clootie Dumpling

DESCRIPTION:

A PUDDING STEAMED IN A CLOTH (CLOOT) – A ROUND, FLATTENED BALL-LIKE SHAPE, MORE CURVED AND ROUNDED ON THE UPPER SIDE WITH A SHINY LEATHER-LIKE SKIN, OFTEN SOLD CUT IN SLICES. A WHOLE DUMPLING WEIGHS APPROXIMATELY 900G (LARGE), 680G (MEDIUM), OR 113G (SMALL). COLOUR: LIGHT BROWN ON OUTSIDE, DARKER INSIDE, DEPTH OF COLOUR DEPENDS ON AMOUNT OF SPICES AND BLACK TREACLE. FLAVOUR AND TEXTURE: SPICY, SWEET, FRUITY.

HISTORY:

This pudding developed as a sweet version of the savoury pudding (haggis) stuffed into sheep's or pig's stomach bags and boiled in a large cauldron. Using instead a cotton or linen cloth, the sweet pudding mixture was made originally as the Scottish alternative to a baked celebration fruit cake for holidays, birthdays and during winter solstice celebrations, known in Scotland as the Daft Days.

Easily made in the common domestic setting where there was no oven and the cooking was done solely over a fire in a large pot, these special-occasion dumplings usually contained a selection of 'surprises': a ring signifying marriage, a coin – wealth, a button – bachelorhood, a thimble – spinsterhood, a wishbone – the heart's desire, a horse-shoe – good luck. Compared with rich celebration fruit cakes, or an English Christmas pudding, the dumpling mixture is much plainer. No hard and fast rules apply to the degree of richness, or even to the exact content since it has always been a rule-of-thumb affair, depending largely on the fortunes of the family.

Clootie dumpling is served with custard, cream or a bowl of soft brown sugar. When cold it is often fried with bacon and eggs for breakfast. Unlike Christmas pudding tradition south of the border it does not have the same strict linkage to mid-winter feasting.

TECHNIQUE:

A typical recipe is 125g self-raising flour, 175g fine white breadcrumbs, 125g beef suet, 2 teaspoons baking powder, 2 teaspoons each of freshly ground cinnamon, ginger and nutmeg, 175g sultanas, 175g California raisins, 2 tablespoons Golden Syrup, 2 tablespoons black treacle, 2 eggs, 1 large cooking apple, grated, 1 large carrot, grated, and milk to mix. Use a cotton or linen cloth 550mm square. To prepare the pot and cloth, fill a large pot with water, place a metal grid or upside-down saucer in the base. Bring to the boil and put in the cloth for a few minutes. Lift out with tongs and spread on a table. Sprinkle with plain flour, shake off excess. Put all the ingredients into a large bowl (add trinkets wrapped in greaseproof paper) and mix to a fairly stiff consistency with orange juice. Put in the centre of the cloth, bring up edges and tie with string, leaving space for expansion. Hold up the tied ends and pat the dumpling into a good round shape. Place in simmering water which should come about halfway up the dumpling, and simmer for 4 hours. Fill a large bowl with cold water. Lift out the dumpling and plunge into the cold water. Keep submerged for about a minute and this will release the cloth from the pudding skin. Put into a bowl about the same size as the dump-ling, untie the string, open out the cloth, place the serving-dish on top and reverse. Peel off the cloth and dry out the outer 'skin' in a warm place. Serve with sweetened double cream.

REGION OF PRODUCTION:

SCOTLAND.

These much-loved Scotch pancakes are small and thickish, served for tea with butter and jam. They were very much a part of my childhood, flipped over on the girdle as I came home from school. Traditionally Scotch pancakes are, of course, made on a girdle (griddle). If you have never used one before, it is easy: you can test it is hot enough by dropping a teaspoonful of the batter on to the surface. It should set almost at once – and, if it begins to bubble after one minute, the girdle is ready. The large bubbles tell you the pancakes are ready to be flipped over.

You can substitute the same amount of self-raising flour for the plain flour/cream of tartar/bicarbonate of soda combination, or use half buckwheat flour and half plain flour (omitting the sugar and adding a pinch of salt) to make cheat's blinis. Serve these with a horseradish cream made by combining a small tub of sour cream or crème fraiche with enough horseradish to taste. Spread this on to the pancakes then top with smoked salmon, caviar or herring roe and a snip of chives.

Sue Lawrence

FROM SUE LAWRENCE'S BOOK OF BAKING

Scotch Pancakes
Makes 12–16

115G/4OZ/1 CUP PLAIN FLOUR, SIFTED
½ TEASPOON CREAM OF TARTAR
¼ TEASPOON BICARBONATE OF SODA
1 TEASPOON GOLDEN CASTER SUGAR
1 MEDIUM FREE RANGE EGG
150ML/5FL OZ/⅔ CUP OF MILK
MELTED BUTTER FOR GREASING

Sift the flour, cream of tartar and bicarbonate of soda into a bowl and stir in the sugar. Add the egg and slowly add the milk, whisking all the time with a balloon whisk. Whisk until smooth.

Heat up a girdle (griddle) or frying pan; it will take at least three minutes. Once hot, smear with a little butter, then drop in four tablespoons of the batter to cook four pancakes at a time. After one and a half minutes you will see large bubbles. Flip the pancakes over and continue to cook for a further one minute or so until just done. Serve Warm.

Petticoat Tails

A SHORTBREAD BISCUIT BAKED IN A ROUND RESEMBLING THAT OF AN OUTSPREAD BELL-HOOP CRINOLINE PETTICOAT – WITH A SMALL CIRCLE CUT OUT OF THE CENTRE. THE BISCUIT IS THEN MARKED OR CUT INTO SEGMENTS. BECAUSE OF THE REMOVAL OF THE INNER CIRCLE, THERE IS NO LONGER A POINTED END TO EACH WEDGE OF BISCUIT, THUS AVOIDING UNTIDY BREAKAGE IN THE CRISP, CRUMBLY SHORTBREAD.

HISTORY:

There are several possible, and fanciful, explanations of the name. Hartley (1954) suggests they were originally called, in the twelfth century, *petty* [little] *cotes* [a small enclosure] *tallis* [a cut-out pattern from the cuts on sticks made for measuring or tallying]. This evolved into *petticote tallis* when the central round was removed and the biscuits formed the pattern of women's gored skirts or petticoats. Another theory is that it could be a corruption of the French *petites gatelles*, which were small French cakes popular with Mary, Queen of Scots, who is said to have brought them from France in 1560. However, *The Annals of The Cleikum Club*, the leading nineteenth-century gastronomic club, opined that 'in Scottish culinary terms there are many corruptions, though we rather think the name petticoat tails has its origin in the shape of the cakes, which is exactly that of the bell-hoop petticoats of our ancient Court ladies'.

Around the time of the Cleikum Club, Meg Dods (1829) wrote: 'Scotch petticoat-tails: Mix a half-ounce of caraway-seeds with the fourth of a peck of flour. Make a hole in the middle of the flour, and pour into it twelve ounces of butter melted in a quarter pint of milk, and three ounces of beat sugar. Knead this, but not too much, or it will become tough; divide it into two, and roll it out round rather thin. Cut out the cake by running a paste-cutter round a dinner pate, or any large round plate. Cut a cake from the centre of this one with a small saucer or large tumbler. Keep this inner circle whole, but cut the outer one into eight petticoat tails. Bake all these on paper laid on tins, serve the round cake in the middle of the plate, and the petticoat-tails as radii round it.'

Today the differences between shortbread and petticoat tails are shape, thickness and texture. Though some producers make both from the same mixture, others make a less gritty, softer, more melting biscuit for petticoat tails. Shortbread manufacturers have exploited the distinctive shape, treating it as a luxury requiring special packaging.

TECHNIQUE:

Although the proportions of flour, butter and sugar are the same as shortbread (approximately 6:4:2), those producers who make a distinction between the texture of shortbread and petticoat tails replace some of the flour with cornflour and some of the sugar with icing sugar. The method is to mix the butter and sugar together and then work them into the flour to make a firm, pliable dough which is rolled out and shaped. It is baked in a slow oven (150°C) until uniformly pale, golden brown.

REGION OF PRODUCTION:

SCOTLAND.

Scone

DESCRIPTION:

GIRDLE AND OVEN SCONES ARE ROUND OR TRIANGULAR (FARL) IN SHAPE; SODA GIRDLE SCONES ARE APPROXIMATELY 150MM ROUNDS, OTHER SCONES ARE 50–70MM DIAMETER. COLOUR: FROM DARK BROWN (MADE WITH TREACLE) TO FLOURY-WHITE.

POTATO SCONES: A FARL (TRIANGULAR) SHAPE IS MOST COMMON, BUT THEY ARE OCCASIONALLY ROUND, 100–150MM ACROSS, ABOUT 5MM THICK. THEY ARE MOTTLED ON THE SURFACE, CREAM OR WHITE INSIDE; THEIR FLAVOUR IS UNSWEETENED, SALTY, REDOLENT OF POTATO AND THEIR TEXTURE IS SMOOTH.

HISTORY:

This is a composite entry for 2 distinct varieties of a single Scottish food type. A scone is a small round piece of dough, more or less enriched and cooked either upon a girdle – a flat iron plate heated on the flame – or baked in an oven. They may be made with barley or wheaten flour, or have an addition of potato. They may be chemically leavened or, in the case of barley, not leavened at all.

The word scone appears to have been adopted first by the Scots though it is also common in England. Scots pronounce it with a short vowel as in 'gone' while the southern English pronunciation is usually with a diphthong rhyming with 'stone'. The word is thought to have been adopted from the Dutch *schoonbrot* meaning fine white bread. The poet Robert Burns refers to them as 'souple [soft] scones, the wale [choicest] of food'. It is most likely his would have been made with barley meal, cooked to a porridge with water and salt, then small spoonfuls removed from the pan, pressed out on a board floured with barley meal and fired on both sides on the girdle until browned – a method described in Clark (1909). What he was referring to was not the soft, baking-powder scone common today, but to the pliability or suppleness which is still the criterion for a good potato scone. The softness was a notable change from hard-tack oatcakes.

The fugitives who 'lay upon the bare top of a rock, like scones upon a girdle,' in Robert Louis Stevenson's *Kidnapped* would have found themselves in the transitional period, between old-fashioned thin barley-meal scones, baked on the girdle, and oven scones. Modern bakers have transferred most, but not all, scones to the oven. Despite this, the demand for girdle-baked scones continues and every Scottish baker has a large hot-plate where daily he girdle-bakes a supply of soda scones, potato scones, pancakes and crumpets. When English supermarket chains started putting in-store bakeries into their Scottish branches, they were obliged to put in hot-plates for girdle-baking. Although early scones were yeast-raised, most of those now produced and eaten in Scotland and the rest of Britain are chemically aerated.

Scones baked in the oven, using wheaten flour and raised with chemical agents, developed as the Scots population acquired baking powder in the 1860s and baking ovens became a more common domestic appliance. With the appearance of a new commercial form – the tea-room – in Glasgow around the same time, these scones became a tea-bread item presented to customers on the decorative 3-tiered stand. Freshly baked scones were essential daily fare for both afternoon and high teas, spread with butter and jam. Modern oven scones comprise the whole gamut of base materials and added flavours or ingredients. They may be made with wheaten flour (wholemeal or white), oatmeal or barley meal, butter or buttermilk, soured milk or fresh milk, treacle, honey, cream, herbs, spices, nuts, dates, fruit or cheese. Although Scotland is properly their region of origin, oven scones are now baked throughout Britain. Few English people would appreciate that this was as Scottish as oatmeal porridge.

It is not clear when the habit of baking scones with mashed potato added to the flour developed. They were certainly known in the 1930s when the novelist Dorothy L. Sayers addressed a foreword in one of her books to a Scottish hotel keeper, remarking that she would 'come back next summer for some more potato scones'. They are also colloquially known as tattie scones. Potato scones are sold in packets, from groceries as well as bakeries, and may be heated and rolled with butter and jam for tea, or fried with bacon for breakfast.

TECHNIQUE:
For girdle scones, the butter is rubbed into the flour and raising agents, and the ingredients mixed to a soft dough with fresh milk (if baking powder) or buttermilk (if baking soda). It is shaped into a large round marked into triangles or cut into individual scones. A scone is distinguished from the large round bannock by its size and shape.

For oven scones, mixing and shaping may be the same as for girdle scones. They are baked in a hot oven (230°C) for 15–20 minutes.

For potato scones, butter is melted with the potatoes which are mashed and mixed into the flour with milk to make a stiff dough. This is rolled out to a large thin round the size of a meat plate, marked into triangles and baked on both sides on a hot girdle.

REGION OF PRODUCTION:
SCOTLAND.

Scottish Cookie

DESCRIPTION:
A ROUND BUN, 90MM DIAMETER, 40–50MM HIGH. COLOUR AND TEXTURE: GOLDEN EGG-GLAZED SURFACE, PALE YELLOWISH, OPEN-TEXTURED INTERIOR. FLAVOUR: YEASTY, SLIGHTLY SWEET.

HISTORY:
The cookie is an enriched yeast dough bun with a glazed top but without the dried fruit usual in English teacakes. If offered plain, it is split and spread with butter and jam. Or it might have a sugar icing on the top, when it becomes an iced cookie; or be split and filled with cream, thus transformed into a cream cookie. Scottish branches of English supermarket chains have taken to offering cream cookies as Devon splits, which is a gross error of nomenclature.

The name appears to have come from the Teutonic *koeck* (Belgian, *koekie*; Dutch, *koekje*), the diminutive of cake. There are various references to cookies over the last 300 years: for example a 'cukie' is mentioned in domestic accounts of the seventeenth century and Sir Walter Scott in The *Antiquary* writes, 'Muckle [much] obliged to ye for your cookies, Mrs Shortcake.' A later appearance is by R.M. Williamson in 1929: 'I want a plain ham and egg tea, … and some cookies and cakes.' The Scots cookie joined other tea breads on the ornamental cake stands which decorated the centre of tables in Glasgow's innovative tea rooms at the turn of the last century. Originally privately owned, these were later taken over by bakery companies, who ran them until the beginning of the Second World War, selling a sophisticated range of Scottish baking including girdle-baked items like crumpets, pancakes and girdle scones which took their place usually on the middle tier. Cream and iced cookies were special treats on the top tier.

The Scottish cookie should not be confused with the flat, round biscuit which goes under the same name in North America.

TECHNIQUE:
A yeasted dough enriched with butter, milk and eggs. The cookies are baked for 10 minutes at 220°C. To make a cream cookie, the bun is split diagonally through the top, slightly to one side of the centre, and filled with piped cream. The whole surface is dusted with icing sugar.

REGION OF PRODUCTION:
SCOTLAND.

Scottish Crumpet

DESCRIPTION:
A ROUND BREAD PITTED WITH HOLES ON ONE SIDE AND A UNIFORM SURFACE ON THE OTHER; 120–150MM DIAMETER, 5MM HIGH. COLOUR: GOLDEN BROWN ON THE UNIFORM SURFACE, PALER ON THE LACY SURFACE. FLAVOUR AND TEXTURE: SWEET.

HISTORY:
The Scottish crumpet is thinner than both a girdle pancake or scone and the English bread that also goes under the name. The derivation is also unlike its southerly cousin. In the seventeenth century, there emerged a cake called the 'crompid cake', that is curled cake, from the verb to crump or crimp, because it curled or bent in the cooking on the girdle. Calling this a 'cake' was no more than the literal use of the word. Cakes were bread, distinguished either by their regularity of shape (and that they were not a great undistinguished loaf) or by their particular, sometimes fanciful, ingredients. The latter distinction is all that matters in modern usage. At first, it was the shape that counted most: thus oatcakes or pancakes, or the statement, 'Scotland is the land of cakes'.

Crumpets' development in Scotland may have a connection with the Shrove Tuesday pancake. It appears likely that they are a progression from the old Scottish car-cakes, mentioned by Sir Walter Scott in *The Bride of Lammermoor*. Car-cakes were made for Fastern's E'en (the Scottish equivalent of Shrove Tuesday) and are described in Jamieson's *Dictionary of the Scottish Language* (1818) as, 'a kind of thin cake, made of milk, meal or flour, eggs beaten up, and sugar'.

The Scots crumpet joined other tea-breads on the ornamental cake stands which decorated the centre of tea tables in Glasgow's tea rooms at the turn of the century. Girdle-baked items like crumpets, pancakes and girdle scones took their place on the middle tier.

TECHNIQUE:
The batter is more runny than for pancakes or drop scones and the crumpet is much the thinner when cooked. The ingredients and method of cooking, however, are the same as the Scottish pancake (see below).

REGION OF PRODUCTION:
SCOTLAND.

Scottish Pancake

A DISC, UNIFORM ON BOTH SIDES, 70–90MM DIAMETER, 15MM HIGH. COLOUR: GOLDEN BROWN.

HISTORY:
This is known as a drop or dropped scone in England, and also sometimes in Scotland. The thick, aerated Scottish version should not be confused with a thin, unleavened English pancake. In Scottish bakeries today the description of pancake for the thick, aerated version is the one generally in use. This is a concept which has now been fairly well fixed in people's minds with the development of the similar (but much larger diameter) American thick pancakes featured in themed pancake-restaurants.

TECHNIQUE:
A thickish batter is mixed with flour, egg, sugar and either buttermilk and bicarbonate of soda or sweet milk and baking powder. It is poured in spoonfuls on a hot girdle and cooked for about 2 minutes, then turned and cooked for another minute. It is wrapped while warm to preserve its freshness. The pancake is a thicker item than the Scots crumpet and made with a thicker batter.

REGION OF PRODUCTION:
SCOTLAND.

Shortbread

DESCRIPTION:
MADE IN MANY SHAPES AND SIZES – SMALL AND LARGE ROUNDS, FINGERS AND WEDGES – THICKNESS 5–25MM. COLOUR: PALE, EVENLY GOLDEN. FLAVOUR AND TEXTURE: BUTTERY-SWEET; CRUMBLY TEXTURE VARYING FROM FINE TO COARSE.

HISTORY:
The term short, used to describe a friable, brittle, crumbling texture, whether of food, soil or metal, has been applied since medieval times (*OED* quotes a cookery manuscript of *c.* 1430). Early examples in printed books include the short-paste that was made for Lent (*Good Huswife's Handmaide*, 1594) or the short paste as an alternative to puff paste used by Robert May (1660). (See Congreve under Shrewsbury cake, p. 175.) Later the word was also prefixed to cake and bread. The first published Scottish cookery book, by Mrs McLintock (1736), says: 'To make Short Bread, Take a Peck of Flour, put three lb of Butter in among a little water, and let it melt, pout it in amongst your Flour, put in a Mutchkin of good Barm; when it is wrought divide it in 3 parts, roll out your cakes longer than broad, and gather from the sides with your Finger, cut through the Middle and job [jab, prick] it on Top, then send it to the oven.' By the 1850s, this yeast-leavened shortbread had been abandoned and the recipe modified to something more akin to modern style: a crumbling biscuit texture more befitting its description.

Although now an everyday food, it was originally a festive treat, flavoured and decorated accordingly. Meg Dods (1826) describes how she put more almonds and butter into a rich shortbread she intended to send 'as a holiday present to England'. Baked about an inch thick to withstand transport, this rich shortbread was flavoured with candied citron and orange peel

'Kissing don't last: cookery do!'

GEORGE MEREDITH

and blanched almonds, the top strewn with caraway comfits. In time, it became known as a Pitcaithly Bannock, made originally by a woman in Pitcaithly (Perthshire). Besides its use as a present, it was also associated with the Yule season, embracing Christmas and Hogmanay, when thick round shortbread, a version of the old Yule bannock, was eaten.

Today, manufacturers continue to exploit shortbread's potential for flavour innovations by adding chocolate, ginger, almonds and so on. Some years ago the Scottish Association of Master Bakers was challenged by a government ruling threatening to classify shortbread as a common biscuit. Arguing rather that it was an item of flour confectionery, an amicable agreement was achieved and shortbread, though indeed eaten mostly as a common biscuit, retains its position as a special confection.

TECHNIQUE:

The ingredients are plain flour, including a small amount of rice flour for the gritty texture, butter and sugar in a ratio of 6:4:2 to make a firm but pliable dough which is rolled out and shaped. It is baked in a slow oven (150°C) until a pale golden brown.

REGION OF PRODUCTION:

SCOTLAND.

Square Loaf

DESCRIPTION:

A LOAF WITH STRAIGHT, SOFT SIDES AND CLOSE-TEXTURED CRUMB; ABOUT 190MM LONG, 60MM WIDE, 80MM TALL. COLOUR: DARK BROWN TO ALMOST BLACK ON TOP AND 'HEEL' END. FLAVOUR: SALTY.

HISTORY:

This loaf shape, also called plain loaf or batch bread, appears to have developed in the cities of Scotland during the industrialization of the late nineteenth and early twentieth centuries. The loaves were 'set so close together in the oven that they touch, in which case crumb instead of crust forms on the sides and the type becomes a crumby loaf' (Banfield, 1947). As modern bakers point out, it was an economical loaf to bake since the loaves rose upwards rather than outwards, giving their characteristic height. Banfield goes on to say that Scotland and Ireland have a 'strong penchant for bread so baked'. Though the loaf itself is not actually square, when a slice is cut in half it forms a square. It was a working-class, city alternative to the crusty country loaf and formed an important part of the diet.

A square loaf was a batch bread. The oven was charged with a group of loaves which touched as they expanded so that they were almost a single mass when cooked. This assured the lack of crust. Because there was a limit to lateral expansion, the loaves rose much higher than bread that had space around it in the oven. This gave it the aerated texture increasingly favoured by the British. Other loaf shapes, for instance the cottage loaf and bloomer, might also be cooked on the batch principle – especially in urban bakeries with strong pressure of trade provoking high productivity and economic prudence. The square loaf may once have been baked on the sole of the oven, each piece of dough lovingly delivered there off the baker's peel. Nowadays, however, the baker is allowed to work in the cool of the kitchen to make up a large tin containing 24 loaves which can be loaded into the oven at once.

A variation on the square is a pan loaf. This is baked in a long tin with a tight-fitting lid. Each tin holds 4 loaves in a line. As they are put into the tin, the surface which touches its neighbour is brushed with fat. When the closed tin is placed in the oven, the rising dough fills it completely and the loaves are perfectly square when removed. The loaves are broken apart when cooled. The pan is a slightly richer bread, made originally with milk powder, sugar and butter (Banfield, 1947). The result is even softer and less crusty than a batch bread.

In city culture, a class distinction developed between those who ate 'plain' and those with aspirations, who ate 'pan'; a distinction which was transferred to speech, when 'pan-loaf' became a common term for those who deliberately changed their city vernacular accent into a more polished, sophisticated form.

These loaves were central to everyday life in Scotland for they were the perfect shape for lunch pieces (sandwiches) packed into square lunch boxes sometimes with a square sausage (see Lorne sausage, above). The Jeely (i.e. jam) 'Piece Song' (Adam McNaughton, *Noise and Smoky Breath*, 1983) describes them being also spread with jam and thrown out of tenement windows by mothers to their children playing in the back courts.

REGION OF PRODUCTION:
SCOTLAND.

Mixed Boilings

DESCRIPTION:
THIS IS A COLLECTION OF BOILED SWEETS, SOLD BY WEIGHT FROM A JAR WHICH CONTAINS A SELECTION OF THE FOLLOWING: BLACK-STRIPPIT (STRIPED) BALLS, A ROUND BALL WITH BLACK AND WHITE STRIPES, STRONGLY FLAVOURED WITH PEPPERMINT; SOOR PLOOMS [SOUR PLUMS], ROUND, BRIGHT GREEN, STRONGLY ACIDIC, LIME-FLAVOURED; ANISEED BALLS, ROUND, ANISEED FLAVOUR; HOREHOUND TOFFEES, USUALLY TRIANGULAR, FLAVOURED WITH ESSENCE OF WHITE HOREHOUND; CINNAMON BALLS, ROUND BALLS, FLAVOURED WITH OIL OF CINNAMON; BUTTERSCOTCH ROCK, SMALL BITE-SIZED PIECES, WITH A RICH BUTTER FLAVOUR; BARLEY SUGAR, A ROUND OR TRIANGULAR BOILING WITH A CLEAR GOLDEN SHINE; LIME ROCK, SHARPLY FLAVOURED; RHUBARB ROCK, SHOCKING PINK WITH A BRIGHT PALE GREEN CENTRE AND SHARP FLAVOUR; RUM TOFFEE, A HARD ROUND BALL, FLAVOURED WITH RUM. COMPOSITION: SUGAR, GLUCOSE, FLAVOURINGS, COLOURINGS.

HISTORY:
These bright mixtures have been made since at least the late nineteenth century. Craftsmen sugar-boilers and itinerant sweet-sellers provided a rich supply of colourful sweeties remembered by F.M. McNeill (1929): 'Besides such homely sweets as gundy, glessie, cheugh jeans and black man, there were bottles of "boilings" (Scotch mixtures) that glittered like rubies, emeralds and topazes and all the jewels of the Orient, and tasted of all the fruits of the orchard and spices of the Indies.' Many of the individual items within the mixtures have been known for as long as Scotland has had sweeties; barley sugar (along with tablet) is one of the earliest. It appears in Mrs McIver's list of Scottish National Dishes (1773), and was made originally with barley water (the water strained from cooking barley). Horehound, *Marrubium vulgare*, is a herb used as an ancient remedy for colds and coughs (see cough candy, p.236). Soor

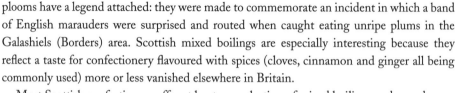

plooms have a legend attached: they were made to commemorate an incident in which a band of English marauders were surprised and routed when caught eating unripe plums in the Galashiels (Borders) area. Scottish mixed boilings are especially interesting because they reflect a taste for confectionery flavoured with spices (cloves, cinnamon and ginger all being commonly used) more or less vanished elsewhere in Britain.

Most Scottish confectioners offer at least one selection of mixed boilings and may do seasonal ones such as 'winter mixtures' of items considered especially warming like clove rock, aniseed balls, ginger drops, lemon rock and farmers' friends. Others offer variations such as 'mixed balls': striped round sweets in various colours and flavours.

A similar habit of selling mixed boiled sweets exists in parts of northern England, where they are known as 'Yorkshire Mixtures'; containing types of rock, mint balls, barley sugar, and fruit-flavoured drops in fish shapes.

TECHNIQUE:
There is little difference between the technique for boiled sweets and for mixed boilings. Sugar, water and glucose are boiled to 148–160°C, depending on the manufacturer and the exact nature of the confection. On removal from the heat, the sugar is poured on to a slab and divided into portions which are coloured and flavoured as required. For sweets such as black striped balls or rhubarb rock, some of the mixture is stretched or 'pulled' and used for striping the remainder of the batch before shaping into balls or sticks. For butterscotch, butter is added to the sugar during boiling.

REGION OF PRODUCTION:
SCOTLAND.

Tablet

DESCRIPTION:
SUGAR CANDY IN OBLONG BLOCKS 15–20MM THICK, MARKED INTO 30MM SQUARES. COLOUR: PALE TO DARK BROWN. FLAVOUR AND TEXTURE: VERY SWEET; CRISP BUT MELTING. COMPOSITION: SUGAR, THIN CREAM OR MILK, SOMETIMES BUTTER. VARIANTS MAY CONTAIN CINNAMON, COCONUT, GINGER, LEMON, ORANGE, PEPPERMINT, VANILLA, WALNUT, CHOCOLATE.

HISTORY:
First used as a sweet vehicle for sour medicines, medicinal tablets were made by apothecaries in both England and Scotland. The term was abandoned in England but continued in Scotland, transferring to an item of confectionery as sugar from the West Indies became plentiful in the nineteenth century. Earlier entries have referred to Scotland's distinctive confectionery but tablet has arguably the longest history. Certainly it is now the most widely made, with national rather than regional repute. Early documentation is in the household book of Lady Grisell Baillie (1692–1733) referring to 'taiblet for the bairns'.

While Grisell Baillie was buying tablet for her children, Mrs McLintock, author of the first published Scottish cookery book, was writing recipes for 'tablets'. To make Orange Tablets with the Grate [zest]; To make Rose Tablets; To make Ginger Tablets; and To make Cinnamon Tablets: 'Take half an ounce of cinnamon, beat and search [sieve] it, or take four Guts [drops] of the Spirit of Cinnamon [distilled bruised cinnamon and rose water] to a pound of sugar; take half a mutchkin of water, clarify it with the white of an egg, put it on a slow fire, and boil it till it be almost candy'd and put in the four Guts of the Spirit of Cinnamon, mix them well together, rub the papers wither with sweet oil or fresh butter and pour it out, and cut them in small four corner's pieces.'

Today tablet is distinguished from fudge by its crisp bite. The degree of bite depends on the richness of the ingredients. Tablet has less butter and glucose than fudge; it is also boiled to a slightly lower temperature.

TECHNIQUE:
Sugar, water, single cream and/or milk (sometimes condensed milk), butter (commercial makers also add glucose and/or fondant while some domestic recipes suggest syrup or vinegar) are boiled to 115°C (soft ball). While still hot, the mixture is beaten until it begins to grain slightly. It is poured into a buttered tray and left until just set before marking into small squares.

REGION OF PRODUCTION:
SCOTLAND.

Grain And Blended Whisky

DESCRIPTION:
WHISKY IS A DISTILLED LIQUOR MADE FROM BARLEY, MALTED FOR MALT WHISKY, BUT NOT FOR GRAIN. EACH HAS ITS DISCRETE MANUFACTURING PROCESS AS WELL AS RAW INGREDIENT. A GRAIN WHISKY HAS A QUIETER PERSONALITY WHICH MAKES IT OFTEN, THOUGH NOT ALWAYS, LESS INTERESTING THAN A MALT. A BLENDED WHISKY IS A BLEND OF BOTH MALT AND GRAIN WHISKIES. IN COLOUR THEY VARY FROM PALE TO DARK GOLD AND ARE USUALLY AROUND 40 PER CENT PROOF. MOST GRAIN WHISKY IS USED TO SOFTEN AND LIGHTEN A BLEND AND THERE ARE ONLY 2 COMPANIES WHICH PUT STATED-AGE SINGLE GRAINS IN A BOTTLE.

HISTORY:
Grain whisky developed after the invention in 1832, by Irishman Aeneas Coffey, of the patent still which allowed distillation to take place in a continuous process in a single still. Whisky could be produced more cheaply but the method yielded a less characterful result than the malted-grain whiskies made in the pot still.

In the 1850s, however, the face of the industry was changed when the Edinburgh merchant, Andrew Usher, who was the agent for Glenlivet, vatted together several casks from his stocks, producing a more consistent product. Vatting was soon extended to the blending of malt and grain, producing a lighter spirit which the English, unused to the much stronger malt, found more palatable. This was timely as the stocks of brandy declined in the 1870s and 1880s as a result of the phylloxera blight in France.

The 1890s was a period of unprecedented growth. New malt distilleries were opened and commercial groups like Distillers and the North British Distillery Company, serving the interests of the grain distillers and the blenders respectively, became phenomenally successful.

Blending whisky is a highly developed skill: each brand is made to a specific recipe. Well-known brands like Famous Grouse and Bell's may have as many as 20–50 different whiskies in their make-up. Blending assembles the best degrees of whisky's richness – flavour, aroma,

texture, mellowness and strength – without allowing any of the intrusive extremes of pungency, high strength, smokiness or blandness to dominate. Like sherry and champagne, the blend aspires to improvement rather than merely making something acceptable out of constituents that are unbalanced or flawed. Whiskies used in blended Scotch are available as whiskies in their own right and good blends will have 45–60 per cent malt content.

Alternative recipes have developed on the safe foundation of mainstream blended Scotch. De luxe blends are recognized as of superior quality, usually with a higher proportion of better-quality, longer-matured malts. They command substantial premiums, especially in export markets. There are also liqueurs based on blended whisky, for instance flavoured with honey, fruits, herbs and spices or cream (Drambuie, Glayva, Heather Cream).

TECHNIQUE:

Grain distilleries use continuous patent stills. The process is similar to that of making malt whisky up to the point of distillation, although everything takes place on a much larger scale and with much less malted barley. Distillation is carried out in 2 large cylindrical columns which are linked by pipes. The wash passes into the first column, the rectifier, in a coiled pipe running through its length. Jets of steam are forced up into the column through a series of perforated plates between which the coiled pipe passes, heating the wash inside before it passes out and into the analyser. In the analyser the wash is no longer in the coiled pipe, and it is now met by another jet of steam passing through more perforated plates.

The steam and evaporated alcohol rise and are passed back into the rectifier, cooling as it moves up, encountering fresh cold wash in the coiled pipe on the way down, until it reaches a cold water coil where it condenses before passing out to the still. The impure alcohols in the first and last part of the distillate can be redistilled while the alcohol which reaches the spirit safe and receiver is very pure. The whisky will mature faster than malt and is less subject to variable factors.

Blended whisky will be married in oak (often sherry) casks for at least a year to allow intermingling and further maturation to take place. As with most malts, the blend is reduced to the correct strength with the addition of water. There are at least 2,000 commercial blends. The major blenders own both grain and malt distilleries. All grain distilleries are located in the Lowlands of Scotland with the exception of Invergordon. Blending occurs throughout the country.

REGION OF PRODUCTION:
SCOTLAND.

Malt Whisky

DESCRIPTION:

MALT WHISKY HAS SPECIFIC, SOMETIMES VERY PRONOUNCED, FLAVOURS AND AROMAS WHICH COME FROM A NUMBER OF FACTORS: THE QUALITY OF THE WATER, THE MALTED BARLEY, THE AMOUNT OF PEAT USED IN DRYING THE GRAIN, THE SHAPE OF THE POT STILL, THE TYPE OF WOOD IN WHICH IT MATURES, THE LENGTH OF TIME IT HAS MATURED AND THE TEMPERATURE AND HUMIDITY CONDITIONS DURING MATURATION. THE RANGE OF CHARACTER GOES FROM DEEP, PUNGENT, SMOKY AND EARTHY TO LIGHT, SUBTLE, GENTLE

AND SWEET. COLOUR IS PALE STRAW TO DEEP GOLD. MALT IS AROUND 40 PER CENT PROOF.

DISTINCTION IS MADE BETWEEN HIGHLAND AND LOWLAND MALTS. THE DIVIDING LINE IS THE HIGHLAND BOUNDARY FAULT WHICH RUNS FROM THE FIRTH OF CLYDE IN THE WEST TO THE FIRTH OF TAY. IN THE HIGHLAND AREA THERE ARE FURTHER DIFFERENCES: SPEYSIDERS HAVE THEIR MELLOW, MALTY SWEETNESS; CAMPBELTOWN'S LIGHTLY PEATY MELLOWNESS COMPARES WITH ISLAY'S NOTABLY STRONGER PEATY FLAVOURS; NORTH HIGHLAND MALTS FROM INVERNESS TO WICK HAVE A DRY FRUITY-SWEETNESS, NOT NOTICEABLY PEATY; THE SOUTHERN MALTS NEAR PERTHSHIRE AND TO THE WEST ARE SOFT, LIGHT IN CHARACTER, OFTEN SWEET BUT SOME QUITE DRY; THE SMALL NUMBER OF WEST HIGHLAND MALTS BETWEEN OBAN AND FORT WILLIAM ARE SMOOTH AND ROUNDED; THE EASTERN HIGHLAND MALTS ALONG THE NORTH SEA COAST FROM BRECHIN TO BANFF HAVE A WIDE RANGE OF STYLES FROM FRUITY-SWEET TO PEATY-DRY; THE ISLAND MALTS OF JURA, MULL, SKYE AND ORKNEY (EXCLUDING ISLAY) HAVE A WIDE RANGE FROM DRY TO FULL, SWEET AND MALTY. LOWLAND MALTS ARE GENERALLY LESS ASSERTIVE; SOFT, LIGHT WITH A GENTLE SWEETNESS.

IN DESCRIBING A BOTTLE, THE TERM SINGLE MALT INDICATES WHISKY PRODUCED BY AN INDIVIDUAL DISTILLERY, WHILE VATTED MALT IS A BLEND FROM 2 OR MORE.

HISTORY:

The Scots word whisky derives from the Gaelic *uisge beatha* meaning water of life – in Latin *aqua vitae* – the common European root words for distilled spirit. While its origins in Scotland are hazy, its fortunes have had some dramatic ups and downs since the first written reference in 1494 in the Scottish Exchequer Rolls as a commercial product made in monasteries: 'eight bolls of malt to Friar John Cor wherewith to make aquavitae.'

The particular connection of malt whisky with the Highlands was a result of enthusiasm for home distilling, to use surplus barley and produce a warming drink against a cold, inhospitable climate. It was drunk with meals at least 3 times a day and commonly given as a restorative to children.

In every Highland glen sacks of barley would be soaked in water, possibly in the burn, for a few days to soften the grain and begin germination. Then the grain would be spread to allow it to sprout, halted by drying over a peat fire. The malted grain would then go into a large tub with boiling water and yeast to ferment. Once fermented, it would be passed twice through the pot still and the middle cut (the drinkable part, without the dangerous methyl alcohols) would be separated from the foreshots and the aftercuts or feints. It was a skilled operation which produced a liquor strongly influenced by the local water and peat and much more highly esteemed than anything distilled in the Lowlands. The Highlanders' distilling activities grew and developed until the Union in 1707 when the government began to tax them. For over 100 years, until the Excise Act in 1823, the Highlanders smuggled their malted whisky illicitly with great ingenuity. But the passing of the act signalled the beginning of a new era of development and success for the Highlanders' malt whisky as old smugglers became legitimate and linked their considerable skills to the business of large-scale production.

For the rest of the century and until about the 1920s the malt distilleries flourished. The First World War, prohibition in America and then the Second World War and its aftermath, meant a slump which lasted until the 1950s. Thereafter, an export-led recovery was under way. New distilleries were built in the 1960s, old ones reopened and the production of malt whisky quadrupled in a decade. This upturn in fortunes has, on the whole, continued, with an emphasis on quality and individual character as the range and variety of distinctive malts has become more widely appreciated.

TECHNIQUE:
The barley is soaked, spread out on the malting floor and turned daily until it sprouts. Germination is stopped by drying over a peat fire in a malt kiln. It is milled roughly and put into a mash tun and mixed with hot water until its sugars are dissolved producing a wort, when the solid remains of the barley are removed. The wort is cooled and mixed with yeast which converts it in about 2 days to a low-strength, alcoholic liquor known as the wash. This passes through first the wash still and then the spirit still, the middle cut is separated from the feints and foreshots and the spirit transferred to a vat to be mixed with water before transferring to casks where it must mature for 3 years before sale. Most will mature 8–15 years.

REGION OF PRODUCTION:
SCOTLAND.

Heather Honey

DESCRIPTION:
THIS IS SELDOM SOLD AS SINGLE-HEATHER HONEY, BUT LING HEATHER HONEY CAN BE DISTINGUISHED FROM THE OTHERS BY ITS THICK, JELLY-LIKE (THIXOTROPIC) CONSISTENCY WITH A STRONG AROMA AND FLAVOUR. HONEY FROM BELL HEATHER IS THINNER, WITH A MORE BITTER EDGE, WHILE CROSSLEAVED GIVES A THIN HONEY WITH LIGHTER FLAVOUR.

HISTORY:
Honey as a sweetener in the Scottish diet combines particularly well with the distinctive flavours of oatmeal and whisky in a number of drinks and dishes. Originally it was collected from wild colonies of bees: 'The boys,' says Osgood Mackenzie in *A Hundred Years in the Highlands* (1921), 'were able to collect large quantities of wild honey, which, by applying heat to it, was run into glass bottles and sold at the Stornoway markets. Hunting for wild-bee nests was one of the great ploys for the boys in the autumn … Cameron tells me that, as a young boy, before he left his home, there was an island in Loch Bhacha Chreamha where there was no necessity for hunting for bees' nests, as the whole island seemed under bees, the nests almost touching each other in the moss at the roots of tall heather … My stalker, too, informs me that his home at Kernsary used to be quite famous for its wild bees, but they finally disappeared.'

Beekeeping, which originated as a hobby or sideline for people running other businesses, continues to attract an enthusiastic following. The flavour of heather honey is highly esteemed for its distinctive character.

TECHNIQUE:
To ensure purity, hives are filled with unused combs and 'flitted' each summer, as the heather comes into bloom around the middle of July, to positions on the heather moors where the bees can collect the maximum nectar in the shortest time. To extract the honey, the outer caps are shaved off and the combs subjected to a Honey Loosener (nylon needles with a bulbous end which disturbs the honey). The combs are then put into a Tangential Swinging Basket

Reversible which extracts by alternating 2 slow swinging movements with 2 fast. The honey is sieved into barrels and seeded (mixed with about a tenth volume of honey of the correct texture from the previous year's harvest) before it is poured into jars. Combs are cut and boxed.

PRODUCTION:
An average amount of honey per hive can vary from 350g to 69kg with the average working out at 23–30kg. A medium to large producer will have 300–400 hives.

REGION OF PRODUCTION:
SCOTLAND.

Oatmeal

DESCRIPTION:
COMPOSITION: WHOLE OATS, LESS THE HUSK. COLOUR: GREYISH-BEIGE. FLAVOUR: SWEET-MEALY, THIS DEPENDS ON THE MOISTURE AND OIL CONTENT, DETERMINED BY THE VARIETY, THE DISTRICT WHERE IT IS GROWN, THE SOIL AND THE CLIMATE.

HISTORY:
It is not known where or when cultivated oats originated. The first evidence of the grain in Scotland is carbonized grain found at archaeological excavations along the Forth and Clyde Canal dated to approximately 100 BC. It is generally agreed that although oats thrive best in cool climates, they originally came from some warmer country to the east. In a climate such as Scotland's, growth is comparatively slow which allows the kernels to fill out and mature better.

Oats became the most important food grain in Scotland towards the end of the seventeenth century when they displaced barley. Oatmeal was more versatile and was generally better liked for its flavour when made into oatcakes, porridge and brose, the staple items of the peasant diet. By the end of the eighteenth century oatmeal had become firmly established as the people's grain. 'Oatmeal with milk, which they cook in different ways, is their constant food, three times a day, throughout the year, Sundays and holidays included,' says Donaldson in *A General View of Agriculture of the Carse of Gowrie* (1794). Throughout the nineteenth century its popularity continued to increase. The figure of the penniless Scottish university scholar, surviving on his sack of oatmeal, is legendary. The mid-term holiday known as 'Meal Monday' was given to allow the student to return home to replenish his supply of oatmeal.

With the industrial revolution and the extension northwards of the English diet of cheap white bread accompanied by tea, the old oatmeal traditions of porridge, brose and oatcakes were seriously under threat. The fact that they have survived is largely to do with a greater understanding of the nutritional value of oatmeal as its role as a popular 'health' food has become established. Rolled oats, or oatflakes, were developed in America by the Quaker Oat company in 1877: they are made by steaming and rolling pinhead oatmeal. Their introduction greatly eased the process of making porridge and other oatmeal dishes.

There are several water-powered stone-ground mills as well as factory mills kiln-drying and stone-grinding oatmeal in the traditional way.

TECHNIQUE:
The traditional method is first to dry or condition the grain to a moisture content of usually around 15 per cent. It is then spread on a kiln floor, consisting of perforated metal sheets, with

a smokeless-fuel furnace some 20–30 feet below. The oats are turned by hand with large shovels until the moisture content is reduced to around 4–5 per cent when the meal has taken on its mild nutty flavour. Milling begins with shelling the husks, then the grains are ground between stones to the required cuts or grades: pinhead (whole grain split into two) – used for haggis; rough – used for porridge, brose and sometimes oatcakes; medium/rough (sometimes known as coarse/medium) – used by butchers for mealie puddings; medium – used for porridge, brose, skirlie and baking; fine and super fine – used in baking and for feeding to babies.

REGION OF PRODUCTION:
SCOTLAND.

***

Also produced in Scotland
SMOKED MACKEREL (P. 16)

Britain: Nationwide

Blackberry

DESCRIPTION:

CULTIVATED BLACKBERRIES ARE BRED TO PRODUCE LARGER FRUIT WHILE RETAINING A FLAVOUR CLOSE TO THE BEST AVAILABLE WILD BLACKBERRIES. A WHITE BLACKBERRY (ACTUALLY A PALE YELLOW) HAS ALSO BEEN BRED.

HISTORY:

Blackberries belong to the genus *Rubus*, native to Britain. In the wild (these are often referred to as brambles), they are a common plant of woodland and waste. Several species are recognized – there are 386 at the very least (Stobart, 1980) – and have contributed to the development of the cultivated blackberry (Roach, 1985). Archaeological and literary evidence suggestthat blackberries have been used for food in Britain since earliest times. However, they do not appear to have been grown in gardens until the nineteenth century, probably due to the wild berries being both common and acceptably sweet.

The development of cultivated varieties first received most encouragement in the USA. North American and European varieties were used for genetic material. By 1900, blackberries were being grown commercially in Kent. The acreage grown in Britain has since much increased, and development of new varieties and hybrids has been the subject of research at the Scottish Crop Research Institute. Stobart (1980) makes some apposite comments: 'Cultivated blackberries suffer in popularity from being no better than the best wild ones, which can be gathered free from the hedgerows in summer. However, wild ones can be so seedy as to be fit only for jelly. Seedy blackberry and apple pie is one of the supreme horrors of British cooking.'

TECHNIQUE:

Blackberries are grown on permanent post-and-wire systems, separating the fruiting canes from the season's new growth (which forms the next year's fruiting wood) by thinning, pruning and training. The canes which have fruited are cut to soil level once the season is over. Blackberries grow best on well-drained, medium soils with a neutral pH, and crop best in full sun. The canes are planted in winter in well-mulched soil; spacing depends on variety. Loch Ness, which has stiffer canes than average, can be planted relatively close together. The fruit are picked by hand, and the season finishes with the arrival of the first frosts.

Alexanders

DESCRIPTION:

A LARGE UMBELLIFEROUS PLANT, GROWING TO ABOUT 1.5 METRES; IT LOOKS RATHER LIKE CELERY, HAS A SOFT TEXTURE WHEN COOKED, AND THE FLAVOUR BEARS SIMILARITIES TO BOTH CELERY AND PARSLEY. ITS VARIANT NAMES OF BLACK LOVAGE AND HORSE PARSLEY SHOW THE LINKS PEOPLE USED TO MAKE TO OTHER PLANTS. IT MAY BE CALLED ANGELICA IN EAST ANGLIA.

HISTORY:

This plant, *Smyrnium olusatrum*, was brought into Britain by the Romans (Mabey, 1978). It was still being eaten in Renaissance Italy (Castelvetro, 1989), and in England it was used as a vegetable and a medicine; John Evelyn included it among his 'plants for the kitchen garden' (1699). It was cultivated until the 1800s, then fell out of favour, displaced by celery. But even as late as Vilmorin-Andrieux (1885), Lord Leconfield's gardener at Petworth (Sussex) provides information on its use as a vegetable and salad. The plant has naturalized and can be found growing on waste land and cliffs, especially along the South coast, where some people collect it to use in the kitchen; it is also cultivated on a very small scale by a few herb growers. The stalks can be boiled for a short time and served with butter as a hot vegetable, or allowed to cool and dressed for salads.

TECHNIQUE:

The wild plants are collected at the appropriate season. If cultivated, alexanders requires a sunny position and is grown from seed in March and April. The plant requires 1 or 2 years' growth to become large enough to yield; it dies back to the roots during the winter. In the past, the stems were blanched by being earthed up at the beginning of March for 3 weeks. Although the plants are grown by a few herb producers, they are regarded primarily as ornaments, and blanching is no longer carried out. The stems are cut from the base of the plant, in which case they may be partially blanched naturally by the presence of the previous year's dead foliage. For the best quality vegetables, the stems are picked just before the flowers open.

Nasturtium

DESCRIPTION:

A TRAILING PLANT WHICH GROWS LARGE, ROUND, DARK GREEN LEAVES AND BRILLIANT RED, ORANGE AND YELLOW FLOWERS ON LONG, THIN STEMS; THE LEAVES AND STEMS BOTH HAVE A PEPPERY, HOT NOTE REMINISCENT OF ENGLISH MUSTARD.

HISTORY:

The word nasturtium was commonly used in English in the past to refer to various plants, including the native watercress, whose leaves have a peppery flavour. Such language is now restricted to botanical science. In common usage, nasturtium has come to describe the genus *Tropaeolum*, either *T. majus*, or the dwarf variant *T. minus*, introduced from Peru in the seventeenth century. The confusion between the names (nasturtiums were sometimes called Indian cress) suggests that the English, who have a fondness for peppery, piquant flavours, classed both types of plant together in the kitchen.

From the seventeenth century onwards, references can be found to the use of nasturtiums for salads. The indications are that this, and the use of fresh flowers as salad ingredients in general, is a peculiarly English habit. An early suggestion comes from John Evelyn's manual for salad-lovers, *Acetaria* (1699), and another from *Adam's Luxury and Eve's Cookery* (1744) whose anonymous author noted, 'There are two or three sorts of this plant cultivated for the Use of the Flowers in Sallets, and the Seeds to pickle.' Hannah Glasse (1747) recommended decorating a dish with 'stertion' buds, and gave instructions for strewing a salmagundi with the flowers. This culinary practice continued: Mrs Beeton (1861) suggested them as a garnish for summer salad, as did Vilmorin-Andrieux (1885). The pre-war writers Dorothy Allhusen and Mrs Leyel were happy to make the same point and so, too, have a succession of authors in the intervening years whose repetition of the idea has borne fruit in its adoption in much commercial and private cookery.

TECHNIQUE:

In their native country, nasturtiums are perennial, but they are susceptible to frost and have to be grown as annuals in Britain. They grow easily from seed and are used as an ornamental garden plant. They are germinated indoors in April and planted out after the danger of frost has passed; or are planted outdoors as seeds in late May. Several varieties are grown. Commercially, nasturtiums are germinated and planted in designated beds. Growers now use polytunnels to extend the growing season, and special packaging to preserve the flowers in good condition for a short period between picking and use. After the first year the plants are cleared off the soil, leaving seeds to germinate the following year.

Spearmint

DESCRIPTION:

Spearmint has long, narrow bright green leaves; it is sweet and clear in flavour.

HISTORY:

The spearmint or common mint of British cookery is *Mentha spicata*. Although some have claimed that it was spread through Europe by the influence of the Ottoman Turks (Kaneva-Johnson, 1995), the genus was either indigenous or long since naturalized and it has always been difficult to sort out the history of individual varieties. Several are known in Britain, including some with scents reminiscent of apple, pineapple or lemon. John Evelyn (1699) recommended orange mint. The *Colloquy* of the Anglo-Saxon Aelfric Bata (fl. 1005) suggests that mint was eaten every day, picked from his garden (Hagen, 1995). References have abounded ever since, even if they do not always make clear the extent to which it was the cook's friend or the apothecary's.

Who would have thought that in the very recent past, mint was one of the few culinary herbs known to the generality of British households – the other being sage? For there is in fact a shortage of recipes in early cookery books that depend on its flavour for success. An old name for spearmint is fish mint, implying it was used in cooking fish, and Hannah Glasse (1747) suggested mackerel should be boiled with mint, parsley and fennel, but the generality of instructions that include mint are for waters, vinegars, cordials and syrups proposed for the still room. Lamb, for example, was served not with mint but with gooseberry or sorrel sauce,

or citrus fruits, or even samphire or laver if a salty or acid cutting edge through its fatty flavour was required. An exception were green peas. These, and their soup, were seasoned with mint by Mrs Raffald (1782). The combination was explained by Mrs Beeton (1861) in medical terms. Mint was anti-spasmodic and stomachic, it was a wise accompaniment, therefore, to the dangerous afflatus induced by too many peas.

Although its use was restricted in the eighteenth century (there is also reference to it flavouring puddings), the energetic cook Martha Bradley (1756) does point to its being an accepted part of the English kitchen garden, while it was probably outlawed from the French. Her ingredients for a *sauce ravigote 'au bourgeois'* included equal quantities of mint, thyme and basil. The advice of *La Cuisinière Bourgeoise* of 1774, published in Brussels, certainly does not admit of mint in a ravigote, even if Bradley wrote as appendix: 'This is a sauce much in Esteem in France, where the People of Fashion, weary of their rich Dishes, are copying the plainer Dressings of the Tradespeople and even of the Peasants.'

What had seemed an unmentionable in the eighteenth century suddenly appears with frequency in the nineteenth. Dr Kitchiner (1817) included a recipe for mint sauce observing then that 'this was a usual accompaniment' to lamb – even if the marriage was folk wisdom rather than written law. Acton (1845) agreed with him. She also joins mint and peas, as already had Maria Rundell (1807). Mrs Beeton sent a whole tureen of mint sauce up with her lamb. The intrepid soldier-cook 'Wyvern', teaching memsahibs a thing or two about French cookery to make their stay in Madras a happy one (*Culinary Jottings for Madras*, 1878), had this to say about mint and the Indian cook: 'Mint as a flavouring agent, save with green peas, in certain wine "cups," and in a bona fide mint sauce, is one of the banes of the cook-room; its use, and that of any parsley except the curled English variety, should be considered absolutely penal.' His aversion to minting serves as reminder that the culinary use of mint was far more general in the Middle East and India than it ever was in Europe or even Britain – although the Romans (*vide* Apicius) had valued the herb.

The culinary proposals of the Victorians have borne fruit. Lamb and mint – as a jelly if not a sauce – now seem inseparable, and mint with new potatoes, if not always peas, is thought essential. The position has become further entrenched as lamb has become more favoured than mutton.

Mint is also popular in Britain as flavouring for sugar confectionery. At one time an industry to distil essential oils from mint and other herbs was located at Mitcham in Surrey. This existed until the 1950s but, despite claims for the superiority of the native product over imports, is now extinct. Peppermint (*Mentha piperata*), pennyroyal (*Mentha pulegium*) and spearmint were all used in this industry, but *M. piperata* was by far the most important, according to the *Pharmaceutical Journal* in 1850.

TECHNIQUE:

The plant grows very easily. Root cuttings are planted in early spring, about 5cm apart and 5cm deep; the plants are mulched with well-rotted manure in winter. Some mint is forced in glass-houses for winter.

Sweet Cicely

DESCRIPTION:

A LARGE PLANT WHICH GROWS TO A HEIGHT OF ABOUT 150CM IN GOOD CONDITIONS; IT HAS BRILLIANT GREEN FERN-LIKE LEAVES AND TINY, WHITE FLOWERS IN LARGE UMBELS. THE PERFUME HAS A DISTINCT ANISEED NOTE AND IS SAID TO BE REMINISCENT OF MYRRH.

HISTORY:

Sweet cicely, *Myrrhis odorata*, can be found growing wild in damp, shady sites in northern England and southern Scotland. It is sometimes called fern-leaved chervil or giant sweet chervil, for it is a cousin of that more delicate herb. It is highly ornamental and is sometimes used as a flowering plant in gardens, but it also has a long history of medicinal and culinary use. Nicholas Culpeper, whose *Herbal* was first published in the seventeenth century, noted the plant was used in salads, that the root could be boiled and eaten with oil and vinegar, or it could be candied, and that the seeds had a very pleasant taste. Florence Ranson (1949) remarked that it had been known for centuries as a useful herb by North-Country people.

It is the leaves which are now mainly used, especially as a visual flourish, or added to salads. Domestic cooks exploit the softening effect it has on the acidity of gooseberries and rhubarb, by adding a few whole leaves during cooking, or by chopping them finely and adding them raw to the cooked fruit. This reduces the amount of sugar required in the dish.

TECHNIQUE:

Sweet Cicely is a perennial, and can be found growing wild in suitable habitats. It is also grown commercially, in which case most growers begin with seeds which are planted in the autumn and over-wintered in cold frames. This is important, as sweet cicely will not germinate without a period of prolonged cold. Once germinated, it is planted outdoors: the plant prefers partial shade. It is easy to grow, and will flower 3 times in a year by cutting back after each flowering. Once established, it grows every year with little further attention.

Mutton

HISTORY:

In theory, any sheep older than 12 months becomes mutton when killed for meat. In practice, young mutton does reach the market but is rarely described as such. Nor would it have been described as mutton in centuries past. Then, the word implied sheep several years old. According to William Kitchiner in *The Housekeeper's Oracle* (1817), fat mutton was the best, and the finest came from a 5-year-old wether, or castrated ram. Kitchiner was writing when sheep had value for their fleeces as well as their meat; wethers could be kept for several years simply to grow wool, before being fattened for slaughter. Although all breeds were killed for the table, the Victorians favoured Southdown above most (Beeton, 1861).

Over the last century, English wool has had much competition from foreign production and the value of the fleece has declined. Furthermore, the British palate has shifted its preference from mutton to lamb – particularly as frozen lamb from Australasia greatly improved availability and price. Mutton's strength of flavour, fat and toughness have militated against it. There is now a growing return towards young mutton although it is more likely to come from ewes, as 5-year-old wethers are rarely kept. Two producers in the South-West are particularly interested in this market, one of whom concentrates on using a breed specific to the area.

TECHNIQUE:

One producer in Devon does specialize in mutton, using his flock of White Faced Dartmoor sheep. The historical centre for these is Widecombe-in-the-Moor. A breed society was only formed in the 1950s, but they are accepted as close to the primitive sheep of the Devon hills (Hall & Clutton-Brock, 1989). They are farmed in the traditional manner, grazed on the native vegetation of the common land during the summer, and kept in enclosed farmland on grass, hay or root crops during winter. For mutton, the ewes (rams are not used for meat) are culled at 6–10 years. Carcasses are hung for 14 days. The White Faced Dartmoor tends to have large fat deposits on the forequarters, and the producer sells only the haunches and loins as joints; the shoulders are trimmed of fat and the lean meat minced.

Anne Petch, also in Devon, has wether mutton from primitive and rare-breed sheep reared to her specifications, slaughtered at 2–3 years, and hung for 2 weeks before sale.

Goose

DESCRIPTION:

A DRESSED CARCASS WEIGHT OF 4–6KG GENERALLY SEEMS PREFERRED. DOMESTIC CONSUMERS LIKE A RELATIVELY SHORT-BODIED BIRD, WITH A HIGH RATIO OF MEAT TO BONE, AS FOUND IN THE BRECON BUFF.

HISTORY:

Goose only sacrificed its undisputed place at British Christmas dinner in post-war years. It was an autumn and winter speciality and, being the largest domestic fowl apart from turkey (which at first was by no means common), was perfect festive fare, with links to particular days and particular regions.

Geese were much farmed in eastern England, especially East Anglia. Autumn goose fairs were held at several places, the most famous being Nottingham. Originating in the 1200s, it was well-established by the 1600s when geese from the East Midlands and Norfolk were sold. Mrs Beeton (1861) wrote, 'the best geese are found on the borders of Suffolk, and in Norfolk and Berkshire; but the largest flocks are reared in the fens of Lincolnshire and Cambridge … large herds of them are sent every year to London'. In this arable region, the geese were fattened on stubble after the corn harvest. Before the railways, they were shod by walking them over hot tar, then driven on foot to the city. Michaelmas (29 September), was a date on which geese were eaten; it was one of the quarter-days of the English business year, when cottagers paid their rents and presented a goose to their landlords. Martha Bradley (1756) wrote, 'it would no more be Christmas day without [minced pie], than Michaelmas Day if a Goose were wanting'.

According to Mrs Glasse (1747), boned goose enclosing other birds and game was sealed with butter inside a pastry crust and sent from Yorkshire to London at Christmas. Goose fat was valued for pastry as well as medicines; the quills and feathers had domestic uses.

There were different names for geese of various ages. Green geese were under 6 weeks and stubble geese were those killed after harvest. A medieval household account contains an entry recording the purchase of 'grenegeys' for Easter; the satirical poem *The Art of Cookery* by

William King (1708) contains the couplet,

'So Stubble Geese at Michaelmas are seen,
Upon the Spit, next May produces Green.'

The British farmyard goose, represented by the white geese now found in the West of England and in the Shetland Islands, does not appear to have received much attention from improvers, although in the early 1900s, another truly indigenous British type, the Brecon Buff, was evolved from stock collected in central Wales by poultry breeder Rhys Llewellyn. A medium goose with buff feathers and pink beak and feet, birds of this type have remained popular on the Welsh Marches. Most breeds that are now in current use owe their origins to foreign varieties such as Roman (Italian), Pilgrim (North American), Toulouse (French) and Emden (German). These were brought into the country during the Victorian period. Several commercial hybrids have now been developed. Since the 1960s, Wessex Geese have been bred using Roman and Emden stock, and the Legarth, a Danish hybrid, is another major source of British goose flesh. In the 1950s many birds from Ireland were imported for finishing in Britain.

TECHNIQUE:

Geese were once kept on small, mixed farms. A few goslings were raised each year, feeding on grass during the summer, fattened with grain and killed and sold for Christmas. 'Brecons are the ideal farm geese,' because they sit (brood), convert food to meat more economically than large breeds, and produce an attractive table bird (Ashton, 1994). This trade depended on small producers who carried out preparation of the birds for the table in domestic buildings. Strict implementation of food hygiene legislation has almost extinguished the tradition.

East Anglia is still the place for geese, even if from foreign strains. A large hatchery in southern Norfolk sells approximately half its stock to East Anglia or the East Midlands.

Goslings are housed for the first 4 weeks, then kept on grass, with housing provided at night. They still roam the stubble on some farms, although modern harvesting methods mean there is less grain left than formerly. Large producers use machines to pluck and prepare the geese, but many still adhere to the practice of hanging for 7–10 days.

Grey Partridge

DESCRIPTION:

MINIMUM WEIGHT IN FEATHER ABOUT 350G. THEY HAVE GREY-BROWN PLUMAGE WITH CHESTNUT MARKINGS ON BREAST; PALE FLESH.

HISTORY:

After the battle of Agincourt (1415), the French prisoner Charles, Duke of Orleans was held at Pontefract castle. He was allowed on excursions, for example to nearby Methley, a manor belonging to Robert Waterton, where he hunted for game. Some of Waterton's household accounts survive. They include entries that tell of the sale of 182 partridges, and the purchase of another 56 birds. Some years later, the poet-duke allegedly wrote *The Debate between the Heralds of France and England* which poured scorn on this island for having no true partridges. He, and many other cooks and gormandizers, preferred the larger red-legged bird which lived happily in France, barely recognizing the creatures he hunted at Methley as food at all. The grey partridge (*Perdix cinerea*) is native to Britain, but is now less common than its continental relative, the red-legged, or French partridge (*Caccabis rufa*).

The red-legged partridge was introduced to this country after the return of Charles II from exile in France in 1660. However, the rate of introduction mushroomed in the years after 1770. The birds like different habitats. The grey prefers arable and is said to have greatly increased its numbers in the years of the Napoleonic wars when so much more land was brought into cultivation. The red-legged is happier on heaths and was thus a candidate for those creating shooting estates. They also have different habits: while the grey is keen to take to the air – and thus give good sport – the red-leg is loath to do other than walk or run. British shooters prefer the native.

There was a thought that the red-leg was pushing out the grey – as grey squirrels have ousted the red – but as they need different surroundings, the claim is false. More likely, the population of grey partridges has gone through a cycle of increase and decline as farming methods have changed; at present, the use of herbicides and insecticides probably has an adverse effect by reducing the number of insects available for the young birds.

There are several references in early texts to rearing partridges – either for the table or for release and subsequent sport – but the British cook was not as inventive as the French in the treatment of this bird. Many's the dismissal of the monotonous English roast in favour of the French braises, such as *perdrix aux choux*. Martha Bradley (1756) wrote of the partridge pie for Christmas, 'which in peaceful times we could employ the French to make for us'.

The highest population now is thought to be in north Norfolk, but they are found especially in areas which have a drier climate, sandy soils, and arable land: the Sussex Downs, Lincolnshire, Yorkshire, and eastern Scotland all support relatively large numbers. The season runs from 1 September to 1 February.

TECHNIQUE:

Grey partridges can be reared but are more difficult to hold in an area than the red-legged. The chicks are hand-fed until about 8 weeks and released into areas of suitable field crops; small patches of farmland may be specially prepared for them in some cases. In the season, they are collected together by beaters and driven from open fields into the cover of root crops, then sent up over the guns. Grey partridge are regarded as good sport for shooters, they fly well and fast. The birds are hung for about a week and sold by licensed dealers.

Gulls' Eggs

DESCRIPTION:

GULLS' EGGS WEIGH ABOUT 35G. THE SHELLS ARE GREENISH WITH SPECKLES; THE WHITE HAS A BLUE TINGE AND THE YOLK IS OCHRE YELLOW.

HISTORY:

The eggs of several species of wild bird have been gathered and eaten. Plovers' eggs were considered a delicacy and the eggs of several seabirds were collected and eaten around the British coast – on St Kilda, they were part of the staple diet. Each species had its own advocates – tastes varied from community to community (Baldwin, 1974). Eggs were also sold to urban markets.

One English district where harvesting of wild nests took place was Bempton, on the Yorkshire coast (Dent, 1980). Here, until the 1930s, the eggs of guillemot and razorbill were taken. Rights to the cliff face were vested in the riparian owners, who might dispose of the right to collect eggs. Men worked in groups of 5, using ropes and harnesses to reach the nests. By custom, landowners were paid with baskets of eggs. Laws protecting wild birds and changes in taste began a decline in the trade; the disruption caused to the labour force and to local customs by World War II more or less extinguished it. Egg collection at Bempton ceased in 1953 (Atkinson, 1993).

Today, only the eggs of black-headed gulls, a common species under no threat, are available on a restricted basis, mostly from sites on the Scottish Borders and around the Solent on the south coast of England.

TECHNIQUE:

The black-headed gull is widely distributed. It nests in large colonies, on the coast and at inland marsh sites. Formerly, the eggs were collected by many people living near the nesting grounds; they were eaten by locals or sold to game dealers who took them further afield. A licence is now required for anyone who wishes to collect the eggs for, despite being common, black-headed gulls are protected by the Wildlife and Countryside Act (1981). Legislation and lack of interest, rather than geographical location, are the limiting factors.

During the season, the nests are observed. As the gulls begin to lay, the single eggs are removed each day, to ensure the eggs are fresh. As further check on freshness, eggs are immersed in water and any which float removed. Collection from any particular nest ceases after 12–14 days, to allow the gulls to lay and hatch full clutches of eggs, which will mean the return of the birds the following year. The eggs are sold through licensed game dealers, most finding their way to London. Collection licences are issued annually. The number of licences, and the number of eggs allowed to be taken with each, is adjusted annually in line with the estimated population of the birds. The season generally runs from late March for about 4 weeks.

Red Grouse

DESCRIPTION:

THIS IS A MEDIUM-SIZED GAME BIRD WITH REDDISH-BROWN PLUMAGE SPECKLED WITH WHITE AND BLACK. WEIGHT IS ABOUT 500G. IT HAS A DISTINCTIVE RED COMB OVER THE EYE, WHICH IS MORE PROMINENT IN THE COCK. GROUSE HAVE DARKER FLESH AND STRONGER FLAVOUR THAN OTHER GAME BIRDS.

HISTORY:

The red grouse (*Lagopus lagopus Scoticus*) is native to the British Isles, and is considered the finest British game bird. It is also unique, being 'generally regarded as an insular form of the Willow Grouse' (Simon, 1960). It inhabits most areas of heather moorland. Simon notes that grouse vary in flavour from area to area, depending on soil and climate rather as do wines. However, the bird is closely identified with the Highlands, and McNeill (1929) cites numerous references about the culinary use of this bird in the region.

It was during the mid-nineteenth century that grouse really became famous as a speciality and integral to the food habits of the English aristocracy and mercantile bourgeoisie. This was due largely to the manner in which grouse-shooting developed as a fashionable sport. Queen Victoria's move to Balmoral in late summer every year for the shooting season had popularized the Highlands to such an extent that the high heather moors became the Englishman's playground. Many purchased estates and the landscape became populated with shooting parties for the Glorious Twelfth. This day opened the season: grouse and snipe were the first permitted quarries after summer breeding – the full season runs from 12 August to 10 December. Grouse became the rich gourmet's delight: 'Nothing is better,' says Shand (1902), 'for a spartan lunch by the spring on the hillside than half a cold grouse with oatcake, and a beaker or two of whisky and water.' Though it had previously, as with other wild game, been eaten by native Highlanders (see Red Deer Venison p. 345), it no longer entered the diet of the people – unless illegally poached.

The black grouse (blackcock), wood or great grouse (capercaillie) and white grouse (ptarmigan) all belong to the same family but are rarely used for food today.

TECHNIQUE:

Grouse are wild birds, and no attempt is made to rear chicks by hand. However, their survival is enhanced by management of the areas in which they live. This requires considerable skill, and, in country where grouse are encouraged, has produced a unique landscape. This is essentially a heather monoculture, which would not exist without the commercial value placed on these birds. The heather moorland is burnt in small patches on a rotation basis at intervals of 10–20 years. As the different areas selected for burning each year regenerate, they create a mosaic of heather plants at various stages of growth which benefits the highly territorial grouse. The system provides plenty of young shoots, which are an important part of the diet, plus older, well-grown plants for nesting birds. Their principal foods are the flowers, seeds and young green shoots of ling heathers, which is thought to be why grouse meat tends to be darker and stronger-flavoured than other game birds. They also eat blaeberries and the seeds of sorrel which may add further distinctive flavours. As the taste of the flesh depends on diet, so it also varies according to its hanging time. This may be from 2–3 days up to a fortnight, depending on weather conditions, temperature and humidity.

The habitats of black grouse, capercaillie and ptarmigan are much more restricted; they are mixed woodland, pine woods, and exposed mountain tops respectively. All these birds are less commonly shot and rarely reach the market. Capercaillie has a strong pine flavour and it is said that instead of hanging, the method for ageing the birds was to bury them for several days.

Game Pie

DESCRIPTION:

A COOKED PIE OF GAME, USUALLY QUITE LARGE, 30–40CM DIAMETER, 8–10CM HIGH, WEIGH-ING ABOUT 3KG. FORM: ROUND; SOMETIMES ELABORATE POINTED OVAL MOULDS WITH DISHED SIDES ARE USED; THE TOP IS OFTEN HEAVILY DECORATED WITH CRIMPED EDGES AND PASTRY LEAVES. COLOUR: GLAZED, DEEP GOLD-BROWN PASTRY; A SELECTION OF DARK AND LIGHT MEAT, OFTEN MIXED WITH BACON OR BRINED PORK.

HISTORY:

Game of various kinds was a large part of the diet of the rich in medieval Britain. Venison was especially popular and was often made into pasties. There was a London ordinance in 1379 forbidding pie-bakers to 'bake beef in a pasty for sale, and sell it as venison' (Henisch, 1976). The taste for venison pasties was permanent, only matched by that for pies of game of all sorts. These, and many other pies, were often made of several species at once. Thus, in the same London ordinance, pastry cooks were upbraided for making pasties of 'rabbits, geese, and garbage, not befitting, and sometimes stinking'. They were henceforth forbidden to buy from the kitchens of great households, 'any garbage [leftovers] from capons, hens, or geese, to bake in a pasty, and sell'.

A famous pie containing game was the 'Yorkshire Christmas Pie', a standing pie with a thick crust, filled with spiced poultry and game birds which had been boned and tucked one inside another, smallest first, from a pigeon up to a turkey. These were sent from Yorkshire to London at Christmas time. Hannah Glasse (1747) gives such a recipe, enclosing the meat in a puff pastry crust without a mould to keep the shape – they had to be stoutly constructed, she advised. Doubters should refer to a report in the *Newcastle Chronicle* for January 1770 that Sir Henry Grey had recently been sent by his housekeeper a raised pie of '4 geese, 2 turkies, 2 rabbits, 4 wild ducks, 2 woodcocks, 6 snipes, and 4 partridges; 2 neat's tongues, 2 curlews, 7 blackbirds, and 6 pigeons'. It measured 9 feet round, took 2 men to lift, and was equipped with a travelling box with 4 small wheels. It weighed about 170lb (75kg).

Not all were so extravagant. Eliza Acton (1845) gave a recipe for a 'good common English game pie'; whilst Mrs Beeton's (1861) was for a moulded standing pie. The habit of adding pork, either as fat bacon or in the form of forcemeat (replaced by sausage meat in some mod-ern recipes) can be traced back at least to the middle of the nineteenth century.

There are several manufacturers and shops who produce raised game pies.

TECHNIQUE:

Either shortcrust pastry (made with flour and butter, in the proportions 2:1, plus egg yolks) or a hot-water crust (for raised pies) is used. Whatever game is available, depending on the area and the season, is boned, cut into slices or cubes and used to fill the pastry; a layer of ham, bacon or sausage meat is often added. The top of the pie is covered with a circle of pastry; the trimmings cut into decorative shapes for the top, usually leaves, but sometimes animals and flowers. After baking, whilst the pie is still hot, heated stock or well-reduced gravy is poured through a hole in the lid. The pie is cooled overnight before unmoulding.

Potted Meat

DESCRIPTION:

COOKED AND GROUND MEAT (USUALLY BEEF) PRESERVED IN BUTTER OR FAT, BOUGHT BY
WEIGHT IN TUBS OF 100–200G. FLAVOUR: STRONGLY BEEF; FINE, SMOOTH TEXTURE.

HISTORY:

Potting was an important way of preserving perishable food such as beef, ham, tongue, hare,
salmon, char or game birds. The cooked meat was removed from the bone, drained of any
liquor (which might spoil), pounded with butter and spices, and packed into wide, shallow
pots, often made specially for the purpose. The smooth, dense pastes were sealed with a thick
layer of melted butter or suet. During the 1800s, many recipes were commercialized to give
cheap, highly flavoured pastes packed in small jars. They were immensely popular as sandwich
fillings though lacking the finesse of hand-crafted production. *Law's Grocer's Manual* (*c.* 1895)
described the ordinary kinds as made from meat, well-boiled, chopped, spiced, mixed with
gelatine and set in moulds. They were were intended more as relishes than foods in their own
right. This history has been regretted, as well as described, by David (1968). The development
of other preservation methods has affected the demand for potted meats, as has the latter-day
taste for pâtés made to continental European recipes.

These meats were part of a national cookery tradition, known and made all over Britain.
Potted fish was often a means of exporting a delicacy from a single district to the wider
market, but meat and game did not fall into this category. In their survival, however, a
regional tendency has developed, especially for potted beef, found mainly in the East
Midlands (Mabey, 1978) and northwards into Scotland. Potted game and ham are less
widely available.

TECHNIQUE:

Lean beef is sometimes pickled in brine for a short time before cooking. It is simmered in
stock for several hours, then minced finely and seasoned. Pepper and mace are usual seasonings for potted meats of all types; others might be ginger, cayenne, or nutmeg. The mixture is
put into containers whilst hot and covered with a layer of melted clarified butter or suet, then
allowed to cool before sale.

Steak and Kidney Pie

DESCRIPTION:

A COOKED PIE OF VARYING DIMENSIONS AND SHAPE, FILLED WITH BEEF AND KIDNEY IN A
GRAVY. UNLIKE A RAISED PIE, THE PASTRY WAS USUALLY PUFF AND THE PIE WAS SOLD TO BE
SERVED HOT. IT WAS NOT THE CONVENIENT HAND-HELD SNACK THAT MIGHT BE THE
UNDERLYING REASON FOR THE SURVIVAL AND POPULARITY OF THE PORK PIE.

HISTORY:

Hot pies were a food of London and other big cities, hawked through the streets by itinerants
whose individual cries have been celebrated or excoriated since the fifteenth century. Beef, mutton,
eels and fruit are all recorded as fillings. The modern steak pie is always understood to contain
beef, although not of a quality that would necessarily qualify as steak. The precise combination of
steak and kidney, however, does not seem to be mentioned until early in the 1900s (*OED*).

'Kill no more pigeons than you can eat.'

Benjamin Franklin

Domestic 'Beefsteak Pies', such as those described by Eliza Acton (1845), were filled with strips of rump steak placed uncooked in the bottom of a pie dish, seasoned with salt, pepper and cayenne, with onions if desired. Some water was added to help produce gravy; the dish was covered with a puff-pastry crust and baked. More elaborate concoctions of steak rolled around diced sheep's kidney (or oysters, or chopped mushrooms), seasoned with parsley, allspice and mushroom ketchup, then covered with a handsome decorated pastry, are also quoted. These were recipes for those with time and money. They were viewed as preternaturally British. When des Esseintes, the hero of the decadent novel *A Rebours* (1884), visited an English restaurant in Paris, he passed a table of women, 'who were unaccompanied, were dining together, facing each other, hearty English women who had boyish faces, teeth as broad as shovels, apple-coloured cheeks, with long hands and feet. They were making violent assaults on a beef-steak pie, which contained hot meat cooked in a mushroom sauce and covered in crust like a pâté.'

The hot pies sold as street-food or served in common eating-houses were filled with less distinguished meat. The urban working class made simpler pies at home, and demanded cheaper pies when buying them. A butcher's recipe from the 1930s stipulates cheap forequarter cuts, which were cooked for a little time before the other ingredients were added and the pies made up. This is the type which has survived. The meat is now often a fully-cooked stew used as a filling. The invariable conjunction of steak and kidney may well have arisen as a source of guaranteed flavour to these otherwise tough and watery mixtures. Oysters (once a favourite) became too expensive but, like them, the kidney afforded welcome variation of texture as well as taste. Steak and kidney pie is the traditional New Year's day dinner in Scotland; beef sausages may be used as a cheap replacement for kidney.

TECHNIQUE:
Modern recipes are a stew of beef and kidney, cooked with liquid and flavourings – water or beef stock is usually used, but beer, especially porter or stout, is often added. Worcestershire or some other proprietary sauces are quite often added. The gravy is starch-thickened. The mixture is placed in tinfoil dishes and topped with pastry (usually puff, although a double-crust version may be made using shortcrust). The top may be decorated, but is more frequently left plain; it is always egg-washed. The pies are baked at about 140°C; one of 500g needs 45 minutes.

Steak and Kidney Pudding

DESCRIPTION:
A COOKED, SUET-CRUST BEEF PUDDING MADE IN A DEEP BASIN SHAPED LIKE A TRUNCATED CONE. COLOUR: THE PASTRY IS VERY PALE, ALMOST WHITE; THE FILLING IS A RICH BROWN. FLAVOUR: BEEF AND KIDNEY FLAVOURS PREDOMINATE; THE SAUCE IS OFTEN QUITE AROMATIC AND HIGHLY SEASONED WITH ONE OR ANOTHER ENGLISH STORE SAUCE AND BLACK PEPPER.

HISTORY:
It is not clear when and where steak and kidney first met in a savoury pudding. Evidence so far discovered points towards the south-east of England in the late eighteenth or early nineteenth centuries. Steak puddings, using either beef or mutton, are found in cookery books like

Hannah Glasse (1747). A century later, Eliza Acton gave a recipe for 'Beef-Steak, or John Bull's Pudding'. This is a suet-crust pudding made in a basin filled with rump steak and steamed. She observes it was a favourite with many, especially sportsmen, as it didn't spoil if cooked for longer than strictly necessary; oysters could be added; and the paste was best made with suet from around the veal kidney. Kidneys as an ingredient for the inside of the pudding are not called for with beef, but are mentioned for a mutton pudding. In a footnote she says that in Kent and Sussex a special type of pudding basin, resembling a large, deep saucer, was sold expressly for steaming meat puddings. Mrs Beeton's (1861) recipe for a beef-steak and kidney pudding came from a Sussex lady, 'in which county the inhabitants are noted for their savoury puddings'. She notes that it differs from the general method in cutting the meat smaller and using a shallower dish.

Such puddings are now made in private households throughout the land and may also be bought ready-cooked. The pudding has less of a sale than the pie.

TECHNIQUE:

A mixture of beefsteak, cut in cubes of about 2cm, and smaller pieces of beef kidney, is prepared (this mixture can be bought ready-cut from some butchers). It is browned, with chopped onions; a little flour is stirred in, then liquid (often beef stock or a dark beer such as stout or porter) added, plus seasonings such as Worcestershire sauce, thin Yorkshire Relish, or mushroom ketchup. The stew is cooked for about 90 minutes, then cooled. A suet crust (pastry which employs shredded suet as a shortening) is rolled out to line a pudding basin then filled with the meat mixture. At this stage, shelled oysters may be added. A portion of the pastry is reserved to cover the top. The basin is covered with tinfoil, or greaseproof paper and a cloth, and lowered into a pan of water which is kept boiling for between 2–3 hours (for a large pudding). Such recipes are generally adjusted to include a generous proportion of gravy. A domestic or restaurant cook retains some of the gravy from the stew to serve with the finished product; alternatively, an incision is made in the top of the cooked pudding and boiling stock added to augment the juices it contains.

Venison Pie

DESCRIPTION:

THE MOST TRADITIONAL SHAPE IS THE RAISED PIE, 7–9CM DIAMETER, 3–4CM HIGH. USUALLY THESE ARE VERY PLAIN, WITH A FILLING OF LIGHTLY SEASONED MEAT, BUT SOME RECIPES CALL FOR A TOP LAYER OF CRANBERRY OR REDCURRANT JELLY.

HISTORY:

Venison once indicated game in general but is now restricted to the flesh of various deer. In England, deer hunting has always been strictly controlled. The animals were emparked in large areas designated for hunting, a system originally brought to Britain by the Romans, consolidated by the Anglo-Norman monarchy and which has been extended and developed to embrace modern deer-farming techniques.

The meat was used in many ways. The best was roasted, but stews and pies and pasties were also made. Venison pasties appear to have been very large, and to have consisted of venison joints wrapped in sturdy flour-and-water crusts or, by the eighteenth century, butter-enriched shortcrust and baked; sometimes a strong bone stock was poured into the pasty after cooking. Pies were made using similar ingredients or, in versions for the servants, from the umbles or internal organs – the original humble pie. Umbles and trimmings might also go into haggis or puddings, a tradition which modern venison farmers have built upon.

Because of venison's association with the aristocracy, dishes achieved wide geographical spread but those entitled (at least in theory) to consume them were limited. Generally, venison entered mainstream diet as a result of gifts from landowners to friends or dependants. Pepys's appetite for venison pasties is well attested. In 1662, 'I having some venison given me a day or two ago, and so I had a shoulder roasted, another baked, and the umbles baked in a pie, and all very well done.' However, some meat must have gone into the wider meat market.

TECHNIQUE:

The raised pie is closest to the old-fashioned pasty made from hot-water crust or sturdy short-crust. The pastry is moulded, by hand or machine for small pies, or by hand in large, elaborate fluted moulds for large pies. A filling of roughly chopped or coarsely minced venison is used; shin is quoted as a good cut. Black pepper and salt are the usual seasonings; other spices may be added to the maker's taste, and some recipes include redcurrant jelly. A strong stock made from venison bones was usually poured into the pies in the past, but it is not clear if this method is still used.

Dripping

DESCRIPTION:

ANIMAL FAT, USUALLY BEEF OR PORK, RENDERED DURING ROASTING, SOLD BY WEIGHT. DRIPPING IS COMPOSED OF TWO LAYERS: A DARK BROWN, JELLIED GRAVY UNDERNEATH, PALE BROWN FAT ON TOP.

HISTORY:

Dripping, the fat and juices from roast meat of any sort, has always been carefully conserved by British cooks. The word has been in use since the middle of the fifteenth century (*OED*). It should be distinguished from lard, which is the rendered fat of the pig, particularly the internal fat of the abdomen. English cooks have always been famed for their roasting, it was the one culinary skill for which they were accorded supremacy, even by the French. Small wonder, therefore, that dripping – the natural by-product of the art – should have been so highly esteemed. Cookery books such as Hannah Glasse (1747) show that fat, especially from cooking beef, was sometimes clarified and flavoured with herbs, then stored and used for pastry or as a medium for deep-frying. Dripping spread on toast was considered an excellent dish, and dripping cakes were made in the nineteenth century (Hartley, 1954). Toast and dripping and a cup of warm ale made a substantial snack for a working man. This was rarely fat derived from mutton or lamb, as that had commercial value for other products.

In smaller households with lower rates of meat consumption, 'dripping' became a debased and rather unpleasant mixture of fat from different kinds of meat, especially during the Second World War when meat and fats of all kinds were severely rationed. On a commercial level, dripping is now sold by pork butchers who deal in cooked meat, especially pork and ham. The dripping is simply a by-product, but it is valued for the flavour and the jellied stock that comes with it. In Scotland, it is sold by butchers for flavouring stovies (a stew of potatoes and onions).

TECHNIQUE:

Dripping is collected in roasting-trays under meat during cooking, poured into clean dishes, and allowed to cool.

Suet

DESCRIPTION:

SUET IS FAT FROM THE LOIN AND KIDNEY REGION IN A BEEF CARCASS; IT IS CREAM-COLOURED, HARD AND BLAND TASTING. NOW USUALLY BOUGHT SHREDDED (CUT INTO SMALL PELLETS) AND PACKED IN BOXES OF 250G OR 500G.

HISTORY:

Formerly, the word suet described the fat of sheep or deer but this usage is now archaic. The culinary use of these fats can be seen in some of the earliest English cookery texts. A primary use of suet was, and still is, chopped small, and combined with cereals, seasonings and meat or fruit to make puddings. Originally filling sausage skins, these mixtures developed into bag-puddings (enclosed in a cloth and boiled) during the seventeenth century. At this time, suet must have been of great importance in the British kitchen, for these dishes were part of the staple diet. They were served with meat, or instead of it in very poor households, before potatoes became common. Suet was also incorporated into dumplings and used for making pastry, which was rolled up with a filling of meat, fruit or jam to make a 'roly poly' in the nineteenth and twentieth centuries.

The relative importance of suet on a regional scale is difficult to assess as it has long been required for Christmas pudding eaten by almost every household in Britain. However, a huge range of suet-based dishes is to be found in the south and east of England: steak-and-kidney or oyster puddings in London and the surrounding area, lemon- and brown-sugar-filled Sussex pond puddings, Norfolk dumplings, clootie dumplings in Scotland (see p. 366, 379) and the bacon- or jam-filled clangers and suet rolls traditional to farm labourers' diets in the South and East Midlands. Although their importance has declined, as both animal fats and slow-cooked dishes have become less commonly used, they are still made.

Shredded suet was first prepared on an industrial scale in Manchester at the end of the 1800s by Gabriel Hugon, of French origin. This was marketed as Atora. The brand was bought by Rank Hovis McDougall in 1963.

TECHNIQUE:

Beef suet can be bought in pieces from small butchers but as it is tedious to prepare it is more commonly sold ready-prepared. Atora comes from beef kidney fat which has been processed to remove connective tissue before it arrives at the factory. The suet blocks are melted down, the fat is cooled then pumped to a machine which cools it further until it begins to solidify, at which point it is extruded through plates with small circular holes. The shreds are dusted with flour to prevent them from adhering. They are then passed through a series of sieves to remove excess flour and oversized particles. A vegetarian alternative, based on hydrogenated vegetable oils, has recently been developed.

Hot Cross Bun

DESCRIPTION:

A CIRCULAR BUN ABOUT 100MM DIAMETER, 50–60MM HIGH. WEIGHT: ABOUT 50G. COLOUR: GOLDEN BROWN, HIGHLY GLAZED, WITH A WHITE CROSS MARKED ON THE SURFACE. FLAVOUR: LIGHTLY SPICED.

HISTORY:

'Hot Cross buns; Hot Cross buns.
One a penny, two a penny, Hot Cross buns.
Smoking hot, piping hot,
Just come out of the baker's shop;
One a penny poker; two a penny tongs;
Three a penny fire-shovel, Hot Cross buns.'

Hot cross buns are baked for Good Friday in Britain. Their early history is unknown. Speculations have been made about possible pagan origins, but no firm conclusions have been reached. Whatever their origins, the buns are deeply embedded in folk traditions. It was commonly believed that breads baked on Good Friday never went stale or mouldy. They were hung as good luck charms in the corner of the kitchen. Steeped in water, crumbs from the same bun were thought curative. Such traditions are parallelled on mainland Europe.

David (1977) observes that hot cross buns are made from a spiced fruit dough which is also made for ordinary buns. Such recipes have been used since at least the fifteenth century for making large and small cakes. In the sixteenth century, bakers were limited by law to the times at which these doughs could be produced and sold; one of these occasions was Good Friday.

Hot cross buns were produced in great quantity in the London region during the eighteenth century by the Chelsea Bun House. At Easter 1792 so many people gathered outside that there was almost a riot (Spicer, 1948). Few recipes for hot cross buns are given in domestic cookery books before the twentieth century. When made at home, the dough is lightly sweetened, enriched and spiced. Allspice, nutmeg, cinnamon and cloves are common additions. The cross can be made by cutting the dough, or by laying on strips of pastry or candied peel.

Brandy Snap

DESCRIPTION:

A THIN, LACY, ROLLED WAFER, ABOUT 80MM LONG, 20MM DIAMETER. WEIGHT: ABOUT 14G. COLOUR: LIGHT GOLD-BROWN. FLAVOUR AND TEXTURE: SWEET, MILDLY SPICY, VERY CRUNCHY.

HISTORY:

A brandy snap is a wafer, which are thin biscuits made in wafering irons. Waffles are made in the same way, but have leavening and are light and puffy. Wafers are a European form that have a history as long as the Catholic Church that used them as Host in the Mass. Every country has traditional patterns, recipes and customs pertaining to them – many still alive today. This link to religious observance puts wafers plumb in the middle of the idea of festival food; it is small coincidence that many were called fairings in England – those little mouthfuls that people bought and gave away on high days and holidays. Mid-Lent or

Mothering Sunday, particularly in the South, was also called Wafering Sunday (White, 1932).

Brandy snaps have preserved some connections with festivals, as has their more substantial cousin gingerbread. At the Marlborough Mop fair in the 1970s, David Mabey (1978) found them on sale as a fairing. Here, they were not rolled or curled (as we know them on most encounters) but flat like a true wafer.

If this ties the brandy snap to a tradition of British baking, what of the name? Is the snap reflection of texture, or some other attribute? The word snap meant a light meal, a snack, its use current from the early seventeenth century. The use of snap to denote a thin, crisp ginger biscuit seems first to have appeared in the Victorian period, especially in Scots and Northumbrian usage. There is, however, some difference between a thin ginger biscuit (which we still know as a snap) and the lacy ephemera that are brandy snaps. These do not have a recorded history much beyond the 1800s.

In their modern form, brandy snaps cannot date much earlier than the introduction of Golden Syrup (1870s), now thought essential to the recipe. However, there was nothing to stop them being made with honey or treacle (Simon 1960). *Law's Grocer's Manual* (*c.* 1895) describes them as wafer-like ginger biscuits, generally curled, and gives a recipe involving treacle; it is not as rich as the modern version. Jack (*c.* 1910) gives a recipe identical to that still used. Harris and Borella (*c.* 1900) give a ginger snap recipe and remark that the biscuits made from it look best if curled. Their advice to bakers, for they were writing a trade manual, was to make brandy snaps on a set day of the week: 'The old-fashioned way was on Brandy Snap day to use all the peel handles in the bakehouse, set them on supports, and fill them as fast as the snaps came from the oven.' The baker would roll them round the long, thin handles to make a tidy curl – domestic cooks simply roll them round wooden spoon handles. Until modern airtight wrappings were introduced, brandy snaps were sold as soon as they were made as they soften rapidly after cooling.

TECHNIQUE:

Equal quantities of Golden Syrup, butter, sugar and flour are used. The syrup, butter and sugar are melted together, and the flour added, together with a little salt, ground ginger, lemon juice and brandy. Small amounts of the mixture are dropped at widely spaced intervals on to paper-lined baking trays. They are baked at 200°C for 8–10 minutes then removed from the trays and cooled. On removal from the oven, the biscuits are allowed to cool for a few seconds then rolled around a wooden stick and allowed to set.

Cheese Straw

DESCRIPTION:

A LONG, NARROW BISCUIT BASED EITHER ON PUFF PASTRY OR SHORTBREAD, 60–160MM LONG, 7–20MM WIDE; PUFF PASTRY 10–15MM DEEP, SHORTBREAD 3–4MM. WEIGHT: APPROXIMATELY 15G. COLOUR: PUFF PASTRY-TYPE, GOLDEN ON TOP WITH PALER SIDES; SHORTBREAD-TYPE, AN EVEN GOLD. FLAVOUR AND TEXTURE: STRONG CHEESE FLAVOUR, CRISP TEXTURE.

HISTORY:

The first mention of cheese straws dates to about 1870 (*OED*). Rich pastry recipes involving cheese as a flavouring are to be found prior to this but it seems that dishes such as soufflés and toasted cheese were more popular. Cheese straws and related biscuits made from mixtures flavoured with Parmesan or Cheddar came into their own during the late nineteenth century when the British developed a habit of taking a savoury as the final course of an elaborate meal. This consisted of some small, highly flavoured, salty item of meat, fish or cheese. The intention was, according to Sir Henry Thompson, to clean the palate, or to take away the sweet taste of the dessert, allowing for better appreciation of a final glass of wine.

It is from this that cheese straws and other cheese-flavoured biscuits and pastries descend. They have remained popular as an appetizer and accompaniment to cocktails even though the habit of eating savouries at the end of a formal meal has atrophied. They are still made by many bakers. Both puff-pastry and shortbread types are still available. There are also a few artisan bakers who make high-quality products in this tradition. A modern development is Dorset Cheddar Wafers, made by a family bakery near Sherborne in Dorset, using local cheese, butter and cream.

TECHNIQUE:

Puff pastry is folded and rolled with grated cheese; a mature Cheddar is usually preferred. Shortbread cheese straws and biscuits require flour, butter and cheese in the proportions 3:2:2. Parmesan (which has been imported and used in British cookery for over 300 years) is often named but may be replaced by a strong English cheese. Cayenne, mustard and salt are added to the mixture, which is bound with egg yolk and a little water. Dorset Cheddar Wafers are unique, and based on a different principle.

Christmas Pudding

DESCRIPTION:

A BOILED FRUIT PUDDING, USUALLY PRESENTED IN A DEEP BASIN, BUT SOMETIMES MADE AS A SPHERE WRAPPED IN CLOTH, AN OLDER METHOD. A PUDDING WEIGHING 1LB (ABOUT 500G) PACKED IN A BASIN IS 60–70MM DEEP, ABOUT 110MM DIAMETER AT THE TOP, AND 70MM AT THE BASE. WEIGHT: 500G–1KG. COLOUR: FROM CHESTNUT TO RICH, DARK BROWN; SPECKLED WITH DRIED FRUIT AND NUTS. FLAVOUR AND TEXTURE: RICH, SWEET, SLIGHTLY ALCOHOLIC.

HISTORY:

This is a representative of a group of foods which were formerly much more important to the British: suet puddings enclosed in a floured cloth and cooked by steaming. Food has been wrapped in animal guts or skins from the very first sausages, but the suet pudding – and by inevitable progress, the sweet pudding – was only sensibly practicable with the development of the pudding cloth, first identified in a recipe for Cambridge or College pudding in 1617 (Wilson, 1973). An immense variety of puddings was then created.

Plum (or plumb) puddings – the plum referring to the dried fruit – are mentioned in a pamphlet *Christmas Entertainments* (1740), as is plum porridge, which is sometimes quoted as a forerunner of the pudding. A plum porridge recipe given by Mrs Glasse (1747) shows that, like the filling for mince pies, plum porridge contained meat; it was thickened with bread crumbs and flavoured with spices, wine, sugar, and large quantities of dried fruit. Plum puddings contained suet, dried fruit, eggs, bread crumbs, flour and spices and the relationship between the dishes is unclear. Wilson noted that early plum puddings never included alcohol amongst the ingredients. By the nineteenth century, recipes for plum porridge had vanished from cookery books, but many were given for plum pudding, ranging from plain to very rich. Some are specifically intended for Christmas, but it is clear from Mrs Beeton (1861) that plum puddings generally were seasonable in winter, presumably because the dried fruit appeared in the shops during the late autumn. In the twentieth century, the term plum pudding became archaic and the name Christmas pudding now ties the dish to that festival.

The plum pudding is one of the most distinctive British foods, a guaranteed marker of nationality. The French, for example, cannot accept the idea of using suet in the way it is deployed in a plum pudding. When Lady Mary Wortley Montagu was living in Padua in the 1750s she educated her neighbours in the delights of English cookery: wheaten breads, butter, custard, syllabub, mince pies and plum puddings were her great successes. When Casanova wished to impress an Englishwoman of his undoubted charms, he ordered her a dinner cooked by an Italian innkeeper to his instructions. It consisted of a pudding and some fillet of beef broiled on a grill.

Today, the suet pudding's attractions have waned. The style of cookery – long boiling – and the very substantial nature of the food are less attuned with the national taste than they were. The plum pudding has become a calendar food, eaten at one season. Many people still do make their own puddings but more buy them from large manufacturers, artisan bakers or speciality cooks. The standard of those from commercial makers is as varied as the prices they charge and the skills they deploy.

Although the tradition is of no great antiquity, the making and serving of Christmas pudding (and Christmas cake) has attracted much folklore and superstition. Some of these have been transferred from the now archaic celebration of Twelfth Night. The pudding is reheated by steaming and brought to the Christmas table flaming with warm brandy and decorated with holly. Accompaniments are rum or brandy butter, cream, custard or a sweet roux-based sauce flavoured with rum. Lucky tokens are added to the mixture for home-made puddings; once, silver threepenny or sixpenny pieces were the choice. Sometimes special silver charms, reserved for the purpose, were used instead; they were made in sets, each one a different shape, and were supposed to indicate the finder's fortune in marriage and money matters. This is parallelled by many similar European customs relating to festive foods.

TECHNIQUE:

Recipes are based on a mixture of bread crumbs and shredded suet. Sugar, currants, sultanas, raisins and candied peel are incorporated. Flour, prunes, grated raw or cooked, mashed carrots are quoted in some modern recipes. Mixed sweet spice (cinnamon, nutmeg and allspice), brandy and a little salt are added. These dry ingredients are mixed thoroughly together. Milk, eggs or beer are used to bind the mixture. Brandy or whisky may be added. Then it is allowed to stand for some hours. Bag puddings are made by smearing a cotton pudding cloth with butter, liberally dusting this with flour, and then placing the mixture in the centre. The edges of the cloth are drawn up around it and tied by a string. Alternatively, the mixture is measured into basins, covered with greaseproof paper and foil or cloth. A 500g pudding is steamed for about 5 hours. When cooled, the pudding is covered with fresh paper and stored for at least a month before reheating. If correctly made and stored, a pudding will keep for up to 2 years. Leftover Christmas pudding is often reheated by frying it in butter.

Madeira Cake

DESCRIPTION:

A PLAIN SPONGE, LIGHTLY FLAVOURED WITH LEMON, ABOUT 220MM ACROSS, 60–80MM DEEP. WEIGHT: ABOUT 900G. COLOUR: DEEP GOLD, RICH YELLOW CRUMB; IT MAY BE DECORATED WITH CANDIED CITRON PEEL. FLAVOUR: RICH, BUTTERY, NOT SWEET.

HISTORY:

The name was given this cake because it was thought a perfect companion to the wine. Madeira was much imported from the 1600s, if not earlier, and highly esteemed thereafter. The drinking of wine accompanied by cake was the eighteenth century's version of the modern meal of lunch – dinner was then much earlier in the day. It was a custom of the leisured classes. Come the Victorians, the wine and cake remained as a snack.

The name itself is not especially early. Ayrton (1975) claims to have found it in a manuscript of the 1700s but its first use in print is in Eliza Acton (1845). What she describes is reminiscent of earlier 'biscuits' for she suggests whisking the eggs and adding the rest of the ingredients slowly to avoid curdling. Other major Victorian writers do not include recipes by the name of 'Madeira' cake. It is only widely used from the early 1900s. By then, the method is identical to a rich sponge. The essential component, from Acton onwards, is the flavouring of lemon; the decoration with citron peel is also almost invariable.

TECHNIQUE:

The ingredients are butter, sugar, eggs and flour. Higher quantities of sugar are called for in early recipes; modern ones contain more egg. Butter is essential to the close texture and rich flavour. Butter and sugar are creamed, the eggs whisked over hot water until pale and thick and then beaten into the creamed mixture; sifted flour is folded in with grated lemon rind. It is baked in tins at 180°C for 2 hours. The top is decorated with thin strips of candied citron peel.

Rich Fruit Cake

DESCRIPTION:

A CAKE: VERY DARK BROWN, FLECKED WITH DRIED FRUIT, OFTEN HIGHLY DECORATED WITH LAYERS OF MARZIPAN OR ALMOND PASTE, AND A COATING OF STIFF WHITE ICING, TO WHICH PIPING, RIBBONS AND OTHER THINGS MAY BE ADDED AS THE OCCASION REQUIRES.

HISTORY:

The history of the rich fruit cake is interwoven with that of many other fruited, spiced bakery specialities in Britain. These share a common origin in the habit of enriching bread doughs with butter or lard, sugar, eggs and adding dried fruit, candied peel and spices to make special celebration affairs. Their immediate ancestors can be seen in the 'plum' cakes (plum in this context referred to the dried fruit, and the term occurs from the mid-seventeenth century onwards) and 'bride cakes' (known from the mid-sixteenth century onwards). These were probably rich yeast-leavened doughs. Marzipan, ornamented with icing, was a separate entity, served at the

end of the meal as part of a banquet of sweetmeats (Wilson, 1991). By the eighteenth century, recipes for bride cakes show them to be yeast doughs, much enriched with eggs, butter, cream, spices, dried and candied fruit, sugar and wine or brandy. Mrs Raffald (1769) gives several examples. She also gives instructions for making almond and sugar icing for the cake, illustrating how this formerly separate item had become integral. At some stage during the nineteenth century, the yeast vanished from the recipe and cooks relied upon thoroughly beating the eggs to leaven the mixture. Up until the late 1800s, such cakes seem to have been mostly used for weddings, and are found under the title of bride cake or wedding cake in standard works such as Mrs Beeton (1861) and Florence Jack (*c.* 1910).

At what stage fruit cakes became part of the Christmas feast is not clear. At first, puddings and pies were more important. A cake was often part of the Twelfth Night celebrations but it was not necessarily a fruit cake (Henisch, 1984). However, plum cake is mentioned amongst Christmas foods in a chapbook dated 1740, so the association is probably of long standing.

TECHNIQUE:

Many people use formulae which have been handed down by several generations in a family. However, they produce results which are recognizably similar. Flour, butter and soft brown sugar are used in equal proportions; the weight of dried fruit is about equivalent to the total weight of basic ingredients and is a mixture of sultanas, raisins, currants, candied peel and glacé cherries; spices, usually cinnamon and nutmeg, are also added, plus lemon or orange juice and zest, a small proportion of ground almonds and a high ratio of eggs. Baking powder is sometimes used. The butter and sugar are creamed; the eggs added; the flour and spices are folded in; all other ingredients are added. It is baked in a tin at 175°C for 2–4 hours. The cakes are wrapped and stored for 1–6 months; it is common practice to sprinkle them from time to time with brandy or rum. Decoration, with a layer of marzipan and then icing, is often elaborate and will depend on the skill of the baker and on the event being celebrated.

Seed Cake

DESCRIPTION:

A CIRCULAR CAKE, DECORATED WITH WHOLE ALMONDS, 140MM DIAMETER, 60–70MM DEEP. WEIGHT: ABOUT 750G. COLOUR: LIGHT BROWN OUTSIDE, PALE GOLD CRUMB INSIDE, FLECKED WITH CARAWAY SEEDS AND PIECES OF CANDIED PEEL. FLAVOUR: RICH, BUTTERY, WITH CARAWAY AND LEMON.

HISTORY:

Caraway occurred not just in seed cakes, but in every sort of bun, bread and sweet confection imaginable. One of the great divides in the history of British cookery is its disappearance from everyday flavours. Cakes well perfumed with this spice were universal in English households. Eliza Smith (1758) gave several recipes. They could be divided between a 'common', plain and yeast-raised seed cake and a much richer affair. The latter may have developed from the caraway-flavoured 'Prince bisket', an early type of sponge cake composed of beaten eggs, sugar and flour, for which recipes can be found in early seventeenth-century cookery books. The very richest version was known as 'the Nun's cake'. Some of these cakes used plain caraway seeds, others called for caraway comfits (dragées or sugar-coated seeds).

'Let us eat and drink; for tomorrow we shall die.'

Isaiah, 22:13

Rich (egg-raised) and plain (yeasted) seed cakes persisted until the early part of the twentieth century, by which time baking powder was becoming the raising agent of choice. Modern seed cakes are in reality no more than caraway-flavoured sponges.

TECHNIQUE:

Meg Rivers Cakes of Middle Tysoe (Warwickshire), the only company located making seed cakes at the present time, uses a recipe based on a conventional creamed cake mixture. Caraway seeds are soaked in lemon juice for some hours before the batter is prepared. Ground almonds and candied peel give additional flavour and texture.

Treacle Tart

DESCRIPTION:

A CIRCULAR OPEN TART, SOMETIMES DECORATED WITH TWISTED STRIPS OF PASTRY OR A LATTICE; USUALLY BETWEEN 120–240MM ACROSS, ABOUT 15MM DEEP. FLAVOUR: VERY SWEET, SLIGHTLY LEMON.

HISTORY:

Treacle, in modern English, refers to the uncrystallizable syrup which is a by-product of sugar refining. It most commonly refers to black treacle and is often used as a synonym of molasses (in American English). Pale treacle, known under the trade name Golden Syrup, was obtained by a different industrial process and was not sold in Britain until the 1880s. It is this which is used in 'treacle' tart. The history of the recipe is largely unknown, but in its modern form it cannot date back earlier than the introduction of Golden Syrup.

It is possible that Golden Syrup was a late substitute. The lexicographer Joseph Wright (1896–1905) records a Hertfordshire dialect term, 'treacle waddies', stating they were made of breadcrumbs and treacle; and the first recipe so far located, Jack (c. 1910), cites either syrup or treacle as the filling. It is still a favourite pudding. Grigson (1984) considers treacle tarts to be typical of a Northern tradition of baking for high tea, in which 'plate pies' have formed an important element, especially for poorer people, for well over a hundred years. She remarks, 'A plate pie is frugal, much pastry, little filling, the art is all in the pastry.' The ratio of pastry to filling distinguishes plate pies from the deeper pies made in the south of England.

TECHNIQUE:

A plain short-crust pastry, typically made of plain flour and lard in the proportion 2:1 is used for the case. This is filled with a mixture made from warmed Golden Syrup, bread-crumbs and lemon juice, decorated with a pastry lattice or twisted pastry strips and baked at about 180°C for 30–40 minutes.

Butterscotch

DESCRIPTION:

THE BEST-KNOWN VERSION OF BUTTERSCOTCH NOW AVAILABLE IS SOLD IN SMALL OBLONG BLOCKS, 25 X 15 X 9MM, EACH WEIGHING 8G. COLOUR: A SLIGHTLY TRANSLUCENT TAWNY BROWN. FLAVOUR: RICH, BUTTERY, A HARD, BRITTLE, CRUNCHY TEXTURE. COMPOSITION: SUGAR, BUTTER, FLAVOURING.

HISTORY:

Although the term butterscotch has not been identified in use before about 1850, Everton toffee was very similar – short-textured, buttery, high-boiled. This appears to have been known a hundred years before. Skuse (*c.* 1892) thought Doncaster butterscotch and Everton toffee were identical except in presentation. Butterscotch was cut into small bars and Everton toffee left in a slab. Everton toffee's origins lie in the mid-eighteenth century, when it is said to have been made by one Molly Bushell in what is now a suburb of Liverpool. Once famous, it is no longer made commercially, although an old-fashioned toffee of this type is still made in the Yorkshire town of Harrogate by a company established in 1840 (Farrah's – recently defunct, but now revived under new ownership).

In Doncaster itself, a variation on Everton toffee was made by the confectioner Samuel Parkinson from about 1817. This was called butterscotch. The business (which became Parkinson and Son in 1840) was soon renowned for its creation, which was sold to crowds who came to the horse races in the town and gained approval from Queen Victoria and other members of the royal family.

This type of sweet always seems to have had a northern bias but the name has no specific connection with Scotland, despite the fame enjoyed by Dundee (Tayside) butterscotch. The derivation is obscure. It owes its flavour largely to the use of salted butter, and it is possible that scotch in this context means scorched, as the butter browns during boiling. (The word is also a culinary term meaning cuts or slashes made on meat before broiling.)

TECHNIQUE:

Any sweet including the word butter in its title must by law contain at least 4 per cent butter-fat. White sugar (light brown was once used) is dissolved in water and boiled, glucose syrup is added and the batch cooked to 146°C. The butter, melted or cut into small pieces, is added and small quantities of salt and oil of lemon stirred through. The mixture is poured on to oiled marble and cut or moulded into small bars, while still plastic. The sweet is packed as soon as possible in foil and waxed paper.

Fudge

DESCRIPTION:

FUDGE IS USUALLY CUT INTO CUBES OF 20MM. COLOUR: A PLAIN FUDGE IS LIGHT BROWN. FLAVOUR: PLAIN FUDGE IS VERY SWEET, WITH A CARAMELIZED MILK NOTE. FUDGES FLAVOURED WITH NUTS, CHOCOLATE, COFFEE OR FRUIT ARE ALSO MADE. COMPOSITION: SUGAR, MILK, GLUCOSE, BUTTER, FLAVOURINGS.

HISTORY:

The word fudge with reference to confectionery is a relative newcomer to the English language. Its first known use dates from the early years of the twentieth century. Nor can the confection it describes, a mixture of sugar and dairy produce boiled together and then stirred, claim much greater antiquity. There are precedents for the ingredients, which are the same as in toffee, and for the technique, which is employed in making fondant. But the origins of fudge itself remain obscure. It is probably related to Scottish tablet, which also uses similar ingredients and techniques. It is now well-established in many parts of the country, especially in areas which have a tourist industry and where good cream and butter are found. One of the longest-established fudge-makers, the Toffee Shop in Penrith, uses a recipe dating from the early twentieth century.

TECHNIQUE:

Exact recipes and techniques vary from maker to maker. The ingredients are refined sugar, butter and milk. Cream, clotted cream or evaporated milk can all be added; some recipes require glucose syrup. The sugar and dairy produce are combined, heated and stirred continuously until the sugar is dissolved; then it is heated to 116°C. This may vary by one or two degrees either side and, as temperature is part of the special knowledge involved in making fudges, the exact figure is rarely revealed. It affects the final texture of the product, a slightly higher temperature giving a slightly harder confection. The sugar syrup is now grained, either by stirring it to induce crystals to form or by adding a small quantity of fondant especially prepared to have a particular texture. The fondant method is more common. In the past, the syrup was beaten; again, temperature was vital to the outcome. If hot, the syrup produced larger sugar crystals and a coarser result; a cool syrup gave small crystals and a smooth texture. Once grained, the mixture is poured on to a slab or into metal trays and left to set before cutting into cubes or slices.

Humbugs

DESCRIPTION:

HUMBUGS ARE SMALL SUGAR SWEETS SHAPED BY CUTTING PIECES FROM LONG STICKS OF BOILED SUGAR WHILE THEY ARE STILL HOT AND MALLEABLE. THE STICK IS TURNED A QUARTER TURN AS EACH CUT IS MADE, SO THAT A TETRAHEDRON IS FORMED. COLOUR: STRIPED BLACK AND WHITE OR BEIGE AND BROWN. FLAVOUR: STRONGLY PEPPERMINT. COMPOSITION: SUGAR, GLUCOSE, FLAVOURING.

HISTORY:

These sweets share a common origin with many of the pulled and striped confections so popular in the British Isles. They developed from small, flavoured, pulled-sugar sticks known as pennets. These had been made until the 1800s, when they either disappeared completely, were replaced by modern forms, or were renamed humbugs. The word humbug (which carries another meaning of deception and sham) has been used for sweets since at least the early nineteenth century, when it was remembered as being in common use in Gloucestershire (*OED*). Many early references to the sweet come from the north of England, and one, from the novelist Mrs Gaskell, describes them as well-flavoured with mint – still a characteristic. Fifty years on, Skuse (*c.* 1892) described a method identical to that used to make humbugs, but called the sweets 'cushions'. It is clear that several types were known. It was not until a later (1957) edition of Skuse that the name changed to humbug.

TECHNIQUE:

Sugar and glucose (proportions 3:1) are dissolved in water and boiled to 149°C. The batch is poured on to a marble or steel table and divided; one portion is left clear, the other coloured black; both are flavoured with peppermint. The clear portion is pulled until opaque and satin-smooth and is then used to stripe the black portion. Subsequently, the mass is spun out, cut into appropriate lengths, cooled and packed. Occasionally batches are made with brown sugar, one portion being left clear and brown, and the other, used for striping, pulled or worked until a very pale beige.

Earl Grey Tea

DESCRIPTION:

A BLACK LEAF TEA FLAVOURED WITH OIL OF BERGAMOT.

HISTORY:

Tea-drinking became fashionable in Britain during the eighteenth century; it has flourished ever since. Merchants blended teas according to the tastes of particular customers, and kept these blends secret. Occasionally they were commercialized, made available to a wider public. This is what has happened to Earl Grey.

The person who gave his name to the blend is reputed to have been Charles, second Earl Grey (1764–1854). The link between the person and the tea is still matter for debate. The Earl spent some time as a diplomat in China, and the commonly accepted story is that he was given the recipe whilst working there. However, Norwood Pratt (1982) points out the Chinese themselves 'are not now and never have been Earl Grey Tea drinkers'. Two of the greatest London tea companies, Jackson's of Piccadilly and Twining's, claim to be the owners of the original formula, although Pratt remarks that Twining's claim is much weakened by the fact it uses a blend of China and Darjeeling teas. Tea was not planted in Darjeeling at the time the Earl was meant to have obtained the recipe.

Earl Grey was, apparently, the first scented tea known in the West, and has been a best-seller since the 1930s, if not before.

TECHNIQUE:

The British market accounts for a substantial part of the world tea crop every year. It is now regarded as the national drink. The British were responsible for introducing tea-growing to India, Ceylon and Kenya.

Although the raw material is grown and dried abroad, the final step, blending, is carried out in Britain. In the country of origin, samples are taken each day by tea growers and sent to the London brokers for comparison with earlier batches; the remainder of the day's output is packed in tea chests. When the sample arrives in London, it is tasted and a decision made on where the tea is to be sold. The tea in chests is imported (usually to Felixstowe) and kept in the tea clearing houses; small samples are circulated to all tea auctions and potential buyers, who taste before bidding at auction for particular lots. The auctions, which depended on personal contact and interaction, have been superseded (as has the ritual of the London Stock Exchange) by electronic trading.

Speciality teas – of which Earl Grey is one – form a very small sector. The dried leaves are sprayed with a very small proportion of oil of bergamot, to produce a delicately flavoured mild tea. Although the tea trade is concentrated on London, about 25 companies blend and pack speciality teas in the UK as a whole.

Elderberry Cordial

DESCRIPTION:
A FRUITY, WINY FLAVOUR, REMINISCENT OF PORT.

HISTORY:
Cordials – which were supposedly good for the heart – were usually made with alcohol. It both revived the flagging breast and acted as a preservative. They were made by countless home apothecaries in their still-rooms, the essential harvest of a thousand plants and trees. Juices from wild or cultivated fruit were also mixed with honey or sugar boiled to a syrup. They were known as rob in the seventeenth and eighteenth centuries. They were a medicinal rather than culinary preparation (as, indeed, might be cordials). The sugar, like the alcohol, acted as a preservative. Until sugar became spectacularly cheap in the nineteenth century, the alcoholic essences outnumbered the syrups.

Elderberries have long been appreciated as a base for wine and alcoholic drinks. They gave not much taste, but spectacular colour; and they were free. Recipes survive from the earliest period of cookery books.

The manufacture of sugar-based cordials was eventually industrialized at the beginning of last century and received a tremendous fillip in the period 1939–45 when black currant was identified as a ready source of vitamin C. The most famous cordial, Ribena, owes its success to this. Specialist producers cast about for other fruit to emulate Ribena. Elderberry is one.

TECHNIQUE:
The berries are cleaned and pressed to extract the juice, which is heated with sugar, citric acid and other ingredients before bottling.

Gooseberry Wine

DESCRIPTION:
THESE WINES ARE 10–12 PER CENT ALCOHOL BY VOLUME.

HISTORY:
Fruit, vegetable and floral wines in Britain include elderberry, blackberry, raspberry, damson, parsnip, elderflower and meadowsweet flower. Gooseberries have been grown in Britain for over 400 years, and it seems probable that a fermented drink has been made with them for almost as long. In the late nineteenth century, Kettner remarked that an alternative name for the gooseberry was wineberry, 'because of the wine it made'. It was also a wine of the people, for ease of cultivation meant gooseberries were grown in cottage gardens, especially in northern England and Scotland.

Recipes were passed down through families or published in texts such as Mrs Beeton's (1861), where an effervescing version was suggested. It is evident that sparkling gooseberry wine was made and passed off as champagne by the unscrupulous. English wines were usually produced at home, not by large enterprises. However, there were exceptions. Gooseberry wine was produced in Sussex shortly after the Second World War by the cider and wine company Merrydown. Other companies in fruit-growing areas have followed suit. There are 10 companies making fruit-based country wines in the South-East.

TECHNIQUE:

The gooseberries (preferably slightly underripe) are pulped, often with the addition of some water, then strained to yield their juice; a sweetening agent – which may be sugar, honey, grape or apple juice – is added and the mixture fermented using a wine yeast. Gooseberry wine is matured for up to 10 months before bottling. A sparkling version, using the champagne method, is produced by at least one company.

Sweet Stout

DESCRIPTION:

THESE STOUTS ARE DARK. MACKESON'S HAS 'A DARK HEAD AND AN ALMOST BLACK COLOUR WITH CLARET HIGHLIGHTS' (JACKSON, 1993). MACKESON'S IS A SWEET BEER WITH COFFEE-CHOCOLATE NOTES.

STOUTS ARE USUALLY LOW IN ALCOHOL, TYPICALLY 3–3.5 PER CENT ALCOHOL BY VOLUME. THE USE OF THE WORDS 'MILK' OR 'CREAM' ON THE LABELS OF SWEET STOUTS IS NOT ALLOWED IN MAINLAND BRITAIN, ALTHOUGH THEY CAN BE USED ON GUERNSEY.

HISTORY:

In 1875 John Henry Johnson of Lincoln's Inn Fields, London, sought a patent for a milk beer based on whey, lactose and hops. Several applications for similar brews were filed by different people over the next 30 years, and one, by a dietician, went into commercial production at Mackeson's Brewery, Hythe (Kent) in 1907. This was available nationally by the 1930s and was emulated by many other brewers. The health aspects of these beers were emphasized, although they probably just contained more sugar and calories than ordinary ales.

Overall success of the recipe was dealt a blow by rationing during and after 1939–45. Brewers were discouraged from using milk. Furthermore, sweet stouts have become less popular; they are viewed as old-fashioned.

Mackeson's is still the most important brand, although a regional variant survives on Guernsey. Mackeson's is owned by Whitbread, who produce sweet stout in Lancashire.

TECHNIQUE:

At Mackeson's, brewing commences with a mixture of pale ale and chocolate malts mixed with water at about 70°C. The wort is strained off and boiled in a brew kettle for 60–90 minutes; hops (Targets), brewer's caramel and lactose, the latter representing at least 9 per cent of the grist, are added; the beer is fermented, racked, fined, primed, pasteurized and bottled.

Guernsey milk stout is brewed using invert sugar and primed with candy sugar before bottling.

Apple Chutney

HISTORY:

This illustrates a particular aspect of British food culture. The word is derived from *chatni*, Hindi for a hot or spiced relish, reflecting the influence of Indian food and ingredients on the British. The imperial connection gives a common source for chutneys, which show little regional variation in their new home. The families of retired civil servants and soldiers adapted them to local orchard fruit in place of mangoes and tamarinds. With a show of culinary realism, however, *Law's Grocer's Manual* (*c*. 1895) states the best chutneys were imported from India though imitations were produced in Britain. Mrs Beeton's 'Indian Chetney Sauce' (1861) of apples, tomatoes, salt, brown sugar, raisins, cayenne, ginger, garlic and vinegar is similar to modern recipes except the mixture was left in a jar in the sun, not boiled as is now the practice.

The new condiment must have offered a welcome addition to the jams and sour pickles produced in Britain. Recently, some specialists have evolved their own specific products based on family recipes and regional materials such as the Suffolk Chutney now made in East Anglia.

TECHNIQUE:

Ingredients are generally fruit, sugar and vinegar in the proportions 3:2:1. Spirit vinegar, which is colourless, is preferred to malt, though cider vinegar is also popular. Demerara or dark brown sugar is normally used.

Fruit and vegetables are peeled, cored or stoned, then diced or sliced. More sophisticated recipes call for the fruit to be salted, left overnight and drained. Vinegar may be flavoured with peppercorns, cloves, chillies and allspice. Sugar, garlic or shallots, sultanas, ground ginger and turmeric or mustard are added as required. This is all simmered until soft. Some recipes have been commercialized; one of the best known is a spiced vegetable mixture made under the name Branston Pickle. There are several similar products on the market, made by large manufacturers.

Curry Powder

DESCRIPTION:

AN AROMATIC YELLOW-BROWN POWDER OFTEN GRADED ACCORDING TO 'HEAT' (CHILLI CONTENT). BLENDS ARE BASED ON CORIANDER, FENUGREEK, TURMERIC, CUMIN AND PEPPER COMBINED WITH SMALLER AMOUNTS OF MORE AROMATIC SPICES.

HISTORY:

The British Empire is reflected strongly in a few foodstuffs. Exotic recipes returned with merchants, civil servants and administrators and have become naturalized. Curry has become, through the interaction of British and Indian culinary traditions, a dish which the British regard as part of their heritage. The word curry may derive from Tamil *kari*, meaning sauce; the first known reference in English dates to the end of the sixteenth century (*OED*). In modern usage, curry powder refers to particular spice blends used for flavouring dishes of meat, fish and vegetables. It is generally assumed that the mixtures marketed as curry powder are some mysterious Indian compound. This is not true. On the Indian sub-continent, cooks make up their own spice mixtures as required. Whilst curry powder obviously developed from Indian influence, long-standing British brands bear little resemblance to blends used in the Orient.

Recipes for curry 'the Indian way' appeared in cookery books such as Hannah Glasse (1747). Martin Muggeridge of Lion Foods Ltd, a spice company with a history stretching back to the mid-eighteenth century, observes that many of the formulae used by spice companies date from this time. Curry powders themselves are mentioned from the early 1800s, when Britons in India packed up their own favoured blends to send to their families in England. They were also made in England: Kitchiner (1817) stated his recipe had been selected for him by a friend at India House. It required 3 ounces (75g) coriander seed, 3 ounces (75g) turmeric, 1 ounce (25g) each of black pepper, mustard and ginger, half an ounce (14g) each of allspice and 'lesser' cardamoms, and a quarter of an ounce (7g) of cumin seed.

Many early curry powders, which may at that stage have been imported ready-prepared from India, were criticized for their balance of flavours. *Law's Grocer's Manual* (*c.* 1895) commented on poor quality and adulteration. These factors may have been the driving force behind a trend towards milling and blending of spices for curry in Britain itself. London was, and remains, a very important centre for spice importing, milling and blending and the ports of Liverpool and Bristol carried on this trade. Manufacture is concentrated in such districts.

As Indian food has gained a greater slice of British restaurant business, so curries have entered the national diet. While Indian and Bangladeshi cooks may use their own pastes and flavouring mixes, there has arisen a considerable modern trade with India for condiments and powders.

TECHNIQUE:

Spices for curry powder are selected for the British market from various countries according to quality, availability, exchange rates, and climatic conditions. India remains the most important supplier. Hygiene is now a major consideration. Spices are tested and, if necessary, treated to ensure low microbial levels. Ethylene oxide gas was used for this in the past. As this is now illegal under EU law, heat treatments which reduce the microbiological burden whilst leaving the flavour unaffected have been developed. In the last 20 years, a market for pastes, blends for specified dishes made up as semi-solid mixtures, has expanded.

Gooseberry And Elderflower Jam

DESCRIPTION:

COLOUR: TRANSLUCENT, DARK PINKISH-BROWN. FLAVOUR: SWEET-ACID, WITH PRONOUNCED GOOSEBERRY FLAVOUR AND MUSKY FLORAL OVERTONES. COMPOSITION: GOOSEBERRIES, SUGAR, ELDERFLOWERS.

HISTORY:

Gooseberries (*Rubes uvacrispa*) are the fruit of a wild plant native to northern Europe. We know they have been eaten in Britain since the fifteenth century and have remained popular here and in other Northern European countries such as Germany. Their flavour is less appreciated further south, for example in France beyond the north-western provinces of Normandy and Brittany. The elder (*Sambucus nigra*) is native to the British Isles and common in southern and lowland England, but rarer in areas of high altitude and the north of Scotland. Elderflowers have been used for drinks and herbal remedies for centuries. Elderflower wine was likened to the muscat wine Frontignan (Bradley, 1756). The same author, and others, proposed elderflower fritters as a sweet dish.

Recipes for gooseberry preserves and puddings appear in cookery books from the early eighteenth century and floral flavourings were proposed in some of these. John Nott (1726) has instructions that are very close to a modern jam recipe and another for candying gooseberries with rose-flavoured sugar. Hannah Glasse (1747) favoured orange flower water or sack (a sherry-like wine) for flavouring. Early evidence of the combination of gooseberry and elderflower is not forthcoming and owes much of its popularity to the writings of the late Jane Grigson, for example in *Good Things* (1971).

TECHNIQUE:

This type of jam is the product of domestic and artisan jam-makers. Small green gooseberries from early in the season make the best jam; this coincides with the flowering season of the elder tree. Gooseberries are prepared by topping and tailing. Elderflower heads are collected as they come into full blossom – on a sunny morning after the dew has evaporated for the best perfume. Domestic cooks simply mix fruit, water and sugar, and boil together, adding the elderflowers in a muslin bag. Commercial jam makers prefer to cook the gooseberries briefly with a little water and the bag of elderflowers; the latter is removed before the sugar is added.

Alternatively, a jelly can be made, cooking the fruit and flowers and straining the juice before adding the sugar.

Horseradish Sauce

DESCRIPTION:

CREAM-COLOURED OR GREYISH-WHITE; SLIVERS OF GRATED ROOT ARE USUALLY APPARENT. THE FLAVOUR IS ACID, ACRID, PIQUANT.

HISTORY:

Roast beef accompanied by horseradish sauce is considered by the English to be one of their best dishes. The combination has been popular since at least the middle of the nineteenth century.

Early reference to horseradish (*Cochlearia armoracia*) as a condiment ties it to Germany where, in the seventeenth century, it was apparently boiled with beef. (Germany remains an important source of the raw root for sauce manufacturers.) At this time, the English were more likely to put horseradish in mustard. Although references to horseradish vinegar and horseradish powder (the dried roots) are found in the early nineteenth century, for instance in Kitchiner (1817), its use in a sauce seems to have escaped mention until Eliza Acton (1845) gave a recipe for an Excellent Horseradish Sauce, compounded mostly of grated horseradish and cream. Essentially, this is the one still used in the domestic kitchen. Mrs Beeton (1861) remarked that horseradish had been for many years a favourite partner of roast beef.

By the late nineteenth century, horseradish sauce was bottled for sale. Some of the responsibility for commercialization of the sauce must lie with the Heinz company of North America in the 1870s. It was one of their first products. *Law's Grocer's Manual* gave a recipe for horseradish sauce showing it to be essentially a mixture of horseradish and vinegar mixed to a cream paste. The 4th edition of *Law's*, published just after the Second World War, observes that before 1940 a high-grade horseradish sauce was made in Oxford.

For the best sauces, fresh horseradish root is cleaned, peeled and grated, mixed with fresh cream, stabilizer and antioxidant, and filled into sterile jars. Cheaper grades include more stabilizers, sugar, and may rely on dried horseradish or horseradish powder for flavour and include other roots such as turnip. Much fresh horseradish root has been imported from Germany, although domestic supplies of mature roots (the older the root, the stronger the flavour) can still be obtained, for example at the mouth of the River Humber.

Lemon Curd

DESCRIPTION:

A SMOOTH, TRANSLUCENT SEMI-SOLID. COLOUR: BRIGHT YELLOW. FLAVOUR: AROMATIC, SHARP-SWEET. COMPOSITION: LEMONS, SUGAR, EGGS, BUTTER.

HISTORY:

The modern form of lemon curd developed in England in the later 1800s. When it gained acceptance, it was described as 'lemon curd for cheesecakes' – both in the Army and Navy Stores catalogue of 1895 and in Florence Jack's cookery book (c. 1910). However, the cheesecakes familiar to cooks of the 1700s were curds of milk or cream mixed with egg yolks, put into tart cases and baked until set. The lemon butter thickened with egg, lemon curd as we understand it, was more precisely a transparent pudding (Raffald, 1769). The thought that this mixture might be bottled and stored for later use, or even for sale, was of a piece with the industrialization of food production during the late Victorian period.

TECHNIQUE:

The zest of lemons is grated finely, or rubbed with sugar lumps to remove the oils; the juice is squeezed and strained. Juice, zest, sugar and butter are heated together until the butter is melted and the sugar dissolved; the eggs are beaten and the hot lemon mixture strained into them; the mixture then receives further gentle cooking until thickened.

Mincemeat and Mince Pies

DESCRIPTION:

COLOUR: BROWN, MOTTLED WITH PALE SUET AND DARK FRUIT. FLAVOUR: RICH, SWEET, WITH DRIED FRUIT AND SPIRITS. COMPOSITION: CURRANTS, SULTANAS, CANDIED PEEL, SUGAR, APPLES, SPICES, SUET, BUTTER, RUM. MINCE PIES ARE A ROUND, DOUBLE-CRUST PIE FILLED WITH MINCEMEAT.

HISTORY:

Mincemeat, in modern English, refers to a mixture of dried fruit and candied peel with spices and other ingredients. Grated raw apple is often included, as is sugar and brandy or rum or other strong spirit. Some type of fat is always present: butter or vegetable fat, but usually beef suet. In the past, most recipes required finely shredded fresh meat. This was presumably a development of medieval dishes of richly spiced and sweetened meat. Exactly when people began to prepare a spiced fruit and fat mixture as a long-keeping preserve is not clear. Hannah Glasse (1747) gave such a recipe under 'to make Mince-Pies the best Way', instructing the cook to put the mixture in a close-covered pot in which it would keep for months. When the mixture was used for pies, adding tongue or sirloin of beef was left to the cook's discretion. It is clear from the recipe that the name mincemeat had already transferred to the fruit mixture without any meat being present at all. However, the habit of using a proportion of meat in mincemeat persisted for some time after that. Eliza Acton (1845) thought minced raw steak was an improvement, and *Law's Grocer's Manual* (*c.* 1895) gave a recipe for the grocery trade which included cooked beef fillet. Some families maintain the tradition to the present day, although it is now unusual.

Meat in mincemeat survived longest in the sheep-rearing district of Cumbria, where lamb or mutton was used in preference to beef. Recipes are quoted by the Women's Institute (1937), Joan Poulson (1979), and Peter Brears (1991). An interesting line of development is evident in the Lake District custom of eating 'hackin' on Christmas morning, reported to the botanist Richard Bradley (1736). Hackin was a sort of sweet haggis, prepared by the maids of the household. If the pudding was not ready by daylight, 'the Maid is led through the Town, between two Men, as fast as they can run with her, up Hill and down Hill, which she accounts a great shame … all I can say to you of it, is, that it eats somewhat like a Christmas-Pye'. This hackin seems to have disappeared by the last years of Victoria to be replaced by a 'sweet pie' or a 'sweet lamb pie' – our mince pie with meat.

Although mincemeat was never confined to Christmas feasting, the close link between the food and festival is long-standing. Samuel Pepys records his Christmas eating in 1662: 'a mess of plum-porridge and roasted pullet for dinner; and I sent for a mince-pie abroad, my wife not being well to make any herself yet'. Martha Bradley (1756) wrote, 'it would no more be Christmas without [minced pie], than Michaelmas Day without Goose'. George Woodward wrote in a letter of 1754, 'Tom is come to us this Christmas, who is no enemy to minced pies.' Mincemeat at Christmas is now almost universal. There are many manufacturers and the variation in recipes – allowing for cost, dietary preference and taste – is great.

TECHNIQUE:
The ingredients – usually raisins, currants, shredded beef suet, chopped candied peel, peeled, cored minced apple and dark brown sugar – are mixed thoroughly together with spices and flavourings (grated nutmeg is the commonest). Lemon zest is sometimes added. So is brandy or rum. If required, raw lean meat is shredded or minced and mixed thoroughly with the other ingredients. The mincemeat is put in jars for keeping.

Mint and Apple Jelly

HISTORY:
Mint and apple is perhaps the best known jelly to use herbs or flowers – rosemary, thyme, marjoram, elderflower, lavender, clove pinks, marigolds, geranium and rose are others. The type developed from preserves that rely on fruit pectin (generally apples, although gooseberries are also used). They are related to jam rather than to gelatine-based dessert jellies. The use of flower flavourings, particularly rose and clove pinks (clove gilly-flowers) has a long history, with many recipes from at least the sixteenth century. Changing tastes have led to more emphasis on jellies eaten as condiments with meat. Mint jelly appears to have been commer-

cialized in the 1920s (*OED*). A specific recipe was published by Leyel and Hartley (1925). Subsequent interest in these products from preserve-makers in general has led to the large-scale introduction of apple and mint jelly and enthusiasm for other flower and herb jellies.

TECHNIQUE:

Originally, apple jellies were sweet and intended for the dessert course; lemon juice was added to nineteenth-century recipes, and vinegar is now used to sharpen their flavours. The prepared fruit is simmered with water, vinegar (cider, wine or spirit) and flavouring until the fruit disintegrates. The juice is drained through a jelly bag for 12 hours. The pulp is discarded, the juice measured. Sugar (about 500g to 660ml) is added and stirred until dissolved. It is brought to the boil and cooked rapidly until setting point is reached; a pectin extract may be added at this stage if necessary.

Mint Sauce

DESCRIPTION:

MINT SAUCE IS DARK GREEN-BROWN, DEPENDING ON THE RECIPE, AND SWEET-ACID IN FLAVOUR WITH STRONG MINT TASTE.

HISTORY:

The combination of sweet and sour and the extensive use of the herb mint are a specifically British addiction: they run counter to the separation of flavours that was a mark of the French style of cookery from the seventeenth century onwards. Other British store sauces, for example Cumberland, perpetuate the fruit-acid flavours. Although records of specific recipes and processes often do not extend further back than the eighteenth century, the spectrum of flavours they represent has many connections to the palette of tastes deployed by medieval cooks. Mint sauce is mentioned from the eighteenth century onwards (Glasse, 1747). At the end of her instructions on how to roast the hindquarter of a pig in imitation of young lamb, she remarks that 'it will eat like Lamb with mint sauce'. It seems that everyone knew what mint sauce was and how it was made, to the extent that a recipe was not thought necessary. Kitchiner (1817) does give a recipe: very similar to the modern one, a mixture of fresh mint, vinegar and brown sugar. His contemporary Frederick Accum (1820) comments, 'In some parts of the north of England, it is customary for the innkeepers to prepare mint-salad by bruising and grinding the vegetable in a large wooden bowl with a ball of lead of twelve or fourteen pounds weight. In this operation the mint is cut and portions of lead are ground off at every revolution of the ponderous instrument.' Accum's concern was with food purity, and his horrified observation about the use of lead has left a useful record of how mint was prepared for something he calls 'salad'; the mint must have been so crushed by the process that it yielded a texture similar to that of the modern sauce. Mint vinegar is mentioned as a substitute for fresh mint by Kitchiner.

TECHNIQUE:

Manufacturers use either fresh or dried mint. A variety known in English as spearmint (*Mentha spicata*) is used. Fresh mint has to be prepared by stripping it from the stalks and chopping. A mixture of sugar, salt, vinegar, water (and colouring if desired) is boiled together and poured over the mint.

'A cucumber should be well sliced, and dressed with pepper and vinegar, and then thrown out, as good for nothing.'

SAMUEL JOHNSON IN BOSWELL, *JOURNAL OF A TOUR TO THE HEBRIDES*

Piccalilli

DESCRIPTION:

PICCALILLI IS BRIGHT YELLOW, THANKS TO TURMERIC AND MUSTARD, WITH IDENTIFIABLE PIECES OF VEGETABLE. ITS FLAVOUR IS SWEET-ACID AND SPICY, THE TURMERIC PARTICULARLY APPARENT.

HISTORY:

The term piccalilli first entered English in the middle of the eighteenth century. Its origin is unknown, and may simply be a play upon 'pickle'. Mrs Raffald (1769) instructs the reader how to make 'Indian Pickle or Piccalillo'. Her recipe shows similarities to piccalilli made now, calling for mixed vegetables to be salted and preserved with mustard seed, turmeric, vinegar and spices. It shows the influence of the East-India trade, using imported spices and home-grown vegetables to imitate exotics. The pickle subsequently became a standard part of the English repertoire, used for preserving gluts of vegetables. Customary ingredients are cauliflower, beans, vegetable marrow, cucumber and small onions. *Law's Grocer's Manual* (c. 1895) described it as 'ordinary mixed pickles immersed in a special liquor'. It is the liquor of vinegar, turmeric and mustard which distinguishes piccalilli. Since at least the end of the nineteenth century, this has been made rather thick.

TECHNIQUE:

In the domestic method a selection of vegetables is prepared. Large items are cut or broken to give cubes of about 1–1.5cm, then soaked in a strong brine for 24 hours or longer. A mixture of spirit vinegar, sugar, ground mustard, ginger and other spices is prepared, the vegetables drained, added and simmered for 20 minutes. Turmeric and a little flour are blended with some cold vinegar and added to the mixture, then cooked to thicken it. The pickle is stored for 2 months before use. Small, artisan factory methods are essentially a scaled-up version of this process.

Pickled Onion

DESCRIPTION:

ONIONS ABOUT 3–4CM IN DIAMETER ARE USED. BRITISH PICKLES ARE MADE FROM LARGER ONIONS THAN THOSE OF OTHER COUNTRIES. THE PICKLE ASSUMES A BROWNISH CREAM COLOUR. THE TASTE OF THE PICKLE IS OFTEN STRONG FROM THE SPIRIT, MALT OR CIDER VINEGAR, WITH PEPPERCORNS AND ALLSPICE.

HISTORY:

It is not clear when the tradition of pickling fairly large onions in spiced vinegar began. They were certainly being made in the 1740s when Mrs Glasse instructed her readers to take onions about as large as a big walnut, blanch them and preserve them in spiced brine. Eliza Acton (1845) called for white-wine vinegar for her pickled onions, and observed that the Reading onion was the proper one to use. Mrs Beeton (1861) gave a recipe close to that still used by domestic producers, in which the onions were peeled, put in jars, covered with spiced vinegar and stored.

Commercial production of pickles was already well established. London had become a great centre of the trade. *Law's Grocer's Manual* noted that both imported and local onions from around Sandy in Bedfordshire were used. More recently, special varieties of pickling onions have been developed for the trade, as opposed to the small ungraded onions culled from ordinary crops which were formerly used.

Since the 1960s, pickled onions are often served with bread, cheese and salad under the name 'ploughman's lunch'. There is no evidence that such a combination was commonly eaten by ploughmen in the past or that ploughmen ate lunch in the modern sense of the word.

TECHNIQUE:

In industry, onions are peeled mechanically, finished by hand and brined for 24 hours. Washed and drained, they are put in jars and covered with spiced vinegar (often spirit vinegar). The jars are capped and pasteurized. Domestic makers brine and may also blanch the onions then pour over hot, spiced vinegar. They are matured for some weeks.

Pickled Walnut

DESCRIPTION:

THE WALNUTS LOOK ALMOST BLACK IN THE PICKLE, AND ARE GREY-BROWN INSIDE. THEIR FLAVOUR IS ACID, MILDLY SWEET AND SPICED. THEIR TEXTURE IS FIRM.

HISTORY:

Pickled walnuts became fashionable in the eighteenth century. The first detected reference to them is Eliza Smith (1727). They were used as garnishes and their liquor was also used in meat dishes. Recipes often called for large quantities of spices. The walnuts were picked at midsummer, steeped in brine, then covered with spiced vinegar for keeping. Such recipes must have been very useful for cooks in the British climate, where walnuts seldom ripen properly. *Law's Manual* (*c.* 1895) described how walnuts arrived at the pickling factory, barrelled up in brine (which was used for making walnut ketchup after the nuts had been removed), then were exposed to the sun to blacken before being soaked in vinegar and bottled with vinegar and spices. The result was 'one of our most esteemed condiments'.

TECHNIQUE:

Craft methods are broadly similar. The nuts must be picked before the shell forms, generally the second half of June. They are pricked and submerged in strong brine for 9–42 days, then removed and exposed to daylight for 2 or 3 days. After putting into jars, they are covered with vinegar (usually malt) and flavoured with spices. They are usually stored for at least a month for the flavour to mature. Commercial pickles use nuts imported from Italy.

Rhubarb and Ginger Jam

DESCRIPTION:

RHUBARB YIELDS A REDDISH OR BROWNISH JAM. THE GINGER IS USUALLY SMALL, TRANSLUCENT PIECES OF CANDIED ROOT.

HISTORY:

Sweet ginger-flavoured preserves of rhubarb or vegetable marrows are now considered humble examples of the jam-maker's craft. Unlike other jams, they do not use fruit; the basic ingredients are so easily grown that they are often disregarded, and the addition of ginger is seen as a simple method of adding flavour. To some extent this is true, but interesting precedents exist for these jams in the British tradition of preserving. These include the use of sugar syrups to preserve cucumbers – found in recipe collections of the seventeenth century onwards. An example is quoted by Mrs Beeton (1861), and the formula includes ginger. There are also seventeenth-century recipes for preserving the stems of plants, such as lettuces, in syrup, so the idea of rhubarb (technically a vegetable) in jam was not entirely strange. Added to this, the British have exhibited a persistent taste for sweet preserves of ginger very much in the style of seventeenth-century 'suckets' of fruit, stems or roots in syrup. Jarrin (1820) talked of preserved ginger, and Mrs Beeton noted imports of West Indian ginger in syrup. However, the development of a ginger jam (sugar-preserved green ginger, in a pectin gel) dates only to the 1920s, when it was known as ginger marmalade (Wilson, 1985).

TECHNIQUE:

Neither rhubarb nor marrow contains significant quantities of pectin, and preserving sugar (with added pectin) is sometimes recommended. Rhubarb is cut into small pieces, covered with the sugar and left for 24 hours for the sugar to draw out the juice and produce a syrup; this is strained and boiled with candied ginger and lemon peel. The rhubarb is added and everything cooked to 104–106°C. Marrow for jam is sometimes cubed, salted, then rinsed; otherwise, the high water-content produces an unsatisfactory jam.

***

Also produced nationwide

CUMBERLAND SAUCE (P. 108)
DOUBLE-CRUST FRUIT PIE (P. 47-48)
GINGER CAKE (P. 100-101)
MEDLAR (FRUIT) JELLY (P. 136-138)
MUFFIN (P. 255-256)
PIG'S TROTTERS (P. 238)
SIMNEL CAKES (P. 177)
SLOE GIN (P. 106)
WHEY BUTTER (P. 14)

Enjoying
British Food

A British Cheeseboard

CHEESES:

Derby, Leicester, Stilton, Coverdale, Swaledale, Wensleydale, Cotherstone, Cheshire, Lancashire, Ribblesdale, Carolina, Sussex Slipcote, Wellington, Bath, Baydon Hill, Beenleigh Blue, Caerphilly, West Country Farmhouse Cheddar, Cornish Yarg, Curworthy, Herefordshire Hops, Double and Single Gloucester, Dorset Blue Vinney, Sharpham, Vulscombe, Kelsae, Caboc, Crowdie, Orkney Farmhouse, Dunlop, Dunsyre Blue, Lanark Blue, Scottish Cheddar.

BISCUITS FOR CHEESE:

Bath Oliver, Scottish Oatcake, Dorset and Norfolk Knobs, Beremeal Bannock, Orkney Water Biscuit

APPLES FOR CHEESE:

Cox's Orange Pippin, Egremont Russet, Blenheim Orange, D'Arcy Spice, Ribston Pippin, Worcester Pearmain, Discovery, James Grieve

A Picnic Hamper

Melton Mowbray Pork Pie, Potted Shrimps, Potted Crab, Pressed Tongue, Pressed Beef, Suffolk Ham, Brawn, Lincolnshire Stuffed Chine, Bath Chaps, Fidget Pie, Cornish Pasty, Devonshire Ham, Potted Hough, Scotch Pie, Forfar Bridie, Smoked Game, Smoked Mackerel

Breads and biscuits:

Cottage Loaf, Channel Island Butter, Bap, Aberdeen Rowie, Stotty Cake, Glasgow Roll, Crusty Swansea, Softie

Seasoning:

Pickled Damsons, Taylor's Original Mustard, Apple Chutney, Colman's Mustard, Cider Vinegar, Marmite, Maldon Sea Salt, Piccalilli, Pickled Onion

Sweet:

Custard Tart, Yorkshire Curd Tart, Banbury Cake, Yorkshire Parkin, Eccles Cake, Lardy Cake, Apple Cake, Cornish Heavy Cake, Kendal Mint Cake, Double Crust Fruit Pie [listed under Blueberry Pie], Border Tart, Cumnock Tart, Oldbury Tart, Treacle Tart, Wilfra Tart, Yorkshire Mint Pastry

Fruits and vegetables:

Egremont Russet, Cox's Orange Pippin, Blenheim Orange Apple, Cherry, Conference Pear, Victoria Plum, Strawberry, Tomato, Watercress

Drinks:

Cider, Bitter Beer, Heather Ale, Newcastle Brown Ale, Silver Birch Wine, Dandelion and Burdock, Oatmeal Stout, Single Variety Apple Juice, Irn Bru, Tizer, Vimto

An Afternoon Tea

Earl Grey Tea

FOR SPREADING:

Yorkshire Tea Cake, Pikelet, Scone, Scottish Pancake and Crumpet, English Crumpet and Muffin, Devon Split with Clotted Cream, Medlar Jelly, Sea Lavender Honey, Marmite, Black Butter, Channel Island Butter, Lemon Curd, Rhubarb and Ginger Jam, Mint and Apple Jelly

CAKES AND TEABREADS:

Colston Bun, Cornish Fairing, Dorset Knob, Norfolk Knob, Dough Cake, Oldbury Tart, Sally Lunn, Welsh Cake, Welsh Plate Cake, Fat Rascal, Isle of Wight Doughnut, Ripon Spice Cake, Bath Bun, Whitby Lemon Bun, Whitby Gingerbread, Borrowdale Teabread, Chorley Cake, Wilfra Tart, Market Drayton Gingerbread, Ashbourne Gingerbread, Kirriemuir Gingerbread, Grantham Gingerbread, Lincolnshire Plum Bread, Melton Hunt Cake, Shrewsbury Cake, Goosnargh Cake, Madeira Cake, Grasmere Gingerbread, Bara Brith, Hawkshead Wig, Kendal Pepper Cake, Ormskirk Gingerbread, Cider Cake, Chelsea Bun, Maids of Honour, Abernethy Biscuit, Petticoat Tails, Parkin Biscuit, Puggie Bun, Raggy Biscuit

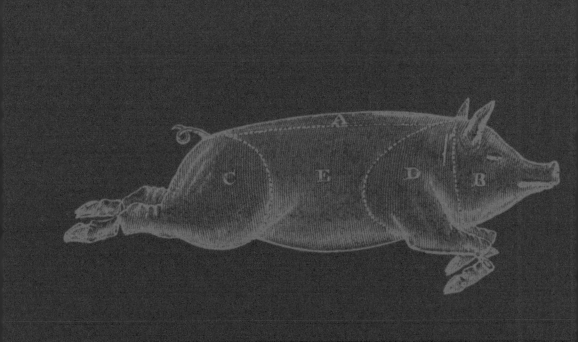

A Christmas Hamper

Cumberland Ham, York Ham, Suffolk Ham, Welsh Ham, Smoked Salmon, Smoked Eel, Spiced Beef, Cumbria Air-Dried Ham, Game Pie, Pork Pie, Venison Pie

Sweet:

Christmas Pudding, Clootie Dumpling, Shortbread, Rich Fruit Cake, Selkirk Bannock, Black Bun, Dundee Cake, Brandy Snap, Cheese Straws

Seasoning:

Patum Peperium, Tewkesbury Mustard, Urchfont Chilli Mustard, Heather Honey, Cumberland Rum Butter, Cumberland Sauce, Tablet, Dundee Marmalade, Spiced Damson, Pickled Walnuts, Rowan Jelly

Drinks:

Malt Whisky, Elderflower Cordial, Ginger Wine, Mead, Plymouth Gin, Sloe Gin

Address Book

Trade Associations and Interest Groups

ASPARAGUS GROWERS ASSOCIATON www.british-asparagus.co.uk

ASSOCIATION OF MASTER BAKERS www.masterbakers.co.uk

ASSOCIATION OF SCOTTISH SHELLFISH GROWERS www.assg.co.uk

BEE FARMERS ASSOCIATION www.beefarmers.co.uk

BISCUIT, CAKE, CHOCOLATE AND CONFECTIONARY ALLIANCE www.bcca.org.

BRAMLEY APPLE INFORMATION SERVICE www.bramleyapples.co.uk

BEE KEEPERS ASSOCIATION www.bbka.org.uk

BRITISH CARROT GROWERS ASSOCIATION www.bcga.info

BRITISH CHEESE BOARD www.cheeseboard.co.uk

BRITISH DEER FARMERS ASSOCIATION www.bdfa.co.uk

BRITISH GOOSE PRODUCERS ASSOCIATION www.goose.cc

BRITISH HERB TRADE ASSOCIATION www.bhta.org.uk

BRITISH PIG ASSOCIATION www.britishpigs.co.uk

BRITISH SUMMER FRUITS www.britishsummerfruits.co.uk

BRITISH SOFT DRINKS ASSOCIATION www.britishsoftdrinks.com

BRITISH WATERFOWL ASSOCIATION www.waterfowl.org.uk

BROGDALE HORTICULTURAL TRUST www.brogdale.org

CAMPAIGN FOR REAL ALE www.camra.org.uk

CARROT GROWERS ASSOCIATION www.bcga.info

COMMON GROUND www.england-in-particular.info

CURRY CLUB www.thecurryclub.org.uk

DAIRY TRADE FEDERATION www.dairyuk.org

ENGLISH APPLES AND PEARS www.englishapplesandpears.co.uk

ENGLISH FARM CIDER CENTRE www.middlefarm.com

FOOD FROM BRITAIN www.foodfrombritain.co.uk

FOOD AND DRINK FEDERATION www.fdf.org.uk

GAME CONSERVANCY TRUST www.gct.org.uk

GIN AND VODKA ASSOCIATION OF GREAT BRITAIN www.ginvodka.org

GUILD OF Q BUTCHERS www.guildofqbutchers.com

HENRY DOUBLEDAY RESEARCH ASSOCIATION (organic gardening and food)
www.gardenorganic.org.uk

HERB SOCIETY www.herbsociety.co.uk

KENTISH COBNUTS ASSOCIATION www.kentishcobnutsassciation.co.uk

MEAT AND LIVESTOCK COMMISSION www.mlc.org.uk

NATIONAL FRUIT COLLECTION www.webvalley.co.uk

NATIONAL ASSOCIATION OF CIDER MAKERS www.cideruk.com

NATIONAL FARMERS UNION www.nfuonline.com

NATIONAL FEDERATION OF WOMEN'S INSTITUTES www.womens-institute.co.uk

NATIONAL MARKET TRADERS FEDERATION www.nmtf.co.uk

NATIONAL SHEEP ASSOCIATION www.nationalsheep.org.uk

QUALITY MEAT SCOTLAND www.qmscotland.co.uk

RARE BREEDS SURVIVAL TRUST www.rbst.org.uk

SAUSAGE APPRECIATION SOCIETY www.sausagefans.com

SCOTCH MALT WHISKY SOCIETY www.smws.com

SCOTTISH ASSOCIATION OF MASTER BAKERS www.samb.co.uk

SCOTTISH ASSOCIATION OF MEAT WHOLESALERS www.scottish-meat-wholesalers.org.uk

SCOTTISH CROP RESEARCH INSTITUTE www.scri.sari.ac.uk

SCOTTISH FEDERATION OF MEAT TRADERS ASSOCIATION www.sfmta.co.uk

SCOTTISH QUALITY SALMON www.scottishsalmon.co.uk

SEA FISH INDUSTRY AUTHORITY www.seafish.org.uk

SEASONING AND SPICE ASSOCIATION (UK) www.seasoningandspice.org.uk

SHELLFISH ASSOCIATION OF GREAT BRITAIN www.shellfish.org.uk

SOIL ASSOCIATION www.soilassociation.org

SOUTH-WEST OF ENGLAND CIDER MAKERS ASSOCIATION http://tinyurl.com/pylmg

SPECIALIST CHEESEMAKERS ASSOCIATION www.specialistcheesemakers.co.uk

TASTE OF SHROPSHIRE www.shropshiretourism.info/food-and-drink/

TASTE OF THE WEST www.tasteofthewest.co.uk

TASTE OF WALES LTD www.wela.co.uk

TASTES OF ANGLIA LTD www.tastesofanglia.com

THREE COUNTIES CIDER AND PERRY ASSOCIATION
     www.thethreecountiesciderandperryassociation.co.uk

TRADITIONAL FARM FRESH TURKEY ASSOCIATION www.golden-promise.co.uk

UK TEA COUNCIL www.teacouncil.co.uk

UNITED KINGDOM VINEYARDS ASSOCIATION www.englishwineproducers.com

WATERCRESS GROWERS ASSOCIATION www.watercress.co.uk

WINE AND SPIRIT TRADE ASSOCIATION www.wsta.co.uk

PRODUCERS, SUPPLIERS AND PARTICULAR INTEREST GROUPS

This is by no means an exhaustive list, but this list will point readers wishing to sample a taste of Britain in the right direction. Where possible, a website is given. For smaller organizations or individuals without a functioning website, a postal address is given.

The address book echoes the structure of the text, organized into categories that roughly reflect the natural order of a visit to market: fruit and vegetables, dairy, fishmonger, butchery, bakery, confectioners, drinks and condiments.

Fruit

BLACK WORCESTER PEAR

Countryside and Conservation Section, Environmental Services Department, Hereford & Worcester County Council www.worcestershire.gov.uk

BLUEBERRY (HIGH BUSH)

Trehane Blueberries http://tinyurl.com/pazyv

Scottish Crop Research Institute, (SCRI), Invergowrie, Dundee DD2 5DA.

BLENHEIM ORANGE APPLE

Sepham Farm, Filston Lane, Shoreham, Kent TN14 5JT.

CAMBRIDGE GAGE

Wilkin and Sons Ltd www.tiptree.com

The English Fruit Co, River House, Stour Street, Canterbury CT1 2PA.

CARELESS GOOSEBERRY

Mr Preston, Egton Bridge Old Gooseberry Society, 10 St Johns Croft, Wakefield, WF1 2QR.

G. Cragg, The Gooseberry Association Show, The Crown Pub, Lower Peover, Cheshire

DAMSON

The Mason's Arms at Cartmel Fell www.strawberrybank.com

DITTISHAM PLUM

Dittisham Fruit Farm, Capton, Dartmouth, Devon TQ6 0JE.

FORCED RHUBARB

The National Rhubarb Collection, Harlow Carr Gardens, Harrogate, North Yorkshire HG3 1QB.

RIBSTONE PIPPIN

Ampleforth Abbey Orchards, Ampleforth Abbey, Ampleforth, Yorkshire YO6 4HA.

SCOTTISH RASPBERRY

Scottish Crop Research Institute, (SCRI), Invergowrie, Dundee DD2 5DA.

STRAWBERRY

Darby Brothers, Darby Bros Farms Ltd, Bam's Hall Farm, West Dereham, Kings Lynn, Norfolk PE33 3RP.

Hugh Lowe Farms www.hlf.co.uk

Vegetables

ALEXANDERS
R.T. Herbs, Orange Farm, Kilmersdon, Bath, Somerset BA3 5TD.
DOCK PUDDING
Mytholmroyd Community Centre, Elphaborough, Mytholmroyd, Hebden Bridge HX7 5DY.
GLAMORGAN SAUSAGE
Bryson Craske, Abergavenny Fine Foods, Unit 14 Castle Meadows Park, Abergavenny, Gwent NP7 7R2.
JERSEY ROYAL POTATO
Jersey Produce Marketing Organisation www.jerseyroyals.co.uk
KALE
Scottish Crop Research Institute, (SCRI), Invergowrie, Dundee DD2 5DA.
LAVERBREAD
Selwyn's Penclawdd Seafoods www.selwynseasfoods.co.uk
SEAKALE
Michael Paske Farms Ltd, The Estate Office, Honington, Grantham, Lincolnshire NG32 2PG.
TOMATOES (SCOTLAND)
Scottish Crop Research Institute, (SCRI), Invergowrie, Dundee DD2 5DA.
British Tomato Growers Association, Pollards Nursery, Lake Lane, Barnham, W Sussex PO22 0AD.
VEGETARIAN HAGGIS
MacSween   www.macsween.co.uk

Dairy Produce

i: Milk, Cream, Butter And Ice Cream

AYRSHIRE MILK
Ayrshire Cattle Society www.ayrshirescs.org
CHANNEL ISLAND MILK
Quality Milk Producers Ltd, The Bury Farm, Pednor Road, Chesham, Buckinghamshire HP5 2JY.
CLOTTED CREAM BUTTER
R.A. Duckett & Co, Walnut Tree Farm, Heath House, Wedmore, Somerset BS28 4UJ.
THE TALLY'S ICE-CREAM
Rizza's www.rizza.co.uk

ii: Cheese

BATH CHEESE
Bath soft cheese company www.parkfarm.co.uk

BAYDON HILL CHEESE
J. Hale, Eventide, Baydon Hill Farm, Aldbourne, Wiltshire SN8 2DJ.

BEENLEIGH BLUE CHEESE
Ticklemore Cheese Company, 1 Ticklemore Street, Totnes, Devon TQ9 5EJ.

CABOC CHEESE
Highland Fine Cheeses, Knockbreck, Tain, Easter Ross 1V19 1LZ.

CAERPHILLY CHEESE
Caws Cenarth Cheese www.cawscenarth.co.uk
Caws Nantybwla Farmhouse Cheese, College Rd, Caermarthen SA31 3QS.
J. Savage, Teifi Cheese, Glynhynod Farm, Ffostrasol, Llandysul, Dyfed SA44 5JY.
Trethowan's Dairy Ltd, Gorwydd Farm, Llanddewi Brefi, Tregaron, Ceredigion, Wales SW725 6NY.
R.A. Duckett and Co, Walnut Tree Farm, Heath House, Wedmore, Somerset BS28 4UJ.

CAROLINA CHEESE
Nepicar Farm www.nepicarfarm.co.uk

CHESHIRE CHEESE
Appleby's www.applebysofhawstone.co.uk
H. S. Bourne www.hsbourne.co.uk

CORNISH YARG CHEESE
Lynher Dairies Cheese Company www.cornishyarg.co.uk

COTHERSTONE CHEESE
Joan Cross, Quarry House, Marwood, Barnard Castle, County Durham DL12 9Q.

COVERDALE CHEESE
N. Reaks, Fountains Dairy Products, Kirkby Malzeard, Ripon, North Yorkshire HG4 3QD.

CROWDIE CHEESE
Highland Fine Cheeses, Knockbreck, Tain, Easter Ross 1V19 1LZ.

CURWORTHY CHEESE
Stockbeare Farm www.curworthycheese.co.uk

DERBY CHEESE
Fowler's of Earlswood www.traditionalcheeses.co.uk

DORSET BLUE VINNEY CHEESE
The Dorset Blue Soup Company at Woodbridge Farm www.dorsetblue.com

DOUBLE GLOUCESTER CHEESE
Smart's Traditional Gloucester Cheese www.fmiv.co.uk
C. Martell and Sons, Laurel Farm, Dymock, Gloucestershire GL18 2DP.

DUNLOP CHEESE
Ann Dorward, West Clerkland Farm Stewarton, Ayrshire KA3 5LP.
Scottish Handmakers Association, Walston Braehead Farm, Carnwath, Lanarkshire ML11 8NE.

Dunsyre Blue cheese
Handmade Cheeses of Scotland, Walston Braehead Farm, Carnwath, Lanarkshire ML11 8NE.

Hereford Hops cheese
Malvern Cheesewrights, Manor house, Malvern Road, Lower Wick, Worcester WR2 4BS.

Kelsae cheese
Brenda Leddy, Garden Cottage Farm, Stitchill, Kelso TD5 7TL.

Ribblesdale cheese
I. and C. Hill, Ashes Farm, Horton in Ribblesdale, Settle, North Yorkshire, BD24 0JB.

Sharpham cheese
M. Sharman www.sharpham.com

Single Gloucester cheese
Diana Smart, Old Ley Court, Chapel Lane, Birdwood Churcham, Gloucestershire GL2 8AR.
C. Martell and Sons, Laurel Farm, Dymock, Gloucestershire GL18 2DP.

Stilton cheese
Olive Middleton, The Stilton Cheesemakers Association, PO Box 11, Buxton, Derby SK17 6DD.

Sussex Slipcote cheese
Sussex High Weald Dairy www.highwealddairy.co.uk

Swaledale cheese
The Swaledale Cheese Company www.swaledalecheese.co.uk

Vulscombe cheese
G. Townsend, Higher Vulscombe, Cruwys Morchard, near Tiverton EX16 8NB.

Wellington cheese
Village Maid Cheeses, The Cottage, Basingstoke Road, Riseley, Reading, Berkshire RG7 1QD.

Wensleydale cheese
S. Stirke, Fortmayne Farm Dairy, Newton-le-Willows, Bedale, Yorkshire DL8 1SL.
Wensleydale Dairy Products www.wensleydale.co.uk
Fountains Dairy Products Ltd, Kirkby Malzeard, Ripon, North Yorkshire HG4 3QD.

Fish & Seafood

Air-dried salted fish
MacCallum's of Troon, 71 Holdsworth St, Finnieston, Glasgow.

Arbroath smokie
R.R. Spink www.rrspink.com

Cockle (Stiffkey Blues)
The North Norfolk Fisherman's Association, 104 Overstrand Road, Cromer, Norfolk.

Cockle (Penclawdd)
The South Wales Sea Fisheries Committee www.swsfc.org.uk

CROMER CRAB

R. & J. Davies, 7 Garden Street, Cromer, Norfolk NR7 9HN.

ELVERS

The Severn River Authority, Tewkesbury, Gloucestershire.

FINNAN HADDOCK

Andy Race, Fish Merchants Ltd www.andyrace.co.uk

KIPPER (CRASTER)

L. Robson and Sons www.kipper.co.uk

Swallow Fish www.swallowfish.co.uk

KIPPER (MANX)

George Devereaux and Son www.isleofmankippers.com

John Curtis www.manxkippers.com

KIPPER (SCOTTISH CURE)

Summer Isles Foods www.summerislesfoods.com

Loch Fyne Smokehouse www.lochfyne.com

KIPPER (WHITBY)

Fortunes, 22 Henrietta Street, Whitby, Yorkshire YO22 4DW.

R.J. Noble, 113, Church Street, Whitby, Yorkshire YO21.

MORECAMBE BAY SHRIMP

Martin Boyce, NW and N Wales Sea Fisheries Committee www.nwnwsfc.org

MUSSEL

Eastern Sea Fisheries Joint Committee www.esfjc.co.uk

Brancaster Staithe Fisherman's Society, The Retreat, King's Lynn, Norfolk PE31 8BX.

MUSSEL (SCOTLAND)

The Scottish Shellfish Marketing Group www.scottishshellfish.co.uk

OYSTER

Colchester Oyster Fishery Ltd. www.colchesteroysterfishery.com

Seasalter Shellfish www.seacaps.com

OYSTER (SCOTLAND)

Loch Fyne Oysters www.lochfyne.com

PATUM PEPERIUM

Elsenham Quality Foods Ltd, Bishop's Stortford, Hertfordshire CM22 6DT.

POTTED CRAB

The North Norfolk Shellfisherman's Association, 104 Overstrand Road, Cromer, Norfolk.

POTTED SHRIMP

James Baxter and Son, Thornton Road, Morecambe, Lancashire LA4 5PB.

RED HERRING

H.S. Fishing Ltd, Sutton Road, Great Yarmouth NR30 3NA.

SCALLOP

Dr A.R. Brand, Port Erin Marine Laboratory, University of Liverpool, Port Erin, Isle of Man.

SMOKED EEL

The Teviot Game Fare Smokery www.teviotgamefaresmokery.co.uk

Summer Isles Foods www.summerislesfoods.com

SMOKED MACKEREL

Andy Race, Fish Merchants Ltd www.andyrace.co.uk

SMOKED SALMON (LONDON CURE)

H. Forman and Son www.formans.co.uk

SMOKED SALMON (SCOTLAND)

Scotfood Ltd, Clachan, Locheport, Lochmaddy, North Uist PA82 5ET.

Summer Isles Foods www.summerislesfoods.com

Hebridean Smokehouse Ltd www.hebrideansmokehouse.com

SMOKED SPRAT

Butley Orford Oysterage www.butleyorfordoysterage.co.uk

SPOOT

Orkney Fishermen's Society www.ofsorkney.co.uk

YARMOUTH BLOATER

The Lowestoft Laboratory, Centre for Environment, Fisheries and Aquaculture Science www.cefas.co.uk

Meat

i: Cattle

ABERDEEN-ANGUS CATTLE

Aberdeen-Angus Cattle Society www.aberdeen-angus.co.uk

BEEF SHORTHORN CATTLE

Beef Shorthorn Society www.shorthorn.co.uk/beef_shorthorn/home.htm

DEVON CATTLE

The Devon Cattle Breeders Society www.redruby.devon.co.uk

GALLOWAY CATTLE

The Galloway Cattle Society www.gallowaycattlesociety.co.uk

HIGHLAND CATTLE

The Highland Cattle Society www.highlandcattlesociety.com

MacBeth, Butchers www.macbeths.com

LINCOLN RED CATTLE

The Lincoln Red Cattle Society www.lincolnredcattlesociety.co.uk

OLD HORNED HEREFORD CATTLE

The Hereford Cattle Society www.herefordcattle.org

Lower Hurst Farm www.lowerhurstfarm.co.uk

SUSSEX CATTLE

The Sussex Cattle Society www.sussexcattlesociety.org.uk

James Wickens Butchers, Castle Street, Winchelsea, Nr Rye, East Sussex TN36 4HU.

Welsh Black cattle
The Welsh Black Cattle Societywww.welshblackcattlesociety.org

ii: Sheep

Cheviot sheep
P. Francis, Secretary, Brecknock Hill Cheviot Sheep Society, 13 Lion Street, Brecon, Powys LD3 7HY.
Cheviot Sheep Society www.cheviotscheep.org
North Country Cheviot Sheep Societywww.nc-cheviot.co.uk/public.index.php
Dorset Horn sheep
The Dorset Horn and Poll Sheep Breeders Association www.dorsetsheep.org
Herdwick sheep
Herdwick Sheep Breeders Association www.herdwick-sheep.com
Agnus Farm Meats, Low Wool Oaks, Penrith, Cumbria CA11 9SZ.
Manx Loghtan sheep
Manx Loaghtan Breeders Group
http://vts2.dnsalias.com/manxbreeders/html/000index3.html
Mutton
S. Baker, Lingcombe Farm, Chagford, Devon TQ13 8EF.
North Ronaldsay sheep
The National Farmers Union www.nfuonline.com/x11.xml
Romney sheep
Romney Sheep Breeders Society www.romneysheepuk.co.uk
Shetland sheep
The Shetland Sheep Society www.users.zetnet.co.uk/ssbg/index.html
Southdown sheep
The Southdown Sheep Society www.southdownsheepsociety.co.uk
Welsh Mountain sheep
Welsh Lamb and Beef Promotions Ltd. www.welshlambandbeef.co.uk

iii: Pigs

Berkshire pig
The Berkshire Breeder's Club www.berkshirepigs.co.uk
Gloucestershire Old Spots pig
Gloucestershire Old Spots Breeders Club www.oldspots.com

Middle White pig

M. Squire The Middle White Breeder's Club, Benson Lodge, 50 Old Slade Lane, Iver, Buckinghamshire SL0 9DR.

Tamworth pig

Chesterton Farm Shop www.chestertonfarm.freeserve.co.uk

Tamworth Pig Breeders' Club www.tamworthbreedersclub.co.uk

iv: Poultry

Aylesbury duck

R. Waller, Long Grove Wood Farm, 234 Chartridge Lane, Chesham, Buckinghamshire HP5 2SG.

Norfolk Black turkey

Kelly Turkey Farms www.kelly-turkeys.com

v: Snails And Game

Mendip wallfish

North Nethercleave Farm & South West Snails www.south-west-snails.co.uk/devon-farms.htm

Red deer venison and Red Grouse

Weatherall Foods Ltd. www.blackface.co.uk

Highland Game www.highlandgame.com

Meat Products

Ayrshire bacon

Ramsay of Carluke www.ramsayofcarluke.co.uk

Bath chap

Sandridge Farmhouse Bacon www.sandridgefarmhousebacon.co.uk

Farmhouse Fresh Foods, 61 Northgate Street, Gloucester GL1 2AG.

Bedfordshire clanger

Gunns Bakers, 8 Market Square, Sandy, Bedfordshire.

Black pudding

Morris Pork Butchers, 120 Market Street, Farnworth, Bolton BL4 9AE.

Bradenham ham (Fortnum Black Ham)

Fortnum and Mason www.fortnumandmason.com

CUMBERLAND AIR-DRIED HAM

Richard Woodall www.richardwoodall.com

Sillfield Farm www.sillfield.co.uk

CUMBERLAND SAUSAGES

Richard Woodall www.richardwoodall.com

J. Cranston, Cranston's Butchers, Brampton, Cumbria.

DENBY DALE PIE

The Denby Dale Pie Company www.denbydalepie.co.uk

DEVONSHIRE HAM

Heal Farm Meats www.healfarm.co.uk

FIDGETT PIE

R. & J. Lodge, Greens End Road, Meltham, Huddersfield, Yorkshire HD7 3NW.

FORFAR BRIDIES

JAS McLaren & Sons, 22 Market Street, Forfar, Scotland.

GLOUCESTER SAUSAGES

The Butts Farm Shop www.thebuttsfarmshop.com

The Gloucester Sausage Company, Unit 1 Knightsbridge Business Centre, Knightsbridge Green, Knightsbridge, Cheltenham, Gloucestershire GL51 9TA.

HAGGIS

MacSween www.acsween.co.uk

LINCOLNSHIRE SAUSAGE

A.W. Curtis & Sons Ltd, Long Leys Road, Lincoln, Lincolnshire LN1 1DX.

MELTON MOWBRAY PORK PIE

Dickinson & Morris www.porkpie.co.uk

NEWMARKET SAUSAGES

Musk's www.musks.com

Powter's www.powters.co.uk

OXFORD SAUSAGE

Stroff's, 96 Covered Market, Oxford OX1 3DY.

POTTED MEAT

Heal Farm www.healfarm.co.uk

PRESSED TONGUE (SUFFOLK CURE)

Emmett's Stores www.emmettsham.co.uk

REESTIT MUTTON

Globe Butchers, Lerwick, Shetland www.globebutchers.co.uk

SCOTCH PIES

Scotsmeat www.scotsmeat.com

H. R. Bradsfords Bakers, 70 Spiersbridge Road, Thornliebank, Glasgow G46 7SN.

SMOKED GAME

Rannoch Smokery www.rannocksmokery.co.uk

Summer Isles Foods, Achiltibuie, Ullapool, Wester Ross IV26 2YG.

SPICED BEEF

Heal Farm www.healfarm.co.uk

SUFFOLK HAM

Emmett's Stores www.emmettsham.co.uk

F.E. Neave and Son www.feneave.co.uk

Rolfe's of Walsham, The High Street, Walsham-le-Willows, Nr Bury-St-Edmunds, Suffolk IP31 3AZ.

SUFFOLK SWEET-CURED BACON

Emmett's Stores www.emmettsham.co.uk

F.E. Neave and Son www.feneave.co.uk

Rolfe's of Walsham, The High Street, Walsham-le-Willows, Nr Bury-St-Edmunds, Suffolk IP31 3AZ.

WELSH BACON

Carmarthen Ham www.carmarthenham.co.uk

WELSH HAM

Carmarthen Ham www.carmarthenham.co.uk

WILTSHIRE BACON

Sandridge Farmhouse Bacon www.sandridgefarmhousebacon.co.uk

Eastbrook Farm Organic Meats www.helenbrowningorganics.co.uk

YORK HAM

Harris-Leeming Bar, Leases Road, Leeming Bar, Northallerton, DL7 9AW.

George Scott, 81 Low Petergate, York, YO1 7HY.

Radford Butchers, 81 Coach Road, Sleights, Whitby YO21 5EH.

Breads

BATH BUN

Mountstevens Ltd, The Bakery, Fishponds Trading Estate, Clay Hill, Bristol BS5 7ES

BEREMEAL BANNOCKS

Orkney Quality Food and Drink Ltd www.oqfd.co.uk

BORROWDALE TEA BREAD

The Village Bakery www.village-bakery.com

GLASGOW ROLLS

Morton's Rolls, 2 Allardyce Road, Glasgow G15 6RX.

GUERNSEY GÂCHE

L.S. Warry and Sons, PO Box 111, St Peter Port, Guernsey GY1 3EU.

New Senners Bakery, St Martins, Guernsey.

KENTISH HUFFKINS

The Baker's Oven www.bakersoven.co.uk

PUGGIE BUNS

Fisher and Donaldson www.fisheranddonaldson.com

Ripon spice cakes

Davill's Patisserie, 24 Westgate, Ripon, North Yorkshire HG4 2BQ.

Sally Lunn

The Sally Lunn Shop www.sallylunns.co.uk

Selkirk bannocks

A. Dalgetty & Sons www.alex-dalgetty.co.uk

Softie

Chalmers Bakery, Auchmill Road, Bucksburn, Aberdeen AB21 9LB.

Square loaf

Chalmers Bakery, Auchmill Road, Bucksburn, Aberdeen AB21 9LB.

Stotty cakes

Gregg's Bakers www.greggs.co.uk

Whitby lemon buns

Elizabeth Botham and Sons www.botham.co.uk

Ainsley's of Leeds www.ainsleys.co.uk

Griddle-breads, biscuits & Puddings

Abernethy biscuit

Simmers www.nairns-oatcakes.com/simmers/simmers_index.html

Ashbourne gingerbread

Spencers Original Ashbourne Gingerbread, William Spencer & Son, 37/39 Market Place, Ashbourne, Derbyshire DE6 1EU.

Cheese straw

Fudges www.fudges.co.uk

Treloars, 38 High Street, Crediton.

Betty's www.bettysandtaylors.com

Clootie dumpling

A. Dalgetty & Sons Bakers www.alex-dalgetty.co.uk

Speyside Heather Centre Clootie Dumpling

http://heathercentre.com/acatalog/Clootie_Dumplings.html

Cornish fairings

Furniss of Cornwall www.furniss-foods.co.uk

Grasmere gingerbread

The Gingerbread Gingerbread Shop www.grasmeregingerbread.co.uk

Kirriemuir gingerbread

Bells Bakers www.bellbakers.co.uk

MARKET DRAYTON GINGERBREAD

The Gingerbread Sanctuary, Pell Wall House, Market Drayton, Shropshire TF9 2AB.

MUFFIN

Betty's & Taylors of Harrogate www.bettysandtaylors.com

PAVING STONE

Fisher and Donaldson www.fisheranddonaldson.com

PETTICOAT TAILS

The Shortbread House of Edinburgh www.shortbreadhouse.com

RAGGY BISCUIT

Fisher and Donaldson www.fisheranddonaldson.com

SCOTTISH OATCAKE

Stockan & Gardens www.stockan-and-gardens.co.uk

SHORTBREAD

The Shortbread House of Edinburgh www.shortbreadhouse.com

Walkers Shortbread www.walkersshortbread.com

SUET CAKE

Southam's of Haworth Ltd, Fairfax Street, Haworth, Keighley, West Yorkshire.

WHITBY GINGERBREAD

Elizabeth Botham and Sons www.botham.co.uk

Cakes & Pies

APPLE CAKE

Mrs M. Stewart, Lower Farmhouse, Sandford Orchas, Sherborne, Dorset.

BAKEWELL PUDDING

The Old Original Bakewell Pudding Shopwww.bakewellspuddingshop.co.uk

The Bakewell Pudding Parlour, Water Street, Bakewell DE14EW.

Bloomer's Original Bakewell Puddings, Water Street, Water Lane, Bakewell, Berbushire DE45 2LX.

CIDER CAKE

R. Peel, Berryhill Farm, Coedkernew, Newport, Gwent NP10 8UD.

Suffolk Larder www.suffolklarder.co.uk

CUMNOCK TART

H.R. Bradford (Bakers) 70 Spiersbridge Road, Thornliebank, Glasgow G46 7SN.

DORSET KNOBS

Moores www.moores-biscuits.co.uk

DUNDEE CAKE

Goodfellow & Steven www.scottishbaking.co.uk

FAT RASCALS

Betty's Café Tea Rooms www.bettys.co.uk

KENDAL PEPPER CAKE

J. R. Birkett and Sons Ltd, Hutton Hall Bakery, Benson Row, Penrith, Cumbria CA11 7YN.

MAIDS OF HONOUR

Newens Bakers, The Original Maids of Honour, 288 Kew Road, Kew Gardens, Surrey TW9 3DU.

MELTON HUNT CAKE

Ye Olde Pork Pie Shoppe www.porkpie.co.uk

NORFOLK KNOBS

Merv's Hot Bread Kitchen, 38 Market Place, Wymondham, Norfolk NR17 0AX.

SEED CAKES

Meg Rivers Cakes www.megrivers.com

WELSH PLATE CAKE

Miss E. Marks, Popty Bach-y-Wlad, Court Farm, Pentrecourt, Llandyssul, Dyfed.

WILFRA TART

Davill's Patisserie, 24 Westgate, Ripon, North Yorkshire, HG4 2BQ.

YORKSHIRE MINT PASTY

Southams Bakers, Fairfax Street, Haworth, Keighley, West Yorkshire BD22 8JA.

Confectionery

BERWICK COCKLES

Gibbs, Fort Matilda, Greenock PA16 7SZ.

James Ross and Son, Pentland Industrial Estate, Loanhead, Midlothian, Scotland EH20 9QR.

BITTERMINTS

Bendicks of Mayfair Ltd www.bendicks.co.ul

BLACK BULLETS

Maxons Ltd www.maxons.co.uk

COLTSFOOT ROCK

Stockley Sweets Ltd www.stockleys-sweets.co.uk

EDINBURGH ROCK

Gibbs, Fort Matilda, Greenock PA16 7SZ.

Ross's of Edinburgh, Pentland Industrial Estate, Loanhead, Edinburgh EH20 9QR.

FISHERMEN'S FRIENDS

Lofthouse of Fleetwood Ltd www.fishermansfriend.com

FUDGE

The Toffee Shop www.thetoffeeshop.co.uk

GOOSEBERRY AND ELDERFLOWER JAM

Garden of Suffolk Preserves, 119 Plumstead Road, Norwich NR1 4JT.

Rosebud Preserves, Rosebud Farm, Healey, Ripon, Yorkshire HG4 4LH

Wendy Brandon www.wendybrandon.co.uk

HAWICK BALLS

Gibbs, Fort Matilda, Greenock PA16 7SZ.

Humbugs Traditional Sweet Shop www.humbuguk.co.uk

JETHART SNAILS

Millers, 10 High Street, Jedburgh, Roxburghshire TD8 6AG.

KENDAL MINT CAKE

Romney's Kendal Mint Cake www.kendal.mintcake.co.uk

J.E. Wilson and Sons www.funchocs.com

D. Quiggin and Son www.quiggins.co.uk

LILY OF THE VALLEY CREAMS

J. Fairbank, Bonnet's, 38–40 Huntriss Row, Scarborough YO1 1ES.

MARMALADE

Pettigrews of Kelso www.pettigrews.com

MOFFAT TOFFEE

The Moffat Toffee Shop www.dalbeattie.com/moffat/traders/moffat-toffee/index.html

PONTEFRACT CAKES

Dunhill's www.haribo.com/planet/uk/info/frameset.php

Monkhill Confectionery www.cadbury.co.uk

RHUBARB AND GINGER JAM

Stonham Hedgerow Products www.stonhamhedgerow.co.uk

Rosebud Preserves, Rosebud Farm, Healey, Ripon, Yorkshire HG4 4LH.

Melanie Knibbs, St Nicholas, Bevis Way, King's Lynn, Norfolk, PE30 3AG.

STARRY ROCK

The Star Rock Shop www.thestarrockshop.co.uk

TABLET

The Moffat Toffee Shop, High Street, Moffat, Scotland DG10 9DW.

TOFFEE APPLES

Evan's Toffee Apples www.evanstoffeeapples.co.uk

Aromatics & Condiments

APPLE CHUTNEY

Stonham Hedgerow Products www.stonhamhedgerow.co.uk

CHELSEA PHYSIC GARDEN HONEY

The Chelsea Physic Garden www.chelseaphysicgarden.co.uk

CIDER VINEGAR

C. Collins, The Cyder House, Aspall Hall, Stowmarket, Suffolk IP14 6PD.

Merrydown www.merrydown.co.uk

Franklin's Cider Farm, The Cliffs, Little Hereford, Ludlow, Shropshire S78 4LW.

COLMAN'S MUSTARD

Colmans of Norwich www.colmansmustardshop.com

Colman's Mustard Museum, 3 Bridewell Alley, Norwich.

CUMBERLAND SAUCE

The Tracklement Co Ltd www.tracklement.co.uk

MALDON SEA SALT

The Maldon Crystal Salt Co Ltd www.maldonsalt.co.uk

MARMITE

Unilever www.marmite.com

MEDLAR JELLY

Stonham Hedgerow Products www.stonhamhedgerow.co.uk

Garden of Suffolk Preserves, 119 Plumstead Road, Norwich NR1 4JT.

Melanie Knibbs, St Nicholas, Bevis Way, King's Lynn, Norfolk PE30 3AG.

Elsenham Quality Foods, Bishop's Stortford, Hertfordshire, CM22 6DT.

Wilkin and Sons Ltd, Tiptree www.tiptree.com

MINT AND APPLE JELLY

Les Fines Herbes, 8 St Mary's Hill, Stamford, Lincolnshire PE9 2DP.

Womersley Famous Fruit and Herb Delicacies www.womersleyfinefoods.co.uk

MUSHROOM KETCHUP

Peter Mushrooms www.petermushrooms.co.uk

PICKLED WALNUTS

Opies www.b-opie.com

RASPBERRY VINEGAR

Seldom Seen Farm www.seldomseenfarm.co.uk

Les Fines Herbes, 8 St Mary's Hill, Stamfor,d Lincolnshire PE9 2DP.

Womersley Famous Fruit and Herb Delicacies www.womersleyfinefoods.co.uk

Spring Farm Shop, The Moor, Trowell, Nottinghamshire NG9 3PQ

ROWAN JELLY

Moniack Castle and Highland Wineries www.moniackcastle.co.uk

SEA LAVENDER HONEY

Margaret Thomas, 25 Tyrone Road, Southend-on-Sea, Essex SS1 3HE

TEWKESBURY MUSTARD

Kitchen Garden Preserves www.kitchengardenpreserves.co.uk

URCHFONT MUSTARD

The Tracklement Co Ltd www.tracklements.co.uk

Flours

BEREMEAL
Golspie Mill Sutherland www.golspiemill.co.uk
Barony Mill, Birsay, Orkney KW17 2LY.
OATMEAL
The Oatmeal of Alford www.oatmealofalford.com

Fats

SUET
RHM Foods, Greatham, Hartlepool TS25 2HD.

Beverages

APPLE JUICE
Hebling, The Ruffett Duskin Farm, Covert Lane, Kingston, Canterbury, Kent CT4 6JS.
BARLEY WINE
Young's www.youngs.co.uk
BITTER BEER (BURTON-UPON-TRENT)
Marston's Beer www.marstonsdontcompromise.co.uk
BITTER BEER (KENT)
Shepherd Neame Ltd www.shepherd-neame.co.uk
P. and D.J. Goacher, Unit 8, Tovil Green Business Park, Tovil, Maidstone, Kent ME15 6TA.
Larkins Brewery Ltd, Larkins Farm Hampkins Hill Road, Chiddingstone, Edenbridge, Kent TN8 7BB.
BITTER BEER (TADCASTER)
Samuel Smith's Old Brewery www.merchantduvin.com/pages/5_breweries/samsmith.html
The Black Sheep Brewery www.blacksheepbrewery.com
BLACK BEER
J.E. Mather and Sons Ltd, Barchester Winery, Silver Royd Hill, Leeds LS12 4JL.
Matthew Clark Gaymer Ltd www.matthewclark.co.uk
BROWN ALE
Scottish and Newcastle Breweries www.scottish-newcastle.com
CIDER (WEST COUNTRY)
The Hereford Cider Museum www.cidermuseum.co.uk
John Hallam, 27 Fraser Street, Windmill Hill, Bedminster, Bristol BS3 4LZ.
H. Weston and Sons, The Bounds, Much Marcle, Herefordshire HR8 2NQ.

Cider (Eastern tradition)
John Hallam, 27 Fraser Street, Windmill Hill, Bedminster, Bristol BS3 4LZ.

Cider brandy
The Hereford Cider Museum www.cidermuseum.co.uk

The Somerset Distillery www.ciderbrandy.co.uk

Dandelion and burdock
Ben Shaw Ltd www.benshaws.com

A.G. Barr plc www.agbarr.co.uk

Fitzpatrick's Herbal Health Shop www.fitzpatricks1890.co.uk

Elderberry cordial
The Original Drinks Co. www.originaldrinks.com

Elderflower cordial
Belvoir Fruit Farms www.belvoirfruitfarms.co.uk

Bottlegreen www.bottle-green.co.uk

Thorncroft www.thorncroftdrinks.co.uk

The Original Drinks Co. www.originaldrinks.com

Fentiman's ginger brew
Fentiman's www.botanically-brewed-soft-drinks.co.uk

Ginger wine
Stone's of London www.stonesgingerwine.com

Matthew Clark www.matthewclark.co.uk

Heather ale
Heather Ale, New Alloa Brewery, Kelliebank, Alloa FK10 1NU.

Imperial Russian stout
Courage Ltd, John Smith's Brewery, Tadcaster, North Yorkshire LS24 9SA.

Samuel Smith's Old Brewery www.merchantduvin.com/pages/5_breweries/samsmith.html

McMullen & Sons Ltd www.mcmullens.co.uk

Irn-Bru
A.G. Barr plc www.agbarr.co.uk

Malt whisky
Bowmore Distillery www.morrisonbowmore.com

Mead
St Aidan's Winery www.lindisfarne-mead.co.uk

Mild
Bank's www.banksbeer.co.uk

Oatmeal stout
Samuel Smith's Old Brewery www.merchantduvin.com/pages/5_breweries/samsmith.html

Old ale
Greene King www.abbotale.co.uk

Old ale (Yorkshire)
T.& R. Theakston Ltd www.theakston.co.uk

Plymouth gin
The Blackfriars Distillery www.plymouthgin.com

MENU

SILVER BIRCH WINE

Highland Wineries www.moniackcastle.co.uk

Broadland Wineries Ltdwww.broadland-wineries.co.uk

SLOE GIN

Gordon's Gin www.gordons-gin.co.uk

TIZER

A.G. Barr plc www.agbarr.co.uk

VIMTO

J.N. Nichols plc www.nicholsplc.co.uk

Fitzpatrick's Herbal Health Shop www.fitzpatricks1890.co.uk

PGOs AND PGIs

Britain and continental Europe possess an enormous range of wonderful food. When a product's reputation extends beyond national borders, however, it can find itself in competition with products using the same name and passing themselves off as genuine. This unfair competition discourages producers and misleads consumers, and for this reason the European Union in 1992 created systems known as Protected Designation of Origin and Protected Geographical Indication to promote and protect regionally important food products.

A Protected Designation of Origin (PDO) describes a food that is produced, processed and prepared in a given geographical area, using a recognised skill. A Protected Geographical Indication (PGI) demonstrates a geographical link between a foodstuff and a specific region in at least one of the stages of production, processing or preparation.

For more information, visit http://ec.europa.eu/agriculture/qual/en/uk_en.htm

Bibliography

Unless otherwise indicated, the place of publication is London and the country of publication is the United Kingdom.

Aberdeen-Angus Cattle Society (1994), *Aberdeen Angus Review*, October.

Accum, F. (1820), *A Treatise on the Adulterations of Food*, facsimile ed.1966, Mallinckrodt Collection of Food Classics, USA.

Acton, Eliza (1845), *Modern Cookery for Private Families*, facsimile ed., introduction by Elizabeth Ray, 1993, Southover Press, Lewes.

Aflalo, F.G. (1904), *The Sea-Fishing Industry of England and Wales*, Stanford.

Allen, Brigid (1994) ed., *Food*, Oxford University Press.

Allhusen, D. (1926), *A Book of Scents and Dishes*, Williams and Norgate.

Anon. (*c.* 1450–1500), Manuscript XVI.O.10, York Minster Library.

—— (1740), *Christmas Entertainments*, facsimile ed. 1991, Pryor Publications, Whitstable.

—— (1744), *Adam's Luxury and Eve's Cookery*, facsimile ed. 1983, Prospect Books.

—— (1812), *Family Cookery Book*, by a Lady, Coventry.

—— (1838), 'Bacon and Ham', *The Magazine of Domestic Economy*, vol. 4.

—— (*c.* 1949), *The Pontefract Liquorice Industry*.

Ashton, C. (1994), 'Brecon Buffs', *Country Garden Magazine*, December.

Atkinson, F. (1960), 'Oatbread in Northern England', *Gwerin*, vol. 3, No. 2.

—— (1993), *Pictures From the Past*, *Northern Life*, Selecta Books, Devizes.

Austen, Jane (1995), *Jane Austen's Letters*, ed. D. Le Faye, Oxford.

A.W. (1587), *A Book of Cookerye*.

Ayrshire Cattle Society (1977), *The History of the Ayrshire Breed*.

Ayrton, Elizabeth (1975), *The Cookery of England*, André Deutsch.

—— (1980), *English Provincial Cooking*, Mitchell Beazley.

Baldwin, J.R. (1974), 'Seabird Fowling in Scotland and Faroe', *Folk Life*, vol. 12.

Banbury Local Historical Society, *Cake and Cockhorse*, Summer 1967.

Banfield, W.T. (1947), 'Manna', *A Comprehensive Treatise on Bread Manufacture* (2nd ed.), Maclaren.

Barr, A.G., plc (n.d.), *The Soft Drink Market, an overview*, AG Barr, Atherton.

Bateman, M. (1993), 'No Ham Like an Old Ham', *Independent on Sunday*, 29.8.93.

Baxter, E. (1974), *Ena Baxter's Scottish Cookbook*, Johnston and Bacon.

Beeton, Isabella (1861), *Beeton's Book of Household Management*, facsimile ed. 1982, Chancellor Press.

Black, M. (1989), *Paxton and Whitfield's Fine Cheese*, Little Brown.

Bond, R. (1923), *The Ship's Baker*, Munro, Glasgow.

Borrow, George (1862), *Wild Wales*.

Bostwick, D. (1988), 'The Denby Dale Pies', *Folk Life*.

Bowness, W. (1868), *Rustic Studies*.

Boyd, Lizzie (1976), *British Cookery*, Croom Helm, Bromley.

Bradley, Richard (1736), *The Country Housewife and Lady's Director*, ed. Caroline Davidson, 1982, Prospect Books.

Bradley, Martha (1756), *The British Housewife*, facsimile ed. 1997-8, Prospect Books, Totnes.

Brears, P. (1984), *The Gentlewoman's Kitchen*, Wakefield Historical Publications, Wakefield.

—— (1987), *Traditional Food in Yorkshire*, John Donald, Edinburgh.

—— (1991), 'Food in the Lake Counties', *Traditional Food East and West of the Pennines*, ed. C.A. Wilson, Edinburgh University Press.

—— (1998), *The Old Devon Farmhouse*, Devon Books, Tiverton.

British Medical Association, (*c.* 1950), 'All about Tripe', *Family Doctor Magazine*.

Brown, Catherine (1981), *Scottish Regional Recipes*, Drew, Glasgow.

—— (1985), *Scottish Cookery*, Drew, Glasgow.

—— (1990), *Broths to Bannocks*, John Murray.

Brown, G (1993), *The Whisky Trails*, Prion.

Brown, Lynda (1987), 'Elder, a good udder to dinner', *Petits Propos Culinaires* 26.

Brown, M. (1986), 'Cider Making in the Channel Isles', *Folk Life*, vol. 25.

Buchanan, G. (1629), *Description of Scotland*.

Burdett, O. (1935), *A Little Book of Cheese*, Gerald Howe Ltd.

Burgess, G.H.O. (1965), *Fish Handling and Processing*, HMSO.

Cassell's (1896), *Cassell's Dictionary of Cookery* (first ed. *c.* 1875).

Castelvetro, Giacomo (1989), *The Fruit, Herbs & Vegetables of Italy*, translated and edited by Gillian Riley from the manuscript of 1614, Viking.

Cheke, V. (1959), *The Story of Cheesemaking in Britain*, Routledge and Kegan Paul.

Cherfas, J. (1995), 'Vanishing Potatoes, not an illusion', *Disappearing Foods*, Oxford Symposium on Food and Cookery, ed. Harlan Walker, Prospect Books, Totnes.

Clapham A.R., Tutin T.G., & Warburg E.F. (1962), *Flora of the British Isles*, Cambridge University Press.

Clark, Lady (1909), *The Cookery Book of Lady Clark of Tillypronie*, ed. 1994, Southover Press, Lewes.

Clark, Colette, ed. (1960), *Home at Grasmere*, Penguin Books.

Cleland, E. (1755), *A New and Easy Method of Cookery*, Edinburgh.

Cleveland-Peck, P. (1980), *Making Cheeses, Butters, Cream and Yoghurt at Home*, Thorsons Ltd, Wellingborough.

Cookson, R. (1888), *Goosnargh Past and Present*, Preston, H. Oakey.

Copsey, W.G. (*c.* 1949), *Law's Grocer's Manual*, 4th ed., William Clowes.

Cox, J. Stevens (1971), *Guernsey Dishes of Bygone Days*, St Peter Port, Guernsey.

CPC (UK) Ltd (n.d.), *The Marmite Story*, Burton upon Trent.

—— (n.d.), *Marmite, brief notes on its history, production and value*, Burton upon Trent.

Craig, E. (1956), *The Scottish Cookery Book*, Deutsch.

Crew, B. (1933), 'Recollections of Chorley', *The Chorley Guardian*, 1.7.1933.

Crossing, William (1911), *Folk Rhymes of Devon*.

Cumbria Magazine (1957), correspondence from H.MacKinnon Adams.

Cutting, C.L. (1955), *Fish Saving, A History of Fish Processing from Ancient to Modern Times*, Hill.

Dalesman (1975), 'Lakeland Cookery', *The Dalesman Magazine*.

Dallas, E.S. (1877), *Kettner's Book of The Table*, facsimile ed.1968, Centaur Press.

Dalton, P. (*c.* 1930), *Dalton's Meat Recipes*, Leeds.

Davy, Sir Humphry (1813), *Elements of Agricultural Chemistry*.

David, Elizabeth (1968), *English Potted Meats and Fish Pastes*, reprinted in *An Omelette and a Glass of Wine*, (1984), Robert Hale.

—— (1970), *Spices, Salt and Aromatics in the English Kitchen*, Penguin Books.

—— (1977), *English Bread and Yeast Cookery*, Allen Lane.

—— (1992), 'Anglo-American Tomato Ketchup', *Petits Propos Culinaires* 40.

Davidson, Alan E. (1979) *North Atlantic Seafood*, Macmillan.

—— (1988) *Seafood, A Connoisseur's Guide and Cookbook*, Mitchell Beazley.

—— (1991), *Fruit*, Mitchell Beazley.

—— (1993) 'Sherbets', *Liquid Nourishment*, ed. C.A. Wilson, Edinburgh University Press.

Davies, G. (1989), *Lamb, Leeks and Laverbread*, Grafton Books.

Davies, S. (1993), 'Vinetum Britannicum, Cider and Perry in the seventeenth century', *Liquid Nourishment*, ed. C.A. Wilson, Edinburgh University Press.

Dawson, Thomas (1596), *The Good Huswifes Jewell*, ed. Maggie Black, 1996, Southover Press, Lewes.

Defoe, Daniel (1724–6), *A Tour Through the Whole Island of Great Britain*, Penguin ed. 1971.

Dent, J.G. (1980), 'Egg Gathering at Bempton, 1935–39', *Folk Life*, vol. 18.

Department of Scientific and Industrial Research (1951), *The General Principles of Smoke curing of Fish*, Food Investigation Leaflet No. 13, HMSO.

de Selincourt, E. (1959), *The Journals of Dorothy Wordsworth*, Macmillan.

Digby, Sir Kenelm (1669), *The Closet of … Sir Kenelme Digbie, Kt. Opened*, new edition 1997, Prospect Books, Totnes.

'Dods, Meg'['Dods, Mrs Margaret, of the Cleikum Inn, St Ronan's'] (1826), *The Cook and House-wife's Manual*, Edinburgh. (Written anonymously by Christian Isobel Johnstone.)

Douglas, W. (*c.* 1906), *Douglas's Encyclopaedia*, (2nd ed.).

Driver, Christopher and Berriedale-Johnson, M. (1984), *Pepys at Table*, Bell & Hyman.

Dunkling, L. (1992), *The Guinness Drinking Companion*, Guinness Publishing, Enfield.

Dyson, John (1977), *Business in Great Waters*, Angus and Robertson.

Eales, M. (1733), *Receipts*, facsimile ed. 1985, Prospect Books.

Economist Intelligence Unit (1993), *Retail Business Market Survey* 426, August.

—— (1993), *Retail Business Market Survey* 429, November.

Eden, R. (1991), *The Sporting Epicure*, Kyle Cathie.

Edlin, A. (1805), *A Treatise on the Art of Breadmaking*, reprinted 1992, Prospect Books, Totnes.

Ellis, W. (1750), *The Country Housewife's Family Companion*.

Elsenham Quality Foods Ltd (n.d.), *Patum Peperium, a brief history*, Bishop's Stortford.

Emmins, C. (1991), *Soft Drinks*, Shire Publications, Princes Risborough.

Evans, J. (1994), *The Good Beer Guide* (1995), CAMRA Books, St Albans.

Evelyn, John (1699), *Acetaria. A Discourse of Sallets*, new edition, 1996, Prospect Books, Totnes.

Farley, John (1783), *The London Art of Cookery*.

Farmers Weekly (1963), *Farmhouse Fare*, Countrywise Books.

Farndale, N. (1995) 'Queen of the Orchard', *Country Life*, 11 November.

Fenton, A. (1973), 'Traditional Elements in the diet of the Northern Isles of Scotland',
    Reports from the Second International Symposium for Ethnological Food Research, Helsinki.

Festing, S. (1977), *Fishermen, a community living from the sea*, David and Charles, Newton
    Abbot.

Finlinson, S. (1993), *Newcastle Brown Ale, the one and only*, Scottish & Newcastle Breweries.

Finney, Thomas B. (1915), *Handy Guide for Pork Butchers*, Finney & Co, Manchester.

FitzGibbon, Theodora (1965), *The Art of British Cooking*, Phoenix House.

—— (1971), *A Taste of Wales*, Pan Books.

—— (1972), *A Taste of England, The West Country*, Dent.

—— (1980), *Taste of the Lakes*, Pan Books.

Forth, Mrs (c. 1794), MS recipe book, York City Archives.

France, W.J. (1968), *The International Confectioner*, Virtue and Company.

Freeman, Bobby (1980), *First Catch Your Peacock*, Image Imprint, Griffithstown.

French, R.K. (1982), *The History and Virtues of Cyder*, Robert Hale.

Fussell, G.E. (1966), *The English Dairy Farmer 1500–1900*, Frank Cass and Co Ltd.

Gailey A (1986), 'Cultural Connections and Cheese', *Folk Life*, vol. 25.

Galloway Cattle Society (1994), *Galloway Journal* (December).

Gathorne-Hardy, A.E. (1898), *The Salmon* (Fur, Feather and Fin Series), Longmans.

Gauldie, E. (1981), *The Scottish Country Miller 1700–1900*, John Donald, Edinburgh.

Gerard, John (1597), *The Herball*.

Gibson, Donald (1983), ed., *A Parson in the Vale of the White Horse, George Woodward's Letters
    from East Hendred, 1753–1761*, Alan Sutton, Gloucester.

Giles, R.A. (1970) *Forced Rhubarb in the West Riding of Yorkshire*, Department of
    Agricultural Economics, Leeds University.

Glasse, Hannah (1747), *The Art of Cookery Made Plain and Easy*, facsimile 1983, Prospect Books.

—— (1772), *The Compleat Confectioner*.

Gomar, A. (1988), *Hampshire Country Recipes*, Ravette Books, Horsham.

Grant, E. (1898), *Memoirs of a Highland Lady*.

Green, Henrietta (1993), *Food Lover's Guide to Britain*, BBC Books.

Grigson, Jane (1971), *Good Things*, Michael Joseph.

—— (1974), *English Food*, Macmillan.

—— (1975), *Fish Cookery*, Penguin Books.

—— (1982), *Fruit*, Michael Joseph.

—— (1984), *Observer Guide to British Cookery*, Michael Joseph.

Hagen, Ann (1995), *A Second Handbook of Anglo-Saxon Food & Drink. Production and
    Distribution*, Anglo-Saxon Books, Hockwold cum Wilton.

Hall, S.J.G. and Clutton-Brock, J. (1989), *Two Hundred Years of British Farm Livestock*,
    British Museum.

Hallam, J. (1979), *The Gingerbread Ladies*.

Hammonds Ltd (n.d.), *Hammonds, a brief history*.

Hancock, D. (1967), *Whelks*, MAFF Laboratory Leaflet No. 15, Burnham-on-Crouch.

Harbutt, J. (1992), *A Guide to the Finest Cheeses of Great Britain and Ireland*, Specialist Cheese-makers Association, Thames Ditton.

Harris, H.G. and Borella, S.P. (c. 1900), *All about Pastries*.

———— (c. 1900), *All About Biscuits*.

Hartley, Dorothy (1954), *Food in England*, Macdonald and Janes.

Henderson, W.A. (c. 1790), *The Housekeeper's Instructor*.

Henisch, B.A. (1976), *Fast and Feast, Food in Medieval Society*, Pennsylvania State University Press, Pennsylvania, USA.

Hess, Karen (1981), *Martha Washington's Booke of Cookery*, Columbia University Press, New York, USA.

Hieatt, Constance A. (1986), *An Ordinance of Pottage*, Prospect Books.

Hodgson, W.C. (1957), *The Herring and Its Fishery*, Routledge and Kegan Paul.

Hogan, W. (1978), *The Complete Book of Bacon*, Northwood Publications.

Holmyard, Nicki (1993), *Shellfish Farming in Scotland – from crofting to big business*, Fish Trader Yearbook, (1993).

Hood, Dr A. (1993), 'Kentish Food, or Food of Kent', *Petits Propos Culinaires* 45.

Hope, Annette (1987), *A Caledonian Feast*, Mainstream Publishing, Edinburgh.

Houlihan, H. (1988), *A Most Excellent Dish, tales of the Lancashire tripe trade*, Salford City Museum, Manchester.

Howes, F.N. (1979), *Plants and Beekeeping*, Faber and Faber.

Hughes, Edward (1952), *North Country Life in the Eighteenth Century, The North East 1700–1750*, Oxford University Press.

ICA Test Kitchen (1971), *Swedish Cooking*, Vasteras, Sweden.

Irons, J.R. (*c.* 1935), *Breadcraft*, privately published.

Jack, Florence (*c.* 1910), *Cookery for every Household*, Thomas Nelson and Sons, Edinburgh.

Jackson, Michael (1989), *Malt Whisky Companion*, Dorling Kindersley.

———— (1993), *Michael Jackson's Beer Companion*, Mitchell Beazley.

Jacob & Co. (n.d.), *Fortt's company history*, Jacob and Co., Reading.

Jamieson, Dr J. (1818), *Dictionary of the Scottish Language*.

Jarrin, G.A. (1820), *The Italian Confectioner*.

Jenkins, J,G. (1971), 'Commercial Salmon Fishing in Welsh Rivers', *Folk Life*, vol. 9.

———— (1977), '*Cockles and Mussels, aspects of shellfish gathering in South Wales*', *Folk Life*, vol. 15.

Jesse, J.H. (1901), *George Selwyn and his Contemporaries*, Nimmo.

Johnston, J.P. (1977), *A Hundred Years of Eating*, Gill and Macmillan, Dublin.

Jones, A. (1957). 'The Cheese from Caerphilly', *The Milk Producer*, vol. 4, 1.

Kaneva-Johnson, Maria (1995), *The Melting Pot*, Prospect Books, Totnes.

Kenrick, J. (1981), 'Elderflower', *Petits Propos Culinaires* 7.

Kinchin, P. (1991), *Tea and Taste, The Glasgow Tea Rooms 1875–1975*, White Cockade, Oxon.

Kirkland, J. (1907), *The Modern Baker, Confectioner and Caterer*, Gresham Publishing Company.

Kitchiner, W. (1817), *The Cook's Oracle* (1829 ed.).

Larousse Gastronomique (1938), Paris.

Law, J.T. (*c.* 1895), *Law's Grocer's Manual*, Liverpool.

Lea & Perrins (n.d.), *The History of Lea & Perrins*.

Lees, R. (1988), *A History of Sweet and Chocolate Manufacture*, Specialised Publications, Surbiton.

Leyel, C.F. and Hartley, O. (1929), *The Gentle Art of Cookery*, Chatto & Windus.

Liddle, C. and Weir, R. (1993), *Ices, The Definitive Guide*, Hodder & Stoughton.

Little, C. (1988), *The Game Cookbook*, Crowood Press, Wiltshire.

Lloyd, L.C. and A.J. (1931), *Shrewsbury Cakes, the story of a famous delicacy*.

Lockhart, R.B. (1951), *Scotch*, Putnam.

Lofthouse of Fleetwood (n.d.), *The History of Fisherman's Friend*.

Lutes, Della (1938), *The Country Kitchen*, 1985 ed., Bell & Hyman.

Mabey, David (1978), *In Search of Food, traditional eating and drinking in Britain*, Macdonald and Jane's.

MacCarthy, D. (1989), *Food Focus 1*, Food From Britain.

MacClure, Victor (1955), *Good Appetite, My Companion*, Odhams.

Mackay, C. (1888), *Dictionary of Lowland Scots*.

McKee, R. (1991), 'Ice Cream Vendors', *Public Eating*, Oxford Symposium on Food and Cookery, ed. Harlan Walker, Prospect Books, Totnes.

Mackenzie, Compton (1954), *Echoes*, Chatto & Windus.

MacLean, Donald (n.d.), *Potato Varieties, a Fact sheet on Special Properties*.

McLintock, Mrs (1736), *Mrs McLintock's Receipts for Cookery and Pastry Work*, facsimile ed., Aberdeen University Press with an introduction by Iseabail Macleod.

McNeill, F.M. (1929), *The Scots Kitchen*, Blackie, Glasgow.

——— (1946), *Recipes from Scotland*, Albyn, Edinburgh.

——— (1956), *The Scots Cellar*, Lochar, Moffat (1992).

——— (1963), *The Scots Kitchen* (2nd ed.), Blackie, Glasgow.

Maddever, K.D. (1988), *Farmhouse Cheddarmakers' Manual*, Milk Marketing Board, Thames Ditton.

Magazine of Domestic Economy (1840), vol. 5.

Maldon Crystal Salt Company, (n.d.), *The Magic of Salt*.

Man, R. and Weir, R. (1988), *The Compleat Mustard*, Constable.

Marine Laboratory, Aberdeen (1993), *Scottish Shellfish Farms, Annual Production Survey*.

Markham, Gervase (1615), *The English Hus-wife*.

Mars, Valerie (1998), 'Little Fish and Large Appetites', *Fish, Food from the Waters*, Oxford Symposium on Food and Cookery, ed. Harlan Walker, Prospect Books, Totnes.

Marshall, Mrs A.B. (1887), *Mrs A.B. Marshall's Cookery Book*, 1st ed. (n.d.)

Marshall, M.W. (1987), *Fishing, the coastal tradition*, BT Batsford Ltd.

Martin, C. (1993), *Our Daily Bread*, Tabb House, Padstow.

Mason, Laura (1994), 'Everything Stops for Tea', Luncheon, Nuncheon and Other Meals, ed. C.A. Wilson, Alan Sutton, Stroud.

——— (1998), *Sugar-Plums and Sherbet*, Prospect Books, Totnes.

Matthews, P. (1994), (ed.) *The Guinness Book of Records*, Guinness Publishing.

May, Robert (1660), *The Accomplisht Cook*, facsimile ed., 1994, Prospect Books, Totnes.

Mayhew, Henry (1861), *London Labour and the London Poor*.

Merrick, Heather (1990), *Pasties and Cream*, Helston.

Ministry of Agriculture, Fisheries and Food (1959), Bulletin no. 43, *Cheesemaking*, HMSO.

—— (1994), *Basic Horticultural Statistics for the UK*, MAFF.

Mitchell, W.R. March (1986), 'A Taste of Swaledale Cheese', *The Dalesman*.

Montagu, F. (1938), *Gleanings in Craven*.

Moore's Biscuits (n.d.), *Biscuits from a Dorset Village*.

Morgan, Joan and Richards, Alison (1993), *A Book of Apples*, Ebury Press.

Morris, C. (1949), (ed.) *The Journeys of Celia Fiennes*, The Cresset Press.

Moss, M. (1991), *Scotch Whisky*, Chambers, Edinburgh.

Murray, P. and C. (1974), *Oatcakes in Staffordshire*, Staffordshire County Museum.

Murrell, John (1638), *Murrels Two books of Cookerie and Carving 1638*, facsimile ed.1985, Jackson's of Ilkley.

National Sheep Association (1992), *British Sheep*, Malvern.

Neild, Robert (1995), *The English, the French and the Oyster*, Quiller Press.

Neufville-Taylor, J. (1965), 'Elver Fishing on the River Severn', *Folk Life*, vol. 3.

Newens Bakers (n.d.), *The Original Maids of Honour, a short history*, Newens, Kew.

Newton, L. (1931), *A Handbook of British Seaweeds*, British Museum, Natural History.

Nichols, S. (1994), *Vimto: The Story of a Soft Drink*, Carnegie Publishing, Preston.

Nicholson and Burn, (1777), *The History of Cumberland and Westmoreland*.

Nilson, Bee (1975), *The WI Diamond Jubilee Cookbook*.

Norwak, M. (1988), *A Taste of Norfolk*, Jarrold and Sons, Norwich.

Norwood-Pratt, J. (1982), *Tea Lover's Treasury*, 101 Productions, San Francisco, USA.

Nott, J. (1726), *Cook's and Confectioner's Dictionary*, facsimile ed. 1980, Lawrence Rivington.

Penrose, John (1983), *Letters from Bath, 1766–1767*, ed. Brigitte Mitchell and Hubert Penrose, Alan Sutton, Gloucester.

Phillips, R. (1983), *Wild Food*, Pan Books.

—— (1987), *Seaweeds and Seashells*, Hamilton.

Plat, Sir Hugh (1602), *Delightes for Ladies*, modern ed. 1948, Crosby Lockwood.

Pointer, M. (1980), *The Grantham Book of Recipes*, Bygone Grantham, Grantham.

Pollard, Helen (1991), 'Lancashire's Heritage', *Traditional Food East and West of the Pennines*, ed. C.A. Wilson, Edinburgh University Press.

Poulson, J. (1978), *Lakeland Recipes Old and New*, Countryside Publications, Chorley.

Pybus, M. (1988), *Shropshire's Spicy Secret*, Newport, Shropshire.

Quinion, M.B. (1982), *Cidermaking*, Shire Publications, Princes Risborough.

Race, M. (1990), *The Story of Blackpool Rock*, Blackpool.

Raffael, Michael (1994), 'Deluxe Ducks that flourish in Bucks', *Sunday Telegraph*, 29 March.

—— (1997), *West Country Cooking, Baking*, Halsgrove, Tiverton.

Raffald, E. (1769), *The Experienced English Housekeeper*, facsimile of 1782 ed. 1970, E&W Books.

Rance, Patrick (1982), *The Great British Cheese Book*, Macmillan.

Ranken, M.D. and Krill, R.C. (1993), *Food Industries Manual*, Chapman and Hall.

Ranson, F. (1949), *British Herbs*, Pelican Books.

Rare Breeds Survival Trust (1994), *Rare Breeds Facts and Figures*, RBST, National Agricultural Centre, Warwickshire.

RHM Foods (n.d.), *The History of Suet*.

Riley, Gillian (1995), 'Parsnips, now you see them–now you don't', *Disappearing Foods*, Oxford Symposium on Food and Cookery, ed. Harlan Walker, Prospect Books, Totnes.

Roach, F.A. (1985), *Cultivated Fruits of Britain*, Basil Blackwell, Oxford.

Roberts, M. and V. (1994), *British Large Fowl*, The Domestic Fowl Trust, Stratford-upon-Avon.

Roberts, Robert (1971), *The Classic Slum*, (Penguin Books ed., 1973).

[Rundell, Maria Eliza] (1807), *A New System of Domestic Cookery, by a Lady*.

Russel, J. (1460), *Boke of Nurture*.

Sala, G.A. (1859), *Twice Round the Clock*, reprint, 1971, Leicester University Press.

Salaman, R. (1970), *The History and Social Influence of the Potato*, Cambridge University Press.

Samuel, S. (1860), (ed.), *The Pig*, by William Youatt.

Schnebbelie, J.C. (1804), *The Housekeeper's Instructor by W.A. Henderson, corrected revised and considerably improved by Jacob Christopher Schnebbelie*.

Schofield, E.M. (1973), 'Working Class Food and Cooking in 1900', *Folk Life*, vol. 13.

Scottish Crop Research Institute (n.d.), *Soft Fruit Research*, Invergowrie, Dundee.

Shand, A.I. (1902), *Shooting*.

Shaw, C. (1993), *Collins Gem Whisky*, Harper Collins, Glasgow .

Shaw's, Ben (n.d.), *Great Grandfather had a Wheelbarrow*, Ben Shaw's, Huddersfield.

Shipperbottom, R.(1995), 'The Decline of Tripe', *Disappearing Foods*, Oxford Symposium on Food and Cookery, ed. Harlan Walker, Prospect Books, Totnes.

Shorthorn Society (1993), *Shorthorns, Two Centuries of Breed Development*.

Simmons, J. (1978), *A Shetland Cookbook*, Thuleprint, Shetland.

Simon, A.L. (1960), *The Concise Encyclopaedia of Gastronomy*, Collins (1983 ed., Penguin Books).

—— (1960), *Cheeses of the World*, Faber and Faber.

Sinclair, Sir J. (1799) (ed.), *The Statistical Account of Scotland 1791–1799*, VI, Ayrshire, reissue, Wakefield, 1982.

Skuse, E. (*c.* 1892), *The Confectioner's Handbook*.

—— (*c.* 1910), *Skuse's Complete Confectioner* (10th ed.), W.J. Bush.

—— (1957), *Skuse's Complete Confectioner* (13th ed.), W.J. Bush.

Smith, C. (1951), 'My Lady's Caprice', *The Critic*, October.

Smith, Eliza (1758), *The Compleat Housewife*, first published 1727, facsimile of the 16th ed., 1983, Arlon House Publishing, Kings Langley.

Smith, J. (1989), *Fairs, Feasts and Frolics, customs and traditions in Yorkshire*, Smith Settle, Otley.

Smith, M.W.G. (1978), *A Catalogue of the Plums at the National Fruit Trials*, HMSO.

Spencer, Colin, and Claire Clifton (1993) eds., *The Faber Book of Food*, Faber and Faber.

Spencer, Colin (1994), 'The Magical Samphire', *Disappearing Foods*, Oxford Symposium on Food and Cookery, ed. Harlan Walker, Prospect Books, Totnes.

Spicer, D.G. (1949), *From an English Oven*, The Women's Press, New York, USA.

Spurling, Hilary (1987), *Elinor Fettiplace's Receipt Book*, Penguin Books.

Stavely, S.W. (1830) *The Whole New Art of Confectionary*, Derby.

Stead, Jennifer (1991), 'Prodigal Frugality', *Traditional Food East and West of the Pennines*, ed. C.A. Wilson, Edinburgh University Press.

Stobart, Tom (1977), *Herbs, Spices and Flavourings*, Penguin.

——— (1980), *The Cook's Encyclopaedia*, Batsford.

Stocker, D. (1988), *Potted Tales, Recollections and views of Morecambe Bay Fishermen*, Lancaster City Museums, Lancaster.

Stout, M.B. (1968), *Shetland Cookery Book*, Manson, Lerwick.

Stuart-Wortley, A. (1895), *The Grouse* (Fur, Feather and Fin Series), Longmans.

Tea Council (n.d.), *File on Tea*.

Tee, George (1983), 'Samphire', *Petits Propos Culinaires* 15.

Thear, K. (1888), *Home and Farm Dairying*, Broad Leys Publishing, Essex.

Thick, Malcolm (1998), *The Neat House Gardens*, Prospect Books, Totnes.

Thompson, C. (1870), *Food and Feeding*.

Thompson, E.P. (1975), *Whigs and Hunters*, Penguin Books.

Thompson, Flora (1939), *Lark Rise to Candleford*, Guild Books.

Thomson, G. (1980), *The Other Orkney Book*, Edinburgh.

Thomson, M.G. (1992), *The Situation, Tendencies and Prospects for the Cultivation of Soft Fruit in Great Britain*, Scottish Soft Fruit Growers, Blairgowrie.

Thorpe, L. (1921), *Bonbons and Simple Sugar Sweets*, Pitman and Sons.

Tibbott, Minwel (1976), *Welsh Fare*, The National Museum of Wales, Cardiff.

——— (1986) 'Liberality and Hospitality, food as communication in Wales', *Folk Life*, vol. 24.

Tuer, A. (1885), *Old London Street Cries*, facsimile ed.1982, Pryor Publications, Whitstable.

Tusser, Thomas (1573), *Five Hundred Points of Good Husbandry*, 1984 ed., Oxford University Press.

Vancouver, C. (1813), *General View of the Agriculture of the County of Devon*.

Vilmorin-Andrieux (1885), *The Vegetable Garden*, reprinted 1976 Jeavons-Leler, Palo Alto, USA.

Walton, C. (n.d.), *The Changing Face of Doncaster*.

Webb, Mrs A. (*c.* 1930), *Farmhouse Cookery*, George Newnes.

Westmoreland County Federation of Women's Institutes (1937), *Westmoreland Cookery Book*, The National Federation of Women's Institutes.

Wheatley-Hubbard, C. (1995), 'Pig Bloodline Survey', *The Ark*, February.

White, Florence (1932), *Good Things in England*, Jonathan Cape.

Whitley, John (1994), 'Nest eggs that are going to waste', *Sunday Telegraph*, 9 May.

Whyte, M. (*c.* 1910), *Highclass Sweetmaking*, Birkenhead.

Williams, R.R.(n.d.), (ed.), *Cider and Juice Apples, Growing and Processing*, University of Bristol.

Wilson, C. Anne (1973), *Food and Drink in Britain*, Constable.

——— (1985), 'I'll to Thee a Simnel Bring', *Petits Propos Culinaires* 19.

——— (1985), *The Book of Marmalade*, Constable.

——— (1991), (ed.), *Banquetting Stuffe*, Edinburgh University Press.

Wolfe, E. (1978), *Recipes from the Orkney Islands*, Gordon Wright, Orkney.

Women's Institute and Michael Smith (1984), *A Cook's Tour of Britain*, Willow Books.

Wondrausch, Mary (1995), 'Potted Char', *Disappearing Foods*, Oxford Symposium on Food and Cookery, ed. Harlan Walker, Prospect Books, Totnes.

Woolgar, V.M. (1992), *Household Accounts from Medieval England*, 2 vols, The British Academy.

Wordsworth, Dorothy (1803), *Recollections of a Tour Made in Scotland*.

Wright, C. (1975), *Cassell's Country Cookbooks, The West Country*, Cassell.

Wright, Joseph (1896–1905), *The English Dialect Dictionary*, Henry Frowde.

W.S. (1864), *The Art and Mystery of Curing, Preserving and Potting All Kinds of Meat, Game and Fish*.

Youatt, W. (1834), *Cattle*.

——— (1837), *Sheep*.

——— (1860), *The Pig* (ed. S. Samuel).

Acknowledgements

Particular thanks to the following chefs, authors and journalists who generously contributed pieces on the following pages:

John Burton Race (p. 17), Matthew Fort (p. 31), Raymond Blanc (p. 66), Prue Leith (p. 75), Delia Smith (p. 119), Galton Blackiston (pp. 130-1), John Torode (p. 149), Fergus Henderson (p. 171), Mark Hix (p. 193), Bruce Poole (p. 212), Simmon Rimmer (p. 239), Rose Prince (pp. 280-1), Gordon Ramsay (pp. 338-9), Catherine Brown (pp. 342-3), Tom Lewis (p. 366) and Sue Lawrence (pp. 380-1).

The following people have kindly given the compilers information about particular foods and trades. This book could not have been completed without their assistance.

J. Adlard, Norfolk; T. Alty, Preston, Lancashire; J. Ashworth, Wymondham, Norfolk; C. Askew, London; C. Beach, King's Lynn, Norfolk; A. Beer, Barnstaple, Devon; C. Bench, Thistleton, Rutland; B. Bertram, Kirriemuir, Scotland; P. Brears, Leeds, West Yorkshire; E. Biltoft, Ripon, North Yorkshire; J. Botham, Whitby, Yorkshire; A.R. Brand, Port Erin, Isle of Man; C. Bray, Herefordshire and Worcestershire County Council; G. Bulmer, Hereford; P. Canipa, Douglas, Isle of Man; G. Chubb, Taunton, Somerset; A. Churchward, Severn-Trent River Authority, Tewkesbury; G. Cloke, Solihull, West Midlands; A. Cook, Sandwich, Kent; F. Cooke, Cooke's, Dalston Junction, London; G. Davies, Cardiff, South Wales; P.D. Davies, Lowestoft; K. Davill, Ripon, North Yorkshire; A. de Gruchy, St Mary's, Jersey; M. Dorman, Middle Tysoe, Warwickshire; D. Eastwood, Great Yarmouth; J. Edwards, Cobham, Kent; E. Elder, Barton-on-Humber; A. Elliott, Ambleside, Cumbria; J. Elmhurst, Barnsley, Yorkshire; T. Evans, Barnstaple, Devon; Trevor Fawcett, Bath; S. Featherstone, Winchester, Hampshire; N. Fletcher, Auchtermuchty, Fife; W. Fortune, Whitby, Yorkshire; M. French, Langport, Somerset; S. Fudge, Sherborne, Dorset; L. Garrad, Douglas, Isle of Man; J. Gibson, Whitstable, Kent; W. Gosling, Swindon, Wiltshire; C. Gough, Cardiff, South Wales; P. Graham, Hawkshead, Cumbria; T. Grayson, Leeds, West Yorkshire; H. Green, London; J. Griffiths, Denbigh, North Wales; R. Groves, Billingshurst, Sussex; M. Hackett, Lindisfarne, Northumberland; J. Hale, Aldbourne, Wiltshire; D. Hall, Bristol; M. Hall, Southam's Bakery, Haworth; S. Hallam, Melton Mowbray, Leicestershire; J. Hamilton, Annan, Scotland; F. Hams, Canterbury, Kent; B. Harrison, Nottingham; E. Hawksley-Beesley, Stamford Bridge, Lincolnshire; R. Hayes, Bristol; G. Hepburn, Chelmsford, Essex; N. Hodgetts, Worcester; P. Holmes, Upper Denby, West Yorkshire; D. Hopper, Herne Bay, Kent; J. Huggins, Southwold, Suffolk; N. Jerrey, Emmett's Stores, Suffolk; N. Johns, Bristol; B. Jones, Penclawdd, South Wales; B. Keen, Peel, Isle of Man; R. Keen, Chippenham, Wiltshire; S. Kennedy, Robertsbridge, Sussex; C. Kerrison, Colchester, Essex; P. King, Kenilworth, Warwickshire; E. Kirkaldy, Whitstable, Kent; B. Knights, University of Westminster, London; B. Lake, Launceston, Cornwall;

P. Lawson, Cornwall; P. Lawson, Stockley's, Accrington, Lancashire; R. Lutwyche, Cirencester, Gloucestershire; R.S. Malcolm, Banbury, Oxfordshire; C. Margrave, Harrogate, North Yorkshire; R. Marsh, Lewes, Sussex; K. Mason, Ilkley, West Yorkshire; B. Matthews, Crediton, Devon; K. Mold, Bangor, North Wales; W. Morrison, Tain, Rossshire; M. Muggeridge, Runcorn, Cheshire; A. Muller, The Lizard, Cornwall; D. Myers, Horncastle, Lincolnshire; K. Neuteboom, Hemingstone, Suffolk; L. Newboult, Lincoln; D. Newton, Boston, Lincolnshire; G. Padfield, Bath; L. Patterson, Gosforth, Tyne & Wear; D. Payne, Plymouth, Devon; D. Pennell, Faversham, Kent; A. Petch, Heal's Farm, Devon; E. Phipps, Boston, Lincolnshire; J.R. Pitchfork, Sheffield; M. Pitts-Tucker, London; G. Powter, Newmarket, Suffolk; H. Pollard, Kendal, Cumbria; N. Pooley, Chewton Mendip, Somerset; D. Powell, Ledbury, Hereford & Worcester; N. Pugh, Pembrokeshire; K. Pybus, Market Drayton, Shropshire; Quality Milk Producers, Chesham, Buckinghamshire; D. Reed, Richmond, Yorkshire; A. Rees, Carmarthen, Dyfed; R. Reynolds, Priddy, Somerset; J.A. Rivis and staff, Helmsley, North Yorkshire; D. Roberts, St Mary in the Marsh, Kent; C. Robinson, Grange-over-Sands, Cumbria; A. Robson, Craster, Northumberland; D. Rossiter, Kingsbridge, Devon; G. Ross, Edinburgh; S. Saunders, Blackpool, Lancashire; Dr Scofield, Cardiff; A. Sebire, Hartington, Derbyshire; F.W. Shepherd, Newcastle and District Allotment Society, Newcastle upon Tyne; the late R. Shipperbottom, Stockport, Cheshire; D. Smart, Churcham, Gloucestershire; F. Smith, Appledore, Kent; N. Smith, Tiptree, Essex; S. Smith, Leeming Bar; Spencers, Ashbourne, Derbyshire; J. Stead, Leeds, Yorkshire; M. Stewart, Sherborne, Dorset; S. Stirke, Bedale, North Yorkshire; C. Sutherland, Brancaster, Norfolk; P. Symonds, Hereford, Hereford & Worcester; A. Tann, Colchester, Essex; R. Taulbman, Brighton, Sussex; J. Temperley, Kingsbury Episcopi, Somerset; D. Thomas, Aberystwyth; M. Thomas, Southend-on-Sea, Essex; D. Thomasson, Dorchester; M. Tibbot, Cardiff; G. Townsend, Tiverton, Devon; J. Trehane, Wimborne, Dorset; J. Tullberg, Malmesbury, Wiltshire; P. van Reale, Pontefract, West Yorkshire; E. Vigeon, Manchester; B. Waddington, Rawtenstall, Lancashire; D. Walker, Oxford; R. Waller, Chesham, Buckinghamshire; H. Watkins, Sandy, Bedfordshire; C. Westhead, Ide Hill, Kent; R. Westwood, Wolverhampton; J. Whitehouse, Swansea, South Wales; J. Wickens, Winchelsea, Sussex; S. Wickham, Mytholmroyd, West Yorkshire; A. Wigmore, Reading, Berkshire; B. Williams, Glasgow; H. Williams, Laindon, Essex; J. Williams, Bristol; A. Winter, University of Liverpool; N. Wood, Sherborne, Dorset; G. Woodall, Thorncroft Ltd, Leatherhead, Surrey; R. Woodall, Waberthwaite, Cumbria; H. Woolley, Sevenoaks, Kent; B. Wordsworth, Barnoldswick, Lancashire; P. Zissler, Darlington, County Durham.

Index

Laura Mason was raised on a farm in Wharfedale, Yorkshire. A food historian, her books include *Sugar-Plums and Sherbet: The Prehistory of Sweets, Food and the Rites of Passage* (as editor), *Food Culture in Great Britain* and *Farmhouse Cookery*. She is also active in the Slow Food movement, and has contributed regularly to the Leeds Symposium on Cookery and Food History.

Catherine Brown grew up in a Glasgow tenement and began her catering career at sixteen in a Clydeside docker's canteen. A professional chef, food writer, critic and author of seven books on Scotland's food culture, she is also a fellow of the Society of Antiquaries of Scotland. She has received three Glenfiddich Food Writing Awards and was the 2001 Guild of Food Writers' Food Journalist of the Year.